Frank Loffland

Thomas P. O'Neill

EAMON DE VALERA

EAMON DE VALERA

The Earl of Longford &
Thomas P. O'Neill

GILL AND MACMILLAN
in association with
Hutchinson of London

GILL AND MACMILLAN LTD.
2 Belvedere Place, Dublin 1

First published 1970

This book has been set in Ehrhardt type, printed and bound in Ireland
on antique wove paper by Hely Thom, Dublin
SBN 7171 0485 0

TO ELIZABETH
AND MARIE

CONTENTS

ILLUSTRATIONS

Frontispiece: Eamon de Valera

Between pages 62 *and* 63
Childhood at Limerick.
Vivion and Catherine de Valera (Eamon's parents).
Edward Coll and Pat Coll (Eamon's uncles) and his home at Bruree.
Eamon and Sinéad de Valera: wedding day (1910) and diamond jubilee (1970).
The only family group of all the children.
The British Army recruiting drive in Dublin.
The 'Asgard' discharges Mauser rifles at Howth.*
Easter 1916: the surrender demand*; de Valera in uniform; Clanwilliam House*; leading his troops after surrender*; under close arrest.

Between pages 222 *and* 223
Countess Markiewicz*; Michael Collins*; Professor Eóin MacNeill*; Arthur Griffith*; W. T. Cosgrave*.
1917: the prisoners return*; de Valera elected to the Dáil*.
1921: the Irish delegation at the Grosvenor Hotel, London, in July.
De Valera in Limerick on the day the treaty was signed in November.
De Valera disguised after the Civil War.
Arbour Hill and Kilmainham Gaol*.
Arrested in Newry (1924).
Deputies try to take their seats in the Dáil (1927).
The first Fianna Fáil cabinet (1932).

Between pages 350 *and* 351
De Valera on the platform.
With Col. Lindbergh; with Mr. and Mrs. Jack B. Yeats.
Presiding at the Disarmament Conference, Geneva, 1932.
With Anthony Eden and Sean T. O'Kelly in Dublin (1938).
The election of May 1951.

Greeted by Churchill in Downing Street (1953).
With Nehru in India (1948).
With Attlee and other Labour leaders in London (1947).
Visits to the Vatican: Pope Pius (1958) and Pope John (1962).
President Kennedy (1963) and President Johnson (1964).
De Valera 'has always revelled in physical exercise'.

*Photographs restored by George Morrison

ACKNOWLEDGEMENTS

This book could not have been written without the co-operation of President de Valera himself. He has always steadfastly refused to write an autobiography, but once he had agreed to the suggestion that an authoritative biography be written he could not have been more helpful. The authors wish to express their gratitude to him not only for making his huge library of private papers freely available to them, but giving them the benefit of his personal recollections of the great events in which he has played so prominent a part. But he made it clear at a a very early stage that, if they ever found a discrepancy between his memory of events and contemporary documents, it was the documents that must be trusted. The authors would like to record that such discrepancies were almost non-existent.

As well as thanking the President for his co-operation in preparing the text, the authors owe him a great debt for his generosity in making available many private photographs of himself and his family. *The Irish Press* has also been extremely generous in making available many of the photographs used in this book which have come from their extensive library. The authors would like to express their appreciation to Mr George Morrison, who has restored so many historical photographs which would not be otherwise available. The authors are most grateful to Mr Colman Doyle for the coloured photograph of the President which has been used on the jacket and as a frontispiece.

We are very grateful to many others, most of whom cannot be mentioned by name. They include the authors of numerous books of which a considerable number are referred to in the text. We are grateful to Mrs Lloyd for permission to publish letters from her father, Mr Neville Chamberlain, to Mr de Valera, and to C. & T. Publications Ltd. for permission to publish extracts from letters from Sir Winston Churchill. Extracts which are not specifically recorded in the list of sources came from Mr de Valera's private papers.

We have benefited much from the endless patience and helpfulness of Miss Marie O'Kelly, the President's personal secretary. Mr Frank Aiken, Dr Maurice Moynihan, Professor Kevin Nowlan, and Professor

Desmond Williams are among those who have read the proofs. The large number of those with whom we have enjoyed fruitful conversations include in particular members of Mr de Valera's Cabinets and, in in England, Sir John Wheeler-Bennett.

We are especially grateful to Mr Malcolm MacDonald for his vivid recollections of his crucial dealings with Mr de Valera.

We warmly thank the members of the President's family for their invaluable contributions, and our own families for their long-suffering encouragement.

No list of acknowledgements, however, would be complete without reference to the untiring labours of Mr Harold Harris.

None of these persons from the President downwards has, of course, any responsibility for any statements appearing in this book.

AUTHORS' NOTE

Many persons who appear in this book have used two forms of their names, the Irish form and an English one. In an effort to avoid confusion, the English form has been followed in most instances by the authors, but in some cases consistency would have been impossible to achieve without interfering with quotations. In the index the references to these persons are presented under one form only, with a cross-reference from the other form. As a help to readers, a very brief biographical note has been included in the personal references in the index.

PROLOGUE

Eamon de Valera was re-elected at the age of eighty-four to be President of Ireland for another seven years. As he entered on his second term of office it could hardly be said of him as it was of Moses at the time of his death that 'his eye was not dimmed nor his natural force abated'. For many years de Valera had been able to see very little in the physical sense. But his vigour of body remained impressive, his clarity and acuteness of mind were undiminished. So were his breadth of vision and interest in all things human, public and personal.

His alertness and keen hearing did much to compensate for his handicap of sight. A visitor who brought his son to see him was surprised to find de Valera estimating correctly that the son was half an inch the taller of the two. He suggested that the visitor himself had been suffering from a slight cold in a recent broadcast—a point overlooked by others. Many friends and acquaintances of the President have been heard to say that the great pleasure of talking to him has increased if anything with the years. A formidable quality has never left him. He has never been a man to be taken lightly. Professor Nowlan has described him admiringly as 'a great eagle with lovely gloves on his claws', but in these later years the overwhelming impression is one of deep mellow benignity.

He was thirty-three years old, a lecturer in a teachers' training college, at the time of the 1916 Rising. Condemned to death and reprieved, he was the senior commandant to survive. After a year of militant defiance inside various British prisons, he emerged a symbolic hero and was accepted with acclamation as the leader of the forces of independence. For over forty years until he 'retired' to the Presidency in 1959, he was either the Head of the Irish Government (twenty-four years) or Leader of the Opposition (sixteen years). In both roles he dominated, directly or indirectly, the Irish scene.

The century offers no parallel to such sustained pre-eminence. When de Valera came to the top after the 1916 Rising, Asquith was still the Prime Minister of Britain. He and eight successors, Lloyd George, Bonar Law, Baldwin, MacDonald, Chamberlain, Churchill, Attlee and Eden were all to pass from office before de Valera handed over control. Harold

Wilson was born in that year of de Valera's first appearance (1916). Few in England outside the London Library knew of the existence of Lenin. Mussolini, Hitler, Stalin and De Gaulle were still figures of the future. In the last case, the distant future. Only one active life in politics at or near the top level offers a span in any way comparable. Winston Churchill had become a national hero eight years earlier. He finally retired from the premiership in 1955, four years before de Valera's similar withdrawal. But he never attained the highest office of all until 1940. De Valera preceded him there by twenty-three years. De Valera has displayed an extraordinary degree of perseverance and ability to command public confidence. It is true of him, if it is true of any man of our time, that he has been fashioned of the stuff that endures.

For half a century his appearance and manner combined to make a lasting impression on all who met him. Six feet one in height, he always looked even taller by reason of an exceptionally upright carriage which remains to him. An athletic frame—he once received a rugby trial for Munster, and always revelled in physical exercise—sharply delineated features, the mouth and chin especially powerful. Dark, deep-set eyes could still, behind the spectacles worn since his youth and in spite of all their limitations in old age, express a whole range of grave or gay emotions. Reference was made in *Peace by Ordeal*[1] to his 'meditative sorrow-lined face'. Meditative, yes. Even more so perhaps in the later days. But by then the sorrow seemed merged in serenity as executive anxieties were laid aside. His courtesy has always been acknowledged even by hostile critics. Denis Gwynn, author of many admirable works, published an unfavourable book about de Valera in 1935. Even so Gwynn paid tribute to the simplicity and unfailing courtesy of his dealings with all who approached him.

Lloyd George in 1921 did not take to de Valera nor de Valera to him. Lloyd George reported to his private secretary, Tom Jones, who recorded his opinion, that de Valera was 'not a big man', but even Lloyd George admitted that 'he was a sincere man, a white man and an agreeable personality'. Courtesy in itself can be a rather chilling quality. Throughout his public life de Valera possessed in addition a winning charm. If one says that this was frequently held in reserve, one does not mean that it was used or not used to suit his convenience as is the case with many notables. One would say rather that he was guarded, reluctant to give himself away until he was sure that a basis for confidence existed. Yet he prided himself, rightly one would think, on his habitual efforts to put himself in 'the other fellow's place' whether friend or foe. Sympathy was a word, for example, that he could use to Chamberlain at the beginning of the war. Indeed he expressed sympathy for Britain throughout the war when few British people were able to feel much sympathy for him. This quality of putting himself in someone else's place should not be seen only as a diplomatic asset but as an important element behind his personal charm.

W. B. Yeats, as will be found in Joseph Hone's biography, recorded a slight feeling of disappointment when taken to a big meeting addressed by de Valera in New York (May 11th, 1920). He had been impressed by a saying reported of de Valera after the suppression of the Rising: 'If the people had only come out with knives and forks'—the words used were 'hay forks'—but after the meeting he noted: 'A living argument rather than a living man. All propaganda, no human life, but not bitter or hysterical or unjust. I judged him persistent, being both patient and energetic, but that he will fail through not having enough human life to judge the human life in others. He will ask too much of everyone and will ask it without charm. He will be pushed aside by others'. The last judgement reads curiously today; and yet in 1922 during the Civil War or in 1924 while de Valera was still in prison it might have seemed quite prescient. But Yeats, when he met de Valera some years later (1932) found 'a charm in the personal contact' which did not appear in the speeches. After his first meeting Yeats wrote: 'I was impressed by his simplicity and honesty though we differed throughout. It was a curious experience. Each recognised the other's point of view so completely. I had gone there full of suspicion but my suspicion vanished at once'. Since then a multiplicity of visitors has been won over in the same way.

His personality as it impinged on the world and his achievements on the plane of history were deeply rooted in his moral nature. No famous statesman of our time can have centred his life more completely, or perhaps so completely, on religion. It represented the very core of his being. Certainly in later years, and perhaps always, he has drawn his ultimate strength and direction from there.

Here, as elsewhere, but here most of all, his reticence and reserve at a certain point bring down the shutter absolutely. The interpreter is left to speculate as best he may. Not for him the self-accusations of a Gladstone, or other forms of self-exposure. Concerning his religion and its significance to him, he concealed nothing, but revealed very little directly. No more in fact than was necessary to perform his public functions and testify to his beliefs on occasion.

There are no sources available for tracing a spiritual Aeneid and, in any case, it is unlikely that there has been much deviation or wandering. As President, in spite of his disability of vision, he probably had more opportunities for ardent religious practice than ever previously. A deepening process can be assumed, and even detected. But there is reason to regard his religious development as a consistent story and his later attitudes and performance as providing a fair clue to his life as a whole.

He had long been known as a daily communicant. Once installed in the President's Residence he usually visited the Oratory five times a day. One of his first steps was to obtain permission for the Blessed Sacrament to be reserved. He was characteristically scrupulous about its custody. He felt strong personal satisfaction when it was decided that his desk was the safest place for the key of the Tabernacle. His preoccupation with the Blessed Sacrament was striking indeed. In that, and in his overall devotion to the Mass, he represented a whole world of Irish Catholicism at its simplest and purest.

His appetite for the Gospels was insatiable and he insisted that they be read to him again and again. He could not be described, least of all by himself, as a theologian. But his absorption in the life and teaching of Jesus might qualify him as an amateur Christologist. Religious discussions with selected clergy made a strong appeal to him. He has been described by one such priest as a man *intellectum quaerens*, a man seeking to extract a full rational meaning from the official teaching of the church. But all this with a practical rather than a speculative bent, a general rather than an egocentric purpose. Such would be the flavour of his discussion, for example, of the arguments for the immortality of the soul.

His attitude to the church itself would be easier to understand in Ireland than in most other countries. In all that concerns faith and morals, he might fairly be called docile. In such matters he was prepared to accept unreservedly the teaching of the church. The controversies flowing from Vatican II did not appear to have disturbed him or stirred him greatly. Nor would they be likely to have done so in his younger days.

He could be proud to have been received in private audience by four Popes, to have attended three Papal coronations and to have been decorated with the highest order in the Church, the Supreme Order of Christ. But in line with one Irish Catholic tradition, though not the only one, he set a sharp limit to the guidance he would accept from the clergy. Daniel O'Connell said, 'I take my religion from Rome, but my politics from Ireland'—a phrase de Valera himself could have coined. The debt of the Irish Independence movement to the clergy, especially the lower clergy, is immeasurable. But in the long years of struggle and emergence, the hierarchy was more often a restraining rather than a revolutionary force.

During the Civil War (1922–3) de Valera, like other Republicans, was denied the Sacraments as 'not worthy to receive them', though he was not excommunicated. It is said that de Valera could have found plenty of priests to defy the ban. At the cost of much spiritual anguish, he refused to expose them to the risk of official censureship. For all his acknowledged piety he could never be defined as a clerical statesman.

It would not be difficult to collect public and private tributes from Protestant leaders to his concern for their communities' well-being. They were well pleased on the whole with their treatment by him under the 1937 Constitution. His appearance at the Presbyterian Assembly, 1969, was one illustration among many available of his determination to act as a President for all Irishmen. As long ago as 1921 Lord Midleton, then Leader of the Southern Unionists, appreciated that this was his purpose.

Various strands of thought may here be distinguished. On the political level he was always acutely aware that the Protestants of the North must be reassured about the treatment of their faith, if they were ever to be won. On the plane of democratic theory he would be the last to ignore the contributions of Tone, Davis, Parnell and other Irish Protestants to the thought and achievements of Irish nationalism. He was always proud to share a birthday, October 14th, with Thomas Davis.

Against his own background of humble beginnings and life-long struggle he identified himself easily and naturally with the under-dog. The very idea of religious discrimination, above all of religious perse-cution, filled him with automatic revulsion. There remains a more hypothetical factor. A profound admirer of his catholicism at close quarters, after describing his exceptional devotion to the church, has added a startling comment. 'He would have made such a good Protestant'. He meant, no doubt, that outside the sphere of Catholic dogma, de Valera always remained a man of ineradicable private judgement; a man not only with a most sensitive conscience, but with the self-confidence to live and die by what it told him.

Along with a great tolerance has gone an endemic conviction of the rightness of his own decisions once they were taken. Perhaps on the deepest level the two attitudes, the self-confidence and the tolerance, at first contrasted, sprang from a common source. Was not this a humility which told him that all the good in him and all the wisdom in him came from God? That similar possibilities of goodness and wisdom could be found in all men living, whose personalities he found no difficulty in believing were as dear to God as his own?

Part I

1882-1916

THE CALL TO SERVE

THE EARLY YEARS

1882-1903

Looking back over a long life, Eamon de Valera, President of Ireland, retains one vivid memory of his early childhood. It comes from America: a large room in a New York apartment, 1885. Beside the fireplace sits a man. On the floor lies a small, fair-haired boy. A slim, pale-faced young woman is bending over him, dressed in black. The child's eyes are fixed wonderingly on the shiny metal fittings which ornament her handbag. This snapshot of the past is all that de Valera remembers of his American origins. But the events preceding it provide the background. To get it in its frame we must turn the family album thirty years further back. It is a story which starts in Ireland.

Four days before Christmas, 1856, Patrick Coll, a farm labourer, and Elizabeth Carroll had their first child—a girl. She was christened Catherine, and known as Kate. The Colls lived at Knockmore, a townland a mile or so north of the village of Bruree, Co. Limerick.

In 1874 Patrick Coll died leaving four children. Ireland was still struggling after the famine of the '40s. For five years Kate Coll worked for neighbouring farmers, but as famine threatened once more in the harvest of 1879 she decided to give herself a new start.

On October 2nd, 1879, New York saw one more Irish immigrant arrive. Like all the others, Kate was tired and almost penniless, but full of hope and carrying a letter to a relative. Kate Coll had an aunt living in Brooklyn. Soon she was at domestic work, first at Bennets in Park Avenue, Brooklyn, and then with a French family, named Giraud, of Myrtle Avenue and later of Gold Street. It was here she first met Vivion Juan de Valera, a delicate young man who used to visit the Girauds. They were together in exile. He had been born in Spain. His father, Juan de Valera, was engaged in the sugar trade between Cuba and Spain and the United States, but his mother, Amelia Acosta, had died when he was young. Vivion had studied to be a sculptor but a chip of marble had injured one of his eyes. Then he took to book-keeping but his health deteriorated and he lived by teaching music.

The acquaintance continued after Kate left the Girauds and went to work in Greenville, New Jersey. On September 19th, 1881, they were married at the Catholic church of St Patrick, Greenville.

They moved into an apartment at 61 East 41st Street, Manhattan, near the site of the Chrysler Buildings. Almost twelve months later Eamon de Valera was born. The date, October 14th, 1882; the place, the New York Nursery and Child's Hospital in Lexington Avenue, between 51st and 52nd streets. Although registered as George, he was baptized Edward of which he used the Irish form Eamon from the time he entered public life. The eve of his birthday was the feast of St Edward the Confessor. His birth certificate was not altered to Edward until 1916 when his mother saw a copy of it while trying to get him released from Dartmoor Prison.

Kate de Valera had reserves of inner strength which carried her through many crises. Her husband's health soon became so bad that his father offered to send him again to the healthy air of Denver. They had to part in 1884 after less than three years of marriage. He never returned; for in the Spring of the next year, 1885, he was dead. Mrs de Valera put the child Eamon in the care of another Bruree immigrant, Mrs Doyle, and went out to work again.

So the young woman in black was de Valera's widowed mother and his mental picture was of the occasions when she came from work to visit him. This arrangement was hardly ideal; the little boy would be much happier in the friendly Bruree atmosphere. Mrs de Valera's brother, Ned Coll, who had joined her in America was about to return home. He could take his nephew across the Atlantic to his grandmother. De Valera remembers leaning over the teak rail of the ship and watching the blue-green of the sea spreading out in a broad tail behind him. And he remembers asking where they were when they got off the boat and being told 'Queenstown'. This replaced the old Irish name in honour of Queen Victoria who had stepped ashore there on her first visit to Ireland.

The Coll house at Knockmore was a typical survivor of pre-famine times. Consisting of one large room, it was mud-walled and thatched, with the fire at one end and a window nearby facing west. The child's bed was in the end furthest from the fireplace. The household consisted of his grandmother, an energetic woman who was not yet fifty, his Uncle Pat, just twenty-one, and Aunt Hannie, a slender fifteen-year-old.

The day after his arrival the whole household moved into one of the first agricultural labourers' cottages built by the Liberals. De Valera always remembered his single night in the old house because he woke up in the morning to find the whole place deserted. Everyone had gone to the new house nearby leaving him behind while they did the work of changing. He was very proud to have been the last occupant of his family home.

The new house was a palace compared with the old, but by that

150 Australian Avenue, West Palm Beach, Florida 33406   Telephone 407-684-9400
Reservations 1-800-HILTONS

standard only. The kitchen occupied more than half the floor space. It had no ceiling but the slated roof. The rest of the floor space was occupied by two small rooms with a loft above, reached by a ladder. This ladder was nearly young Eddie's downfall. One morning his grandmother left him upstairs with his uncle who was still in bed. Then she went off to deliver the milk. Coming back a little later she prepared to give the little boy a bath. She found Eddie crumpled up at the bottom of the ladder. As he descended his attention had been diverted by the bloody end of a goosewing used for dusting and he had crashed to the gound. He came to, to hear his grandmother saying, 'Is he dead?'

He grew particularly fond of his young Aunt Hannie. She used to lace his boots for him, and on special occasions dressed him up in the velvet suit he had brought with him from America. But soon she too, like her sister and her brother, had to go to America. So she laced Eddie's boots for the last time, warned him he would have to do it for himself in future and departed from Bruree station. Grandmother and child waved her goodbye, tearfully.

America must have seemed no further away than Dublin to a child in Bruree, for the next year there was another arrival off the boat from New York. It was Kate de Valera home for a visit. There were a few glorious weeks and a trip to Limerick and then she went back again. Soon after her return she married Charles Wheelwright—Uncle Charlie to her son.

By now, 1888, Eddie was old enough for school. Earlier efforts to send him had failed; it was difficult to find a companion to take him to Bruree and back. But now he was six and could walk the mile or so by himself. His first day at the National School was May 7th. The teacher was a dapper little man who dressed as befitted 'the master' in an Irish rural community. He was elderly and walked about with his head stuck in the air. His name was John Kelly; he wished de Valera's was as easy. But Uncle Pat wrote it in the boy's exercise books, which resolved the difficulty.

To the boys at school, John Daly, Tim Hannon, Paddy Horgan, Paddy Ruddle, he was Eddie Coll. So there was no difficulty over the name de Valera here. It was Uncle Pat's name that was the problem. He had to compete with 'Big Pat', 'Black Pat' and 'Foxy Pat' who all lived round about. But when the boys took to calling him 'the Dane Coll' it was too much. Related to the Norse invaders who had ravaged Ireland? Never. De Valera fought many a battle by the pump at the Bruree crossroads. The loose stones which filled the pot-holes were telling ammunition. Later de Valera heard that the name 'Dane Coll' (Dean) was bestowed upon his grandfather by some local wags because he used to give out the rosary in chapel. Or was it because his grandfather Coll was the nephew of Dean Coll of Newcastle West?

The rural village of Bruree was still a very self-sufficient community. The railway had opened it up to industrial goods but it still had its fascinating craftsmen. The most interesting of the houses in the village were the forge and the cooper's yard, producing an endless supply of firkins and barrels. There were three bootmakers, though Connors was only for fine boots, and there was Rourkes further down where a big blackbird was being trained to whistle 'Harvey Duff'. Then of course the barracks where Sneider carbines and bayonets hung forbiddingly, but beautifully polished.

The barracks was by no means a popular place. De Valera's first political memory is of the attitude towards the police after three people had been shot in Mitchelstown in 1887. The issue came nearer home. In order to extend his meagre grazing area, Uncle Pat allowed his cattle on to 'the long acre', the grass at either side of the road. One of Eddie's jobs was to keep a look-out for the police.

Politics ranged round the national issues in the 1880s. The Parnell split had not yet embittered feelings and de Valera remembers his joy at hearing his uncle announce to his grandmother that Parnell's name was cleared and later that the forger Pigott had shot himself. The walls of the loft were covered with political cartoons from the *Weekly Freeman*. Soon there would be a new one to record the discomfiture of the *Times* and of the Tories, both of whom had believed the worst of Parnell.

Uncle Pat's politics spread beyond the national issues to other problems. He became a member of the Land and Labour League, the first organisation of rural workers, and was for a time on the Kilmallock board of poor law guardians.

One land dispute made a deep impression on Eddie, though not in precisely a political sense. A local landowner and horse-breeder John Gubbins was to be boycotted, i.e. ostracized. Eddie, in petticoats, watched from an upstairs window as the people assembled in the village. On a wagonette the Fedamore brass band had left the biggest drum he had ever seen. De Valera never forgot the pomp and glory which that drum represented for him.

Bruree village church was a centre of much excitement, for the parish priest was Father Eugene Sheehy whose support of the Land League had earlier landed him in prison. The well-to-do in the galleries or pews and the poor standing or kneeling on the tiled floor listened to a variety of fiery sermons.

Occasionally on St Munchin's Day, a parish holiday, he delivered his most famous sermons based on local Bruree history. Little de Valera sat with the other servers on the side steps of the altar drinking in every historic detail. Father Sheehy, eyes closed and long nose reaching his lips, retailed the golden exploits of bygone days, as if in ecstasy. By the time he checked his gold watch for the last time, Bruree seemed not only the capital of Limerick but of Munster and of Ireland. Who knows what seeds of patriotism he sowed?

For eight years Eddie walked the mile or so to Bruree, carrying with him a couple of quarts of milk for customers in the village. He had many jobs to do round the house, and with the cows, particularly after his grandmother's death in 1895, and also with neighbouring farmers in the summer time. Years later he claimed that the only farm work which he did not learn while growing up was how to handle a plough.

Partly because of these duties Eddie's attendance at school was never very regular. In class II he was present on thirty-six fewer days than the most regular boy. In his last year, as his home tasks became heavier, he was away even more often. Nevertheless, he was always passed for promotion each year. One year he rose from his bed of measles to be there when the inspector held the examination and drew up the promotion list.

Uncle Pat was quite severe with his nephew; he disapproved of wasting time with such games as hurling. He thrashed Eddie when he went 'on the slinge' (played truant) or, as he did once, used the donkey's Sunday pair of reins to make a swing. But Eddie's pleasures were not all stolen. The race-meeting at Athlacca with its 'thimble riggers', 'three-card tricksters', the man in the barrel who kept bobbing his head up and down while people tried to hit him with a thrown wattle, 'pigs crubeens', more sweets and cakes and, of course, the races themselves—all this was top entertainment.

At school, teacher succeeded teacher, although three of the four were from the Kelly family. They were helped by an assistant and 'monitors', boys who had just left school and hoped to become teachers themselves later. Uncle Pat occasionally sent Eddie's writing exercise books to his mother in America. In these hand-writing books he assiduously copied out such bald statements as that 'Queen Victoria was born on 24th May, 1819',[1] He had to depend on Father Sheehy's sermons for his Irish history. In 1892 he received his first communion and two years later was confirmed by the Bishop of Limerick, Dr Edward Thomas O'Dwyer. Soon the question of Eddie's future arose. Uncle Pat, who was a determined man, felt that he should become a school monitor. But de Valera thought this a dead end unless he had enough money to pay for his teacher's training later. The return of Aunt Hannie to nurse her mother had given him some support. After she went back to America again they continued to correspond. In the spring of 1896 he wrote her a firm letter.[2]

Would she persuade his mother to arrange for him to come to America? Bruree could never satisfy him. His closest friend had moved out of the neighbourhood and his uncle was about to get married. In fact this last development should have been good news for de Valera as he did most of their bachelor housekeeping; he even cooked his uncle's wedding breakfast. Nevertheless ahead of him was the life of a monitor or a farm labourer. Neither was at all attractive.

But there was a third plan which he tried to persuade his uncle to accept. Paddy Shea, who was a few years older than de Valera, and had been at the National School in Bruree with him, had gone to the Christian Brothers School in Charleville and had won a junior grade exhibition which paid for his further education at St Munchin's College, Limerick. Could he not do the same? But he forgot that Paddy Shea lived about three miles nearer to Charleville than Knockmore and there was no suitable transport; the Colls could not even afford a bicycle. At length Uncle Pat agreed to the scheme since de Valera was willing to walk the seven miles there when necessary.

De Valera started at the school on November 2nd, 1896, despite an unfortunate interview with the head brother at which Uncle Pat protested his nephew's ability to do arithmetic, algebra and geometry, but de Valera failed to give to the brother correctly the factors of a^3-b^3. At Charleville he took Latin and Greek; arithmetic, geometry and algebra; and English and French. No history. He progressed quickly and was allowed to take the junior grade examination the following June. Though it was considered a trial attempt, he passed with honours but was young enough to take it again the next year. Often on the long walk home from Knockmore he would rest exhausted against a fence, longing to throw away the heavy pile of school books. But he persisted as so often later in life.

One day, as he and another boy were leaving the town to walk home, a race-horse passed them being ridden by a tipsy rider. It looked as if he might fall off but there was nothing they could do. Further down the road they found he had been stopped by the aforementioned horse-breeder John Gubbins who asked de Valera to take the rider's place. Gubbins later owned two horses that won the Derby. Thus originated the story that de Valera had ridden Galtymore, one of the two. In fact it was neither.

In 1898 he sat for the junior grade a second time and got honours in all his subjects. He also won his main objective—an exhibition of twenty pounds a year retainable for three years. This meant he was likely to secure a place in a college although the £20 might not cover the full fee. Although not accepted at St Munchin's or Mungret Colleges, he was accepted at Blackrock College, Dublin. Now sixteen years old, de Valera considered becoming a priest. But the President of the College, Father Larry Healy, advised him to go as a lay boarder first. Later, if he still wanted to, he could join the scholastics—that is, those intended for the priesthood.

De Valera left by train from Kilmallock station in September with a little tin trunk bought by Uncle Pat and a new sixteen-shilling suit. Destination Dublin. Blackrock was slightly outside the city and everything was strange to the country-bred boy. He travelled partly by horse tram, partly by electric tram and partly on foot. He crossed over O'Connell Bridge and saw the beautiful Merrion Square. He could hardly guess that these same streets would later be for him a field of battle.

Blackrock was not America but was still a new world. De Valera was happy that the seven-mile walk was over. He was amazed by the boys who cried at night from loneliness. He was determined to work hard and get a better place in the middle grade than he had in the junior grade.

The school was run on a strict routine. Up at six thirty, down to the study hall for half an hour, then mass followed by breakfast and a short recreation, then class work, meal, recreation, class work, meal, recreation, plus four or five hours in the study hall outside class hours. De Valera did not find the work easy. At first he found difficulty adapting himself to the new grammar textbooks, then he became terribly burdened by the number of Latin exercises. At one time he even considered giving up and leaving the college altogether. Luckily he quickly became fascinated by mathematics in which subject the teaching was particularly good.

Elocution lessons were included in the school curriculum. Junior and senior boys collected together in the study hall one hour each week and de Valera was astounded by the whole performance. A boy stood up and recited with extraordinary clarity and repressed energy a piece from 'Bell's Elocutionist'. As he reached the climax and declaimed 'I am not mad' at the top of his voice, de Valera wondered whom he was trying to convince. But he laughed too soon. The following week, he himself was called out to recite. At first he could think of no piece of any kind. On being pressed by the teacher, however, he remembered some lines from his old 6th book on 'The Downfall of Poland' by Thomas Campbell. He stood up, shut his eyes tightly and began: 'O sacred truth that triumphed ceased a while . . .' and concluded:

> Warsaw's last champion from her height surveyed,
> Wide o'er the fields, a waste of ruin laid,—
> 'O Heaven!', he cried, 'my bleeding country save!—
> Is there no hand on high to shield the brave?

Yet though destruction sweep those lovely plains,
Rise, fellow-men! Our country yet remains!
By that dread name, we wave the sword on high
And swear for her to live!—with her to die!'

De Valera as he finished relaxed from the rigid position he had held throughout the recitation and opened his eyes. The elocution teacher turned to the class and said jokingly, 'I didn't think we had an O'Connell here'. A truer word than he knew.

In his first year de Valera worked hard and was rewarded by coming out top in the college from the middle grade examinations with honours in all his subjects. He had eighth place in Ireland and a new scholarship worth thirty pounds a year for two years. He had won no medals for first place in any individual subject but he had the best aggregate of marks in the middle grade in the college.

Success brought duties and privileges—the sort common to any Catholic education. He read the morning and night prayers, led the rosary and read in the refectory during the annual spiritual retreat. One glorious lunchtime he found a passage from St Alphonsus on death including a long and detailed description of a corpse devoured by worms. As the boys choked over their food he dwelt lovingly on every detail.

The following year he took the senior grade examination but this time was disappointed in the results. He won no new exhibition. Among those whom he was beaten by was John d'Alton, later Cardinal Archbishop of Armagh. That Christmas de Valera had described him in a letter to his half-brother as 'a very holy and intelligent boy and a great friend of mine'. He wrote to this half-brother, Tom Wheelwright, with a sort of paternal affection although he had never met him.

The next stage in his career was university. Luckily the continuance of his old exhibition made it possible for him to go to University College, Blackrock. But in those days the path of a devout Catholic seeking higher education was far from easy. On the one hand Trinity College, Dublin, was almost exclusively a Protestant institution. On the other, the Royal University of Ireland, the alternative choice, was a purely examining body. The examining professors were all from the Queen's Colleges, which, because of their non-denominational charters, were dubbed 'Godless Colleges'. Catholic colleges, such as Blackrock, were severely handicapped, taking the same examination but with none of their teachers examining.

Hard work, it was hoped, could overcome any disadvantages. A time-table he jotted on the back of a sports programme[3] is perhaps slightly optimistic:

5.45	Rising
6–7½	Euclid
8–11½	Algeb[ra] 2 hrs (–10½) Euclid 1 hr.
12–2½	Conics
5–7	Nat[ural] Philos[ophy]
7–10½	Trig. and theory of equations

By this time he had realised that mathematics was his strongest subject although he always loved the classics. He took the honours matriculation in mathematics, obtaining second-class honours. He obtained a place and won a new £24 exhibition. This meant that his position was once more financially adequate.

De Valera's politics as he reached the age of twenty were hardly radical. He was a committee member of the College debating society and spoke often. On the motion 'That the policy of free trade is preferable to protection' he did not feel strongly one way or the other, or, as the minutes put it, 'was in favour of a little of both'. But on the motion 'That a constitutional monarchy as a form of government is preferable to republicanism' he was frankly committed. He maintained 'that constant elections disturb a nation and are thus not conducive to the prosperity of the people'. With the French Revolution in mind, which he had attacked in an earlier debate, he held that no rule could be more tyrannical than majority rule.

De Valera put most work into a speech on the Irish University question.[4] He proposed that Dublin University should no longer be confined to Trinity College and that two other University Colleges, one Presbyterian and one Catholic, should be established in the city. He also argued that the clergy badly needed a university education. A priest who spoke to the paper pointedly observed that he did not know that they had a 'Frankeen Hugh O'Donnell in their midst'. O'Donnell was a Nationalist M.P. whose views on education were at variance with those of his fellow Catholics. But de Valera's argument was a well worked out argument, built on a considerable basis of research.

Sport did not figure largely in his life at University College. Yet he was an athletic youth who used to run round the playing-fields in the early morning and drink a glass of milk before getting down to work. He missed his great chance of athletic fame through an excess of humanity, or perhaps just a lack of sporting ambition, although he does not tell the story by any means in his own favour.

He had won the mile race and was going strong in the half-mile for the President's cup, but whenever he tried to pass the front runner on the right or on the left, the latter kept using his elbows to block him. De Valera gritted his teeth: 'I will break his heart', he said to himself, and at that moment the leader crashed to the ground unconscious. The spectators were flabbergasted. De Valera stopped dead and went back to help him. He, of course, lost the race. There was a curious sequel. Soon afterwards he found himself opposite the same opponent at rugger. Again this young man used his elbows all too vigorously. This time de Valera reacted remorselessly. 'I hopped on him,' he used to say, 'knees and all'.

Although the years at Blackrock did not make de Valera a priest, they further strengthened his religious convictions. He especially respected the priests for their work in African missions in a climate which was then considered almost fatal. He took part in the regular religious exercises and the annual retreats; he was enrolled into such sodalities as the Children of Mary.

He was also secretary and then president of the College branch of The St Vincent de Paul Society, just then established as the first college branch in Ireland. The society was devoted to visiting and assisting the poor of the parish. This brought de Valera into direct contact with the problems of city life—pain and suffering such as he had never dreamt of.

His charitable work had one rather unfortunate effect on him. During one visit he came in contact with a smallpox suspect and consequently had to be vaccinated. As a result he was so ill that it made him a lifelong enemy of vaccination.

Meanwhile examinations continued. In 1902 de Valera took his first arts examination and got second-class honours in mathematics and a second-class exhibition of £15. He also won a much sought-after scholarship from the Royal University, worth £20 for three years. The following year he again got second-class honours and a further exhibition of £18.

Although these exhibitions were insufficient to meet the full College fee, de Valera was allowed to continue at Blackrock. He decided, however, to make up the difference by teaching without payment. He made an excellent start. Two pupils were helped by him through all subjects in the solicitor's preliminary examinations. (They showed their appreciation by presenting him with a ticket for the Rugby International—between England and Wales!) A year or two later he was excited to hear of a teaching vacancy in Rockwell College, near Cashel, which was, like Blackrock, owned by the Holy Ghost Fathers. So after a summer holiday in Bruree, at the age of twenty-one de Valera set off for his first full-time job. It certainly seemed that teaching was to be his life's vocation.

YOUTH

1903-1913

A good name had preceded him to Rockwell. The President, Father Nicholas Brennan, C.S.Sp., had been impressed by reports from Blackrock and appointed him professor of mathematics for senior classes. Most of the staff were priests of the order; there were few lay professors there. Among them, however, was a man who was to become one of de Valera's closest friends: Jack Barrett. De Valera intended to continue his studies for the degree of the Royal University of Ireland, but in the rural surroundings of Rockwell he found many distractions. His pupils were more interested in his athletic ability than in his academic distinctions.

He rapidly won their approbation when he gained his place in the combined Rugby team of masters and boys. The famous internationals Mick and Jack Ryan were members of the team. With Jack Barrett he helped to form a three-quarter combination which helped Rockwell to the final in the Munster cup and earned for him a place in a Munster trial for the inter-provincial team. It is possible that he came closer to an Irish cap than was realised at the time. Ireland was looking for a full-back and de Valera was tried out of his usual place in that position. His opposite number later played full-back for Ireland for several years. But de Valera's great chance eluded him. A high kick came his way with the field spread-eagled. If he could have caught it, he would almost certainly have scored a spectacular try. But it bounced off his chest and the opportunity did not return.

Looking back, he realised that this was the first indication of defective eyesight. A little later he found himself unable to read the blackboard clearly and took to glasses, which he always wore subsequently. He was nonetheless for many years an excellent shot and an omnivorous student. It was much later that he had serious trouble with his eyes.

Admiring schoolboys circulated a pleasant story that everything he did was governed by mathematical calculations. Once, when he missed a free kick at goal, it was ascribed to false trigonometrical calculations. It is true of his Rugby, as of everything else in which he engaged, that he committed himself totally. The local shoemaker, Jim Griffin, reported that de Valera visited him every other day with his football boots asking him to put a little bit of leather here and another bit there 'to balance the pressure'.[1]

On going to Rockwell he still was not twenty-one years old. But prowess on the football field gave him status in the College beyond his years. In Rockwell and in the nearby town of Cashel, de Valera made many friends. It was a fellow teacher called O'Donnell who was the first to contract de Valera's name to 'Dev', a form which has stuck to him throughout his life. They were a happy couple of years to which de Valera always looks back with pleasant memories. But he did not succeed in giving the time which he had hoped to his mathematical studies. He had to work for his university examination without the help of expert tuition and, in 1904, he was disappointed when he only obtained a pass degree. He felt he was likely to stagnate if he remained in Rockwell. In the summer of 1905 he reluctantly left and returned once more to Dublin to seek another post. One interview for a teaching position took him to Liverpool, but after one look round he returned the very next day, determined to accept whatever post he could obtain in Ireland.

Eventually he became a member of the staff of the Jesuit college of Belvedere on the north side of the city, soon becoming immersed in highly varied activities. McHardy-Flint, an elocution teacher at a number of Dublin schools, and his wife had written an old-fashioned domestic drama called *A Christmas Hamper* and planned to stage it at the Abbey Theatre. The actor who was supposed to play the part of a doctor fell ill and McHardy-Flint appealed to de Valera to help him out of the difficulty. So de Valera appeared on the stage. The indomitable first-nighter, Joseph Holloway, noted in his diary that 'the tall thin appearance of Mr E. de Valera as he made his entrance as Dr Kelly at the end of Act II caused many to laugh', although he did allow that 'he fitted in better at the death scene'.[2] The *Irish Times* critic was more lenient. He mentioned that de Valera acted capably. De Valera himself was far from satisfied with his histrionic ability, though he knew that two short rehearsals in McHardy-Flint's drawing-room and no dress rehearsal at all made his performance scarcely a fair test. The experience killed any budding notions of a stage career he might have possessed.

Towards the end of the school year de Valera learned of the vacancy for a professor of mathematics in the Training College of Our Lady of Mercy, Carysfort, Blackrock; the college was in the charge of nuns of the Order of Mercy. It was recognised by the Board of Education for the training of young women teachers for primary schools. He applied for the position, was appointed and began work in September, 1906.

De Valera's interest in rugby had not waned. From the time of his return to Dublin he became a member of the Blackrock College Rugby

Football Club. He was called on occasionally as a three-quarter in the senior team, but for the most part he played with the second fifteen, which he captained in 1908. In the same year he was secretary of the club. The following year appears to have been the last in which he played football. At his last practice his companions learnt that he intended to marry.

In Carysfort the young professor found the young women, training to be teachers, a new sort of challenge. Their course was a two-year one and the subjects in which he was supposed to lecture them were arithmetic and mensuration. He was assiduous in preparing his lectures and found the actual lecturing was a pleasure. The girls were as quick and as intelligent as boys. He was, however, highly critical of the way they were taught. Mathematics, he believed, led to precise and accurate modes of thought and enabled a person to apply analytical methods to the problems of everyday life. He found himself sorely hampered. He knew that examinations were a necessary evil, but he could see all too clearly how they restricted him as a professor. If he strayed in his lectures into an aside, he felt immediately the anxiety of the class. Had this or hadn't it a value in examination terms?

He was strongly of the opinion that unless the students in the training college were given a genuine understanding of their subject, they could not be expected to teach it properly. They were being made mechanical teachers of mechanical methods; for this he largely blamed the inspectors of schools. They carried out the examination of the training college students; and Professor de Valera, sitting in at the oral examinations, inwardly railed at the system.

He was far too original in his approach to care for the existing text-books. He often wished that some first-class mathematician would find time, in the interval of his higher researches, to write a textbook on elementary arithmetic. To aid his pupils, and as a companion to his lectures, he himself prepared a book made up of notes and also problems arranged to illustrate the topics with which he dealt.[3] These were privately printed for the use of his students in 1907, but the limited edition soon went out of print and he found that, because of a misunderstanding, the printers had distributed the type.

The young professor made every effort to advance his own knowledge. The foundations of his mathematical knowledge had been laid in his degree course but, after his return to Dublin in 1905, he continued to study. He attended mathematical lectures by Professors H. C. McWeeney and A. W. Conway of the newly-founded University College, Dublin. From 1906 to 1908 he attended the course of Edmund T. Whittaker, Professor of Astronomy at Trinity College, Dublin, and Royal Astronomer

of Ireland, on spectroscopy, astro-physics and electro-optics; later he
attended lectures on metaphysics. He was intrigued by certain mathematical difficulties for which he felt there might be a metaphysical
explanation.

Before the founding of the National University of Ireland in 1909,
de Valera gave lectures for the Royal University first and second arts
examinations in mathematics, mathematical physics and experimental
physics in the Dominican College, Eccles Street, Loreto College, St
Stephen's Green, Holy Cross College, Clonliffe, and in the Catholic
University College, St Stephen's Green. Because of the demands of this
work he had to cut down on some of his classes. He decided to discontinue
teaching experimental physics as he felt that he had too little laboratory
experience to teach it well. Nevertheless he was continually in a hurry,
cycling from one college to another. This perhaps explains how he cycled
into a gate which he found unexpectedly closed across the avenue of
Clonliffe one night. He somersaulted the gate and landed on his hands at
the other side with his toes on the gate.

With the establishment of the National University his lectures in these
colleges ceased. He supplemented his income from his position in the
training college by acting as an examiner in mathematics at the intermediate board examinations and as an assistant examiner in the National
University. Secondary school teachers at that time had no pension rights,
no security and an average salary of £82 6s. 7d. a year. In these circumstances the Association of Secondary Teachers of Ireland was formed.
De Valera joined it. The post in the training college was not, strictly
speaking, that of a secondary teacher but was closely analogous to it. He
took an active interest in the work of the association. He participated in
public meetings organised to protest at the salaries and conditions of the
teachers.

By now he was able to submit impressive testimonials from the heads
of the colleges in which he had taught and from professors under whom
he had studied. He was disappointed, however, on the two occasions when
he applied for professorships in the constituent colleges of the National
University. He was a candidate for the chair of mathematics in University
College, Galway, in April, 1912, but withdrew, and was a candidate for
the chair of mathematical physics in University College, Cork, twelve
months later. But in St Patrick's College, Maynooth, an associate college
of the National University, he got a part-time and temporary appointment
as lecturer in mathematics and mathematical physics in October of 1912.[4]
This association with Maynooth was to be of great value to him in
subsequent years. On the staff there he met young priests who were later

to become members of the Irish hierarchy. Notable among them was the future Cardinal Archbishop of Armagh, Dr Joseph MacRory.

But at this time mathematics and mathematical physics were far from monopolising his energies or aspirations. A new passion, uniting mind and heart, had grown up alongside. At Bruree he had heard the old people, including his grandmother, converse in Irish but its use was rapidly declining. Neither his uncle, Pat Coll, nor he himself learned more than the words and phrases which survived among the English speakers of their own ages. When, in 1896, Father Eugene O'Growney's Irish lessons began to appear in the *Weekly Freeman*, Pat Coll and his nephew thought that they would study them week by week. The uncle's enthusiasm did not last beyond the first lesson and de Valera was unable to continue the studies alone. From then on, however, he was inspired with an interest in the native language. The Gaelic League, which had been founded three years before, had already begun to awaken a new interest in the cultural past and had instigated an effort to stem the decline in the use of Irish. By 1908 de Valera had begun to regret that he had not been able to take advantage of the opportunity of attending Irish classes in Blackrock. In that year he joined the Central Branch, or Ard-Chraobh, of the Gaelic League.

In the fifteen years of the league's existence the movement for the revival of Irish had gone from strength to strength. Pressure on the National Board of Education and on other educational bodies to find a proper place for Irish in the curriculum was increasing. Professor de Valera agreed with this outlook and felt that, in the training college at Carysfort, Irish should be taught to the future teachers of the country. He was determined that he himself must be proficient in the language.

Among his teachers was a young woman, Sinéad Flanagan. She was about four years older than he and a primary school teacher. For a number of years she had devoted most of her spare time to studying and teaching Irish. In 1907 she had won the gold medal in the Oireachtas teaching competition. Soon he found that he was numbered among her many admirers. He studied diligently and, in the summer of 1909, he passed the intermediate examinations in Irish of the Leinster College. He decided to spend his summer holidays at Tourmakeady, an Irish-speaking district between the western shore of Lough Mask and the Partry mountains in County Mayo. From here he cycled to Spiddal, Co. Galway, for the unveiling of a memorial plaque to Micheál Breathnach, the Irish teacher and writer. He was accompanied by Liam Ó Briain and Pádraig Ó Domhnalláin. They ran into a tremendous thunderstorm. Drenched to the skin they called on an unofficial distiller in the district who gave them a drink of poteen and goat's milk as an antidote to the chill which it appeared certain they would get from the wetting. Later on they collected a bottle or so to take back to friends, though the old lady of the house was somewhat reluctant to sell it, as she had already spent a month in prison for selling illicit spirits. Perhaps it was the extra risk with strangers which made her prices higher than usual, though when Ó Domhnalláin protested she gave the excuse that it was because of Lloyd George's budget!

It was no accident that de Valera chose to spend his holidays in Tourmakeady, for Sinéad Flanagan had been associated with it for some years and was attending the Irish College there in 1909. They were already engaged and, some months after their return to Dublin, on January 8th, 1910, he and Sinéad Flanagan were married in St Paul's Church, Arran Quay, Dublin. Both wished the ceremony to be performed in Irish and, since the priest did not know the language, de Valera insisted on teaching him the sentences necessary. These seemed on the short side, and the anxious bridegroom, a day or two before the wedding, decided to compare them with a ritual in Gill's shop in O'Connell Street. Down he cycled on a new bicycle, complete with all the latest gadgets including gears and chain guard. He had bought it a day or so before and parked it carefully in a hallway at Gill's. He spent too long, however, comparing the Irish and English rituals for, when he came out, his bicycle had been stolen.

This marriage proved the happiest of partnerships. Through long years of trouble and struggle, the enduring patience and understanding of Mrs de Valera played an immense part in the life of her husband. She was a born teacher with a wonderful love for children and for her home. Her husband's duties in office or out of office were for him alone. She did not interfere. Her duties were to her family and she did all in her power to free her husband from domestic anxieties. Although she had taken a leading part in Gaelic League activities before her marriage she always avoided the limelight. In her own unassuming way she played her part for Ireland far more effectively than those who were prominently before the public. The charm of her youth stayed with her through life and was still captivating men who met her over fifty years after she married. The late President Kennedy's gesture as he left Dublin Airport in 1963, when he had said farewell to all his Irish friends, was to give a special hug to Mrs de Valera. He showed that he too had come under her spell.

Eamon de Valera was still not well known, even in Gaelic League circles, at the time of his wedding. In fact the organisation's paper in referring to that event did not give his Christian name and gave his surname as 'Devalaro'. He continued his Irish studies throughout the year at the Leinster College, gaining first place for the teaching diploma in Irish, and at the same time he attended lectures by Professor Corcoran for the Irish diploma in teaching at the Royal University, which he was awarded the following autumn. Having completed these formal courses, de Valera began to take a larger part in the activities of the Gaelic League, especially in its educational aspects. He recognised that its founders, Douglas Hyde, Eoin MacNeill and others, were attempting to revive the Irish language so as 'first to go back to that point at which the nation was forced to wander, to make our own the ideals of our forefathers as embodied in their language, that imbued with a true Celtic spirit we might advance in that faith as they would have advanced'.[5]

On the committee of the Ard-Chraobh, to which he was elected in 1910, he supported a suggestion that the branch establish a history society to foster the study of Irish history which found little place in the curricula for public examinations. His idea was that a number of members of the branch would meet and arrange between themselves to write a series of papers on incidents in history. De Valera agreed to prepare one of these supposedly informal papers but, to his horror, found himself billed to give one of the public lectures arranged by the Ard-Chraobh, normally given by experts and specialists. The professor of mathematics felt deeply embarrassed as he set out to deliver his lecture with the formal title, as given in the *Claidheamh Solais* that morning of 'A study in early Irish history'. Apologetically he explained to the audience what had happened. He had never read an ancient text in his life, was ignorant of both philology and archaeology, and was on the rostrum through his own ignorance of the subject which he had hoped to rectify in forming a private discussion group. He went on, however, to give an interesting discourse on a scientific approach to the study of history.[6]

The following summer de Valera was chosen as one of the delegates from the Ard-Chraobh to the annual convention or Ard Fheis of the Gaelic League and his name was put forward for membership of the executive committee. At that time, however, the secret militant national organisation, the Irish Republican Brotherhood, which had existed since Fenian times a generation before, was eager to gain a footing in the Gaelic League. The influence of this body was thrown behind selected candidates for the executive committee and, when de Valera was defeated, he felt that a hidden hand was responsible. He did not realise that the IRB even existed but sensed instinctively that the elections had been managed by a small group. He wrongly blamed Sinn Féin, the political organisation which had been founded by Arthur Griffith in 1905 with a more independent national policy than the Irish parliamentary party, and vowed that he would never have anything to do with it. He continued to represent the Ard-Chraobh at subsequent conventions but never again let his name go forward for election to the executive.

About this time Ernest R. McClintock Dix, a Dublin solicitor and well-known bibliophile, approached de Valera to take charge of an Irish language summer school in Tawin, an Irish-speaking district, near Galway. De Valera, though he had got the highest certificate for his ability to teach Irish from the Leinster College, did not feel competent but, when pressed, agreed to direct the school provided he had native speakers to help him in the oral teaching. For three years de Valera was director of the summer school at Tawin, an island off the eastern coast of Galway Bay joined to the mainland by a bridge. In an advertisement for the school among the island's attractions was noted: 'It has neither public houses nor policemen and requires neither'. To the abstemious and nationally-minded de Valera these were attractions indeed, and there he brought his wife and infant son, Vivion, then seven or eight months old, in August, 1911.

On the opening of the summer school at Tawin in 1912, Roger Casement, who was patron of it and of most of the colleges of Irish, paid it a visit. He was much impressed by the director and, after he left, sent him five pounds as a contribution towards prizes at a sports meeting to be held at the end of the school course. He insisted in his letter 'that all competitions be in Irish not English—the judgments in Irish—and so far as practicable the prizes of Irish make'.[7] In general, de Valera looked after the organisation of the school and saw that there was entertainment as well as study.

After 1913 de Valera, because of other commitments, gave less time to Gaelic League activities though he attended the annual Ard Fheis in Killarney in 1914 and that in Dundalk in 1915. The Dundalk Ard Fheis was an important one which changed substantially the character of the Gaelic League since, through IRB pressure, a resolution was now passed abolishing the rule that the Gaelic League be non-political. While the resolution was not a personal one aimed at Douglas Hyde, he refused to continue as president of the league in the changed circumstances. De Valera was very reluctant to see Hyde resign, though he considered MacNeill, who was elected in his place, a more effective chairman. De Valera was in favour of the change in the rules. He felt that it lent essential solidarity to the whole national emergence. By this time, as will be seen, he was an ardent Volunteer.

Inspired originally by the Gaelic League, like many another at that time, he had advanced by 1915 far in thought and action. The resolution at Dundalk helped to identify the Gaelic League with the national movement and linked together the joint aims of a free and of a Gaelic Ireland.

THE IRISH VOLUNTEERS

1913-1916

But we must return to 1913. A Home Rule Bill conferring very limited powers on a parliament for the whole of Ireland had passed through the British Parliament by the beginning of the year. The House of Lords rejected it by ten to one and it could not pass into law until the summer of 1914. This year (1913) was to see a relentless movement towards planned military resistance among the Ulster Protestants. Armed parades and drilling became ever more widespread and blatant. A provisional government was set up in the North with a military committee attached. These events affected de Valera profoundly.

Up to this point, though so active in the Irish language revival, he had taken no part in politics. He knew of Sinn Féin which, under Arthur Griffith, was seeking to educate the Irish people in a philosophy of self-reliance. It drew its method from the Hungarian example of passive resistance and its goal, a dual monarchy with England, from the same source. De Valera, however, left politics to the Irish Parliamentary Party. In general he supported John Redmond and his fellow members of parliament in their parliamentary approach and their piecemeal approach to Irish freedom. The events of 1912 and 1913, however, turned his mind to political problems and, at the same time, to much more drastic solutions.

The founding of the Ulster Volunteers and the support which they received from the English Conservative Party convinced him that home rule would be won 'not by ballots but by bullets'. He had read somewhere a statement made in 1833 by Macaulay:

The repeal of the Union we regard as fatal to the Empire, and we will never consent to it—never, though the country should be surrounded by dangers . . . never till all has been staked and lost, never till the four quarters of the world have been convulsed by the last struggle of the great English people for their place among the nations.

He became convinced that Ireland would not win any measure of self-government without a show of force. It is noticeable that here, as with so many later decisions, he did not need to be indoctrinated. He reached his conclusion on his own.

An article, destined to become famous, by Eoin MacNeill in the Gaelic League paper, *An Claidheamh Solais*, at the beginning of November, 1913, brought the possibility of an Irish armed force to de Valera's attention.

He saw the announcement of a public meeting to be held in the Rotunda Rink in Dublin to found a volunteer force. On Thursday evening, November 25th, 1913, he went to that meeting and, when he entered the hall and took his seat, he found, to his surprise, sitting directly in front of him, his former parish priest, Father Eugene Sheehy of Bruree, and with him Larry Roche, noted hurler and athlete from that parish. He was reluctant to intrude on them. The future President of the Irish Republic took his seat alone.

The Irish Volunteers were, on the face of it, completely independent. They owed much to the stirring of national consciousness by Sinn Féin, the Gaelic League, the Gaelic Athletic Association and, it may fairly be argued, the Irish literary revival. Unknown, however, to most of the force the majority of its inspirers and founders were members of the Irish Republican Brotherhood. The IRB was secret, oathbound, republican or nothing, with physical force and an armed rising an essential part of their creed. There was much interweaving and overlapping between these various bodies. Michael Collins' biographer, Piaras Béaslaí, records that Collins, then a young clerk in London, had joined all of them by 1914. By 1915 plans for a rising were to be jointly concerted with James Connolly, Leader of the Irish Transport and General Workers' Union and his Citizen Army. Connolly himself attended meetings of the IRB.

Eamon de Valera, some fifty years later, offered his own analysis. He considered that three main currents of thought led to the foundation of the Irish Volunteers. There were those who saw the nation being robbed of the fruits of years of patient constitutional endeavour by an arrogant defiance of the constitution. There were others who looked on this as an opportunity to repair the error of the late eighteenth century when the volunteers of that era were allowed to lapse. Finally, there were those who thought that the occasion should be seized to form a force which would be ready at any time to strike another blow for Irish freedom.

These currents intermingled in de Valera's own mind and inspired his attendance on that night. He had still no clear-cut commitment to any solution for Ireland beyond a full measure of Home Rule. He listened to the speeches of MacNeill, Patrick Pearse and young Michael Davitt. He scarcely heard what Laurence J. Kettle had to say, owing to vociferous Labour supporters who accused Kettle's brother of employing 'scabs' on his farm in north county Dublin. The great strike was nearly three months old at this stage and a party of hurlers who appeared in front of the platform to protect Kettle could do little to quell the organised tumult of angry strikers.

During the meeting enrolment forms were issued to those present and de Valera was profoundly troubled by the decision with which he was faced. He was a married man with a wife and children and was fully sensible of his responsibilities. His third child, Éamonn, had been born only six weeks before, while the eldest, Vivion, was not yet three years of age. The movement being launched was one which, to his mind, could end only in armed conflict. He came to the conclusion, however, that all the able-bodied men in Ireland would be necessary to make any struggle successful. The unmarried men alone would not be sufficient. He filled in the form with some misgivings and so took the irrevocable step. On Saturday evening, December 6th, the Volunteers of Rathmines and Pembroke districts met for the first time.

From the time de Valera enrolled he was an enthusiastic and whole-hearted Volunteer. Not only did he attend his weekly drill meetings regularly; he also went to the voluntary Saturday afternoon exercises in Larkfield, at Kimmage. These were open to all Volunteers and were specially designed for picked men who would become future NCOs. Under Sergeant-Major Merry of the British Army, Volunteers from all over the city gathered to do more advanced exercises in company and battalion drill. 'Selected men' also attended special lectures on military theory on Wednesday nights. De Valera was little known when he joined. His name as written on the membership card issued to him was in a mangled form, 'Emin Dilvara'. He paid his threepence weekly like the rest of the recruits, but soon his diligence began to bring him to a more important position. He was first promoted to be squad leader, that is something like corporal, in charge of twelve men, and then a section commander, or sergeant, in charge of two such squads. Later he was elected a second lieutenant.

When the Donnybrook company was formed, he was elected captain of the company and had, as his first and second lieutenants, a tram driver, who was a former British guardsman, and a solicitor. De Valera was in charge of recruitment, of collecting subscriptions and of arranging for instruction in drill. The drill was based on that set out in British army manuals and there were difficulties in making it simple for part-time soldiers. De Valera wrote, on request, during 1915 a manual of drill suitable for the Volunteers. He urged, however, that as a rising was imminent, the top priority should be given to training in the use of weapons.

It was in keeping with his enthusiasm that de Valera should strive at an early stage to equip himself properly as a soldier. When the design of the uniform of the Irish Volunteers was decided on in the first half of 1914, he bought one. He also bought, for £5, a Mauser carbine from the O'Rahilly. A military force without arms was, of course, completely useless and it is not surprising that efforts were made to supply the deficiency. Liam Mellows, Joseph M. Plunkett and de Valera, as early as March, 1914, co-operated in storing and distributing some gelignite taken from Kynock's explosives factory in Arklow and some four thousand rounds of ·303 ammunition acquired from English soldiers on the Curragh. Secret preparations were afoot to bring off a *coup* which would have a great moral effect on the Volunteers and on the public in general—the importation of arms in a manner somewhat similar to the Ulster Volunteers' gun-running at Larne.

The story has been told many times of the landing of the arms at Howth from Erskine Childers' yacht *The Asgard*, the intervention by British troops as the arms were being brought back to Dublin and the civilian loss of life that followed. The role played by de Valera is less well known. His company were the last to receive their arms and when the British troops were encountered on the way back, they acted as part of a defensive screen while the other Volunteers dispersed. By this time it seemed impossible to get back to Donnybrook. The only hope of crossing the Liffey seemed to be to make a wide detour and with that in mind he led his company to Santry. But they had marched about twenty miles that day, each had a heavy Mauser rifle from Howth. De Valera soon realised that they would never manage to circle the city by the following morning, so he changed his plan.

He dismissed two-thirds of his company, making each man leave his rifle with someone in the section left behind. Then he set out to cross the city alone. When he arrived at Donnybrook he took out his motor bicycle and side-car and returned to Santry. Each one of his remaining men was by now in charge of three rifles and de Valera ferried them one by one with their rifles hidden under the apron of the side-car through the city to their homes. The operation lasted all night. Dawn was breaking when he delivered the last man to his home at Clonskea.

The result of the Howth gun-running was a considerable increase in the number of recruits, but other events were occurring which would put an end to progress. John Redmond was not unnaturally taking an interest in the control of the Volunteers and an uneasy peace was reached in June, 1914, when twenty-five nominees of Redmond were added to the executive committee. De Valera avoided all controversy at the time, though he felt that Redmond, in attempting to take control of the

Volunteers, was acting without political acumen. A strong armed force behind Redmond, for which he was not directly responsible, could have been a powerful lever in extracting Home Rule from British statesmen. A split was avoided at the time, but the outbreak of war in 1914 soon brought matters to a head.

In September Redmond was inspecting a Volunteer parade at Wooden-bridge, County Wicklow. The Home Rule Bill had been put on the Statute Book accompanied, however, by a suspensory act which postponed its operation until the end of the war. Redmond, full of loyalty and gratitude for the gift so quickly retracted, exhorted the Volunteers, 'Go on drilling and make yourselves efficient for the work and then assert yourselves as men, not only in Ireland itself but wherever the firing line extends in defence of right, freedom and religion in this war'.

This was too much for the original provisional committee who dissolved forthwith their unwilling marriage with Redmond's nominees. The central committee was split and the division went right down through the ranks. De Valera soon made it plain that he was loyal to the original founders. He did not, however, see any immediate necessity for splitting into two parties a body of men who had worked together cordially.

But at the weekly drill meeting of his company on September 28th the issue was forced and de Valera decided that he must candidly address his men. He told them that the time for a split had apparently come and explained his view that the Volunteers could be more effective if not tied to a political party. He permitted other views to be expressed, but ultimately called on those who intended to remain faithful to their signed declarations to fall in. A majority followed him out of the hall. As they left de Valera cried to the Redmondites who owned the hall and stayed behind, 'You will need us before you get Home Rule'.

The split had a disastrous effect on public enthusiasm. The thirty or forty who followed de Valera soon dwindled. At subsequent parades seven men only turned up. An alternative meeting place was hard to find. Drilling and training continued for a time in an open field off Donnybrook Road. Then the captain issued a notice that the company would meet in a basement in 41 York Street.

Yet he was determined to rebuild the strength of his company. He got a special task assigned to it. It was to be a scouting corps for the South City battalions. The programme of training was to include musketry and bayonet fighting, scout training and, on Sunday afternoons, field work. He invited young men to join under the slogan: 'Wanted: eyes and ears for the South City battalions'.[1] The company began to grow in strength again. A portion of P. H. Pearse's school at Oakley Road, Ranelagh, was acquired as new headquarters. Soon de Valera's company

was once more a thriving body, and his work had apparently attracted
the notice of higher authority.

Meanwhile he was devoting considerable attention to the study of
military manuals. When lectures were arranged for officers in early 1915,
Thomas MacDonagh dealt with reports, orders and despatches and James
Connolly, revolutionary socialist, with street fighting. There was a
symposium in which de Valera took part on scouting, map reading and
map drawing. He had the chance of some interesting talks with Connolly.
In particular Connolly held that British officers would not call on their
men to use cannon and destroy buildings in the main streets of Dublin if
a conflict took place. The power of the capitalists would see to that.
De Valera did not agree. The Rising was to prove Connolly strikingly
wrong, but de Valera found him a sympathetic and understanding man
who argued about his opinions without any trace of conceit.

On March 10th, the higher command of the Volunteers was reorgan-
ised. Pearse, the O'Rahilly, Joseph Plunkett and Bulmer Hobson were
appointed commandants on the headquarters staff, while Edward Daly,
Thomas MacDonagh, Eamonn Ceannt and de Valera himself were raised
to the rank of commandant, each in charge of one of the four Dublin
battalions. De Valera's command was the third battalion, which included
the companies on the south-east of the city. On the following day Pearse
questioned de Valera as they walked together up Kildare Street as to
what his attitude would be if a rising took place. De Valera answered that
as a soldier he was willing to accept any orders from his superiors which
might be given. Pearse was evidently satisfied. He drew from his pocket
a letter which not only formally appointed de Valera to his new position,
but requested him to attend a meeting of the four battalion commandants
on the following Saturday evening—clearly an affair of importance.[2]

Pearse presided over this meeting held on March 13th, 1915. The
possibility of a rising in September was frankly discussed. De Valera felt
that he was the only one at the meeting who did not expect to survive.
Pearse showed the officers a letter on grey note-paper, which he said
would be given to them as a signal. The messenger delivering it would
give the password 'Howth'. Each commandant settled with Pearse his
own reply to the password. De Valera's choice was 'Bruree'.

The general strategic plan was outlined by Pearse. Each battalion was
to cut off one of the military barracks from the city centre and to take up
positions where food would be obtainable. De Valera was told that the
task of the third battalion would be the containment of Beggars Bush
Barracks. It must have been shortly afterwards that de Valera was made
adjutant of the Dublin brigade. In this capacity he came directly under

Thomas MacDonagh, now the brigade commander, while retaining command of the third battalion.

The position of the IRB as a secret agency, guiding the Irish Volunteers, led to difficulties for Commandant de Valera. He was not a member of the secret organisation, never liking secret societies at any time. On one occasion, when walking home from drill, his neighbour Batt O'Connor had invited him to join what he called 'the physical force boys'. De Valera had declined. The Volunteers were, on the face of it, an open body governed by an executive elected at conventions. He hated to bind himself to obey orders given by persons unknown. In 1915, however, with serious preparations being made for a rising, de Valera was perturbed to learn that some members of his battalion knew more about the plans of the Volunteers than he did. They had information which he, as battalion commander, should have been given. He duly complained to MacDonagh.

MacDonagh explained that, while de Valera was not a member of the IRB, those who got secret information were. If he would take the oath there would be no further difficulty. To this de Valera objected that he was an officer of the Irish Volunteers and subject to its executive. He could not serve two masters. MacDonagh said that, in fact, there were not two masters, that the central executive was controlled by the IRB and that whatever orders were given would be those initiated by the IRB. He pointed out that taking the oath would not involve more than accepting the orders of the executive of the Volunteers. If he wished to have the information which he required he would have to become a member of the IRB. De Valera then agreed to take the oath. He made it clear, however, that he would attend no meetings. He did not want to know the names of any of the members or share any of the secrets of the organisation except those essential for the proper exercise of his command in the Volunteers. Thus he was sworn into the secret organisation by Thomas MacDonagh.

Later MacDonagh pressed him strenuously to allow himself to be nominated as a member of the Volunteer executive, but de Valera absolutely refused. He had been taken from his company and made commandant of the third battalion and then made adjutant of the brigade all too quickly. He wished to concentrate on the tasks allotted to him. At this stage of his life he was above all a soldier and little concerned with politics.

From the time he was informed that, in the event of a rising, his battalion would be assigned to the Westland Row–Grand Canal Street area, de Valera made a close study of the district, surveying its military possibilities. With his son Vivion, then about five years old, he walked several times from Baggot Street to Grand Canal Street along the banks of the canal. These walks seemed to be the innocent recreation of a father and son, but they helped de Valera to reconnoitre the area carefully. The railway was an important link passing through the area from Kingstown (soon to be restored to the name which graced it before the visit of George IV, Dun Laoghaire). Unless the line could be disrupted, the holding of the canal bridges would not prevent troops from pouring in through Westland Row station. De Valera would travel on the train from Lansdowne Road past the Grand Canal basin, checking as he did so the means of immobilising the railway.

His eldest daughter Máirín, born April, 1912, now Professor of Botany at Galway University, recalls this period vividly.

My earliest memory of my parents.

Christmas 1915—a small front room, greenery, silver paper, a doll, a golliwog, chocolates and my mother's red gold hair gleaming in the firelight. My father and brother playing with lead soldiers on the floor—then my father showing me how he filled his fountain-pen and 'stylo'. For years I considered him to be the world's outstanding expert on fountain-pens!

A roll-top desk, foolscap paper (unused pages of examination scripts), books, notebooks and of course fountain-pens, and 'Daddy busy mustn't be disturbed'.

Walking with him down the path of the tiny garden at the back of the house, inspecting the vegetables, especially the lovely white cauliflowers which he had grown.

Learning to count pebbles—a basin-full of nice rounded pebbles. This again three years later in Greystones. I hated those pebbles—I know now that he was trying to introduce us to the notions of numbers and arithmetic more or less along the lines that have become popular in the sixties. 'The new mathematics—groups etc.'

His motorbike with its side-car—seeing him standing in the back yard dressed in muddy oilskins and 'pull-ups'—buckets full of water being poured over them (and him). He had just ridden the machine from Maynooth. I am told that I objected strongly to his having to stand still and endure the violent washing down. I don't remember that but I can still picture him towering over me—looking like a giant in those oilskins.

Watching the O'Donovan Rossa funeral on its way to Glasnevin and feeling very proud as my father marched by in his green volunteer uniform.

That green uniform again—but this time I felt more mystified than proud. He wore it as he walked down the street with my Godfather Jack Barrett—my Godfather wearing a British khaki uniform! (I think that he was living in England and had been conscripted—but all I remember is the fact that he had an English uniform).

Preparations for the Rising were being made continuously from the

time of the meeting of commandants in March, 1915. The autumn
went by. No signal came. The Volunteers were mobilised, however, for
parades on St Patrick's Day, 1916. The Dublin brigade turned out in
strength and took over the centre of the city for a parade at which Eoin
MacNeill, in College Green, took the salute. For over two hours, from
11 o'clock to 1 p.m. they stopped all traffic through College Green.
De Valera's third battalion was there to take part in the exercise on the
public thoroughfare.

At one stage a military car from Dublin Castle attempted to force its
way through. De Valera would not allow it. He indicated an alternative route to the driver, but the man insisted that he had the
right and intended to go through College Green where the trams and
other vehicles had already been stopped. De Valera gave an order to
three files of Volunteers to capsize the car if it attempted to move. The
vice-commandant of the battalion, Seán Fitzgibbon, became anxious lest
the incident develop into an attack by the military from the Castle nearby
on the Volunteers and he intervened. He was a member of the executive
of the Volunteers and perhaps felt that he had superior authority.
De Valera ordered him to his place.

The battle of wills lasted a short time. The army driver insisted that
he had a right to go 'the shortest way' from the Castle to his destination.
Ultimately the driver reversed the car and drove off in the direction
indicated by de Valera amid the cheers of the crowd.

The incident had a sequel. De Valera decided that he could not have
officers under him in his battalion who felt that as they were members of
the executive of the Volunteers their authority was superior to his. He
took up the matter with headquarters. Seán Fitzgibbon and also The
O'Rahilly were accordingly transferred.

What appeared to be an official British document, though the British
authorities denounced it as a fabrication, was captured and circulated
among Volunteers early in April. Not only were the Irish Volunteers and
James Connolly's Citizen Army threatened, but so were Redmond's
volunteers, the Gaelic League, Sinn Féin, trade union buildings, St
Enda's College and, most provocative of all, Archbishop's House.
De Valera was convinced that Connolly regarded the document as
genuine, as he did himself. Connolly was certain that unless a rising took
place quickly it would be forestalled by the British. In fact, while always
remaining in the background, the military council of the IRB had already
fixed Easter Sunday, 1916, as the day for a rising, though this information
was closely guarded.

De Valera had joined the Volunteers, well aware that armed conflict
was almost inevitable; and he gave all his energies to training himself and

his men for the fray. The benefits of the military preparation and spartan discipline which he learned in this period were to stay with him throughout his life. The dedication in general terms to a free Ireland had developed into something more definite. Home rule, which he considered a possibility in 1913, had by 1916 lost all reality. The shelving of the Home Rule Act and the British effort to solve Ireland's problems by partition had assured him that the establishment of a republic provided Ireland's one hope of complete freedom.

Before he became a Volunteer he had known little of the Republican movement in Ireland. One evening a few years previously he had passed round the corner of the provost's house at Trinity College and had heard a speaker, using a side-car as a platform, make a plea for an Irish republic. It meant little to him, this being the first time he had heard the idea put forward as a practical political aim. He gave it some thought but put it out of his mind. In the ranks of the Volunteers, however, especially after the split with Redmond in the autumn of 1914, he became steadily more imbued with the ideal. By 1916 he had emerged as a committed Republican.

Part II

1916 - 1924

THE CREST AND THE TROUGH

[4]

THE RISING

Easter, 1916

The Easter Rising of 1916 has assumed a secure and glorious place in the struggle for human freedom. Its appeal has proved universal. Of the seven signatories of the Proclamation of the Republic, it can be said with truth 'The very wind of their name has swept to the ultimate seas'. The world is now unlikely to forget the mystical prophet of nationality, Pearse; the revolutionary Labour leader, Connolly; the old Fenian prisoner and tobacconist, Tom Clarke; the professor of literature, MacDonagh; MacDermott, the tireless organiser despite his polio; the junior municipal officer, Kent; the amateur strategist Plunkett, later to be married an hour before his execution. In purity of motive, drama of incident and astonishing victory through defeat the Rising seems in retrospect the perfect thing. Yet it was almost wrecked in advance by unforeseen accidents and muddle.

The secret IRB had a firm grip on the effective positions in the movement, though the majority of the Irish Volunteers had little idea what was afoot. The IRB were preparing for a national uprising in their own way. Not until those preparations were completed would the signal be given, and much depended on the hope of German aid. Roger Casement, a noble-minded knight errant, had gained world-wide fame by exposing the brutal exploitation of native rubber workers in the Congo and Putamayo. For some years he had been committed heart and soul to the crusade for Irish freedom. Before the uprising of 1916 he was in Germany seeking help for a rising.

But he was a far from expert conspirator. His mission met with little enthusiasm from the German General Staff whose sole interest was military. An uprising in Ireland would create a useful diversion; it would embarrass the British war effort; but it would be defeated. German officers were sceptical of its value. Only after considerable debate and delay was it decided to send arms—20,000 rifles captured on the Russian front, some million rounds of ammunition, ten machine-guns and some fire bombs. These were sent on the steamer *Libau* in April, 1916. The military council of the IRB had by then fixed Easter Sunday, April 23rd, as the date for the Rising.

Easter was an auspicious time for an event which would make a new Ireland. For Pearse, whose national loyalty had the fervour of his religious faith, no more fitting day could be chosen for the resurrection of a nation. To him the odds did not matter—failure could be a glorious renewal of the spirit of Ireland. He had made his decision. As he said in his little poem 'Renunciation':

> I have turned my face
> To this road before me,
> To the deed that I see
> And the death I shall die.

Or, to quote one of the greatest of Irish poets,

> 'But where can we draw water,'
> Said Pearse to Connolly,
> 'When all the wells are parched away?
> O plain as plain can be
> There's nothing but our own red blood
> Can make a right Rose Tree'.[1]

Pearse was inspired by sacrifice and hoped to inspire by it. To others, however, the odds did matter. Some keenly felt their responsibilities and their ordinary duties and were fired by no such transcending inspiration as that of Pearse. Eoin MacNeill was one of them. For him the morality of insurrection depended on its chance of success. Thus, even within the ranks of the Irish Volunteers, there lay fundamental differences. They remained hidden because the IRB acted in secret. Its military council, while perfecting its plans for a rising, kept a close guard on its aim. Through Pearse it exercised a real control on the Irish Volunteers, while MacNeill remained their nominal head. MacNeill had set his face firmly against any insurrection, while Pearse spoke openly and fearlessly about 'the day we rise in arms'.

Unity was maintained by the expedient of keeping MacNeill in the dark as to the actual preparations in hand. Even the mobilisation order issued by Pearse did not enlighten him, since it was an innocuous call to manoeuvres 'following the lines of last year'. This, however, was probably designed to deceive the British rather than MacNeill. The question of insurrection and of divided authority had never been pushed to a conclusion by MacNeill. And so by Holy Week there was both divided opinion and duality of control in the Irish Volunteers. The duality of leadership was to be put to a test when MacNeill learned the real plans for Easter Sunday.

For de Valera there was no doubt as to how he should act. On Wednesday in Holy Week, cycling from the headquarters of the Volunteers to his home he was stopped by Joe Sweeney, a young boy from Pearse's school. Sweeney gave him a note uttering at the same time the fateful password 'Howth'. De Valera replied 'Bruree' and took the letter. It was the notice of the Rising as arranged with Pearse. The hour was fixed—midnight at the end of Easter Sunday. De Valera, one repeats, was a man under military discipline, altogether willing to obey. Immediately he received the order he set about his final preparations.

Throughout his life, on principle, de Valera did not discuss confidential political matters with his wife, though he knew her sympathy was complete and that she could be trusted, if anyone ever could, to keep her counsel. In general he felt that it was sufficient that one of them should be disturbed by these problems. Nevertheless, he felt keenly the troubles which the forthcoming struggle was likely to impose on her and their children. To one of his officers he confided on Holy Saturday, 'We'll be all right, it's the women who will suffer. The worst they can do to us is kill us, but the women will have to remain behind to rear the children'.[2]

He had not much to leave them but, nevertheless, made a simple will leaving whatever he might own to his wife. He called on his neighbours from whom his own home was rented to act as witnesses. His position as an insurgent would not, he felt, invalidate the will, but he was anxious in regard to a small life assurance policy. If he were killed in the Rising, would the assurance company pay the sum assured? In fact he felt that death was almost inevitable. But he hid his emotions as, on Good Friday, he bade goodbye to his wife and four children. The youngest of them, Brian, was still less than a year old. For the first time he told his wife that serious business was pending. Máirín's fourth birthday had occurred a few days earlier. 'I remember my father buying me a doll's pram and my own delight and wonder mingled with a vague anxiety. Such extravagance —a real black shiny *pram*, not a cheaper wicker-work bassinet which was all that I had dared to hope for!' Now he parted from his family and went to University Church on St Stephen's Green. There he sought the consolations of his religion and made what he thought would be his last confession.

In the meantime he had been in consultation with the officers of his battalion. He spent Good Friday night in the home of one of his junior officers, Michael Malone, and the following night at battalion head-quarters where there was a strong Volunteer guard. His briefing of the company officers was detailed. One of them has recorded:

He was able to tell each Company Captain where he would enter on to his area and what he would find to his advantage or disadvantage when he got there. . . . He was able to discuss every detail even to the places where it would be possible to procure an alternative water supply, where we could definitely find tools for such things as loopholing walls and making communications. . . . I cannot remember a query put to him that he was not able to answer immediately.[3]

This mastery was the result of long effort and careful organisation and was undoubtedly a great encouragement to his officers. All were ready for mobilisation on Sunday in his battalion area. Meanwhile battalions throughout the country had received orders which would bring them into action. But the plans had already begun to go wrong.

For the first time, on Holy Thursday night, MacNeill learned by chance that an insurrection was planned for Sunday. The truth that he had for months studiously ignored now stared him in the face as Pearse stood before him, roused from his bed to answer MacNeill's anger. The Gaelic League professor found himself facing a mind made up. Arguments were vain. Logic and reason could make no impression against Pearse's, 'I feel that I am right'. All MacNeill could answer was, 'I will do everything I can to stop this, everything except to ring up Dublin Castle'. Next morning MacDonagh and MacDermott attempted to intervene. They saw MacNeill and told him that a German ship with arms was on its way to Ireland, that it was too late to stop the Rising without disaster. MacNeill's heated anger had abated. Perhaps German aid might at least give some hope of success to the enterprise. It could remove from it the stigma which he most feared, the immorality attaching to futile insurrection. He yielded to the inevitable in which he felt they were all involved.

At the other side of the country the second act of the drama was being played. The *Libau* had arrived off Tralee bay with its name painted over and changed to the *Aud*. It had run the blockade successfully disguised as a Norwegian vessel. But plans to receive the cargo of arms at Fenit pier were not complete. Anxiously it waited in the bay. At the same time a frail boat landed Sir Roger Casement and two companions from a German submarine on the sandhills of Banna Strand a few miles to the north. Ill, exhausted and drenched in the effort of landing, Casement rested in an old fort near the beach while his companions tried to get in touch with the Volunteers in Tralee. Before they could do so Casement was arrested and the *Aud* was intercepted by a British naval vessel. Rather than allow his cargo to fall into the hands of the enemy, the Captain scuttled his ship and with it, sky high, went Irish hopes of German aid.

To MacNeill, sadly miscast in a military role, the disastrous news from Kerry was the last straw. It did not, however, immediately change his decision to participate in a rising. He had come to think that it was by now inevitable. But during Saturday he changed his mind again. A rising did not seem inevitable after all. He could and would stop it. He would assert his authority. He despatched couriers to Cork, Belfast and Limerick, cancelling all orders, and sent notices to the press calling off the Easter Sunday mobilisation. He had been through the agony of a terrible nightmare. Now that he had taken his decision, he did all in his power to make it effective. He thought that his authority was strong enough to stop an insurrection, but he reckoned without the determination of those who would not 'be wise'.

On the morning of Easter Sunday, de Valera at his battalion head-quarters woke up with a clear conscience but a nagging toothache. This was to be the day of destiny. He had all his plans in order. But that tooth could not be gainsaid. Its claims were overriding. He repaired to his wife's cousin, Tom Flanagan, a dentist in Baggot Street. As he sat in Tom Flanagan's chair, however, he was troubled. Something that he had read on a *Sunday Independent* billboard indicated that all was not well. On leaving the dentist he bought a newspaper. In it was an order from MacNeill countermanding all activities for that day. No parades, marches or other movements were to take place. To assert his authority over the heads of any officer who might disagree with him, MacNeill addressed his order to each individual Volunteer.

To de Valera it came as a shocking blow. All that he had prepared for, for two and a half years, was to come to naught. His own spirit had been keyed up for the inevitable logical consummation which was to follow that first step in the Rotunda Rink and the second at Howth. Were they to falter now at the third and decisive step? Were they really to prove, at the time of trial, the tin soldiers which many opponents had called them? If they failed to take the field now they would justify those taunts; if they failed to go into battle now they would never do so. Men had been worked up to a pitch where they either went out to fight or home to wither.

With a newspaper in his hand de Valera returned to battalion head-quarters, puzzled and disappointed. After some hours he received word from MacDonagh that perhaps all was not lost, that a military council was in conclave in the Labour headquarters at Liberty Hall, and that a vital decision would be taken. The meeting that took place that Easter Sunday morning was as historic as any in the whole history of Ireland. Seven brave men sat there: Pearse, Connolly, Clarke, MacDonagh, McDermott, Kent and Plunkett. They had seen their plans fall asunder. They knew, however, that if they drew back now they could never hold their heads high again. 'We would be a disgrace to our generation', said MacDonagh. The majority felt, however, that MacNeill's order had created such confusion that plans must be somewhat rearranged. The effect of MacNeill's order was limited to Easter Sunday, so it was decided to confirm it with the significant added instruction, 'All Volunteers are to stay in Dublin until further orders'.

In the meantime MacNeill, fearful lest his order be disobeyed, sent out instructions in various ways to Volunteer companies throughout the city confirming the cancellation of all activities. To de Valera, in the early afternoon, he addressed a personal letter in his own hand to this effect, ordering him to make it known to his own and other commands.[4] To this de Valera replied by letter stating that, since MacDonagh was his superior officer, he would obey only if the order was countersigned by him.[5] Later MacDonagh's confirmatory order to the Dublin brigade with the significant addition was received and countersigned by de Valera who sent it to the officers of his battalion.

Knowing that further instructions were to come from MacDonagh, de Valera remained at the headquarters of his battalion. It seemed obvious to him and others that the crisis had only been postponed. By this stage it mattered little who struck the first blow, and armed conflict was inevitable. It was inconceivable after the events of Good Friday, showing the contacts with Germany, that the British would continue to allow the Volunteers to keep their arms. The only question was, who would strike first. The Volunteers would allow the whole initiative to pass to the British authorities if they waited for an effort to disarm them. About five o'clock that afternoon, de Valera learned with relief that the Rising was to take place at noon on the next day, Easter Monday.

The immediate problem which faced de Valera was to find some means of undoing the confusion created. The effect of MacNeill's intervention was likely to be serious. The response of the Volunteers to a new mobilisation order might be poor. Nevertheless, he was determined to follow the orders of his senior officer MacDonagh no matter what the circumstances. A concert arranged for that evening at 41 Parnell Square gave him an opportunity of addressing some of the men and restoring some of the spirit which had existed until that very morning. It was not easy. Rumour and disaster had already started to bring disillusionment.

Yet all was not lost. The seven resolute men who met in Liberty Hall that Sunday saw to that. Early the next morning one of them, MacDonagh, issued an order to the Dublin brigade to parade for inspection and a route march at 10 a.m. Full arms and equipment and one day's rations were to be carried. On the copy sent to de Valera, the words 'full arms and equipment', were underlined apparently by Pearse who added a note in his own hand that E company of the third battalion should parade at Beresford Place, outside Liberty Hall, as part of a fifth battalion.

It was this fifth battalion which shortly before noon set out from Liberty Hall to march on the Post Office. Supplemented by a contingent fron Connolly's Citizen Army, the bulk of which had set off for St Stephen's Green, it numbered perhaps 150 men. Not more than a fourth of its members wore the dark green uniform of the Citizen Army or the heather green of the Irish Volunteers, though others wore puttees, riding breeches, bandoliers or yellow brassards to put up some kind of military appearance. The armament was highly variegated—several kinds of rifle, but also shot-guns, pickaxes and pikes. Yet it seems to be agreed that the march was not unimpressive. The military training had borne fruit. To quote one historian of the Rising: 'They had an appreciation of order and discipline despite their ridiculous paraphernalia, despite even the pikes'.

There was not likely to be any faltering in front. James Connolly, perhaps the happiest man in Dublin at that moment, led the column in the full uniform of a commandant general, his leggings splendidly polished. On his left went Plunkett, dying of glandular tuberculosis, his throat still swathed in bandages. On his right was Pearse, dignified and distant, his mood and bearing matching the long awaited hour. Tom Clarke and the limping jesting MacDermott were there, of course. Further back were Seán T. O'Kelly, later to be President of Ireland, Connolly's fifteen-year-old son Roddy and his secretary Winifred Carney, the only woman in the entire procession. Countess Markievicz was second-in-command of the force in St Stephen's Green.

On that Easter bank holiday the streets were far from thronged. There were leisurely sightseers and a few holiday-makers who looked askance at the file which marched out of Abbey Street and wheeled right towards the very centre of Dublin, the hundred foot high Nelson's Pillar. 'Another route march', thought many scoffing onlookers until, suddenly, opposite the General Post Office, Connolly's voice rang out with strident passion, 'Left turn, the G.P.O.—Charge!'

The men who took the Post Office met no resistance. The armed guards surrendered to the onslaught. They had no ammunition for their rifles. Disarmed by MacNeill's countermanding order, Dublin Castle had been caught napping. The G.P.O. building was quickly put into a defensive state and, at three o'clock in the afternoon, a green flag rose to the head of the mast over Prince's Street corner. On it were the words 'Irish Republic'. Above the royal arms of the pediment floated the flag of a new Ireland, the Republican tricolour of green, white and orange. Down on the street, under the portico, a cold and pale Pearse read the Proclamation of the Republic to a largely indifferent crowd. Connolly waved his hand exuberantly but the observer, Stephen MacKenna, 'felt sad for him'. The few perfunctory cheers emphasised the uncomprehending chill with which it was received. Yet it was one of the great documents of Irish history.

> Irish men and Irish women: In the name of God and of the dead generations from which she receives her old tradition of nationhood, Ireland through us summons her children to her flag and fights for her freedom! In every generation the Irish people have asserted their right to national freedom and sovereignty; six times during the past three hundred years they have asserted it in arms. Standing on that fundamental right and again asserting it in arms in the face of the world, we hereby proclaim the Irish Republic as a Sovereign Independent State, and we pledge our lives and the lives of our comrades in arms to the cause of its freedom, of its welfare and of its exaltation among the nation . . .

The phoenix flame was lit once more. The Fenian torch was grasped in the hands of a new generation. De Valera was not a signatory and did not hear the document read. In fact he did not see a copy of it until several months later, but it put into words the ideal which he henceforth was to pursue unceasingly.

The four Dublin battalions were already in their appointed districts. The first was to cover the Four Courts and the Church Street area on the north-west of the city. The fourth the South Dublin Union on the sourth-west. The second at Jacob's Biscuit Factory was to defend the southern approach to the city centre, while the third, de Valera's battalion, tried to close the circle on the south-east of the city.

But in fact the circle could not be closed. The effects of the cancellation order of Sunday were shown in the numbers who mobilised on Easter Monday. In every battalion the same story was told. Where the total number of 1,000 Volunteers were expected, only 200 turned out. In the third battalion, de Valera's experiences were those of the other commandants. A and C companies of his battalion were each about 120 strong, but on Easter Monday the numbers who paraded at Earlsfort Terrace on mobilisation were eighteen and thirty-four respectively.

In all, about six or seven score out of the five hundred men of the battalion answered the call to arms. Some twenty-five members of E company who were intercepted on their way to Liberty Hall helped to make up this number. None of the ladies of Cumann na mBan, the women's auxiliary of the Volunteers, reported for duty. De Valera's decisions had disappointed them. He would be glad of their assistance for commissariat or first aid purposes, but he would not give them arms. He had barely enough for the men.

De Valera informed his men at once that they were taking part in a serious rising. The principal building to be occupied by his battalion was

Boland's Bakery. The heavy task began of putting it into a state of defence. Walls had to be loopholed, houses telescoped, and supplies provided. Initially there was some confusion. A number of officers were among the absentees. Vacancies on the battalion staff as well as in company commands had to be filled by promotions. A more difficult problem was the reorganisation of plans to fit in with the limited number of men available.

As already explained, de Valera's area was intended to cover the south-eastern approaches to the city. The shortage of men prevented him from linking up with the second battalion at Leeson Street on his right flank to the south. Instead, he had to concentrate his men in defence of three bridges over the Grand Canal, Ringsend, Grand Canal Street and Lower Mount Street (named from north-east to south-west). The railway line which ran through the area formed the backbone of his defensive plans, Boland's Bakery overlooked it, and overlooked also the central or Grand Canal bridge. The roads approaching the Grand Canal and Lower Mount Street bridges, Grand Canal Street and Northumberland Road respectively, enclosed the British Military Barracks at Beggars Bush. They were well covered by de Valera's outposts. He hoped indeed to lure the attackers along Grand Canal Street where they would come under the direct fire of Boland's Bakery. (The prospect of a terrible trap and a massacre at Grand Canal Street bridge caused de Valera certain qualms.)

In fact, the main fighting followed quite a different course. The principal attack was directed along Northumberland Road with a view to a passage of the canal at Lower Mount Street bridge. Northumberland Road was well defended. De Valera had organised outposts at No. 25 (on the corner of Haddington Road) which also dominated the gate of the barracks, at the Parochial Hall, halfway between them and Lower Mount Street bridge, and finally at Clanwilliam House on the city side of the canal.

For de Valera the activities of Monday, the supervision of the plan of operations, the setting up of his own headquarters in the little dispensary beside the bakery, were a relief after the long hours of indecision and waiting. He personally saw to the removal of some essential parts from the gas works and the electricity supply station in Ringsend. He had himself studied textbooks and brought with him some qualified men. He wished to immobilise the electric trams lest they be of assistance to the British. Cutting off the gas supply was a precaution against an explosion which could endanger civilian life. Even in this time of anxiety, his kindness for animals was seen. He arranged that the horses belonging to the bakery were to be fed as long as food was available. Later in the week, when food ran out, he had them let loose on the streets to avoid suffering.

The animals in the nearby cats and dogs home he also liberated when it was clear that there was no one to tend to them.

Going into action did not worry him personally since he accepted it fully as part of his duties. What caused him most anxiety was the effect it might have on his men. They had little military training despite their weekly exercises. He feared that they would not realise the importance of precautions which full-time soldiers would take for granted. Ceaselessly he moved among the men along the railway seeing that sentries were posted and were on the alert. He gave orders to the company officers to keep the men occupied so as to divert their minds from fear. Yet he was careful to warn against overwork, for he knew the rigours which were facing them with numbers so few that rest periods would be difficult to arrange. In the distance the sound of rifle shots from St Stephen's Green told of severe fighting in that area.

As he strode among his men, his mind was working on possible schemes which might help in the event of an attack. A railway engine would, he thought, prove useful for bringing men out along the railway line to Merrion Gates. They might launch a surprise attack on British troops approaching from Dun Laoghaire, a natural landing place for British reinforcements. This plan was not feasible owing to the absence of an engine-driver, but others, more practical, were put into operation during the week. For example, he found that the signal wires at the side of the railway line could be pulled across the tracks and would thus make useful trip wires in case of a night assault.

At night de Valera was as active as by day. Without the support of experienced battalion officers, with newly promoted company officers and a terrible shortage of manpower, he felt that a heavy responsibility for discipline rested on him. At one post on the railway, as he went his rounds, he found a part of his Volunteers saying the rosary. He passed by and found to his horror that the sentries were missing. They were with their comrades at the rosary. Devout though he was, he insisted that they go back to their posts.

Monday and Tuesday saw a good deal of sniping. Morale remained high. Michael Malone and James Grace formed the essential outpost at 25 Northumberland Road. Dressed in a spruce overcoat and carrying an umbrella, Malone reported to Commandant de Valera that he and Grace had only single shot rifles. In their outpost they would need a fast-firing weapon. De Valera unbuckled his treasured Mauser pistol and gave it to Malone together with some four hundred or more rounds of ammunition. Rather surprisingly the assault expected from the Beggars Bush Barracks did not materialise. The Rising had taken the British so much by surprise that the barracks were nearly empty. More troops, however, were on their way. One of de Valera's difficulties was that he had no scouting parties to tell him what was happening. That was the greatest weakness in his scheme of defence. Equally important, perhaps, was the lack of a good communications system. This applied not alone to his command but to all the other commands in Dublin. Each had to act independently, largely isolated from the other Volunteer battalions. In fact throughout the week the third battalion fought without knowing whether any of the country brigades had risen or not.

Wednesday dawned—a critical day for the insurgents. Already the Irish Republic proclaimed at the General Post Office had lasted longer than any Irish rising since 1798. But Wednesday was the day of the great test. Up to this point the British troops had been primarily concerned with taking up positions to break resistance. Now, however, the grey shape of the *Helga*, a converted fisheries protection vessel, came threateningly up the Liffey. The guns of the *Helga* boomed out the information to all Volunteers that their ramshackle weapons would be answered by artillery, that in the long run there could be but one result—artillery must win.

Meanwhile, eight miles to the south-east, the first reinforcements from Britain were landing at Dun Laoghaire. A couple of thousand men of the Sherwood Foresters were soon marching along the Blackrock road towards the city—a direct threat to de Valera's positions, which lay between them and the city centre. The Sherwood Foresters divided into two contingents; about half went through Donnybrook, by-passing de Valera on his right or south-west side, while the other half marched to Ballsbridge where they paused. Two sections now broke off from the main body at Ballsbridge; one party approached the canal at Ringsend bridge (the most north-easterly of his three bridges) where they were driven back by the small garrison in Boland's Mill (to be distinguished from Boland's Bakery). A second party made their way into Beggars Bush Barracks and thence attacked the railway line and the canal. Captain Joseph O'Connor, with only six men, drove them back. He begged de Valera for reinforcements, but de Valera, attacked now along three lines of approach, had none to send.

The main assault was aimed at Mount Street bridge and directed along Northumberland Road. The defence of Mount Street bridge was carried to the limits of courage. One cannot but recall Horatio of ancient days or Custume, the Irish equivalent, at Athlone in 1691. Michael Malone and his companion held the house on the corner of Haddington Road against extraordinary odds. They were helped by rifle fire from Clanwilliam House on Mount Street bridge. The corner house was taken only when Malone fell dead at his post, his comrade making his escape.

The Sherwood Foresters now launched their full assault on Clanwilliam House commanding the bridge, but they faced a long straight road up to it and they were met by a withering fusillade. Three Volunteers in the Parochial Hall inflicted further losses as they passed. When at last they reached the bridge, they came under fire from various vantage points as well as Clanwilliam House, from a builders' yard, from the works room of the railway workshop, and from Boland's Bakery itself.

Friend and foe alike have paid tribute to the indomitable men who held the approach to Mount Street bridge. It was not until Clanwilliam House was a burnt out shell that the bridge fell into British hands. Fourteen men aided by crossfire from other positions held up the Sherwood Foresters for nine hours. They had inflicted heavy casualties. The total killed and wounded was 234 officers and men, almost exactly half the total British military casualties in the Rising. The deaths among the Volunteers amounted to four. The resistance had been so stubborn that the Sherwood Foresters did not push forward to their destination at Trinity College that night. Instead, they retired to the Royal Dublin Society's showgrounds.

Wednesday had been a day of action along the three lines of approach to the city which the third battalion held. Commandant de Valera was tireless in moving round among the positions occupied by his men along the railway. His aim was always to help those under fire by bringing supporting crossfire to bear on the attackers. The strain on him was immense. Because of the absence of both his vice-commandant and his battalion adjutant he was left without battalion officers. De Valera was forced to promote Joseph O'Connor, captain of A company, to be vice-commandant, still leaving him with his company.

Thursday was a day of incessant firing on the positions held by the third battalion. The high houses in Mount Street gave British snipers a valuable field of fire from which they kept Boland's Bakery and the positions along the railway covered. When some of his men were shot at between the bakery and the railway, de Valera was very angry. The only point from which the snipers could cover this spot was the roof of Sir Patrick Dun's Hospital. G. F. Mackay was a British army cadet who had been taken prisoner early on Easter Monday. De Valera told him that he was sending a message to the British officer in charge that they would shoot the cadet if the hospital was used by British snipers. Lest the cadet be unduly worried, de Valera informed him that he had no intention of carrying out the threat!

The shriek of bullets was almost continuous. About mid-day a new and more ominous sound was heard—the British had turned the artillery on to the area. The target was Boland's Bakery, a very vulnerable position because the roof was largely glass.

One tall building in the area was not occupied by the Volunteers through lack of men. It was a distillery in Ringsend adjacent to Boland's Mill. A tower rose above the building and de Valera feared that if occupied by the enemy it would dominate the area. He resorted, therefore, to a trick to give the impression that it was occupied in force. Accompanied by some of his men, he climbed from the roof of the distillery up an iron ladder on to the outside of the tower. Though silhouetted and an open target for the many bullets which were flying around him, he was surprised to find that his principal fear was the height. He carefully fixed a pike on a corner of the tower and attached to it a green flag with a gold harp on its centre. The ruse was brilliantly successful. The enemy's fire was diverted and the post destroyed—a post which might have been highly dangerous.

But de Valera felt that at any moment the artillery fire would again turn on the bakery. Men who had to evacuate it for fear of flying glass at the time of the bombardment found themselves on the railway line, and they saw for the first time the flames which were eating the heart out of the city centre. Incendiary shells had wrought havoc around the General Post Office. De Valera discussed plans with his vice-commandant, O'Connor, for a retreat to the Dublin mountains if their own position became untenable and they could no longer render help to their comrades in other battalions. Methodical as ever, he tried to arrange as much rest as possible for his men with this possibility in mind. At the same time he was thinking hard about a last fighting stand where he was. The attacks so far had been launched on outposts. His main defences along the railway and his base at Boland's Bakery were still intact. If a last stand were to be made, it would be in Guinness's granary or malthouse with its back to the canal basin.

The sniping was continued throughout Thursday and Friday, but these days passed without the expected assault on the bakery. On Friday evening de Valera was at last persuaded to rest. In the office of his head-quarters at the dispensary, he got his first real sleep since Easter Sunday. He slept soundly enough despite the fact, unknown to him, that the Rising was near collapse. It had become a series of separate sieges.

The British Forces, by now outnumbering the Irish by perhaps twenty to one, had driven a wedge across the city along the general line of the Liffey. O'Connell Street was blazing. Amidst the ruins of the G.P.O., Pearse had issued his valedictory message to the Irish people.

He paid homage to the gallantry 'of the soldiers of Irish free men who have during the past four days been writing with fire and steel the most glorious chapter in the later history of Ireland . . . They have redeemed Dublin from many shames and made her name splendid among the names of cities'. He went on to mention Commandant General James Connolly commanding the Dublin division: 'He lies wounded but is still the guiding brain of our resistance'. And the last reference was perhaps the most generous of all. He said he would not speak further of the fatal countermanding order which prevented the plans for a rising of the whole country from being carried out. 'Both Eoin MacNeill and we have acted in the best interests of Ireland'.

But the hardest battles had already been fought. De Valera, of course, did not know this, but already Pearse and the other leaders in the G.P.O. were satisfied that they had 'saved Ireland's honour', that, in the face of overwhelming force, their positions would soon be untenable and there would soon be little more that they could do.

After his rest, de Valera moved about on Saturday with renewed energy preparing his men for the coming assault. In the heat of the April sunshine he threw away his puttees. Many also noticed the unmilitary stocking which showed between the lacing of his knee breeches and the tops of his boots.

The British snipers on the high houses of Lower Mount Street were by now having matters all their own way. De Valera feared that the ammunition of the third battalion would run out. He ordered that none be wasted. The major assault must come soon and they should be ready. By Saturday evening surrender was the thought furthest from his mind, yet by Saturday afternoon, again without his knowing it, Patrick Pearse, President of the Provisional Republic of Ireland, and the survivors had been forced to evacuate the burning G.P.O. Pearse had tried to enter into negotiations with the British for a conditional surrender. Having failed, he and his colleagues had surrendered unconditionally. Shortly before four o'clock on Saturday, Pearse signed an order to all commandants:

> In order to prevent the further slaughter of Dublin citizens and in the hope of saving the lives of our followers now surrounded and hopelessly out-numbered . . . the Commandants of the various districts in the City and County will order their commands to lay down arms.

The Rising was over, but de Valera was still quite unaware of this.

On Sunday morning he ordered that all weapons be thoroughly cleaned and he even set up a target. Those who had had little chance of using their guns during the week should have an opportunity of learning how to use them properly. He was thus preparing for a final stand. He himself decided to shave. As he did so a messenger, Miss Elizabeth O'Farrell of

Cumann na mBan, the women's auxiliary of the Irish Volunteers, arrived with a message. She handed de Valera the order signed by P. H. Pearse. De Valera did not accept it at once. It was not countersigned by the commandant of the Dublin brigade, Thomas MacDonagh, and de Valera feared that it might not be genuine. With his main positions still intact, there was no immediate need for him to give in. He feared that the order might be some kind of British trick. He was terribly concerned lest he let down MacDonagh and other battalions who might be battling on. Miss O'Farrell went off to get MacDonagh's signature while de Valera consulted with his vice-commandant, Joseph O'Connor. Ultimately he was convinced that the order was genuine and that they must obey it.

This was something which de Valera had not foreseen. He had thought of a fight to the finish, but not surrender. It brought new thoughts and worries to his mind. While up to then his course was simple and easily mapped out, now he was assailed with problems. In particular he was worried for the safety of his men who had fought so gallantly. Tales had been told of the shooting of prisoners who had surrendered at the front in France. He feared that after the havoc his men had wrought among British troops on Wednesday, they might now be shot in cold blood. Accompanied by Cadet Mackay, the English prisoner who had been held for a week in Boland's, he crossed the road to Sir Patrick Dun's Hospital to arrange the surrender.[5] For himself he had no hope of surviving and he gave Mackay his Browning automatic with the request that, at some time, he give it to his eldest son, Vivion.

Within the bakery his troops were being gathered together from their various outposts, and heard the news with incredulity. Their spirit was unbroken, they would fight on. Only when they understood that they had received an order from headquarters were they satisfied. Then, in accordance with military manuals, they put out of action most of their arms in case they should be of use to the enemy.

The vice-commandant, O'Connor, led them out of the bakery, having persuaded a Red Cross worker to carry a white flag, a task which none of the Volunteers was willing to undertake. At Grattan Street he handed over command to de Valera who gave the despondent order to 'ground arms'. He still remembers the angry crunch with which the rifles hit the street. Afterwards they marched into Lower Mount Street where they were searched and then they set off, four abreast, with British soldiers at each side. De Valera, a tall hatless figure in the bedraggled uniform which he had not removed for a week, walked behind the white flag, with two British officers beside him, at the head of his men.

As they passed over the bloodied Mount Street bridge and through Northumberland Road, de Valera felt that the onlookers and indeed the people of Ireland did not understand. It galled him to find that people who were rushing to their doors to give cups of tea to British soldiers could not see that they had a *right* to freedom, that Ireland was a nation with *rights* like Belgium's. It would take a new renaissance to waken people out of their slumber and he did not see any hope of that. The Rising had failed and it need not have done so if the people of Ireland had come out even 'though armed with hay forks only'. He did not see the dawn on the horizon. He was no Pearse with a vision of a new nation rising out of the sacrifice of a generation. For de Valera that hope was vain. A young Unionist woman who saw the prisoners pass was surprised to find that the leader in Boland's was 'a fine looking man who was educated and speaks like a gentleman'. Her general reaction she recorded in her diary:

> . . . fine-looking fellows, swinging along in good step. Of course they looked shabby and dirty, they had been fighting for seven days. Until I saw them I thought they ought to be shot, but I don't know—it would be terrible waste of material, if it was nothing else—it made one miserable to see them.[7]

In the showgrounds 117 Volunteers were herded together in horse-boxes. De Valera, however, was treated as an officer and placed under guard in the Weights and Measures office of the Town Hall. He sat there wondering what the position was in the city, even now somewhat haunted by the fear that he had left others in the lurch by his surrender. Two offers of escape were made to him. One involved a leap on to a fire-engine, but an armed corporal made it plain he would shoot. In the other case a British soldier offered to let him have a British army uniform. De Valera considered this a ruse to take his own uniform from him. He feared that it might be worn by a decoy. He tore the facings and officer's rank marks from the already bedraggled outfit lest they be of any help to the British.

The bewildering march of events that occurred during the next few days was jotted down by de Valera on the back of Pearse's order to surrender. Despite the strain, there is no hint of emotion in the terse notes he made at the time. The diary, if diary it can be called, merely recorded his movements as he was being moved from one point to another. It is worth reproducing here, partly because it shows de Valera's extraordinary powers of calm and objectivity—after all, he felt that he would be facing death in a few hours—but also because it is almost the only personal document of his about 1916 that survives:

Diary: Ap. 30th Surrender order recd. & executed
1 p.m.
Sunday Ap. 30th 2 p.m., to Tuesday May 2nd
(Ballsbridge).

Tuesday   May 2nd to May 5th (morning) (Richmond Bks.
            Detent. cells.)
Friday May 5th (morning) to Sat (afternoon) Gymnasium,
R. Barracks.
Sat 6th to Monday 8th Room 4 (L block) R. Bks.
Monday 8th 9.45 Trial with Ashe, 2 Lawlesses and Dr Hayes
and a couple of others.
Mond 8th Kilmainham—cell No. 59.

What these entries mean is that from Sunday until Tuesday he and
his men were detained at Ballsbridge. At midday on Tuesday they were
marched through Dublin to Richmond Barracks at the western extremity
of the city. The prisoners were preceded and followed by machine-guns
mounted on lorries while armed troops marched on each side of them.
Passing through Dame Street and Thomas Street they received a hostile
reception from people along the sidewalks. De Valera was overwhelmed
with sadness that these Irish men and women should misunderstand the
Volunteers' fight for Irish liberty just as he felt a pang of disappointment
when he saw the people of Northumberland Road feeding the British
soldiers.

In Richmond he was lodged in the detention cells. As de Valera and
his comrades moved into Richmond Barracks the first prisoners were
being court martialled. Next morning at 3.45 the shots of the first firing
squads woke many of the prisoners. Pearse, MacDonagh and Clarke had
been executed. De Valera expected to be executed but he was not
wakened by the shots. While others could face death with the calmness
of self-sacrifice to revitalise the nation, de Valera was not inspired by a
similar feeling. Death was to him a fearsome thing and the prisoners'
discussions on the volleys of the previous night heightened the tension.

In that room with him was the venerable looking Count Plunkett
whose son, Joseph, had been executed on the previous Thursday. Two
other sons were sentenced to death on Saturday but their sentences were
commuted to penal servitude for life. Count Plunkett's wife was also
arrested. Seán T. O'Kelly, later to be President of Ireland, big John
O'Mahony, Larry O'Neill, a future Lord Mayor of Dublin, were also
with him. Years before de Valera had read with incredulity of the morbid
game which occupied the time of Thomas Francis Meagher and his
Young Ireland colleagues in Clonmel Jail while they awaited trial for
treason in 1848. Now he was to find the scene re-enacted with himself in
the leading part.

With death but a short distance away, a mock trial does not appear to
be the most happy of pastimes, but the irrepressible John O'Mahony
insisted. The bearded Count acted as a sombre judge and Larry O'Neill

was advocate for the defence. Seán T. O'Kelly prosecuted, since none of the others relished this task, and de Valera was charged with being a pretender to the throne of the Muglins, the rocky island on which a lighthouse stood off Dalkey Island. The verdict, as expected, was against the commandant. But the judge stopped short at pronouncing the frightening sentence, despite the urgings of one of the prisoners who had a black cap ready for the occasion.[8] None of this gave de Valera much comfort and the grim game almost unnerved Larry O'Neill. Quietly that night, as they lay on the floor hoping for the oblivion of sleep, he moved over to the man whose doom appeared to be sealed, and whispered, 'This is terrible,' and pressed a crucifix into de Valera's hand.

On Monday morning, May 8th, de Valera was told that his trial would take place that day, and shortly before two o'clock that afternoon he was taken from his companions. As he was leaving them, Seán T. O'Kelly asked him for a souvenir. It was all too obvious that he did not expect to see him again in this life. De Valera gave him his pen. Seán T. O'Kelly recalled that it was stolen from him before he left Richmond Barracks.

The court martial was short and businesslike. De Valera did not deny his identity or make any such difficulties. His wife had, a few days before, approached the American Consul in Dublin to make representations that he was an American citizen and the Consul had written to the Under Secretary, Sir Mathew Nathan, on the point. At his court martial, however, he did not make any claim on this basis. When questioned, he stated that he understood that he was born in New York, but he could not say whether his father was a Spanish subject or a naturalised American citizen. On one point he was firm. He said that he always regarded himself as an Irishman and not a British subject. Captain Hitzen was there to prove that de Valera had surrendered to him and that the men in the Boland's Bakery area obeyed him. Cadet Mackay corroborated that de Valera was in command in that district during Easter Week and added that he himself had been well treated while a prisoner in the bakery. The court martial ended, he was taken to cell number 59 in Kilmainham Jail. In the yard outside, the executions had been carried out throughout the preceding week. There he awaited his fate.

He sent some letters to his friends announcing that his execution was certain, but he did not write to either his wife or his mother because there was still no definite news. To the nun in charge at the training college where he had taught mathematics he wrote:

Dear Sister Gonzaga,

I have just been told that I am to be shot for my part in the rebellion.

Just a parting line then to thank you and all the sisters (especially Mother Attracta) for your unvarying kindness to me in the past and to ask you to

pray for my soul and for my poor wife and little children whom I leave un-
provided for behind.

Ask the girls to remember me in their prayers.

Goodbye. I hope I'll be in heaven to meet you.

Yours faithfully,
(Sgd) E. de Valera

I expect you will have no difficulty filling my place.

To Mick Ryan, the friend of his Rugby-playing days at Rockwell who
had been in the Irish Triple Crown team of 1899, he wrote:

My dear Mick,

Just a line to say I played my last match last week and lost. Tomorrow I
am to be shot—so pray for me—an old sport who unselfishly played the game.

Remember me to Pat, Jack, Nora, Margaret and the Mrs. Tell Colgan
we will never have another game of Nap together, or beat Rice's bog.

Farewell old friends.
You are in my last thoughts,
(Sgd) de Valera

Not long ago, when de Valera saw these letters again, he was shocked
by what he thought was the levity with which he wrote to Mick Ryan.
Outsiders may well feel moved by his efforts to soften the sadness.

Already the executions had begun a revulsion of feeling. In Ireland
few had sympathised with the Rising, but the daily bulletins listing those
executed that morning had a marked effect on public opinion. In Britain
too the policy of military executions was being questioned. The Dublin
executions ceased for some days after the morning of de Valera's court
martial. The British Government was reviewing General Maxwell's
military policy and had apparently reached the conclusion that the
executions should stop, except in the cases of 'ringleaders'. This phrase
seems to have been directed principally against Connolly and MacDermott,
the two surviving signatories of the Proclamation, but few felt much hope
for de Valera whose command had been responsible for so many British
casualties. In his cell in Kilmainham de Valera waited for the verdict in
his trial. He did not find the thought of death easy, but it was even harder
to wait for it. The following day an officer arrived and read to him the
verdict of the court. He was convicted and sentenced to death. De Valera
had expected this and had steeled himself to show no emotion. To his
surprise, after an interval, the officer then read a second document
commuting the sentence to penal servitude for life. De Valera decided
to receive the tidings in exactly the same way as he had received the
sentence of death. He listened to the officer with an unchanging
countenance.

The Rising was over. Two further leaders, however, signatories of the Proclamation, were executed, James Connolly and Seán MacDermott. Their deaths helped to accentuate the change of feeling among the people of Ireland which the other executions had begun. Two commandants escaped the firing squad because of the delay in bringing them to trial. They were Thomas Ashe and Eamon de Valera. It has been suggested that the latter was reprieved because of his American birth. There is no evidence of this, and the fact that he and Ashe were both tried and reprieved on the same day supports the view that it was the effect of the executions on public opinion and the delay which saved them. De Valera was the senior officer of the Irish Volunteers who took part in the Rising and escaped. The exploits in the area under his command were soon to win him a high renown among the Irish people as they learned of the events of Easter week. But the unyielding tenacity of his men was something which he himself had, at the beginning, scarcely counted on. He had expected those on the outposts to hold out for a while and then withdraw before superior forces. In fact they held out till their outposts were shattered or they were dead.

It is often said that British official folly turned the men of 1916 into martyrs. That is no doubt true, but they had already proved themselves heroes and Ireland, before very long, began to recognise them as such. In the prophetic words of Pearse, 'My sons were faithful and they fought'. Execution or no execution, this would surely have come to be the Irish and the world opinion.

FELONS OF OUR LAND

April, 1916 – June, 1917

De Valera was now removed from Kilmainham to the more comfortable Mountjoy Prison. Here he was given prison clothes and his first bath since the uprising. The prison chaplain offered him for his diversion a book on mathematics: unfortunately, on arrival, it turned out to be a school book of elementary algebraic problems. He also got him a copy of *The Imitation of Christ* in Irish. During prison exercises, as he and about a hundred other Volunteers marched in circles, he saw amid the crowd Thomas Ashe and the irrepressible Harry Boland. Soon the regulations were being evaded and tales of the Rising exchanged.

Máirín remembers very little about Easter week itself.

There was the maid who was working for my mother and held me up on the wall at the end of the garden and pointed in the direction of the city, telling me to look at the fires. I could see no fires.

Being taken care of by an English neighbour.

Being told, I don't know by whom, that my father was not going to be shot after all, but that he was going to be taken away to a big house with high walls and little windows with bars on them.

De Valera was visited by his wife and two eldest children. Vivion proudly showed him his new toy pistol. Máirín continues:

Going with my mother and brother to see my father in prison, before he was taken to Dartmoor. He looked stern and indignant—I don't think I ever hated anything (certainly I never hated anyone) as I hated the warder on duty—but my parents did not seem to take any notice of him.

At the time of the Easter Rising, Vivion was five, Eamon two and a half and Brian not yet one year old. We were all too young to understand the strain and worry which my mother endured. We only knew that she was altogether committed to the cause of Irish Freedom though of course we didn't understand what that was all about. At that time and throughout the years that followed she shielded us from fear and anxiety. She often repeated what little Éamonn had said to her during Easter week: 'Ta Deaidí imithe ach fillfidh sé. (Daddy is gone away, but he will come back again).

But he was not to be left long in Mountjoy. After a week he was given his own clothes and sent with a batch of other prisoners to England, under military escort. The long journey was enlivened by the high spirits of some of the men. The Fenians had been prisoners for up to twenty years; they could hardly expect much less. They had been given permission to smoke, normally forbidden, and as they approached the desolate moorlands of Dartmoor and caught sight of the prison, one man jokingly resolved to give up smoking until his five years' sentence had passed, another until Ireland would be free. De Valera, taking the pipe out of his mouth, announced that he would never smoke again. Harry Boland quipped that he was certainly making preparations for his life sentence.

Once within Dartmoor, de Valera was given prison clothes and became 'convict q95'. The warders were gruff and spoke threateningly to the Irish prisoners. Obviously they felt that the Irishmen were an extra dangerous type of convict. They were more likely than most to act in unison. So the prison staff early set about teaching them to obey orders without question.

The prison library was not well stocked. De Valera asked for a Spanish grammar or dictionary, intending to learn his forefathers' language. A member of the prison staff, a teacher, managed to find him a Spanish anthology. The first piece in it was by the fifteenth-century Diego de Valera. Eamon de Valera, however, decided that his Spanish studies would have to wait for adequate books. Silence was rigorously imposed. Prisoners were allowed one letter in four months.

Faced with a life sentence, de Valera did not expect release within the foreseeable future. In the United States of America, his half brother, Father Wheelwright, and other Redemptorist fathers bombarded senators and congressmen with letters. They sought President Wilson's intervention to reduce de Valera's sentence. President and State Department refused. In July, the latter wrote: 'The fact that Mr de Valera may be an American citizen constitutes no reason for clemency in his case, or for a request by this Government for clemency on the part of the British Government'.[1]

Assisted, however, by his military rank, de Valera was now beginning to emerge as a leader. One evening he heard a new arrival being questioned outside his cell. It was Eoin MacNeill whom he had admired both as vice-president of the Gaelic League and as chairman of the executive of the Irish Volunteers. MacNeill, however, had issued the countermanding order on Easter Sunday and there was little love for him at that moment among his imprisoned compatriots. De Valera was determined to show him that he would not be isolated. The next morning the prisoners were lined up in the hall before going out to exercise, de Valera at the extreme right. Suddenly he glimpsed the unmistakable and still bearded MacNeill descending the staircase on the left. Immediately de Valera stepped forward and ordered the prisoners to attention. Facing towards MacNeill he saluted, at the same time commanding the Volunteers to 'Eyes left'. His orders were obeyed as if on a ceremonial parade. He was immediately sent to his cell and the Governor warned him that what he had done was mutiny—an offence for which he could be flogged.

Work did little to relieve the tedium of Dartmoor. He later wrote from Lewes Jail:

> Labour, as labour, we rather welcome for its own sake and as an employment, be it digging, carting manure, carrying sacks of coke on our back, or scrubbing our halls. Efficient at it, considering our previous training, is more than some of us can hope to be.
>
> Labour immediately associated in our minds with the tasks of the criminal and his debasement, monotonous and soul-killing as such labour generally is in itself, we cannot be expected to take to very kindly. In Dartmoor, fully realizing the consequences, I refused to pick oakum, because it was degrading. If other men similarly regard the stitch-stitch of the mailbag, I at any rate can understand and appreciate their feelings.[2]

Regulations were strict, news from outside infrequent. But de Valera was not the man to bow the knee. On one occasion he needed a pencil to record the results of some mathematical formula he had been allowed to work out on his slate. Lead pencils were forbidden. De Valera noticed that the workshop superintendent, a fellow prisoner, had a pencil with a particularly long point. Leaning forward, he broke the lead and pocketed it. He avoided the daily search of all the prisoners by hiding it in a piece of fluff on the floor of his cell.

On another occasion de Valera was not so lucky. A warder caught him throwing bread to a prisoner in the cell opposite. The dimly lit hall did not hide the throwing. Receiver and donor were sentenced to three days' confinement on bread and water. The traditional protest weapon was the hunger strike. De Valera considered the prospect. He remembered how some years before cycling back from a dance, with Frank Hughes, he had suddenly been overcome by the most terrible hunger and weakness; how, with the aid of his friend, he dragged himself to the nearest town, and before he could go on he consumed four raw eggs, four whiskeys, and a vast amount of bread and butter. All this raised doubts in his own mind about his capacity for this kind of endurance. It was all too real in his memory. For three or four days the food and water remained untouched.

Finally the worried and uncomprehending Governor told him he was to be transferred to the infirmary and then to Maidstone with two others. On the journey to Maidstone he was chained to his two companions, and so his first entrance into London was in chains.

He was only a few weeks in Maidstone before being again transferred, this time to Lewes—part of a large-scale movement to bring together Irish prisoners.

De Valera and his colleagues in Lewes knew little of the changing trend of political feeling in Ireland, England and America. In Ireland the military role of General Maxwell had ended. In Britain untried prisoners held at Frongoch and other detention centres were allowed to go home at Christmas. Lloyd George, now taking the place of Asquith, wished to mollify Irish-American feeling, so much roused by the executions, in the hope of American support in the war. If the convicted prisoners were not allowed home, at least they were granted better conditions. The wooden floors in Lewes replaced the hard flags of Dartmoor and Maidstone. Prisoners were allowed to talk freely when on exercise. The Governor, Major Marriott, was interested in geology. He approached MacNeill for some advice. But MacNeill told him that the professor of early Irish history from University College, Dublin, would be less help than the professor of mathematics from Carysfort. De Valera was allowed, through the Governor, to obtain a work of Poincaré's, so he was able to study some mathematics. The Governor was certainly lenient but was apparently reproved by higher authority. In Lewes de Valera read his first full account of the Rising in an Italian pamphlet.[3]

The prisoners made various attempts to get information on events outside. The Christmastide release of the untried prisoners had brought a new impulse to the 1916 spirit. In many of the letters from Lewes questions were asked about Kathleen Ni Houlihan, an allegorical name for Ireland used by the poets, and oblique answers received. The unsuspecting Governor, faced with Home Office orders to black out all references to this popular figure, drew the obvious conclusion. Was she, he asked one of the prisoners, a 'bad woman'?

De Valera sought a more reliable means of communication. He wrote to Simon Donnelly about the matter at Easter, 1917, in a dispatch smuggled out in scapulars worn by Gerald Crofts who was released because of ill-health:

> The only chance would be to draw up a detailed account and give it to trustworthy visitors coming here, with instructions that they were to endeavour to pass it to one of our men (in convict dress) who is often at the gate.

De Valera considered a knowledge of the political position essential for the prisoners:

> We regard ourselves as at present, in a very special way, identified with the cause, the ideals and aspirations for which our comrades died last Easter. We feel that any important action of ours will, too, have a reflex effect on last Easter's sacrifice and on any advantages which have been secured by that sacrifice. To do anything which would be liable to be misinterpreted and misrepresented—to create a wrong impression as to the ideals, principles and opinions which prompted last Easter's action would, it seems to us, be a national calamity.[4]

From the time he stepped forward at Dartmoor to order the salute for MacNeill, de Valera had been accepted as the leader of the prisoners. He now showed his attitude to prison discipline by framing a petition about the food. From an article in the *Catholic Bulletin* he calculated the calorific value of the prison diet. He claimed it was insufficient to maintain health even in idleness. Separate petitions were signed by de Valera, MacNeill and Éamonn Duggan. In this, de Valera was trying to make difficulties not for the Governor of the prison but for the British officials in the Home Office and for the Government. As a result, the prisoners were allowed a kippered herring three times a week. The Governor, however, soon became involved in trouble when a prisoner was sent to the punishment cell on bread and water for talking during work, and the prisoners, on de Valera's orders, refused to work. The Governor came to terms and released the man. Discipline was being broken down.

An inspector from the Home Office spent a week in the prison. De Valera, feeling that the inspector would recommend the dispersal of the prisoners, ordered that in that event they should continue to act in unison. If transferred, they should:

1. Refuse to put on civilian clothes for the journey—we must therefore be taken in convict garb.
2. Refuse to give parole for the journey—we will therefore be chained or they will have to send a very strong escort—we will sing songs on the journey if we go in groups.
3. Refuse at any time to go home on 'ticket of leave'.
4. Refuse to associate with other prisoners at work or at exercise—this will mean confinement for us.
5. Refuse to act as orderlies—(i.e. take around dinners, take up slops, etc.) —we will empty our own slops.
6. Refuse to use closets used by other prisoners—have chambers used in cells, I expect.
7. Refuse to do any labour in cell or out of it.[5]

The punishment which this involved could be severe; a loss of privileges, such as letters, a reduction to half rations and solitary confinement.

He was eager, however, to avoid useless suffering. He stopped prisoners on punishment from hunger striking. He advised:

> You may be tempted to Hunger Strike. As a body do not attempt it whilst the war lasts unless you were assured from outside that the death of two or three of you would help the cause. As soldiers I know you would not shrink from the sacrifice, but remember how precious a human life is . . .

In this document he also gave a list of nine men who might take over the leadership if he and others were removed. He also advised that 'as long as Eoin MacNeill is here, the committee should *always* consult with him'.

De Valera did not think that the Government would release them until, at the earliest, the end of the war. His primary concern was with the future of the Irish Volunteers. At Easter he wrote to Simon Donnelly:

> The armed force started in 1913 must not be allowed to disappear. The Irish Volunteers, or whatever else you like to call them, must be kept as a permanent force at the country's back. That it seems to us is our mission as a body and we must allow nothing to make us forget it.

Regarding the wisdom of contesting by-elections against members of the Irish Parliamentary Party, he had grave doubts. He felt that, left alone, the party would crumble, but if attacked it would reform itself and recover its prestige. Count Plunkett, however, was proposed as candidate for a by-election in Roscommon. Father Michael O'Flanagan made unambiguous speeches on his behalf, reminding audiences of the participation of Plunkett's sons in the Rising. Yet the policy was not defined. It was only some time after he had won the seat that Plunkett made it clear that he would not attend the British Parliament. On St Patrick's Day he issued an invitation to public bodies and national organisations to meet in the Mansion House, Dublin. His aim was that Ireland's claim to independence should be heard at the peace conference which would follow the war.

De Valera and the prisoners in Lewes still did not know how far their comrades who had been released at Christmas were united. Or whether as an organisation they supported Count Plunkett's policy. Naturally, they hoped he would win. But de Valera wished to clarify their position:

> It is a question whether it is good tactics (or strategy if you will) to provoke a contest in which *defeat* may well mean *ruin* . . . As soldiers (Irish Volunteers, etc.) we should abstain *officially* from taking sides in these contests and no candidates should in future be *officially* recognized as standing in our interests

or as representing our ideals. We can individually help all those who are striving for Ireland's freedom by other means—there will never be any lack of these—but we should *as a body* keep to our own special sphere.

On Count Plunkett's policy he asked:

How far is it a reversion to the old Sinn Féin *political* movement? With his movement, or that part of it which aims at getting representative men to draw up a statement on Ireland's case for presentation at the Peace Conference, we are heartily in accord, and it seems to us that if his policy were limited to this one (and new) issue it would be endorsed by the majority of the Irish people.[6]

Through these means, he thought the national forces in Ireland might be united. America's entry into the war would, he considered, make the peace conference more favourable to Ireland's standpoint.

De Valera's letters had not yet got through to Donnelly when the prisoners were faced with a political decision. A parliamentary seat for Longford became vacant and a Lewes prisoner, Joseph McGuiness, was proposed by friends outside. Count Plunkett sought his consent. The prisoners took counsel. De Valera wrote:

As regards the contesting of elections question, it is so extremely dangerous from several points of view that most of us here consider it very unwise.

Regarding the appeal to the post-war peace conference, he was emphatic that they should demand nothing less than absolute independence:

If delegates are sent and are admitted they should be given no powers of agreeing to anything less.[7]

His principal fear was that something would be done in the name of the prisoners which might be considered as a retreat from the position taken up in the 1916 Proclamation of the Republic.

MacGuiness' letter refusing the nomination was drafted by de Valera. Other drafts were proposed by Thomas Ashe and Diarmuid Lynch. Despite this, MacGuiness' candidature went ahead and, after a recount, he won by thirty-seven votes. The men outside had calculated rightly the chance of success. The appeal which they had made to the public had, however, not stated any clearly defined aim. 'Put him in to get him out' was a slogan which won sympathy for the prisoner, but it did not necessarily keep the Republican flag flying.

At this time the Irish Nation League, an anti-partition body formed in Ireland in September, 1916, began to press that the Irish prisoners be treated as prisoners-of-war. De Valera decided to call a strike on this question. He arranged that a telegram should be sent to Harry Boland in Lewes which would announce the death of his uncle if those outside agreed with the plan. The sad news arrived; and the chaplain posed a theological problem for the prisoner by offering to say a requiem mass for the non-existent uncle.

Lloyd George meanwhile had announced the setting up of an Irish Convention, wishing to impress the United States which, a month earlier, had entered the war. It was possible that he might try to make a big gesture by releasing the prisoners. De Valera pointed out in his final orders for the strike that in this way they would anticipate England's move and 'deprive her of any credit she may hope to gain from the release'. The order was signed by de Valera, Ashe and Hunter. It ended thus:

> When you form up after exercise, do not move off till I have handed the ultimatum to the warder.
> When I have returned to my place, let each man simultaneously take his cap in hand and give three cheers for Ireland.
> Return to attention—await warder's orders. Shop, garden and painters' parties will not move off to work.

The strike began on Whit Monday, May 28th, 1917. The prisoners, except those in the cleaning squad, refused to work. The cleaning squad, always mobile, could keep them informed on events both inside and outside the prison. The prisoners were marched back to their cells. As arranged, they did no work except that which was personally necessary.

An offer to exercise under convict conditions was refused. De Valera ordered that, on being let out to mass the next Sunday, they should refuse to return to their cells, take possession of the prison and force the authorities to summon the military. This order was discovered and the prisoners were forbidden to attend mass unless they promised not to make a demonstration. Instead they recited the rosary in their cells. This episode was used to represent de Valera as an atheist.[9] The bishop's secretary later told the prisoners that the diocesan bishop's name had been used without authority, and his view misrepresented.[10] De Valera remembered nineteenth-century British policy. Rome was to persuade the people to keep the peace. He would have none of that in prison.

Still there was no reply to the demand for treatment as prisoners-of-war. Plan two was a systematic destruction of the prison cell windows the first night, spyholes the second, lamp screens the third—individual initiative encouraged. Singing 'God save Ireland' they set to work. The prison authorities decided that separation would break this resistance. De Valera and some prisoners were returned to Maidstone; others went to Parkhurst.

De Valera had regretted doing no damage to Maidstone Prison on his former brief visit. Here was a second chance. He was made more determined when the Governor accused him of playing on the good nature of the reasonable Governor at Lewes. He would not meet any softness at Maidstone. His first act of defiance was to strike the windows with a three-legged stool. Unfortunately, after three attempts he could only crack the glass. When a warder arrived he still persisted.

When the Governor interviewed him, de Valera was ordered to attention. He refused. He was ordered to button his jacket. He refused; it was more comfortable open. Warders buttoned it for him. He unbuttoned it with one tug; it was more comfortable that way. De Valera knew that his punishment of solitary confinement and bread and water could not be repeated without a break more than once or twice. There were fewer punishments than there were ways of breaking prison discipline.

A warder entered the cell and ordered him to stand for the Governor. De Valera was more comfortable lying down. He was jerked to his feet. He simply told the Governor that he had no more respect for him standing up than he had lying down. He lay down again.

During his punishments de Valera was moved to a new cell. In Lewes, engaged in horseplay with another prisoner, he had crushed a disc in his spine—although he only found this out years later. The only position which he found at all bearable was to lie on the flagged floor with his feet resting on the wall. In this position he studied the high cell window. It was plain glass. Pain or no pain, he knew his duty. He got up and broke it.

The events in prison were reported with perhaps some exaggeration in the Irish papers. Cathal Brugha and others co-operated by organising protests. Relatives of the prisoners were instructed to bombard the various prison governors with telegrams. On Sunday, June 10th, a protest meeting was held in Dublin. Although it was proclaimed, a huge crowd assembled. The arrest of the speakers led to a mêlée with a tragic outcome. A police inspector was killed with a hurling stick.

Politically, the prisoners' fight was admirably timed. As they had expected, the Prime Minister, with the Convention in mind, decided to release the prisoners. On June 15th, Bonar Law, the Chancellor of the Exchequer and the Leader of the House, announced that the Government had decided to release the prisoners.

The order for release came as a complete surprise to de Valera and his companions in Maidstone. However, they received the news impassively, as they had received their punishments. They were united in the rigid discipline which de Valera had taught them.

All the prisoners were quickly collected in Pentonville where they were given civilian clothes. De Valera kept his badge with 'q 95' on it as a memento. One prisoner managed to take out his whole convict outfit under his new suit. Before leaving the jail, de Valera, MacNeill and a few others said a prayer at the grave of Roger Casement who had been executed there the preceding August.

As he emerged from Pentonville, de Valera was handed a telegram informing him that he had been chosen to contest a parliamentary seat in East Clare. He had decided views against contesting any election, but he resolved to consult the leaders in Dublin before taking a decision.

The Irish in London gave the prisoners a rousing send-off from Euston Station. Girls went round with trays of pipes and tobacco. But de Valera stood by the resolution which he had made on the way to Dartmoor. His refusal to smoke helped to create an image of ascetic dedication which followed him throughout life.

At Westland Row the prisoners had their first taste of the new spirit abroad in Ireland. The same men who had been insulted on Dublin streets after Easter, 1916, were now accorded a tumultuous welcome. De Valera, MacNeill and all the others were hailed as heroes. One of the prisoners wrote of de Valera in particular:

> As the leader of the prisoners, [he] was the hero of the hour . . . He arrived in Dublin the accepted leader of the men of Easter week.[11]

After public recognition came the long-awaited family reunion. Mrs de Valera had had a distressing year since the events of Easter week. Máirín writes:

> We still wonder how my mother lived through the months that followed the Rising. She had no income, and had to leave our home and return to live with her parents, brother and sisters. She had to send Viv and me to stay with her other sister and aunt in Balbriggan—Éamonn joined us later on.
>
> My grandparents were very old and both were semi-invalids. My eldest aunt was living with them and was suffering from a very painful form of cancer. She was bedridden and because money was very scarce a nurse or other hired help was out of the question. My mother had to undertake all the work of nursing her, as well as all the housework, cooking and care of the old and the babies. My younger aunt was a teacher and was out at work most of the day as was my uncle. He was very lame.
>
> My elder aunt died in August 1916, my brother Ruairí was born in November that year and my grandmother died in January 1917.

Máirín can remember her father coming to Balbriggan to take them home. He had been released from jail and had rented a house in Greystones.

I think I can truly say that during all the hard years from 1916 to 1924, the only thing about which I heard my mother complain with any degree of bitterness was the constant stream of well-meaning callers, many of them Job's comforters. She learned to hate the sound of the hall door bell, as to some extent did we children in spite of the sweets that some of the visitors brought us.

Mrs de Valera, always retiring, did not take part in the public celebrations of welcome. She waited patiently at home until a boy whom she had taught at school rushed up shouting that de Valera was arriving over Cross Guns Bridge. With Father Roche he had left the celebrations and come to meet his wife once more.

Left: Aged 4½, wearing, he says,
his aunt's boots.

Right: At about the age of 12.

Vivion and Catherine de Valera,
Eamon's parents.

Left: Uncle Edward Coll, who brought Eamon back from America.

Right: Uncle Pat Coll, who brought him up.

Below: The President revisits his childhood home at Bruree.

EAMON AND SINÉAD DE VALERA

Right and below: Two wedding
day pictures,
1910.

Right: Celebrating their
Diamond Jubilee, 1970.

The only family group of Eamon and Sinéad de Valera and all their children.
Standing (left to right): Ruarí, Vivion, Eamon, Brian; *sitting (left to right):*
Máirín, Sinéad and Eamon de Valera, Emer; *and kneeling in front:* Terry.
Brian died shortly after this picture was taken in 1936.

Above: The British Army recruiting drive in Dublin at the beginning of World War One.

Below: The 'Asgard' discharges her cargo of Mauser rifles at Howth. In the centre is the Hon. Mary Spring-Rice, daughter of Lord Monteagle, and on her right is Erskine Childers.

From Commander of Dublin forces
To P. H. Pearce
29. April/16
1.40 P.M.
A woman has come in and tells me
you wish to negotiate with me.
I am prepared to receive you in
BRITAIN ST at the North End of
MOORE ST provided that you
surrender unconditionally.
You will proceed up MOORE ST
accompanied only by the woman who
brings you this note under a white
flag.
W. H. Lowe
B. Genl.

EASTER 1916

Above: The surrender demand, signed
by Brigadier General Lowe.

Right: De Valera in uniform.

Below: Clanwilliam House, the outpost of de Valera's command where the
fiercest resistance took place.

Above: Behind the white flag, de Valera leads his surviving troops after the surrender.

Below: Under close arrest before his court martial.

[6]

NATIONAL RESURGENCE

June, 1917 – May, 1918

At a meeting of the Irish Volunteers de Valera took one of the most momentous decisions of his life. He agreed to contest the East Clare by-election, making the condition that Eoin MacNeill should accompany him. So the healing process continued, and a promising soldier took the first step towards becoming a world-famous statesman.

The name Sinn Féin pervaded everything. Derogatively it had been attached to the Rising of the previous year, now all opposed to Redmond were looked on as Sinn Féiners. De Valera found himself included in their number.

On the Friday following his release de Valera travelled to Bruree, his home town, before beginning a weekend's electioneering. Contingents from Charleville and Kilfinane, Ballylanders and Bruff, waited to meet him. They formed an enthusiastic procession. Eager admirers replaced the horse between the shafts of his cart. De Valera was reminded of how, as a child, he had been entranced by the Fedamore big drum as the local bands played martial airs through the village.

From Bruree de Valera went to Ennis, the capital of Clare. He and MacNeill spoke all over the county. A listener at Tulla wrote to the *Irish Times:*

> I have never heard a cause pleaded with more transparent honesty and loftier patriotism. With them, be they right or wrong, it was Ireland first, last and all the time.[1]

De Valera fought the campaign on clearly defined issues. He appealed for a revival of the national language, an object close to his heart. He wanted Ireland's case heard at the post-war peace conference. He made it clear that he would not attend the British Parliament and that on the Ulster question the majority would not surrender their rights to a minority. 'Ulster was entitled to justice and she should have it, but she should not be petted and the interests of the majority sacrificed to please her.'[2]

Above all he stood by the principles of the Easter Rising. 'Mr de Valera,'

4

wrote one newspaper, 'has declared for complete and absolute independence—for an Irish Republic.'[3] In a draft for one speech he wrote:

> Political platforms have little attraction for me, but in this case I considered that the principles for which my comrades died were at stake and that it was my duty, seeing I still adhered to these principles, to avail of every opportunity to vindicate and advance them.

The draft then quoted part of the Proclamation of the Irish Republic read by Pearse at the beginning of the Rising. He went on:

> That proclamation was sealed . . . by . . . the life blood of all its members . . . To that government, when in visible shape, I offered my allegiance and to its spirit I owe my allegiance still.

He described the shape of his allegiance:

> To assert it in arms, were there a fair chance of a military success, I would consider a sacred duty.[4]

At Scarrif and Killaloe, as elsewhere, he spoke of the Republican ideal of wanting an Irish Republic because if Ireland had her freedom it was the most likely form of government. So long as it was an Irish government, he would not put in a word against it.[5] He appealed to the Irish Nationalist spirit:

> Every voter amongst you knows in his heart of hearts that his aspirations are ours—it will be the glorious privilege of each to boldly proclaim the truth.[6]

The Irish Party candidate, Patrick Lynch, K.C., came from one of the best thought of families in Clare. However, as former Crown prosecutor he was not so attractive a figure as the 'Crown prosecuted'. Moreover the Irish Party was by now much discredited. The carrot of the long-delayed Home Rule seemed even further beyond their reach. The threat of partition had not been dealt with firmly by John Redmond and there was a growing fear of conscription.

De Valera wanted a clean fight without personal vituperation: 'The depths to which the party machine has dragged public life is almost inconceivable.'[7]

De Valera's supporters were organised with military precision. Irish Volunteers came from all over the country. They canvassed votes and eventually manned the polling-booths. Every instruction was treated as a military order. Their hotel rooms were like military camps.

Feelings ran high. The wife of one of the Munster Fusiliers was seen in the streets of Ennis challenging every Sinn Féiner with her husband's drawn sword. De Valera and Lynch kept the conflict on a high plane. Peace was secured by Volunteers nominated by both candidates.

The election result was overwhelming. Mrs de Valera received this telegram: 'De Valera 5010, Lynch 2035. Dev.' De Valera heard the results dressed in his Volunteer uniform. He proclaimed, amid loud cheers, his solidarity with the comrades of Easter week, saying that 'this election would always be historic, a monument to those glorious men.'[8]

The resounding victory was hailed jubilantly. From Sligo to Vinegar Hill bonfires blazed in celebration. De Valera's return from Clare was a triumphal procession. In Dublin he told the crowds that in order that Ireland's case might be heard at the peace conference she should first claim absolute independence.[9] De Valera's success in Clare dramatically illustrated that no Irish Party seat could be counted on. The Irish Convention which Lloyd George had called was already anachronistic. As one paper put it:

> The Convention, in the light of East Clare, has the promise of Dead Sea fruit and the stability of an inverted pyramid.[10]

The political initiative, almost overnight, had passed into the hands of the opponents of the Irish Parliamentary Party. These opponents still lacked co-ordination and a formulated policy, but while de Valera was still in prison some attempts at unity had been made. Representatives of the Irish Nation League, the Labour Party and of Sinn Féin came together. A joint committee was formed. In June 1917, Brugha, with Thomas Dillon, now secretary of the joint committee, decided that unity throughout Sinn Féin was imperative.

Arthur Griffith agreed to a new provisional executive of six representatives from the existing Sinn Féin committee, six from Count Plunkett's newly formed Liberty Clubs and six from the joint committee. The objects and officers were to remain unchanged until a general meeting. For the moment, the aim of Sinn Féin as stated in its constitution was still the restoration of the Irish Parliament under the Crown.

But the aims of the Irish Volunteers were clearly far removed from 'the restoration of the king, lords and commons.' The papers were already pointing to de Valera as the 'real leader of Sinn Féin'[11]—a new Sinn Féin, fast becoming a Volunteer body. Grants paid from the relief fund for resettlement of the released prisoners left them free to enter politics. De Valera's importance as their acknowledged but unofficial leader was recognised when he became a member of the Sinn Féin national council and of the provisional executive of the Irish Volunteers.[12] At his first meeting of the Volunteer executive, Cathal Brugha was in the chair when he arrived. Brugha immediately insisted that de Valera, as senior officer, take his place.

De Valera did not resume relations with the secret Irish Republican Brotherhood. He had argued in Lewes that the secret organisation was no longer necessary. The Volunteers could work openly for Irish independence. This was also the view of Cathal Brugha. The contradictory orders at Easter exemplified the problems arising between a public and a secret organisation. He also disliked swearing to obey an executive of unidentified members. Because his attitude was well known, he was not apparently approached to continue his membership.

At the same time he helped win another by-election, in Kilkenny City. The Sinn Féin candidate, nominated at de Valera's suggestion, was W. T. Cosgrave, one of the 1916 men who had been sentenced to death and reprieved. He polled almost twice as many votes as his opponent. For ten years (1922–32) he was to be Prime Minister of the Irish Free State and he was referred to by Winston Churchill in *The Aftermath* as a 'chieftain of higher quality than any who had yet appeared'.

On his release from prison de Valera had looked around for a suitable teaching post. But a grant of £250 from the National Aid Fund and Griffith's persuasions decided him to devote all his time to the national cause. He had felt that it was in the military sphere rather than the political that he could be of most use to the country. Something in his nature was now drawing him towards political leadership. But politics and soldiering were not yet fully sorted out in his mind. At that stage he felt that a strong Volunteer movement could direct any political organisation into the principles of the Easter week proclamation. At a Sinn Féin meeting, he stated clearly that politics could actually be run on military lines. He apparently envisaged the use of the military body as the basis for political clubs and of the communication system of the Volunteers for political purposes. At a Dublin meeting he demanded the return of the bodies of the leaders executed the previous year. He visited Longford and Ballaghadereen, and at Tullamore addressed an audience of some ten thousand. Despite a British military order he always wore his Volunteer uniform.

The enthusiasm for the policy of putting Ireland's case before the peace conference was growing. Moreover the Irish demand was not for a whittled-down form of Home Rule, but for full independence. The electoral results started the tide of public opinion flowing against the Irish Party. One event strengthened it greatly. In late September Thomas Ashe, one of the Lewes prisoners now in Mountjoy Prison, died under forcible feeding. Ashe was one of the eighty-four Republicans arrested for making 'speeches calculated to cause disaffection'. He was on hunger strike for prisoner-of-war treatment. Two days before Ashe collapsed in the surgeon's chair de Valera proposed a resolution at a public meeting in Smithfield calling the attention of the European powers and of the United States to the treatment of Irishmen. He referred to President Wilson's statement 'that no people shall be forced to live under a sovereignty under which it does not desire to live.'[13]

Ashe's death showed that the 1916 Volunteer spirit still lived. His funeral and lying-in-state were the occasion for an immense demonstration of public sympathy with the young man and with his cause. De Valera's speeches became ever more militant. After a fortnight's campaign in Clare, one newspaper correspondent wrote at the beginning of October:

> He has a strenuous time. There seems to be no limit to his energy. It is ostensibly a political campaign, but it is worked on military lines. The idol is, *de facto,* the general. The general's army of young Sinn Féiners, capable, well-equipped and most skilfully trained, has been playing at soldiers in intense earnestness.[14]

De Valera returned to Dublin about the middle of the month. The English correspondent who followed him everywhere wrote—'they are all in dead earnest . . . they are feverishly, but quietly, at work; their organisation becomes better every day, their enthusiasm keener, and their confidence firmer. The Irish Republic is to them a dream no longer.'[15]

What now became crucial was the relationship between Sinn Féin and the Volunteers. The latter were determined on the reform of the constitution of the former. It was arranged to hold a convention on October 25th in the Mansion House, Dublin.

Would the political and military movements again separate? De Valera realised that the Republican movement must be above all a movement of people. Not for the last time he succeeded in producing a definition of aims: 'Sinn Féin', he announced, 'aims at securing the international recognition of Ireland as an independent Irish Republic. Having achieved that status, the Irish people may, by referendum, freely choose their own form of government.'

With this formula de Valera reconciled two apparently irreconcilable elements. He was one important step closer towards formal leadership. Dr Thomas Dillon has recorded that at those meetings 'a split would have been inevitable only for de Valera.' People got up and walked out, but de Valera brought them back again.

About a week before the convention de Valera met Griffith over coffee in the D.B.C. restaurant near the top of Grafton Street. The principal problem was the presidency of the new organisation, Sinn Féin. De Valera, Griffith and Count Plunkett would all be nominated. The Irish Volunteers and the IRB (mainly composed of Volunteers) supported de Valera. The Volunteers knew him for a 1916 man, and the IRB for a staunch Republican. Griffith was supported by old Sinn Féin adherents. Plunkett had the backing of Liberty Clubs. The discussion with Griffith was friendly, but de Valera was firm. He insisted if he went forward he would win, since the new Sinn Féin was largely a Volunteer movement. But it would be better if there were no contest. Griffith agreed and decided not only to withdraw his name, but to propose de Valera. It was a magnanimous gesture from the older man, the existing president who was not yet certain of defeat.

The convention, which lasted for two days, was lively. Some 1,700 delegates attended. The committee's draft for the new constitution was proposed. De Valera explained his idea of a referendum on the final form of government.

> The only banner under which our freedom can be won at the present time is the Republican banner. It is as an Irish Republic that we have a chance of getting international recognition . . . Some might have faults to find with that and prefer other forms of government. But we are all united on this— that we want complete and absolute independence . . . This is not the time for discussion on the best forms of government. This is the time to get freedom. Then we can settle by the most democratic means what particular form of government we may have. I only wish to say in reference to the last clause that there is no contemplation in it of having a monarchy in which the monarch would be of the House of Windsor.

Unity was ensured when Arthur Griffith proposed Eamon de Valera as president. He praised his sincerity, courage, determination and judgement. His election would secure a leader who was statesman as well as soldier. Count Plunkett then withdrew his candidature. De Valera was elected unopposed. A presidential salary of £500 left de Valera free to devote all his energies to the struggle for independence. Returning thanks for his election, de Valera said, amidst prolonged applause, that it was a monument to the dead: 'I believe that this is proof that they were right'. He added that what they fought for, the complete and absolute freedom and separation from England, was the pious wish of every Irish heart.

During the election of the council and other officers, Countess Markievicz bitterly attacked Eoin MacNeill. Both de Valera and Griffith defended him and he was elected at the head of the executive poll. Michael Collins had circulated to IRB members a list of candidates to be supported. Darrell Figgis had done the same for the more conservative element. Many spoke against these 'Irish Party methods'. De Valera said, 'Beginning a new Ireland it will not be necessary to resort to such methods any more.' Collins was the last member of the executive to be elected. As yet he was little known.[16]

Griffith considered that this convention, the tenth Ard Fheis of Sinn Féin as he regarded it, continued the life of his old organisation, but the new constitution fundamentally altered its aims. Its immediate object was international recognition of an Irish Republic. Yet it was committed to 'make use of any and every means available to render impotent the power of England to hold Ireland in subjection.' It is true that de Valera explained that only moral means were intended and Brugha excluded assassination.

The constitution preserved, however, the original Sinn Féin idea of a constituent assembly to carry on the functions of government. And this retention made the other changes more palatable to Griffith. A detailed revision of organisation and rules drafted by de Valera was passed. *Dáil Éireann* first appears here as the name of the proposed constituent assembly. Sinn Féin membership was open to all adults of Irish birth or parentage, except members or pensioners of the British armed forces or those who held positions involving an oath of allegiance to the British Monarch.

The unity of the convention surprised and impressed its opponents. It was thought that the British Government only permitted the meeting because it could precipitate a split in the organisation. Newspapers, though completely unsympathetic, unanimously recognised the importance of the new Sinn Féin.

The military organisation held a separate convention in the Gaelic Athletic Association's grounds on the day after the Sinn Féin Ard Fheis. Many were delegates to both conventions. The meeting place was a great change from the impressive Round Room of the Mansion House. De Valera was still in the chair, but the platform was a bench of hay behind him on which lay the leaders of new Ireland, Brugha, Collins, Stack, and others. Rows of country delegates faced them, seated on planks and crude forms. In the result the aims of the 1914 constitution were unchanged:

1. To secure and maintain the rights and liberties common to all the people of Ireland.

2. To train, discipline and equip for this purpose an Irish Volunteer force.

3. To unite in the service of Ireland Irishmen of every creed and of every party and class.

Unlike the original Sinn Féin, the constitution of the Volunteers already embraced the Republican ideal. The Irish Volunteers were so basically Republican that it was unnecessary to incorporate it into their constitution.

The election returned most of the provisional executive. Collins was elected mainly through the influence of de Valera who recognised his excellent executive qualities. De Valera himself was elected President. Later, Cathal Brugha was appointed Chief of Staff and Collins Director of Organisation.

The military and political wings of the National movement were now combined under one man, Eamon de Valera. The Prime Minister, Lloyd George, watched de Valera's progress as a politician. He commented on his speeches in the House of Commons: 'They are not excited and, so far as language is concerned, they are not violent. They are plain, deliberate, and I might also say cold-blooded incitements to rebellion . . . This is not a case of violent, abusive and excitable language. It is the case of a man of great ability, of considerable influence, deliberately going down to the district . . . to stir people up to rebellion against the authorities.'[17] But de Valera's arrest was not expected. One English paper reported that the Government proposed to establish a council in Ireland to advise the Lord Lieutenant on policy. This council would gradually take over executive functions and act as a cabinet to a convention which would assume the role of a parliament. De Valera and MacNeill were listed as probable members.[18]

Lloyd George had set up an 'Irish Convention' supposedly representative. But ignored by Sinn Féin it lacked the people's confidence or interest. It showed no signs of being the nucleus of a parliament. De Valera reiterated the Sinn Féin attitude to the convention and rejected the proposed council: 'I would never allow myself to become a tool or an instrument for enforcing British law in Ireland.'[19]

Many arrests followed the Ard Fheis. Meetings at Newbridge and Waterford were proclaimed. De Valera merely altered their location and carried on. Food shortage was one outcome of the war in Ireland. Sinn Féin set up a food committee to arrange for the retention of necessary food then being exported to England.

At this time de Valera was faced with growing criticism from the more conservative Catholic clergy. The question of the ethics of insurrection was raised by Dr Gilmartin, Archbishop of Tuam. At Athy de Valera spoke on Sinn Féin morality. There were two steps towards setting up a real government in Ireland. The first was to repudiate English authority. The second was to build up a self-reliant nation.[20]

Cardinal Logue, speaking to the priests of his diocese, attacked Sinn Féin and described the demand for an Irish Republic as 'ill-considered and Utopian.' And 'a dream which no man in his sober senses can hope to see realised.'[21] Next evening, at a concert in Roscommon, de Valera answered the Cardinal's charge of immorality. He cited Pope Leo XIII to prove that it was not necessarily wrong to prefer a democratic form of government. The critics' objection to the Sinn Féin programme was that they considered it Utopian and because it was Utopian they said it was immoral. But no one considered Belgium's resistance to Germany immoral. However, de Valera did not want a direct controversy with the Cardinal, and refused a statement to the papers.

In spring, 1918, Sinn Féin lost three by-elections. Two, South Armagh and East Tyrone, were in Ulster. Here the Orangemen and the Hibernians combined against Sinn Féin where the Cardinal had his greatest influence. The third, Waterford, was an old Redmondite stronghold. De Valera's views on the Ulster question were distorted by the newspapers. In a draft for one letter he wrote:

> See the unnatural combination of Orangeman and Hibernian. Ask yourself what does it mean. Why has the Unionist candidate retired? Why all this anxiety by the Unionist press to keep Sinn Féin out of Ulster? I say it is because Sinn Féin is the only power to deal with the Orangeman. Let the Orangemen fall back on their fortress of the two races, their fortress of partition—that has no terrors for us. Let them fall back on it, they will find it a Metz. It is after all only an old fortress of crumbled masonry—held together with a plaster of fiction.[22]

From the beginning he was sure that the fight for Irish freedom would not leave an insoluble problem in the north-east.

The triumph of Sinn Féin was hastened through the inconceivable stupidity, as it must seem to us now, of British policy. A successful German offensive on the Western Front led to the extension of the age limit for compulsory military service in England. By March, 1918, there was a widespread demand in England for the extension of conscription to Ireland. The Irish bishops passed a resolution warning the British Government against such a course. Yet the same evening Lloyd George announced to the House that Ireland's exclusion could no longer be justified. Immediately Ireland was ablaze. It was a brutal shock to followers of the Irish Party. Men, women and children determined to fight. But only Sinn Féin and the Volunteers were organised. The bishops' statement dissolved the doubts about the morality of physical force which had hampered Sinn Féin. Moreover, the bishops secretly decided that if the clergy were included in the Conscription Bill, a general meeting of the Irish hierarchy would be summoned.

Dublin Corporation was equally resolute. The Lord Mayor, Laurence O'Neill, invited representative leaders to meet at the Mansion House 'to arrange for a united opposition to conscription and to consider the advisability of establishing an all-Ireland Covenant on the subject.'

De Valera and Griffith were invited on behalf of Sinn Féin. Many of its members advised them to boycott the meeting, as they had the Irish Convention. But this was no handpicked meeting of Lloyd George's. De Valera accepted, but suggested that representatives of the All-For-Ireland League and the Irish Unionists should also be invited.

The Lord Mayor's meeting was held on April 18th. Old animosities between the two parliamentary groups did not spoil it. Healy was reported as 'considerate and conciliatory to a degree that took away the breath of Mr Dillon himself.' It was de Valera's first meeting with the men whose faces had decorated the walls near his bed in Bruree. The fiery young Dillon of the Land War was now the respected and conservative parliamentarian. O'Brien and Healy still carried some of the vehemence of their youth, but their methods did not impress the younger man. At the meeting he showed no awe. O'Brien recorded:

His transparent sincerity, his gentleness and equability captured the hearts of us all. His gaunt frame and sad eyes deeply buried in their sockets had much of the Dantesque suggestion of 'the man who had been in hell'. His was that subtle blend of virility and emotion which the Americans mean when they speak of 'a magnetic man'. Even the obstinacy (and it was sometimes trying) with which he would defend a thesis, as though it were a point in pure mathematics, with more than French bigotry for logic, became tolerable enough when, with a boyish smile, he would say: 'You will bear with me won't you? You know I am an old schoolmaster?'[23]

The delegates agreed unanimously to a form of pledge drafted by de Valera; 'Denying the right of the British Government to enforce compulsory service in this country, we pledge ourselves solemnly to one another to resist conscription by the most effective means at our disposal.' Now came the task of winning the support of the bishops who were holding their own meeting at the same time. De Valera had risen early that morning to call on Archbishop Walsh who sympathised with Sinn Féin and strongly opposed conscription. A deputation set out from the Mansion House conference.

Healy was asked to share a hackney cab with his old antagonist, Dillon. It was too much. He said to Harry Boland, who was arranging the transport—'I can eat crow, but I don't hanker after it.' So de Valera took Dillon's place. On the way, Healy tried to persuade de Valera against the Sinn Féin policy of abstention. Finally, de Valera declared that nobody would ever see him in the House of Commons at Westminster. To which the warrior of the parliamentary battles of the 1880s answered rather nostalgically: 'It is the breath of my nostrils.'

The delegation was received immediately on arrival. Some of the members may not have felt too comfortable in the ecclesiastical atmosphere of the college. But de Valera as an ex-collegiate lecturer had grown used to it and was acquainted with a number of bishops. De Valera spoke after the Lord Mayor. He argued that passive resistance was a fantasy. It must anyway lead to physical force if conscription were applied. The British Government had a right to know the outcome if they went ahead. The morality of the use of physical force had its counterpart: the immorality of the effort to conscript the Irish nation. John Dillon, to de Valera's relief, also stated that a determination to resist by all means in their power was necessary. The Cardinal was brought forward step by reluctant step to agree to firm action.

The manifesto which the bishops finally published was a courageous one. Unanimously they declared: 'We consider that conscription forced in this way upon Ireland is an oppressive and inhuman law which the Irish people have a right to resist by every means that are consonant with the law of God.' They ordered that arrangements for taking the conference's pledge should be announced at all masses in every parish on the following Sunday. Subscriptions for a fund to fight conscription would be collected outside the church gates.

The result was an unrivalled exhibition of public feeling. The pledge was signed throughout the country. Subscriptions rolled in. De Valera had earlier agreed with the Irish Volunteers executive that they would resist by force. But he put off the final decision till April 26th, so that they could think seriously on all its implications. On that day he presented the executive with a written pledge of resistance. Each member must read it and either sign or reject it, stating his reasons. Thus de Valera emphasised the seriousness of the occasion.

The crisis finally undermined the Irish Party's position. The members' decision to leave the House of Commons and fight conscription in Ireland helped them not at all and seemed to justify the original Sinn Féin policy of abstention. Again, many of the members of the Parliamentary Party had appeared in khaki on recruiting platforms. Their policy of waiting for home rule until after the war had been met by a cynical threat to all Irish manhood. Their inability at this time to field a candidate against MacCartan, the Sinn Féin nominee in north King's County (now Offaly) was a further indication that their three earlier wins were exceptions to a general trend.

The Sinn Féin policy of physical force now seemed justified. Out of the crisis de Valera's stature grew. The *Daily Chronicle* reported, 'Mr de Valera is now the Irish leader.' Meanwhile the Irish people were changing their attitude towards Home Rule. One English paper remarked:

A fortnight ago it was quite an extreme thing in Ireland to hint at the Colonial form of self-government. To-day the moderate men demand nothing less, and in view of what has already happened we must not be surprised to find them in another week or two repeating Mr de Valera's demand for an independent republic. [24]

The members of the anti-conscription conference worked in harmony. Some felt that the circumstances called for complete unity amongst the various groups. But Sinn Féin was committed to the Republican ideal. It could not accept the kind of unity which would mean a compromise with the Home Rule policy of the Irish Party. A by-election in East Cavan highlighted the problem. The Sinn Féin chosen candidate was Arthur Griffith. Dillon wanted the Lord Mayor of Dublin to be nominated by both parties to avoid a contest. Sinn Féin refused.

Early in May de Valera and Dillon appeared on the platform together at a large anti-conscription meeting in Ballaghadereen. De Valera knew that Dillon would raise the question of unity. He wanted the opportunity to reply to him. Though invited to speak first, he insisted that Dillon, the sitting M.P. for that area, had the honour. In pointed fashion, Dillon appealed for unity. When de Valera rose, he agreed with Dillon on the need for unity against conscription. Then he mentioned the election campaign in Cavan. A loud shout interrupted him, 'Bad work there'. Immediately he answered that on the contrary, 'there is in this cry of unity a tyranny as great in its way as the tyranny that is often exercised under the cry of liberty. We have the right unity, the unity of co-operation. The unity of amalgamation would be no unity and that we cannot have.' [25] Adroitly he put Dillon in the position of trying to foist an M.P. on East Cavan by an inter-party deal. De Valera was showing that he was an astute politician as well as a revolutionary leader.

Significantly, de Valera gave his first interview to a foreign newspaper at this time. It was to *The Christian Science Monitor* of Boston. He received the correspondent in his office at Sinn Féin headquarters, 6 Harcourt Street, Dublin. On the walls were a few maps and pictures of Young Ireland and Fenian leaders of the previous century and three large warning notices such as, 'Walls have ears'. De Valera made a strong case for Irish independence based on the principles of allied leaders in the war. 'As a nation Ireland in its present position should stand neutral as regards all powers but England. Ireland's enemy is the power that denies Ireland self-determination.'

The question was asked, 'If you were free tomorrow you would not hand over your ports to Germany?' His answer was uncompromising. 'To be free means to be free, not to have a master. If England took away her troops and our independence were acknowledged, we would fight to the last man to maintain that independence. It is not a change of masters we want, though I do not know that the change would be for the worse'.

Finally, de Valera expressed the hope that his views would not be misrepresented, as they so often were. He called the press 'the devil's chief agency in the modern world.'[26] His suspicion of newspapers was deep-rooted. In 1919 he wrote to George Lansbury, editor of the emergent *Daily Herald*: 'What might be a very minister of Heaven is used daily as a minister of Hell! . . . An honest press has a big mission in England.'[27] This distrust remained with him all his life. It accounted not a little for the care which he put into the preparation of every public utterance. The time was to come when he was to found a paper of his own.

De Valera devoted some time to preparing a statement on conscription for submission to the President of the United States. The statement was unfinished when the executives of Sinn Féin and the Irish Volunteers met on May 17th. Michael Collins warned them that the Dublin Castle authorities intended a 'round up' of their leaders. But such warnings were frequent. Besides, the alternative to 'go on the run' would make work for independence very difficult. De Valera therefore decided to carry on his work openly.

After the meeting he caught a train to his house at Greystones, a secluded seaside village just south of Dublin. He held second-class season tickets for himself and for the bicycle he used in the city. At Bray Head some men of the Royal Irish Constabulary got into the carriage adjoining his. At Greystones a force of armed police waited for the train. De Valera was arrested as his foot touched the platform.

LINCOLN JAIL

May, 1918 – February, 1919

On being arrested de Valera was immediately searched.[1] It is remarkable that the police took no notice of de Valera's walking-cane, and he was allowed to retain it. They never realised that it was a sword-cane which had been presented to him in Tullamore the previous year, and he retained it throughout his imprisonment. The bulk of the documents in his attaché case were quotations from British ministers on the maltreatment of Ireland through the centuries. These he had been collecting to put as an appendix to the statement which he was preparing against conscription. A letter which he had been handed during one of the meetings that evening dealt with the probable methods which would be used to enforce conscription and suggestions as to how to defeat them. De Valera had barely glanced at it, but had realised that it was a dangerous document and had carefully pinched off the signature so as to protect the writer. Another document gave lists of places which had been suggested to him as a basis for a system of communications. None of them contained any evidence that he was in contact with Germany, but the Government was determined to justify the wholesale arrests of Sinn Féin leaders which began with that of de Valera on the plea of a German plot. Few people gave any credence to the preposterous charges made but all kinds of evidence was pressed into service to prove the case. The fact that a brother-in-law of Mrs de Valera was found boating in Dublin Bay, contrary to Admiralty regulations, was given as proof that he was in contact with a German submarine. When the documents were finally published some years later[2] the Government described a document on the organisation of an Irish army as being in de Valera's handwriting. This was not true and de Valera challenged the Government on the point. He did not deny that he was aware of the document, but it is quite clear that it was a scheme of organisation which could only be brought into operation if Ireland were independent.[3] It was probably drafted by J. J. (Ginger) O'Connell.

At Greystones de Valera was handed over to the military and was driven in a Crossley tender which was waiting outside the station to Kingstown, now Dun Laoghaire, where he was put on board an Admiralty cruiser or sloop of war. He was amused to see on each side of the door of the hold in which he was to be confined piratical looking sailors standing with drawn cutlasses and two guns stuck in their belts. It gave an air of unreality to the events, which was soon dispersed.

He had been informed that he was to be interned by order of the Home Secretary under a regulation of the Defence of the Realm Act because, in the words of the Order, 'he is a person suspected of acting, having acted or being about to act in a manner prejudicial to the public safety and the defence of the realm.' As dawn was breaking, the loneliness of his vigil was broken by the arrival of other prisoners. Among them were colleagues who had attended the meetings with him the evening before— Griffith, Cosgrave and many others. By nine o'clock in the morning, fifty-one prisoners were aboard and throughout the day the number grew. The last group, which brought the total to seventy-three, arrived after five in the afternoon. Among them was one woman, Countess Markievicz. Despite police precautions a large crowd gathered on the West pier, and as the ship moved off at about six o'clock the prisoners were given a hearty send-off.[4]

On arrival at Holyhead, the male prisoners were sent for a few days to an internment camp nearby, but on the following Monday they were separated into two groups, some to go to Usk prison and the remainder to Gloucester. Griffith and de Valera were among the latter, travelling by train with a strong military escort. The soldiers belonged to a Welsh regiment and were friendly to the Irishmen in their custody. One of the officers indeed went around among them to collect their autographs; he had no doubt that they were not criminals but men whose principles he admired. At Gloucester the prisoners held a sports meeting. De Valera showed that he was still in good athletic trim by winning the mile.

In the meantime, relatives of the prisoners had little or no information as to where they had been taken. It was not until June 6th that de Valera was able to send a telegram, stating that he and twelve others had now reached Lincoln Jail.[5] In Lincoln de Valera and his colleagues reached a decision at an early stage that they would not accept food parcels which, as unconvicted internees, they were allowed. In a letter to his secretary, Patrick Sheehan, at Sinn Féin headquarters, he wrote, 'It is for the English Government to feed us properly.'[6]

Conditions within Lincoln were less rigorous than those which had obtained in Dartmoor and Lewes during his earlier imprisonment. The prisoners were not treated as convicts and were allowed to associate freely together.[7] They played handball, an exercise which de Valera enjoyed. De Valera organised Irish classes for his colleagues and devoted much of his own solitude to continuing his study of mathematics and history for which he was allowed to acquire the necessary books. He also obtained the loan of a typewriter and practised typing.

The typewriter was an unusual model on which the letters were not attached to ordinary keys but were arranged on a cylinder. De Valera devoted a considerable amount of time to devising means of typing in code if the cylinder were inserted in certain incorrect positions.

Outside, the places of those arrested were filled by equally single-minded men and women. Indeed, the arrests turned out unhappily for the British Government. They had made charges of complicity in a German plot but these had failed to 'stick'. It looked as if the main purpose was to silence the opposition to conscription. Moreover, by picking on the Sinn Féin leaders, the British had made it plain to the Irish people that it was that party which was the main bulwark against the conscription and thus rendered them an invaluable service. The Government's action ruined any standing the Irish Party still possessed among the people of Ireland. The final blow to that body came at the end of the war when Lloyd George announced that the Home Rule Act of 1914, which had lain dormant on the Statute Book for the four war years, was now to be further postponed. The organising ability of Michael Collins among the Irish Volunteers and of Harry Boland, who was acting as secretary of Sinn Féin found a fertile soil of disappointment in which to spread the roots of the revolutionary movement.

In Lincoln the prisoners had looked forward to the end of World War I as the time at which they might expect release. They were soon disappointed. When they heard that Bob Brennan had been arrested on November 20th, 1918, they realised that the Government had no intention of freeing them to stand for parliament. They were to fight the election with their hands tied behind their backs. In Ireland, however, there were eager workers carrying on the campaign. Sinn Féin candidates, many of them in prison, were nominated for almost all the constituencies in Ireland. De Valera was selected to contest four seats, West Belfast, South Down, East Mayo and the seat which he already held, East Clare. But, after some rather unsatisfactory negotiations between Eoin MacNeill and Cardinal Logue, de Valera's candidature in South Down was withdrawn in favour of the Irish Party nominee, Jeremiah McVeagh.

Censorship hampered the Sinn Féin election campaign considerably. The election manifesto issued beforehand by the executive was mutilated by the censor. Only about one half of it could be published. The manifesto was published, however, with black leading showing the amount excised and was perhaps even more potent in that form. Even in its mutilated shape it stated that Sinn Féin aimed at establishing an Irish Republic by abstaining from attendance at Westminster and forming a constituent assembly in Ireland of the members returned in the coming election. De Valera's own election address was stopped by the prison censor. He wrote from prison early in December:

> It is improbable that we will be released for the elections. Silence is preferable to mutilated statements.

He would not issue an address which would be acceptable to the prison censor, but he asked the Director of Elections to see that this was explained to the electors. At the time, he was making a careful study of the electoral acts, but his letter had to be very circumspect in the advice he could offer. The one point which he stressed was that abstention from Westminster should not be allowed to become the main issue. It was only a corollary to the establishment of the Republic.[8]

In the meantime, the ending of the war had brought a sense of relief to the world. To his mother de Valera wrote at the end of November:

> If America holds to the principles enunciated by her President during the war she will have a noble place in the history of nations—her sons will have every reason to be proud of their motherland. These principles too are the basis of true statecraft—a firm basis that will bear the stress of time—but will the President be able to get them accepted by others whose entry into the war was on motives less unselfish?

He realised that a spirit of vengeance had been aroused by the horrors of war and that militated against future peace.

> What an achievement [he wrote] should he [President Wilson] succeed in getting established a common law for nations—resting on the will of the nations—making national duels as rare as duels between individual persons are at present: if that be truly his aim, may God steady his hand. To me it seemed that a complete victory for either side would have made it impossible almost.

His time in Lincoln gave him an opportunity for reading. Among the books which he read with special interest was Lecky's *Democracy and Liberty*—to him the most impressive of Lecky's works. He continued his mathematical studies and also studied the international situation carefully in the English newspapers. The *Manchester Guardian* he considered a journal of which an Englishman might well be proud. Its views he considered better balanced than those of other papers which came his way. He did not, however, agree with its outlook on Ireland.[9]

Throughout his imprisonment, de Valera was, according to one of his colleagues, Seán Etchingham, 'unbending and unbreakable'. When Etchingham fell ill, de Valera had not only been kind in his attentions, making toast and Bovril drinks for him, but told the Governor of the prison that if anything happened to Etchingham the prisoners would create trouble. When Etchingham showed no signs of improvement, de Valera had a number of interviews with the Governor and these culminated in Etchingham's release. While the prisoners were still confined, the general election was held and, despite the fact that many of the Sinn Féin candidates could take no part in the election, the results were overwhelmingly favourable. The Irish Parliamentary Party was reduced to six seats and Sinn Féin won seventy-three.

The parliamentary leader, John Dillon, was defeated by de Valera in Mayo; de Valera's seat in East Clare was uncontested, but in West Belfast he failed to dislodge Joseph Devlin. In Lincoln Jail the results were received with colossal enthusiasm when they were read out from the balcony.

The dashing of hopes of an early release at the end of the war had turned de Valera's mind, from late November, to the possibility of making his escape. He realised that such a *coup* would be of immense publicity value to the Irish cause and would be a serious setback to the British Government. The first problem lay in getting a key which meant, in the first place, obtaining a copy.

De Valera had been a devoted server at all the masses celebrated in the prison. One day he noticed that the chaplain never carried his key with him to the altar but left it in the sacristy. He now turned his attention to getting an accurate impression of it. Wax, the remains of burnt candles, lay in a drawer in the sacristy and de Valera collected it. From one of his fellow-prisoners he got a Capstan tobacco tin, and in one end of it he made a nick large enough to let the shank of the key sink into it. Then he warmed the butts of the candles and filled the tin with the white wax.

The next step was to get an opportunity of taking an impression of the key. One Sunday he got one of his colleagues to take his usual place as principal server. De Valera, who acted as sacristan, conveniently omitted to put out one of the cruets. Thus, after the priest went on the altar, he had an excuse to enter the sacristy. Before mass he had warmed the wax by the common-room fire. Unfortunately it had cooled and become so hard that he could not get the impression. He returned to the altar, however, and warmed the wax with friction and the heat of his body. Before mass ended he made a second attempt and this time he was successful. Carefully he took two impressions, one of the flat surface of the key and the other of the end showing its thickness. Then he returned once more to the altar. Later he cut pieces of paper into the shape of the impressions, so that they fitted exactly. These were models from which the key could be drawn.

Now that he had the dimensions and shape of the key, de Valera's next problem was to transmit this information to friends in Ireland. Seán Milroy, later a Sinn Féin M.P., had already shown his ability as an artist in drawing the programme for a concert staged by the prisoners in honour of de Valera's thirty-sixth birthday. It was a 'grand opera' entitled 'The Linking Girl', performed by 'The Lincoln Grimy Opera Company'. De Valera had heard the words of a popular music-hall song of the early years of the century, 'I couldn't get the latch-key in—upon my word, I couldn't'. It gave him an idea. He got Milroy to draw a Christmas card showing a tipsy Seán McGarry, another Sinn Féin prisoner, with a huge key trying to put it into a small keyhole. Underneath was written 'Xmas 1917 can't get in.' In a lower inset was drawn a picture of McGarry in a prison cell, looking at a large keyhole in his cell door. It was captioned 'Xmas 1918 can't get out'. Inside John O'Mahony, another prisoner, wrote a short note composed by de Valera:

> My dear Tommie,
> The best wishes I can send are those de Valera wrote in my autograph book. Field will translate.

(Field was Michael Collins' pseudonym.) Then followed, in de Valera's handwriting, an explanation in Irish that the key in the picture was an exact drawing of the prison key and that the keyhole showed a cross-section of it. It would open the inner doors and the back gate on the north side of the prison. He asked that a key, made to these dimensions, and some files be sent in a cake, and that arrangements be made to meet him outside the prison. The date could be fixed well in advance by sending a letter to Seán McGarry saying, 'Billie got up the —th of last month—Is now quite well'. The date would be understood as the date in January on which the escape would be attempted.

The card was duly delivered to Seán McGarry's wife. She, however, does not appear to have passed it on to any of the Sinn Féin leaders at that time, probably because she thought it all a joke.

The prisoners were getting anxious when no message came, and on Christmas Eve de Valera composed another letter which he got John O'Mahony to write to Father Kavanagh, a curate in Leeds, with an instruction in Latin written with the help of Sam Flaherty, one of the prisoners who was a student of the classics. It was veiled as if it were a quotation from the ancient classics:

> We all greet you. In the words of the old Roman, 'Hanc epistolam in toto ut per nuntium fidelem statim mittas ad illam mulierem cujus domicilium notavi, rogat et orat dux noster Hibernicus'.[10]

A rough translation of this would be, 'Our Irish Chief asks and prays that you send this letter complete by a faithful messenger immediately to that woman whose address I have indicated'. The Latin words have an interest apart from the Lincoln adventure. All his life de Valera remained a student of languages, although he would never describe himself as a classical scholar. Years later, for instance, when he was recovering from a serious eye operation in Utrecht, a friend was reading the psalms to him in Latin. Suddenly de Valera interrupted to ask why a certain noun was used in an unfamiliar case. It is not for nothing that one of de Valera's favourite books is the dictionary.

The letter went on to recount those ordinary complaints which might be expected of a lonely prisoner, but it was replete with details of the prison and its surroundings, laying particular stress on the possible escape route. He even mentioned how the prisoners at a high window could give or receive a signal:

I smoke a cigar and de Valera watches the plough revolve around the Polar Star. He studies the stars, I watch the lights on earth, the motor and cycle lights coming along the road from the East, or perhaps North East, towards the town and blinking as the objects get between them and us—my cigar must look like an evening star, if it can be seen as far as the road perched up in the sky as we are in this window.

References to de Valera as an amateur astronomer covered a number of useful tips about the dark periods at the time of a new moon and ended with what, for any Irishman, would be the broadest of broad hints:

Xmas is a dull time with us. Dev last night told me a story of a famous Xmas in Irish History. There was snow on the ground as usual of course. I said I thought that a bad thing and he nearly hit me when he saw the kind of interest I was taking in it; even the mention of Dublin Castle in the story did not win my attention. This story will give you an idea of the line in which our thoughts are running.

Every Irish child knows the story of the escape of Hugh Roe O'Donnell and two companions from Dublin Castle on Christmas Eve, 1592, but the kindly warder who posted the letter was unaware of the implications of the apparently innocuous missive. Enclosed with this letter of O'Mahony's was a note from Seán McGarry to his wife in Irish asking if she had received the Christmas card at all. This also was composed by de Valera. The instructions about sending the key were given and he arranged that, if it fitted, he would mention in his next letter, 'Your last cake was a treat'.

By January 10th, 1919, no response to the request for the key had been received and John O'Mahony wrote once more. This time a little piece of Latin in the middle of his letter was in de Valera's handwriting; a key was duly made by Gerry Boland, later a minister in de Valera's cabinet.

(Collins and Harry Boland, Gerry's brother, were by now in Manchester making arrangements for the escape.) The first man to deliver a cake was Fintan Murphy who went through agonising minutes as the chief warder prodded it suspiciously with a long knife. Luckily he hit nothing harder than raisin seeds.

The prisoners inside were delighted. Then came disappointment; the key was found to be defective. A second one was made and sent disguised in a cake delivered by Frank Kelly on January 24th, the day originally fixed for the escape. Misfortune again! Not only was it too small, but it was not a master key and the chief warder's master key put a double lock on the doors. In a note added in Irish to an outgoing letter, Seán McGarry explained the difficulty to the collaborator outside and said that if a blank key and files could be smuggled in they would make the key themselves. This time the heavily laden cake was handed in by Boland himself. Again there was difficulty. The blank keys sent in had a slot in the centre so could not be fashioned to fit the locks. Another letter had to be sent out. Another cake was delivered, this time by an Irish school teacher, Kathleen Talty. On the following Friday there was the good news that the new blank key was perfect. McGarry wrote, on de Valera's instructions, to Michael Collins that they would be ready on the evening arranged.

The long delays and various mishaps which had taken six weeks or more to overcome were at an end. De Valera at last had a key which worked like a charm in every lock. Each time he tried it he got a feeling of exhilaration. Indeed his great fear at this moment was that the Government might decide to release him before he could escape.

Collins was devoting his attention to laying plans for the escape route. This he did with his usual thoroughness. He and Boland were acting under instructions from Cathal Brugha in Dublin, and he sent to the prisoners word from Brugha that if there was a military guard on the prison they were not to attempt to escape. Harry Boland was more specific in one of the last notes smuggled in: 'C[athal] B[rugha] assumes', he wrote, 'that ye can do the job on your side without risk of being shot.'

While Brugha was anxious about de Valera's safety, the latter was perturbed by the fact that two such important men as Collins and Boland should be risking their freedom to get him out. He feared that if the plan failed and if Boland and Collins were caught, the organisation in Ireland would suffer severely and the British have a great triumph. In Dublin, however, it had apparently been agreed that the freeing of de Valera was of such importance that it should be handled by the best men. Within the prison de Valera's anxieties were raised when some girls innocently mentioned Boland's movements in Manchester in letters to the prisoners, which passed through the hands of the prison censor. He even suggested, in a letter written by Seán McGarry, that perhaps those outside might consider it better to postpone the plan lest the prison authorities had laid a trap for them. Collins and Boland, however, decided to carry on.

Once all the preparations were completed, it was decided that instead of the escape attempt being initiated from within the prison, the signal should come from those outside. If the attempt were not made by Monday, February 3rd, 1919, it would have to be postponed for a fortnight until the moon would be well on the wane. Each evening over the weekend de Valera took up his position at the window on the stairs which was a couple of floors above ground level. He waited anxiously at the appointed times, 6.40 p.m. on Saturday and 7.30 p.m. on Sunday. The hours had to be fixed according to the times at which the moon rose. The escape had to be made before the cell doors were locked as it was impossible to open these from the inside. Escape by 7 p.m. would allow two hours or so before he was likely to be missed.

On that evening of February 3rd de Valera stood at the window and at 7.40 sharp a beam of light from a torch cut through the sky. For what seemed like an age it shone and de Valera felt that everyone would see it. In fact, Harry Boland could not switch it off as the catch had stuck. With relief de Valera saw the light disappear. Boland had doused it by putting the lighted torch in his pocket. Immediately de Valera gave his signal in reply—he struck a match and lit four or five matches held together to make a flare. The attempt was on.

De Valera untied the key which he had kept hidden hanging from his braces and quickly set off with his two companions, Seán McGarry and Seán Milroy. To avoid making any noise he had socks over his shoes. Milroy had sandshoes for the same reason, but as one of the soles had come away from the upper, it flapped noisily along the flagged passages. Each door and gate opened easily, and carefully de Valera locked them again after him. He did not want to leave any clue behind as to how he had gone.

At last the trio reached the back gate. Again it opened easily, but they found themselves faced by yet another one. There was, in fact, a double gate through the wall. The outer gate was sheeted to the ground with corrugated iron. Collins and Boland were outside. In horrified tones Boland whispered that a duplicate key which he had brought had got stuck in the lock from the outside and that the shank had broken. It was the first major hitch.

All, however, was not yet lost. In accordance with de Valera's instructions, Collins and Boland had brought a rope ladder. Using it to climb the wall, however, would have caused considerable delay and, therefore, de Valera decided to try to push out Boland's key with his. He pressed lightly first and then, with a prayer, a little more heavily; he had to be careful not to break his own key. Luckily Boland's had not turned. Under the pressure it fell outwards and, as de Valera turned the key, the lock opened smoothly. The gate was rusted and made a noise that sounded to the prisoners like thunder as they slowly pushed it sufficiently open to allow them through. Reluctantly de Valera abandoned the idea of locking it again—it would make too much noise to close it. He was free at last, but there were many hazards still to face.

The barbed wire had already been cut by Collins and Boland. Together the five men crossed the field to a gate on to Wragby Road. This was much frequented by soldiers from the nearby military hospital, and many of them were bidding loving farewells to their girl friends who had escorted them to the hospital gates.

It was decided that time was precious and that a chance would have to be taken. Boland put his heavy fur-lined coat on de Valera and donned his own light raincoat. Arm-in-arm, like a fond couple, they ran the gauntlet—Harry, the supposed lady, adding to the pretence with an occasional 'Good night, chums' to soldiers who were too engrossed to take any notice. They all got through safely, only to find that the taxi which was waiting to take the prisoners away could not be found.

At last the car was located outside the Adam and Eve Inn. Here the prisoners parted company with Collins and Boland and set out on the journey to Worksop, some twenty-five miles away. Collins and Boland planned to take another car and to pick up a train for London.

At Worksop, Fintan Murphy had yet another car waiting on the Sheffield road. Arrived in Sheffield, de Valera and his companions were guided to a taxi which was waiting to take them to Manchester. According to Collins's plans, they were to be there at midnight and, despite the various delays, they were only five minutes late in arriving. It was a fine tribute to Collins's extraordinary organising ability that the journey was completed so smoothly, despite many difficulties. Not the least of these were the wartime restrictions on taxis and the petrol shortage.

In Lincoln Jail the escape went unnoticed for some time. John O'Mahony helped to delay the discovery by inviting the warder who was locking the cells to share a little whiskey with him. By about 9.30 p.m., however, the hue and cry was raised. The public did not learn of the event until the following afternoon when stop press editions of the Irish papers were put on sale in Dublin. The people of Ireland were delirious with joy. De Valera was not only a leader, he was a wizard who could out-smart the British any time he wished. Among the British authorities there was consternation and continuous speculation. Various reports were printed regarding his whereabouts.

The world press looked on in wonder and gave the Irish cause much-needed publicity. De Valera was said by some to have been seen in Skibbereen, a remote village in Cork. Others thought that he was on his way to Paris to attend the Peace Conference. In fact, he remained in Manchester for some weeks. On arriving there he had parted company with McGarry and Milroy outside Liam McMahon's house and walked with a guide to the house of Father Charles O'Mahony, chaplain to the work-house in Crumpsall. He stayed with Father O'Mahony for a week, during which Cathal Brugha arrived from Dublin to confer with him. He stayed from Friday, February 7th, until the following Sunday, bringing de Valera up-to-date with the progress made in establishing an Irish legislature and on conditions in Ireland.

One of the matters raised by Brugha was the possibility, if war were waged by Britain against the forces of the newly-elected legislature, of shooting cabinet ministers in London in retaliation. Theoretically, if the cabinet forced a war on the Irish people, de Valera felt that any defensive action against the members of that cabinet was justified and would have agreed in principle with Brugha on that point. Whether such an attempt would damage rather than help the Irish cause was another matter, but de Valera did not feel called upon to argue the question too closely since it was not an immediate issue. It was raised again a few times by Brugha, once in a letter to de Valera in America. De Valera's reply to Brugha's question on that occasion as to possible ill-effects of assassination on American opinion does not appear to have survived. Though it has been suggested that at some stage he gave his consent to the plan, there is no evidence that he did so. More likely his usual caution would have restrained him from endorsing it.[11]

Despite the fact that most of the elected representatives were in jail, the constituent assembly, or Dáil Éireann, promised in the Sinn Féin election manifesto, had met in Dublin on January 21st. Brugha had been elected temporary President in the absence of de Valera and one of its first acts had been the reading of the Declaration of Independence. The Government of the Irish Republic was formally established and a beginning was being made in the effort to put government departments to work, but the principal aim at that stage was to get Ireland's case heard at the Peace Conference. The first meeting of the Dáil had nominated de Valera, Griffith and Count Plunkett as delegates to the Conference, but there seemed little chance that they would succeed in attending. Passport regulations made it unlikely. He moved, accordingly, towards a far-reaching decision. He began to think that the place in which he could best work for Ireland was the USA where he could bring Irish-American pressure to bear on President Wilson.

The enforced inactivity of hiding was a greater strain than prison life. De Valera feared that the prestige gained by his escape and the national morale raised by it would be lost if he were recaptured. A week after his arrival in Manchester he had to change his place of concealment. Detective Sergeant Thomas Walsh of the Manchester police informed Liam McMahon that Father O'Mahony's residence was under suspicion. Fitted out in a colonial uniform, complete with a wide-brimmed hat turned up at one side, de Valera was escorted by Kathleen Talty from Crumpsall. They walked arm-in-arm for six or seven miles to Victoria Park as he feared to take a taxi. There de Valera was taken to a house in Fallowfield. For a week he stayed there, but he did not venture out in the uniform again. Having seen how pale his skin was after his long imprisonment, he could not understand that someone had not questioned him.

He was waiting for word from Ireland about arrangements for travelling home. On February 18th, word came from Collins that all was ready and that he was to go at once to Liverpool. Paddy O'Donoghue, Kathleen Talty and another girl, Mary Healy, took him there by taxi, dressed as a priest, to the house of a Mrs McCarthy near the docks in Liverpool. Next night he was taken on board the *Cambria* by Seamus Donaghue, the second mate, and Con Murray, one of the sailors, and was hidden in Donaghue's cabin.

At one o'clock, on the morning of February 20th, de Valera landed in Dublin and was immediately taken to the house of Dr Farnan in Merrion Square. At that time he gave an interview to an American journalist, Ralph F. Couch, a United Press correspondent. Couch, after a harassing blindfolded journey, was impressed to find himself in a stately Georgian room. De Valera, he noticed, looked very much at home in his surroundings. He wore a black silk handkerchief round his neck instead of a collar and the final touch of informality was his rubber-soled carpet slippers. Certainly he did not seem like a man 'on the run'. A trimly-uniformed maid appeared with a tray and silver tea service while de Valera discussed the prospects of successfully defeating British forces in Ireland. To Couch, thus suitably impressed, de Valera gave a statement in which he stressed that the world was looking to Paris for justice; that President Wilson was their main hope; that the Machiavellis, Lloyd George among them, might scoff, but the people of America would help to keep their President firmly to his principles.[12] Indeed, quite a few politicians were Machiavellian in his eyes. He advised the Chief of Staff of the Irish Volunteers, Richard Mulcahy, that if he entered politics he should study Machiavelli and read economics.

In the meantime, Harry Boland and Michael Collins had been searching for a more suitable and permanent hiding-place. On Sunday de Valera was moved to the Dublin Whiskey Distillery premises on the north side of the city near Clonliffe College; and under cover of darkness the next evening he was brought to an unused gate in the eastern wall of the college. A plaintive curlew's call by Boland brought Father (later Monsignor) Michael Curran hurrying from the table of Archbishop Walsh to open the gate. As de Valera parted from his companions, Boland and the owner of the distillery, Denis Lynch, he gave hurried instructions to Boland to get him a large-size fountain-pen for use on board ship, for the idea of an American mission had now taken firm root. His return to Ireland was to be purely temporary and would last only while arrangements were being made for the voyage across the Atlantic.

Through the deserted college grounds Father Curran, who was Archbishop Walsh's secretary, led de Valera and put him into a bed-sitting-room in the gate lodge in the grounds of the Archbishop's House. The Archbishop was quite unaware of the presence of de Valera, who spent most of his time revising the text of a statement of Ireland's case for presentation in Paris. Many hands had contributed to the first draft of this—the historical section having been the joint work of Father Curran and of two Jesuits, Professor Tim Corcoran and Father John McErlean.

Each evening, after dark, de Valera and Father Curran walked together in the grounds. On one occasion de Valera went beyond the walls, back again to the distillery. There he attended a meeting of the ministers of Dáil Éireann. The demand for the Irish case to be heard in Paris was encountering heavy weather. Seán T. O'Kelly had succeeded in getting a passport and had arrived in the French capital. He was finding, however, that President Wilson's fourteen points were being applied only to nations held in bondage by those defeated in the war. National questions involving the victors were simply 'domestic issues' in which Wilson could not interfere. The British delegation had succeeded in preventing the application of principles of self-determination to Ireland. At this time de Valera got word that he was to move. The ship for America would soon be ready, so he crossed to Liverpool to wait for it, hiding once more in Mrs McCarthy's house. He was there only a day or two when Arthur Griffith and the rest of the 'German plot' prisoners were released.

De Valera, for a while, was not sure that the British would allow him to remain unmolested. While waiting he drafted a constitution for an Irish organisation in Britain to support the Irish cause.

In the meantime, the executive of Sinn Féin decided that de Valera could return in safety to Ireland and arranged that he be given an official reception never surpassed hitherto. He was to be met at one of the bridges over the canal—fittingly enough Mount Street bridge—by the Lord Mayor and was to be presented with the keys of the City of Dublin. The honour had never been bestowed before except to royalty and the occasion would have been one of great national rejoicing. In preparation for the day, de Valera drafted a speech in uncompromising terms in which he paid tribute to Mick Malone and the men who fell defending that bridge three years before. He argued, as he had argued before, that the success of Sinn Féin in the elections showed that the men of 1916 'were justified in regarding themselves not as a clique or faction or praetorian guard but as genuine representatives of the nation'. Of the supposed 'German plot' he denied that it ever existed but he asserted that 'some of us would gladly have availed of German help if, by that help, we might deprive England of the further power of harming us'.[13]

The occasion for delivering this speech, however, did not arise. On the day before the planned reception it was prohibited by the British authorities. They might be prepared for a safe return but not for a public triumph. Many took this to be a challenge to the Irish Volunteers and P. S. O'Hegarty wrote to Harry Boland that 'a withdrawal would be as fatal to the morale, and I believe to the success of Sinn Féin, as was the Clontarf withdrawal to O'Connell's Repeal Movement'.[14] De Valera was much less belligerent in his outlook. He did not consider that there was any reason why a public reception for himself should be a *casus belli*. To the Sinn Féin executive he wrote that he did not consider it an occasion on which they would be justified in risking the lives of the citizens. Matters of greater principle would arise. 'We who have waited', he wrote, 'know how to wait. Many a heavy fish is caught even with a fine line if the angler is patient.'[15] So the reception was cancelled and de Valera returned to Ireland quietly.

The calm of his return to Dublin was not, however, an indication that he was weakening in his resolve to continue the struggle. In a hard-hitting article in the *Daily Herald*[16] he made it clear that there was no question of Irish acceptance of, or acquiescence in, English rule. For English readers he gave the translation of Sinn Féin as 'We ourselves' and explained that it was a motto of self-reliance. Those who translated it as 'Ourselves alone' were twisting it to misrepresent it as a doctrine of selfish isolation.

> So far are we [he wrote], from desiring isolation that our whole struggle is to get Ireland out of the cage in which the selfish statecraft of England would confine her—to get Ireland back into the free world from which she was ravished—to get her recognised as an independent unit in a world-league of nations, so that she might freely give of her gifts to, and receive in return of their gifts from, her sister nations of the world over.

This broad view of the Irish national struggle he brought before the Dáil about the same time. He proposed a motion announcing that the Irish Republic was willing to enter into any world league of nations which was based on equality of rights. 'We are willing', the motion stated, 'to accept all the duties, responsibilities and burdens which inclusion in such a League implies.' The Covenant of the League of Nations which was emerging from the Peace Conference in Paris, however, was a profound disappointment:

It simply meant an association to perpetuate power for those who had got it, and to keep for ever in slavery those who had been kept in slavery by international rules, as they were called, but which were simply the rules of thieves for regulating their conduct amongst themselves.

He foresaw the dangers of an imposed peace—a natural outcome of the bitterness of war. France had suffered much, but she should be restrained from taking revenge. If the imposed treaty was a vengeful one, he warned that another war of revenge must surely follow.[17] The international history of the following twenty years may be felt to vindicate his forebodings.

The meetings of Dáil Éireann early in April, 1919, were devoted principally to making the rule of that assembly effective throughout Ireland. Brugha, who had been unanimously elected President, in a temporary capacity, in January, resigned in favour of de Valera, who was unanimously chosen for the position on April 1st. The following day he announced his ministry in which Arthur Griffith was in charge of Home Affairs and Cathal Brugha the Department of Defence. Michael Collins was placed in the all-important post of Finance Minister in place of Eoin MacNeill who had held it in Brugha's temporary cabinet. Count Plunkett was left in charge of Foreign Affairs and W. T. Cosgrave and Countess Markievicz held the portfolios of Local Government and Labour respectively.

In statements on policy, de Valera set out as their first aim the obtaining of international recognition for the Government of the Irish Republic. It was by no means their only one. They would apply for safe conducts for Irish representatives to attend the Paris Peace Conference. They would send ambassadors and consuls throughout the world to speak for Ireland and to co-ordinate the work of the various bodies working voluntarily on Ireland's behalf. The attitude which should be maintained to the British administration in Ireland should be that recommended to the Belgians in the face of German occupation. The President said:

We shall conduct ourselves towards them in such a way as will make it clear to the world that we acknowledge no right of theirs. Such use of their laws as we shall make will be dictated solely by necessity and only in so far as we deem them for the public good.

Against the Royal Irish Constabulary he directed his most vigorous attack. It was an armed force, 'the eyes and ears of the enemy'. Moved by an account of the imprisonment and questioning of two Tipperary children, one aged eleven years and the other eight, the President advised that the police force be ostracized. They were Irishmen who were being used to keep Ireland in servitude. It was they who had placed many of the Sinn Féin leaders in prison; and though he said he spoke without passion his words carried in them deep feeling for those who still lay in confinement.[18] On social policy, he pointed out that the democratic programme adopted by the Dáil in January contemplated a different situation from that in which they found themselves. The Ministry for Labour would consult with the trade union leaders and they would do what they could to improve the conditions under which people worked but 'while the enemy was within their gates, the immediate question was to get possession of their country'.[19]

The principal endeavours of the months of April and May were directed to putting the new administrative machinery to work. The first, and most essential, problem was finance. The Dáil sanctioned the floating of loans in Ireland and in the United States and Collins threw himself wholeheartedly into making these successful. An urgent and thorny problem, too, was the definition of the authority of Dáil Éireann in relation to the Irish Volunteers. Ultimately, by August, 1919, it was agreed that members of Dáil Éireann would take an oath of loyalty to the Republic, and the Volunteers agreed to take the same oath which committed them to loyalty to the Dáil.[20]

But the first task was to make an international issue of the Irish Question. From America, where a monster Irish Race Convention was held in February, 1919, three delegates were sent to Paris to press President Wilson to have the Irish case heard there. They visited Ireland early in May, addressed a special meeting of Dáil Éireann, and were welcomed by the President. He described America as 'the nation which the whole world recognises as its only hope, that nation on which depends whether the principles of right and justice are to prevail, or whether, as formerly, might and might only is to be right.[21]

The proud principles of President Wilson were the hope of struggling nations. President de Valera looked to the American people to see that their President lived up to them.

In private, however, he learned from the delegates that the British and French Premiers, Lloyd George and Clemenceau, would almost certainly be too much for Wilson and would manage to prevent the hearing of Ireland's case. American public opinion was, therefore, becoming of paramount importance. President de Valera had already sent Harry Boland as an Irish official envoy to the United States to launch the Dáil Éireann external loan and, at the same time, to compose differences which had arisen in Irish-American circles. De Valera had been informed of these differences by an Irish priest on the American mission whom he had met at Gill's shop in O'Connell Street. While the American delegates were in Ireland, President de Valera discussed with them the possibility of getting banks to underwrite the Irish loan in America. One of them, a prominent banker in Philadelphia, Michael Ryan, asserted that this was impossible and that, if the loan were to be a success, de Valera himself should go to America to launch it.

While in hiding, de Valera had had considerable difficulty in deciding where he could best serve Ireland. He saw that great work could be done, at that time, both outside and inside the country. He had returned to Ireland so as to be available to present the Irish cause to the Peace Conference. If the statesmen in Paris refused to receive him and the other Irish representatives, it would be clear to the world that all their altruistic professions were no more than a wartime ruse to delude their own people. By May, 1919, it was becoming clear that the Irish case would not be heard. On May 17th President de Valera, Arthur Griffith and Count Plunkett wrote to Clemenceau, President of the Peace Conference, denying the right of British representatives to sign any treaty on behalf of Ireland. Nine days later they wrote again, formally requesting consideration of Ireland's claim to be recognised as an independent sovereign state and submitting a memorandum on the case. This was done to put the claim on record. It was already known that the Conference would not hear the Irish delegates and thus the League of Nations Covenant, which was being made part of the Peace Treaty, was all too likely to leave existing injustices intact. President de Valera decided to revert to his original plan of going to America and of appealing to the people above the head of Woodrow Wilson. The necessity for an American mission was never fully out of his mind.

AMERICAN MISSION

February, 1919 – June, 1920

The President originally intended that his American visit should be brief. In fact, he stayed in the United States from June, 1919, to December, 1920, for reasons that will emerge. Why was the visit ever decided on? Before the general release of prisoners, it was considered that the moral effect of his escape would be nullified were he to be recaptured. But this was far from all, as we know.

Many years later, in 1964, when he gave an address to the United States Congress, he summarised his mandate:

> I was sent here with a threefold mission. First to ask for official recognition of the independence and the Republic . . . I was sent here also to try to float an external loan . . . and finally, I was asked to plead with the American people that the United States would make it clear that 'notwithstanding Article 10 of the Covenant of the League of Nations', the United States was not pledging itself to maintain Ireland as an integral part of British territory.

The need for an American loan was apparent if the new Government were to operate at all effectively. Again, in the broader international field, American support was crucial. The Peace Treaty being evolved in Paris between Lloyd George, Clemenceau and Wilson incorporated a scheme for a League of Nations. American public opinion must be induced to realise the relevance of the case of Ireland.

These two purposes, the financial and the international, were interwoven in the months that followed. If the loan were to be a success he himself must go to America. The President acted upon this conviction and, in doing so, had the full support of the Cabinet. Arthur Griffith made this latter point clear in a statement to Dáil Éireann which removed any conceivable suggestion that the President was retreating from the front line.

By this time, it had become clear that all hope of having the Irish case heard at the Peace Conference itself could be abandoned. It seemed an opportune time, nevertheless, to appeal to the American people on behalf of a small nation fighting for freedom. The principles for which America had entered the war were being lost sight of in Paris, but there were grounds for hoping that they were still alive in the minds of the people of the United States.

Sunday, June 1st, was set aside as a day of family celebration in the de Valera household in Greystones. It was Mrs de Valera's birthday and, for the first time in four years, her husband could celebrate it out of jail. Since his escape he had been able to spend little time with his family and for this one day he made no engagements. But it was not to be. Before lunch a messenger made his ominous appearance. The President had to leave at once for America. All arrangements had been completed by Michael Collins for his voyage. He made a hurried departure to Dublin, where he met some of the Cabinet; then took the mailboat for Holyhead.

The President bought a return ticket to Manchester, trying to create the impression that he intended to visit Austin Stack and others still confined in Manchester Jail. His plan seemed in danger from the outset. On the boat he met Father McCarthy, who had been chaplain in Kilmainham Jail in 1916, and who was travelling with James McMahon, the Under-Secretary for Ireland. Father McCarthy wanted to bring him to the state cabin to meet McMahon. McMahon was an old Blackrock man and de Valera knew him well. De Valera refused. He also thought unwise Father McCarthy's suggestion that McMahon could make representations to the jail authorities in Manchester to admit de Valera.

He avoided the two of them on landing and went straight to Liverpool where friends helped to smuggle him on board the S.S. *Lapland*. It was a miserable voyage. He was violently sick for eight days and scarcely ate. Secreted away, he could only lie on his coffin-like bunk all day. On June 11th the ship arrived in New York. As the stowaway waited to be taken off, all traces of sea-sickness vanished and he gazed through the porthole at the bright sunshine. His first sight of New York since leaving it at the age of two and a half remained impressed upon his mind—a city of 'straw hats and sunshine'.

That night he disembarked and was met by Harry Boland, who took him to Liam Mellows's flat. Boland had been sent to the USA to float a loan there simultaneously with the floating of a loan in Ireland. Mellows had escaped to the United States after leading a rising in Galway in 1916. The President was immediately taken on to Joe McGarrity's home in Philadelphia where he was warmly welcomed.

For some time he wished to keep his presence in America secret. He did not want it to be known how he had crossed the Atlantic, for fear that the British authorities might trace the sailors who had helped him. About a week after his arrival the President wrote to Collins:

I have been trotting about—Rochester, Philadelphia, Washington, Boston, New York, back and forward and broke all my appointments.[1]

At his mother's home in Rochester, however, he was greeted by a cousin, Mary Connolly, one of his Aunt Hannah's daughters, who immediately ran to tell all her family. When he realised where she had gone, he knew that the news would soon spread and that the reporters would be on his trail. Harry Boland had made the situation yet more difficult by announcing, a week beforehand, that de Valera would appear in New York at the Waldorf-Astoria Hotel at 5.30 p.m. on June 23rd, and at the same time challenging the reporters to find him.

During these first days, de Valera discussed many problems with Boland. The latter had written two reports to Dublin, but they had not arrived before de Valera sailed. The first, sent towards the end of May, gave the impression that the differences of opinion in Irish-American ranks were not serious. He wrote:

> Most opportune that I got here at the moment as I may be able to harmonise the little differences that have arisen on policy, finance, etc.[2]

The situation, however, was much more awkward than Boland first realised. The Friends of Irish Freedom had launched, at the third Irish Race Convention in February, 1919, the Irish Victory Fund. Immediately pledges came in for over one million dollars, but the use to which that money was to be put caused immense difficulty. In his second report Boland had written that $250,000 would be sent to Ireland. He said:

> I had a very, very stiff fight to get any money for home and it will be necessary to inform you as to the attitude of the men here on this question. An ambiguous resolution was passed at Philadelphia Convention pledging the delegates to collect two million dollars. One of the delegates asked as to how the money would be expended. The Chairman, Judge C., answered, 'For educational propaganda in America', and it passed at that.[3]

In this same letter Boland said that Michael J. Ryan, the member of the American Commission on Irish independence who had returned from Paris, had stated that he could not see how Dáil Éireann could spend more than $50,000. Apparently he, like many of the Irish-American leaders, did not understand the magnitude of the programme of Dáil Éireann; or that it was seriously intended to establish a government with active departments taking over work up till then administered by the British.

At the same time there were other differences unsolved. Dr Patrick MacCartan had been in the United States for a couple of years. He had been sent as an envoy by the IRB in 1917 and had been officially appointed as the representative of Dáil Éireann in April, 1919. But disagreement had already arisen with John Devoy and Judge Cohalan, the two leading Irish-Americans.

As announced, President de Valera arrived at the Waldorf-Astoria on June 23rd at 5.30 p.m. A great crowd awaited him, making Thirty-third Street almost impassable. As he stepped from a car he was met by Devoy and Cohalan, one carrying the green, white and orange tricolour of the Irish Republic and the other the Stars and Stripes, and shouts of greeting rose from the throng. The President told a press conference that his journey was undertaken to seek American aid for the republic established by the will of the Irish people. All questions as to how he had arrived in America he refused to answer, but he made it clear that he intended, as one of his primary duties, to float a Dáil Éireann loan. The size of the loan was not yet decided.

After this public appearance the President was extremely busy. Invitations poured in from all parts of the country. A young Irish girl from Cahirdaniel, Co. Kerry, was taken on as a typist. She was Kathleen O'Connell, who was to be his faithful personal secretary for thirty-seven years until her death in 1956.

His first anxiety, however, was to float the loan. He found that the scheme was not popular. Cohalan and Devoy opposed it on the grounds that a bond issue would contravene the 'blue sky' laws of the United States which were designed to prevent fraud. They also feared that the loan would interfere with the Victory Fund which the Friends of Irish Freedom were collecting and they did not think the loan could be floated successfully. The President, however, announced that he was determined to go ahead with the project.

The President, in a letter to Arthur Griffith early in July wrote:

My three present objectives are (1) Pressing unofficial recognition of the Republic and preparing campaign re the Treaty [of Versailles]. (2) The interest of wealthy men of the race in the industrial development of Ireland. (3) The floating of the bonds.

He went on to say that the sympathy for Ireland was widespread, but it was difficult to harness it to a definite purpose. The press he did not find hostile, but he feared the effect of large-scale British propaganda. Of President Wilson's attitude he was uncertain. 'I am waiting', he wrote, 'till we have got the people properly first—then even were he to attack, it would not be deadly.'[4]

The tenacity of purpose which de Valera displayed in his floating the loan had little effect on those opposed to it, with the exception of Judge Goff, who, seeing that the President had made up his mind, agreed to support him. Engagements, however, were pressing in. Making his first public appearance outside New York on June 29th at Boston, he was received with wonderful enthusiasm and spoke on the Treaty which had been signed two days before at Versailles:

Peace has been nominally signed between the two great combatting sides. Peace! Peace that gives us twenty new wars instead of the one that it nominally ends, and this is the peace treaty the world has been asked to look forward to as the treaty that could end wars, and establish a stable, lasting peace . . . A new Holy Alliance cannot save democracy; a just League of Nations, founded on the only basis on which it can be just—the equality of right amongst nations, small no less than great—can.[5]

But this hopeful attitude towards the League of Nations differed significantly from that of Wilson's principal opponents in America. Reaction to the war had resulted in an upsurge of feeling in favour of the old American policy of isolation. Cohalan and Devoy supported this outlook and denounced the League as an alliance with Britain. They were against it in any form. De Valera was much less rigid in his opposition. He told Griffith:

The political situation here is obscure for the moment. Am trying to give Wilson to know that if he goes for his 14 points as they were and a true League of Nations, Irishmen and men and women of Irish blood will be behind him. So Democrats and Republicans are bidding for our support— Democrats by amending the Covenant and Republicans by destroying it.[6]

The article in the League of Nations Covenant to which de Valera took particular exception was Article X by which members undertook to preserve the existing territorial boundaries of member nations. This article, it was feared, would prevent any international recognition of Irish independence. In the months which followed, the President, in speech after speech, concentrated his attack on the article. The return to America from Paris of Frank P. Walsh and Governor Dunne on July 8th brought home to de Valera that the hope of Ireland's case being heard in Paris was finally ended. As he entertained them to lunch in the Waldorf, he and his colleagues saw, from the hotel window, President Wilson pass down Fifth Avenue standing in his open car and bowing to the greetings of the crowd. Wilson had returned from Paris that day and was opening his campaign in favour of the League.[7]

De Valera had not intended to open a campaign for recognition of the Irish Republic so soon. His first task was to get money to put the Government of Dáil Éireann into effective operation. Circumstances, however, pushed him forward. In dealing with the League of Nations he had to state clearly what his purpose was. In August he wrote to Griffith:

You may be surprised that I took the big step here of openly asking for recognition so soon. I haven't yet sent any formal demand to Washington but said to the people generally that was what I was here for.[8]

The President felt that if he was successful in raising the loan, it would not alone supply money for home needs but would also be a proof that a large number of Americans recognised the Republic. The Dáil Éireann Cabinet had originally decided that the loan to be floated in the United States should be for $1,250,000. The President was soon persuaded that the loan should be for a much greater sum. Joe McGarrity said: 'Look for $100,000,000 and $50,000,000 will be subscribed'.

Delays persisted, but de Valera pushed ahead impatiently during July and August. He had little help from Irish-Americans, partly because it was holiday time. De Valera, apart from his prison sojourns, had had little rest since Easter, 1916, but holidays were out of the question while Ireland's freedom was at stake.

Joe McGarrity, alone of the leaders, stood by him. He made preparations for the issuing of bonds and submitted the text to a New York lawyer, Martin Conboy, in case of any illegality. Conboy reported favourably but, fearing that his judgement might be clouded by his Irish sympathies, he advised that the President consult someone whose opinion would be completely unbiased. As a result, de Valera submitted the matter to Franklin D. Roosevelt, at that time a partner in the New York law firm of Emmet, Marvin and Martin. Roosevelt met de Valera and pronounced his formula safe.

In September de Valera decided to make a new approach to the Friends of Irish Freedom. Surely they would at least cover the cost of launching the bond drive: the scheme could not be a success without some initial capital. The Friends had controlled the Irish Victory Fund and had agreed that twenty-five per cent of it be sent to Ireland. The expenses of floating the loan, de Valera foresaw, might be as much as ten per cent of the total loan, and he asked that the Friends of Irish Freedom give in advance their subscription for the amount in certificates which the organisation proposed to take.[9]

As a result, on September 29th, the trustees of the Friends recommended a loan of $100,000 to President de Valera and a few days later this was approved by the national council of the organisation. This was to lead to difficulties later. The Friends considered this money as part of the twenty-five per cent which it was agreed would be sent to Ireland, though they still claimed that it was a loan.

In drafting documents relating to the loan, de Valera encountered a problem which he submitted to Michael Collins, who was floating the internal loan in Ireland:

Only today when I was drafting the form of application for American issue did I notice (realise) that you propose that interest should be calculated from the day on which the certificate is fully paid—It should be of course from the date of the recognition and evacuation. I hope you have not made that mistake in your proposed issue in Ireland.[10]

Obviously de Valera did not expect early settlement of Ireland's claim. He considered it was foolish to commit Dáil Éireann to paying interest while the struggle was still in progress. He feared that the accumulated debt might become so great that it would be difficult to keep faith with the bond-holders.

By August he had already visited many centres, mainly around the east coast where he received enthusiastic receptions. His first public meeting at Boston was one of the most outstanding. He was accorded full civic honours and ended by addressing the Massachusetts State Legislature. These meetings were not, however, confined to the east. He visited Chicago and San Francisco, where he unveiled a statue of Robert Emmett, in late July and spoke in Salt Lake City, Butte and other centres on his way back to New York.

His presence in the United States was having a tremendous public appeal and proving an effective answer to British propaganda. The Prince of Wales was on a goodwill visit at this time to help to defeat some of the anti-British feeling which was gaining strength in post-war reaction. To Griffith the President sent a message:

The mayor of Newport and Governor of Rhode Island sent me an invitation to go to Newport. I am waiting till the Crown Prince of England gets there and he is waiting till I leave there—Meanwhile all the ball dresses of the aristocracy who are ready to receive him are getting musty—most amusing![11]

He now undertook a systematic grand tour. It took the President right across the northern states of the Union, then south through California to Arizona on the Mexican border. Everywhere he made Ireland's right to recognition the chief topic of his speeches and he stressed the weaknesses in Article X of the League of Nations Covenant. He also made arrangements, as he went, for the establishment of local committees to support the bond drive.

The journey from New York to Los Angeles took over seven weeks, and everywhere the President was greeted in a manner fitting to his position as head of state, even in some unexpected places. In Kansas City on October 25th he recorded in his diary: 'Visited courtroom and interrupted murder trial.' He sat beside the judge who invited everyone present to shake de Valera's hand, and the entry added: 'Shook hands with condemned woman who said, "Glad to meet you, Mr President, you are the first President I ever met. So glad you came." '

Probably the most colourful reception was given to him at Chippewa Reserve, Spooner, Wisconsin, where he was entertained by Indian chiefs. They adopted him as a chief of the Chippewa nation. He was given the name 'Nay, nay, ong, ga, be', which meant 'Dressing Feather'.[12]

The President met Henry Ford at Detroit where they argued hotly about the League of Nations. Ford maintained that the vast majority of the people were in favour of the League; a bad League was better than no League. After a long meeting the President did not think that Ford was very favourable to the Irish cause. At Portland, Oregon, on November 15th, the President was joined by James O'Mara from Ireland.

The arrival of O'Mara made an immense difference to the bond drive. He organised a headquarters office in New York and committees throughout the country. Soon de Valera felt happy enough about the position to leave the organisation of the loan in his competent hands. He was equally concerned to promote the loan and to state the wider case of Ireland. On January 31st, 1920, he attended a luncheon under the auspices of 'The League of Free Nations' in a New York hotel, to debate with Sir Horace Plunkett the merits of dominion home rule as compared with a republic. The hall was bedecked with flags of the world, but no Irish tricolour. The President refused to participate in the debate or to touch the soup set before him unless the Irish flag was hung among the others. The hotel manager pleaded that he had none. De Valera offered to get one from the nearby Waldorf. Then a compromise was reached. He would remain if all the flags, including the Union Jack, were removed. The Stars and Stripes was the only flag which decorated the hall when the President began to eat.

The subsequent debate was heated. Sir Horace Plunkett did not speak to the point but spoke about agricultural co-operatives. When he sat down the chairman called on St John Ervine to speak. His name had never been mentioned in connection with the debate. He abused de Valera and said his views did not represent Irish opinion. Ervine's attitude was so insulting that de Valera, much to the astonishment and disapproval of the audience, called him a liar and said he would prove it. Fortified by the results of the municipal elections in Ireland, the President was able to win the sympathies of the audience which had at first been shocked by the directness of his attack on the previous speaker.

In the mid-winter months the President stayed mainly in New York or Washington. Christmas he spent with his mother at Rochester, but was quickly at work again in Washington where the Irish delegation opened headquarters. He held impressive meetings at Washington and Hartford, Connecticut, but few occasions were as triumphant as January 17th when he was granted the freedom of New York. Many Irish-

American leaders, including Devoy, Cohalan and Austin Ford, accompanied the President to the City Hall. He considered these displays, not as a personal triumph but as a public acknowledgement of the Republic.

Early in February he set out on a short expedition through the states of New England. He was accompanied by Dr Patrick McCartan and they left New York in an inauspicious snowstorm. But it was nothing compared to the storm caused by an interview which de Valera had given W. J. Hernan, correspondent of the *Westminster Gazette*, before his departure.

The sequence of events was peculiar. The President gave the interview to Hernan, thinking that it would first appear in the *Westminster Gazette* which would arrive in Ireland on the evening before its publication in America. He expected that the first comments on it would come from Ireland where he knew his argument would be understood. Little did he realise that the New York *Globe* had an arrangement for obtaining Hernan's reports. Consequently the interview appeared in the *Globe* first and the headlines which accompanied it were sensational.

In the interview, which was in fact an extract from the draft pamphlet which Hernan was shown, de Valera insisted that Britain could safeguard her security without infringing on Ireland's right to independence. He asked the question:

> Why doesn't Britain do with Ireland as the United States did with Cuba? Why doesn't Britain declare a Monroe Doctrine for the two neighbouring islands?

The interview appeared in the *Globe* on February 6th, a day before the *Westminster Gazette* carried it. In fact the latter incorporated in its report the comments of the *Globe* that the interview was a

> withdrawal by the official head of the Irish Republic of the demand that Ireland be set free to decide her own international relations.[14]

This was a complete travesty. De Valera simply meant that Ireland would give a guarantee not to enter into a treaty with any power which might impair the independence of Ireland or allow the country to be used as a base for an attack on Britain. Britain would equally guarantee that Ireland's independence was preserved. The document regarding Cuba, from which de Valera had quoted the first clause, was known as the Platt Amendment. There were other clauses in the same document which made Cuba a United States Protectorate, but de Valera did not refer to them in any way. A denial by the President that he had intended to suggest that he would accept the other clauses of the Platt Amendment was rejected vociferously by his antagonists.

The strain of the work which he had been doing and the nervous

tension caused by bitter newspaper controversies over his Cuban interview caused the President to show signs, for the first time, of physical
exhaustion. During February Harry Boland noted the growing strain and,
on March 1st, entered in his diary: 'Chief far from well'.

Nevertheless, he continued to work and results were showing. In
Washington he met many senators engaged in the final debate on the
Covenant of the League of Nations. On March 18th the Senate passed
a resolution in favour of Ireland. The day before, St Patrick's Day,
de Valera had reviewed the annual parade in New York. On the review
platform with him were the Governor of the State of N.Y., the Mayor
of the City and the Archbishop. He had been accorded the highest
honours by the church in the cathedral that morning. No wonder he
could feel that his mission was proving successful.

Harry Boland, however, prevailed upon him, with much difficulty, to
take a rest. The holiday was a short one—only four or five days. The
President was accompanied by Seán Nunan and they passed the time
rifle shooting, walking and going to the cinema. They even saw a play
which he described in his diary as 'a racing story and the Republican
colours win'.

By the end of March, 1920, he was again in Washington. A southern
tour was planned, but after the first part of it was completed events
conspired to make the remainder impossible. These arose out of divided
counsels among the Irish-Americans.

THE MISSION UNDER STRAIN

January, 1920 – December, 1920

We must cast our eyes back for a moment.

The President had arrived in America fully aware of differences among the Irish-Americans but hopeful that all would unite behind him. As time went on he realised increasingly that Judge Cohalan and John Devoy were far from giving him the support which he had expected. The first manifestations of trouble were contained in a letter of John Devoy's which he received early in September, 1919. Devoy had a fanatical distrust of Dr W. J. A. Maloney, a friend of Dr MacCartan, and later the author of a book in defence of Roger Casement. Today there is no doubt about the sincerity of Maloney's work for Ireland in America, but Devoy for some extraordinary reason considered him a British agent and had no hesitation in saying so. He claimed that Maloney was responsible for dissension among Irish-Americans and that he was influencing the President through MacCartan and Joe McGarrity.

De Valera, from the time of his arrival in America, was very careful in dealing with Maloney because of the rumours. In fact he met him no more than twice during the whole of his time in America. But this in no way appeased Devoy. The floating of the loan was one cause of division, but only one.

For six months or so the dissensions were 'kept within the family'. Then came the *Westminster Gazette* interview in February, 1920, and public controversy flared up. The *Gaelic American*, Devoy's paper, accused the President of compromising on Ireland's claim. 'It will be hailed in England', he wrote, 'as an offer of surrender.'[1] Immediately the President issued a statement clarifying his position. He pointed out that he had quoted but one clause of the Platt Amendment relating to Cuba and had not referred to any other clause. The *Gaelic American*, though it printed his statement, continued the attack:

You cannot cite the Platt Amendment without bringing in the whole text of it, which gives the United States rights in Cuba which it would be suicidal to give to England in Ireland.[2]

This article made it quite clear that John Devoy was spoiling for a fight.

It is possible that de Valera's interview had been genuinely misunderstood but his subsequent statement should have cleared the air. Devoy, however, continued his attack unabated. He argued that 'when a part of a document is offered in evidence in court, or in negotiations, the whole document becomes a subject for consideration', and promptly quoted sections from the interview. He put into large capitals sentences which, taken out of context, could mislead.[3] On this somewhat specious argument de Valera commented that acceptance of the first of the 'Thirty-Nine Articles' did not make him a Protestant.

The attack at this time was all the more unfortunate because the bond drive was making such progress. De Valera was both disturbed and angry. He wrote to the Cabinet at home that if they doubted him they should let him know. But they knew well that he would say nothing in America which he would not be willing to say at home.

Today it is not difficult to see the possibility of a clash between Irish and Irish-American interests. As the President wrote at the time: 'Fundamentally Irish-Americans differ from us in this—they being Americans first would sacrifice Irish interests, if need be, to American interests—we, Irish first, would do the reverse.'[4] Strained relations existed between America and Britain at this time. If war came Devoy, following long-standing Fenian policy, would welcome it and hope for an alliance of American and Irish interests. De Valera's suggestion of a guaranteed Irish neutrality would make such an alliance impossible.

It was not, however, over fundamentals that the real differences arose. It was largely a question of personalities. Judge Cohalan, for example, had supreme confidence in his own abilities. He had controlled the Irish-American movement for many years. Young President de Valera seemed to provide a challenge to his position. But in fact had he backed the President he would have been all the stronger in Irish-American circles when de Valera returned to Ireland. Instead he set himself to oppose him at every point. The success of the Irish bond drive proved that Cohalan was not infallible on the American position. It made de Valera more steadfast in following the dictates of his own judgement.

The open breach in February, 1920, arose out of an accumulation of ill-feeling and mistrust which John Devoy had nursed through the preceding months. Cohalan was in no way publicly connected with it though it was known that he and Devoy worked in collaboration. In a letter late in February Devoy listed his grievances, real and imagined.[5] The circulation of a pamphlet written by Maloney, the calling of a meeting at the Lexington Theatre, New York, by Joe McGarrity, MacCartan and Maloney, such occurrences were looked upon as evidence of de Valera's ill-will. Even McGarrity's proposal that a large share of the Irish Victory

Fund be sent to Ireland was interpreted as a ruse to deplete the funds of the Friends of Irish Freedom. McGarrity had opposed Cohalan on a number of occasions and Devoy resented the fact that de Valera was in any way associated with him. In fact McGarrity and Frank P. Walsh were the only Irish-American leaders who, from the beginning, threw themselves whole-heartedly into the bond drive and McGarrity worked so hard that he became seriously ill.

The articles in the *Gaelic American* angered the President. This was especially true of the second one, which refused to accept his denial that he intended any more than the first article of the Platt Amendment to be considered. He was persuaded that Cohalan was behind the attack and that he should be forced into the open and declare his position in regard to the *Gaelic American* articles. With that in mind the President wrote to the judge privately:

> I am led to understand that these articles in the *Gaelic American* have your consent and approval. Is this so? . . .[6]

The President soon realised that he was unwise to have written this letter as it gave Cohalan an opportunity to reply. Cohalan, in a stinging letter, avoided the question which was put to him. 'Into any controversy you may have with Mr Devoy or others', he wrote, 'I refuse to be drawn.' He went on to stress that he always acted as 'an American, whose only allegiance is to America' even when advocating the Irish cause. He accused the President of interfering in purely American affairs and of endangering the unity of opinion which, he claimed, had existed on the Irish question before de Valera's mission. He suggested that the Cuban interview policy would 'make Ireland the ally of England and thus buttress the falling British Empire so as to further oppress India and Egypt and other subject lands'.[7]

Efforts by Boland to persuade John Devoy to be reasonable were no more effective and de Valera decided that he would have to send Dr MacCartan to Ireland to explain the situation to the Cabinet. He also wrote to them his side of the story of his clash with Cohalan:

> Our first clash came about the bonds. He pooh poohed the idea of bonds in any shape . . . Then I wanted to be let into the political steps which he was going to take . . . He didn't want me to go near the political end at all—anyhow the rift was developing. I did my best to stop it.

He went on to admit that he did not weigh every word and every sentence of a speech and of an interview as if it were a legal document. He claimed that his statement had done considerable good in America among those who thought that the Irish mainly wanted their independence to take revenge on Britain.

The President surmised that the *Gaelic American* attack had a double aim. They hoped either to make him return to Ireland to put out a fire which they hoped to kindle there or force him to make a public withdrawal of the Cuba interview. In one way the limelight would once more centre on the judge, in the other the President would be made to look like a puppet pulled into line by the great Irish-American leader.

> The moment that the judge can make it appear, or anyone else can make it appear that I am definitely under their thumb, then good-bye to any effective work we can do.[8]

The Cabinet, on March 11th, decided that Arthur Griffith should send the President an assurance of full support, leaving it to his discretion as to the propriety of publishing it. In fact he did not publish it because he felt that it might be taken as a sign of weakness if he were depending on a vote of confidence. Griffith's personal letter was a great consolation:

> Have no fear for Ireland. No such misrepresentation as that you have suffered will shake the national solidarity, but the men responsible for it have little realisation of how England sought to exploit their action over here and how indignant Ireland is at their thoughtlessness.[9]

And now the antagonism was flaunted publicly. Judge Cohalan called a meeting of a number of his supporters and a few other distinguished Irish-Americans for March 19th in the Park Avenue Hotel, New York.

At the last moment Harry Boland learned of Cohalan's 'caucus meeting', as he called it, and he asked Joe McGarrity to attend. The meeting was arranged for a day on which de Valera was scheduled to attend a function in Chicago. On McGarrity's advice he postponed his trip. When the moment arrived every effort was made to make McGarrity leave the meeting, but he persisted in remaining and nobody had the nerve to expel him. Cohalan made several charges against the President, claiming that he had alienated the support of those who had spent a lifetime in the services of Ireland and that he was placing the people of Ireland on the side of England against the United States of America. He accused him also of squandering money collected for Ireland. McGarrity interrupted and soon had the meeting in uproar. He suggested that, since de Valera was on trial, he should be heard in his own defence. Cohalan thought that he had left for Chicago but, when told that he was still in New York, Bishop Turner and Judge Goff insisted that he be invited. In response to a telephone call de Valera was quickly on the scene, accompanied by James O'Mara and Harry Boland.

Melodrama took over. The meeting became an occasion of cheers and challenges and ended in an emotional scene. Boland announced that he could produce a letter written by John Devoy which would confirm

McGarrity's statement that the Cuban interview was being used to force the President to leave America. The effect of this threat was electrifying. Bishop Turner called on Cohalan and the President to shake hands and all knelt down to receive his episcopal blessing on the peace so quickly achieved.

Outwardly there was a truce, but de Valera knew there was no change of heart as he continued to press Ireland's case. He wrote:

> Heretofore everything was left to the judge in this line. I never knew after he had left me that he wouldn't go and do something quite different from that he had led me to believe he intended doing.[10]

The hostilities were renewed when the Republican Convention was held in Chicago early in June. The President had long fixed his eyes on the party conventions, at which presidential candidates would be selected, as important platforms for proposing recognition of the Irish Republic. A resolution was passed by the Friends of Irish Freedom that a committee be appointed to 'wait on the Republican and Democratic Conventions to request a plank in the party platforms favouring recognition of the Republic of Ireland'. De Valera left matters to Cohalan and the Friends, thinking that they would comply with the resolution. As the convention date at Chicago approached, however, de Valera was warned that Cohalan had no intention of pressing the cause of recognition. Cohalan had promised that he would go to Chicago. He did not do so immediately and the President decided to visit the city in person.

It is difficult to assess Cohalan's motives for not pressing Ireland's claims. It was undoubtedly linked with his whole-hearted support of Hiram Johnson as presidential candidate. Many thought that if Johnson succeeded, Cohalan was assured of office in his administration. The President thought that the judge had made some bargain with Johnson and his supporters. 'Of course', he wrote, 'the bargain was too sacred for me to be let into.'[11] What Judge Cohalan had to barter was Irish sentiment in America and de Valera felt that Ireland had a claim on that.

The President thought that the question could be presented to the convention in several ways. He himself could, if invited, offer a plea on behalf of Ireland asking for recognition. The Irish-American plea could be presented by Senator Mason and the purely party case by Judge Crowe. The President arrived in Chicago on June 3rd; Judge Cohalan did not get there until two days later. A suggested plank had been prepared by de Valera and had won some support among delegates to the convention. Once Cohalan arrived, however, de Valera found that efforts were being made to undermine it. According to John E. Milholland, Cohalan had let it be known that he did not want the Irish cause raised at the convention at all.

Milholland gives a plausible explanation of the motives of Judge Cohalan.[12] He had supported Johnson for the presidential nomination so strongly that Johnson had been in danger of being identified with the Irish cause. Irish support was being counterbalanced by English propaganda against him. As a result Johnson asked Cohalan to moderate his open support for the Irish cause, not to press it at the convention, but trust him, if he became President of the United States, to do his best for Ireland. Despite the resolution of the Friends of Irish Freedom, Cohalan was intent on fulfilling his promise to Johnson and ultimately underbid the de Valera resolution with a proposed 'statement of sympathy' with Ireland's cause. In the end neither was accepted as a plank in the Republican platform.

The President was very angry at the attitude of Cohalan and his supporters. He felt that he had to press forward with Ireland's full claim for recognition: 'It was necessary to get the Republican Party', he wrote, 'to declare themselves.' He went on that if an Irish plank had been adopted it would have made it easier for Johnson, or any Republican president, to support the Irish cause. The failure of the plank at the convention did not preclude the presidential candidates from adopting it themselves if they thought it good policy. 'In any case it was a serving of notice', wrote the President, 'that this question was one which would come up again and again and was a legitimate question for Americans to deal with.'[13]

Next came the Democratic Convention which was to be held in San Francisco. De Valera had more time to make preparations for this convention. Through Frank P. Walsh he made contact with leading Irish-Americans in various states to put pressure on the state delegates to support an Irish plank.

The plank prepared for submission to the Democratic Convention was a straight proposal for recognition. It had a rough passage and was defeated by the resolutions committee. Nevertheless it was decided to present it as a minority resolution to the body of the convention. It was with difficulty that a delegate was found who was willing to present it, but Edward L. Doheny, the Californian oil magnate, put it forward forcibly. In his speech he made it clear that what he wanted was recognition of the Irish Republic. So, too, did the speakers who followed. President Wilson had his machine at work on the negative side. Nevertheless the resolution received 402½ votes against 675½ for the opposition.

Meanwhile de Valera was ready for any possible outcome. He had prepared drafts of statements, one of which he could issue if the convention rejected an Irish plank completely, another in case the plank, if adopted, did not go the whole way in supporting recognition of the Irish

Republic, and a third for the unlikely eventuality of the Irish cause getting full support.[14] In the statement which he issued he said:

> Rejection of the plank pledging the Democratic Party to the recognition of the Republic of Ireland merely indicates that it has not yet realised how great is the volume of public sentiment in this country behind the demand for justice in Ireland.

From San Francisco the President returned to Chicago where a third party was holding a convention. This was a labour grouping and de Valera on invitation addressed it on July 12th. Here at last was a party which was ready to pledge itself to recognition of the Irish Republic, although there was no hope whatever that they would win the presidential election.

The Chicago Republican Convention and the differences arising out of it caused a renewal of the attacks on de Valera. The seizure by the British of some dispatches from the Irish delegation to their colleagues in Dublin and their publication in the newspapers brought a new intensity of vituperation. In particular a letter from Seán Nunan in de Valera's party giving an account of the events at the Chicago convention made John Devoy's pen even more venomous.[15]

De Valera went on undismayed. From the spring of 1920 he had been considering the preparation of a brief for submission to the State Department in connection with the official recognition demand. During September a brief was drafted, much of it by the President himself. It consisted of a letter to the President of the United States, signed by de Valera and asking for recognition. The basis of the argument was:

1. That the people of Ireland constitute a distinct and separate nation.
2. That Ireland never voluntarily accepted British domination.
3. That the people had in general election and in local elections declared their choice to be an independent republic, and had set up this republic in accordance with the principle of self-determination.
4. That the people's representatives had formally declared a republic.
5. That Dáil Éireann had set up a government which, on democratic principles, was *de jure* and which was in fact functioning as a government.
6. That the rival British authority in Ireland was an alien usurpation.
7. That the standards and principles approved by United States practice entitled Ireland to recognition.[16]

Much of the brief was based on the wartime statements of President Wilson, so it was deemed advisable to present the case before the presidential elections. It was presented, at the end of October, by a committee headed by Frank P. Walsh to the Secretary of State, Bainbridge Colby, but no reply was ever given.

While the presidential election was in progress de Valera took no steps about the Friends of Irish Freedom. He was biding his time. After the election he gave an interview to the press, saying that he intended to hold conferences in a number of centres to promote the recognition of the Irish Republic. He wished to discuss the furtherance of his aim with leaders of American opinion.

At a meeting on November 16th at the Hotel Raleigh in Washington he insisted on fresh initiative or some concerted action in favour of Ireland. If a new organisation were established, and he could not see how they could work without a new organisation, he appealed to them to found it on fully democratic principles. It should be broad enough to embrace every sympathiser with Ireland's cause and the officers should be elected for short terms. Its policy should be to act in unison with the policy of Ireland's elected government.[17]

Those present then went ahead to found an organisation. The title chosen was cumbersome—The American Association for the Recognition of the Irish Republic. De Valera thought that a title proclaiming the association's purpose would get useful publicity each time it was used; in fact the length of the title meant that it was always reduced to the meaningless initials, A.A.R.I.R. To further the development of this new body, de Valera set out on another tour, choosing points at which representatives from surrounding areas could easily be present. He spoke in Rochester, Albany, Cleveland, Chicago and St Paul, Minnesota. At St Paul he received important news. Arrangements, he learnt, were nearly complete for his return to Ireland. He had heard of Arthur Griffith's arrest in Dublin and had indicated his desire to come home at once. He urged that the necessary arrangements for his journey be made. It looked as if he could now do far more for Ireland by coming back and resuming the leadership of the Cabinet. Rumours were reaching America, too, that peace moves were being made in Dublin and de Valera felt sure that he would be urgently needed in any negotiations impending.

Indeed he had been anxious to return to Dublin for a long time. When he went to America he thought, as we have seen, that his visit would be short, but the failure of the executive of the Friends of Irish Freedom to co-operate in the bond drive much prolonged it. Then, at the end of 1919, the Cabinet in Dublin became aware that if he returned he was to be arrested. Collins wrote to him, enclosing a copy of an order issued to immigration officers at British and Irish ports.[18] In December, 1919, Griffith sent a formal order to the President:

> At its last meeting the ministry unanimously decided to request you to remain for the present in the United States and consolidate the great work you are performing.[19]

This insistence on his staying in America lasted throughout 1920. In June and October, 1920, the views of the Cabinet were reiterated to the President by Diarmuid O'Hegarty.[20] In October de Valera was informed that he should not return to Ireland until after the presentation of the formal demand for recognition of the Republic of Ireland. The Irish Cabinet made it quite clear that they considered that his principal work should be in the United States but that, if time could be spared, they would not be opposed to a South American tour.

Occasionally in his diary Harry Boland reveals glimpses of how keenly de Valera felt the long separation from his family. When Boland returned to Ireland in May, 1920, he decided to ask Mrs de Valera to visit America for a few weeks. The President did not think this wise and Mrs de Valera was reluctant to leave the young children. Somehow Boland persuaded her. She arrived in America in the middle of August and she stayed there for six weeks. In Washington de Valera was very surprised and perturbed, one day in August, to get a telegram that 'Flanagan' had arrived. Despite Boland's talk, he did not believe that Mrs de Valera would be persuaded to travel and he took it that the volatile Father Michael O'Flanagan, vice-president of Sinn Féin, had landed in New York, to add to the troubles already mounting up in Irish-American circles. He was so taken up with the serious strife with Devoy and Cohalan during his wife's visit, and was so busy with meetings and work on the Irish cause, that they had little time together. The publicity and ceaseless activity had few attractions for Mrs de Valera, who longed to return to the quiet of her Greystones home. She returned to Ireland early in November.

Máirín was observing matters in her own way:

> My elder brother and I had of course a vivid recollection of my father and naturally my mother often spoke to us and to the younger children about him and about the struggle for Irish freedom. She also worked hard at trying to teach us Irish.
>
> The younger children could not remember my father—my mother overheard Brian and Ruairí discussing him. 'Who is Dev?' 'I think he's Mummy's father.' And baby Emer began to know that she could raise a laugh by taking up the newspaper and asking 'Is Mr 'Lera in the paper today?'

The President's work in America was almost at an end. In spite of all the disputes, the bond drive had been a wonderful success; five times the amount initially contemplated by the Irish Cabinet had been collected.

The case for recognition of the Irish Republic had been officially presented; and he had seen Diarmuid Fawsitt established as Irish trade consul in New York.

The wider propagandist effect of de Valera's work was incalculable but far-reaching. For eighteen months he kept the cause of Ireland before the American public. Publicity which would have cost millions to buy was attained in the American press by his indefatigable efforts. He won the goodwill of William Randolph Hearst and his chain of newspapers for the support of the Irish cause and gained a platform which greatly hampered the continuance or extension of British repression. For all the embarrassment he caused to the British Foreign Office, he never could be accused of interference with American internal politics. Above all, in anything he said and did he showed that the Irish were in deadly earnest and engaged in a life and death struggle from which there would be no turning back.

The split with Cohalan and Devoy was the one dark spot, but even this had its compensations. He had laid the basis of a new organisation, more clearly committed to supporting the decisions of the Irish Cabinet. Branches of the Friends of Irish Freedom left the Cohalan–Devoy body and affiliated to the new association, which went from strength to strength. By April, 1921, the American Association for the Recognition of the Irish Republic had over half a million members and by the end of the year this had risen to 700,000. In the meantime the older organisation had lost ground considerably. Only one-tenth of its original 200,000 members remained affiiliated to it. It was so small that it had little influence.

Among other struggling nations, too, de Valera had built up goodwill which could have helpful consequences. As George Washington had said to Ireland, 'Patriots of Ireland, your cause is identical with mine', so de Valera repeated that Ireland's cause was the cause of India, of Egypt and of Persia.

Arrangements for the President's return to Ireland were completed in December, 1920. He was smuggled on board the S.S. *Celtic*, and as he waited in a storeroom he composed his farewell address to the American people. He left behind him an immense task to be accomplished. The Irish Republic had still to be recognised. But he brought back with him to Ireland a message of hope to those who were carrying on the struggle at home. The rousing receptions and magnificent ovations which he had received had shown how much sympathy the American people felt for Ireland's cause. He told them:

> You will not need to be assured that Ireland will not forget and that Ireland will not be ungrateful.

A PRESIDENT IN HIDING

December, 1920 – June, 1921

The President entered on a strange inheritance. When he arrived in Dublin at the Custom House Quay on the morning of December 23rd, 1920, he was met at the boat by Tom Cullen and was taken by car to Doctor Farnan's house at 5 Merrion Square. Here Mrs de Valera visited him on Christmas Eve. His first visit, however, on the evening before, was from Cathal Brugha carrying, to the President's surprise, a Mauser pistol in his coat pocket. Brugha could not be persuaded to give it up. He had every intention of using it if he were stopped. This was the President's introduction to the conditions prevailing in Dublin at that time.

The British side of the story is best described in Sir John Wheeler-Bennett's authoritative *Life of Lord Waverley*, at that time the chief British official in Dublin Castle. Sir John suggests, incidentally, that the President returned to Dublin from America 'with the connivance of the British authorities'; this has since been disproved by the minutes of the British Cabinet made available since Sir John wrote.

The Cabinet had, in fact, decided that de Valera was not to be allowed to return to Ireland and instructed the British Embassy in Washington:

> If he applies for a visa to a passport it is to be refused. If he returns clandestinely he will be deported to his country of origin . . . In any communication to the United States Government you should emphasise the fact that he is not a British subject . . .

This decision so moved an unidentified civil servant that he minuted on the file:

> It is an astonishing revelation, after all the bullying H.M. Govt. have put up with from this man, to find out that he is not even technically a British subject.[1]

It is true, however, that the British Cabinet soon learned of his return and decided against arresting him, supposing he could be found, until they could bring some definite criminal charge against him.[2] Not knowing this, he stayed in hiding. In any case, he could not have fulfilled his function as President if his whereabouts had been known and his visitors had been watched.

De Valera soon learned from Brugha that he and Michael Collins were not seeing eye-to-eye. There was more than one point at issue here. Collins was acting President since the arrest of Griffith in November, and Brugha in terms of seniority would have seemed the natural choice. But Brugha admitted that he had declined the position. There were also more awkward questions of military jurisdiction. Brugha as Minister of Defence was seeking, not unnaturally, to maintain the control of the army by the Dáil to whom he, as Minister, was responsible. But many of the leading GHQ officers were members of the IRB and recognised prior allegiance to that body in which Collins was dominant.

Again, Collins, as Director of Military Intelligence, was nominally a subordinate of Brugha, Minister of Defence. But as Minister of Finance he was Brugha's cabinet colleague with far-reaching powers. The President made a mental note to keep an eye on this personal problem, but he attributed it to the normal human frictions and probably under-rated its gravity. In later years he put it this way: 'In military matters Collins should have acted as Brugha's subordinate, but as Cabinet Minister he was Brugha's equal. It is difficult to be an equal and a subordinate at the same time, and it rarely works well.' On this occasion it worked extremely badly. By October, 1921, the relations between de Valera and Collins had come under strain, but at the time he returned to Ireland de Valera looked on Collins as someone who had already rendered exceptional service to the Irish cause and shown much help-fulness and loyalty to himself. They had hitherto, to use his own expression, 'been good pals' bearing in mind that de Valera was about twelve years younger than Griffith but seven years older than Collins. None of these leaders, it should be remembered, had come together before 1916. Since then their various prison sentences and de Valera's absence in America had cut down their period of intimate co-operation to months rather than years.

Be all that as it may, no one could have been more helpful to de Valera than was Collins in finding him, for example, a place to live and work in. On New Year's Day, 1921, he moved into Loughnavale a detached late-Georgian house on Strand Road, Merrion, near the sea. Passers-by could not easily see from the road what was going on. The elected President of his country had to lie very low. In front of Loughnavale were two stone figures of lions as if to guard him.

Already he had met most of the cabinet ministers and become im-mersed in business. He concentrated first on the recent peace negotiations initiated by Lloyd George through Archbishop Clune of Perth, who had been in touch with Griffith and Collins about a possible truce. On January 3rd de Valera saw Father O'Flanagan, vice-president of Sinn Féin, whose intervention was supposed to have weakened Lloyd George's interest in the negotiations. De Valera told Father O'Flanagan that if Lloyd George were genuinely anxious for a truce 'the best way to expedite matters is for us to hang up the receiver.' Let the British Government come out openly and make an offer.[3]

The household at Loughnavale now settled down with Miss Maeve McGarry as housekeeper and Miss Kathleen O'Connell, returned from America, as private secretary. The President communicated actively with ministers about their departments and saw as many members of the Dáil as possible. But he decided, in consultation with Michael Collins, that this was insufficient. A meeting of the Dáil must be called. With his usual respect for anniversaries he wrote to Collins: 'It would be well to hold the meeting on or before the Dáil anniversary. Will you please see that arrangements for it are made.'[4]

In fact the Dáil met in strict secrecy on January 21st, 1921, the second anniversary of the meeting of the first Dáil. But under last-minute pressure from Brugha, who feared that there would be widespread arrests, the President and other ministers did not attend. The Dáil was far from satisfied and a second meeting was held, in Mr Walter Cole's house in Mountjoy Square, on January 25th, with the President and his colleagues present.

The President made a considered statement. Since his return he had been trying to assess the extent to which the strain of the struggle was telling on the people. The enemy possessed superior forces and equipment. All that Ireland had in the last resort was the power of endurance and moral resistance. He felt that the main purpose should be to keep up the spirit of the people. Delaying tactics were their best policy: they could not defeat the British 'in the field', and they should not therefore seek a decision 'in the field'. A strong aggressive policy to bring a decision would be right if they were strong enough, but seeing they were *not* strong enough, the delaying policy was the right one. Their policy should be to 'stick on', to show no change 'on the outside' as far as possible, and at the same time to minimise the burden on the people.[5]

This policy, of course, was interpreted as 'lightening the war' and in a sense this is what was meant. But its real object was to ensure the continuation of the war by reducing the sufferings of the people as far as possible. The ultimate success of the struggle depended on their support. The President insisted more than once that any *external* sign of a change in policy would be disastrous. It would give the impression that the country was admitting defeat, which it most certainly was not. He went on to detail the history of the negotiations for peace and how they had broken down.

The President succeeded in holding three meetings of the Dáil in the five months after his return, as many as in the whole of the preceding year. He called his first cabinet meeting on January 9th, and meetings were thereafter held monthly except that two meetings were called in April. All meetings of both bodies were, of course, clandestine. It was agreed that the President could summon any minister for consultation.

At this time the Ministries of Finance, Defence, Home Affairs and Trade and Commerce were manned by Collins, Brugha, Stack and Blythe. Local Government was in the hands of W. T. Cosgrave, who was staying some distance outside Dublin. De Valera decided to appoint as Assistant Minister for Local Government Kevin O'Higgins, and Joseph McDonagh as Minister of Labour, in the absence of the imprisoned Countess Markievicz.

Among all these Michael Collins was the outstanding personality. Bearing in mind his age (thirty-one) and his conditions of work, he was something of an administrative genius. Making perhaps inadequate allowances, he took a poor view of the efficiency of most of his colleagues. De Valera himself was far from satisfied that all the departments were working as they should, but he felt it necessary to calm down Collins and wrote to him early in January: 'I would be sorry to think that your feeling discontented and dissatisfied and fed-up was due to anything more than natural physical reaction after the terrible strain you have been subjected to.'[6]

Cathal Brugha, Minister of Defence, was a quieter but no less determined figure. A director of a firm of candle manufacturers, he was able, without salary, to devote himself to the work of his department. Collins' criticism of other departments might be dismissed as the impatience of an extremely efficient young man with any form of inefficiency. But his differences with Cathal Brugha were of a different character. It has been already suggested that a conflict of authority was partly responsible. The anomalous position of the IRB had much to do with it. Brugha could be forgiven for wanting complete control of his own department, unimpeded by a secret society.

A letter from Harry Boland to Collins, his great friend, demonstrates that the problem was no hallucination of Brugha's. He wrote to Collins on May 16th: 'I regret very much at this stage of the proceedings there should be the slightest question between Porter [Brugha] and Gould [Collins]. . . . I understand of course the question at issue between you and Porter and am fully alive to the situation as it is paralleled over here as between Woods and Cowe.' This referred to the dual position in which Boland, then in America, found himself. Woods was his code name in IRB correspondence. Cowe was his code name in correspondence relating to Dáil Éireann.

Because of the later differences between Brugha and Collins, the earlier disputes take on added significance. At the time the President did not find that they impaired the work of the Cabinet. Collins and Brugha were the most effective ministers and the antagonism was never open. He was more concerned about the danger to the national cause if the whole Cabinet should be caught and imprisoned, and wrote to Collins suggesting that he should go to America: 'We will not have here, so to speak, all our eggs in one basket, and whatever coup the English may attempt the line of succession is safe and the future provided for.'⁷

There were indeed several reasons for sending Collins. There were money and munitions to be obtained, a boycott of British goods to be organised, and de Valera was hopeful that Collins might help to restore unity in the Irish-American forces. The Cabinet agreed and Collins, at first reluctant, became reconciled to the idea. He was somewhat disappointed when Lord Derby's visit in April made the President feel that, with the possibility of serious negotiations, Michael Collins could not be spared from Ireland.

Throughout these first months of 1921, the President took a ceaseless interest in the activities of the various departments. Every effort appealed to him which might display the authority of Dáil Éireann and the powerlessness of Dublin Castle. Early in 1921 it was proposed that the Minister for Home Affairs, Austin Stack, should make an order prohibiting the taking of a census by the British authorities. The President commented: 'We are on fairly safe ground in giving an order here inasmuch as we can be certain to make it effective. Don't you think so? Our policy in my mind ought always to be to give *orders* where we are sure that the effort as a whole will be successful, but to make *appeals* only where there is any doubt.'⁸ The order was duly made and the census rendered impossible.

Despite his own personal reserve and the fact that he had to keep in hiding, de Valera fully understood the importance of publicity. He had thought a great deal about this in America. Desmond Fitzgerald, gay and gifted, was Director of Propaganda, but he was arrested in February and the President looked round for someone to succeed him. The man he chose—a fateful choice—was Erskine Childers, who had been introduced by Michael Collins. From the first de Valera was deeply impressed by Childers. Of all the men he ever met in politics he had the highest regard for him. He said much later that if he could choose a person along whose lines of character he would like to have modelled himself, that person would have been Childers. Childers was both thinker and writer, a bold adventurous spirit and, above all, an inflexible idealist.

Childers had served with distinction with the British Army in the Boer War, had later become a Liberal, and had resigned his post as clerk in the House of Commons to advocate the cause of Irish Home Rule in an important book and otherwise. In 1914 he brought in the arms for the Irish Volunteers in his yacht *The Asgard*. During World War I he served again in the British forces, being decorated for valour. His first cousin was Robert Barton, educated at Rugby and Christ Church, Oxford, landowner, agricultural expert, now imprisoned as a Sinn Féiner in Portland. Childers had always looked on Barton's house in Co. Wicklow as his home. From early 1919 he lived in Ireland and, with his dedicated, inspiring American wife, was admitted to an active part in Irish affairs. To quote *Peace by Ordeal*: 'Literary and political circles were well aware that here was a notable addition to the Irish ranks and a wider public followed with a morbid fascination the author of *The Riddle of the Sands*.'

When de Valera brought Childers's name before a meeting of the Dáil, there was a certain amount of opposition. The constitutional position was questioned. How could a man be head of a department who was not a member of the House? De Valera pointed out that the new director was not a member of the Cabinet; he was merely the civil service head of the department, for which the President would be responsible to the Dáil.

De Valera wrote to Childers about interviews which he would give to the press. Details of arrangements were left in the hands of the press officer of the Volunteers, Piaras Béaslaí, who was informed of his duties in April, 1921: 'I shall take it as fixed that all arrangements for my interviews with press men (home and foreign) will be made by you; this includes place and time for the appointments, conducting the journalists to the appointed place in such a way that they will not be shadowed, and taking any other precautionary measures that may be necessary.'[9] In these interviews he dealt with any talk of peace negotiations, but with all sorts of other matters as well. For example, he wrote to Erskine Childers on May 26th, 1921: 'I would be glad if you arrange for that interview with the editors of *The Freeman* and *Independent* early next week. The general tone of these papers is not at all what it should be.' It was, however, through the Foreign Affairs Department that he issued an answer to an attack on him in the official Dublin Castle Weekly Summary. 'Valera', it proclaimed, 'belongs to a race of treacherous murderers and he has inducted Ireland into the murderous treachery of his race.' De Valera gave a good deal of thought to a reply. Finally the press were informed that he had sent a letter to the Spanish Ambassador in London, with a copy of Sir Hamar Greenwood's Weekly Summary. He had marked a passage which he thought would interest the Ambassador as affecting the honour of the Spanish race and the Spanish nation. The Dublin Castle attack on the President was turned against its authors and the reply was used with great effect in the Spanish-speaking nations of South America as well as in Spain itself.

De Valera was actively concerned with the elections for the new Six County Parliament, which took place in May, 1921. The Nationalists and Republicans won 12 of the 52 seats in the six county area. Among the Republicans elected were President de Valera for S. Down, Arthur Griffith for Fermanagh and Tyrone, and Michael Collins for Armagh. No elections took place in the rest of Ireland. All the Sinn Féin candidates were returned unopposed. The four university representatives of Trinity College were Unionists.

From the time of his return to Ireland the President was anxious about the military situation and the strength of the Volunteers throughout the country. He was in close and continuous contact with Cathal Brugha, though any correspondence would appear to have been destroyed, no doubt for security reasons. He realised that outside Ireland many of the attacks by the Irish Volunteers were being interpreted as 'small incidents or murders'. He propounded the idea of larger actions in which up to five hundred men might be involved; failing that, an attack on Beggars Bush Barracks, the headquarters of the auxiliaries. Neither plan was considered practicable. He was, however, present when the decision to attack the Custom House was reached. He had many qualms about destroying the beautiful building, but it was important politically to carry out a large-scale action, and to destroy the local government and revenue commissioners' records. And these results were achieved.

Another matter to which he gave special attention was acceptance of a state of war. The Dáil in March, 1921, empowered him to issue a statement that the Dáil took full responsibility for all the acts of the army. 'These actions', he declared, in response to hostile propaganda, 'are not the acts of irresponsible individuals or groups, nor is the Irish Republican Army, as the enemy would have us believe, a praetorian guard. It is the national army of defence.'[10] From the moment he returned from America, he was determined to secure international belligerent rights for the soldiers of the IRA. Irish Volunteers, captured in action, were still being 'executed' by the British.

Whenever possible, amid the ceaseless hazards, he interviewed the guerrilla leaders. It was arranged that he should travel to Cork, disguised as a fireman on a train, but Lord Derby's visit suspended the project. Not only was the President worried about the military situation, but also about the ability of the population to hold out against military terrorism and economic pressure. But he had no intention whatsoever of calling off the fight; it was a question of conserving energies and making the struggle last as long as possible.

His political aim throughout was to consolidate the unity of the Irish people in their demand for a republic. Time and again he warned individuals who came forward with peace proposals, or offered to act as intermediaries, that they were only playing the game of Lloyd George and fermenting possible divisions that might arise in Ireland. He was particularly worried at the time of Lord Derby's visit.

Lord Derby came secretly in the rather thin disguise of horn-rimmed spectacles. The President was disquieted to know that he would first be seeing the Cardinal at Armagh. The 'line' of the latter was somewhat unpredictable. De Valera tried to impress on him, through the Bishop of Dromore, the need for a united front. Why could not the Cardinal say flatly that the Irish people were fighting for a republic and on the principle of self-determination were entitled to what they had voted for? Failing that, he could say, simply, that it was a matter for the temporal authorities, the Republican Government, and that discussions should be with them. The President himself met Lord Derby at the house of James O'Mara, 43 Fitzwilliam Place. They had tea together and a long political talk.

Derby seemed to be trying to find out how far the Dáil Cabinet was prepared to go to meet the British position. The Cardinal seemed to have given the impression that the Irish would be satisfied with some form of Dominion home rule. A week after the meeting De Valera wrote to Boland in America:

> You won't, of course, be misled by any of the British peace dodge reports. I wouldn't be surprised if before you get this a definite move were made by the British to split the country on the basis of fiscal autonomy; they are intriguing to make this an issue between ourselves and the Church—that is the real meaning of the Derby affair.[11]

The ever-active Alfred Cope at Dublin Castle was making efforts to bring together de Valera and Sir James Craig. In the end he achieved a meeting on May 5th, at the house of Tom Greene, a solicitor, on Howth Road, Dublin. When the two men met they were both rather surprised to find they had been misled by Cope. Each had been given the impression the other wanted to see him. As it was, there were no specific proposals to discuss and no conclusion was arrived at.

It has been said more than once that de Valera lectured Sir James

Craig on history. This is hardly fair. Craig suggested that the Act of Union was a treaty morally binding on the Irish people. De Valera discussed the moral basis of that argument and the morality of the methods by which the Act was passed. Craig was a man of courage beyond question, but he had just been carried hither and thither by Irish Volunteers through the City of Dublin, so as to conceal his destination. He seemed to the President anxious and ill at ease. De Valera wrote at this time to Judge O'Connor:

I do not see any hope of ending the struggle with England through a prior agreement with a Unionist minority. At bottom the question is an Irish/English one and the solution must be sought in the larger general play of English interest.[12]

Throughout these months de Valera never left the city of Dublin except for a couple of surreptitious visits to his home at Greystones. He attended cabinet meetings, meetings of GHQ and of the Sinn Féin executive and occasional conferences at various houses throughout the city, but always with the utmost circumspection. He wrote to Childers in May, 1921: 'Yesterday some colleagues thought it unwise for me to go to your place. One promised to arrange for you to meet me elsewhere at 6 o'clock. I called at the house, but found the family away. I suppose you had the same experience.'[13] He had more than one close shave. On his way to Madame O'Rahilly's house at Herbert Park to attend a meeting of GHQ to discuss the attack on the Custom House, he was crossing Ballsbridge in a taxi. Suddenly he found himself held up by an armoured-car with a machine-gun pointing at him. He was ordered to get out of the car and put his hands up. When one was in jail, this order meant that one must put one's arms outstretched almost horizontally, and that is what de Valera did automatically as a result of his prison experience. A moment later he realised his mistake. If any of those searching him knew the prison practice they would suspect him at once. As it was, they let him pass after searching him, and de Valera continued on his journey with the firm resolve that next time he was ordered to put his hands up he would do so literally.

On another occasion, on the way back to Loughnavale, his taxi was held up at Ailesbury Road. He was ordered out and questioned. The questioner remarked that his boots were muddy and asked for an explanation. The President had, in fact, come out of the muddy avenue from Loughnavale, a point to be concealed at all costs. He made up some hurried excuse about the weather. These episodes were normal features of Dublin life at the time and de Valera was lucky to be questioned only twice. Many others were questioned much more frequently, but he kept very closely to Loughnavale and his various hiding-places and hence was seldom interrogated.

His visits to his home were infrequent. Máirín writes:

> I remember the excitement when my father paid a secret visit home when he was 'on the run'. Viv and I were allowed to see him because we were old enough to understand, but the younger children could not. He had to wait until they were asleep to go and look at them. During the day we were all very careful 'not to disturb the important visitor in the dining room'.

In fact, he had realised by mid-April that he could not stay at Loughnavale much longer. One day he was told, as a matter of no special significance, that two of his landlady's houses had been raided by British forces. They had got 'nothing of value' he was told. A few papers, old receipts, a rent receipt for Loughnavale perhaps. Nothing of value? He saw the danger at once. He made hurried arrangements to meet the situation and an equally hurried flight to Dr Farnan's. Three days later the Black and Tans crashed in to Loughnavale. They found a pair of gloves with the President's name inside them, but otherwise obtained no satisfaction.

A month later, on May 18th, the President moved into Glenvar, a big house in its own grounds off Merrion Avenue, Blackrock. By now he was working on how to secure the recognition of the Republic by the Irish bishops. His object was in part achieved when the bishops' statement was published on June 22nd and included the following:

> We are now threatened with even darker doings because our countrymen spurn, as they rightly do, the sham settlement devised by the British Government. Until repression ceases and the right of Ireland to choose her own form of government is recognised there is no prospect that peace will reign among us.

On that same bright summer's evening, about 9 o'clock, a Lancia open lorry with eight or ten men of the Worcestershire Regiment arrived at the gate of Glenvar. De Valera was in the grounds. He had been working on army documents during the day. In his pocket was a document signed by members of his Cabinet and leading members of GHQ. In reply to charges made by John Devoy, it guaranteed that there was no trace of any split among the Irish leaders. Worse documents could have been found on him but these were sufficiently incriminating. De Valera's first impulse was to try to escape through a small gate into the garden at the back of the house. But the gate was closed and locked. He was indubitably trapped. Under the guns of the soldiers he was made prisoner.

From Glenvar he was taken in the Lancia to the Bridewell, where he was treated roughly and put into a cell which was filthy. On being questioned, he admitted that he was de Valera. He had spent three or four unpleasant hours in the Bridewell, and there seemed no reason why he should not prepare himself for another long spell of imprisonment, when suddenly the door opened. A man in evening dress entered, a stranger to de Valera but clearly a person of authority, in fact Sir Alfred Cope, Assistant Under-Secretary. The prisoner was rapidly transferred to Portobello Barracks, where he was put into an officer's room for the night, an agreeable change. Its usual occupant, a captain, swore horribly at having to give up his room to a 'bloody rebel'. The President found there a book on war by Marshal Foch which he read.

Next morning he saw out of the window the funeral of a British officer who had been killed in an ambush in the Dublin mountains. At that moment an officer of high rank—the President thought that he was a general—came in and told him that it was terrible, 'this firing from behind hedges and ditches at British soldiers'. De Valera pointed to a tank just outside. Wasn't that, he asked, just as good a protection as the stone walls or the hedges? If the military gentleman was fighting to defend his country, would he not take what protection was available? History does not record the rest of the dialogue.

Later in the morning de Valera was told that he could go, that he was being released. He was taken aback. He did not know what it meant. He couldn't guess the intentions of the military or Dublin Castle officials. In his diary that day, June 23rd, 1921, he made the laconic entry— 'Released: did not know what to make of it. Went to Greystones.'

FENCING WITH THE WELSH WIZARD

June – September, 1921

De Valera walked confusedly out of Portobello Barracks on to Rathmines Road. His release made nonsense of his arrest. There must be some definite political purpose behind it. What on earth was open to him now?

It was clearly impossible for him to lead the Government in the same way as before. His movements would now be known and anyone who tried to get in touch with him would be suspect. The most obvious reason for his release seemed to be a desire to undermine his authority, to make little of him, and even to make him suspect among his own followers. In the circumstances, he thought that the news of his arrest and release should be issued immediately through the Publicity Department of Dáil Éireann. After that there seemed little he could do for the cause of Irish freedom but to go south to Munster and join the Irish Army.

His political usefulness seemed over. All he could give now were his services as a soldier. Before leaving Dublin he met Collins, Brugha and Stack for a final gloomy discussion. Among the papers taken from Glenvar was a copy of code names then in use in official correspondence. These should all be changed at once. Those whose names might be found in the correspondence should be warned. He wrote: 'I am going to move about freely for a few days, going only where no harm can come of it— Gills would be a good place to leave messages for me.'[1] But even moving around was doubtful policy; as the cabinet secretary O'Hegarty cheeringly put it: 'There is such a thing as a murder gang here in Ireland.'[2] Once again de Valera took the train for his home at Greystones. It was little consolation to know that this time, unlike 1918, he could be sure of arriving. It seemed the end. In fact it was the beginning.

By a strange coincidence, de Valera's arrest occurred on the very day chosen by Lloyd George to initiate a new era of conciliation. It had all come about rather suddenly. Dr Thomas Jones records a cabinet meeting on May 12th, in which nine cabinet ministers, including the Prime Minister, opposed a truce against five who supported it. On May 19th, he was writing to Bonar Law, 'There is no change in the policy of the Government and there is to be "no sign of weakness".' But by June 14th 'a new chance of opening negotiations presents itself.' On that day,

General Smuts wrote to Lloyd George suggesting that the Government should use the opportunity presented by King George V's speech at the state opening of the newly elected Ulster Parliament, in order to 'foreshadow the grant of Dominion status to Ireland'. He enclosed a draft which might be used in the King's Speech.

As the Irish President was thrown roughly into a dirty cell, the Belfast Parliament was still echoing with King George's opening speech:

> I speak from a full heart [he said with profound emotion] when I pray that my coming to Ireland today may prove to be the first step towards the end of strife among her peoples, whatever their race or creed. In that hope I appeal to all Irishmen to pause to stretch out the hand of forbearance and conciliation, to forgive and forget, and to join in making for the land which they love a new era of peace, contentment and goodwill.

Whatever the precise parts played by others, the personal initiative and instinct of the King himself have never been disputed, nor has the extraordinary impact of the speech. King George, on his return to London, was welcomed at the railway station by the Prime Minister and members of the Cabinet. To quote Frank Owen's Life of Lloyd George: 'From the tremendous acclamation which the citizens of London gave him as he drove to Buckingham Palace, it was plain that peace with Ireland was the most popular policy of the day.' Or so it seemed at that moment.

The British Government could hardly negotiate for peace with the Irish Republican President a prisoner. But it was only with some difficulty that Sir Nevil Macready, Commander-in-Chief of the British forces in Ireland, was persuaded to release his notable captive. To quote Sir John Wheeler-Bennett:

> Hamar Greenwood and John Anderson had gone to the North for the opening of Parliament and were still in Belfast. The telephone wire buzzed between the two Irish capitals with the result that, armed with an imperative order from Anderson, Cope personally effected de Valera's release over the protests of the military.

Later the British military claimed that they had known de Valera's whereabouts all through the first half of 1921 and only did not arrest him because of a continuing cabinet decision to leave de Valera free. It is almost certainly untrue that the British knew where he was. Collins, Brugha and Mulcahy, whom they were undeniably pursuing, frequently visited de Valera. They could easily have been arrested if the President's whereabouts had been known.

But de Valera knew what the British intended only when he was handed a letter from Lloyd George by Dr Mulhern, Bishop of Dromore, two days after his release, 'The British Government felt it incumbent upon them to make a final appeal, in the spirit of the King's words, for a conference between themselves and representatives of Southern and Northern Ireland.'[3] The letter proposed that de Valera, Craig and Lloyd George should meet in London. The present Lord Birkenhead rightly reminds us that this offer 'burst on an astonished world'. The constant talk of force, the ruthlessness of the Black and Tans and the Prime Minister's grim promise 'to take murder by the throat' had all 'occluded from the public mind the possibility of negotiation.' Sir Winston Churchill in *The Aftermath* went still further: 'No British Government in modern times has ever appeared to make so sudden and complete a reversal of policy.'

From de Valera's point of view the letter could not fail to be welcome, but as drafted it contained one quite unacceptable facet. It implied that the President should accept equality with Craig, the leader of the recalcitrant minority at whose demand Ireland had been partitioned. De Valera said, in his reply, that he wished first to consult with the principal representatives of the Irish nation. 'We most earnestly desire to help in bringing about a lasting peace between the peoples of these islands,' he wrote, 'but see no avenue by which it can be reached if you deny Ireland's essential unity and set aside the principle of national self-determination.' This letter was sent on June 28th, three days after the receipt of Lloyd George's invitation. Mr Owen considers that in his reply 'de Valera defined that "Rock of the Republic", independent and indivisible, from which he never budged throughout the Truce, the Treaty, the Peace, the Second World War and anything that has ever happened since.'

De Valera realised that now he could work openly. Lloyd George's letter had recognised his status to some extent; it was important to consolidate it. He moved into an office in the Mansion House. It was from this address that the answer to Lloyd George was sent and it was also from there that invitations to a conference were issued to Irish Unionists, Sir James Craig, the Earl of Midleton, Sir Maurice Dockrell, Sir Robert H. Woods and Andrew Jameson. The invitations stressed the importance of the proposed meetings:

> The reply which I, as spokesman for the Irish nation shall make to Mr Lloyd George will affect the lives and fortunes of the political minority in this island, no less than those of the majority. Before sending that reply, therefore, I would like to confer with you and to learn from you at first hand the views of a certain section of our people of whom you are representative. I am confident that you will not refuse this service to Ireland.

Everybody accepted, bar Sir James Craig, who sent a telegram saying that he would not be able to attend. De Valera meanwhile replied saying that Lloyd George's proposal could not be accepted in its existing form. 'Irish political differences,' he went on, 'ought to be adjusted . . . on Irish soil. But it is obvious that in negotiating peace with Great Britain the Irish delegation ought not to be divided, but should act as a unit on some common principle.' Despite Craig's persistent refusal to attend, the meeting came together on an auspicious day, July 4th, with the flag of the United States of America flying overhead at the Mansion House in honour of Independence Day. At that first conference Lord Midleton suggested that if peace were to be achieved, the first requisite was a truce. He undertook to raise the question with Lloyd George. The meeting then adjourned for a few days.

The Imperial Conference in London at this time was a factor of high relevance. Among the Prime Ministers of the self-governing Dominions General Smuts was especially influential. After much preliminary spade-work, initiated by de Valera, Smuts and his secretary arrived in Dublin on July 5th. They were met in Dr Farnan's house at 5 Merrion Square by President de Valera, Griffith, Barton and Duggan.

Smuts argued strongly against the demand for a Republic. Dominion status, he maintained, was much better, as it would be guaranteed by all the other Dominions. A written agreement would be more confining than the greater freedom and looseness of Dominion status. The full implica-tions of this de Valera did not accept, but he was genuinely impressed by Smuts. He considered him the cleverest of all the leaders he met in that period, not excluding Lloyd George. 'We argued,' said Smuts later, 'most fiercely all the morning, all afternoon until late into the night and the men I found most difficult to convince were de Valera and Childers. I couldn't convince them.'[4] He certainly could not convince Childers, who was not present. But de Valera felt that there had been no real argument: the Irishmen listened rather than argued.

Smuts later surmised that Griffith, who characteristically hardly spoke during the meeting, 'was with him' but this view was probably arrived at in the light of subsequent events. 'Irish peace chances not so rosy as de Valera's poses' the *Sketch* commented on July 8th, and continued in black print: 'General Smuts was astounded at the attitude of some of the Sinn Féin leaders he met in Dublin. Arthur Griffith was the most reasonable, but the posturing of de Valera was a revelation to the South African Premier.' So said the *Sketch*. Jones noted in his diary: 'Smuts had met de Valera, Griffith and others, and found them deeply suspicious of a meeting at which Ulster would be represented. Smuts took great pains to persuade them, and asked them to consider seriously the proposal of Dominion status. This, he thought, had impressed them, but they continually harped on visionary aims and believed that they could win the Republic by force of arms.' Smuts did not abandon his interest in an Irish settlement. His South African experiences enabled him to sympathise with the Irish desire for freedom but seemed, if anything, to hamper his understanding of their reasons for demanding a Republic rather than Dominion status.

Meanwhile de Valera was drafting a reply to Lloyd George and the conference with the Southern Unionists reconvened in the Mansion House on the morning of July 8th. In England on that day the press speculated on an Irish peace. *The Times*, which took a strongly optimistic view of an early Irish settlement, carried the headline, 'A good omen'. *The Telegraph*, more worried over Ulster than Ireland, felt that they could only support the phrase, 'moderately hopeful'. Three days later the editorial contained this paragraph:

> Ireland must remain within the Empire; Sinn Féin cannot be allowed to impose her will upon Ulster. These, stated in the broadest terms, are the two conditions upon which no British Government can give way, and on which no illusions should be cherished.

Lord Midleton reported that Lloyd George concurred in a truce, and General Macready arrived in uniform at the Mansion House to clear up outstanding difficulties. For the purposes of the truce, the President appointed Eamonn Duggan and Robert Barton as liaison officers between the British and Irish armies, and valued their status. The British military authorities seemed to be giving thereby some official recognition to the Irish Volunteers—a dearly sought objective.

At the meeting with the Unionists, de Valera read to them the text of the reply which he was sending to Lloyd George. It welcomed the effort to bring about harmony between the peoples of the two islands and stated: 'I am ready to meet and discuss with you on what basis such a conference as that proposed can reasonably hope to achieve the object desired.' When the President told Lord Midleton that he proposed to go to meet Lloyd George alone, Midleton said 'Surely not alone.' 'Yes,' said de Valera. 'Then you must be a very brave man,' rejoined Midleton. Lloyd George's reputation was such that many people thought it dangerous to go into conference with him without witnesses. But de Valera felt that his word would stand a better chance of being believed than Lloyd George's if any conflict arose as to the conference. To the Unionists de Valera stressed the necessity for a settlement for the whole of Ireland. Any settlement based on less than this would be impermanent and cause great problems later.

On the day following this meeting the President issued a proclamation regarding the cessation of hostilities which was to come into operation on July 11th:

> During the period of the truce each individual soldier and citizen must regard himself as a custodian of the nation's honour . . . should force be resumed against our nation you must be ready on your part once more to resist. Thus alone will you secure the final abandonment of force, and the acceptance of justice and reason as the arbiter.

On Sunday, July 10th, de Valera was working at Glenvar when Cathal Brugha and Robert Barton arrived with a telegram from Lloyd George asking him to fix a date for the meeting. The President replied that he would be in London on the following Thursday.

The President decided to take a formidable retinue, in keeping with the dignity of an official visit. He picked out three members of his cabinet, Griffith, Stack and Barton, and, in addition, Doctor and Mrs Farnan, Kathleen O'Connell and Erskine Childers. When the names of those who were to accompany the President were announced, Michael Collins came out at once to Glenvar. He looked upon his omission from the delegation as a slight. For several hours he walked up and down the garden arguing heatedly with the President. Collins, in a letter written to the President a few days later, referred in a half apologetic tone to the 'little unpleasant things on Monday evening.'[5] The President explained that he feared that the discussions might end in a stalemate and that war might be resumed, so he saw no reason why photographers should, at this stage, be given too many opportunities of taking pictures of Collins.

The delegation arrived in London on July 12th. The city was sweltering in a heat-wave which contributed, perhaps, to the frenzy that greeted the Irish arrival at Euston. Excited women, who far outnumbered the men, surged and fought to get near de Valera. An eye-witness reported: 'They stopped not to cheer. They just howled and screamed in the extremity of their enthusiasm.' 'Oh isn't he lovely,' was a general comment. Meanwhile, de Valera, hatless and dishevelled, was being protected from the violent affection of the Irish crowd by a number of stalwart policemen.

The delegation made their headquarters at the Grosvenor Hotel. The President, Dr and Mrs Farnan and Kathleen O'Connell stayed at 5 West Halkin Street, the home of a Major Loftus. In the course of a short message to the people of England on his arrival the President asserted his hope for peace based on justice.

The meeting with Lloyd George was fixed for 4.30 on the afternoon of July 14th at 10 Downing Street. It was agreed that they should meet alone.

Crowds filled the streets, saying the rosary when they were not shouting or singing. The emotional build-up was intense. Lloyd George's secretary,

Miss Frances Stevenson, who was later to become his wife, has recorded in her diary his anxiety and excitement in preparing for the discussion.

> Indeed I have never seen D so excited as he was before de Valera arrived. He kept walking in and out of my room and I could see he was working out the best way of dealing with de V. As I told him afterwards, he was bringing up all his guns.[6]

The meeting when it occurred was a kind of dramatic anti-climax. Sir Winston Churchill has described Lloyd George as 'never a greater artist than in the first moments of a fateful interview.' But his own account of this particular interview, which was first in the field, has long since been superseded.[7] Lloyd George would never have set out, as Sir Winston implies, to embarrass his visitor or make him feel a fool. His tactics while, in fact, unsuccessful were much more carefully calculated.

Everything was done to impress on the young Irishman (de Valera was under forty and Lloyd George was close on sixty) the strength and magnificence of the British Empire. A map of the world extensively coloured with the red of British possessions was hung on the wall of the cabinet room. Pitt, Palmerston, Gladstone—Lloyd George intoned the names of some of those who, from this prime ministerial seat, acquired for the Crown such vast dominions. The British did not mind who occupied the seat, he said. Trying to build up a sort of Celtic camaraderie, he added: 'Campbell Bannerman was a Scot. I, Welsh.' But de Valera was totally unimpressed. His school-master's eye noted that it was a map based on Mercator's projection, which exaggerated the red markings. In any case, it was proof to him of British rapacity and certainly not an argument for re-entering the Empire.

But Lloyd George's appeal had more to it than that. He began reflecting on the amazing change that in these last fifty years had transformed the relationship of the Colonies to the Mother Country. The chairs were still laid out as they had been for the Imperial Conference then in session, and Lloyd George pointed out where each Dominion Premier sat. There had been Smuts, there Meighen, there Hughes, and so on. There was one vacant chair facing Lloyd George. As he finished he seemed to be expecting a question: whose chair was that? But de Valera had no intention of playing the game required of him. Again Lloyd George repeated his list and still no question. Finally, he was driven to supply his own answer: 'One chair remains vacant—waiting for Ireland.' The chair was Ireland's right and destiny when she wished to take her place in this great sisterhood of nations.

At the conference de Valera spoke little. He wished to let Lloyd George reveal himself. The Prime Minister later said that he had a more limited vocabulary than any Irish man he had ever met. The first meeting lasted for more than two hours and another was arranged for the following day. On the evening of that second meeting the President wrote to Michael Collins:

> I am sure you are anxious to hear whether any important developments have taken place. The position is simply this—that Lloyd George is developing a proposal which he wishes me to bring in my pocket as a proposal to the Irish nation for its consideration. The meetings have been between us two alone as principals. The idea on which we, the Ministry, started out remains unchanged. You will be glad to know that I am not dissatisfied with the general situation. The proposal will be theirs—we will be free to consider it without prejudice. I hope to see you about the middle of the week.[8]

The President, who wore for this meeting a sombre suit of black with a black tie, despite the heat, was set and grave when he entered Downing Street, according to one newspaper, but coming out 'he was distinctly cheerful. The clouds seemed to have disappeared and the sun shone again.' Three days elapsed between that second meeting with Lloyd George and the third meeting. In the meantime General Smuts called on de Valera to advise him and to offer any assistance. On Sunday de Valera and the delegates went to mass at St George's Cathedral, where the crowd roared and sang and lifted two of the delegates shoulder high. Afterwards they drove out to Oxford.

The newspapers at this time give the impression that, in these early meetings, de Valera had put forward some form of compromise. To counteract this he issued a statement saying:

> The press gives the impression that I have been making certain compromise demands. I have made no demand but the one I am entitled to make: the self-determination of the Irish nation to be recognized.[9]

When the meetings between the Prime Minister and the President were resumed on July 18th, the question of Ulster was the principal topic discussed. Smuts had reported to Lloyd George that de Valera did not appreciate that the British Government had any real difficulty in regard to Ulster, but seemed to think that Lloyd George was just using Ulster to frighten him. On the other hand, Lloyd George had seen Craig and was finding him quite obstinate. On his side, Craig felt that the British Premier was using Sinn Féin to force the Unionists into concessions. It has become clear since then, in the works of Lord Beaverbrook and others, that Lloyd George's position in his own cabinet at that time was much weaker than the Irish leader thought. But de Valera would, in any case, have felt that if the Irish issue were put fairly to the people of Great Britain by Lloyd George he would overcome the 'die-hards'.

At this meeting the President made it quite clear that the Irish people wanted a republic; Lloyd George was anxious to avoid this term. He picked up the headed notepaper on which de Valera's letters to him were written and asked about the Irish word 'saorstát' which was used on it. He said there was no Welsh equivalent for 'republic'. The President explained that there were two schools of thought among Gaelic scholars regarding the translation of 'republic'. Some preferred the word 'poblacht' while others favoured 'saorstát' which meant, literally, 'free state'. Lloyd George jumped at this solution to his problem and said 'Yes, there is the South African Orange Free State' and the title 'Free State' could be given to Ireland. De Valera is convinced that the name Irish Free State originated in this incident.

Sir James Craig had counselled prudence. He had stated to a press representative that 'the slightest indiscretion may easily cause incalculable harm. In my opinion what will best help to the attainment of peace is for everyone concerned to maintain, outside of the official consultation, a rigid silence on the whole subject.' He did not, however, mince his own words. In a message to his followers at Castle Dawson, Co. Derry, he proclaimed:

> You may all rest assured that I will see to it that the Empire in whose cause our heroes so nobly laid down their lives is not weakened by any cause of mine. They trusted us to give nothing away, and their trust will never be betrayed.

On the next day he challenged de Valera's statement on the right of Ireland to self-determination by making a similar claim for the six counties of the north-east. De Valera wrote a strong letter of protest to Lloyd George, pointing out that Craig's statements were issued after a meeting with Lloyd George:

> Our answer to this wholly inadmissible claim is not a mere negation. I have made it clear in public statements which reflect the views of the Irish people that Ireland, so far from disregarding the special position of the minority in north-east Ulster, would be willing to sanction any measure of local autonomy which they might desire, provided that it were just and were consistent with the unity and integrity of our island. It is plain, however, that if the claim of Sir James Craig is concurred in and supported by the British government, there can be no purpose in pursuing our conversations which would cease at once to be consistent with justice and honour and the interest of my country.

In view of Craig's public statements, de Valera asked whether Lloyd George supported him in his outlook? Lloyd George's reply was curt, but disclaimed all responsibility for Craig's statements.[10]

De Valera's fears were, however, aroused. He wrote to Collins:

Things may burst up suddenly here so be prepared. I intend adhering to our original plan as closely as possible, but the changes in the situation have to be met as they arise.[11]

To this Collins replied that he had been expecting that the negotiations might break down. The British military were preparing for it in Ireland.

I don't know whether anything tangible has been referred to up to the present, but I should say that in the final result it would be worth while stipulating that no matter how bad the terms are they would be submitted to a full meeting. You will know my object in this.[12]

This admonition of Collins referred to the plan decided on by the Irish Cabinet. It was intended that the negotiations should be prolonged into the late autumn if possible so that, if hostilities did recommence, the advantage of the long winter evenings would favour the guerrilla tactics of the Irish.

On the evening of July 20th, at 11 p.m., Lloyd George's proposals were finally delivered to President de Valera at West Halkin Street. Since they were to meet the following morning, this did not leave much time for discussion and thought. The proposals, which purported to offer Dominion status, at first sight gave an impression of large concessions, but these were hedged in by qualifying clauses which undermined their significance. It was proposed:

That Ireland shall assume forthwith the status of a Dominion with all the powers and privileges set forth in this document . . . That she shall exercise all those powers and privileges upon which the autonomy of the self-governing Dominions is based, subject only to the considerations set out in the ensuing paragraphs.

De Valera had always maintained that Dominion status for Ireland would never be real. Ireland's proximity to Britain would not allow it to develop as dominions thousands of miles away could. Lloyd George's limitations on the Dominion status confirmed his opinion. The Royal Navy was to control the Irish seas and have full access to Irish coasts and harbours. Britain was to have the use of Irish soil for defence and for air communications. Ireland would not be able to impose tariffs on British products, and the position of Northern Ireland under the Government of Ireland Act would be confirmed.

De Valera at once conferred with his colleagues. When he met the British Premier next morning he flatly rejected the proposals. He said that he would not recommend them either to the Cabinet or the Dáil. Lloyd George then brought out the threat which he had partially uncovered at the first meeting, but which he was to use again and again.

'But you realise that this means war? Do you realise that the responsibility for it will rest on your shoulders alone?'

De Valera ridiculed the threat. 'No, Mr Lloyd George,' he retorted, 'if you insist on attacking us, it is you, not I, who will be responsible, because you will be the aggressor.'

Lloyd George answered: 'I could put a soldier in Ireland for every man, woman and child in it.'

De Valera replied, 'Very well. But you would have to keep them there.'

Lloyd George tried a different stratagem. 'I will publish these terms immediately for the Irish people to see. I will leave the Irish people the chance of knowing what is being offered them.'

This plan, in flat defiance of previous arrangements, would have placed de Valera in a quandary; for the world would expect an immediate official reply to the British terms; and how could he produce anything adequate on the spur of the moment, with most of his colleagues absent in Dublin?

'Go ahead,' said de Valera, 'but I thought that nothing would be published unless we both agreed.'

Lloyd George would have brushed the pedantry aside, 'That was a little matter. We are dealing with big things now.'

De Valera answered him: 'So I must assume that is how you keep your promises. But have your way. You publish your terms and I will publish my refusal of them.'

During this altercation both men had stood up and de Valera was by now at the door, having left the document lying on the table. He said he could not be seen 'taking these things home with me.'

'Aren't you going to give me a considered reply?' Lloyd George asked.

De Valera replied, 'I'll give you a considered reply if you keep your part of the bargain.' By that he meant if the truce were extended.

Lloyd George agreed. But by this time de Valera could not pick up the document without going back into the room. He left without it but, to Lloyd George's relief, he sent a messenger for it in the evening. He could not give a considered reply without it.

Both the *Times* and the *Telegraph* described him as leaving Downing Street that day 'in a particularly good humour'. Perhaps it had been a relief to take a strong line for once. Lloyd George felt otherwise. Miss Stevenson (later Lady Lloyd George) wrote:

D. was very depressed. De V. had not even taken the terms away with him, but now we find this was a mistake and he has sent for them—how Irish![13]

De Valera managed to send a final message to General Smuts:

I regret that I cannot see you before I leave, to thank you for the interest you have shown in our cause. I was greatly disappointed with the British Government's proposals. They seem quite unable to understand the temper of our people, or appear not to have the will to realise the opportunity that is now presented to them.

Much suffering would seem to be in store for our people but God will, I trust, strengthen them to endure as they have endured the sufferings of the past.[14]

De Valera and his party left London that evening amidst a 'swarm of pretty girls, sacred emblems and Sinn Féin colours.' Described as usual as 'looking pale', de Valera got into the railway carriage which had been specially decorated in green and seated himself composedly before a collection of morning papers. He was entitled to relax—for a brief moment. It was doubtful whether he had gained anything; certain that he had given nothing away. The negotiating novice had confronted an acknowledged master of diplomatic wile. He had emerged intact and unmarked from the first round. But he had no illusions about the next one.

The British records and impressions of the visit are not easy to piece together. Jones, on the 22nd July, wrote to Bonar Law giving what he calls 'the P.M.'s account of de Valera'. According to this, de Valera then was 'not a big man, but a sincere man, a white man and an agreeable personality. He has a limited vocabulary, talks chiefly of ideals and constantly recurs to the same few dominating notions'. What follows is perhaps the only ludicrous sentence in a very distinguished diary. According to Lloyd George (Jones is of course reporting at second-hand): 'De Valera agreed to drop the "Republic", the P.M. telling him that there was no Irish or Welsh word for it and therefore it was alien to the spirit of the Celt.'

The Cabinet record for July 20th, also deriving from Lloyd George, has a somewhat truer ring.

> The Prime Minister informed the Cabinet that after three interviews with Mr de Valera, aggregating several hours, he found it difficult to say exactly where the Irish leader stood.
>
> Mr de Valera, who had an agreeable personality, had reached the stage of asking questions in regard to such matters as the entry of Southern Ireland into the Empire, swearing allegiance in the form of an oath, the name of the new State and so forth. What he wanted was a Republic, but the Prime Minister said this was impossible, being inconsistent with the Monarchy. Mr de Valera did not admit the inconsistency.

Erskine Childers drafted a reply, but the President thought it too argumentative. The solution propounded by de Valera to his Cabinet was very much his own. It was a subtle and revolutionary idea which might bridge British and Irish differences, incorporating as it did a plan for the association of Ireland as a republic with the British Commonwealth.

But the first reaction of the Dáil Cabinet to his draft was disappointing; it aroused little enthusiasm. The idea itself was novel and no sharp phrase had been produced to illuminate its meaning. The President proposed that they think over the matter further and meet again two days later. Meanwhile he did some hard and fundamental thinking.

As he arose on the morning of July 27th, an idea came to him vividly. He was tying his bootlaces, sitting on the side of his bed at Glenvar, when the word 'external' flashed into his mind. It would clarify all that he had been trying to say. Soon he was explaining his proposition diagrammatically to his friends. The British Commonwealth was represented by a large circle within which were five smaller circles, each representing one of the self-governing countries of that group of nations. The President sketched in Ireland as a circle outside the large circle but touching it. The whole idea was that Ireland would be *associated with* the Commonwealth but not a *member* of the Commonwealth.

The word 'external' was incorporated in the draft which was submitted to the resumed meeting in the Mansion House. It announced that the Irish people believed that they could best realise their destiny as a neutral independent state in political isolation like certain of the small states of Europe. But just as they had been ready to enter the League of Nations, 'so it is our belief,' the statement went on, 'that the Irish people would be ready to attach themselves as an external associate to that partial league known as the British Commonwealth of Nations.' All this was on the understanding that Ireland's independence was not imperilled or obligations assumed to take part in aggressive action against any other nation or people. This document was received with unanimous approval by the ministers. One intervention alone surprised the President. Eoin MacNeill, who was considered one of the most moderate of those present, said he trusted that the association would be *external* only. The President replied, 'It will be external only.'

Having won cabinet approval for external association, the President was now in no hurry to answer Lloyd George. Militarily delay was desirable and politically he felt that all the implications of his new idea should be well understood. He soon came to the conclusion that the document submitted to the Cabinet was a fundamental definition of policy which would be too revealing if sent to Lloyd George in that form. De Valera drafted a third letter, which contained a much less definite offer of association, and obtained cabinet approval for it on August 6th. It was based largely on Childer's draft. This was the letter finally sent, though the President continued to make verbal amendments to it until it was actually out of his hands. It was read by Griffith, MacNeill and Childers immediately before despatch. More argumentative in tone than the second draft, it was designed to initiate a long correspondence. The suggestion of external association was indicated, but vaguely and not under that precise name.

A certain treaty of free association with the British Commonwealth group, as with a partial League of Nations, we would have been ready to recommend, and as a government to negotiate and take responsibility for, had we an assurance that the entry of the nation as a whole into such association would secure for it the allegiance of the present dissenting minority, to meet whose sentiment alone this step could be contemplated.

Dáil Éireann was to meet to consider the British offer, and all the imprisoned deputies, except Seán MacEoin, who was under sentence of death, were released. Some members of the cabinet felt that to insist on his release, as de Valera wanted, would jeopardise the negotiations. Any effort to get MacEoin freed would, they felt, reduce their status to that of an amnesty association. De Valera thought differently. He knew that the British could not afford to let the fate of the peace talks depend on holding one particular prisoner. MacEoin was under death sentence; his position was more critical than that of any other prisoner. As he was an elected member of Dáil Éireann, de Valera felt that the British could not refuse to let him out. On August 8th the President issued a statement:

If the detention of Commandant MacEoin is persisted in, I cannot accept responsibility for proceeding further with the negotiations.

That evening Seán MacEoin was released; and two days later de Valera sent Barton and Duggan to London with the reply to Lloyd George.

An Irish version, prepared by J. J. O'Kelly (Sceilg), was sent together with the English form, which was called the official translation. Three days later they returned with a further letter from the Prime Minister.

Lloyd George made it quite clear that he totally refused to accept de Valera's standpoint. He said that no British government could consider 'the claim that we should acknowledge the right of Ireland to secede from her allegiance to the King'. There could be no compromise on this. He claimed that history proved that the destinies of Ireland and Great Britain were indissolubly linked and that the propinquity of the two islands made this necessary. The English press, however, continued to be hopeful, though a headline 'De Valera ready to drop Republic—on terms' cannot have pleased the President, despite its qualification.

De Valera replied to Lloyd George on August 24th. He discussed the effects of the Prime Minister's principle of 'geographical propinquity' on other small nations:

We cannot believe that your Government intend to commit itself to a principle of sheer militarism destructive of international morality and fatal to the world's peace . . . We long to end the conflict between Britain and Ireland.

The *Irish Bulletin* pointed out the absurdity of a policy which threatened war if Ireland declined 'as a free Dominion to join voluntarily a free association of free nations.' De Valera once again cited the principle of government by consent of the governed as a basis for lasting peace. To negotiate it Dáil Éireann would be willing to appoint plenipotentiaries. Once more he was not closing the door.

Lloyd George's reply was long and rich in historical dialectics. He quoted Daniel O'Connell and Thomas Davis, great nineteenth-century nationalists, to prove that the British offer of July 20th went further than anything ever demanded by them for Ireland. He cited Abraham Lincoln on the American Civil War to prove the unreasonableness of the demand for complete separation of Ireland from Great Britain.

Jones gives a vivid account of how the letter was concocted:

We sat up until three a.m., going through my Irish books. I dug out the passage in Thomas Davis' letter to the Duke of Wellington, which was used, but we had throughout an uncomfortable feeling that a contradictory quotation could be got from each writer, especially from speeches delivered in America. On my way home, I called on Chamberlain to borrow Lecky's *Leaders of Irish Opinion* but he hadn't a copy.

The previous answers of President de Valera had been delivered after some delay, while Lloyd George's letters were sent almost by return. De Valera had been gaining time. Now he speeded up the correspondence. But his continuing theme of government by consent of the governed was still unacceptable to Lloyd George. Lloyd George asked instead for a definite reply to the suggestion that they enter into conference 'to ascertain how the association of Ireland with the community of nations known as the British Empire can best be reconciled with Irish National aspirations', and suggested that it take place at Inverness on September 20th. De Valera agreed, but reaffirmed the Irish position. He was determined to give no ground, but he must have been aware that to state the Irish position so conclusively as he did would endanger the whole possibility of negotiations. His second paragraph read:

Our nation has formally declared its independence and recognises itself as a sovereign State. It is only as the representatives of that State and as its chosen guardians that we have any authority or powers to act on behalf of our people.

This letter was taken by Harry Boland and Joseph McGrath to Gairloch in Scotland where Lloyd George was enjoying a fishing holiday. When they handed the letter to the Prime Minister he was in good humour. He had been lucky in fishing the Scottish streams; he hoped now that he had something Irish on his hook at last. His good humour disappeared when he read the letter. 'It won't do,' he said a couple of times. The second paragraph was the difficulty. Lloyd George complained to the couriers that it was he who had given way each time to meet de Valera's intransigence:

> In the case of a big and a small nation, the big nation should not have to give all and get nothing. No, I have dealt with all nations and all men, M. Clemenceau, M. Briand, etc. We all have to give something but Mr de Valera will give nothing. I am done, done.

He left the couriers for a few minutes. When he returned he said that he would not accept the letter. He asked the couriers to take it back and withhold publication. He would accept it only if the second paragraph were struck out. The couriers refused to take the letter back, but they agreed to withhold publication until they had telephoned Dublin.[15]

In Dublin de Valera was perturbed by the telephone message which was, apparently, very indistinct. Fearing that they were bringing the letter back, he sent Robert Brennan to intercept them at Holyhead. But he found that they had not after all displayed any weakness. At a secret session of Dáil Éireann held on September 14th, the President placed the correspondence before it for approval. He warned them of the dangers involved in the now famous second paragraph. It could mean war. He admitted that he could have been more diplomatic by stating simply that the Irish position was unchanged, but he felt that a firm statement was needed at that stage. Lest the letter be taken as the end of the negotiations, he got the Dáil to ratify the names of the plenipotentiaries chosen by the Cabinet. To make it more difficult for Lloyd George to break off the correspondence at this stage, the names were announced in the evening papers.

In fact Lloyd George, in his telegraphed letter of September 15th, nearly did end the correspondence. He would not negotiate with de Valera as 'the representative of an independent and sovereign state'. That would be an official recognition by the British Government of the severance of Ireland from the Empire. It was de Valera this time who averted the break. He telegraphed his reply, reiterating:

> It should be obvious that in a case like this, if there is to be any result, the negotiators must meet without prejudice and untrammelled by any conditions whatever except those imposed by the facts as they know them.

And on they went again.

Lloyd George continued, for a fortnight, in an exchange of telegrams, to try to force de Valera from his position. Fifteen letters and telegrams were exchanged between the leaders after de Valera returned to Dublin. On September 29th, Lloyd George gave up. He ended the correspondence by saying that it provided no basis which the British Government could accept for a conference. However, he was ready to make a new start altogether. He sent a fresh invitation to a conference on October 11th in London

> where we can meet your delegates as spokesmen of the people whom you represent, with a view to ascertaining how the association of Ireland with the community of nations known as the British Empire may be reconciled with Irish national aspirations.

De Valera's reply was diplomatic, but firm:

> Our respective positions have been stated and are understood, and we agree that conference, not correspondence, is the most practical and hopeful way to an understanding. We accept the invitation . . .

De Valera had won his point; a conference without prior conditions. He had secured a conference without surrendering the position taken up when the Irish Republic was declared. The demand that the Republic be renounced in advance had been at issue when Lord Derby visited Ireland in April, but had not been raised when Lloyd George wrote to de Valera in June. It had been resurrected, but dropped again by the British Premier.

He had warned the Cabinet at Inverness, on September 7th, that the problems of allegiance to the Crown and membership of the Empire were vital, and that if a break was to come on these, it would be better then than later.[16] But shrewder counsels had prevailed.

In the debate on rights, the President had surely the better of the argument; and tactically he had won a breathing space, which his soldiers thought essential. The long summer evenings had passed, the winter nights fast approached. So much was sheer gain.

On one matter, however, he had not made his position clear. He had preserved intact the republican position, but had not shown himself irreconcilably committed. In fact, in all his messages he only mentions the Republic twice. He had shown his willingness to negotiate without restrictions, and world opinion took this to mean that he was willing to make some retreat from 'the Republic', in the only sense in which that conception had hitherto been known to them. By hiding his hand from Lloyd George, he had also hidden it from the public. External association, with its distinction between the isolated and the externally associated republic was something not easy to grasp immediately. The idea was as yet known only to a few and it would mean a campaign of education to make it understood. Rightly or wrongly, of necessity or otherwise, the chance to propagate it and commend it to the public was passed over in that crucial period.

De Valera's major success was in keeping unity in the Dáil and in his Cabinet. He had forced Lloyd George to modify his position by sheer firmness. Neither in the Cabinet nor in the Dáil was there a split when the correspondence appeared in danger of collapsing. When this danger was greatest he warded it off by, at one time, offering to appoint plenipotentiaries and, at the next, by appointing them. He had shown great political prescience as to how far he could go without spoiling everything. In one way, however, he realised that the Irish position was weaker in September than it had been in June. Despite gaining valuable time for the army, he was deeply conscious that the truce made the resumption of hostilities more difficult for the weaker side. Efforts to drill, train and recruit could have some effect but, on the other hand, British Intelligence had the opportunity to become much better informed.

THE BEST LAID PLANS

October – November, 1921

Meanwhile a good deal had been going on in the Dublin Cabinet and the secret sessions in the Dáil. In these discussions the President could be much more outspoken about the situation than in public. In secret session he warned the members of the dangers involved in the negotiations ahead. There could be no question of their being in a position to dictate their own terms to the British. Differences of opinion on their own side were therefore inevitable. These might be sharp and painful. The principles of united cabinet responsibility would be honoured in anything put to the Dáil. If the final proposals sponsored by the Cabinet were not acceptable to Dáil Éireann—well, they could always elect a new cabinet.

Much more significant than any verbal warning or precautions was the decision that the President should not himself be a member of the delegation to the London conference. This decision, which was to provoke much controversy later and has puzzled many history students, did not cause much stir at the time.

It was at the cabinet meeting of August 23rd that de Valera first indicated that he did not wish to be one of the plenipotentiaries in London. But he did not explain his reasons fully at that stage. Three days later he discussed in the Dáil the powers of the delegation whose appointment would be made by the Cabinet and ratified by the Dáil. On this occasion a motion was passed, giving the delegates at the peace conference a free hand in the negotiations as far as the Dáil was concerned. At the cabinet meeting on September 9th the names of the delegates were settled. The President left no one in any doubt that he did not wish to be one of them. Probably a majority of the Cabinet would have liked him to go, but when he pressed the point his colleagues divided evenly and he decided this important issue by his own vote. However, the matter was not quite disposed of. When the Dáil met on September 14th to ratify the appointment of the plenipotentiaries, Cosgrave proposed that de Valera should lead the delegation. He argued that it was a pity to have 'their best player among the reserves'. Though the Cabinet had decided the issue already, the President felt that the Dáil should be able to discuss the question; after all the Cabinet had not been unanimous. But Cosgrave's motion received no support. The English press did not give any indication of the narrowness of the Cabinet's decision or of the discussion in the Dáil. The *Daily Telegraph* reported 'The omission from the list of delegates of Mr de Valera occasions no great surprise for it had been assumed that he would not take part in any negotiations.'

It is worth lingering for a moment on de Valera's reasons. He explained his position some months later in a letter to Joe McGarrity. First of all he was the symbol of the Republic as its President. At a conference talk, dealing with Lloyd George, it might be necessary to finesse a little. The President, of all men, should not give rise to even the remotest suspicion of 'letting down' the Republic. He felt that by remaining in Ireland he could act as a reserve against any tricks of the Prime Minister. Even more important was the need for strong leadership at home should external association prove acceptable to the British. External association was a new concept. All de Valera's influence might be necessary to commend it to uncompromising isolationist republicans. He felt that his influence with Brugha, Stack, Mrs Clarke and others would be much greater if he were not a party to the negotiations. We must remind ourselves repeatedly that unity on his own side was his overriding objective.[1]

There were other considerations which weighed with him. In the first place, the delegation would be forced by his remaining in Ireland to refer home before decisions were taken. This should strengthen their position as negotiators and gain them time for careful consideration at critical points. It would give an opportunity for the submission of the final draft to independent legal opinion. The plan would also enable the members of the Cabinet at home to make their contribution remote from the pressures of the conference table. All this again should help to guarantee a united Cabinet.

Again, should no agreement be reached and the negotiations break down, their situation would be far more easily accepted if the delegation had been led by Griffith, who was considered a moderate. No one would accuse *him* of intransigence. The President, because of his conference with Lloyd George and the subsequent correspondence, had come to be looked upon as an uncompromising extremist.

Finally, by remaining in Dublin he could give free expression to national feeling and help to guide it. Thus the British would be made to realise that they were facing a determined and united nation. Psychologically and physically his absence from the conference would give him the opportunity during the negotiations to strengthen the nation in the event of any resumption of war.

The President's decision to stay at home made it obvious that Griffith and Collins would have to go to London. Brugha was unwilling to go.

It was equally obvious that Griffith must be chairman of the delegation. From a strictly Republican standpoint, this combination was not quite satisfactory. Griffith, since 1917, had shown no sign of weakening in his support of the republican aims of the new Sinn Féin. Nevertheless, for many years previously he had propounded with extreme devotion and efficiency the dual monarchy solution. The President felt that if Arthur Griffith followed his own preference, that is to say had the ordering of things in his own hands, he could accept 'the Crown' under pressure. But as a member of a team, he felt he could be absolutely relied on to act in accordance with Cabinet decisions.

Griffith's appointment was warmly received by the English press. For example:

> The selection of Mr Arthur Griffith as Chairman . . . may be said to afford widespread satisfaction. He is generally regarded as a very able man, and as possessing excellent qualifications for such an important position.

Collins was a different case. A leader indeed, by that time *the* leader of the IRB, he was much more firmly committed to the republican ideal than Griffith. At first sight it would be very difficult for him to accept Dominion status. Yet an escape route was open to him if he could persuade himself that Dominion status was only a stepping stone on the way to an independent republic. In a settlement of that kind there might even be a temptation for him to emerge after the settlement as the leader of an extreme republican party. A temptation to him which, rightly or wrongly, de Valera feared.

Information had reached the President which suggested that Collins was already contemplating the acceptance of 'the Crown'. At a meeting of the supreme council of the executive of the IRB on September 1st, 1921, the question of peace or war, of what would and would not be an honourable peace, was debated. No decision was reached at the meeting, but the discussion gave a clue to the way Collins's thoughts were running. In fairness to Collins one must rebut any suggestion that he was preparing to 'do a deal' in London. He was strongly opposed to being a member of the delegation at all and said so clearly in the Cabinet and the Dáil. His reluctance surprised de Valera, who recalled Collins's protests when he had not been included in the mission to London in July. His state of mind has been made more intelligible since. A little later, October 11th, the day of the first session of the conference, it now appears that Collins was writing: 'You know the way it is. Either way it will be wrong. You might say the trap is sprung'. This, while no doubt sincerely believed, was far from the truth. It illustrates all too perfectly what Frank O'Connor has written in his life of Collins:

One of the most amazing things revealed by the Treaty split was that none of the team of delegates and secretaries seemed to have the least notion what the other fellow was thinking of, and all were equally bemused when it came to the question of what de Valera and the rest of the Cabinet at home were planning.[2]

Collins's suspicions of a plot against him were quite unjustified. Yet it would be an affectation to pretend that by October de Valera's feelings towards him and personal confidence in him were what they had been previously. De Valera, in later years, has been very reluctant to analyse, let alone to criticise, his old comrades in the struggle for independence. If asked about Collins he would always begin by insisting that 'Collins was a very fine revolutionary leader and a splendid executive. He got at once to the heart of things and saw to it that what was important was done'. He would recall that shortly after coming out of prison 'I recognised his fine qualities. I made him Minister of Finance and Director of Information and Communications. These were the key posts which gave him the power which he exercised later to the full.' He preferred to dwell on his amazing efficiency, never failing to mention his punctuality, and leave it there.

He would admit, however, that he had never ceased to feel concern over Collins's high and even dominant position in the IRB. Two points seem to arise there. Between the arrest of Griffith and the arrival of de Valera in Ireland (November to December, 1920) Collins was acting-President at a time when he was looked on in the IRB as their own effective leader. De Valera was under the impression, in later years, that a strong element in the IRB would have preferred Collins to be President instead of himself. Whether or not for this reason de Valera recalled later that from April, 1921, onwards 'Collins did not seem to accept my view of things as he had done before and was inclined to give public expression to his own opinions even when they differed from mine, for example, in connection with the release of Seán McKeown.' In this last case de Valera in fact felt that Collins was 'not acting loyally'. But in de Valera's mind it was no trivial accident that, after 1916, he and Brugha severed their very tenuous connections with the IRB and Collins went on to become its life and soul. For de Valera the outlook of a civil secret society was incompatible with his kind of scrupulous fidelity to principle. Collins, serving the cause no doubt devotedly in his own fashion, 'was inclined to take the course immediately convenient and trust to be able in the future to make modifications or changes when they became necessary'.

In happier circumstances these contrasts of mind and spirit might have been overcome. By October, 1921, they were already contributing to an astonishing degree of mutual ignorance.

This weakness, in due course to prove fatal, was already present in embryo by the start of the negotiations in London. To offset any suspicions of Republican frailty in the delegation, the President was resolved to send with them a strong republican. Cathal Brugha's refusal to go seemed just as well on account of their different opinions. If he went the delegation might spend its time wrangling. There would not be the necessary team-work. Collins and Griffith would be tempted to out-manoeuvre rather than convince him, and it would lead to endless trouble. Stack also declined. Mary MacSwiney, sister of Terence MacSwiney, the Lord Mayor of Cork who had died on hunger-strike, was considered by de Valera as a possible delegate. Because of the attitude, as he understood it, of Griffith and Collins to women in politics, he did not propose her name.

The suitable staunch republican to balance Griffith and Collins was not easily discernible. Robert Barton was the man whom de Valera finally selected for the role. Of him de Valera wrote: 'I felt that he would be strong and stubborn enough as a retarding force to any precipitate giving way by the Delegation.' He nominated Erskine Childers, experienced, dedicated, indomitable, as secretary, to give added strength to his cousin and close friend Robert Barton. Two lawyers were added as delegates, Éamonn Duggan and George Gavan Duffy, later to be an Irish judge. Duggan was likely to support Collins while Duffy would be favourable to Barton and Childers. An adequate balance seemed to be provided.

In ultimate human values the Irish delegation had nothing to fear, but confronted with the subtle diplomacy, traditional self-confidence and vast experience they must expect from the British, their limitations for the job were manifest. De Valera took precautions intended to strengthen their hands. While the plenipotentiaries were not to be bound by restrictions imposed by Dáil Éireann, they were to be subject to certain cabinet instructions. The President explained to the Dáil that the delegates would set off not only with a cabinet policy, but also on the understanding that any large question would be referred home before it was decided.

Besides their letters of credence as plenipotentiaries, the delegates were given a letter with the Cabinet's instructions. In view of later controversies these must be given in full and special attention called to number 3.

Instructions to Plenipotentiaries from Cabinet
7th October 1921

1. The plenipotentiaries have full powers as defined in their credentials.
2. It is understood, however, that before decisions are finally reached on the main questions that a dispatch notifying the intention of making these decisions will be sent to the members of the Cabinet in Dublin and that a

reply will be awaited by the plenipotentiaries before the final decision is made.

3. *It is also understood that the complete text of the draft treaty about to be signed will be similarly submitted to Dublin and reply awaited.*

4. In case of break the text of final proposals from our side will be similarly submitted.

5. It is understood that the Cabinet in Dublin will be kept regularly informed of the progress of the negotiations.

Thus did de Valera feel that cabinet unity would be preserved and that those who remained in Dublin would have a guarantee that nothing would be signed in London without their knowledge and consent. While Barton in his eyes would be the anchor man among the delegates, the instructions gave the cabinet ministers the power of 'hanging on to their coat-tails' in the expected tug-of-war with the British.

The plenipotentiaries left for London in the second week of October, taking with them the draft of a treaty which had been prepared by de Valera, Duffy and Childers. It was intended to be a guide to the principles which could be accepted. External association was a fundamental feature of the draft treaty. The President expected that as the negotiations proceeded it would be revised and kept up-to-date. It would always be ready for publication as a series of counter proposals if the negotiations broke down and British proposals were published. In the eyes of the general public in both countries there seemed to be a clear choice between Ireland being a republic and outside the British Empire, or a dominion inside it. De Valera had worked out a third possibility—a republic externally associated *with* the Empire, but still *outside* it and certainly not a dominion with allegiance to the Crown. It was not until 1949, in the case of India, that it was found to be possible to be a republic and yet remain inside what, by then, had become the Commonwealth. No solution of this kind had crossed the mind of the author of *Peace by Ordeal*, who wrote in 1935, 'It was agreed by both sides that it was impossible to be at once a republic and a member of, or inside, the British Empire.'

The Irish strategy arranged in consultation with de Valera avoided an immediate head-on collision. External association was held in reserve while the British offer of dominion status and its various qualifications was examined. Half a century later, it is not impossible, though even now far from easy, to propose a different tactic. De Valera must share responsibility for the initiation of this 'circumspect' policy, though very early in the conference he attempted to check the lengths to which it was being carried by Griffith.

From the end of October, it acquired a special twist under a particular

THE BEST LAID PLANS

handling of the Ulster issue. If a break must come, let it be on the refusal of Ulster to 'come in' to a united Ireland, rather than on the refusal of the Irish delegates to accept inclusion in the Empire. In the Ulster case the Irish and British delegates would, on paper at least, be aiming at the same thing—the unity of Ireland. In the event of a breakdown on Ulster it was inconceivable that war would follow. In the second case (republic versus dominion) the two sides were sharply opposed. In the event of a breakdown, war was a distinct possibility.

Whether this line of diplomacy could ever have succeeded is highly doubtful. How it was counteracted by the British is set out at length in various works, which also deal fully with the correspondence between de Valera, in Dublin, and Griffith, in London.[3]

It is not proposed below to recapitulate the full story of the negotiations, but to place ourselves in de Valera's situation in Dublin, as he felt the impact of events and tried to interpret and guide them.

The delegations confronted one another for the first time on October 11th. Lloyd George tactfully effected group introductions without the necessity for handshakes, or presentation of credentials, and the two teams got down to work.

Ironically enough, the first threat to the continuance of the conference arose from a telegram from the Pope wishing it well. This telegram, sent to George V on October 19th, began:

We rejoice at the resumption of the Anglo-Irish negotiations, and pray to the Lord, with all our heart, that He may bless them and grant to your Majesty the great joy and imperishable glory of bringing to an end the age long dissension.

The King's reply, written for him by Lloyd George, read:

I have received the message of Your Holiness with much pleasure, and with all my heart I join in your prayer that the Conference, now sitting in London, may achieve a permanent settlement of the troubles in Ireland and may initiate a new era of peace and happiness for my people.

As soon as de Valera learnt of the Pope's telegram and the King's reply, he immediately sent one to the Pope himself:

The people of Ireland have read the message sent by Your Holiness to the King of Great Britain and appreciate the kindly interest in their welfare and the paternal regard which suggested it. I tender to your Holiness their gratitude. They are confident that the ambiguities in the reply sent in the name of King George V will not mislead you, as they may the uninformed, into believing that the troubles are 'in' Ireland or that the people of Ireland owe allegiance to the British King.

... The trouble is between Ireland and Britain and its source that the rulers of Britain have sought to impose their will upon Ireland and by brutal force have endeavoured to rob her people of the liberty which is their natural right and heritage.

Lloyd George at the next meeting of the conference described de Valera's telegram as 'challenging, defiant, and if I may say so, ill-conditioned.' The British press 'threw herself into one of her paroxysms of patriotic righteousness'. According to the *Times* de Valera was 'impertinent' to the Pope. The *Daily Express* considered that the telegram betrayed 'a spirit of irresponsible mischief scarcely credible in a serious leader.' The Dublin correspondent of the *Daily Telegraph* wrote: 'It is generally felt that Mr de Valera's message to the Pope has seriously imperilled Irish peace.'

Over the conference table Arthur Griffith answered for his President:

Mr de Valera only stated public facts. I should say that this message was called for by the phrase in King George's letter in which he refers to 'troubles in Ireland'. The trouble is not a trouble in Ireland but is one between Ireland and Great Britain.

Frank Gallagher considers that 'These words were more courageous even than they read now, because Griffith, supported by Collins and Duggan, privately thought the President's telegram inopportune, whereas Barton and Duffy thought it timely.' The incident passed.

But the next one produced an explosion. On the same day, October 21st, the delegates met in London to review the progress of the negotiations. They realised that the question of the Crown would come up at the next meeting and they instructed Erskine Childers to write to the President:

Two courses are open to the delegates, (*a*) to refuse allegiance to the Crown, (*b*) neither to refuse nor accept it at the present stage, but to say that if they are satisfied on other points—Ulster, defence, trade, etc.—they would be prepared to consider the question of the Crown: in other words to obtain a field of manoeuvre and delay the crucial question. They request instructions as to which course to adopt.[5]

Griffith followed this up a few days later with a report of the conference:

They pressed me to say that I would accept the Crown provided we came to other agreements. It was evident they wanted something to assure themselves against the Diehards. I told them that I had no authority. If we came to an agreement on all other points I could recommend some form of Association with the Crown.[6]

De Valera's reply to these letters was firm:

We are all here at one that there can be no question of our asking the Irish people to enter an arrangement which could make them subject to the Crown, or demand from them allegiance to the British King. If war is the alternative we can only face it, and I think that the sooner the other side is made to realise that the better.[7]

In the same letter the President mentioned that Collins, visiting Dublin the previous weekend, had warned him to hold himself in readiness to go to London. De Valera therefore continued:

You understand fully the considerations of tactical advantage which determined me in holding the view that I should remain here. If any new considerations arise it would be well that we should know them exactly so that we may all weigh them and, if possible, secure unanimity for whatever action is taken. My own position is I am loath to go unless the position imperatively calls for it.

And now a strange thing happened. The earlier paragraph of de Valera's letter produced a storm. Griffith, Collins, and Duggan were incensed. They looked upon it as an unjustifiable interference with their freedom of action. After all, they would have to discuss some form of association and some recognition of the Crown in raising the official policy of external association. Were they to understand that this was now being denied them?

Griffith wrote a strong letter which each member of the delegation signed, protesting against the letter of the President. It was, they claimed, inconsistent with the powers set out in their instructions. These powers, they pointed out, had been granted by the Cabinet as a whole and could only be varied by the same body. If they could not continue under the powers granted them they would have to break off negotiations and return to Dublin.

The President was attending a meeting of the Sinn Féin Ard Fheis when he received this letter. He wrote back immediately that the intention of his letter had been misunderstood. He had no intention of tying the hands of the plenipotentiaries further than they had been tied by the original instructions. He went on, 'The delegation must understand these memos of mine, except I explicitly state otherwise, are nothing more than an attempt to keep you in touch with the views of members of the Cabinet here on the various points as they arise. I think it most important that you should be kept aware of these views.'[8]

This exchange of letters increased, if anything, the chances of misunderstanding later. The tone of the joint letter from London surprised the President who felt that the delegates were becoming nervous and overwrought. After that he was much more careful about making suggestions and sending advice. This incident, however, also passed off at the time, like the affair of the Pope's telegram. On November 13th, the cabinet members in Dublin decided to confirm the original instructions and powers given to the delegates.

All this while de Valera was using his influence to commend external association to leaders of opinion in Ireland. From August onwards he had been impressing on a number of people, including the redoubtable Mary MacSwiney, that it would prove an honourable settlement and, in particular, that it preserved the Republic. There were, however, some aspects of the idea which were in need of much more working out. Of these the distinction between *allegiance* to the British Crown and *recognition* as head of the association for certain purposes was the most significant.

It was always clear that no *allegiance* to the British Crown was tolerable. On the very day that the delegates in London sent the letter of protest to Dublin, the cabinet members there discussed this precise question. O'Higgins, Cosgrave, Stack and Brugha were all in line with de Valera at this stage. O'Higgins said later that they would have gone back to war rather than recommend a settlement involving allegiance.

Nevertheless, the letter from London called for some new and clear thinking on what could and what could not be accepted. Allegiance to the Crown unanimously ruled out, de Valera continued to seek a formula which would fit in with the scheme of external association, preserve the Republic and yet be tolerable to the British. He was as convinced as ever that there could be no question of recognising the King's authority *inside* Ireland, but he came to the same conclusion as his colleagues in London that there need be no objection in principle to recognising the King as head of the British Commonwealth with which Ireland would be associated. He would not recognise him as the head of each individual state, *but as the head of the association of states.* He explained this to Cathal Brugha whom he was taking great pains to conciliate and asked Brugha after the explanation to go and write down exactly what he was willing to accept.

Next day Brugha brought the President a pencilled note in his own handwriting.

> All other matters being satisfactorily settled, we are prepared to recommend to our people that the accepted head of Great Britain be recognised as the head of the new association. We are prepared to co-operate with, and send a representative to, whatever council is appointed to conduct the affairs of the group. In matters that do not affect the group we continue to act independently; our form of government remains the same as at present, and can only be altered by the Irish people themselves.

This statement by Cathal Brugha brought immense encouragement to de Valera. Perhaps for the first time he now saw the way to an agreement with Britain. Brugha represented the most extreme republican element in Ireland and here he was accepting external association in its entirety.

The delegates in London had said on October 24th that they were willing to accept the King of Great Britain as head of the association of states. De Valera, on his side, had now satisfied himself that this was a logical corollary of his own ideas and, what is more, had persuaded Brugha to accept it.

At the private meeting of the Sinn Féin Ard Fheis, de Valera made a speech in which he prepared the delegates for the type of settlement which he envisaged. 'You will never' he said, 'be asked by us to subscribe to a lie. Whatever concession our representatives at present in London may feel constrained to offer, an offer of allegiance will not be one of them.' He gave a solemn pledge, 'even though the awful alternative be war, a war of extermination against our comparatively defenceless people, we shall not, even to avoid war, forswear the truth, or the principles we stand for.'

One question the President told them, the allegiance question, was closed from the Irish point of view, but the question of some form of association with the states of the British Empire was 'open'. There was no reason why Ireland should not associate itself with the other nations 'provided the association was one a self-respecting nation might enter' and that it was not against her interests to do so.[9]

By the end of October, then, the President had achieved unity among cabinet members in Dublin and, it appeared, among those in London also, on the thorny questions of allegiance to and recognition of the Crown. Allegiance was totally rejected. Recognition of the King as head of a group of states, the Commonwealth, of which Ireland would be an external associate, was acceptable. He had committed himself to facing a renewal of the war rather than accept an oath which would involve forswearing his principles. The delegation in London, however, had become restive at his letters and henceforward, partly because of their letter of protest, he wrote much less frequently. He continued to trust the delegates to act in accordance with their instructions, which they had cited to him even in their letter of protest. He still felt safe against any precipitate action.

Griffith continued to keep him well informed of the official discussions. Collins returned to Dublin almost every weekend and had frequent consultations with cabinet members. Other delegates, too, returned from time to time.

It was through the secretary of the delegation, Erskine Childers, that de Valera received copies of minutes of the early meetings at which

Childers was present. These were occasionally accompanied by some covering letter in which Childers gave his impressions of the British attitude as revealed at the sessions. They contained nothing to suggest that Childers was acting in any but the most correct fashion as secretary. At no stage did he refer to the division which took place within the delegation from the end of October onwards. One sees now, however, that the split, always potentially present, had become actual from about this time. It was Collins, Griffith and Duggan on one side and Barton and Duffy on the other.

[13]

THE THUMBSCREW

December 1st – 6th, 1921

There had all along been differences of approach among the Irishmen. They had been aggravated by discussions with the British. And now the fissures went deeper. Lloyd George decided, towards the end of October, that meetings with the full complement of delegates were too cumbersome and that more progress would be made if the Prime Minister and one or two of his colleagues met Griffith and Collins. In *The Anglo-Irish Treaty*, Frank Gallagher writes:

> It is true that Barton and Gavan Duffy resented the change since they were henceforth almost wholly excluded from the discussions. But they saw no way of resisting the proposal when it was made. What inspired the British seems to have been that they detected the cleavage in the delegation over the telegram to the Pope and had a better chance of working with (one would almost say 'on') Griffith and Collins if they were separated from Gavan Duffy and Barton. Certainly it was a result of these private meetings, or meetings in sub-conference as they were called, that Griffith was persuaded to compromise himself.

More fuel was soon added to the fire. Griffith, on October 30th, visited Winston Churchill's home after dinner for a discussion with Lloyd George. The Prime Minister faced a vote of censure the next day in the House of Commons from the Die-Hards. Lloyd George (according to Griffith's letter to de Valera) said that, 'If I could give him personal assurances on these matters' (the Crown, free partnership with the Empire and naval facilities) 'he would go down to smite the Die-Hards and would fight on the Ulster matter to secure "essential unity".' Griffith assured the Prime Minister that, on the Crown, he would be prepared to recommend recognition provided that they were satisfied with the other points at issue.

The other delegates learnt of this assurance on November 1st when Griffith showed them the letter he proposed to send to Lloyd George. Angry scenes followed this disclosure. Collins and Duggan did not take sides, but Duffy and Barton, with Childers's support, were vehemently opposed to the letter being sent in its present form or as a personal communication. Griffith was head of the Irish delegation and could only write as such. The next day Griffith re-wrote the letter, but the delegates did not forget this further incident.

On November 4th Gavan Duffy went to Dublin at the request of Barton and Childers. He told the President what was happening. Yet, curious as it may seem today, de Valera saw no grounds for alarm. He trusted Griffith and Collins. He felt that in similar circumstances he might easily have gone to see Lloyd George alone. Griffith and Collins were the leading figures of the delegation. Had Lloyd George selected any other two delegates the President would have been more suspicious of his intentions. Yet the President had taken great trouble to select a strong republican in Barton, who was now excluded from the vital talks.

The anxieties of Barton and Duffy about the attitudes of Griffith and Collins are intelligible enough. Sympathetic and well-informed biographers of Collins, and various other writers, have dealt with his attitude, during these weeks, to the Republic and dominion status. According to Frank O'Connor:

> Both Collins and Griffith put up as good a show as could be expected with de Valera's plan of external association. Unfortunately neither took it seriously.[1]

It is difficult to resist Rex Taylor's conclusion:

> It is beyond question that Collins as early as the beginning of November had put his mind to Dominion status as being the best temporary settlement, though he placed particular emphasis on the fact of it being only a temporary settlement or, as he was to call it later, the freedom to achieve freedom.[2]

But all this remained hidden from de Valera. So was Griffith's personal assent to a British document, on November 13th, without the knowledge of his colleagues. Formally it did not depart from official policy, but it was to be used against him by Lloyd George with crushing effect on the last afternoon. Barton and Childers, though unaware of the document of November 13th, remained anxious to open the President's eyes, and on November 14th Childers saw the President in Dublin. He had only five minutes with him alone, and failed to impress him with the seriousness of the matter. Yet he probably respected Childers as much as any man alive.

By the end of November, the conference seemed to be drawing towards a conclusion. The Irish had undertaken to prepare and submit a formula expressing the limited sense in which they were prepared to recognise the Crown. This called for a consultation in Dublin and a cabinet meeting was fixed for November 25th. Collins had returned almost every weekend, but it was Griffith's first encounter with the President since the negotiations had started. The two went for a drive together in the Dublin mountains where they discussed at length how the talks were progressing. The President was reassured and satisfied with Griffith's report on the position.

The main purpose of the delegates' visit was the formula they brought with them for a form of external association.

> The proposal is that Ireland shall agree to be associated with the British Commonwealth for purposes of common concern such as defence, peace and war; and she shall recognise the British Crown as head of the association; and that, as a token of that recognition, she shall vote an annual sum to the King's Civil List. Her legislative and executive authority shall be derived exclusively from her elected representatives.[3]

At the cabinet meeting it was agreed that the grant of the annual sum could be reasonably conceded. It was looked upon as a means of paying for any service which the head of the association might render. At this stage the Cabinet still seemed united. There was no indication visible to the President, in spite of earlier apprehensions, that any members of the Cabinet in London or Dublin were weakening. The formula brought from London was acceptable all round to the Irish.

It was plain, very soon after the delegates returned to London, that the proposal was far from acceptable to the British. Lloyd George seemed willing to insert a phrase in the proposed treaty that the Crown would have no more authority in Ireland than in Canada and he even agreed to modify the oath. But he was adamant against the exclusion of the Crown from purely Irish affairs and the omission of an oath of allegiance. The real conflict was revealed.

De Valera made no attempt to minimise the problem when he wrote to Harry Boland on November 29th:

> As things stand today it means war. The British ultimatum is allegiance to their King. We will never recommend that such allegiance be rendered . . .
>
> Without explanation you will understand that if I appear with those who choose war it is only because the alternative is impossible without dishonour. As far as I am concerned it is now, External Association, YES; Internal Association involving Allegiance, NO.

He was fully prepared for a breakdown in the negotiations.

The preservation of cabinet unity was not the President's only activity during the negotiations. He made every effort to prevent any slackening off in the functioning of the departments of Dáil Éireann. In particular, he was concerned that the army should be strengthened during the truce. Preparations must be made for all contingencies.

At the end of November he began a tour of inspection. Cathal Brugha and Richard Mulcahy set off with him to Limerick, Clare and Galway

7

areas, but almost immediately (December 2nd) they had to return to Dublin; Griffith and the other delegates were bringing the final British proposals. The President had to return from Clare by car. He insisted on driving all the way. If hostilities were soon to break out again, he wanted all the driving practice he could fit in. It was no doubt valuable practice, but the President was very tired when they arrived back at Kenilworth Square at 10.30 p.m. The roads were very slippery.

Griffith arrived half an hour later and remained for two hours. He showed de Valera the British proposals. The President said 'we could never accept these proposals'. Griffith reminded him that he had always said that he, Griffith, would not break on the Crown, which was what the President now seemed to expect of him.

The President felt too tired to argue satisfactorily. He decided that the questions could be fully discussed at the cabinet meeting fixed for the next day. Later he was to regret the adjournment bitterly. He always reproached himself for having missed his most favourable chance of persuading Griffith of the consequences of acceptance. But, fatigued as he was, it is hard to know what, if anything, he might have achieved that night.

He was still clinging to the hope, which the Cabinet clung to next day, that if a break must come it could be brought about on Ulster and not the Crown. In other words, the British terms should be rejected on the grounds that they perpetuated the partition of Ireland, to which in theory at least the British were also opposed; not on the grounds that they imposed allegiance to the Crown, where the British and Irish views were opposed in principle.

The cabinet meeting next day, December 3rd, was supremely critical. Three weeks later the President wrote an account of it to Joe McGarrity:

> I criticised the British proposals in detail. They meant . . . Dominion status nominally, with an oath of allegiance to the British King as an organic part of the Irish Constitution, and a recognition of him as head of the Irish state. The oath crystallised in itself the main things we objected to—inclusion in the Empire, the British King as King in Ireland, chief executive of the Irish state, and the source from which all authority in Ireland must be derived.

But to all objections the plenipotentiaries had answered that the British were insisting upon an oath. He himself, he continued to McGarrity, had 'insisted that we should stand on our own proposals, and if necessary break with the British on them'. If the worst came to the worst, though, he was prepared to accept 'recognition of the British King as head of the whole association, that is, we could swear to recognise him as a sort of President of the whole league'.

Griffith repeated what he had said to me—that he would not break on the Crown. It was pointed out to him that the acceptance of allegiance meant a certain split—the greatest of all dangers. There was a question of my going over in person to London. The objection to this was that the British would think I had gone because I was anxious to prevent a breakdown. They would accordingly not make any further advance to me but might stiffen instead.

The next sentence is crucial for an understanding of de Valera's moral and tactical position:

I probably would have gone nevertheless had not Griffith on being shown that if he accepted the Crown he would split the country, given an *express undertaking* that he would not sign a document accepting allegiance but would bring it back and refer the matter to Dáil Éireann. This made us all satisfied; we were certain for our part that Dáil Éireann would reject it.[4]

Other accounts of the seven-hour-long meeting show it to have been less orderly than the President's letter might suggest. The setting was not the most propitious. Many of those participating in the discussion were terribly tired. Three of them had had a gruelling experience on the journey from London. They had left at 8.15 on the previous evening, but owing to a collision with a fishing-smack, killing three fishermen, their boat had had to return to Holyhead. Collins, Duffy and Childers did not reach Dun Laoghaire until 10.15 a.m. and the cabinet meeting began at the Mansion House at 11 o'clock. The President and Cathal Brugha were far from fresh after the journey from Clare the previous night.

At an early stage, reference had been made to the selection by Lloyd George of Arthur Griffith and Michael Collins to attend all the sub-conferences. According to the acting secretary of the cabinet, Colm Ó Murchadha, who recorded his impressions of the discussion and on the decisions reached, 'The Minister of Defence here remarked that the British Government selected its men.' In Brugha's own account:

In saying this I did not mean to cast any reflection on the honour of these two men . . . My meaning was this: because they knew they were the two weakest men we had in the team and Lloyd George and his friends pretty soon discovered that; and that is how they came to select them out of the five.

The whole atmosphere immediately became marred and embittered. Antagonisms which had with difficulty been suppressed now came undisguisedly into the open. Griffith rose from his place at the table and went up to Brugha to make him withdraw the charge. Brugha with typical stubbornness refused. Griffith insisted that it be recorded in the minutes; ultimately it was withdrawn but the damage was done.

In the exchange of views the Cabinet divided into two groups with Griffith, Collins and Duggan on the one side and Barton, Gavan Duffy and Childers on the other. The President, who was naturally Chairman, endeavoured to find a *via media*.[5]

Ó Murchadha recalled that the President believed the delegates had done their utmost; and it now remained to them to show that if the document was not amended, they were prepared to take the consequences—war or no war.

Griffith's recent experience had taught him enough to know that this would not be accepted by the British Government. He did not like the British document but did not think it dishonourable. It would practically recognise the Republic and the first allegiance (in the oath) would be to Ireland.

Suddenly Brugha turned to him, saying, 'Don't you realise that if you sign this thing, you will split Ireland from top to bottom?' The force of this seemed to strike Griffith, and he said, 'I suppose that's so. I'll tell you what I'll do. I'll go back to London. I'll not sign that document, but I'll bring it back and submit it to the Dáil.' This pledge satisfied everybody present at the meeting. It has been usually interpreted, and rightly, as an undertaking not to sign any document involving allegiance to the Crown or inclusion within the Empire. There was felt to be no necessity now for substitute delegates to go over and break off the negotiations. De Valera, in particular, abandoned the idea of going over himself, reassured as he was by Griffith's pledge. (Compare his letter to McGarrity above).

There were only minutes left before the delegates were to cross back to London that night. Somehow Ó Murchadha was able to record six points of apparent agreement before they broke up.

(*a*) Delegates to carry out their original instructions with same powers.

(*b*) Delegation to return and say that Cabinet won't accept Oath of Allegiance if not amended and to face the consequences, assuming that England will declare war.

(*c*) Decided unanimously that present Oath of Allegiance could not be subscribed to.

(*d*) Mr Griffith to inform Mr Lloyd George that the document could not be signed, to state that it is now a matter for the Dáil, and to try and put the blame on Ulster.

(*e*) On a majority vote, it was decided that the Delegation be empowered to meet Sir James Craig if they should think necessary . . .

(*f*) It was decided that the President would not join the Delegation in London at this stage of the negotiations.

With nearly fifty years' hindsight to help us, one comment cannot be resisted. No student can fail to be aware today that by this time the possibility of breaking on Ulster (compare above 'put the blame on Ulster') had been almost totally eroded.

Immediately after the conclusion of the cabinet meeting, the delegates set out for London, while the President, with Brugha and Mulcahy, went westwards to resume his tour.

He had said at the cabinet meeting that they were prepared to face the consequences—war or no war. To the people of Galway he said on December 4th:

> There are things, no matter what the alternative, that those who are charged with the direction of affairs in this country can never give up. When we started out in our programme, we knew what it meant, and we counted the cost. We are not going to quail now, even if it be certain that the full price of our freedom has to be paid.[6]

From Galway the party travelled to Ennis and reviewed a number of Irish Volunteer brigades on the agricultural show grounds. The President warned them:

> At any moment they might be called upon by the national Government to stand by the principles they held.[7]

At Limerick, in thanking the people for honouring him with the freedom of the City, he was equally unequivocal:

> No offer will be accepted by the nation if that offer deprives us of the essentials of freedom. Now, it is not a hard thing to know what are the essentials of freedom. Freedom is a thing that you cannot cut in two—you are either all free or you are not free. It is, therefore, for complete freedom that we are struggling, and we tell everybody that this nation will continue to struggle for its freedom until it has got the whole of it.[8]

In this atmosphere the English press was understandably pessimistic. The *Daily Chronicle* reported on December 5th, 'Little hope of settlement now entertained'. The *Daily Express* dared the headline 'IRISH CONFERENCE FAILS'. The *Times* was less dramatic and felt only able to say, 'The negotiations are not broken off'.

It now appears from British cabinet records that, at a cabinet meeting on December 5th, the prospect of an immediate settlement seemed poor:

> It was clear that the Irish Cabinet had no intention of coming within the British Empire, but wished Ireland to remain an independent republic, associated with the British Empire for certain specific purposes, and bearing no allegiance to the King, but merely recognising him as the head of the associated states. The Cabinet were informed that Mr Arthur Griffith and

Mr Michael Collins were greatly disappointed at the rejection of the British proposals.

The latter information no doubt came from Jones.[9]

That night the President and his party stayed with Stephen O'Mara in Limerick. Inevitably their thoughts and feelings centred on their colleagues in London. They would have given much to know how they were faring. Was it to be war again, or peace?

Today it seems astounding that any use of the telephone between the President and the delegates in London should not have been contemplated. In 1921 telephones were few and far between in Ireland and dangerous for 'freedom fighters' to use. The delegation in London and the cabinet in Dublin must have accepted their mutual isolation as a law of nature.

The group in Limerick were totally unaware that the climax had been reached in London. They could not visualise Lloyd George withdrawing from the council chamber, far less his secretaries searching desperately through all his suits for a piece of paper that Arthur Griffith had personally agreed to on November 13th; nor Lloyd George returning to exploit it to the uttermost; nor Griffith stung in his tenderest spot, rising to his feet in his excitement.

Shaking his pencil across the table at Lloyd George, this strong man, usually so quiet, repudiated with staggering emphasis the charge that he would ever break faith. 'I have never let a man down in my whole life and I never will.' If he had given his word he would keep it. And that meant that the attempt to stage the 'break on Ulster', on which the whole Irish strategy hinged, had gone by the board.

They were all unconscious in Limerick of the ultimatum from Lloyd George that followed, with the assurance of 'immediate and terrible' war, unless signature were forthcoming that night. They could not hear Lloyd George stating bluntly, 'The British could concede no more and debate no further. The Irish delegates must settle now; they must sign the agreement for a treaty or else quit, and both sides would be free to resume whatever warfare they could wage against each other'.[10] They could hardly have imagined the reply of the leader of the delegation, spoken quietly and modestly. 'I will give the answer of the Irish Delegation at nine tonight; but Mr Prime Minister, I personally will sign this agreement and recommend it to my countrymen.'

'Do I understand Mr Griffith that though everyone else refuses, you will nevertheless agree to sign?'

'Yes, that is so Mr Prime Minister.'

They could have understood the agony of the silence that followed Lloyd George's putting the question to the other delegates, his impatience increasing.

'Every delegate must sign the document and undertake to recommend it, or there can be no agreement. We as a body have hazarded our political futures; you must do likewise and take the same risks.'

The leaders in Limerick were far removed from the magic pressures as Lloyd George held up a letter in each hand:

'I have to communicate with Sir James Craig tonight. Here are the alternative letters which I have prepared, one enclosing Articles of Agreement reached by His Majesty's Government and yourselves, and the other saying that the Sinn Féin representatives refuse to come within the Empire. If I send this letter it is war, and war within three days. Which letter am I to send? Whichever letter you choose travels by special train to Holyhead, and by destroyer to Belfast. The train is waiting with steam up at Euston. Mr Shakespeare is ready. If he is to reach Sir James Craig in time we must know your answer by 10 p.m. tonight. You have until then, but no longer, to decide whether you will give peace or war to your country.'

They were all-unaware in Limerick, as indeed were the Irish delegates in London, of the exhaustion of the English. 'They had taken grave risks, heavily compromised themselves and now it appeared to them that they had failed.' So the present Lord Birkenhead assures us in the life of his father; and Sir Winston Churchill has testified likewise.

They were equally oblivious in Limerick of the shattering wrangle at the Irish headquarters from 9 to 11.15 p.m. Duggan in tears, as he decided to join Griffith and Collins in agreeing to sign; Gavan Duffy and Barton condemning any betrayal of the Republic, but both feeling eventually there was no alternative but to sign.

There was the return to Downing Street, the confrontation with Lloyd George, the pause and then the calm, quiet words of Arthur Griffith. 'Mr Prime Minister, the Delegation is willing to sign the agreement.'

The summary of the final stages given in the Jones *Diary* is presumably the verdict of Jones himself. No one on the British side was so well placed to make an assessment. No one perhaps on either side could read so well between the lines.

In the afternoon, Lloyd George played a masterful hand, relying on the knowledge of Griffith's mind which he had had from T.J., and steadily wearing down the Irish delegation by alternate threats and persuasion, to the position where first Griffith, then the others, agreed to sign.

The Limerick party had been long asleep by the time Collins was sitting down to write in the small hours.

When you have sweated, toiled, had mad dreams, hopeless nightmares you find yourself in London streets, cold and dank in the night air. Think—what have I got for Ireland? Something which she has wanted these past 700 years. Will anyone be satisfied at the bargain? I tell you this—early this morning I signed my death warrant—a bullet might just as well have done the job five years ago.

Then an utterly sincere expression of fellow feeling across the 'havoc of war'.

I believe Birkenhead may have said an end to his political life. With him it has been my honour to work.

And then his whole reason for signing in a nutshell:

These signatures are the first real step for Ireland. If people will only re-member that—the first real step.

Was the ultimatum a bluff? Would war have followed if the Irish delegates had not signed there and then? Mr Frank Gallagher points out shrewdly:

On the morning of December 6th, the Treaty having been signed too late to influence the political commentators, the *Times* and the *Daily Chronicle* both believed that the negotiations had broken down—the *Times* declared war to be 'unthinkable'; the *Daily Chronicle* said outright: 'If the negotiators prove still unable to sign a compact let them adjourn their negotiations for a fixed period of weeks.'

And the *Daily Chronicle* was Lloyd George's own paper. Gallagher continues: 'It seems clear that Britain would not have made war had the Irish stood firm to the last.' Very likely that is so. But it is impossible to be dogmatic about one of the great might-have-beens of history.

Next morning in Limerick the first news appeared cheerful. As the President left for the railway station he was told that a telephone message had been received from Dublin saying that a treaty had been signed. His immediate reaction was one of joy and surprise. He had assumed all along that the delegates would carry out their instructions and sign no agreement that had not been submitted to Dublin in its final form. Still, he could imagine circumstances in which the delegates might have risked a formal rebuke for the sake of some dazzling bargain to be clinched immediately if at all. Under some lucky combination of circumstances the British must have collapsed. 'I did not think they would give in so soon,' he said.

The President arrived in Dublin at 2.30 p.m. He lunched at 53 Kenilworth Square and then motored out to his home at Greystones for a few hours. He returned to Dublin in the evening for the Dante celebration at which he was to take the chair; a symposium to be held in the Mansion House to commemorate the sixth centenary of the poet's death. It was due to begin at 7.30 p.m. At 7.15 he arrived and was met by Cathal Brugha and Austin Stack. Stack records the meeting:

> The first question the President asked was, 'Any news?' I said, 'Yes.' 'Good or bad?' 'Bad.'

De Valera glanced at the *Evening Mail* Stack had been holding and read:

> I . . . do solemnly swear true faith and allegiance to the constitution of the Irish Free State as by law established and that I will be faithful to H.M. King George V his heirs and successors by law in virtue of the common citizenship of Ireland with Great Britain and her adherence to and membership of the group of nations forming the British Commonwealth of Nations.

Stack's record continues:

> He donned his gown [university] and was about to lead the way into the Round Room when who should arrive but Mr E. J. Duggan and Mr Desmond Fitzgerald. Duggan reached the President an envelope which the President ignored. Duggan asked him to read the contents. 'What should I read it for?' 'Oh,' said Duggan, 'it is arranged that the thing be published in London and Dublin simultaneously at 8 o'clock, and it is near that hour now.' 'What', said the President, 'to be published whether I have seen it or not— whether I approve or not.' 'Oh, well, that's the arrangement,' Duggan replied. The President took up the envelope, opened, glanced over the contents . . . At that moment he appeared to me to be an almost broken man.

De Valera's own account is less revealing. In his diary he wrote: 'Showed me a copy of *Evening Mail*—incredible.'

By now the President was due on the stage in the Round Room, the scene of the first meeting of Dáil Éireann almost three years before. There he spent one of the most miserable evenings of his life, pondering over the news which he had received and trying to keep himself from showing any emotion. All his plans had been defeated. The instructions, which gave him and his colleagues the supposed 'grip on the coat-tails' of the delegates in London, had been ignored. The unity, which he had made every effort to maintain, was shattered. A few weeks later he wrote:

> Thus, a chance greater than I had dared to hope for was lost—England's imperial needs and her consequent desire for peace, Lloyd George's political needs and his political imagination, the British Coalition which precluded the usual Tory opposition—all this on the one hand and on the other the desire of our own people for peace and the readiness of even extreme Republicans, like Cathal Brugha and Stack, to accept the compromise of

external association—all these made a combination of factors that occurs but once in history. It was lost because Lloyd George wanted not merely all the best trumps but the joker as well for his political hand, and our plenipotentiaries were not bold enough to dare 'to make one heap of all their winnings' and stake it.[11]

The newspapers of Wednesday, December 7th, carried the full text of the treaty and plenty of comment. The *Times* led the way:

Reason has prevailed . . . the beginning of a new era of happiness and mutual understanding.

The *Manchester Guardian:*

It is a splendid achievement.

The *Daily Express:*

Their names will live for ever because the pact that brings to an end the centuries of Irish strife is one of the most memorable documents in history.

The *Freeman's Journal* in Dublin believed:

In the articles of settlement will be found every essential of that freedom which the Irish people have sought for over seven long and sorrowful centuries.

The views expressed in the Mansion House that morning were very different. Kathleen O'Connell wrote in her diary: 'P[resident] in an awful state. What a fiasco.'

At 11.30 a.m. the cabinet members who were in Dublin came together: the President, Austin Stack, Cathal Brugha, W. T. Cosgrave and Kevin O'Higgins. De Valera at once announced that he was intending to call for the resignation of Griffith, Collins and Barton, the three cabinet members of the delegation. But at this stage Cosgrave intervened. He held that the President should not dismiss them without hearing their side of the story. The President felt that the point was a fair one. The thought also struck him that this was the first indication that Cosgrave was not in agreement with him. Caution was necessary. If Cosgrave favoured the Treaty, then four out of the seven members of the inner cabinet would be supporting it. Instead of taking drastic action the President decided to issue a statement:

In view of the nature of the proposed treaty with Great Britain, President de Valera has sent an urgent summons to the members of the Cabinet in London to report at once so that a full cabinet decision may be taken. The hour of the meeting is fixed for 12 noon tomorrow, Thursday. A meeting of the Dáil will be summoned later.

On December 8th the President received a deputation from Ulster, who feared that there would be weakness on the question of partition. From them he went to meet his colleagues of the cabinet, now fully mustered, and an agonising post-mortem began.

The Treaty was examined clause by clause. The President pointed out where, and how far, it departed from cabinet policy. The first four clauses in particular brought Ireland firmly back into the British Empire. The oath would mean that they would have to swear 'to be faithful to H.M. King George V, his heirs and successors'. The King would be part of the constitution to which they would have to swear allegiance; they would be compelled to take an oath which precluded them from advancing any further along the road of independence. The delegates insisted that the alternative was war.

Frank Gallagher gives some indication of the tone of the meeting. He was in the adjoining room talking to journalists:

Just as the room filled with enquiring journalists, came angry voices . . . To every question from the pressmen I gave a voluble answer. They did not perceive the raised voices, which in my ears were again and again an orchestration to what I was saying . . . As de Valera struggled a few feet from them, to draw back a united Cabinet to solid ground, they were as yet unaware of any division.[11]

No progress was made in the turbulent cabinet meeting. Griffith was adamant about the merits of the Treaty and would recommend its acceptance by Dáil Éireann and the Irish people. Collins, Barton and Cosgrave would recommend it, not on its merits 'but as something to be signed'. Only de Valera, Brugha and Stack opposed it. The President refused to recommend it to the Dáil.

The only decisions reached at the meeting were that the President should issue a statement to the press, defining his own position and that of Brugha and Stack, and that a public session of the Dáil should be called for December 14th in the Mansion House. In the meanwhile Ministers were to continue in charge of their departments.

That night the President worked until midnight preparing a proclamation for publication the next day:

The terms of this agreement are in violent conflict with the wishes of the majority of this nation, as expressed freely in successive elections during the past three years. I feel it my duty to inform you immediately that I cannot recommend the acceptance of this treaty either to Dáil Éireann or to the country. In this attitude I am supported by the Ministers of Home Affairs and Defence . . . The greatest test of our people has come. Let us face it worthily without bitterness, and above all, without recriminations. There is a definite constitutional way of resolving our political differences—let us not depart from it, and let the conduct of the Cabinet in this matter be an example to the whole nation.

The benevolent, self-satisfied and optimistic writings in the newspapers were forgotten. The *Daily Telegraph* wrote on December 8th:

That the Cabinet will unanimously approve the terms accepted by the plenipotentiaries admits of no doubt.

The Times on December 9th felt only able to admit that

Some Irishmen have not yet adapted themselves to the reality of Thursday's achievement of their dreams.

But the next day, under the headline 'De Valera's challenge' their Dublin correspondent wrote:

There is much speculation in Ireland as to the outcome of the split in the Sinn Féin Cabinet. The statement made by Mr de Valera came as a bombshell and everyone is wondering what is going to happen next. Is it peace or is it war?

The *Daily Express*, never a friend to de Valera, was incredulous:

Rejection utterly deplorable, we cannot believe that this firebrand will carry with him any considerable section of the Irish people.

And on his side how did he feel? No moral guilt assuredly. He had followed his conscience throughout, and standing where he did would have betrayed his beliefs and his solemn public declarations if he had not rejected the Treaty. But his distress for Ireland's sake and his foreboding were profound and poignant. His whole attitude can be summed up all too well in Kathleen O'Connell's diary: 'What a fiasco!' How had it—how could it have come about? The President had apparently prepared his plan for the negotiations with infinite care. But while he was concentrating on bringing Brugha and Stack along the road of external association, he had lost touch with the minds of the London delegation, or with some of them at least. The mistake which he made was in his over-estimating the power of the instructions and in his assuming that all the delegates would treat them as binding in every circumstance.

The arguments for and against the Treaty of 1921 and for signing it there and then will be debated *ad infinitum*. No one can dispute the high ideals of those who took either side in the face of a cruel dilemma. It was part of the tragedy of those who signed the Treaty that they could not be unaware of the split that was almost bound to follow in the cabinet, the Dáil and the country.

PEACE v. PRINCIPLE—THE TREATY DEBATE

December, 1921 – January, 1922

Pro-Treaty propaganda had got off to a flying start. In his efforts to avoid a public disruption, the President had allowed three precious days to pass. His principal anxiety was to ensure that the split would not affect the army. He impressed on the general headquarters staff the necessity for continued loyalty to the Dáil and to whomever was Minister for Defence. A cabinet meeting fixed for three o'clock that afternoon (the 9th) was cancelled. The split was too deep for concerted action.

The President spent a desperate weekend, straining after some solution which would reunite the divided nation. No light dawned till the following Tuesday, December 13th, the eve of the fateful meeting of Dáil Éireann. It came irresistibly home to him that, at all costs, he must produce alternative proposals. Somehow he must get Dáil Éireann to reject the Treaty and to publish at the same time an agreed alternative which looked as like it as possible. The British people could hardly support Lloyd George in going to war for the seeming difference.

His object clear, he sat down in Kenilworth Square to draft his alternative, completing it all too hurriedly. The draft was based partly on the proposals put forward by the delegation in London after the final cabinet meeting in Dublin, partly on the Treaty itself. The first seven articles of the new document were fundamentally at variance with the Treaty and contained the essence of his idea of external association. They contained no oath and were, in fact, a re-statement of the demand which de Valera had stood by since July.

When the Dáil met in the morning, the President began with a statement on the position which had arisen. In particular, he stressed the fact that the delegates had not complied with the third article of their instructions. This had laid down in black and white that the complete text of any draft treaty to be signed must be submitted to Dublin. In the tenseness of the situation it is remarkable how little bitterness was shown. The President was indeed studiously avoiding it. Privately, however, he felt that he had been badly let down. He wrote about that time:

Not only did the delegation break their word, given a few days previously, that they would not sign any such document and disobey their instructions in not submitting the final text to Dublin, they were guilty further of an act of disloyalty to their President and to their colleagues in the Cabinet, such as is probably without parallel in history. They not merely signed the document but, in order to make the *fait accompli* doubly secure, they published it hours before the President or their colleagues saw it, and were already giving interviews in London and proclaiming its merits and prejudicing the issue at the time it was being read in Dublin.[1]

Nevertheless, despite his personal feelings, he still hoped to restore unity. Ultimately it was decided that the Dáil go into private session, so as to allow the members to examine and debate some confidential documents which could not be made available to the public.

At the private session that evening de Valera circulated his alternative to the Treaty. He knew well that he would have a dire struggle to get his proposals accepted. On the one side, they would be opposed by those who supported the Treaty; he already knew that Michael Collins was bringing the full force of the IRB behind it. On the other, the supporters of an isolated republic would not like them. By putting them forward in a private session, he hoped to have them discussed calmly and in confidence, as a means of restoring unity.

De Valera explained in his speech that his proposals were tentative and designed to form the basis for a document on which they could all agree. They were far from perfect. He was not happy, for example, with the Ulster clauses as they stood. He stressed, however, the advantages of his proposals, even from the British point of view. He maintained that they could lead to a permanent settlement, in which the vast majority of the people could be united. The Treaty would be of little value to Britain if there were a strong minority in Ireland determined to carry on the struggle for the Republic. He saw, however, that if his proposals were to have any value, the Dáil must be more or less unanimously in favour of them. Then they could once more face Britain with a united people. 'It is my last effort,' he said, 'and it is a poor one. It is only a bad best.'

Almost immediately, the proposals were given a name. The exigencies of debate called for comparisons between de Valera's alternative and the Treaty. References to 'this document' and 'that document' lacked clarity. Michael Collins, on the very evening it was circulated, referred to it as 'Document No. 2' and the name stuck. The Treaty was nominally 'Document No. 1', though seldom referred to as such.

On December 15th, still in private session, the President gave a detailed exposition of Document No. 2 to the Dáil. He explained the fundamental points of difference between it and the Treaty. He pointed out that it embodied the policy of external association, by which the internal republic would not be affected, but would be associated with the British Commonwealth. When he came to the Ulster clauses, he said they were engaged, not in a fight with Ulster, but in a fight with Britain. He was ready to grant Ulster all the rights they received under the Treaty, so long as there were a declaratory clause which safeguarded the supreme authority of the Dáil over the whole national territory. Later he amended the Ulster proposals; the basic ideas remained, however, the same.

But already, early in the debate, de Valera was finding that his tactics had been ill-advised. The very similarity in form to the Treaty which he had so patiently worked out did much to undermine the value of the second document. Those in favour of the Treaty asked: 'Is Ireland going to go to war for the difference of these two documents?' External association was decried. 'Do not let us go sideways into the British Empire,' said one speaker. 'If we are going to go in, let us go in with our heads erect and not try to get in dodging around a corner when no one is looking.' Among the pro-Treaty speakers there were two different lines of attack on Document No. 2. One was that the differences between it and the Treaty were so slight that no one should go to war for them. The other was that the difference was too great for the British Government to swallow—that the British *would* go to war for the difference.

While the document got no support from those in favour of the Treaty, the President found that it served to split rather than reconcile the Republicans. Some of these, it is true, spoke in favour of Document No. 2 as against the Treaty, but quite a number of others took their stand very definitely on the solid rock of the isolated republic. They were not willing to accept a compromise of any kind. Seán Etchingham, Séamus Robinson and Liam Mellows made this patent. One of the reasons for their attitude, of course, was that they were mainly concerned to kill the Treaty and they thought that they could best do so by opposing it thoroughly without compromise.

Hitherto the Dáil had consisted of members of one united party and de Valera had never tried to organise a caucus within it to support a particular line. The Treaty introduced a new situation. Those in favour of it began to organise a party within the Dáil from the time of the return of the delegates from London. De Valera wrote to Joe McGarrity:

The only hope is to try in private session to get the Dáil to turn down by a large majority the Treaty as signed, and to offer our counter-proposals to the British. But M.C. [Collins] had got the IRB machine working. The Dáil members of the IRB were told that acceptance of the Treaty would be the quickest way to the Republic, and a lot of other stuff which time alone will explode. It was a case of Cohalan and his machine over again. The personal credit of the plenipotentiaries was at stake—the Treaty was a bird in the hand, the Treaty must be ratified. Though the rank and file of the army is right, the headquarter staff has gone clean wrong—a part of the machine. Curse secret societies.[2]

When Collins and Griffith signed the Treaty, they must have reckoned with the prospect of a split—which is not the same as saying that a civil war seemed to them certain. The likelihood of a split had been pointed out at the cabinet meeting on December 3rd. By the time he signed, Collins not unnaturally was calculating how many members of the Dáil he could count on. He realised that a large section of the Irish Volunteers would take the anti-Treaty side. He even noted: 'situation could be extremely dangerous'.[3] When he returned from London, he called a meeting of the supreme council of the IRB for December 12th. This body decided that the Treaty should be supported—a crucial event. Those members of the Dáil who were also members of the IRB were given freedom of action as to how they would vote, but the influence of the organisation was powerfully used to secure an acceptance of the settlement.[4]

These debates in the private sessions of the Dáil, which lasted from the 14th to the 17th December, were not as well arranged as the public sessions which followed. In the end there was considerable confusion, made worse by the number of documents presented to the members. The question of the oath, for example, was the key difficulty which de Valera found in the Treaty. Other concessions could be made in the last resort under duress and undone at a more opportune time. In conscience, he thought that the oath would bind for *all* time, and create a moral obstacle against the steps which he knew would have to be taken later, before the Irish national demands were satisfied. Yet amid the welter of rumours emerging from the private sessions and the misrepresentations of Document No. 2 when it was published later, there was considerable bewilderment as to where de Valera stood on this relatively simple issue.

When the Dáil went into public session on December 19th, the debates became more formal. Arthur Griffith proposed a resolution that Dáil Éireann approve the Treaty. At first he had intended to move the ratification of the Treaty, but the President had pointed out that the Dáil had no power to ratify it, as it would be beyond their constitutional powers as a republican body. On the orders of the day, there was also a motion in the name of the President. This insisted that the Treaty would not reconcile Irish national aspirations and the association of Ireland with the British Commonwealth, and that Dáil Éireann should make to the British Government an alternative proposal. Griffith refused to allow the President's motion to be taken as an amendment to his resolution. He insisted on a straight vote for or against the Treaty.

The debate continued until December 22nd and, at that stage, showed little sign of concluding. The session was adjourned to January 3rd. Those opposed to the Treaty calculated that, had the vote been taken before Christmas, the Treaty would have been beaten. But once the Dáil adjourned, the deputies became subject to great local pressures. The press was enthusiastic about the terms brought back from London, encouraging local bodies to pass resolutions of endorsement. The Church, too, was giving strong support to this outlook, and the IRB was using its influence.

When the debate resumed after Christmas, there was a noticeable change in the attitude of some of the deputies. One deputy was so opposed to the Treaty that he resigned his seat rather than obey his constituents and vote for it. Two other deputies admitted that, if the vote had been taken before Christmas, they would have voted against the Treaty, but they had decided, because of local pressure over the recess, to vote in favour.

By this time both sides were full of mutual suspicion. Griffith handed both the original and final version of Document No. 2 to the *Freeman's Journal* and the *Irish Independent*. De Valera was learning that the secrecy of secret sessions was no longer sacred. The confidence which had been built up in the Black and Tan war among members of Dáil Éireann was not surviving the difficulties of the Treaty debate. He was not ashamed of his original document, but it had been nothing more than a draft hurriedly prepared. Its publication added to the confusion and profusion of documents.

In the debates on the Treaty, the outstanding figures were de Valera and Griffith, each of them fully equal to the occasion in his own way. The President spoke with great emotion on the high hopes which he had held:

> I wanted, and the Cabinet wanted, to get a document we could stand by, a document that could enable Irishmen to meet Englishmen and shake hands with them as fellow-citizens of the world. That document [the Treaty] makes British authority our masters in Ireland. It was said that they had only an oath to the British King in virtue of common citizenship, but you have an oath to the Irish Constitution which will have the King of Great Britain as Head of Ireland. You will swear allegiance to that Constitution and to that King.

He went on to say how difficult the oath made the position and he drew a comparison from his own experience:

> When I was in prison in solitary confinement our warders told us that we could go from our cells into the hall, which was about fifty feet by forty. We

did go out from the cells to the hall, but we did not give our word to the British jailer that he had the right to detain us in prison because we got that privilege. Again, on another occasion, we were told that we could get out on a 'garden party', where we could see the flowers and the hills, but we did not for the privilege of going out on garden parties sign a document handing over our souls and bodies to the jailers. Rather than sign a document which would give Britain authority in Ireland, they should be ready to go into slavery until the Almighty had blotted out their tyrants. If the British Government passed a Home Rule Act or something of that kind, I would not have said to the Irish people: 'Do not take it.' I would have said: 'Very well; this is a case of the jailer leading you from the cell to the hall,' but by getting that, we do not sign away our right to whatever form of government we pleased.

He maintained that the oath would put a barrier in the way of a final settlement and that the Treaty was something which fell far short of what the Irish people wanted. He felt that he knew the aspirations of the Irish people.

I have been brought up amongst the Irish people. I was reared in a labourer's cottage here in Ireland. I have not lived solely amongst the intellectuals. The first fifteen years of my life that formed my character were lived amongst the Irish people down in Limerick; therefore I know what I am talking about; and whenever I wanted to know what the Irish people wanted, I had only to examine my own heart and it told me straight off what the Irish people wanted.

Few indeed are the leaders who could say this and not be laughed out of politics.

He went on to point out that even the supporters of the Treaty did not like it. The Irish people desired something more, no matter how many might be willing to make a temporary compromise. De Valera warned:

As sure as this other Treaty goes through, so sure will there be rebels against British authority, because they will not be British subjects. We will be living an absolute lie.

He knew that it would never be accepted by anyone committed to republican ideals, and that it would not bring peace. He stood for republican principles himself:

I am not a member of the Irish Republican Brotherhood, but I hope when I die I will get a Fenian grave . . . I would not let personal considerations of that sort have anything to do with the situation. I am doing this and acting on this principle, because I believe it is the only policy that can save Ireland at this moment.[5]

The debate was orderly, but for de Valera it contained many heartbreaks. The things that hurt him most were the suggestions that it was he who had gone back on the Republic. Charges like these roused his anger. Document No. 2 was paraded in the newspapers in its original draft form and in its final form, as if the President had been trying to hide something.[6] The old Devoy dispute about Cuba was resurrected and cast in de Valera's face by people who knew that it had not been a retreat from the republican position, but who now wanted a stick to beat him with. The attempts to confuse the issue by insisting that Document No. 2 contained an oath appeared to have a similar purpose.

The President's speeches, however, were not incisive enough or persuasive enough to convince either those in favour of the Treaty or those loyal to the ideal of an isolated republic that he had found a true *via media*. His speeches were too prudent. To avoid hurting those who signed the Treaty, and thus antagonising them irrevocably, he tried to tone down any attacks on them for violating their instructions. The result was almost like playing with words. 'Paragraph three,' he said, 'was not exceeded; but paragraph three was not carried out.' There were, it is true, occasional remarks which he regretted and withdrew, but they were not seriously hurtful to his opponents or himself. The trouble was of a different kind. His whole effort was too subtle, especially when he was denied an opportunity to propose 'Document No. 2' in a formal speech at the public sessions. It needed explanation, and it met with nothing but hostility in the papers. He was made to appear as a fanatic who had already compromised the position. His speeches, hampered by the subtlety of his ideas on external association and the need for a conciliatory restraint, lacked the forcefulness to maximize support.

A private session on the morning of January 6th brought violent language from Michael Collins and Cathal Brugha. The strain of the long debate was by now telling on tempers. The cabinet was so split that, after the meeting of December 8th, it met on only one more occasion. Arthur Griffith and de Valera appealed to the Irish people to show restraint and discipline while the debate proceeded. But by now de Valera was finding his position as President intolerable. The publication of cabinet and other private documents as party propaganda showed him that the divisions had ended all semblance of united cabinet responsibility. When a pro-Treaty minister interfered in the work of other ministers, he had no means of controlling him. In the circumstances, on January 6th, he tendered his resignation to the Dáil.

Immediately there was an outcry that he was forcing a personal issue, so as to influence the debate on the Treaty. Under the pressure of this criticism, having been given a guarantee that the vote on the Treaty would be taken within forty-eight hours, de Valera did not press the point. He had no desire to do anything which could be misinterpreted as underhand, despite his feeling that those in favour of the Treaty were not themselves acting fairly.

> I am sick and tired of politics, [he said] so sick that, no matter what happens, I would go back to private life. I have only seen politics within the last three weeks or a month. It is the first time I have seen them, and I am sick to the heart of them. Now I am told this is a special political manoeuvre. . . .
>
> Insinuations about me have hurt me—because every man and woman who has dealt with me here known that I am standing exactly where I stood. I tried to reconcile very difficult things and tried to solve the problem as far as I was able. I know what others didn't know; where the verge of the precipice was, and nothing would have pulled me beyond it—not even Lloyd George and all his Empire could have brought me over it. Therefore, I am straight with everybody and I am not a person for political trickery.

At another point, he showed his exasperation with the accusation that he was drawing a red herring across the debate:

> It is because I am straight that I meet crookedness with straight dealing. If I tried to beat crookedness with similar methods, we are undone.[8]

As regards the position of President which he held, he did not want to see it tarnished. He felt every attack on Document No. 2 as an assault on his loyalty to the position he held. It was an accusation of being dishonourable, of lowering the republican standard which he had been elected to maintain. The London *Times* understood Document No. 2 better than its Irish critics:

> This, we say at once, is not a proposal which will appear to Englishmen as a mere modification of the existing Articles of Agreement. The status that it contemplates for Ireland is not that of a Dominion, but of an Independent Power in loose treaty relationship with this country.[9]

In Ireland, however, it did not receive calm consideration. It was doomed from the beginning to be viewed in an atmosphere clouded by a fog of political contentions. Before the vote was taken on the Treaty, the President rose to make a last protest:

> That document will rise in judgment against the men who say there is only a shadow of difference . . .[10]

Then he was interrupted.

The vote was taken on January 7th, in the Council Chamber of University College, Dublin, where the historic debate took place. The result was close: 64 votes in favour of the Treaty, 57 against. It might have been even closer. Larry Ginnell, who was absent, had sent a cable asking that his vote be registered against the Treaty, but this was not allowed. Had Drohan not resigned and had others followed their own original instincts, the result would have gone the other way.

Once the vote was taken, de Valera rose to speak. He affirmed that the Dáil had done no more than give its approval to the Treaty. It had not disestablished the Republic. That had been established by the Irish people and could be disestablished by them alone. The Dáil continued to be the supreme government and it would remain so until the people disestablished it. Collins made a manly speech and de Valera asked those who had voted against the Treaty to meet him the next day. Finally, as the meeting adjourned, the anguish told on him. The official record tells the story:

> I would like my last word here to be this: we have had a glorious record for four years; it has been four years of magnificent discipline in our nation. The world is looking at us now—[The President here breaks down.][11]

In the course of the Treaty debate, the President lost a great deal of the power which he had hitherto wielded. The initiative had passed from his hands to those of Griffith and Collins. He had not asked for the resignations from the cabinet of Griffith and Collins because he still hoped to work with them. He thought he could persuade them to lay the Treaty before the Dáil but not to use all their influence to get it accepted. It is easy to see now that this was asking too much of human nature once they had signed. He could also have forestalled Griffith's resolution approving the Treaty, by one rejecting it. This would have given him the great tactical advantage of holding the initiative and it would have carried with it the opportunity of replying to the debate. Had he known parliamentary procedure as well at that stage as he did later, he would not have allowed the situation to develop as it did.

The most remarkable feature of the debates, including the President's speeches, was the lack of emphasis on the partition clauses of the Treaty. Almost everyone seemed to accept the contention of Griffith and Collins that the boundary commission clause would mean the ending of partition, by cutting off so much of the northern area as to make the rest non-viable. It was difficult to argue against this without prophetic vision. De Valera objected, in the private sessions, to the explicit recognition in the Treaty of the right of any part of Ireland, in this case the North, to secede from the rest of the country. In Document No. 2 he tried to eliminate the Ulster question altogether from the settlement with Britain, by treating it as an internal Irish affair. He was willing that Dáil Éireann should grant to the minority in the North-East a separate legislature which would have all the powers accorded under the Treaty. But there must be a declaration, firm and clear, which safeguarded an overriding Irish unity. A probing attack on the Ulster clauses of the Treaty might well have revealed their weaknesses and might conceivably have made an issue on which the whole agreement could have been defeated.

But supposing he had defeated the Treaty, was his alternative practical politics at the time? Would it have prevented war? Had it been backed up by a united Dáil and a united country, one could argue that it might have been. De Valera was convinced that it was. He felt sure that the reality of external association could have been achieved if speaker after speaker had said in the debate, as Miss MacSwiney said later, that they were willing to die for the difference between Document No. 2 and the Treaty. But this they were far from saying. De Valera did not believe that the rejection of the Treaty by the Dáil and its acceptance of Document No. 2 would have led inevitably to war. Who could say then, who could say now, whether he was right?

THE DRIFT TO DISASTER

January – June, 1922

The acceptance of the Treaty by the Dáil created a new situation. During the course of the debate, the President had avoided any kind of sectional action. He had warned the Dáil that the Irish Republic had been established by the votes of the Irish people and could only be disestablished by them. The same was true of Dáil Éireann, the supreme government of the nation. In the circumstances, he must resign from the presidency, a step which he took forthwith.

This produced a kind of hiatus. There was an obvious reluctance among the pro-Treaty deputies to nominate a president. Eventually Mrs Tom Clarke proposed that de Valera be re-elected. His candid statement of his policy made it more or less impossible for the pro-Treaty group to accept him. Yet when it came to the test, he was only defeated by two votes, he himself not voting—a remarkable tribute to the strength of his personal appeal. Two of those who had voted for the Treaty abstained, while two others voted for de Valera.

The next day, a new motion appeared on the agenda in Collins's name: that Mr Arthur Griffith be appointed President of Dáil Éireann.

And now the constitutional difficulties were becoming ever more obvious. It is easy to lose one's way amidst the intricacies of the argument, but de Valera's object was simple. He was determined to see that the Dáil was preserved until such time as the Treaty could be put before the people in a free election. He was determined, in other words, that the Dáil should not disestablish itself on its own. By their votes in December, 1918, the people had brought the Dáil into existence. The election of May, 1921, had confirmed the position of the Republic, and any departure from Republican principles would have to be decided by the people, not by the Dáil. Naturally he called on Griffith, as candidate for the presidency, to produce a statement of policy. Under pressure, Griffith assured him: 'Whatever the position that the President resigned from yesterday I will, if I am elected, occupy the same position until the Irish people have an opportunity of deciding for themselves'.[1] That sounded satisfactory. But Griffith later made it clear that he wanted the Republic to remain in existence only until the people had made their choice (as he hoped they would in an early election) in favour of the Treaty.

To de Valera, the whole thing had become completely anomalous. The report from the official records must be given verbatim:

> De Valera: 'As a protest against the election, as President of the Irish Republic, of the Chairman of the Delegation, who is bound by the Treaty conditions to set up a State which is to subvert the Republic and who, in the interim period instead of using the office as it should be used, to support the Republic will, of necessity, have to be taking action which will tend to its destruction,—I, while this vote is being taken, am going to leave the House.'

He left the House, followed by the mass of his supporters. As they left, the exchanges continued:

> Collins: 'Deserters all! We will now call on the Irish people to rally to us. Deserters all!'
> Ceannt: 'Up the Republic!'
> Collins: 'Deserters all to the Irish nation in her hour of trial. We will stand by her.'
> Countess Markievicz: 'Oath breakers and cowards!'
> Collins: 'Foreigners! Americans! English!'
> Countess Markievicz: 'Lloyd Georgeites!'

Whereupon Arthur Griffith was elected President of Dáil Éireann.[2]

The constitutional developments that followed need not be elaborated once again in these pages. The complexities were endless, most of all perhaps those affecting the position of the Irish Volunteers or Irish Republican Army. The key to the difficulty was that there were two parts of the Volunteer oath—first allegiance to the Republic, and second, acceptance of the authority of the Dáil. When these became inconsistent, a kind of schizophrenia resulted. The new Minister of Defence, Richard Mulcahy, put immediate doubts at rest when he said that the army would continue to be the army of the Irish Republic. It would occupy the same position as previously in relation to the Minister and the Dáil. In the circumstances, de Valera strongly urged the HQ staff and the divisional commandants that they give the same loyalty to the new Minister as they had previously given to Cathal Brugha. But all this was papering over the cracks.

Soon, however, a diversion occurred. His time became taken up with the Irish Race Congress—a meeting in Paris of representatives of Irish organisations throughout the world. De Valera was one of the eight delegates from Ireland, and he decided to travel from London to Paris in the guise of Father Patrick Walsh, a priest of the Holy Ghost Congregation, with whom he had been friendly in Rockwell. He devoted proper care to his new identity, and jotted down vital pieces of information regarding Father Walsh in his diary. In a studio near Charing Cross he was photographed in clerical garb. The picture was attached to a passport which was forged or, at least, had been tampered with.

The Paris congress, which met in the shadow of the Treaty argument, was not at first acrimonious. De Valera was unanimously elected president, but later controversy broke out over the appointment of an executive secretary. The organisation was finally swamped by the events which followed in Ireland. Behind a confessional in Notre Dame Cathedral, de Valera put on once more the Roman collar and set off for London, via Antwerp. By February 3rd he was back at his home in Greystones. Feelings, already divided before he left for Paris, were becoming more bitter with every day that passed.

The Provisional Government under the Treaty which was to 'take over from the British' had been set up on January 14th at a meeting of the representatives of the twenty-six counties who had voted for the Treaty. This 'parliament' was not attended by de Valera or other Republican deputies and was never, in fact, called together again. Confusion between the Provisional Government and the Dáil cabinet, with considerable overlapping of personnel, was probably inevitable, but Republican suspicions grew ever stronger. It appeared that the Dáil departments were being allowed to lapse, instead of being strengthened by the gradual take-over from the British. It was the Provisional Government which was becoming powerful and acting without the control of any elected body. There was bitterness in Brugha's voice as he protested: 'I suppose it is for the purpose of maintaining unity all this thing is gone on with'.

De Valera continued to play his part manfully in the public argument. On February 12th he spoke at the first of a series of anti-Treaty meetings. It was held on O'Connell Street, in sight of the General Post Office, at which the Republic had been proclaimed by Pearse in 1916, and Pearse's mother was on the platform to endorse de Valera. He vehemently addressed a vast enthusiastic crowd from three platforms, and with all the vigour of his spirit assailed the London agreement. The big anti-Treaty rally in Dublin was followed, a week later, by another in Cork. This time he laid main emphasis on the Constitution, throwing out a challenge to Griffith and his cabinet. They were saying they could frame a constitution which could give the Irish people complete freedom. 'Let them make the boast good,' he said, 'frame it, and then come before the people and they would know what they were voting on'.[3]

A week after he was in Ennis and later in Limerick, urging the people to stand by the Republic. 'We are asking you to stick it out,' he concluded, 'to cross the desert and don't listen too much to those who tell you of your own weakness. Think of your own strength and the weakness of your enemy—that is the way to win, and please God, we will win and there will be an end to the Free State'.[4]

Meanwhile, a meeting of the Ard Fheis of Sinn Féin was held on February 21st. The united party, which had dominated the Irish political scene since it committed itself in 1917 to securing the international recognition of Ireland as an independent Irish Republic, was facing the same problem which had faced and divided the Dáil. But on this occasion, a unity of a kind was preserved. It seems likely that de Valera could have carried a motion confirming the aim of Sinn Féin to be the upholding of the Republic. Griffith, in moving an amendment to approve the Treaty, had something of a rough passage until de Valera, as chairman, intervened to protect him. Collins put forward a powerful plea for unity; there was an adjournment till the next morning; when the leaders reappeared an hour and a half later an agreed statement was read out. The Ard Fheis was to stand adjourned for three months. In the meanwhile Dáil Éireann would meet regularly and continue to function in all its departments as before. No parliamentary elections would be held during this period. But when they were held, the Constitution of the Free State would be put before the people in its final form, at the same time as the Treaty.

The agreement met with almost unanimous approval from the delegates, but many Republicans thought that in the interests of unity and in his desire to avoid a snap election, de Valera had conceded too much. Even the faithful Kathleen O'Connell on this occasion doubted his wisdom. In her diary she wrote: 'The vast majority were Republicans. What a pity a division wasn't taken. We could start a new Republican Party clean. Delays are dangerous. Many may change before the Ard Fheis meets again.'[5] She might have added that the unity of Sinn Féin achieved at the Ard Fheis was basically unreal. Nevertheless, it played a large part in keeping the peace for several months and at the time that ranked high as a duty of statesmanship.

There would be time, it seemed, to prepare for an election. De Valera immediately turned his attention to putting the Republican Party on an organised basis. Early in March, the republican deputies met and formally established Cumann na Poblachta, with de Valera as President and Stack, Brugha and Mary MacSwiney as vice-Presidents. De Valera was most anxious to postpone the election until the Constitution was ready to be placed before the people. Then, but not till then, would it be clear whether the pro-Treaty party had succeeded in doing, within the terms of the Treaty, something which he considered impossible. Regarding the possibility of reaching unity in this way, he wrote to Stack:

Honestly, I am afraid that this is a dream pure and simple. I don't believe the other side will make any advance beyond the strict terms of the Treaty which, of course, precludes a Constitution which we could agree to.[6]

When asked by an American correspondent if he saw any way by which the two sides could unite without the complete capitulation of one of the parties, he answered: 'Frankly, I do not.' Nevertheless the hope lived on.

Week after week de Valera travelled throughout the country, to state the anti-Treaty case. It was all too easy for pro-Treaty speakers to say that it gave freedom to achieve freedom, he said. There was the man who said, 'If, for instance, a British soldier during the last half dozen years offered me a rifle on condition that I would take this oath, I would take it.' Some might have 'a very elastic mind' on oaths, but to de Valera international documents were not things to be signed and later torn up. Many years later[7] he wrote to Malcolm Macdonald, who claimed to have learned lessons in the art of politics and diplomacy from him:

I do not know of any art in these matters, and indeed doubt if there is any other than a sincere desire and a corresponding effort to find a just solution for such problems as present themselves. This is, I think, particularly true of problems that have proved intractable. Half measures are frequently proposed for these. I have never had faith in such measures. They rarely provide even the temporary easement which prompts their adoption.

There was one line of argument against the Treaty which led to some misunderstanding and still more misrepresentation later. He used it in several speeches, but the words most often quoted were uttered from a platform in a square in Thurles. He looked down at the Volunteers in the crowd who had just been told that the Volunteer Convention had been prohibited. He issued this grave warning. If they accepted the Treaty and if the Volunteers of the future tried to complete the work the Volunteers of the last four years had been attempting, they would have to complete it, not over the bodies of foreign soldiers, but over the dead bodies of their own countrymen. They would have to wade through Irish blood, through the blood of the soldiers of the Irish Government and through, perhaps, the blood of some of the members of the Government to get freedom.[8]

These awful warnings were quickly seized upon by the *Irish Independent* and others, not as prophecies but as incitements. Mr de Valera described the paper's editorial as villainous and went on: 'You cannot be unaware that your representing me as inciting to civil war has on your readers precisely the same effect as if the inciting words were really mine.'[9] For fear of future misrepresentations, however, he left aside this argument in later speeches.

There is no evidence that his speeches, in fact, stirred up the violence they were said to encourage. On the other hand, vehement statements by British politicians threatening war in Ireland if the Treaty were not pushed through, caused much more emotion and excitement among the Volunteers. Churchill informed Collins that a Republic would be 'followed by a state of war with the British Empire'.[10] Collins said at the Sinn Féin Ard Fheis: 'I know the English can go to war with us, and will go to war with us, and are at this moment watching an opportunity to go to war with us.'[11] This kind of threat of war from the British Government, said de Valera, was intimidation operating on the side of Mr Griffith and Mr Collins, as sure and as definite as if these gentlemen were using it themselves.[12] But the moral problems involved for de Valera and, indeed, for all concerned, were far from easy.

He was giving much thought to the moral issues involved in majority rule. The foundation of his whole position, then and always, was democratic:

> Not merely do I hold that this nation, *taking away all force,* should have the right to do with itself what it wants, but I would say further that, even in the circumstances of the moment, even with the threat of war, the Irish people would have the right, if they wanted to, to avoid war by taking another course.[13]

That language suggests that he conceded the right of the Irish people to disestablish the Republic even under British duress, but his position as a whole was too complex to be expressed in a single isolated quotation. It is doubtful whether he ever stated the problem as clearly at the time as some years later when he wrote:

> The conflict between the two principles, majority rule on the one hand and the inalienability of the national sovereignty on the other, that was the dilemma of the Treaty.[14]

That, indeed, was the dilemma which was dividing the Irish people in the spring of 1922 and it was a dilemma out of which there seemed little hope of escape. Whatever the theoretical morality of armed resistance to an Irish government representing an actual or supposed majority, de Valera warned unceasingly that there were people in Ireland who would rather die than acknowledge Britain's King as their king. He feared division in this country, he said, more than he feared England. This was not to argue that the will of a minority, rather than that of a majority, must prevail. It was rather to claim that a majority must show some consideration at least for the conscientious feelings of such a minority. But this, in his view, the pro-Treaty majority seemed quite unable or unwilling to realise.

His actual dilemma was still more agonising than any on the plane of democratic theory. He himself had no control over the army. As Leader of the Opposition, he refrained from interfering or coming between the soldiers and the Minister of Defence. In fact, the Republican part of the army went on their way with complete indifference to any views of his.

In the middle of March, Rory O'Connor and other anti-Treaty officers decided to proceed with an army convention despite a Government ban. Indeed O'Connor went much further. In a press interview, he explicitly repudiated the authority of the Dáil. This extreme step placed de Valera in an appalling situation.

It is true that O'Connor and his officers made it clear that they had no time for politicians of either party. The interview, however, was given at 23 Suffolk Street, in which de Valera's own Party, Cumann na Poblachta, and de Valera himself had their headquarters. The anti-Treaty army leaders were in no way in consultation with him, but their presence in the same building in Suffolk Street was a painful embarrassment for him when he heartily disagreed with O'Connor's action and outlook.

And, of course, his dilemma was not allowed to rest there. His relationship with the Republican officers and his attitude to their policy led, not surprisingly, to sharp cross-examination. In an interview with the *Manchester Guardian*, in April, he tried hard to avoid revealing any rift in the solidarity of the anti-Treaty forces. He pointed out that the military leaders were quite independent of his political party and that they acted entirely on their own initiative. But when asked if the army was entitled to use force to prevent an election, he answered:

If Britain were to remove the threat of force and were to pledge herself to respect whatever decision the Irish people arrived at, and if the register were a valid one, then I would say, but not till then, that intervention by the army would be tyrannical and immoral.

On another occasion he was asked whether he would consider it justifiable to use these armed forces for the achievement of his political aims in relation to the Treaty. His answer was that if the army could save the nation from the calamities which he considered to flow from that agreement, he would consider it justifiable for it to use its strength to do so.[15] De Valera admitted later that at this interview he was straining his own views in order to avoid the appearance of a split. For reasons alike of honour and prudence, he avoided any denunciation of Rory O'Connor's repudiation of the Dáil, although he thought that it was altogether wrong.

He was, in fact, in a nightmarish position, with little influence on events in practice. On the one hand the pro-Treaty government authorities held the initiative. On the other, the Republican section of the army, comprising probably more than half the Volunteers, were taking independent action. In spite of one or two meetings with Liam Mellows and Rory O'Connor, de Valera had little relationship with Republican members of the army and little information about them. It came therefore as a complete surprise to him to learn that the Volunteers had occupied the Four Courts in the early hours of April 14th. He had no part whatever in this step. But he felt that the dispute was a matter for the Minister for Defence and any interference by him would be unwelcome to either party.

Meanwhile, armed clashes were recurring and deaths resulted on both sides, with the prospect steadily deteriorating.

But a nation was not to be sold into civil war, without lifting a finger to save itself. Throughout April, efforts of many different kinds were made to bring about a peaceful settlement. The Labour Party and the bishops exerted themselves without immediate benefit. But in May, Michael Collins responded to a conciliatory speech of de Valera's and the way was open for a final peace-making effort. On May 20th, an agreement, the famous pact, was reached between de Valera and Collins, and presented to the Dáil.

This pact was to mean so much to republicans later that its terms should be noted carefully. It provided that a national coalition panel for the third Dáil, representing both parties, should be put forward by Sinn Féin. The number from each party was to be proportional to their strength in the existing Dáil. It was also agreed that any interest would be free to contest the election against the national Sinn Féin panel (Labour or farmer, for example). After the election, a coalition cabinet would be formed, consisting of the President, elected as formerly, the Minister of Defence representing the army, and nine other ministers, five from the majority party and four from the minority, each party to choose its own nominees.

This agreement, which meant that the Treaty would not be debated at the hustings, was received with great enthusiasm throughout Ireland. De Valera thought that he had come close to unity with this agreement. He had avoided the holding of an election, under the threat of British guns, in which the independence of Ireland might be surrendered. He had provided a basis for reunification of the army and had arranged for the government of the country for some time ahead. The acceptance of the agreement by the Dáil, despite Arthur Griffith's obvious lack of enthusiasm, was an indication of unanimous support for it. Collins's statement, recommending the agreement to the Ard Fheis of Sinn Féin on May 23rd, was immensely reassuring to republicans. The value of the agreement, he said, was not that it secured unity in the Dáil, but that it secured unity in the nation.[16] His heart now seemed to be back in the right place.

But it was hardly to be expected, in the harsh world of international politics, that the British would take these developments and this kind of language lying down. In the next weeks, the Irish cabinet and their advisers were preoccupied with producing a constitution which the British cabinet would accept. Many of them, including Michael Collins, crossed from Dublin to London more than once. As the Irish delegation sat in the visitors' gallery of the House of Commons on June 1st, they got the full blast of a Churchillian broadside. Ratification of the Treaty would be withheld by Britain if the Constitution was not in accordance with the Treaty; if the Treaty was broken by any act such as the inclusion of ministers in an Irish government who had not signed the declaration under Article 17; if the election was such that it could not be said in reasonable common sense to have any effective validity; if the constitution as it emerged from the provisional parliament was amended in such a way as to be no fulfilment of the Treaty.

In spite of the public words, de Valera continued sanguine, little realising the appalling pressure to which Collins, in particular, was being subjected behind the scenes. After the adjournment of the Dáil on June 8th, de Valera went on a whirlwind campaign through the country, speaking impartially for the panel candidates both pro- and anti-Treaty. In the three days, June 11th–13th, for example, he addressed fifteen gatherings.

But now the whole picture changed once more. Collins returned to Ireland from London and spoke at a pre-election rally in Cork. He struck a new and shattering note. He called on the people to vote, but made no appeal for support for the panel candidates. In fact he did the opposite and cast the pact aside. The next morning, polling-day, Friday, June 16th, the newspapers carried the draft Constitution, which had been agreed to by the British cabinet. The draft, containing an oath of allegiance to the King, came as a severe shock, not only to those who opposed the Treaty, but to those who favoured it, in the belief that Collins would not embody such an oath in the Constitution. But it had little influence on the election. Only a handful of electors knew of its contents before voting.

The results of the election, however, indicated that public opinion was definitely in favour of the Treaty, although the pre-election agreement had officially precluded that issue from the hustings. The new Dáil would consist of 58 pro-Treaty deputies, 35 anti-Treaty and 35 others. These last were all to some extent committed to accepting the Treaty. It could also be argued that a clear mandate had been given by the Irish people for the establishment of a coalition government. Yet it was difficult to see how a coalition could be formed in view of the draft Constitution and Collins's fateful speech at Cork on the eve of the poll.

Something unforeseen, but drastic, had obviously occurred at the last moment. The draft Constitution was widely different from anything de Valera had expected. De Valera and the Republicans were most strongly opposed to the clauses which imposed the oath of fealty to the King and gave him executive and legislative authority. 'As it stands,' he stated a few days later, 'it will exclude from the public service, and practically disfranchise every honest Republican . . . Dáil Éireann will not dishonour itself by passing it.'[17]

Despite all this, de Valera did not give up hope that the coalition would come into being. He clung to the idea that it might be possible to prove parts of the Constitution invalid before Republican courts. He waited, therefore, for an approach from Collins regarding the proposed coalition. He understood that he would be acceptable to sections of the army as minister for defence. Harry Boland wrote later to Joe McGarrity:

> As you know, I was the liaison or medium acting between our party and Collins, I expected a call from Mick as to the men on our side who would be required to fill the posts in the Cabinet in accordance with the agreement. No word came.[18]

On the evening of June 22nd, de Valera was having a meal in Jammet's Restaurant with Boland and Stephen O'Mara, Mayor of Limerick. The election results were now complete, Boland noting in his diary on that day: 'Labour and Treaty sweep the country'. As they discussed the situation regarding the election and the prospects of the coalition during their meal, they obtained an evening paper. It carried sensational news. Sir Henry Wilson, chief protagonist of the Orange elements and a die-hard opponent of Ireland's claims, had been assassinated on his own doorstep in London. De Valera was stunned. His instinct told him at once that the assassination would give the British Government a chance to stop a coalition.

The shooting of Wilson was the final act which made Collins's position untenable. Rory O'Connor, on behalf of the Republican wing of the army, denied all knowledge of it. Griffith denounced it. Collins's connection with it has often been asserted, but never established. De Valera was approached for a statement and, mindful of the daily pogroms in Belfast, which were so closely associated with Wilson's name, he said these considered words:

> The killing of any human being is an awful act, but as awful when the victim is the humble worker or the peasant unknown outside his own im-

mediate neighbourhood, as when the victim is placed in the seat of the mighty, and his name known in every corner of the earth.

It is characteristic of our hypocritical civilisation that it is in the latter case only we are expected to cry out and express our horror and condemnation. For my part, I have nothing but loathing for such conventional expressions when the plain means to secure that such awful happenings will not occur are deliberately put aside.

He went on dispassionately, but unambiguously:

I do not know who they were who shot Sir Henry Wilson, or why they shot him. I do not approve, but I must not pretend to misunderstand.

It all, he felt, arose from the half measure of the Treaty. He drew a moral from the situation:

It is idle to look for peace between nations or domestic peace within a nation, except on a foundation of justice. At Versailles, a regard for justice would have given us a world peace. In London, last December, a regard for justice would have secured a lasting peace between Ireland and England, which would have set the two nations heading in a parallel course of friendliness and cooperation. But so-called political expediency and threats of war intervened and we have what we have.

He saw, too, the injustice of the partition of Ireland and the consequences of it when he pointed out:

A regard for justice in the matter of the North-East settlement would have given Ireland internal peace. But in selecting an arbitrary area of six counties for the Northern State in defiance of the desires of the majorities in several areas within these counties justice was flouted and injustice as usual has been compelled to maintain itself by force.

His final sentence was for him a fundamental principle: 'For peace and the end of all such horrors, it is only necessary for statesmen to have the will to be fearlessly just.'

The outlook for a coalition now indeed seemed hopeless, though de Valera still did not believe that the idea should be cast aside completely. The cabinet was under ever heavier pressure from Britain, especially after Wilson's death. On the day following that event, Griffith was called into conference with the former Dublin Castle official, A. W. Cope, and two British army officers, regarding the continued occupation of the Four Courts 'by Rory O'Connor and his men'. On that same day, a letter was received in Dublin from Lloyd George which put strong pressure on Collins to attack the Four Courts. Collins had gone to Cork, and a reply was sent on his behalf by Diarmuid O'Hegarty, secretary to the cabinet. O'Hegarty set out the attitude of the Provisional Government to the occupation of the Four Courts by Republicans:

8

The Government was satisfied that these forces contained within themselves elements of disruption which, given time, would accomplish their complete disintegration, and relieve the Government of the necessity of employing methods of suppression which would have perhaps evoked a certain amount of misplaced sympathy for them.

The Provisional Government was not going to allow itself to be stampeded easily.

Lloyd George had said that the British Government had got information on plans of Republicans to start a campaign of attacks in Britain and in the six counties of the North-East. To this O'Hegarty replied tartly that the Provisional Government

requests your Government to assist them in dealing with the situation by placing at their disposal the information to which you refer. They will then be able to call upon the newly-elected Parliament which meets on 1st proximo to support them in such measures as may be considered adequate.

At this stage it seems clear that the Provisional Government had no intention of attacking the Four Courts without a mandate from the newly-elected assembly. British pressure continued to be exerted, however, and it was apparently decided that, if the Provisional Government did not act, the British forces which still remained in the vicinity of Dublin would attack the Four Courts themselves. General Macready was called to London and given orders to this effect. He found the British cabinet intent on taking dramatic steps to offset the assassination of Sir Henry Wilson. But, on Sunday, June 25th, the British cabinet cancelled the orders. Next day, in the House of Commons, Lloyd George, while denying that he was menacing the Provisional Government in Dublin, insisted that the occupation of the Four Courts be ended. He accepted, however, that a decision would not be taken by the cabinet in Dublin until the Dáil met on July 1st. 'This,' he said, 'is the first thing they will take into their consideration.'

But events in Dublin waited for no man, although the precise sequence has never been fully clarified. There is evidence that on this same day, June 26th, the Dublin cabinet decided to attack the Four Courts without waiting for a meeting of the Dáil. No formal decision, however, was taken till the next day the 27th. In the meantime the Four Courts garrison, in reprisal for the arrest of one of their men, captured the assistant chief of staff of the Government forces, Major General ('Ginger') O'Connell and provided the Provisional Government with some justification for action.

A sudden attack which could cause surrender within a few hours was confidently hoped for by the Government. At 3.40 a.m., on the morning of June 28th, 1922, an ultimatum was delivered to the forces in the Four

Courts. They were to evacuate by 4 a.m. Apparently it was hoped to have the buildings cleared by morning. Shortly after 4 o'clock, the artillery borrowed by the forces of the Provisional Government from the British forces still in Kilmainham opened fire on the Four Courts. The Civil War had begun—two days before the new Dáil was due to meet.

THE WAR OF BROTHERS

July – October, 1922

The booming guns in the early morning of June 28th, 1922, sounded the death knell of the Collins–de Valera pact. But the warning sounds did not reach the de Valera home twenty miles away in Greystones.

De Valera, driving an old Ford model which Mellows had given him, was passing through the village of Stillorgan when men, who were standing at the cross, rushed out to stop him. They told him that people had been killing each other in Dublin since the early morning, and that he should not go into the city. De Valera replied that if they were right, it was all the greater reason why he should go in at once.

At the bottom of Foster Avenue, near the gate of St Helen's, he noticed a barricade held by the army, with only a small passage through. As de Valera approached, the officer recognised him, saluted and let him pass at once.

As soon as he arrived at his office, he called an impromptu conference of republican delegates and issued an urgent statement:

> At the last meeting of Dáil Éireann, an agreement was ratified which, if faithfully observed, would have given us an opportunity of working for internal peace and of taking steps which would make the Nation strong against the only enemy it has to fear, the enemy from outside. At the bidding of the English, Irishmen are today shooting down, on the streets of our capital, brother Irishmen—old comrades in arms, companions in the recent struggle for Ireland's independence and its embodiment—the Republic.

He showed his sympathy with the Four Courts' garrison now under attack. He described them as 'the best and bravest of our Nation' and said of them that they were

> the men who have refused to forswear their allegiance to the Republic, who have refused to sacrifice honour for expediency and sell their country to a foreign King. In Rory O'Connor and his comrades lives the unbought indomitable soul of Ireland.

And he appealed: 'Irish citizens! Give them support! Irish soldiers! Bring them aid!'[1]

De Valera later described his own most unenviable position after the attack on the Four Courts. He admitted his helplessness, which indeed was to continue throughout the coming months. All hopes of effective political action seemed to have been ended by the Provisional Government. He was unable any longer to prevent the terrible state of things which they had hoped by the electoral pact with Collins to avoid. The Republican politicians dropped their hands by their sides and said to themselves, through pure inability to prevent it, this thing has to be— So, having to choose, they preferred to stand with those who, whatever the differences on other matters, were yet true to their pledges and professions and to the traditional national faith.[2]

For himself, de Valera decided that there was nothing left but to join up again. He repaired to the very house in York Street where he had first joined the Volunteers in 1913, and there re-enlisted as a private in his old battalion, the third, swearing the Volunteer oath of allegiance to the Republic. At no time during the Civil War did he rank as a military leader. Each man had now to make his own decision. Brugha and Boland, like de Valera, joined the Republican Army, and Boland was sent south to Mallow, to obtain reinforcements for the Republicans in Dublin. To them the attack by the Provisional Government was a *coup d'état*. During the preceding six months, they had anxiously watched the position of the Dáil being undermined, despite Griffith's guarantee that he would maintain the Republic until it was disestablished by the people. The election campaign had been fought on the basis of the pact and it was only on the eve of the election itself that the pact was broken. In Republican eyes, the election gave authority for no government except a coalition government, least of all for a violent assault of this kind.

A peace move was initiated by the Labour Party, and de Valera hastened to his brigade headquarters at the Gresham, to support proposals for an armistice. All efforts at peace failed, however, since Griffith and Collins insisted that there could be no truce until the Republicans surrendered their arms. It was on this condition of complete surrender of arms that peace talks were to break down repeatedly. Still more objectionable to de Valera was the Cabinet's decision to postpone the meeting of the Dáil. There seemed no hope now of constitutional opposition to the Government.

After two days under heavy fire in the Hammam Hotel, the Republican leaders made their escape across the Liffey to No. 11 Mount Street. Cathal Brugha was left behind for the moment with a small garrison. It was intended that Brugha should leave like the others later, but he had apparently made up his mind to fight with them to the last. The moment came when he dismissed the garrison and walked across the lane alone, where he came under the fire of the Free State troops. He was fatally wounded and died two days later in the Mater Hospital. Some say he was returning the fire of the Free State troops when he fell.

Michael Collins, with whom he had quarrelled violently, was none the less moved to write: 'I would forgive him anything. Because of his sincerity I would forgive him anything.'

In July, de Valera left Dublin for the south, pushing on to Clonmel, the general headquarters of the Republican forces, where he was appointed adjutant to Seán Moylan, the Director of Operations. Harry Boland, a friend equally dear to de Valera and Michael Collins, wrote of him at this time:

> The Chief is at GHQ, hale and well, the same gentle, honest, straight-forward, unpurchaseable man that you knew. All the calumny that has been heaped upon him is British inspired; they failed to bribe or intimidate him, they now try the weapon of slander.[3]

But de Valera was in no way happy about the military situation. All along he found a reluctance on the part of the men to fight. They had little stomach for opposing their former colleagues. Their previous experience had been in guerilla tactics. This gave them no training in the house-to-house defence of towns, and they had no cannon. Yet while there was any chance of success, de Valera plunged whole-heartedly into the war. As he saw it, the Republican Army was throwing itself 'across the stampede of the nation'.

De Valera and his comrades were hustled from one position to another. In Cahir, they camped for a few days in the fine residence of Colonel Charteris, which had been taken over by the Republicans. He was asked by the butler to put his name in the visitors' book. He wrote his name, but a large question mark was all he could put in the column for his address.

The Free State Government forces had the equipment, including cannon, the recruits and the machinery of the State, with British support behind them. They soon succeeded by using coastal shipping in landing troops at strategic points along the coast. The Republican forces broke up into separate columns and aimed at harassing Free State garrisons, instead of trying to defend their now untenable positions. In August, de Valera, tired and depressed, arrived in the mess-room in Fermoy Barracks—about to be abandoned by the army. There he learned of Harry Boland's death. Kathleen O'Connell recorded: 'He felt it terribly—crushed and broken. He lost his most faithful friend.' In this, the last stronghold in the possession of the Republicans, he wrote in an improvised diary: 'Waiting in Fermoy Barracks to leave. One of the most miserable days I have ever spent. Thoughts, thoughts . . .'.[4]

That night, Fermoy Barracks was evacuated and burnt, and the first phase of the Civil War was over.

Three days later, at Kilpeddar, near Ballincollig, de Valera wrote in his diary: 'Went for a walk in a field. Meditation. Any chance of winning? If there was any chance, duty to hold on to secure it. If none, duty to try to get the men to quit—for the present. The people must be won to the cause before any successful fighting can be done. The men dead and gloomy—just holding on. How long will it last?'[5] All were disheartened.

On that day too, he heard that Arthur Griffith had died on the previous day in Dublin of a heart attack. The news brought back memories of their years together since 1917, and the differences of the last eight months. He wrote: 'He was, I believe, unselfishly patriotic—and courageously'. But the shocking denunciation of Childers, and the misrepresentations still rankled. 'If only he had not stooped to the methods he employed to win.' The next day, he was still thinking of Griffith and his reasons for signing the Treaty without referring back to Dublin. He wished he could know why he had done it. 'Did he think when it was signed, I'd accept the fait accompli?'[6]

He would not have quarrelled later with an estimate such as that of Terence de Vere White: 'Arthur Griffith left behind him an unmatched record of selfless devotion to his country. His qualities were not of the kind that excite the imagination; he made no appeal to the passions: he was not less great for that.'[7] De Valera saw him as a man who, at the supreme crisis, put peace before everything.

At this time, one of de Valera's American friends, Peter Golden, succeeded in locating him in the neat, whitewashed kitchen of a house in the hills, near Gougane Barra. When Golden arrived, he found the household saying the rosary in Irish, de Valera kneeling against the back of a sugán chair, his face buried in his hands. The prayers ended, the man who was now reviled and denounced, even from the altars, as a fomentor of civil war, rose and greeted the visitor with his habitual courtesy. Golden wrote:

> He seemed a man heartsick and distraught at the terrible things which had come to the nation and its people . . . not a word of bitterness escapes this man against any of those now so bitterly opposed to him—not even against those who certainly have not in any way spared him . . . he is overweighed with grief. He speaks with great kindness of Arthur Griffith and of his fine pioneer work for Ireland. He is fearful that the next step will be a military dictatorship set up by Mick Collins, taking his orders from England.[8]

De Valera was, no doubt, over-fearful of the plans of Collins who, in fact, would appear at this time to have been much more anxious to quench rather than to stoke up the flames. At no stage was any approach made on Collins's behalf to de Valera. Looking back on the situation later, however, de Valera believed that Collins may well have intended to negotiate, but with others such as Liam Lynch, Chief of Staff, rather than himself. Such an approach, if it was indeed in Collins's mind, was based on a realistic appraisal, for de Valera's influence with the army was slight. Lynch, however, was determined to fight on, so long as he had a man or gun.

Now calamity struck a mortal blow. On the morning of August 22nd, Collins travelled in an armoured convoy into west Cork. De Valera was also in the district, on his way up to Dublin, to be there in time for the meeting of the Dáil. At one house where he called at Béalnabláth, he was told that Collins had been there an hour before. Next day he learnt that Collins had been killed in an ambush near Béalnabláth, on his return journey from west Cork the previous evening.

Collins was aged thirty-three, with a whole world of promise in front of him. At his graveside General Mulcahy spoke in noble eulogy and with inflexible purpose:

Men and women of Ireland, we are all mariners on the deep, bound for a port still seen only through storm and spray, sailing still on a sea 'full of dangers and hardships, and bitter toil'. But the Great Sleeper lies smiling in the stern of the boat, and we shall be filled with that spirit which will walk bravely upon the waters.

If the deaths of Cathal Brugha and Harry Boland put iron into the souls of the Republicans, the death of Collins had a similar effect on his Free State colleagues, already shocked by the loss of Griffith. Violent death brings little peace to the living, and that of Collins appears to have ended all hope of compromise.

Travelling by side roads and avoiding the towns, de Valera continued his hazardous journey to Dublin, which took him altogether about a fortnight. Now he was back again in 11 Upper Mount Street, where he had sheltered after escaping from the Hammam Hotel at the beginning of July. Still bent on reconciliation, de Valera agreed to meet General Mulcahy, Commander-in-Chief of the Free State forces, in Dr Farnan's house in Merrion Square. Just eighteen months earlier, the hunted President of the Irish Republic had met Lord Derby here. Now, still hunted, but this time by former colleagues, de Valera greeted his erstwhile chief-of-staff, now resplendent in top boots and in full uniform. They found little ground for agreement or even discussion.

De Valera noted in his diary: 'Couldn't find a basis. Mulcahy was looking for a basis in acceptance of the Treaty—we in revision of the Treaty.'[9] He was left with the impression that the pro-Treaty party had little desire at that stage to translate the struggle from the military field, where lay their hopes of peace. When Peter Golden suggested a further meeting at this same time, to propose a settlement with Mulcahy, de Valera saw no hope, unless some positive proposals from the Government were put in writing first. Yet Britain's grave international difficulties (the crisis with Turkey) offered in de Valera's eyes an opportunity for revising the Treaty—if only the Irish were united. When Lloyd George's resignation was forced in October, de Valera commented: 'What a position we would have been in, had the Pact been kept.'[10]

The meeting of the Provisional Parliament on September 9th had finally clarified the constitutional position for de Valera. It was clear that it derived its authority from British Acts, rather than from the Second Dáil. In de Valera's eyes the Republic was still therefore the existing State. With greater indignation than ever, he denounced the Provisional Government as a junta using British powers, not Irish, and acting in an arbitrary and irresponsible manner. Its whole assumption of power represented a usurpation. Once again he added that it broke Irish law by not abiding by the pact which had been ratified by a decree of Dáil Éireann.

Nevertheless, he did not immediately fall in with proposals put forward by a number of Republicans for setting up a rival government. His reluctance was not due to any constitutional doubts, but rather to physical and military inability to maintain it. 'If we were now in the position we were in when we held a portion of Cork,' he wrote, 'I'd certainly favour it.' Nevertheless, 'if the Army Executive were at hand and would definitely give allegiance to that government, I'd think it wise to try it.'[11]

During September and early October, he waited anxiously for a meeting of the Army Executive. Finally, on October 17th, it met at Mrs Nugent's house, Poulatar, Ballybacon. The whole question of establishing a government was discussed in the light of a letter received from de Valera. He proposed that the Army Executive should issue a proclamation as follows:

> We, on behalf of the soldiers of the Republic in concert with such faithful members of Dáil Éireann as are at liberty, acting in the spirit of our oath as the final custodians of the Republic, have called upon the former President, Eamon de Valera, to resume the Presidency and to form a government which shall preserve inviolate the sacred trust of National Sovereignty and Independence.

With certain reservations the proclamation was agreed to. Considerable difficulties, both psychological and physical had to be overcome before the President could emerge with a cabinet acceptable to the military and civilian wings of the Republican movement. But by early November the task was accomplished. The Emergency Government came into being. De Valera nominated Austin Stack as Minister for Finance, P. J. Ruttledge was put in charge of Home Affairs, Seán T. O'Kelly nominated

Minister for Local Government, Robert Barton, Minister for Economic Affairs and Liam Mellows, Minister for Defence. The last-named, however, was a prisoner in Mountjoy Jail.

It was arranged that documents from the Defence Department would be signed for the time being both by de Valera, as President, and by Liam Lynch, Chief of Staff. It is worth noticing that in asking for the support of the army, de Valera had been at great pains to make clear his views, palatable or otherwise. As he wrote to Joe McGarrity: 'If the army thinks I am too moderate, well let them get a better President and go ahead.' He was determined to avoid a type of situation of which he had had too much experience in the recent past. This time, he was 'going to make provision in advance to prevent any possible misunderstanding among the soldiers of the Republic, or our own people. . . . I would make peace under present conditions, or any conditions that I think likely to prevail in the immediate future, on the basis of that document [i.e. external association], and I do not want the young fellows who are fighting for the Republic to think otherwise.'[12]

But neither on the part of the Free State Government, nor the British Government, was there the slightest sign of a concession.

THE EMERGENCY GOVERNMENT

October, 1922 – February, 1923

A Republican Government was now established as a rival to the Provisional Government, at least in aspiration. It cannot be repeated too often that the Provisional Government was in Republican eyes an illegitimate thing. In Irish law, it could in no sense be regarded as the constitutional successor to the Second Dáil which had decreed that it was to meet on 30th June in order formally to dissolve. There might be two opinions among Republicans as to whether a republic, once declared, could be disestablished at all, or whether any election such as that just held under the threat of British coercion could be valid. There was no doubt whatever in their minds that the actual course pursued by the Free State Government, more especially the repudiation of the de Valera/Collins pact, and their refusal to allow the Dáil to meet until September 9th was quite unconstitutional. The attack on the Four Courts, under British orders, was final proof, so it seemed, that the pro-Treaty leaders were resolved to abandon peaceful methods in favour of force.

On this supposition, the need for a Republican alternative to the Provisional Government was well overdue if the Republican case were not to go by default. This conclusion was reinforced by a pastoral issued by the Catholic bishops of Ireland on October 10th, 1922, in which the Republicans were sternly denounced. 'They carry on,' said the bishops, 'what they call a war, but which in the absence of any legitimate authority to justify it is morally a system of murder and assassination of the National forces.'

The pastoral was certainly loaded against the Republicans. Whatever the provocation, it was the Provisional Government who had attacked the Four Courts, but according to the bishops it was the republicans who had 'chosen to attack their own country'. Many of the statements were at least debatable. The Provisional Government was referred to as being 'set up by the nation' even though, from the Republican point of view, 'the nation' had decisively voted in June for a coalition government. There was not a breath of criticism of the Government's breach of the pact of May 20th. There was no condemnation of murders by Free State troops, though many prisoners had been killed without even the pretext of a trial. Only what was referred to as 'unauthorised murder' was condemned in the pastoral and all who remained members of the Republican forces were prohibited from receiving the sacraments.

The bishops' pastoral seemed to de Valera to lack both charity and foresight. He wrote to Dr Amigo, Bishop of Southwark: 'the good intention which prompted the announcement is not difficult to understand but that means so calculated to defeat these intentions could have been chosen is almost incomprehensible.'[1] The contrast with the obvious wisdom of the Pope's advice given recently in an Italian context was extraordinary. To his old friend, Archbishop Mannix, he was yet more outspoken. 'The late pronouncement of the hierarchy here is most unfortunate,' he wrote. 'Never was charity of judgment so necessary, and apparently so disastrously absent. Ireland and the Church will, I fear, suffer in consequence.' The Treaty which brought the existing situation about must go, he felt, before there could be peace or stable government:

> Human nature must be recast before those Irishmen and Irishwomen who believe in the national right and the national destiny as in a religion, will consent to acquiesce in the selling of the national birthright for an ignoble mess of pottage, as they regard it. Think then of the prospects of a government which can only exist by outlawing the most unselfishly patriotic citizens of the State.

He recalled what Bishop O'Dwyer of Limerick said in 1916:

> as long as grass grows or water runs, men and women will be found ready to dare and give their lives in the cause of Irish freedom, and will deem the sacrifice, virtue and not sin.

All these the Free State must now banish, or execute, or murder. Sadly he looked back at the position as it had been twelve months before. Then there was

> the almost certain prospect of a settlement which all could have accepted, or at least acquiesced in, leaving us a united nation with a future to be freely moulded under God by ourselves. It is sad, but chastening, to realise how they were all blasted within a month.

He realised that party feeling was running too high for calm, dispassionate thinking or for real statesmanship to have any opportunity to influence action. Yet he was not without hope of winning the people to support the institutions which they themselves had established rather than those which derived authority from British statutes. He ended this letter with a request for the Archbishop's blessing and assured him of

> the affection and esteem of all who are striving now that the way may not be closed for those who may be destined to complete the work towards which the hopes of the nation have been set definitely since Easter 1916.[2]

The Republican Government's aim was, in Parnell's immortal phrase, to prevent the setting of 'a boundary to the march of a nation.' But its establishment as the Republican Government was dogged with overwhelming difficulties. The Provisional Government were enforcing ever-stronger repressive measures. At the end of September they had authorised the army to execute prisoners found guilty of possession of firearms or taking part in an attack on the army, or on public or private property. Now came another traumatic step in the sequence—the arrest on November 10th of Erskine Childers, at his cousin Robert Barton's house, at Annamoe, Co. Wicklow.

The arrest of Childers was bitter news. Kathleen O'Connell noted in her diary that de Valera was 'frightfully upset and unhappy about it.'[3] He feared that he would be treated ruthlessly. He had been singled out out for personal attack by Arthur Griffith in the Dáil in April. He was singled out again in the debate on the decree granting the army wide powers of life and death and referred to by Kevin O'Higgins as 'the Englishman' who 'keeps steadily, callously and ghoulishly on his career of striking at the heart of this nation.'[4] Childers had taken no part in the actual fighting but he had, despite the greatest difficulties, continued to issue publicity in favour of the Republic. He had been sent to Dublin by Liam Lynch, who knew that his services would be required by the Republican Government, and from Annamoe he had sent a letter to de Valera saying that he was available. That letter de Valera destroyed at once.

The arrest of Childers heralded indeed the most horrible part of the Civil War. Brugha, Boland and Collins had died during the heat of strife. Childers was tried by court martial for possessing a pistol and, while the trial was still in progress, four young prisoners were executed for having been found with arms. No wonder that Kathleen O'Connell wrote: 'Consternation everywhere. Looks like a forerunner for Childers' execution.' Once again she noted: 'President very upset and unhappy.'[5]

Miss O'Connell's foreboding proved justified when Kevin O'Higgins, Minister for Home Affairs of the Provisional Government, indicated in the Dáil that day that the four young men were executed lest it might be said that the first victim was chosen because he was an Englishman.[6] Childers's trial was not yet over, but the horror of civil war was sinking deep in blood.

De Valera did all in his power to prevent the execution. He was in constant touch with Michael Comyn who acted as counsel for Childers. He advised that it was essential that the Republican position should not be compromised in any way but, short of that, all legal steps should be taken to defend the case. The main point made was that the Provisional Government was acting illegally. He wrote:

A declaration that the Provisional Government, which the Bishops went out of their way to proclaim as the legitimate Government of Ireland, was an illegal body acting illegally, would be of incalculable advantage to us and have world-wide consequences.[7]

Efforts to get this were unsuccessful, as indeed was foreseen with a military court constituted as at that time. He drafted a statement for the nation concerning the trial, but the papers, on the orders of the Provisional Government, refused to print it.[8] A few days later Erskine Childers went to his death serenely in Beggars Bush Barracks, even though an appeal for Habeas Corpus was pending in the courts. Before he died, he shook hands with the firing squad. Kathleen O'Connell recorded the feelings of an ardent Republican in her diary that day:

Stop Press!! Childers executed. Oh God! How can we ever raise our heads again. Oh, the shame of it, shot by Irishmen. Poor Childers who had worn himself out in the service of Ireland.[9]

De Valera, she noted, was heartbroken at the news. To Joe McGarrity he wrote:

He died the Prince that he was. Of all the men I ever met I would say he was the noblest. The gun he had in his possession was an automatic that Mick [Collins] gave him, telling him that it was to defend the Republic. I saw it with him myself—a tiny automatic, little better than a toy and in no sense a war weapon.[10]

No death, since that of Harry Boland, had affected him so deeply.

The death of Childers was not only a severe blow to de Valera, who so fully appreciated his pre-eminent qualities, but to the entire Republican movement. Publicity for the cause was essential and Childers was the most able writer available. De Valera wrote of the difficulties:

Organisation work here is extremely difficult, and *we are sorely in need of funds*. The 'will of the people' cry, abused though it is, for with their lying press they could make the people will anything they chose, is nevertheless a terrible cry to make headway against. The country is so tired of war and fighting, and there is such a natural hatred to turning one's arms against one's own countrymen that some of the very best are standing aside, feeling that we are right but not wishing to be involved themselves.[11]

In general the administration of the Republican Government was not able to make much progress. While the existence of the Government provided a rallying point to some Republicans it failed to attract the allegiance of the people as a whole. The Free State Government formally came into existence on December 6th, 1922, the anniversary of the signing of the Treaty. On that day deputies publicly took the oath, laid down in the Constitution, in the meeting chamber of the Dáil before

Michael Ó hAodha, the Speaker authorised by the Governor-General to administer it. The Republican deputies were absent. The Free State and its Government held the sources of revenue and administration. The full machinery of government lay in their hands. The implementation of the decrees of the Republican Government depended absolutely on the army, but the army, as de Valera noted, was completely taken up with its own military work. 'The old contempt' he was to write 'for civil or semi-civil work apparently persists.'[12] The Republican Government possessed no real control of the army. Liam Lynch, the Chief of Staff, was a determined patriot whose mind was rigid in his allegiance to the Republic. He had been appointed to his position by the elected executive of the army and he acted almost if not entirely independently of the Government.

A large element in the army felt that politicians, as they called all civil leaders, had let them down before and they did not trust the Cabinet with absolute authority. The crucial life and death decisions continued to rest with Lynch, not de Valera, who could do no more than pluck at his sleeve. In the face of the murder of prisoners while in the custody of Free State troops, Liam Lynch had, in September, issued an order strictly prohibiting the Republican forces from carrying out reprisals.[13] But the resort to the official execution of prisoners by the Provisional Government created a new situation. After the first five executions in November, Lynch issued an order to the Dublin brigades that nine members of the Provisional Government were to be executed and two members of the Parliament arrested. He also gave the Commandant of the 1st Dublin brigade permission to deal with those who voted for the decrees. De Valera was not consulted until the orders were issued. Although he had already agreed with the necessity for an extreme warning, now he wrote:

> The efficacy of reprisals is open to doubt, but as I see no other way . . . protect our men, I cannot disapprove.

Troubled in mind as he obviously was, he felt unable in the terrible circumstances of the time to say no. Neither, however, did he give positive approval. He urged moreover that before any such drastic action was taken, at least due notice should be given.[14] Three more executions took place in Dublin on November 30th. In reply, two pro-Treaty deputies were shot at. One of them, Seán Hales, was killed and the other wounded.

A new depth in the struggle was reached. As a reprisal for the shooting of the two deputies, the four leading Republican prisoners, Liam Mellows, Rory O'Connor, Dick Barrett and Joe McKelvey, who had been captured at the fall of the Four Courts five months before, were shot without trial by the Free State Government which had just been formed. Now it was inevitable that further blood should flow. The executions were followed by retaliatory attacks on the property and houses of members of the Free State Parliament and later by the taking of hostages. Every stage of the tragedy brought fresh anguish to de Valera. He was horrified at the ghastly accident in the Republican burning of Seán McGarry's house, when his young son was burned to death. He felt concerned, not alone on humanitarian grounds, but also because of the effect on public feeling. The incident helped to reverse the rising tide of indignation against the Free State which followed the execution of Mellows, O'Connor, Barrett and McKelvey.

De Valera wrote to his Minister for Home Affairs and sent a copy to the Chief of Staff, Liam Lynch:

> I am not against the burning of offices, etc., of Free State officials, particularly if these burnings are done effectively. That is direct legitimate war on the functioning of the enemy Government, but I am against such burnings as that of McGarry's, which was very badly executed and which has all the appearance of a reprisal on his family, and looks mean and petty. . . . Terroristic methods may silence those of our opponents who are cowards, but many of them are very far from being cowards, and attempts at terrorism will only stiffen the bold men amongst them. I am against such methods on principle, and believe we will never win in this war unless we attach the people to our Government by contrast with theirs.[15]

He asked Lynch to cancel the drastic reprisals order. 'The policy of an eye for an eye is not going to win the people to us, and without the people we can never win,' he wrote. Of the Republican reprisals he advised Lynch:

> The recent burnings were, in my opinion, puerile and futile from a military or any other point of view. We must on no account allow our contest to be sullied by stupid and foolish action on the part of individuals who may never look to the consequences, not to speak of the morality or justice of what they are doing.[16]

Liam Lynch, who had consistently ordered that Free Staters captured in action be released unharmed, was shocked by the Provisional Government's policy of executions. In reply to de Valera he explained his position:

> IRA in this war as in the last wish to fight with clean hands, but when the enemy has outraged all rules of warfare—O'Higgins says there are no such rules—we must adopt severe measures or else chuck it at once. I, at least, would not take responsibility for protecting the lives of our forces . . . if we do not cope with enemy barbarous methods.[17]

Once de Valera understood, he sympathised with Liam Lynch's position:

I don't want to tie the hands of our Army, or prevent it from taking the most effective means to defend itself and our cause when it is viciously struck at, and I realise too fully the danger of half measures to try to impose upon you any such policy of futility; but I also see very clearly that the other side is dragging us and the country step by step into the mire with itself. I want to break the vicious circle somewhere, if I can.

His desire was to stop the killing of all who were only indirectly respons- ible for the situation. Those who voted for repressive statutes and who were particularly active or aggressive had chosen their side and must accept the consequences. The Republicans should confine their actions to them. As for the Unionists he considered them far less responsible for the situation than the Free Staters who had formerly been Republicans. It might be argued that action against Unionists could be justified on the grounds that the British Government would listen to them and so might bring pressure on the Free State to make peace.

but [he said] we must be careful not to be tempted ourselves to choose the easy course, or let our soldiers choose it, rather than the just one of getting at the principals.[18]

The executions continued, thirty-four members of the Republican Army being executed during January. It was not surprising that Lynch felt driven to issue a more drastic order early in February. This extended the classes against whom the Republicans were ordered to take action.[19] The army staff was under the impression that the President had agreed to it. The latter protested:

The C/S was wrong in thinking that I had 'agreed' to the order as a definite decision. I merely indicated that I regarded it as possible that we would be forced to adopt as defensive measures some of the drastic proposals which the Staff meeting had agreed to on the understanding that the execution of the orders would be kept strictly under the control of G.H.Q.—liberty of action not being allowed to subordinate commanders.[20]

In all this correspondence the principal difference between Lynch and de Valera lay in the concentration of the former, naturally enough, on the military problem, while de Valera took more cognisance of the political and human effects. He was more fully aware that an outright military victory for the Republicans was remote and that their ultimate success would depend on the support of the people. He was himself far more sensitive about actions which alienated public opinion than was Lynch, who was faced with the desperate problem of protecting his men against relentless and much stronger forces. De Valera seemed also much more alive to the moral issues involved.

The months of horror through which the country passed during that winter were scarcely conducive to thoughts of peace. De Valera was deeply distressed by the course of events in November and early December. The executions and the actual foundation of the Free State Government, on the basis of the objectionable Constitution, ruled out the compromise which he had hoped for in the preceding months—an amendment to the draft Constitution. He felt that his colleagues, particularly P. J. Ruttledge and Liam Lynch, were too sanguine in their hopes of military success. To them he wrote:

> Unless a large section of the Free State Army can be won over, or the people turn overwhelmingly to support us rather than the Free State, there is little prospect of that type of victory which would enable us to dictate terms. . . . What guerilla warfare leads to is a desire on our opponents' part to come to terms with us provided these terms do not mean complete surrender by him to us, which is unfortunately what we require. I do not believe that men who have now so committed themselves as the present Ministry have will ever be got to throw up their hands and quit. Each one will probably say to himself, like Macbeth
> '. . . I am in blood
> Stepp'd in so far that, should I wade no more,
> Returning were as tedious as go o'er.'[21]

Indeed the blood spilt was a hampering restriction on both sides. The Free State Government had committed itself to a course of action from which there was no retreat and Republicans could not give up an ideal for which Brugha, Childers and, indeed, so many others since 1916, had died. As the President wrote early in February: 'Were we to lose all the lives that have been lost and get nothing of national value it would be awful.'[22]

Nevertheless, the President forced his colleagues to think about the way they proposed that the Civil War would be brought to an end. He did not want a surrender, but he wanted the issues involved properly understood. Without the consent of the army he knew that peace was impossible. In December de Valera was still trying unsuccessfully to obtain the military facts. He realised, however, that in the end everything would depend on winning the allegiance of the people to the Republican Government and in mid-January he wrote:

> This situation has not been brought about by my will, nor could my will end it. It has been brought about by a blind and ruthless disregard of the essentials of peace and it will continue as long as these conditions are wilfully ignored.[23]

'The essentials' as he saw them, lay in the strong feelings of loyalty of a large body of people to the Republic, for which they had fought and for which their comrades had died. It was with full understanding of the feelings of both sides in the conflict that de Valera wrote to Miss Edith Ellis in London:

Alas! Our country has been placed in a cruel dilemma out of which she could be rescued only by gentleness, skill and patience, and on all sides a desire for justice and fair-dealing. Instead we find ourselves in the atmosphere of a tempest—every word of reason is suppressed or distorted until it is made to appear the voice of passion. I have been condemned to view the tragedy here for the last year as through a wall of glass, powerless to intervene effectively. I have, however, still the hope that an opportunity may come my way.[24]

This letter was captured and published, with furious comments, by the Free State Publicity Department. The purpose of the publication of this letter was, apparently, to give the impression that de Valera was shirking responsibility and trying to throw it on other Republicans. In fact he felt that the responsibility lay with those who started the Civil War by attacking the Four Courts. In doing so it seemed to him that they had flouted flagrantly the pact of May and the Dáil itself, thus depriving the Republican deputies of any power to intervene.[25]

The support of the press throughout Ireland was one of the most important factors in the struggle. The Republican Government found it almost impossible to get a platform for their point of view, and this persisted not only during the Civil War but for years afterwards. At all times, however, the President paid considerable attention to Republican propaganda productions—and intervened when he considered that they showed any lack of taste. Given the passions of the time, it is understandable that such lapses should occur, but the President's protests kept them to a minimum. In particular he objected to references made to Seán Hales, the pro-Treaty deputy shot on December 7th, and irritated the Director of Publicity by describing one of his bulletins as

exactly like one of the vile issues of the *Gaelic American* with spy, traitor, English gold, etc., etc., running right through it.

The Director was acid in his reply. He claimed that the word 'traitor' was not in that bulletin at all while the word 'spy' occurred but once and that in reference to an Englishman.[26]

In statements prepared by the President at that time, usually for papers abroad, since he was denied any space in Irish papers, he endeavoured to avoid rancour. To the *Irish World*, in January, he explained that, though those who signed the Treaty did so for the highest motives, they had not realised that the young men who were fighting and daily risking their lives to uphold the Republic, and had seen their comrades die for it, would resist to the death any attempt to disestablish it at England's bidding.

He deplored the 'ever rising tide of bitterness' and 'the lowering of the national credit and prestige' which ensued as 'each tried ruthlessly and recklessly by the policy of blood and iron to extricate themselves and the country from an impossible position'. He blamed those who accepted the Treaty not for acting from dishonourable motives but rather for their failure to foresee the consequences.[27]

From the point of view of the members of the Free State Government the position was, of course, critical. They were fighting for their own existence. By December, 1922, there was little use arguing about who had fired the first shot. Two determined forces were ranged against each other. One was happy to have got the English out of most of Ireland and was willing to fight lest, in going under, the English would come back. The other was not satisfied to accept the occupation of Irish ports, the oath and the trappings of British monarchy. They would prefer to 'risk another round with England' to continue the fight rather than compromise on principle, as they would have to compromise if they accepted the oath. One was out to establish the Free State, the other to smash it.

'We have, of course, to face the possibility of the British forces coming back,' wrote de Valera, 'and taking up the fight where the others lay it down—but God is good.'[28] In fact some felt, rather naïvely, that the return of the British would have the effect of restoring the Irish unity which had existed in the previous struggle.

The hell through which Ireland was passing in that terrible winter roused many people to make efforts to intervene. In December, Frank Fahy, on behalf of a Gaelic League Peace Committee, approached Austin Stack in the hope of arranging a truce. De Valera replied to him, after consulting with Liam Lynch:

> With the views you express, anyone who has an eye to see and a heart to feel must in the main agree, but it is useless to ask Republicans to abandon ideals which I know they will surrender only with their lives.

De Valera wrote to Liam Lynch regarding this peace move that it was their duty to meet halfway every honest effort to bring about peace. Lynch, however, was never able to face the possibility of military defeat and was quite unrealistic in his evaluation of the prospects. He insisted that the Republican position was never stronger. He was more convinced than ever that victory was certain.[29] This undue optimism on Lynch's part made the task of the peacemaker doubly difficult.

It must not be thought that de Valera himself was ready for any kind of peace without conditions. Liam Deasy, the captured Deputy Chief of Staff, allowed a document to go out over his name, addressed to de Valera and other Republican leaders and calling for immediate and unconditional surrender. It expressed views that he had formed before his capture but had not yet had time to broach to his colleagues.

De Valera drafted a reply which Lynch sent to Deasy, in which he was told that his proposals could not be considered. At this very time, indeed, the Republican leaders were planning an extension of the war into England. The common enemy, wrote Lynch, 'is waging war against us, if anything more desperate than before.'[30] De Valera agreed with him here and advised 'the first blow should be concerted and big, followed quickly by a number in succession of other blows.' About the same time he wrote: 'were we to abandon the Republic now it would be a greater blow to our ideals and to the prestige of the nation than even the abandonment on December 6th, 1921. In taking upon ourselves to be champions of this cause we have incurred obligations which we must fulfil even to death.'[31]

Yet even now he did not reject the possibility of constitutional instead of military action against the Treaty, for within a few days he wrote to Liam Lynch:

It has always been my view that with anything like goodwill on both sides a constitutional way out of this impasse could be found. We can best serve the nation at this moment by trying to get the constitutional way adopted. In this matter it is all a question of what the Army is prepared to do. If there were no Army we would, of course, have had to resist this 'Treaty' by other methods.

Of course it seemed an unfortunate time for discussion of peace with so much pressure on the army:

But it is very much better to lead in this peace matter in which the whole country is so interested. If we make a decent peace offer which will command the support of reasonable people the others can't proceed and we shall have a victory.[32]

He had no hopes from indirect peace moves and intermediaries. What he wanted was an honourable minimum solution which the Republican Army could be induced to accept.

THE DARKEST HOUR

March – May, 1923

From February to May de Valera laboured to find a way to peace that did not involve unconditional surrender. On the one hand, he had to bargain with the Free State Government who were becoming ever more conscious of their opponents' military weakness. On the other hand, he had to carry with him the Republican Army leaders, among whom the Chief of Staff, Liam Lynch, displayed a noble-spirited optimism, more and more unrealistic.

The re-emergence of Document No. 2 in February illustrates the difficulties that faced de Valera, caught between two fires. The Free State Government issued a pamphlet which was less than fair to his supposed offer to the British Government of the previous year. In his reply, de Valera argued that peace might still be achieved along the lines of the proposals which he had put forward at the time of the debate on the Treaty. 'The fact that these proposals,' he asserted, 'and my statements have been "twisted by knaves to make a trap for fools" doesn't take away from the truth that is in them.'[1]

But this brought him under attack from his own side. The Republican Army leaders reacted most unfavourably. Liam Lynch, the Chief of Staff, wrote: 'Your publicity as to sponsoring Document No. 2 has had a very bad effect on army and should have been avoided. Generally they do not understand such documents. We can arrange peace without referring to past documents.'[2]

To this de Valera replied, with firmness and indeed bluntness, that he was well aware of the dangers when he made the statement.

Fundamentally, this whole question is a political one and the army will have to do one of two things.
(1) Either be definitely subject to the Government and leave all political matters to the Government within the wide range and the understanding with the Executive on which the Government was formed; or
(2) If they want to deal with the political question, and will not confine themselves to the military one, they will have to think intelligently along political lines and discuss the political problems as they would discuss military ones.

He went on to say that he had been dealing for a number of years now with the political question.

> I believe I know what is and what is not possible, as far as Britain is concerned. At any rate I have fixed it definitely in my own mind as a conviction that is likely to be unshaken by anything that I can foresee within my life, whether it were short, or the normal span, and I will take no further responsibility for publicly handling the situation if I have, at every turn, to account for what I say, to people who have not given a moment's thought to the whole question.

Finally de Valera brought the Chief of Staff back to the harsh realities of the military situation. He wrote:

> With the general policy embodied in 'should we be beaten let us quit', I am in complete agreement. Were we to 'compromise' on any essential we would have proved that we were fighting for party—not defending sacred principles.

There would be difficulties in deciding when they were beaten.

> Many good men have come to the conclusion that we have long ago passed the point at which we should have regarded ourselves as beaten so far as actually securing our objective is concerned. And if you were to hold that the objective was the 'isolated' Republic, I would say they were right.[3]

De Valera sent copies of this letter to each member of his cabinet. P. J. Ruttledge approved of it, but felt that the original statement endorsing Document No. 2 had been unwise since some Republicans who were 'mouthing the enemy's summary criticism' of it would claim that the President had let them down. De Valera answered:

> If you want honest consideration for proposals you must throw them in at a crisis which will give them the necessary prominence. The one thing that I am a convinced believer in is the indestructible character of truth and its certainty of ultimate triumph—bad politics it will be said, but to my mind the policy of fooling the gullible is despicable.[4]

He did not believe in leading the army members to think that the policy of the isolated Republic could win at that time. In fact he doubted if he could even get 'external association'.

De Valera's difficulties were not confined to the army leaders and cabinet members. The strong-willed Mary MacSwiney was uncompromising and her frequent letters occasionally wrung from him strong replies. Differences in their appreciation of the situation were to be expected, and in a letter to her de Valera summed up their respective tendencies.

> My personal equation in that respect, tends somewhat to overestimate the strength and determination of the enemy and somewhat underestimating

our own. The personal equation of all you diehards is the reverse of this, and of the two I have no doubt that an omniscient being would rate my error as but a very small fraction of yours—vanity?[5]

Indeed one of de Valera's most remarkable characteristics, then and later, was a quality of detached judgement. Detailed arguments by letter with Mary MacSwiney tended to accentuate differences and this he wished to avoid. He wrote:

When we get away from academic discussions and come down to the real concrete basis of action there is very little difference, and what differences there are can never be adjusted as long as you are you and I am I.[6]

Throughout these debates their relations were always cordial.

De Valera struggled on, endeavouring to extract from the Republican Army chiefs some basis of agreement for achieving peace. But members of the Free State Government were publicly announcing that they would not make any concessions to Republican feeling. Kevin O'Higgins said in the middle of March, 'This is not going to be a draw with a replay in the autumn.'[7] The Leader of the Free State Government announced: 'De Valera hopes to bring about negotiations which will enable him to make a dignified withdrawal from his present position, but we are not going to help anybody in that way.'[8] De Valera was not in fact concerned with personal dignity, his sole interest was to bring the war to an end on tolerable terms. But the chance of this became ever more remote as things went from bad to worse for the Republicans.

On March 23rd, 1923, a crucial meeting of the Republican Army Executive was organised in the South and, despite the considerable hazards, de Valera was determined to go. After many months confined in Dublin with little exercise, he found the journey, some of it on foot over mountains, a great strain. He rode a horse over the last stages. An IRA intelligence report stated that he had been seen crossing the Comeragh mountains on horseback, with a beard down to his toes!

At daybreak on March 23rd they reached the army headquarters at Bliantasour, high upon the western slopes of the Monavullagh mountains in Waterford. De Valera was not however at first admitted to the meeting. He waited impatiently in another room while the members of the Executive decided whether they would allow him to attend or not. His feelings can be imagined rather than stated, but there was nothing that he could do about it except try to hide his anger.

Eventually a proposal was carried unanimously—that the President of the Republican Government attend the meeting—even though without having been given a vote—and de Valera was called in. But the concentration of Free State forces in the district kept the meeting on the move.

First they all marched back to Lyre, where the meeting was resumed and continued until about 2 a.m. Then they went on into the Nire valley and, with Free State troops reported close by, they had to climb up into the mountains where the meeting was continued in the open. De Valera had with him a half loaf of dry bread. Even when the meeting adjourned and the members dispersed to billets, they could not get to sleep before they were roused and forced to move again.

The meeting lasted from March 23rd to the 27th.[9] But it was inconclusive. A crucial resolution ran 'that in the opinion of the executive further armed resistance and operations against F.S. Government will not further the cause of independence of the country'. This was narrowly defeated by six votes to five; in spite of de Valera's arguments a majority still clung to a phantom hope of mountain artillery becoming available.[10] It was decided to wait a little while to see if the guns would come. Another executive meeting was fixed for April 10th and it was agreed that, in the meantime, de Valera should try and find out what the chances were of securing peace on the basis of his stated principles. He was convinced that at the next executive meeting all hope of artillery would be gone and that peace would have to be accepted.

The journey back to Dublin was even more arduous than the journey out. De Valera's diary gives some idea of what he endured:

March 27th. Left before daylight for Rathgormack. Got drenched to the skin through overcoat, leather jerkin, etc. Wildest night I ever experienced. Falling at every step. Misled by the guide. Ignored stepping stones and walked through the streams. Stuck my left leg into a bog hole up to the groin. Arrived in the morning, clothes and leather jacket all ruined.

At Paulstown, on the way back, they found themselves stopped by Free State soldiers who appeared at the front and rear. Luckily their story was well rehearsed and, despite a barrage of questions, they convinced the officer that they were taking Jack Walsh, one of their number, to visit his dying sister who was supposed to be de Valera's wife. De Valera, bearded, was not recognised and they were allowed to pass with a final warning from the officer: 'It's a dangerous hour of the night to be out.'

Back in Dublin he soon found that the Free Staters were as active as in Waterford. Three nights after his return, he was forced once more to take refuge in a hiding-place under the stairs.[11] Fortunately the secret entrance was beside his bed—even more fortunately it went unnoticed.

Abortive discussions followed with Monsignor Luzio, who had been sent by the Pope to study conditions in Ireland. By April 9th de Valera was writing bluntly to P. J. Ruttledge:

To me our duty seems plain, to end the conflict without delay. . . . The phase begun in 1916 has run its course. . . . Those who would continue working for our independence must gird themselves for a long patient effort of reorganisation and education.[12]

To Austin Stack he was just as frank:

The decision lies between 'a quit' by a governmental proclamation and army order to 'cease fire', or a public pronouncement by the Government of the basis on which it is prepared to make peace.[13]

On the very day that he wrote this letter, the Republican Army suffered a crushing blow in the Knockmealdown mountains. The Chief of Staff, Liam Lynch, was shot and died next day while he and other officers were heading towards a rendezvous for a meeting of the Army Executive. Frank Aiken was appointed to fill Liam Lynch's post for the moment. De Valera was now more determined than ever that peace should be made and wrote to Ruttledge.

This is our darkest hour. Do not let my cold way of putting things depress you. I am confident in the ultimate triumph of our cause. My heart and my desires make almost an agonizing appeal to hold on and defy them as long as a rifle and a cartridge remain, but my head and my conscience tell me it would not be justifiable. I am afraid we shall have to face the inevitable sooner or later, bow to force and resort to other methods, either ourselves or those to whom we leave the future of the cause.[14]

Lest, however, the Republican Army should quail under the blows before peace should be negotiated, de Valera issued a rallying address. Aided by their 'royal allies the hills' they had fought bravely. Faced with the desertion of leaders who would lead them into the Empire, they had flung themselves 'across the stampede of a nation'.

It is better to die nobly as your Chief has died than live a slave. Your cause is immortal. Weariness from the exacting struggle, false teachers, temporary losses and defeats may defer but cannot prevail against its ultimate triumph. The sacrifices you are making will ensure it and they who in ignorance calumniate you today, will tomorrow do you honour.[15]

The end was very near, but one or two final attempts at peace by negotiation had still to be completed. At the end of April, Monsignor Luzio departed with nothing positive accomplished. The unfortunate Monsignor incurred the displeasure of the Free State Government without exactly winning the confidence of de Valera, who wrote shortly afterwards:

He came unfortunately at a bad time for us. The peacemaker has always an almost irresistible temptation to try to effect his object by bringing pressure on the weaker side to give in. I am afraid our visitor was succumbing to it when he should have stood rigidly for impartial justice. However his task was almost superhuman and it is easy to criticise.[16]

His personal reply to a friendly parting message from the Monsignor is worthy of remembrance:

Please give to the Holy Father my dutiful homage. Though nominally cut away from the body of Holy Church we are still spiritually and mystically of it, and we refuse to regard ourselves except as his children.[17]

Though it seemed a failure, the visit of the Monsignor had probably done something to influence the atmosphere in favour of peace when the Republican Army Executive met at Poulacappal on April the 20th. There had been serious losses in the preceding week and the mountain artillery had not come. Liam Lynch's successor as Chief of Staff, Frank Aiken, was no less determined a Republican, but had been convinced of the need for peace. At last de Valera obtained the effective agreement of the Army Executive for peace on certain conditions.

Contact was made with two distinguished public men, Senator Douglas and Senator Jameson, who undertook to see W. T. Cosgrave, President of the Executive Council of the Free State Government. The Republicans had issued a proclamation, announcing that they were ready for peace on conditions, and suspending military operations for the time being. Free State activity did not cease. The execution of two Republican prisoners in Ennis on May 2nd brought the total of Republicans executed by the Free Staters to eighty-two in five and a half months. De Valera had been optimistic until he heard of the Ennis executions. This, if anything, was calculated to force the Republicans to fight to the death. Nevertheless, his conversations with Douglas and Jameson continued and Cosgrave saw the two senators on May 2nd.

But peace was not to be. It was perhaps too much to expect significant concessions from the Free State Government in the existing military situation. There were various points of controversy, including the release of prisoners and the surrender of arms, but the principal obstacle in de Valera's view was to be found in the oath of allegiance. At the finish, Cosgrave ruled out all consideration of it and, indeed, of all de Valera's proposals.

On the night of May 13th to 14th the Republican Government and Army Council met at Tower House, Santry, and de Valera laid bare the situation in all its starkness. It was quite evident the Free State Government wanted submission pure and simple. The only alternatives left were to accept Cosgrave's terms or end the struggle unilaterally by 'simple quit'. The advantage of the latter course was that it did not involve any surrender of principles. The Republican leaders unanimously decided that the Chief of Staff should order the army to cease fire and dump their arms.[18]

The preparation of the order took a little time. De Valera was, in the meantime, roundly abused from a number of quarters. The pro-Treaty press continued to blame him for the Civil War and for his failure to surrender to Cosgrave's ultimatum. Some extreme Republicans were violently opposed to his having taken part in the negotiations at all. With these he dealt firmly, perhaps even abruptly. To one such he wrote:

> I can only state that in any decisions I have to make now, as in the past, I shall be guided by what my intelligence tells me is best and by what my conscience approves of. Those who wish for a different line of action can advise it and take upon themselves the responsibility.[19]

To Mary MacSwiney he also wrote in somewhat similar terms. A few days later he explained to her:

> I *was* angry when I wrote you—angry because your criticism, like the others, was in the air without reference to, or knowledge of, the real situation we have to face. You speak as if we were dictating terms and talk later of a military situation. There is no military situation. The situation now is that we have to shepherd the remnant of our forces out of this fight so as not to destroy whatever hope remains in the future by allowing the fight to peter out ignominiously.[20]

The military weakness of the Republicans was the ruling factor. At this time de Valera wrote to Monsignor O'Hagan, the Rector of the Irish College in Rome, to explain his effort to transfer the contest to the political plane. Peace would come only if the Republicans were not pursued and harried, but the transition was fraught with danger:

> For this most dangerous passage, those who could be of value for the steering are for the most part already arrayed as partisans in hostile camps. The moral leaders especially, whose influence in a crisis like this would be beyond price, have allowed themselves to be so entangled in the conflict that they are now useless.[21]

To Monsignor Luzio he wrote:

> A peace by understanding would be by far the best for our nation and would lead most readily to the 'pacification of minds' which the Holy Father desired and was the object of your recent visit amongst us. Our opponents' will for a military 'triumph' has, however, proved too strong and our proposals have been rejected, even as a basis, on the pretence that they were not sincerely made.

He added of the Irish bishops:

Their failure to condemn the ill-treatment, the torturing and the murder of prisoners, and the inflammatory addresses of some of their members . . . are scarcely worthy of representatives of Him who is Charity . . .

He suggested that the Pope should intervene to ease the bitterness. The impression that the Vatican aimed at keeping Ireland subject to England, or at least not independent of her was, he maintained, widespread and was confirmed by the attitude of the bishops. To attain peace now they should help towards a general amnesty of prisoners and to persuade the Free State Government to adopt 'the open-minded generous policy that is the truest wisdom in a case like this.' He feared that instead vindictiveness would predominate. In particular he asked that the Church give a lead and that all the unjust spiritual penalties such as excommunication, which had been imposed on conscientious Republicans, should be removed immediately.[22]

The sorrow of surrender lay heavily upon de Valera at that time. As he examined the orders which the Chief of Staff had to issue, suggesting amendments where he considered it necessary, he turned his mind to framing a message from himself to the soldiers who had fought for the Republic. He devoted great care to the preparation of it, as to all such documents. Even when it had been prepared he was still not satisfied. He wrote to the Chief of Staff:

Looking over the Address to go with the Order of the Day, it seems to me that it is psychologically bad. I was more or less in the dumps when I wrote it. I have brightened up the second paragraph by pointing out what has been achieved.

In the case of duplication, it should be in the revised form.[23]

The newspapers succeeded in getting copies of the unrevised version and it was published with Aiken's order. In either form it was a stirring document which, while accepting military defeat, promised an alternative means of upholding that to which Republicans had dedicated their all. The message ran:

Soldiers of the Republic, Legion of the Rearguard: The Republic can no longer be defended successfully by your arms. Further sacrifice of life would now be vain and continuance of the struggle in arms unwise in the national interest and prejudicial to the future of our cause. Military victory must be allowed to rest for the moment with those who have destroyed the Republic.

He thanked the men who had 'saved the nation's honour' and 'demonstrated in a way there is no mistaking that we are not a nation of willing slaves.' The people of Ireland would again rally to the standard. 'When they are ready, you will be, and your place will be again as of old with the vanguard.' Finally he warned them of the sufferings they would have to

Countess Markiewicz

Michael Collins

Professor Eóin MacNeill

Arthur Griffith

W. T. Cosgrave

Above: A historic picture of prisoners released by the British, setting foot on Irish soil after disembarking in 1917. De Valera is in the left foreground.

Left: East Clare, 1917. De Valera, in Irish Volunteer officer's uniform, hears of his election as a Sinn Féin member of the Dáil.

This page:
In disguise after the Civil War, de Valera grew a beard. These photographs were taken just before the meeting at Ennis where he was arrested in August 1923. First the beard came off, then the moustache.

Opposite above: The Irish delegation at the Grosvenor Hotel during the meetings with Lloyd George in July, 1921.
Left to right, standing: Count Plunkett T.D., Erskine Childers T.D., Laurence O'Neill, Lily O'Brennan, Dr R. Farnan, Mrs Farnan, Robert Barton T.D., Kathleen O'Connell.
Seated: Eamon de Valera, Arthur Griffith.

Opposite below: De Valera photographed in Limerick on the morning of 6 December 1921. Earlier, unknown to him, the Peace Treaty had been signed in London. Cathal Brugha is on the right.

A remarkable picture of de Valera playing chess with Austin Stack in Arbour
Hill barracks, where he was held after being arrested at Ennis.

Left: Kilmainham Gaol, where de Valera was twice held captive: by the British and the Irish.

Below: De Valera arrested by the Royal Constabulary in Newry, 1924.

Above: De Valera, flanked by P. J. Ruttledge and Gerald Boland, with Countess Markiewicz and other deputies on their way to attempt to take their seats in the Dáil, 1927.

Below: De Valera with members of the first Fianna Fáil cabinet, 1932.

face unarmed. He knew that the peace was one-sided and that vindictive-ness on the part of the Free State Government could start civil war again. He asked them to bear these sufferings 'in a manner worthy of men who were ready to give their lives for their cause.' And in conclusion:

> May God guard every one of you and give to our country in all times of need sons who will love her as dearly and devotedly as you.

The Civil War was ended, on the Republican side at least. The bitter-ness, however, was to last a long time. The dilemma which had been created by the Treaty had not been solved, even in blood. De Valera had been thinking of the American—not the Irish—Civil War when he broadcast to the United States of America from Geneva in 1938:

> The most dangerous war is that which has its origin in just claims denied or in a clash of opposing rights—and not merely opposing interests—when each side can see no reason in justice why it should yield its claim to the other.[24]

In many ways it could apply to the Civil War in Ireland.

DE PROFUNDIS

May, 1923 – July, 1924

The militant course which Irish politics had followed from 1916 onwards had drawn to a close. De Valera had meanwhile been preparing for action on the political plane. It was here that his struggle for the Republic must now be continued. From the end of May, 1923, he devoted much of his attention to the reorganization of Sinn Féin. The Republican Army was not dissolved, but its activities were directed towards political rather than military activities. All officers and men were instructed by Frank Aiken, Chief of Staff, to join Sinn Féin. The nation must be represented by men who possessed the Republican ideals and objectives.

De Valera was determined to keep the young Irish Republicans in the country. There was to be no emigration, despite the sufferings which might follow the ending of the war. 'There must be no wild geese this time', he wrote,[1] obviously thinking of the flight of Sarsfield and his men after the Treaty of Limerick in 1691. A general order to all ranks of the Republican Army forbade Volunteers to leave Ireland without a permit from the divisional O Cs at least.[2] The most urgent task was that of getting the men back as quickly as possible into civil employment. Thousands of Republicans were prisoners or internees. Over 2,000 were on the run, trying to evade arrest.

The danger of captured Republicans being murdered without trial was real. Noel Lemass, arrested in July, 1923, by Free State forces, was not heard of again until his body was found in the Dublin mountains three months later. Some officers wished to destroy all arms in return for an amnesty, but de Valera disagreed. The destruction of arms would take away their last protection. While they still had arms, though they were determined not to use them, the Free Staters might feel that too severe a repression could spark off a new civil war. Other Republican leaders tended towards opposite views. The Chief of Staff, Frank Aiken, had to be restrained from allowing himself to be captured by Free State troops. He was anxious to share the trials of the men in prison and to lead them in the hunger strike which he intended to initiate. As a senior officer he felt that he should set an example in the front line. De Valera, however, persuaded him that his duty lay outside and that it was more important to organise an employment and relief bureau.[3]

By July, 1923, a general election was at hand. A convention of Sinn Féin delegates sent a message from Ennis town hall, asking de Valera to stand for their constituency as their unanimous first choice.[4] At the same time the Free State Minister for External Affairs, Desmond Fitzgerald, announced, 'As long as we are in power de Valera and every other enemy of the country will have to be on the run.'[5] De Valera answered Sinn Féin delegates and Desmond Fitzgerald at the same time:

> . . . living or dead, we mean to establish the right of Irish Republicans to live and work openly for the complete liberation of our country. Our opponents make a mistake if they imagine that we are going to remain on the run. If the people of Clare select me as their candidate again I will be with them and nothing but a bullet will stop me.[6]

He was fully aware, of course, of the dangers of appearing in the open. It was said that some of the most vigorous members of the Free State CID, known to the Republicans as 'The Murder Gang', were being roused to assassinate him by being told that he personally had planned Collins's death. De Valera wrote to Mrs Childers, the widow of one who was in his eyes the finest man he had ever met in politics:

> There is of course danger, but I think it is wise nevertheless. . . . I do not err as a rule on the rash side—but I can face the inevitable. The others wanted to come out too but I have forbade that. A reserve must be kept. The M.H.A. [Minister for Home Affairs] will be my substitute.[7]

Before setting out for Clare, de Valera took the precaution of formally appointing his substitute 'until my return or until a new President is elected'. He also drafted a statement which Ruttledge, as acting-President, should issue if he had to take up office. It was designed to counter the Free State claim that the election was genuinely democratic. Of de Valera it was proposed to say:

> The manner of his arrest and renewed harassing of Republicans finally dispose of the claim that the election is free. Such recreant methods will not intimidate faithful citizens of the Republic or bend the unyielding spirit of Irish Independence.

The great publicity which was given to de Valera's forthcoming meeting at Ennis was, in some ways, a protection. While it made the journey to Clare more hazardous, it meant that his place of meeting would be closely watched by the Free State Army. This would make unofficial action difficult. De Valera was advised, however, that 'if possible the meeting should be held in some open place away from houses'.[8]

De Valera felt that by coming out of hiding he would definitely transfer the struggle from the military to the political field. He believed that the Irish people wanted absolute freedom and, under fair conditions, he felt that they would not fear to say so. The conditions in August, 1923, seemed to him far from fair. But in the Sinn Féin manifesto he asked them at all costs to be brave. He had always felt that one of the most degrading events in Irish history had been the submission of princes and prelates to Henry II at the time of the early Normans.

De Valera was up early on August 12th. Among last-minute tasks he made his Will. Then he set out for Clare, guided by an IRA officer, Seán Hyde, who had circulated the rumour that de Valera intended to make the journey by sea. Keeping mainly to the north of the Dublin–Limerick road, they made their way unobtrusively to Toomyvara and Kilcommon and across O'Brien's Bridge over the Shannon, then through the gap at the southern end of the Slieve/Bernagh mountains and on to Knockanira, about five miles south-west of Ennis. De Valera would have preferred to be nearer the meeting-place, to avoid interception next day. Luckily it was decided in the end not to move to a house beside the square in Ennis. It was raided by Free Staters that night.

Tactically it was important, de Valera thought, if he were arrested, that it should be on the platform. His arrest would prove to all that the election was not a free one. If he were arrested beforehand, it might be claimed that he had no intention of coming out of hiding. No doubt for this reason, Free State troops, under the command of Colonel Fallon, were ordered to effect the arrest before he appeared in public. 'Unfortunately he got to the stage before being recognized,' reported a Free State officer that evening.[9] De Valera had, the night before, shaved off his beard. His moustache, too, had come off. He was not going to appear in disguise among the people of Clare.

They gathered in their thousands to greet him and, punctually on the afternoon of August 15, the Feast of Our Lady, he was driven quickly in an open car to the square in Ennis, a crossroads at the business centre of the town. The platform faced the O'Connell memorial. As he mounted the platform, the rousing cheers told the Free State troops that they had been outwitted. The excitement was intense and became overpowering when Colonel Fallon ordered an officer to take a party of soldiers to arrest de Valera on the platform. He had spoken only a few words when firing broke out and the square became a scene of utter confusion.

De Valera, standing at the front of the platform, did not know where the firing was coming from, though he could see the Free Staters in an armoured-car coming through the crowd. A sharp pain in the left leg made him grip the rail of the platform more tightly. He thought his shin-bone had been broken by a bullet. Those on the platform behind him pulled him backwards among them. Gradually the pain eased and life returned to his numbed leg. He rose amid renewed cheering and was able to make his way down the steps to the soldiers and to walk to the barracks with the officers who arrested him. There he examined his leg, to find a small blob of blood beside his shin bone. Forty years later an X-ray revealed that a piece of a bullet, probably from a ricochet, had lodged in the muscle of his leg. What interested de Valera most of all was that he could find no tear in the leg of his trousers.

De Valera did not think that he would be executed out of hand so long after the Civil War had ended. He thought that there might be a state trial. Indeed he was hoping for an opportunity of that kind to expose the various fabrications which some supporters of the Free State were continually enunciating from their platforms, but which they would hesitate to repeat under oath. If there were to be a trial, de Valera was determined that it should not be of himself alone but of the whole system which brought the Free State into existence. Immediately after the arrest, it appeared to have been the intention of the Free State Government to bring him to trial. The Attorney-General was instructed to pursue the matter and the Minister for Defence was asked to make all relevant evidence available. Hugh Kennedy, the Attorney-General, showed no anxiety to press for an immediate trial and was not much impressed by the evidence which the Department of Defence could muster.[10]

In the meantime, Mrs de Valera was anxiously seeking information regarding her husband. To the Adjutant-General of the Free State forces she sent telegram after telegram, with no result. She telephoned his office several times without success until, on August 23rd, she received a telegram that he was in Arbour Hill. She wrote to Kathleen O'Connell:

I was at Arbour Hill today and gave a letter and a cardigan jacket and shirt to Dev. I was told the letter would be given to him after it was sent to G.H.Q. to be censored. But I was told he cannot write to me. I want to make a parcel of his things tomorrow and bring them up.

Then, thoughtful of others who might take rash action to free her husband, she wrote:

For goodness sake don't let anyone take dangerous risks for D's. sake. Write again if you cannot call. I know your poor heart is broken. I, too, am anxious but keep on at the prayers.[11]

That letter was written on polling day in the General Election, before results that were to bring some renewed hope to the sad hearts of the Republicans. In Clare, de Valera headed the poll with more than twice as many first preference votes as his nearest rival, MacNeill. He had received 17,762 votes against MacNeill's 8,196.

Meanwhile in Arbour Hill prison, de Valera was cut off from events outside and was under strict detention. Four Free State army commandants were assigned to guard him in shifts of eight hours each. Mrs de Valera and her eldest son, Vivion, now approaching his thirteenth birthday, came occasionally to the gate with parcels and messages, but were not allowed to see him. He had books to read and study, and the officer sometimes gave Mrs de Valera lists of things which he needed.

One day in October, without warning, he was transferred to Kilmainham Jail, where he had been sent after his court-martial seven years before. He was put in a separate wing from other prisoners; a military policeman guarded the entrance door. Exercise was allowed for one hour each morning and afternoon, but the hours had to vary from day to day lest an escape be planned. He was not allowed to take exercise in any part of the prison where he might be seen by anybody other than the officer on duty. The latter was also the only person to whom de Valera was supposed to talk. Any books which he might receive had to be approved by the Adjutant-General before he could keep them. He was allowed to receive two letters, and to send out two, each week—an improvement on the position in Arbour Hill—but of course they continued to be censored by the military.

Occasionally he would chat with those in charge of him. When one of them cut, in block letters, the name MICK COLLINS over his cell door with the point of a bayonet his schoolmaster's heart was saddened. There were three errors in it. The capital 'i's were dotted and the diagonal of the 'N' was drawn in the wrong direction and the 'S' reversed. He decided to teach the lieutenant how to form his letters!

De Valera remained in solitary confinement, but the solitude itself did not disturb him—a significant facet of his character. To his secretary he wrote:

I am very lonely of course at times and anxious about Sinéad [his wife] and the family but I have no end of work to do.

Among the tasks he attempted was the writing of a book on the adaptation of Gregg shorthand to Irish. He had studied the system and hoped to co-operate with Kathleen O'Connell in preparing the book. Before they had got far, however, he learned that a book by another on the subject had been completed. He was eager, too, to renew his mathematical studies and he asked his secretary to send into prison all his notebooks except those dealing with arithmetic, together with a number of books by Goursat, Niewenglowski, Bromwich and Darboux.

If you want to make me happy, he wrote, send me all of them. It will be living life over again going through them and picking out what is of use. . . . It will be like making the acquaintance of old friends again and what I have forgotten will come back through them more quickly than in any other way.

The number of books he asked for would have been sufficient to keep him working for more than a year and he remarked:

I am afraid Sinéad has grown cynical about my relation to books, and will think this only another of my whims. . . . The privilege of being in jail is that one can ask to be indulged in whims of this sort. I'll be shut off as completely as if I were on another planet and these books, old or new, the only friends at hand.[12]

In the spring he was moved again to Arbour Hill where, according to Vivion, his eldest son, he had better opportunities of studying mathematics than at any time since his youth. His original post-graduate studies with a view to an M.A. had been undertaken under Professor A. W. Conway, who introduced him to quaternions. Thereafter, says Vivion, he had a special interest in Hamilton's work. Then intervened the Gaelic League, the Volunteers and the various ups and downs of his public life. Now, in prison again, he went back to his old interests, especially quaternions.

As time went on, the Free State Government had begun releasing prisoners. Within Arbour Hill, at the end of April, 1924, there was a relaxation in the rules under which de Valera was held. The time for exercise was extended from two to four hours daily, and he was allowed to see Austin Stack and another prisoner, Keegan, during these hours. Though they do not appear to have availed themselves of it, the three were also allowed to meet in a locked cell each evening for a couple of hours. Neither de Valera nor Stack knew much about their colleague, nor why he was picked out for detention with them. They found, however, that he was a good chess player.

Newspapers became more freely available. From the end of June, Mrs de Valera and one of her children were allowed to visit her husband daily. Within the legislature of the Free State, considerable pressure was maintained to secure the release of all political prisoners, and hopes were raised that this event could not be long delayed.

De Valera's mother, in the United States, added to the clamour. She went to Washington to see members of Congress about his continued imprisonment and was the guest-of-honour at a large gathering of the American Association for the Recognition of the Irish Republic. His wife waited patiently. She and her children (by now there were seven) had moved from Greystones to a house in Claremount Road, Sandymount. She wrote to Kathleen O'Connell: 'I am happiest, as you know, when I have them all round me.' She betrayed her thoughts of her husband and of the rumours which were circulating when she said:

I wonder when will we get any good news. . . . I hope something will bring about some good luck. I'll believe he's coming out when I see him.[13]

After months of waiting, he was released on the evening of July 16th, 1924.

Part III

1924 - 1939

THE LONG WAY BACK

IN SEARCH OF A PATH

1924 – 1926

The pro-Treaty elements which went to make up the Government party included disparate elements, ranging from 'stepping-stone' Republicans to conservative ex-Unionists.

But the Republicans themselves were full of potential conflicts. Even before the election and his arrest, there was a difference in outlook between de Valera and Mary MacSwiney as regards attendance of elected deputies at the Dáil. For Mary MacSwiney, and for many other Republicans, entry into the Free State legislature would involve the recognition of an institution completely British in origin. Abstention for them was a principle. De Valera, on the other hand, while not admitting the legitimacy of the Free State legislature, conceded that its recognition by the majority of the Irish people gave it a *de facto* title. So long as the oath of allegiance was administered to members, it effectively excluded him from attendance. But, if the oath were disposed of, he saw no reason in principle why Republicans should not take their seats. Perhaps his absence in prison allowed the more rigid view to take firmer roots. At any rate when de Valera was released in July, 1924, he found the 'Mary MacSwiney' line well established, and a tougher problem ahead of him.

The tide, however, now showed some signs of turning in the Republicans' favour. It was a long time since an Irish bishop had had a good word to say for them when the newly consecrated Bishop of Clonfert, Dr Dignan, forecast at Loughrea that Republicans would soon be returned to power. No wonder Donal O'Callaghan, Republican Minister for Foreign Affairs, wrote: 'Our stock is rising! . . . We're getting quite respectable again.'[1]

A number of questions which Ruttledge had postponed until de Valera was free to give his advice on them were, however, pressingly urgent.

The point of view of the Republicans was that the Second Dáil had never been dissolved. By August, 1924, however, there was an air of fantasy in keeping it in existence. Those who had favoured the Treaty had left it in favour of the Provisional Parliament of September, 1922; while because of deaths there was a gradual decline in the number of Republicans available. Yet the fiction died hard.

At a meeting of all the elected Republican deputies and all the Republican survivors of the Second Dáil on August 7th and 8th, 1924, a suggestion of de Valera's was adopted. 'For formal acts on account of continuity . . . it would be wiser to regard the Second Dáil as the *de jure* government and legislature, but the whole body of elected members, including those just returned, should act as the Council of State and be the actual government of the Country.'[2]

The title Comhairle na dTeachtaí, or Council of Deputies, was given to the larger and more important body. The minutes record:

> The President declared that our policy was to preserve, as far as we can, the Republic—to keep it continually before the minds of the people, and to try to get them to renew the mandate given in 1918. We should help the people economically, yet not stabilize the present Free State position.

The Cabinet was to consist of de Valera, as President, Austin Stack, Minister for Home Affairs and for Finance, Art O'Connor, Minister for Economic Affairs and Local Government, and Frank Aiken, Minister for Defence. The President was also to be Minister for Foreign Affairs, while P. J. Ruttledge and Robert Barton were included as Ministers without Portfolio.

One decision illustrated the evasions imposed by the time. It was decided that members of the army who went on public platforms were not to say that there would be further war or that there would be no further war. They were not to mention war at all.[3]

The new Cabinet formally took office but, in the circumstances, it could do little, if anything. The total finances were negligible as compared with what had been available to the Cabinet of the Dáil between 1919 and 1921. Indeed, the whole Emergency Government was but a shadow.

De Valera addressed his first public meeting outside Dublin since his release in dramatic circumstances. He selected Ennis as the place, and the anniversary of his arrest there as the date. Mrs de Valera was invited to attend, but she declined. She would do exactly as she had done the year before; go to the chapel to pray that all would be well. In the disturbed circumstances of the time there was little knowing what might happen.[4]

At Ennis, de Valera was accorded a tremendous reception on the platform, which had been the scene of violence exactly a year before. There was a touch of irony in his opening words. Volunteers from the three Clare and two South Galway brigades had marched in procession past the saluting-base and formed a cordon around the platform.

'I am afraid,' said de Valera, 'I would disappoint a number here if I were not to start by saying, "Well as I was saying to you when we were interrupted".' Circumstances had changed, but his fundamental principles were unaltered:

> The Sovereignty of Ireland . . . cannot possibly be given away by Irish Republicans. We can never give allegiance to any foreign power or to any foreign people. These are the basic principles on which we stand. Things may be forced upon us, we may have temporarily to submit to certain things, but our assent they can never have. . . . Don't forget for a moment that there is a vast difference between patiently submitting, when you have to, for a time, and putting your signature to a consent or assent to these conditions.

Unity among all sections of the Irish people behind the demand for freedom was necessary to achieve that freedom. The only basis on which such unity could be established had been demonstrated in 1917 when the constitution of Sinn Féin had been revised. The aim of Sinn Féin still held good:

> To secure international recognition of an Irish Republic, it being understood that, having achieved that status the Irish people may, by referendum, freely choose their own form of government.

This was de Valera's answer to the charge of being undemocratic:

> We realise the difficulties of uniting in the cause of freedom. We know that in such a fight there has to be a vanguard, and we know that very often it is only a few choice spirits who can form that vanguard. It was a recognition of that that made us stand out in denial of the fact that elections held as these past elections were held could determine the form of government or freedom that the Irish people wanted.

The next sentence represented his deepest conviction.

> When you are free to determine that, without any pressure from England, or from any outside power, when the form you choose will be the expression truly of your own free will, then we are certainly ready to bow down our heads before it.[5]

The partition of the country was becoming more and more a pressing issue. In his weekend speeches in various parts of the country he reverted to it increasingly. At Dundalk he said:

> You see the so-called Treaty in operation now. . . . Remember, even those who took that Treaty should have had common sense enough to see that that Treaty left three things to the future. It left the constitution of Ireland to the future, and remember that when these foolish men in Dáil Éireann voted for it they thought they would have a Republican constitution. Later on, when it was too late, when they were committed, they were undeceived. . . Not merely was the question of the Constitution left over but there was left over the most important matter of all—the question of political boundaries

within this county. . . . There is also left to the future the question of the financial relations between the two countries. There is not a word of that question just now. But if we should be so unfortunate, if we should be so blind to our own interests, as not to act as if that Treaty did not exist, then, I tell you, very soon you will be up against the realities of that question as today you are up against the realities of Article 12.[6]

Article 12 was the section of the Treaty under which a boundary commission was supposed to define the limits of the jurisdiction of the Belfast Parliament which had opted out of the Free State. Without that clause, Lord Birkenhead had said that the Treaty never would have been signed.

De Valera was still an elected representative of Down, one of the separated counties, though he no more attended the Belfast Parliament than that of the Free State. He soon put the position to the test. On September 1st, 1924, the Minister for Home Affairs in Belfast, Dawson Bates, signed an order prohibiting him from entering not only his constituency of Down but any part of the partitioned area except Co. Antrim. The six counties were still entitled to send members of Parliament to Westminster and a general election was pending. De Valera issued a statement that elections were the only means available of making the wishes of the people clearly known. Abstention from a foreign parliament should not preclude people from registering their views. He was bitterly attacked for splitting the nationalist poll, whereas his intention was that all nationalist opinion, whether Republican or not, should be recorded. In the event, the pro-Treaty nationalists pinned their faith on the Boundary Commission, put up no candidates and issued an official statement advising their followers not to vote at all. At the same time, Dawson Bates announced publicly that de Valera would be arrested if he entered the six counties. Four days later the newspapers carried the news that de Valera was to tour the North.[7]

It was typical of de Valera that he should disregard the threat, just as he had disregarded the threat at Ennis the year before. He knew that he was likely to be imprisoned, but he would do all in his power to speak to his Down constituents. When he arrived at the hall in Newry, where the meeting was being held, on the evening of Friday, October 24th, he was arrested by members of the Royal Ulster Constabulary and detained for the night. The next day he was put across the border, having been served with the order prohibiting his entry.

But he was not to be disposed of so easily. Off he went to Sligo where he announced to a public meeting that he would reassert the right of free speech in Derry. He was interrupted by Free State troops searching some of the crowd. On he went to Derry, slipping across the well-guarded border despite the attentions of the police. But he was arrested again on his way to the platform and taken by rail the next day to Belfast. A hostile Orange mob was at the railway station when he arrived under police escort. It was reported that he would be released once the election was over in three days' time. Protests were sent to the British Prime Minister, Ramsay MacDonald, against his detention when he was contesting an election; they had no effect.

On Saturday, November 1st, de Valera was charged before a magistrate with contravening the order which prohibited him from crossing the border. He refused to recognise the court and was sentenced to one month's imprisonment. It was to be an unpleasant month—the most rigorous incarceration which he ever suffered. The jail at Belfast had not the reputation of Dartmoor, but de Valera found the actual conditions more severe. He was in solitary confinement, under constant surveillance. Obviously he was not going to be allowed to repeat his Lincoln achievement. On November 28th he was taken to a small railway station a mile or so from the border and put on the train for the next station.

Almost at once he was back at work, seeking all the time to convince the Irish people that no path to freedom could be found in adherence to the Treaty. The straight and firm road of the Republican was the only way which could give national unity and strength. At Gorey he pointed out the failure of those who had accepted the Treaty to get from it what they had promised.

Where is their stepping-stone now? They will soon have forgotten that they ever had such an idea. The stepping-stones have been too slippery and they have slipped off. When I think of it, I think of what used to be in some of the old Irish tales about stepping-stones. 'Fuair siad san na clocha. Fuair sinne an t-áth. Do bádh iad san. Do thainig sinne slán.' I am certain it will be so with the Republicans. *They* looked for the stepping-stones and were drowned. *We* found the ford and we came safe.[8]

The method of progress by exhortation, however, was slow and difficult, though de Valera was pleased with the movement of public opinion as shown in the by-elections. This trend in five constituencies was confirmed by a further series of nine by-elections in March, 1925. The Republicans again won two seats from the Government, making a total of forty-eight Sinn Féin deputies who absented themselves from the Free State Parliament.

Yet inevitably, by staying out of the legislature, they were failing to make the impression which their numbers warranted on public affairs. The objections to entering the Dáil were of two kinds; one rested on the alleged illegality of the Dáil itself, the other on the requirement of an intolerable oath. De Valera, while sympathising with the first position, had for a long time occupied the second in his heart. Soon after the end of the Civil War in 1923, he had come to see the oath of allegiance as the one real obstacle to entry into the Free State Parliament.

Politically de Valera could see all too easily the danger of a rigid adherence to the Republican theoretic position. Though the *de jure* authority of the Republic still existed, its *de facto* position was becoming weaker and more unreal. To him it was quite apparent that to remain as they were meant ultimate extinction as an effective political force—reduced to some such position as that of the French monarchists.[9] In any case, there was no question of entering the Free State assembly immediately, even if the oath were removed. At the moment Republican deputies were committed to a policy of abstention by their previous public statements; a change of attitude could not become effective until after a general election and a fresh mandate. Since an election was not immediately pending there was no need to rush a decision on the issue.

In its own weakness the Emergency Government was unable to attract the complete loyalty of the army, which by now had some tradition of independence. Indeed the army tried to assert its control over the political organisation. But de Valera was firm in his refusal to give way to the military. He wrote:

> The discussion of political matters is properly not one for General Head-quarters Staff, and ought never to have been introduced at a Staff meeting. The Headquarters Staff, as such, should confine itself strictly to military matters. Political questions, so far as they affect the Army, are matters for the Army Council to advise the Government on.[10]

To combine the position of Minister for Defence and Chief of Staff was becoming impossible. Frank Aiken decided to resign from the former to concentrate on the latter. He recommended that a suitable successor be appointed Minister for Defence as soon as possible. At the same time he and de Valera, as members of the Army Council, signed an agreement, the first clause of which recognised clearly enough 'That the Government was accepted as the controlling authority for the Army.'[11] A few days later Seán Lemass was appointed Minister for Defence in a temporary capacity. But the difficulties were far from over.

An Irish Republican Army convention was held and a new constitution adopted. Under it the army was to be independent of the Emergency Government—it was, in fact, a casting aside of all semblance of governmental control. In effect the army was going its own way and men like the Chief of Staff, Frank Aiken, were not going with it. Aiken wrote to the Army Council making his position clear.

I will insist on my right to advocate when I think fit, outside Volunteer work, any honourable political policy for strengthening the nation to achieve independence.[12]

At the same time, however, rumours and events in connection with the Boundary Commission were strengthening the desire of others to enter the Free State legislature.

The resignation of Professor Eoin MacNeill, the Free State representative on the Commission, on November 20th, confirmed the worst fears. With great haste, Free State ministers went to London to settle the crisis, and early in December entered into an agreement that the boundary remain unaltered. Combined with this decision were two others, one abolishing the Council of Ireland, an advisory body which had been envisaged under the Government of Ireland Act of 1920, and another releasing the Irish Free State from any liability under Clause V, the financial clause of the Treaty. Thus was to end the promise of the Boundary Commission—in absolute failure and grievous disappointment.

De Valera was utterly incensed with the agreement. He issued an appeal to the Irish people:

When Eoin MacNeill resigned I had hoped that no Irishman, North or South, would be found prepared to put his hand to an instrument dismembering his country; but now that such Irishmen have been found my only hope is that the people will not consent to it.[13]

But he could not agree to taking an oath and breaking his pledges in order to enter the Dáil. In any case, he doubted whether the attendance of Republican deputies at the Free State Parliament would have actually brought down the Government. The highest number of votes registered against the Government at any stage of the boundary crisis was twenty. Even if forty-seven Republicans were added to that number it would not have been a majority of the House.

On December 7th, de Valera invited all the elected Republican deputies to be present at a meeting, called by the Leader of the Labour Party, at the Shelbourne Hotel the next morning:

I welcome the opportunity which I hope the meeting will afford of reuniting the people of all parties throughout the country in effective opposition to partitioning our motherland.

The meeting had no positive result. He and the Republicans withstood the requests of the Labour leaders to enter Leinster House. Instead, on the day on which Parliament met to debate the second reading of the Government proposals, the Republican deputies met at the Rotunda in Dublin.

'In another place tonight,' said de Valera, 'other representatives of the people have met to decide whether or not they will give their consent to the Partition of our country. The sanction of our consent that partition could never have.'[14] Then each deputy signed a protest:

> In the name of the Irish nation and the Irish race, in the name of all who have stood, and will yet stand unflinchingly for the Sovereign Independence of Ireland, we, the duly elected representatives of the Irish people, by our names appended hereto, proclaim and record our unalterable opposition to the partitioning of our country.

It was an ineffectual protest, but at least it represented the detestation of partition felt by the vast majority of Irish people, whatever their party. It represented de Valera's own undying objection. To undo partition would always be one of his major aims:

> It is hard to be calm when one remembers that it is our fairest province that is being cut off. The Ulster that the Irishman of every province loves best next to his own. The Ulster of Cuchulain, the Ulster of the Red Branch Knights. The Ulster of the O'Neills and the O'Donnells. The Ulster of Benburb and the Yellow Ford. The Ulster in whose sacred sod rest the bones of Patrick, Columcille and Brian of the Tributes.[15]

On partition, he and all other Republicans were at one; but the contrasting attitudes to attendance at the Dáil could not be covered up indefinitely. De Valera was preparing by now a large new initiative, though still anxious to educate his party as tactfully as possible. At the Ard Fheis he came right into the open and moved to resolve:

> That once the admission oath of the 26-County and Six-County assemblies is removed, it becomes a question not of principle but of policy whether or not Republican representatives should attend these assemblies.

This was the crucial test and de Valera did not at that time prevail. Father Michael O'Flanagan moved an amendment to the effect that it was incompatible with the fundamental principles of Sinn Féin 'to send representatives into any usurping legislature set up by English law in Ireland.' This amendment was carried by a narrow majority, 223 votes to 218. The next day de Valera announced his resignation as President of Sinn Féin, a position he had held since 1917.

There was not an immediate severance. De Valera and Mary MacSwiney in fact issued a joint message to 'Ireland's friends abroad' that 'Whilst differing in policy we are united in our determination to break the alien power. We ask our friends to take no hasty action.' Indeed, before the adjournment of the Ard Fheis, Father O'Flanagan proposed that the delegates should express their admiration of de Valera. Mary MacSwiney seconded this motion and according to the official report:

The Ard Fheis . . . tried to express by acclamation the deep love and gratitude which each member feels for the man who was described by one delegate as the greatest Irishman for a century.[16]

But the majority of the delegates had taken one decision; de Valera another. Henceforth the ways must part.

FOUNDING A NEW PARTY

1926 – 1927

The time was propitious for a fresh departure. The Free State Government had lost considerably by the Boundary Commission débâcle and a few of its supporters had broken away to found a new party, Clann Éireann. At first it was reported that de Valera and his followers would join it but, in an interview on April 13th, he firmly quashed the rumour:

> The fact is that we are ourselves forming a new organisation. . . . We believe the Republicans ought not to stand aside and allow the country to be utterly ruined, and all except the Imperialists to be driven out of it. We are convinced besides that the ideal of the majority of the Irish people is still broadly the Republican ideal—an Ireland united, free and Irish—and that the people can be banded together for the pursuit of that ideal if a reasonable programme based on the existing conditions be set before them. We intend at any rate to make trial and see.

The next day the provisional organising committee of the new organisation, named Fianna Fáil, issued a circular, asking all who were willing to help in forming branches to communicate with the secretaries.

The choice of name for the new organisation was significant: it indicated a continuity with the movement that had started with the founding of the Irish Volunteers in 1913. The official Irish title of that body had been Óglaigh na hEireann but they were often called by Irish speakers Fianna Fáil and the initials 'F.F.' were incorporated in the Volunteer badge which continued to be used even by the Free State Army. The title had an even older origin, since it was applied to an ancient Irish military organisation of the early sagas. In brackets after the title was the description 'Republican Party'.

On April 17th de Valera gave an interview to a representative of the United Press in which he set out the party's aims:

> The new Republican organisation, Fianna Fáil, has for its purpose the re-uniting of the Irish people and the banding of them together for the tenacious pursuit of the following ultimate aims, using at every moment such means as are rightly available.
>   1. Securing the political independence of a united Ireland as a Republic.

2. The restoration of the Irish language, and the development of a native Irish culture.

3. The development of a social system in which, as far as possible, equal opportunity will be afforded to every Irish citizen to live a noble and useful Christian life.

4. The distribution of the land of Ireland so as to get the greatest number possible of Irish families rooted in the soil of Ireland.

5. The making of Ireland an economic unit, as self-contained and self-sufficient as possible, with a proper balance between agriculture and other essential industries.

He pointed out the need for an acceptable parliament, representative of all the Irish people:

> The Free State Assembly might be used as a nucleus for such an assembly, were it not that the oath of allegiance to the King of England was posed as a political test on all who become members of that assembly. That oath no Republican will take, for it implies acceptance of England's right to overlordship in our country. The Free State oath is then the primary barrier to national unity, and must go if unity is to be attained. The removal of it is the immediate political objective of the new organisation.[1]

Once again the oath was being isolated by de Valera as the first point of attack.

At a large meeting in the La Scala Theatre in Dublin, beside the General Post Office, which ten years before had been the scene of the reading of the Proclamation of the Republic by P. H. Pearse, de Valera publicly launched his new party. He at once adverted to the question as to whether the oath was really an oath in the theological sense:

> For me, it is enough that it is called an 'oath' officially and that it begins with 'I do solemnly swear', and that whenever it suits it will be held to be an oath by those who impose it and will be so understood by the world. I say if it is not an oath why not do away with the mockery? Why not end the whole of this abominable prevarication at once? Why retain it as an instrument for our national and moral degradation and set it as a headline for lying and perjury for the whole country?

He added, indeed, that even if it were not an oath, or in the form of an oath at all—if it were no more than a simple declaration owning allegiance to a foreign power, his opposition to it would not cease.[2]

The forces with which he had to contend, however, were strong. He wrote to Austin Ford, the editor of the *Irish World* in New York:

> The hardest thing to fight against is the weariness and apathy of the people after the long struggle, and the miserable economic condition of the country. Our friends are mostly the poorer section who have suffered most. They

would be quite unable to contribute anything substantial in the way of funds. We are starting here quite empty-handed.[3]

Friends in America were standing by to help the organisation, which gave new hope to Irish Republicans. In May the first subscription of £50 came to Fianna Fáil from the Benjamin Franklin Council in Cleveland, Ohio. It was November before the flow of American support became substantial, with contributions from W. P. Lyndon of Chicago, the treasurer of the American Association for Recognition of the Irish Republic, making up the biggest part of the money. Obviously American assistance could be counted upon, despite Joe McGarrity's pessimistic view that 'no one seems to be willing to help or oppose any side. Frequent disappointments have, I suppose, made them indifferent.'[4]

During the summer and autumn of 1926, the building up of the new party took most of de Valera's time and energy. There were difficulties with those Republicans who had refused to follow his lead; and a demand that those deputies who accepted his policy should resign their seats. De Valera decided to go to Clare to meet his constituents on June 29th. The crowd was enthusiastic, and he cried out to loud applause:

I stand for the Irish Republic, for the full freedom of Ireland, as thoroughly today as I stood nine years ago when I first came before you.

But he warned them that they must face the facts of the existing situation:

If we do not recognise the facts, we cannot make progress. For the moment we have been driven out of the citadel and I am asking our people to attack it again and retake it. I cannot rally the people to a fresh attack if I keep on shouting that I have got the citadel already.

They had to admit, he went on, that there was not a square yard in this country that they could hold and say 'here the Republic exists and no foreign force can drive us out of it'. There was a time a few years ago when they could say that.

But having been driven out of it the task is to win it back and I say we can win back the whole of the country for the Republic if we set about it in the right way and do not hamper ourselves with artificial restrictions.

Concentrating his attack on the oath, he made a point of Clare's part in winning Catholic emancipation in 1829:

Clare had smashed another oath before, and they would now smash the oath of allegiance. If people said they were making too much of the oath, he would remind them of the Oath of Supremacy in former times. To take that would have been a denial of their religious faith and they had refused to take it although it would have helped them materially. The oath of allegiance was a denial of their national faith and they should start out now and smash it.[5]

It was indeed a powerful appeal to local pride on a national issue.

He had no intention of resigning his seat. Why should he? He was utterly convinced that he was not breaking faith with those who had elected him. Republicans, however, who had stayed with Sinn Féin tried to tie him down to specific guarantees as to his future policy. But he was not easily snared.

> To pledge ourselves at this distance ahead as to every step we shall take, and the moment we shall take it, would be absurd. The extent of our majority, the state of public feeling, and a number of other factors determining the tactics of the situation cannot be gauged until the exact moment has arrived, and all the circumstances are fully known.[6]

On November 24th, 1926, Fianna Fáil held its first Ard Fheis. The date chosen had a particular significance—it was the fourth anniversary of the execution of Erskine Childers. In his speech to the Ard Fheis de Valera took up one particular aspect of the political situation at that time. This was the danger of civil war if constitutional means of obtaining liberty were ruled out. He had given the same warning in the maligned speeches which he had made in March, 1922. He warned this time:

> It is vain to think that the natural aspirations of Irishmen for the liberty of their country are going to be stifled now. If the road of peaceful progress and natural evolution be barred, then the road of revolution will beckon and will be taken. Positive law and natural right will be involved in the old conflict. The question of majority rule and minority right will be again bloodily fought out, and when the fight is over it will probably be found out once more that the problem has remained and that force is not the solution.[7]

De Valera was unanimously elected president of the new organisation by the delegates and in that capacity took the chair at meetings of the national executive of Fianna Fáil in the weeks which followed.

The completion of the organisation throughout the country was a prime concern. A general election was expected during 1927. He was under no illusions about the difficulty of obtaining a successful outcome of his policy. He wrote to Joe McGarrity:

> As to the hope of winning through elections, it is not a question of a *choice* of methods—there is no other method at the moment. The acceptance of the 'Treaty' created a situation such as we have never had in Irish history before. The essence of that situation is that we now *appear* to be governed by the wishes of the people as determined by the majority. This is the barrier to freedom that I have been always speaking about and until it is removed the methods of physical force are bound to fail.

And he went on as starkly as ever:

You are not to conclude from this that I have any delusions as to the difficulty of winning at an election, but what I say is that if we cannot win that, then we are not, in the present situation, likely to win any other way.[8]

De Valera's approach to the problem, the break with the existing structure, the construction from zero of a new political party to work along the lines which he proposed—all was thoroughly characteristic. If one attribute more than any other marked his career—and marked it ever more notably as he matured in statesmanship—it was that of perseverance, tempered always with an acute judgement of the politically possible at a given time.

In the early months of 1927, de Valera would have wished to continue his work building up Fianna Fáil without interruption. With a general election approaching, all efforts must be directed to preparing the party for the contest. However, another demand on his time interrupted his efforts. The case taken in the American courts by the Free State Government for possession of the residue of the money collected on bond certificates in 1920 and 1921 had been pending for some time. De Valera, as one of the trustees, was a vital witness. He had consistently refused to hand over the funds to the Free State authorities on the grounds that the subscribers had given the money to the government of the Republic of Ireland and that the Free State Government was not the legitimate successor to that body. De Valera had long felt that the conclusion which any impartial court would reach would be to return the funds to the subscribers in proportion to their original subscriptions. He did not expect that the money would be given to the Republican Emergency Government. For him it would be a victory if the Free State failed to maintain its claim. By February, 1927, the claim for the funds was about to be heard in New York before Supreme Court Justice Peters.

De Valera entered the witness-box in New York about a week after the case opened. According to one New York newspaper, it was 'the moment for which the audience at the trial . . . had been waiting.' The spectators' benches in the courtroom were crowded. For three days he was examined and cross-examined on the details of Irish history from 1913 to 1922. With all his habitual care and precision he answered the questions put to him. The New York newspaper said 'On the witness stand de Valera gave the impression of being meticulously honest. He would decline to identify a paper or vouch for the accuracy of a statement unless he knew of it from his own personal knowledge.' Indeed the deliberation and care which he gave to each question and to his answers appears to have tested the patience of his own lawyers on occasion.[9]

When the judgement of the court became known, de Valera issued a statement:

As a trustee I am not dissatisfied with the decision of the court to return the money to the subscribers.[10]

The law case gave de Valera the opportunity of renewing old acquaintances in the United States. In a tour right across the continent he aroused considerable enthusiasm for the Republican cause. The excitement reached a climax when he ended his visit at Boston on the last day of April. At a meeting on Boston Common more than five thousand cheering men and women had surrounded him, clutching at his coat in their fervour and struggling with each other to grasp his hand. The crowds followed him as he drove away.

> They marched in close formation to Commonwealth Pier where they stood with bared heads chanting 'The Soldier's Song'. . . . It was the most enthusiastic farewell that Boson has seen for years. . . . He boarded the ship to the skirling of the bagpipe music played by the Irish Republican Band. Hundreds followed him to his stateroom on one of the upper decks, and the crowd milled and surged around the decks still trying to get near him. With difficulty the liner was cleared of the enthusiastic visitors and sailed to the strains of 'The Soldier's Song'.[11]

Lest any political significance be thought to attach to the name of the pier from which he sailed, the Commonwealth Pier, it should be noted that the name of the ship in which he travelled was the S.S. *Republic*!

But now he was needed in Ireland; the General Election was to take place in the middle of June. When he landed he threw himself into the election campaign with his habitual zest.

The oath was the keynote of Fianna Fáil's campaign, though other issues, constitutional and economic, were also raised. From the platforms of the Government party, Cumann na nGaedheal, little was now heard of the 'stepping-stone' argument, by which support had been won for the Treaty five years before. Indeed the party leader, W. T. Cosgrave, seemed to de Valera to be carrying out his own (de Valera's) forecast of March, 1922, when he said the Treaty would erect a barrier of the nation's pledged word against future advances. 'We believe in honouring our bond,' said Cosgrave. 'We believe in the sanctity of international agreements. . . . Our honour as the representatives of a nation which has approved of that Treaty is bound to the carrying out of our part of the transaction.'[12] In de Valera's eyes they were tied hand and foot as he had always said they would be.

Even the Catholic clergy joined in the argument. Just before the election, Monsignor Ryan of Cashel gave his answer to a Republican who had asked how would he take the Treaty oath having already taken an oath to the Republic. A man, he said, was bound to his wife by his marriage vow, but when she was dead he was free to make a vow to another. Argument by analogy, however, is always dangerous but doubly so with a man of de Valera's subtlety. Would the Dean, he asked, tell them that they were free to take a vow to a second wife with the intention of proving unfaithful to her, or with a view to compassing her death? The people who told them now to take the oath lightly, and that it meant nothing, would be just the people to tell them when they had them in the trap, that they had taken an oath and must keep it.[13]

The election result was a severe jolt for the Government party, Cumann na nGaedheal, which had won 63 seats in the previous election in 1923 and now won but 46. One member of the party, the Ceann Comhairle, or Speaker, who was returned automatically, brought the party's strength in a legislature of 153 deputies up to 47. Fianna Fáil had polled well, winning 44 seats. Sinn Féin was reduced from 25 to 5 deputies and there were 2 independent republicans, one of whom, almost immediately, joined Fianna Fáil, bringing the strength of that party to 45. The total number of Republican deputies was 51. Even if they did not enter the house, a coalition of the 22 Labour, 14 Independents, 11 Farmers and 8 National League would have unseated the Government. Of course no such coalition was envisaged. The Fianna Fáil party had become a nation-wide party within the short space of thirteen months from its foundation and had succeeded in putting up candidates in every constituency except the universities and North Cork. The party had polled slightly more than 25 per cent of the first preference votes—an excellent start.

The result of the election was inconclusive, but de Valera saw in it a confirmation of his view that if a referendum were held on the single issue of the oath, the oath would go. In his statements after the election he was careful to select his point of attack, the oath, and to concentrate his force on one party, Cumann na nGaedheal. 'Republicans,' he said, 'recognise no opponents save the Imperialist party.'[14]

In a statement which he issued for the *New York Tribune*, de Valera was even quite specific about their attendance at the Dáil.

We intend to claim our seats and to exercise our right to represent our constituents without submitting to an oath of allegiance to any foreign power. If excluded from the assembly by force, it will be at the instance of a party whose strength is less than one third of the whole elected body. If not thus excluded, we believe we can form a strong national government with the support of all the progressive non-imperialist elements.[15]

The rules for administering the oath were not at all clear. In December, 1922, when it was first administered, it was done formally in the Free

State Dáil by the Speaker. In September, 1923, however, when it was feared that Republicans might make a demonstration in the chamber of the House, the procedure was changed. The Clerk of the Free State Dáil was nominated by the Governor-General to carry out the ceremony. This he did in his room before deputies were allowed to enter the chamber of the House. The new Dáil was due to open on June 23rd, 1927. Meanwhile de Valera and the other Fianna Fáil deputies had obtained counsels' opinion, signed by three lawyers, Arthur C. Meredith, K.C., Albert E. Wood, K.C., and George Gavan Duffy.

Counsel advised that there was no authority either under the Constitution or the Treaty for excluding any deputy (whether he had taken the oath or not) from any part of the House before the House was duly constituted and the Speaker elected. The opinion continued:

> In case any such exclusion takes place, we are of opinion that any Ceann Comhairle chosen in the absence of the excluded member or members will not have been validly elected. Any member may be proposed and elected as Ceann Comhairle without taking any oath.[16]

None of the counsel who signed this opinion were members of Fianna Fáil. Two of them might well be considered ex-Unionists.

Armed with this opinion the Fianna Fáil deputies set off for Leinster House on the opening day of the session, June 23rd. They were watched by large crowds as they passed through a strong cordon of police. On entering Leinster House, they were refused access to the chamber by the Clerk, Colm Ó Murchadha, who said that first they must comply with a 'little formality'. On being asked what this was, he read Article 17 of the Free State Constitution, including the text of the oath. De Valera argued in accordance with the legal opinion which he had received, but could make no impression. After a while he and his party withdrew.

The next steps to be taken were already planned by de Valera who had expected to be refused admission. That very evening the national executive of Fianna Fáil decided to support legal proceedings by Seán T. O'Kelly and Seán Lemass against their exclusion. At the same time, de Valera put forward the draft of a petition under Article 48 of the Constitution, with a view to a constitutional amendment abolishing the oath. Under that Article it was obligatory on the legislature, on a petition signed by not less than seventy-five thousand voters, to make provision for submitting the amendment to a referendum of the whole people.[17]

This tactic placed the Free State Government in a quandary. The Constitution for which they had sacrificed so much seemed in jeopardy at a crucial point. W. T. Cosgrave, President of the Executive Council, was determined not to allow any change in the clause which imposed the oath.

A sudden revolting deed showed how close the nation still was to civil war. A fortnight after the Fianna Fáil effort to enter Parliament, Kevin O'Higgins, Vice-President of the Cumann na nGaedheal Government, was assassinated on his way to mass. O'Higgins was considered the hard strong man of the Government.

De Valera was in Clare that weekend and, as soon as he heard the news, he issued a strong denunciation of the murder.

The assassination of Mr O'Higgins is murder, and is inexcusable from any standpoint. I am confident that no Republican organisation was responsible for it or would give it any countenance. It is the duty of every citizen to set his face sternly against anything of this kind. It is a crime that cuts at the root of representative government, and no one who realises what the crime means can do otherwise than deplore and condemn it. Every right-minded individual will deeply sympathise with the bereaved widow in her agony.[18]

In the horrified reaction to O'Higgins's death, the Government introduced three important bills. The first, a public safety bill, gave extensive coercive powers to the Government against any organisation which was involved in treasonable or seditious activities. According to one authority, 'some of the provisions clearly infringed the constitutional guarantees of the liberty of the subject and trial by jury', but this difficulty was overcome by the insertion in the bill of a provision that if any section of the statute contravened the Constitution, it should operate as an amendment to the Constitution.

The other two bills were of more immediate importance in so far as Fianna Fáil policy was concerned. An electoral amendment bill was designed to end the abstentionist policy. It provided that every candidate for election to the legislature should, on nomination, sign an affidavit that he would, if elected take his seat and take the oath prescribed within two months after his election. If he failed to comply he was to be dis-qualified. The second bill was to abolish the clause of the Free State Constitution which allowed the people to initiate by petition a referendum on a constitutional amendment. All doors were being closed by Cosgrave on constitutional action by Fianna Fáil, all except one—that into Leinster House across which lay the barrier of the oath.

De Valera realised the full implications of Cosgrave's policy, but did not see any way out. For some time there had been indications of readiness among members of Fianna Fáil to enter the Free State Dáil. One member, Dan Breen, had resigned from the party to take his seat early in the year. During July Patrick Belton entered the Dáil the moment the new legis-lation was announced. He was expelled from the Fianna Fáil Party. If discipline were to be maintained in the party it was essential that any stand should be unanimous. When de Valera was asked whether, under the new conditions created by the bills introduced by Cosgrave, the Fianna Fáil deputies were likely to change their attitude to the oath, he answered firmly, 'No,' and added:

> After the election, and after our exclusion from the Free State assembly the party met and each member signed a statement reiterating his election pledge and stating that 'under no circumstances whatever' would he subscribe to such an oath. That was final.[19]

But he was becoming painfully conscious that a failure of constitutional republicanism would leave only one road open for Republicans in the future—the road of civil war. If ever a statesman was confronted with a moral dilemma or torn between rival principles it was de Valera at this time.

As the crisis heightened in late July and early August, contacts accumulated with the Labour Party and with the National League founded by Captain W. A. Redmond. Where it would all lead, however, was not too clear. De Valera wrote to Frank P. Walsh and other American friends early in August:

> The political situation here has been completely changed by the projected Free State legislation. A new movement will now be required. The Fianna Fáil way of removing the oath from outside is being made definitely impossible and will, I expect, have to be abandoned. It will take me some time to have the dispositions necessary to meet the new situation made, and it would be premature to indicate the lines I have in mind at the moment for dealing with it.

Yet he still asserted confidence:

> The Free State people at any rate are now for the first time with their backs to the wall so far as the Irish public opinion is concerned. Their regime is going to be henceforth a form of military dictatorship. That cannot last very long.[20]

Meanwhile de Valera went on giving intense thought to the dilemma which faced him. He considered the possibility of an alliance with the Labour Party and with the National League. He held an important and, on the whole, satisfactory meeting with Johnson, the Labour Leader, on August 8th.

On August 9th, the national executive of Fianna Fáil held a special and vital meeting.[21] De Valera put before it his views on the political situation. He explained that he saw no alternative between giving up political action and entry into the Free State Dáil. He could not take an oath, but it was being said that it was not being administered as an oath. The only way to test that was to go to Leinster House again and find out the procedure. A resolution was passed by forty-four votes to seven that the elected deputies of the party as a body be given a free hand in the matter of entering the legislature or not.

The Fianna Fáil deputies met the following evening. During the day de Valera wrote to a friend:

> Not since the 'Treaty' time was any decision so fraught with consequences as that which we have to take now is likely to be. Pray God inspire us to take the right one for the future freedom of Ireland and the general good of the people. . .[22]

At the same time he prepared a draft statement for the newspapers to be submitted to the meeting. It led to a long and heart-searching discussion but only slight amendments. The meeting did not end until midnight when forty-two Fianna Fáil deputies present signed a document whose crucial passages ran thus:

> It has . . . been repeatedly stated, and it is not uncommonly believed, that the required declaration is not an oath; that the signing of it implies no contractual obligation, and that it has no binding significance in conscience or in law, that, in short, it is merely an empty political formula which Deputies could conscientiously sign without becoming involved, or without involving their nation, in obligations of loyalty to the English Crown.
>
> The Fianna Fáil Deputies would certainly not wish to have the feeling that they are allowing themselves to be debarred by nothing more than an empty formula from exercising their functions as public representatives, particularly at a moment like this. They intend, therefore, to present themselves at the Clerk's office of the Free State Dáil 'for the purpose of complying with the provisions of Article 17 of the Constitution', by inscribing their names in the book kept for the purpose, among other signatures appended to the required formula. But, so that there may be no doubt as to their attitude, and no misunderstanding of their action, the Fianna Fáil Deputies hereby give public notice that they propose to regard the declaration as an empty formality and repeat that their only allegiance is to the Irish nation, and that it will be given to no other power or authority.

For de Valera the night which followed was a nightmarish crisis of conscience. It was one of the few nights in his career during which the worry of a decision kept him from sleeping. With a strong conviction that the ultimate consequence of the failure of the Fianna Fáil deputies to take their seats would be civil war, he debated with himself how far he could go. Was it his duty to take that oath to avoid the consequence? Finally he decided that his political duty did not require any violence to his conscience. But if he were made to do anything which he would consider 'taking an oath', he would have no option but to refuse. In that case, instead of entering the legislature, he would devote his energies to the revival of the Irish language.

10

The next day de Valera led the Fianna Fáil deputies to Leinster House. In groups of three they entered the office of the Clerk of the House. With de Valera were Dr James Ryan and Frank Aiken, who were to be witnesses of what took place.

De Valera wrote that day his own account of what happened in the Clerk's office, and included in it the statement he made to the Clerk in Irish. Translated into English this runs:

> I want you to understand that I am not taking any oath nor giving any promise of faithfulness to the King of England or to any power outside the people of Ireland. I am putting my name here merely as a formality to get the permission necessary to enter amongst the other Teachtaí that were elected by the people of Ireland, and I want you to know that no other meaning is to be attached to what I am doing.[23]

De Valera had, in fact, written a pencilled note which he read to the Clerk, so that he had an exact record of what he said. The Clerk said that he was not concerned with these statements. All he wanted was de Valera's 'name in this book', pointing to a volume in front of him. De Valera saw a New Testament lying open face downwards on the volume and asked, 'Then, what is this for?'

The colleagues who were with him wrote a description of what followed:

> Mr de Valera picked up the bible which was lying on the book containing the oath, carried it to the other end of the room, and placed it on the couch there. He then went back, signed his name on the line pointed out by the Clerk, at the same time covering the writing above the line with some papers he held in his hand.[24]

As he left the room, he passed through that occupied by Pádraig Ó Caoimh, a senior Clerk, the former secretary of Sinn Féin. To him de Valera said that he would one day burn that book publicly on the streets of Dublin.[25]

The episode was a turning point in Irish history. It ended abstention as a policy and it brought de Valera and his followers into the Free State legislature. If that was Cosgrave's aim, he had succeeded. De Valera gave him the credit for having instructed Colm Ó Murchadha, the Clerk, to make the test as easy as possible for those with conscientious scruples, but Cosgrave denied this.[26] Certainly Ó Murchadha did not add to the difficulties. He did not read the oath to those signing the book and de Valera did not read it. True he put his signature on that page in a specified place. But he had clearly stated that he was taking no oath and, since he did not see, read, repeat or hear the words involved in the 'oath', the whole thing was indeed treated by him as an empty formality, as it was by all the members of the Fianna Fáil party who 'signed the book'.

Theologians were, in due course, to turn their minds to it. The following year a Jesuit theologian, Father Genicot, included a case like the Irish one, but slightly camouflaged, in his famous *Casus Conscientiae*, published in Brussels. He had no doubt that in the case of 'Edmundus, civis placissimus' there was no oath. There were many others, too, who felt the same way. One man spoke out strongly: Archbishop Mannix of Melbourne:

> There was no perjury where there was no falsehood—and the Republicans proclaimed from the housetops the sense in which they signed the test oath. No one was deceived.[27]

Plenty were found to offer less charitable viewpoints. De Valera had no doubt that he took no oath, but he nevertheless felt deeply the humiliation of the situation. He spoke on the subject with considerable feeling at the time:

> To allow a new civil war to be provoked if we could prevent it would be unpardonable. I grant that what we did was contrary to all our former actions, and to everything we stood for—contrary to our declared policy, and to the explicit pledges we gave at the time of our election. It was a step painful and humiliating for us who had to take it, and for those who had supported us and would suffer in us.

He admitted candidly that it was a step that could easily lower further the standard of public faith. Still, that it was their duty to take the step became increasingly clear as the situation was examined, and being conscious that it was only considerations of the public good that weighed with them, they were able to indulge the hope that such evils as they foresaw resulting would be minimised.

> It is never easy to pass under the yoke, and it was not easy for us with our full understanding of all its baleful significance and the full realisation of the triumphant shout with which the British propagandist in every part of the world, and every enemy of Irish independence would hail this token of our submission.[28]

Perhaps de Valera overstressed the humiliation which he felt. He always preferred to say the awkward things himself rather than have others say them for him—one secret, at least, of advocacy—and he knew what would be said by his opponents. His actions and pronouncements in the preceding year and a half may always startle the historian as they startled so many at the time. Yet no one has ever suggested a better method of extricating himself and his party from a cruel dilemma.

Certainly he rescued the Republican movement from prolonged political impotence. This, Professor Desmond Williams has written, 'was a great turning point in the history of Parliamentary government in Ireland.'[29] De Valera's performance, however one interprets and assesses it, made it certain that parliamentary democracy would in fact prevail.

LEADER OF THE OPPOSITION

1927 – 1931

On August 12th, 1927, de Valera and his Fianna Fáil colleagues took their seats in Leinster House, determined to exercise self-control, to give no occasion for offence. The very first statement of the day, however, almost brought de Valera to his feet. He was highly sensitive as to any accusation that he had taken an oath. As the Clerk reported that Fianna Fáil deputies 'had complied with the provisions of Article 17 of the constitution', de Valera half rose to deny it but then he sank back in his seat thinking, 'If that is his interpretation of the Constitution why should I constitute myself an interpreter of it?' The self-imposed restraint of the Fianna Fáil deputies meant that they made no speeches and barely intervened in the debates on that first day.

There was a strong atmosphere of tension in the House. Not only were men who had taken opposite sides in a civil war facing one another in Parliament for the first time; the whole balance of the chamber was transformed. By combining with the Labour and National League deputies, Fianna Fáil could, on paper, overthrow the Government.

On August 16th, Thomas Johnson, the Leader of the Labour Party, who for five years had played the somewhat thankless, but nevertheless essential role of principal Opposition Leader, moved a vote of no confidence in the Government. On a counting of heads it was clear that the voting would be close. Indeed it looked as if there might be but one vote between the two sides and that vote in favour of the Opposition. There was no question of Fianna Fáil participating in the alternative government but, on the basis of the guarantees which de Valera had received, he was willing to keep a Labour–National League coalition in office.

A debate of five hours followed, of surprisingly little bitterness. The only Fianna Fáil deputy to contribute to it was Seán T. O'Kelly, who spoke in Irish. All he said was that everyone knew the views of Fianna Fáil concerning the Government. To repeat them was unnecessary and would only embitter the debate.

The house divided shortly before eight that evening. The voting was even, seventy-one votes each. But the Speaker gave his casting vote for the Government and against all the odds they were saved. Opposition deputies frantically asked themselves what had gone wrong. Who on earth was missing? Ultimately the mystery was solved. Deputy John Jinks of Sligo, a National League member, was absent. He had been all too well entertained by a pro-Government deputy, Bryan Cooper, and by a Dublin journalist, according to one account, and had taken the train to Sligo, forgetting his obligations to Leinster House. Whatever the reason for his absence it saved the Government for the moment. President Cosgrave moved the adjournment and a few days later this Parliament, then but two months old, was dissolved.

The election campaign was a contest between the two major parties; the smaller groups and independents had depleted their funds. Fianna Fáil themselves found it difficult enough to face a second contest within three months.

To the newspapers de Valera issued an attack on the Government's action:

> The sharp practice of which the Free State Executive is guilty in dissolving the Dáil after adjourning it a few days ago and rushing the country into an unnecessary election during the harvest season does not surprise us. It is exactly what we should expect of them. They will find, however, that Fianna Fáil is not quite as unprepared as they think. . .[1]

Even before the election was announced, he had stated his position on many crucial points. At Blackrock, on August 22nd, he said:

> I want to reply to the suggestion now being put forward that our purpose in entering the Free State Dáil is to destroy it. That is a falsehood. We are entering it in the hope of helping to make it develop to be what it should be ultimately—the sovereign national assembly of the Irish nation. . .
>
> Our purpose is not to destroy but to broaden and widen the Free State assembly, so as to free it from all foreign control or interference, and make it so truly representative of the whole people as to secure for it the necessary authority and influence to have its decisions readily accepted and its laws willingly obeyed.

While he would review all salaries over £1,000 a year in the public service, there would, however, be no dismissals and no replacement of existing officials by others who were Fianna Fáil supporters.

> I for one would not stand for any such policy, and I do not believe that there is any member of our party who would stand for it. I believe in justice to every man, friend or opponent, and I am going to assume that those who took service in the Free State did it believing they were right.[2]

This last assumption was to prove of far-reaching benefit to stable government in Ireland.

One of the factors militating against the success of Fianna Fáil was the public fear, partly because of its revolutionary past and partly because of its opponents' propaganda, that it would attempt too much too quickly. In drafting an election address, de Valera dealt with this point:

> The sinister design of aiming at bringing about a sudden revolutionary upheaval, with which our opponents choose to credit us, is altogether foreign to our purpose and programme. We do not believe in attempting to practice a sleight of hand on the electorate. We shall proceed as a responsible constitutional government acknowledging without reserve that all authority comes through the sovereign people and that, before any important step likely to involve their safety is taken, the people are entitled to be taken into the fullest consultation.[3]

The election campaign which followed was short but vigorous. It was fought not alone by the politicians but by a number of Catholic priests. Canon Slattery, a parish priest in Co. Clare, said that the alternative to voting for Cosgrave's government was to 'hand over the country to be destroyed by the destroyers'.[4] At Clifden, in Galway, Monsignor McAlpine announced that Mr de Valera's policy now was the same as in the past—plunder, devastation and ruin.[5]

These public pronouncements were sometimes made by letter, sometimes in person from Cumann na nGaedheal platforms. The Catholic Dean of Cashel, Monsignor Ryan, addressed the farmers at Cashel Fair and told them not to give their votes to a party that had prostituted a solemn oath, a party that had made a farce of a most solemn religious obligation and turned it into an empty formula.[6]

Many parish priests used even stronger language and they did not confine it to political platforms. They used it even from their altars. Father Thomas O'Hara, a parish priest, ran into a slight altercation in his church as he addressed his congregation on how to vote. A Fianna Fáil candidate, Michael Kilroy, was among the congregation and rose to contradict one of the charges against de Valera.[7]

The Fianna Fáil speeches concentrated largely on economic questions. An attack was launched particularly on the payment of land annuities to the British Treasury. These annuities were paid by tenant farmers purchasing their farms under the Land Purchase Acts which, at the end of the nineteenth century and beginning of the twentieth, had ended landlordism in rural Ireland. Under the Government of Ireland Act of 1920 (abortive in the South) these annuities were to form part of the normal revenue of the two Governments set up in Ireland. The Fianna Fáil claim was that the Treaty did not alter that position and that the Free State Government had been handing over to Britain an annual sum of almost £3,000,000 to which that country had no legal title. The only known commitment to make this payment was an agreement between the Free State Minister for Finance, Ernest Blythe, and the British Chancellor of the Exchequer, Winston Churchill, in March, 1926. This agreement, which involved other annual payments making up a further £2,000,000 a year, had been kept secret for eight months after it was signed and was never ratified by the legislature. The total annual payment being made to Britain was over £5,000,000, or about one-fifth of the total revenue of the Irish Government.

The election took place on September 15th. In the fortnight before it de Valera addressed meetings in many parts of the country, from Wexford to Donegal. He was in Clare for polling-day. The smaller parties came out of the contest much weaker. The National League lost six seats and Labour nine. Sinn Féin found itself unable to put up any official candidates. Alderman John Jinks of Sligo passed from sudden fame to political oblivion, like the racehorse named after him which won the Two Thousand Guineas and failed dramatically in the Derby.

For de Valera the election was a personal victory. He increased his poll in Clare, and brought in a third Fianna Fáil candidate to win three out of the five seats in the constituency. All over the country the party did well, but Clare and Kerry were outstanding. The party won fifty-seven seats, a gain of thirteen on the June figures. Not a single seat held before was lost, and the result was undoubtedly an endorsement of de Valera's policy of entering the Dáil. People who might have considered it futile to vote for abstentionist candidates rallied behind the new departure. Nevertheless the Government party also gained heavily, winning fifteen seats more than in June. With the aid of the Farmers' Party and of most of the Independents, it was clear that Cosgrave would continue to head the Government. His position was, however, precarious.

De Valera's comments after the election were, to put it mildly, forth-right. He referred to the strength of the support given to Cumann na nGaedheal by ex-Unionists and the fact that the daily newspapers were unanimously on their side:

> They conducted their campaign without any regard for truth or fair play. The failure of all the lies, tricks and stratagems shows the resisting power of truth and the strength of a good cause.[8]

These seem strong words, but then elections in those days were fought without gloves. In fact on polling-day one Fianna Fáil election official was shot dead by a former Free State army officer.[9]

When the Dáil met in October it was impossible that the restraint shown when the Fianna Fáil deputies attended in August should continue. There were too many grievances to be aired after five years of bitterness and impotence. The fact that all the Fianna Fáil deputies took their seats made the legislature more representative than it had been, but that in itself did not make it legitimate in their eyes.

'I still hold,' de Valera was to say two years later, 'that your right to be regarded as the legitimate government of this country is faulty, that this House itself is faulty. You have secured a *de facto* position. Very well, there must be somebody in charge to keep order in the community and by virtue of your *de facto* position you are the only people who are in a position to do it. But as to whether you have come by that position legitimately or not, I say you have not come by that position legitimately. You brought off a *coup d'état* in the summer of 1922'.

It was a blunt statement of the Fianna Fáil position and, of course, was not received kindly by other members of the Dáil who saw in it a threat of a new upheaval. Indeed, in the course of his speech de Valera made it clear that he had little respect for the Constitution of the Free State. He said 'As far as I am concerned, the only Constitution I give "that" for,' snapping his fingers, 'the only thing that I think I am morally bound to obey in this House, is a majority vote, because you are all elected by the Irish people.'[10]

Clearly majority rule *de facto* he was accepting, but he would not admit the *de jure* origin of the Government.

This was a difficult position to maintain without being represented before the public as an advocate of anarchy, but he trod his tightrope undaunted. Throughout the lifetime of the assembly which was elected in September, 1927, he was the Leader of the principal Opposition party —a party which was, at one and the same time, constitutional and Republican. Its members saw themselves, in a sense, as the spokesmen of those who continued in Sinn Féin and in the IRA, and were critical of the repressive measures adopted against them by the Government. Because of its Republican aim, the Fianna Fáil party could count on the goodwill of some of those who would not recognise the Free State Dáil, and on benevolent neutrality of others.

In 1929, and the following years, the IRA became active and posed sharp problems for de Valera as leader of a constitutional party. De Valera felt that the policy adopted by the Free State Government had never been based on charity or understanding in regard to those who had maintained their Republican ideals consistently since 1920. The weapon of force neither changed people's principles nor their policies.

Force is the usual remedy to take. Take a stick to hit somebody on the head who doesn't agree with you. That is a very simple remedy. It may do when dealing with an individual, but it does not do when dealing with a situation such as we have here in this country.

He issued this warning to the Government when opposing their drastic legislation against the IRA and other similar groups:

> If you deny people who are animated with honest motives peaceful ways of doing it you are throwing them back upon violent ways of doing it. Once they are denied the peaceful way they will get support for the violent way that they would never get otherwise.

Indeed, here was an extra argument in favour of removing the oath which still remained one of de Valera's primary aims. Repressive legislation, while that barrier to constitutional activity remained was, in his view, to start at the wrong end of the problem. Was this, as was not unnaturally claimed, to give encouragement to the extreme organisations which were gaining strength at this time in Ireland? De Valera sought to rebut this charge:

> I do not want to or be said to give any encouragement to them at all. I say again there is no authority in this country to take life except in so far as the present ruling authority is entitled to take it—no other authority.

That did not exonerate the Government. It was not only the constitutional grievances of the extremist elements that de Valera felt should be tackled before repressive measures were taken. He saw in the upsurge of illegal activity, in 1929 and after, a reaction to lethargy on the part of the Government in economic affairs:

> I recognise that if men are hungry they will not be too particular about the ultimate principles of the organisation they would join, if that organisation promises them bread. . . I say what we have got to do is to remove the breeding ground of attachment to the false principles. That breeding ground is there in the present economic situation.[11]

The relations between the Fianna Fáil party and those organisations which included the IRA and Saor Éire, a body with a left-wing social policy, ranged from friendliness when there was a coincidence of aim to frigid disapproval when there was a clash on means.

While de Valera and his party had a somewhat ambivalent attitude to the more extreme Republicans, they also had a dual attitude to the Free State. The deputies attended the Dáil yet they, and all members of the party, were prohibited by resolutions of the Ard Fheis from attendance in any capacity at social functions organised by Free State ministers. This rule meant, for example, that members of Fianna Fáil were debarred from attending a reception and dinner given by the Government in honour of the Papal Nuncio, Pascal Robinson, who was appointed in 1929. The policy, of course, was open to criticism and might even be construed as an insult to the Pope. De Valera was in the United States at the time, but Seán T. O'Kelly wrote to him about the affair.

I am expecting that there will surely be some religious ceremony, probably a *Te Deum*, at the Pro-Cathedral and, if so, we can all attend there and this should stop the mouths of certain critics.[12]

When Mrs Pearse, mother of the two executed leaders of the 1916 Rising, a faithful follower of de Valera, asked for direction from the Fianna Fáil executive as to what she should do in regard to an invitation which she had received to the opening of the reconstructed General Post Office, she was told that no member of the executive should attend.[13] While this ruling applied only to functions organised by the Free State Government, it was also considered undesirable for members of Fianna Fáil to attend a sports meeting organised by the Civic Guards.[14] The bitterness of the Civil War had gone deep and must be allowed to explain the Fianna Fáil attitude both to other Republicans and to the Free State Government. It might be said, in regard to other Republicans, that they were of them but not with them, while as regards the Free Staters they might be with them but certainly not of them.

As Leader of the Opposition, de Valera's primary objective was to use every constitutional means to abolish the oath of allegiance. The work of collecting signatures to the petition for a referendum on the oath had been interrupted by the General Election but, as soon as it was over, the work was pushed ahead.[15] On May 3rd, 1928, de Valera tried to present the petition which had been signed by 96,000 voters, more than 20,000 more than the number specified in the constitution. Cosgrave immediately objected to the petition being received. Procedural controversy was followed by drastic action by the Government. Sweeping amendments to the Constitution were put before the House by the Government. The most important of these were aimed to abolish the right of public initiative for constitutional amendments as proposed in the previous year.

This new move of the Government was looked upon by de Valera as a cynical effort on their part to override the Constitution. The vaunted guardians of majority rule were abolishing the means of testing the will of the people on a clean-cut issue. Undoubtedly the Government had their back to the wall in their last-ditch fight to save the oath. Apparently they were convinced that any breach in the edifice of the Treaty would be a breach of national faith and they were determined to use every means to prevent it.

De Valera led the attack on the Government's amendments to the Constitution. He even took the unusual course of speaking against the first reading and challenging a division on it. The second reading was passed, together with other constitutional amendments, only after an all-night sitting. De Valera pointed out one conclusion at least which could be drawn from the Government's action; that the will of the people was paramount only when it was in favour of the Free State point of view. It looked for a time as if the abolition of the referendum might mean that the Constitution would become rigid and unalterable after the eight years had elapsed during which it could be amended by ordinary legislation.

Cosgrave, however, gave a guarantee that the period of eight years, which was due to expire in 1930, would be extended, or that some means of amending the Constitution would be left open. With at least that guarantee de Valera had to be content. Though his effort to remove the oath was temporarily blocked, the door was not completely closed.

Another matter on which de Valera took the initiative in the Dáil was Ireland's right to the land annuities, which were being transferred annually to the British exchequer. Senior counsel were consulted by his party on the question but, with his usual caution, he consulted a man whose prejudices, if anything, would make him lean the other way. He called privately on Arthur C. Meredith, a former Unionist, at his home in Upper Mount Street. Meredith was an eminent but conservative lawyer and he was not impressed with de Valera's case until de Valera finally asked him by what right the Belfast Government were retaining similar annuities. He asked for a few more days to look into this aspect of the case. After further deliberation he wrote:

> I must say I can see no flaw in this [your] reasoning, but I am fairly staggered by the result. It may be that I am overlooking some material fact, statutory or otherwise, for I can hardly think that Mr Blythe [the Minister of Finance] would throw away this valuable property.[16]

This letter had a profound effect on de Valera's stand in regard to the annuities. Some years later he wrote to Meredith.

> You are aware, I think, that it was your opinion as expressed in this first letter that gave me the confidence in our case which has supported me through all the controversy in regard to it.[17]

Before receiving this letter de Valera had been careful not to commit himself regarding the annuities, but some of his supporters had done so. Their statements were denounced by Government ministers as dishonest propaganda. 'We have not a shade of right to claim that money,' said Ernest Blythe, Minister of Finance.[18]

De Valera, however, was not long in launching an attack on the existing position. Early in May, in the Dáil, he made a strong speech challenging the arrangements made by the Government for paying the annuities to Britain. It sparked off a strenuous campaign of abuse against de Valera, the tone of which was indicated by the title of a leading article in the *Irish Times*—'A debt of honour.'[19] De Valera was accused of trying to repudiate an existing debt and of undermining the credit of the state. He was not impressed by this latter argument from men who had refused to commit themselves to repaying the American loan which he had raised on behalf of the first Dáil. Once de Valera thought he was right he did not surrender easily. The campaign about the land annuities was only beginning, he warned.[20] It was to become a major point in the next few years.

He intended, however, to attack the Government on a broad economic front. They had shown themselves, he insisted, too conservative in economic matters and timorous in their protectionism. One of de Valera's speeches in the Dáil dealt with the closing down of flour mills, and he referred to the old Sinn Féin policy which both he and Cosgrave had shared in the years before the split:

Food is one of the fundamental necessities of life and, as I understood the policy in the old days anyhow, it was that we would try to make this nation as self-supporting in all essentials as possible. We can make this country self-supporting as far as flour and bread are concerned.

It was not simply that allowing the mills to close would later allow foreign millers to raise the price of flour, but rather that the nation should not be in the position of depending for food on a foreign country. If that happened, he warned:

Whenever there is a war, whenever there is any disturbance in the countries from which we get our chief supplies, we will be cut short of that vital article.[21]

He had already stated his view that in the event of war the right of maintaining Irish neutrality should be insisted on.[22] His economic policy was calculated to make that possible. It was part of a pattern of self-sufficiency. The kernel of this policy lay in the aim of modest comfort for all with no vast differences between rich and poor. Ireland was a small country and should not try to act as if it were the centre of an empire. De Valera, always a frugal man himself, pointed out his view of the choice which had been made by Ireland in seeking independence. He said:

We, as I tried by example long ago to point out, had to make the sort of choice that might be open, for instance, to a servant in a big mansion. If the servant was displeased with the kicks of the young master and wanted to have his freedom, he had to make up his mind whether or not he was going to have that freedom, and give up the luxuries of a certain kind which were available to him by being in that mansion. . . If he goes into the cottage he has to make up his mind to put up with the frugal fare of that cottage.[22]

For him it was a choice between freedom and the luxuries of an imperial administration. His choice was freedom.

De Valera judged each practical issue on what appeared to him its merits. He accused the Government of doing no more than tinker with the question of protection. The country was still being run as an out-farm for the British. He approved, however, of the idea of the electrification scheme pursued by the Department of Industry and Commerce. Its aim, to supply the country with the power necessary to run its industries independently of foreign sources of power, fitted in perfectly with de Valera's self-sufficiency policy. But he disagreed with the choice of the development area. He would have favoured starting with a smaller scheme on the Liffey. He felt that the Shannon scheme would be too big for the country for some time and would involve capital being tied up which could be used to better purpose. The smaller scheme, too, would have the advantage of training Irishmen so that, at a later stage, it would be possible to undertake the larger project without calling in a foreign firm. De Valera, however, was no carping critic. He told the Dáil:

> That is a matter upon which people may differ. They may say 'Very well, the people who are doing it in the other way have the responsibility for it, and we are not going to hamper them in the carrying out of that work. They have taken a certain step; it cannot be undone, and, therefore, our duty should be to make it a success now that the step has been taken.' That is commonsense, and that is the attitude we take towards an enterprise of that kind . . .

He saw that planning was necessary, that a development commission could undertake the task of putting an economic programme into effect, a programme geared to make the country self-contained economically. He was aiming at something which would mean fundamental changes in industry and agriculture. It would need economies. Some people might have to be satisfied with less so that more might benefit. 'The top hats may have to be done without,' he said. But the state would aim deliberately at raising the standards of the poorer sections of the community:

> We believe there ought to be available for every single man in the country employment which will bring him in enough recompense to enable him to maintain his family, and the whole organisation of the State ought to be to that end.[23]

While de Valera was using the years in opposition after 1927 to attack the Free State Government on a broad front of economic and constitutional issues, his outstanding contribution to the growth of his own party was a major break-through in publicity. From the time of the Treaty debates onwards, the daily press and much of the local weekly press was against the Republican cause. The Republican Director of Publicity, in November, 1922, complained that:

> If we could break down the conspiracy of silence in the Daily Press, it would be worth ten times all we could do in handbills.[24]

The Civil War was but a month ended when a proposal was put forward for raising money in the United States to start a Republican daily paper. The project did not begin to take firm shape, however, until after de Valera's release from Arbour Hill in the summer of 1924. De Valera gave his full support to the scheme. In the early stages of the project it had been hoped to buy the *Freeman's Journal*, an old national daily paper, which at this time was in financial difficulties. This plan, however, was upset when another Dublin paper bought it out. Much more money was now needed in order to launch a completely new paper, and it was not at all easy to raise.

De Valera visited America to raise funds in December, 1927, returning to Ireland in February, 1928. He went back again in November, 1929, staying this time for six months and setting up a whole network of committees. In America and Ireland he threw himself into the new venture with a boyish zest which was often noticed in him.

But before his second visit to America he had undergone another unpleasant experience in Northern Ireland. Since his arrest in 1924 he had only crossed the border once, in 1927 for the funeral of Cardinal O'Donnell. In February, 1929, he set out to visit Belfast, unaware that on the 1927 occasion the Free State Government had made a special arrangement with the Northern Government that none of the Dáil deputies would be impeded in any way. There was no such arrangement this time. 'We have no idea what is likely to happen in Belfast this evening,' wrote his secretary. 'It is the general opinion that he will be arrested the moment he reaches the Border. It will be very awkward if that happens, but he has accepted the invitation and is leaving on the 3 o'clock train.'[25]

The meeting which de Valera was to attend was the opening of Aonach na nGaedheal, an Irish fete under the auspices of the Gaelic League and of the Gaelic Athletic Association, and he travelled with a prepared speech on the national aims of these two bodies in his bag. There was nothing 'seditious' about the speech, but that did not protect him. At Goraghwood station he was taken from the train by members of the Royal Ulster Constabulary. He was taken to Belfast, and tried there for crossing the border in contravention of the exclusion order which had been issued against him five years before, and was sentenced to one month's imprisonment in spite of loud protests in Dublin.

The importance of a daily paper was never absent for long from de Valera's mind in those years, but it became more urgent to him when he read statements like that of Ernest Blythe that the Free State Government was a happy member of the British Commonwealth and desired no further freedom than the removal of a few anomalies. De Valera wrote:

> If we had a daily paper at this moment I believe that Blythe's statement could be used to waken up the nation, but the daily press that we have slurs it over and pretends that nothing vital has been said. The English press of course are broadcasting it wherever they can. This is natural enough, for it is Britain's final victory over what remained of the Collins mentality and policy.[26]

The 'stepping stones to freedom' were being forgotten and nothing but a lively national press would force the Government to remember it. De Valera even commented that if ever it came to a choice between leading the party and running the paper he believed that he would choose the latter.

During the summer of 1931 much work went into the final preparations. Concerning the outcome de Valera was careful to make no rash promises:

> The first year in its life is bound to be a critical one. I wish we had more reserve capital than we have. Except for anxiety on this point, I am full of hope that we shall win through, despite the desperate competition of our rivals.[27]

He had taken the closest possible interest in every step of the preparations and he was present in the *Irish Press* building when the presses were tried for the first time in August. As September 5th, the date of publication, approached, the tension mounted. There were trial runs in the last few days. De Valera stayed up till 5 a.m. to supervise them. Then came the first issue.

The leading article in that first number of the *Irish Press* set forth its policy. It was to be the voice of the people giving utterance to Irish ideals and guidance on how to attain them:

> Our services will be to the whole people. We are not the organ of an individual, or a group or a party. We are a national organ in all that the term conveys . . . In national affairs we stand for independence . . . Our ideal culturally is an Irish Ireland.[28]

The other Irish papers had admittedly been hostile to de Valera. This was indeed a great step towards breaking through the wall of antagonism.

Night after night as the paper went through its first teething pains, de Valera worked in the newspaper office to see the paper off the presses. No detail was too small for his attention. Some might claim that he would not delegate authority, but this is an exaggeration. He delegated work in plenty, but to whatever he took personal charge of he gave the closest possible supervision. For example, while he was overseeing preparations for the first edition of the *Irish Press*, he delegated most of the Fianna Fáil party work to others; but within the paper office he saw to everything, including the difficulties of early despatch by train to the country.

The launching of the paper was undoubtedly a big achievement, especially in those years of depression. It reflects a side of de Valera which is sometimes under-estimated, his business acumen. In the years after 1931, the paper had its trying as well as its prosperous times, but its strength was continually growing. The *Irish Press* succeeded in winning the second largest circulation of any Irish daily paper, and its sister papers the *Evening Press* and the *Sunday Press*, both launched in the 1950s, have outstripped all rivals in their fields. Much of this success the company owed to de Valera. As trustee and representative of the American company, Irish Press Incorporated, on the board of directors, he had a controlling interest.

It also owes much to the staff of those pioneer days in the early thirties, above all to the editor, Frank Gallagher, and literary editor, M. J. MacManus, for the standards set and attained. In these and other ways, his period in opposition was abundantly occupied; but these years seemed at the time, and seem in retrospect, to have been years of waiting. De Valera never doubted that before long Fianna Fáil would become the government.

THE COLLISION COURSE

1931 – 1933

With the General Election looming up, the Cosgrave Government might have wished to avoid controversial measures. In the event they followed a different course. Admittedly there was a considerable increase in the activities of the Irish Republican Army; three murders had occurred since the beginning of 1931. For good reasons and bad, the Draconian Bill introduced by the Government in the Dáil in October, 1931, was so severe that it ensured for Fianna Fáil the support of all Republicans in the following months. The Bill was in the form of an amendment to the Constitution. The new Article 2A was, in fact, the most rigorous public safety statute which Ireland had known in a long history of coercion.

A military tribunal of five members was to be established to counter political crime. Its powers included the death penalty. From its decisions there could be no appeal. The Government was empowered to declare associations unlawful; large new powers were given to the police. De Valera was strongly opposed to this measure and denounced it roundly. He knew that he was bound to be misrepresented as encouraging crime. Three months later the Dáil was dissolved and an election campaign fought in the harsh weather of February, 1932.

Not surprisingly the Cumann na nGaedheal party painted de Valera as the close ally of the extremists, whom they dubbed Communists in their turn. A parody of Percy French's ever-popular 'Phil the Fluter's Ball' was issued officially to portray the state of Ireland if de Valera came to power. The chorus indicates the contents, much of which was libellous:

> Och! we'll shoot and we'll loot and with bullets we will riddle oh!
> We'll keep the whole land sizzling like a herring on the griddle oh!

The party's election literature depicted de Valera as the author of one Civil War and seeking another. The Cumann na nGaedheal propaganda indeed concentrated on de Valera as a frightening ogre, whose accession to office would endanger not only the rights of farmers to their land, but the lives of peaceful citizens.

Cosgrave's election manifesto emphasised his party's achievements rather than future policies. On one aspect, however, of genuine progress the manifesto was curiously silent. No mention was made of its strenuous exertions at imperial conferences, which had undoubtedly helped to liberalize the position of all the member states, including the Irish Free State. Free State membership of the Commonwealth, even a liberated Commonwealth, was not apparently a winning card.

On behalf of Fianna Fáil, de Valera issued a manifesto in which the removal of the oath and the withholding of the land annuities were prominent features. In the field of international relations a Fianna Fáil Government would guarantee not to exceed the mandate asked for without again consulting the people. It also felt called on to deny that its members had leanings towards Communism, planned to impose a land tax or would refuse to pay interest due on existing national loans and on savings bank deposits.

A pastoral by the Irish hierarchy some months before the election tended to foster anxiety about Communism and illegal activities. On the other hand, the Government's use of the military tribunal and its prosecution of the editor of the *Irish Press*, Frank Gallagher, under the Public Safety Act, provided excellent propaganda against itself in the last ten days before polling-day.

In Britain, J. H. Thomas, Secretary of State for Dominion Affairs, was warning the cabinet that 'if the General Elections in the Free State should result in the return of Mr de Valera, a difficult situation would be produced, and he might have to consult his colleagues on questions of urgency.'

In the event, Fianna Fáil won 72 seats, as against 57 in the previous election, and emerged as the largest party in the Dáil, though without an overall majority. If it was to take office, it would need the help of the Labour Party, who had now been reduced to seven deputies. De Valera, unfortunately, fell ill, a rare occurrence, and was unable to meet anyone for a week. He was unable to participate in the delayed election in Sligo–Leitrim, which had been postponed for a fortnight, because a Cumann na nGaedheal candidate had been shot dead. The culprit turned out to be a non-political lunatic. De Valera resumed work early in March, but was back in bed again the next day.

By Tuesday morning, March 8th, he was able, with Seán T. O'Kelly and Gerald Boland, to meet the Labour leaders, Tom Johnson, William Norton and William Davin, to explain his programme. He said he thought they would not wish to be represented in the cabinet. They agreed. The resulting independence, de Valera considered, was best for both parties. No conditions were laid down for Labour support, but it was clear that the party would vote for him.

On Wednesday afternoon, the Dáil met; a huge enthusiastic crowd gathered around Leinster House for the momentous occasion. De Valera attended the votive mass at the Cathedral in the morning, and made his way to Leinster House at about 2.30 p.m. He was admittedly anxious. It was clear that he would be elected Head of the Government. He was not sure that the outgoing administration would hand over office peacefully. After what he considered the *coup d'état* of June, 1922, he had felt that there might never be a peaceful transfer of power within the state, even if he won a majority at the elections. He did not rule out the possibility of assassination, but went unarmed. Vivion, his eldest son, was photographed at his side, with a revolver showing all too plainly through his overcoat.

De Valera was nominated to the Presidency by Michael Kilroy, a country deputy, and seconded by Oscar Traynor, who represented a city constituency. The debate was short, a division was challenged and de Valera was elected by 81 votes to 68. He had been supported not only by Fianna Fáil and Labour but by three independents, including James Dillon, later to become leader of Fine Gael.

In the meantime, de Valera was spared a visit to the Viceregal Lodge. The Governor-General, James McNeill, well aware of de Valera's susceptibilities, made matters as easy as possible by himself going to Leinster House and appointing de Valera there as President of the Executive Council, in other terms, Prime Minister.

De Valera assumed, in addition, the portfolio for External Affairs. He always felt that this was a post which should, if possible, be held by the Head of Government, so that there might be no doubt as to the authority with which the Minister spoke. General practice was against him here, but maybe his experience in December, 1921, exerted a lasting influence. After the second World War he had to abandon, as will be seen, the double burden. The number of states represented diplomatically in Dublin became too great, and the international gatherings too many.

His voice was soon raised in public reassurance. 'We heard,' he said, 'of frightful things that would happen the moment the Fianna Fáil Government came into power. We have seen no evidence of these things. . . We have had a peaceful change of Government.'[1] It was indeed the peacefulness of the transfer of power which struck many observers. Rumours were around that a *coup* was planned by the former Government, but such plans, if they ever existed, got no countenance whatever from the Opposition leader. Though some of the new ministers took office with revolvers in their pockets, their fears were in no way realised.

On Thursday, March 10th, he went to meet the heads of the departments. He told them at once that he had no intention of changing any of them. The only immediate appointments he made were the transfer of Maurice Moynihan, a civil servant in the Department of Finance, to his office as private secretary, and the reinstatement as a civil servant of his personal secretary, Kathleen O'Connell. With falling trade and growing unemployment, the new Government took office with the immediate intention of cutting out any unnecessary expenditure. To set an example, the new ministers voluntarily accepted salaries substantially less than those previously in operation. In the case of de Valera, the salary he accepted was £1,500 p.a., exclusive of income tax, equivalent to about £1,700, subject to tax, as against the £2,500 to which he was entitled.

De Valera reiterated the Government's policy in a broadcast to the United States. 'In particular,' he stated, 'the oath will now be removed.' He also referred to the determination to keep the land annuities in Ireland. 'Our annual payments to England,' he pointed out, 'are heavier upon us than a payment of £330,000,000 annually would be on Britain, and that is a sum ten times as great as Britain's annual debt payments to the United States.' The central core of his argument, however, was legal and so it always remained.

He insisted that he was moved, not by hatred of Britain, but by love of his own country. 'My desire,' he said, 'has always been to bring about the friendliest relations between Britain and Ireland, but I know that the only sure foundation for such relations and for a lasting peace, is justice and the recognition of the right of our people to be free. That is what I strove for from 1919 to 1921 when President of the Republic and that is what I intend now to strive for.' And he went on to mention the greatest tragedy of all, 'the partition of our country.'[2]

It was not to be expected that the British Government would sit by with folded hands, although Thomas was at first optimistically advising the Cabinet that 'time is on our side.' Naturally enough, he lost no time in seeking to elucidate de Valera's intentions through J. W. Dulanty, Irish High Commissioner in London, who was forthwith summoned to Dublin. On March 22nd, de Valera informed Thomas that he was in a position to answer him as regards the oath of allegiance, which de Valera was obviously seeking to keep apart from the question of the annuities. 'The oath,' he stated firmly, 'was not mandatory in the Treaty.' Added to which the Irish people had an absolute right to modify their constitution. The Government's decision to remove 'this relic of mediaevalism' was final and irrevocable. He sincerely desired to encourage friendly relations between Ireland and England 'but' he went on, 'there can be no normal relations between us so long as one side insists on imposing on the other a conscience test which has no parallel in Treaty relationships between States.'

There was no going back on the position thus assumed. Thomas stated in the House of Commons, in a somewhat melodramatic speech, that Dulanty had handed him 'a very important and serious document.' De Valera was obviously going to stand on the issue of the oath, but Thomas wished also to find out de Valera's intentions regarding the second part of his election promises, the land annuities. He wrote to de Valera not only denying the right of the Free State to remove the oath from the Constitution, but protesting further against any attempt to withhold the annuities:

> In the view of His Majesty's Government in the United Kingdom, the Irish Free State Government are bound by the most formal and explicit undertaking to continue to pay the land annuities to the National Debt Commissioners.

They were in debt arising from 'an engagement which is binding in law and in honour.'

Now, eleven years after his famous correspondence with Lloyd George, de Valera was once more engaged in argument by letter with a British Minister. He was not frightened of the constitutional issue regarding the oath:

> The real issue is that the oath is an intolerable burden to the people of this State and they have declared in the most formal manner that they desire its instant removal.

He rejected any suggestion that he was breaking faith with the British Government and pointed out many of the Irish objections to the Treaty. It had involved no parity of sacrifice as between Ireland and England and was submitted to only under the threat of immediate and terrible war. British occupation under it of some major Irish ports and their claims to other rights in time of war would make Ireland's right to neutrality a mockery. Its provisions had divided the people of Ireland into two hostile camps. De Valera stood upon the right of the legislature of the Free State to deal with what he described as a purely domestic matter—the elimination of the oath. Regarding the land annuities, he asked Thomas what was 'the formal and explicit undertaking' on which he relied.

While the oath remained the paramount question, it was clear that J. H. Thomas wished to link it with the annuities problem. His reply, sent on April 9th, made the general sanctity of Anglo-Irish agreements the common factor. He was adamant that the oath was an essential part of the Treaty and he surprised de Valera by citing a financial agreement signed by W. T. Cosgrave on February 12th, 1923. This, in addition to the 1926 Agreement, signed and published in 1926 but never ratified by the Dáil, was held to cover the British right to the annuities.[3]

At once, de Valera ordered a search for the 1923 Agreement in the

Government files. It had not been mentioned even in the legal advice which had been given to the previous Free State Government. It was contained in a document marked 'Secret', covering a number of financial matters, and de Valera found that, though it had been referred to on a number of occasions in the preceding nine years, every effort to get it published had been opposed by ministers of the Free State Government. The Attorney-General provided President de Valera with an interesting brief on the ministerial silence regarding the terms of the Agreement. Indeed, the former Minister for Finance, Ernest Blythe, had stipulated on one occasion, when the Agreement had to be produced in a British court, that all the clauses except the one relevant to the law case be pasted over.[4] It was a story replete with political ammunition for use against former ministers. According to de Valera's legal advisers, the 1923 Agreement was no more binding than that of 1926, since it had never been submitted to, or ratified by, Parliament.

His viewpoint stated, the President went straight ahead with legislation to abolish the oath of allegiance. He introduced a bill for this purpose in Dáil Éireann on April 20th, and it was passed by that body on May 19th, despite strong opposition mainly from the Cumann na nGaedheal party. Labour consistently and strongly supported the Government. The burden of the Opposition speeches was the fear of British reprisals, the sanctity of the existing agreements, especially of the Treaty which was felt to be endangered, and the fact that de Valera did not enter into negotiation with Britain on the question of the oath.

De Valera's answer was that the oath was a purely domestic matter. That the oath was not compulsory under the Treaty could be argued on a legalistic level or, more solidly, on the basis of the changes which had taken place in Commonwealth relations since 1922. Indeed, de Valera admitted frankly that the changes culminating in the Statute of Westminster, for which Cumann na nGaedheal claimed credit, were larger than he had anticipated.[5] He sought to disarm the Opposition. If they had won the freedom which they claimed to have won under that statute, he could not see why they should oppose the use of that freedom to get rid of the obnoxious oath.

In Ireland, however, the Opposition was in no mood to reason along those lines. Having opposed every effort to remove the oath while they were the Government, they continued to do so in opposition. Anything else would have seemed to them quite inconsistent.

To de Valera, however, their actions could only appear as giving comfort to the enemy. He was to complain:

Instead of getting help from directions in which we had expected it, we have miserable politics, miserable politics indulged in by people who hope, by the defeat of the Government, they are going to bring back some of their friends.[6]

De Valera did not reopen the question of the annuities with Thomas until the Dáil had passed the bill removing the oath from the Constitution. He was determined that the two things should be kept separate. Negotiations regarding the money might be considered but not, on any account, regarding the oath. Once the Oath Bill had gone to the Senate, he invited Thomas to discuss—specifically—the financial difficulties. Since the beginning of the dispute, the Government had undertaken thorough examination, not alone of the land annuities, but of all the financial payments which were being made to Britain and of the legal basis for them. The financial argument was broadening out.

On Monday, June 6th, 1932, J. H. Thomas arrived in Dublin, accompanied by Lord Hailsham, who held the somewhat ominous portfolio of War. Denis Gwynn recalls the new prestige brought to him by the visit.[7] Other visitors to Dublin that spring and summer recall more vividly the tension and anxiety at a time when the fear of British military measures had not been finally eliminated.

The next day they met de Valera himself in de Valera's office, with the Vice-President, Seán T. O'Kelly. Two days later, de Valera went to London to continue the conversations with the Prime Minister, Ramsay MacDonald, and other members of the British cabinet. Thomas and Hailsham were there and with them Stanley Baldwin and Sir Herbert Samuel.

At the meetings, de Valera carefully explained his views on how to make permanent peace between Ireland and Britain. Peace could be founded only on justice and respect for the rights of both peoples and it would be wrecked if there was any attempt to dominate the Irish people.

I feared [he said later] that the present British Government would not, any more than past Governments, have the courage to face the position and really get down to make a proper peace between the two peoples.

General points made at both the Dublin and London meetings were followed by a reference to the details of the dispute. On the oath, de Valera said that his Government did not believe that its removal from the Constitution was a breach of the Treaty. Come what might, it would be removed. On the question of the land annuities, however, it could not be denied that there were two viewpoints conceivable. The British suggested at this point that there should be a recourse to arbitration.

Arbitration raised a difficult question. The people of Ireland had learned enough from the Boundary Commission to make them chary of accepting the justice of arbitration, yet de Valera was willing to consider such a proposal favourably in principle. The form of arbitration, however, proposed by the British endangered agreement. They suggested not an international, but a British Commonwealth one, such as had been envisaged at the last Imperial Conference. De Valera and his Government accepted the principle of arbitration, but insisted that the tribunal should not, on any account, be limited to members of the British Commonwealth. He also demanded that all the disputed annual payments (of which the annuities were about three-fifths) should be referred to it.[8]

The end of June came and matters were no nearer a solution. The main point of difference remained, the personnel of the tribunal. Early in July, the House of Commons passed a resolution to enable the British Government to make good the money by means of customs duties on imports from Ireland. De Valera was still in correspondence with Thomas when this step was taken without warning. It seemed to the Irish that the punitive measures against Ireland were partly occasioned by the proposed removal of the oath. Thomas in Parliament denied any such purpose:

> I want this House and the great mass of democracy outside not to get confused with the idea that any constitutional issue is involved in this matter, because there is none.[9]

His precipitancy, however, brought him a surprise when Arthur Greenwood revealed to the House that de Valera had not defaulted, but had put the funds in a suspense account pending arbitration. At the insistence of Sir Stafford Cripps, Thomas enquired of the Irish High Commissioner, J. W. Dulanty, who was present at the debate, whether this was true, and Dulanty, after telephoning Dublin, confirmed this statement of Greenwood.[10]

Though it revealed that Thomas had been rather hasty in his actions, Greenwood's revelation did not prevent the resolution from being passed. It was, in fact, a declaration of war, albeit with economic rather than military weapons. To bow to the threat would certainly have far-reaching consequences. De Valera had concluded from his conversations with British ministers that the financial were secondary to the constitutional issues; in other words, he did not accept Thomas's denial that this was so.

By now, preparations were in hand for the holding of an Imperial Conference in Ottawa. An Irish delegation, consisting of Seán T. O'Kelly, Seán Lemass and Dr James Ryan, left Dublin as the crisis heightened. They were at sea when they heard by radio that a 20 per cent *ad valorem* duty was to be imposed on Free State produce entering Britain. Seán Lemass, as Minister for Industry and Commerce, wrote home at once suggesting counter-measures. He singled out British coal as an Irish import from Britain which it might be possible to hit with duties, and even to replace with German or Polish supplies. He and his colleagues saw that the greatest danger from the British measures was their effect on Irish public opinion. However, he was far from pessimistic and wrote:

> I think that the present situation if rightly handled, can prove of permanent benefit to the Free State if our people are prepared to stick out the transition stage.[11]

Back in Dublin, de Valera was thinking along the same lines. But at that point came a last-minute peace effort by the Irish Labour Leader, William Norton. Norton spent much of the early part of July in London interviewing leaders of the British Labour Party. On July 15th, de Valera himself accepted an invitation from the British Prime Minister, Ramsay MacDonald. It was with little hope of achieving anything, however, that he travelled to London, accompanied by his secretary, Maurice Moynihan. He pointed out that there were only two possible ways in which the financial crux could be solved—one was by arbitration, the other by negotiation. If the British imposed the tariffs which had been announced, negotiations would be carried on in an atmosphere of hostility begotten by these impositions and by Irish counter-measures. MacDonald agreed, but insisted that the annuities, then held in a suspense account, be handed over to Britain. Of course de Valera would not agree, and the British duties went into operation next day.

One compensation was visible. The economic policy which Fianna Fáil had intended to pursue had been protectionist, but de Valera had always foreseen that it might cause counter-measures by Britain. The present drastic action of the British Government would make an Irish self-sufficiency policy easier to embark on. In the Senate, two days after his return from London, de Valera announced that it would be possible to make a virtue of necessity and reap an economic benefit from the tariff war. He said:

> The suffering, such as it may be, of certain classes is going to be made up by the foundation here of the sort of economic life that every Irishman who thought nationally in the past hoped for . . .[12]

The imposition of British tariffs was met by emergency legislation in the Free State legislature imposing protective duties. At the same time, de Valera instructed the delegates who had gone to Ottawa not to attend the Imperial Conference pending further guidance. Their main task was to be the exploration of alternative markets for Irish produce and sources of supply for Irish needs.

In fact, the delegates had a number of talks with Thomas and Baldwin during the conference. But these led nowhere.

It was clear, moreover, by this time that the British—despite Thomas's earlier denial—were tying together financial and constitutional issues. Sir Thomas Inskip, the Attorney-General, in a speech at Stranraer, also made this clear:

> It is not money that stands in the way of peace, he said. There is something bigger and deeper. Does Mr de Valera want to be a partner in the Empire, or is he pursuing the will-of-the-wisp of a republic?[13]

In Ireland, an intensive drive was now launched with the aim of self-sufficiency. A series of meetings were begun in September to explain the problems of the economic war to the people of Ireland. In the first of these meetings at College Green, Dublin, de Valera pointed out that the Irish farmers should produce for the home market by turning to tillage, and he appealed to all to buy Irish products. He saw that exports would diminish, but this could be countered by a restriction on imports. In this way, he said, the nation could survive the pressure:

> We are all brothers in this, that no one of us can suffer for any length of time without that suffering reflecting on the rest of us. It is our duty to stand together.

The crisis had made the Government proceed with its protection policy at a much faster rate than had been intended. As a result, there would be more dislocation and hardship than if the change were spread over a number of years. The line of action taken at the present time, he said, was less one of retaliation upon England, than one of construction. It would make the people strong in the future, so that they should never fear a crisis such as the present again. If they approached the crisis in that spirit, then the hardships they might have to endure would prove ultimately for the benefit of the country.[14]

Though issues were being knit, de Valera did not lose all hope of reaching some solution of the financial question. He wrote to Thomas after his return from Ottawa, informing him officially of his acceptance of a proposal put to him by an intermediary who had visited him in August. Thomas, however, was standing firm. The intermediary was not, he said, authorised by the British Government to visit Dublin or to put forward any proposals. De Valera, in a reply on September 26th, summed up the position:

> When arbitration was suggested, I lost no time in declaring my Government's willingness to agree. It was not I, but your Government, that destroyed the hope of a solution in that direction by insisting on an artificial restriction on the selection of arbitrators. When the British Government refused to consent to an unrestricted choice of our nominees on the tribunal, I declared

the readiness of the Irish Free State to seek agreement by negotiation, only to be met by a new difficulty with regard to the disposal of the monies during the period of discussions.

As a way out of this difficulty, I accepted the suggestion of a third party that, in the event of a truce for the period of the negotiations, the Irish Free State should deposit the monies with the Bank for International Settlements. This also has been rejected.

To be precise, it had not been rejected but made impossible by Thomas insisting on a further condition, surely fantastic, that if negotiations failed the deposited funds should automatically go to Britain. It would appear that Thomas was spoiling for a fight, though he did agree to a meeting to make a final effort to solve the financial problems.[15] This was arranged as de Valera passed through London to Geneva early in October. It was a full-scale meeting in which both sides set out their points of view but it did not, in de Valera's opinion, merit the title 'negotiations'. Both sides were adamant in their position. De Valera told the Dáil afterwards:

It is possible that if we were prepared, as they seemed to wish, to go in the role of beggars, hat in hand, asking for consideration and charity, there might be a disposition to make minor modifications and some mitigation of their claim, but simple justice they were not prepared to concede.[16]

The meeting served but to confirm de Valera's conviction that, although nothing apart from financial matters was discussed, political and constitutional matters were fundamental to the British stand.

Indeed, during the spring and summer, a further constitutional question, additional to the oath, had appeared on the scene. Though it was not raised between the governments of the two countries, it obviously affected the other issues. The office of Governor-General was one of the symbols of monarchical authority most repulsive to Irish republicans. The occupant of that office, when de Valera became President of the Executive Council in March, was James McNeill, a prudent and courteous man with a fine record in the Indian Civil Service. While objecting to the symbolism of his office, de Valera had no personal animus against him. He foresaw difficulties, however, and through the Secretary of the Department of External Affairs he advised McNeill of the need for tact. It would be wise to avoid, for the immediate future at least, inviting members of the Government to functions.

Soon, however, de Valera found himself involved in a quarrel not of his or McNeill's making. When McNeill arrived at a dance at the French Legation, the Government ministers who were present left—a fact which did not pass unnoticed in the press. McNeill wrote a letter of protest to de Valera who, in reply, admitted the 'justifiable annoyance' which the

Governor-General felt at the snub. He assured McNeill that it was not 'part of a considered policy that the Governor-General should be treated with deliberate discourtesy.' 'The whole affair,' he wrote, 'was unfortunate and regrettable, and should never have been allowed to occur.' For the future he suggested that it would be well if the Government were kept informed of the Governor-General's public social engagements, as prior knowledge would avoid embarrassments. The situation was admittedly a delicate one and he appealed to McNeill to give understanding and co-operation to the Government. McNeill, however, pressed for an apology, which he did not receive. He was already piqued at delays in receiving the Government's permission to invite guests to the Eucharistic Congress which was to take place in Dublin early in June. Without the Government's consent, and indeed against their direct advice, he sent out invitations.

During the Eucharistic Congress, the President received the principal guests and the representative of the King was kept in the background, but after it was over McNeill challenged the whole authority of the Government by publishing, despite the formal advice of the cabinet, the correspondence which had passed between him and de Valera.[17] De Valera tried to prevent the publication of the correspondence in Irish papers, but once it was published in England there was nothing he could do except allow full publication in Ireland. The whole theory that the Governor-General should act only on the advice of the Irish executive was being challenged and, however one may sympathise with McNeill's personal feelings, the episode brought into question the very foundations of the office as previously understood. To assert the authority of the Government, de Valera saw no option but McNeill's removal from office.

On September 9th, 1932, J. W. Dulanty, the Irish High Commissioner in London, presented a submission from de Valera advising King George V to terminate the appointment of McNeill 'as the representative of Your Majesty in the Irish Free State'. The Government's advice raised immediate problems. Although the King did not challenge the constitutional practice of acting on the advice of the Irish ministers, he asked for information on the facts of the case before approving the submission. Legal difficulties occasioned various delays. Ultimately McNeill was removed by the King from November 1st, without de Valera giving him the reasons which had been sought.

The constitutional problem of who should carry on the functions vested in the Governor-General was not thereby solved. The Dominions Office was quite willing to allow the Chief Justice to give the Royal Assent to bills, but felt that the King himself would have to enter in some way into the procedure of dissolution of parliament. While indifferent as to the way in which the oaths of office should be taken, the British would not agree to their being waived.

As November passed without a solution, the matter became pressing. De Valera was in Geneva at a League of Nations meeting, but before leaving Ireland he already had made arrangements which, in the last resort, would end the difficulty for the time being. He had approached an old supporter, Domhnall Ó Buachalla, and asked him to act if the necessity arose. Ó Buachalla was a 1916 veteran from Maynooth, where he ran a shop, and was a life-long advocate of the Irish revival. The Appropriation Bill had to be signed by November 30th. It was agreed therefore that the King should be advised to appoint Domhnall Ó Buachalla.[18] Instead of living in the Viceregal Lodge, Ó Buachalla took a small suburban house in the city and, by never appearing in public or giving any kind of social lead, he dealt a death blow to the office.

That this and other constitutional questions were predominant in the minds of the British Government was confirmed by Joseph P. Walshe who, at the end of October, had informal talks in London with Sir Edward J. Harding and Sir Henry Batterbee, of the Dominions Office, regarding the issues involved. They put forward the following, in Irish eyes, preposterous requirements:

1). The acceptance by the Irish Free State Government of the 1921 Treaty as valid and to be observed according to its terms unless and until it is altered by agreement;

2). that no further question should be raised by the Irish Free State Government as to the validity of the Financial Settlement, as embodied in the Financial Agreements of 1923 and 1926 and the Boundary Agreement of 1925:

3). that the acceptance of the Treaty should be accompanied on the part of the Irish Free State Government by

a) an undertaking not to proceed further with the Oath Bill,

b) suitable arrangements, in accordance with the Treaty, to take effect on Mr McNeill's relinquishing the office of Governor-General.[19]

If de Valera gave in on all these points, the British Government would be prepared to discuss a modification of the oath, a mitigation of the financial burdens and a trade agreement. Walshe made it clear that these conditions would be completely unacceptable; that de Valera would enter into no negotiations about the oath, and that British pressure on that issue would be the surest way of making Ireland sever its links with the Commonwealth. On the financial question, he stated that the minimum compromise which de Valera would consider was a reduction of £3,000,000 per annum in the £5,000,000 being paid each year to

Britain. This would mean, in effect, that the land annuities, which came to £3,000,000, would not themselves be paid. With the British attitude at that time as it was, a complete impasse was inevitable. Indeed a few days later, they increased the duties then imposed on Irish produce entering Britain, doubling it in most cases.

It was to be some years before J. H. Thomas was to admit that more was involved than the financial questions. In July, 1935, he was to tell the House of Commons that the annuities were not the only difficulty:

> We would soon get over that difficulty if that were the only matter in dispute. But are not the Oath of Allegiance and the Governor-General as the King's representative, 'a foreign king', as defined by Mr de Valera, not fundamental to any settlement?[20]

But already by the end of 1932, the issue was fairly joined on these three questions. De Valera's principal worry was the attitude which the opposition in Ireland was taking. He said in the Dáil in October, 1932:

> I have come to the conclusion that the present British Government, pressed forward as it is by certain anti-Irish feeling in Britain and supported by the attitude of a minority in this country, is not prepared to examine this position on its merits or to yield to claims of simple justice.[21]

The role of a constructive opposition was, in the circumstances of the time, most difficult. Since the Civil War there had been a wide cleavage and a deep mutual distrust between the leaders of the two main parties. Each tended to hear, and not infrequently to believe, the worst of its opponents.

The abolition of the oath and the retention of the annuities had both been submitted to the public in the 1932 election. Opposition tactics in regard to them were considered by de Valera to be completely fractious. He heard from Seán T. O'Kelly that, at the discussion in Ottawa, J. H. Thomas had hopefully referred to the Army Comrades Association and asserted that, in a month or two, there would be civil war in Ireland, and that he would be dealing with a different government.

De Valera indeed became more and more anxious about the activities of Cumann na nGaedheal leaders and their relationship with the Army Comrades Association, an organisation of retired officers and men. In 1932, Colonel Austin Brennan, the President of the association, resigned to be succeeded by a Cumann na nGaedheal deputy, a brother of Kevin O'Higgins, Dr Thomas O'Higgins. In one of his first speeches, he gave a sombre if rather cryptic warning:

> Our objects are peace. We are an army of peace. Policy may, however, not be able to control circumstances. If policy cannot control circumstances in

the future, then policy in the future must be directed to some extent by circumstances.[22]

In governmental eyes the Opposition, instead of presenting a united front against the outside enemy was undermining the national stand.

De Valera decided that the only way to strengthen his hand in dealing with British and internal pressures was to go to the country again. He never had any doubt that he would get the support he needed. On January 2nd, 1933, he dissolved the Dáil. The oath had not yet been abolished. The third reading of the bill for its removal had passed through the Dáil but it was held up by the Senate in which the Opposition had a majority. But de Valera had made it abundantly clear to the people of Ireland what he was engaged on. It could be no fault of his if the issues of the oath, the land annuities and the Governor-General were not as clear to them as they were to J. H. Thomas.

De Valera, at a midnight press interview, pointed out that the Government had been elected on a well-understood programme. Clear proof of popular confidence was required to carry it out successfully. To create doubts on this matter, he went on, had been the systematic policy of the political opponents of the present government. This policy of creating doubt has operated in a manner that has been most damaging to the national interests, both in regard to our external relations and our domestic affairs.[23]

Mistrust had indeed gone very far, for he believed that the Opposition were not only making things difficult in Ireland, but were in actual collusion with British ministers. It is fair to the Opposition of that day to point out that no evidence of this has ever emerged.

The decision to dissolve the Dáil in January, 1933, was taken by de Valera alone. He sent for each minister individually and informed him of his decision. It came to them as a great surprise, as they had not suffered a defeat in the House and a dissolution might in fact jeopardise the position of the party. De Valera, however, threw himself whole-heartedly into the winter election campaign, and was justified by the result. An overall majority made his party independent of the support of the Labour Party on which he had hitherto depended.

Another side of de Valera's life at this time emerges from the recollections of Terry, his youngest son. 'Then,' writes Terry, 'came the 1930s, and our move to Blackrock. This was not only a change of scene but altogether a place of much brighter horizons, such a change from fog-ridden Sandymount and that awful house which I am convinced was haunted.'

11

He remembers well the tense excitement awaiting the result of the General Election of 1932 and how Ruairí, always his counsellor and adviser, explained to him the significance of being 'in power' and the changes it would mean even in their young lives.

'Once father was in power and with our move to dear old Bellevue, haunted as it too was said to be, my father at home became more the accepted order of the day and it was really only then at the age of eleven that I really came to know him.' Whenever time permitted, and this was not too often then, he threw himself into his beloved mathematics, 'a love which the elder boys shared, especially Brian, who was so brilliant in that direction.' Alas, this love and talent was not shared by his youngest. Mathematics however there must be. De Valera showed that there was no avoiding them. Next only to his simple devotion to his faith and his strongly held political convictions, which of course included the Irish language, 'nothing ranked higher in his philosophy.' For Terry, however, it was just like medicine, and mathematics were administered accordingly. 'Not until I matriculated in this subject, and *all* due thanks to Father for that, did I emancipate myself from that dread subject.'

Bellevue was surrounded by some four to five acres, with a long walk around the perimeter. 'Many is the scar those paths bear of countless triangles and other mathematical figures scratched out with a long walking stick.' Many was the hour this youngest son looked vacantly on while the less he understood the deeper the scratch. Unimpressed as his father often was with his poor answers, any gleam of comprehension did not go unrewarded. Times he remembers a hand being thrust down into a dark-coloured trouser pocket and a bright half-crown pressed into his hand. Peace would then reign and that tall figure and 'his very thin youngest' would walk back smilingly to the house with a mutual feeling of satisfaction.

It was in many ways an unusual upbringing, but the strictness of principle was matched by the gaiety and robustness, and the perplexities by the mutual devotion.

FRAMING A NEW CONSTITUTION

1935 - 1937

In the first years of his government, de Valera remained dissatisfied with the existing Free State Constitution, but did not immediately introduce an alternative. The objective of an independent Irish Republic was never out of his mind. He decided, however, to move slowly; he had no wish to alienate the timorous or precipitate international difficulties. At Arbour Hill, on April 23rd, 1933, he revealed his method:

> Let it be made clear that we yield no willing assent to any form or symbol that is out of keeping with Ireland's right as a sovereign nation. Let us remove these forms one by one, so that this State that we control may be a Republic in fact; and that, when the time comes, the proclaiming of the Republic may involve no more than a ceremony the formal confirmation of a status already attained.[1]

The process indicated began with the removal of the oath of allegiance which was accomplished in May, 1933. In November it was carried further when three more amending acts were passed. Two of these transferred from the Governor-General to the Executive Council the functions of recommending money bills and removed his power of withholding assent to bills of all kinds. The third step was in accordance with a policy of the previous administration. It terminated the right of appeal from the Irish courts to the Privy Council in London. The status of the Governor-General had already been whittled down by the removal of James McNeill and the appointment of an unobtrusive substitute. De Valera explained in the Dáil, in July, 1933, that he hoped to abolish the office altogether some day, but since some people feared that this might lead to a renewal of war by England, it was being retained for the moment. Governor-Generals, while they were in office, would do what the Executive Council told them to do. Nothing more and nothing less.[2] Legal difficulties involved in abolition had not yet been surmounted, but they were on the way to solution.

By now he had almost reached the limit of reasonable amendment of the existing Constitution. The extent of the amendments already made by the Cumann na nGaedheal and Fianna Fáil governments had made the state of constitutional law unduly complex. As de Valera pointed out, the Constitution was no longer a fit document to be regarded as the fundamental law. This was in itself a sufficient argument for a new constitution. There were, however, other reasons. Fundamentally, de Valera acknowledged the doubts attaching to the whole basis of the existing Constitution. He could sympathise with those Republicans who still refused to recognise it. By removing the oath of allegiance he had tried to remove an obstacle to entering the Dáil. Most of the conscientious objectors, however, were not appeased so readily. They claimed a constitutional succession from the Second Dáil. No matter how republican the Free State Constitution was made by amendment, it could never escape its basis in British law. What was needed was a new beginning which drew its strength from Irish roots.

On April 30th and May 2nd, 1935, de Valera instructed John J. Hearne, legal adviser to the Department for External Affairs, to prepare a draft of the heads of a new constitution for the State.

From his instructions it was clear that de Valera intended to frame a republican constitution, while leaving it possible to retain a link with the British Commonwealth. This could be effected by using the King in external affairs. In his own mind he was aiming at the form of external association which he had first suggested in 1921. The question which was so crucial at that time—'membership or non-membership of the British Commonwealth'—was not, however, specifically raised.

It was during 1936 that the principal features of the new Constitution took shape. Late in May of that year, de Valera revealed his intentions. He said in the Dáil that he hoped to introduce a measure outlining it in the autumn, though a number of questions were as yet unresolved. About this time, Malcolm MacDonald, the new Dominions Secretary, was launching a peace initiative within the British cabinet. In this and the next chapter, two connected developments present themselves which overlapped each other in time. One, de Valera's constitutional reforms, and two, the movement led by MacDonald, without the knowledge of the public for an Anglo-Irish settlement. The Abdication Crisis impinged on both. It will be found that de Valera was ready to take the initiative in promoting a settlement when his constitutional reforms had been accomplished.

On June 8th, the Irish High Commissioner delivered, on instructions, a memorandum to King Edward VIII. The King was informed:

The Government of Saorstát Éireann, in pursuance of their policy of establishing conditions for permanent peace and harmony amongst the Irish people and providing a more secure basis for friendship and co-operation with the people of Great Britain intend, at the beginning of the Autumn session of Parliament, to introduce a Bill for the purpose of setting up a new constitution. This constitution will deal with the internal affairs of Saorstát

Éireann, leaving unaffected the constitutional usages relating to external affairs. Among the provisions of the new constitution will be the creation of the office of the President, elected by the people and the abolition of the office of Governor-General.

The question of a second Chamber was complex. The Senate which had existed under the Free State Constitution and had been abolished by the Fianna Fáil Government, had not reflected the changes of political complexion in the Dáil. In many eyes it had tended to be a conservative bastion. De Valera was not without hope, however, that a suitable form of bicameral system might be devised.

On June 9th, 1936, a commission was set up to examine the Second Chamber issue. The Chief Justice was chairman; its members included the Attorney-General, seven members of the Dáil; five former senators, four university professors, two civil servants (both intimately associated with the drafting of the proposed constitution), and three others, making a total of twenty-three. But the immediate outcome was somewhat confused. A majority report aimed at the representation of national interests and services. A minority report favoured vocational representation. On the question of powers, the majority were opposed to the right of the Second Chamber to refer legislation to the people, while the minority favoured it. The minority report was certainly closer to views de Valera had already expressed. After prolonged consideration with his colleagues, special attention being given to the advice of the Minister for Finance, Seán MacEntee, and the Secretary of his Department, Seán Moynihan, de Valera announced that he favoured the minority report.[3]

The whole situation was suddenly agitated by the British Abdication crisis. De Valera first learned of the crisis on November 29th, when Sir Henry F. Batterbee arrived with a message from the British Prime Minister, Stanley Baldwin. Baldwin said that the alternatives facing the country were:

(1) that Mrs Simpson be recognised as Queen;

(2) that she should not become Queen but that the King need not abdicate;

(3) that the King abdicate in favour of the Duke of York.

De Valera was asked his views of the course to be followed.[4]

Unlike the Prime Ministers of Canada, Australia and South Africa, he favoured the second course that would allow the marriage to take place without abdication, but not allow Mrs Simpson to become Queen. He explained, however, that the Irish attitude was one of detachment, and that his preference for the course which he suggested was based on the assumption that divorce was a recognised institution in England.[5]

De Valera was kept informed of developments by Baldwin and was particularly perturbed when, on December 4th, he learned that the Abdication was likely within a few days. Shortly after midnight, on the following morning, he sent a telegram to Baldwin urging delay. The main problem was in the legislation which it would be necessary to pass in the Dáil to regularise the position. It was at this stage that the Minister for Finance, Seán MacEntee, presented him with a memorandum suggesting that, as the British had used Irish political divisions to their advantage, the crisis presented a chance of turning the tables.

While, therefore, the Dominions were discussing with Baldwin the course which each proposed to follow, de Valera did not disclose his plans. Baldwin suggested that the Prime Ministers of Dominions should make their views known to the King, but de Valera refrained from offering any advice. In a telegram to the King, all that he asked was that he be informed of the King's intentions. He asked that they be communicated to him directly, and not through the Governor-General. In Dublin, however, he was grasping an unrivalled opportunity of removing the King from any position in regard to the internal affairs of the Irish Free State, while retaining him for certain functions in external affairs. His original intention had been to bring the new Constitution into force and to follow it with an act regarding the use of the Crown in external matters. This, of course, might have led to further difficulties with Britain, for the economic war was still in progress.

De Valera, in view of the Abdication, decided to bring in the External Relations Bill at once and, instead of waiting for the completion of the new Constitution, to amend the existing Constitution by removing all the references to the King and the Governor-General. This course had a tactical advantage in timing, since Britain was so preoccupied with its own crisis that Irish actions seemed of minor importance. England's difficulty was certainly Ireland's opportunity on this occasion at least. De Valera, indeed, saw in the Abdication crisis a means of facilitating what he already had in mind.

On December 10th, de Valera was informed that the Abdication was to take place that day. He had not informed the British Government as to the precise steps which he intended to take, though Sir Harry Batterbee that day had pressed Joseph Walshe, the Secretary of the Irish Department for External Affairs to tell him. Walsh informed him, on de Valera's instructions:

> We intend to make legislative and constitutional provision to meet the situation. In order to do so, we are going to amend the existing constitution, so that the law would exactly express the realities of the constitutional position in regard to the functions exercised directly by the King. The precise manner in which this is to be done, has not yet been determined.[6]

De Valera did not intend to call the legislature together until the following week—a fact which perturbed Batterbee greatly. A lapse of time between the British and Irish Acts would leave an interval during which Edward VIII might be considered as still King in Ireland. In that interval the Free State would be, constitutionally, a completely independent monarchy. Malcolm MacDonald, the British Secretary of State for the Dominions, telephoned to press for an immediate meeting of the Dáil. De Valera decided to get in touch with the party leaders and arranged for the members of the Dáil to be called together by telegram. By post he sent to each member copies of two bills which were to be introduced when they met the following afternoon. Though the British Dominions Office was told the titles of the two bills, de Valera would not give advance information on their contents, fearing that propaganda against them might be initiated in Britain.

When the Dáil met on Friday afternoon, December 11th, the two bills were formally introduced, followed by a drastic guillotine motion whereby all stages of the first bill would be concluded before 11 p.m. that night, and all stages of the second by 10.30 p.m. the following night. De Valera was in a strong position in handling the situation. The abolition of the Senate, which had become effective in May, meant that he had no fear of delays from a Second Chamber. With the Dáil he had a majority. The matter was one of urgency if tactical advantage was to be taken of the Abdication crisis. The first bill deleted all the direct references still remaining in the Free State Constitution to the King and to the Governor-General.

Having eliminated the King from the Constitution, de Valera had still to make provision for the continuance of existing diplomatic relations. All foreign representatives in Ireland at the time were accredited to the King, and to remove him completely would have raised international complications of a high order. The whole question of the continued existence of diplomatic representatives in Ireland was involved, and de Valera was particularly concerned regarding those of the Vatican and of the United States of America. Thus, the retention of the King in foreign affairs was considered prudent. A further factor, too, was de Valera's view that the keeping of this shadowy link with Britain might help towards the ultimate reunification of Ireland. Thus it was that the bill was passed which stated that:

So long as Saorstát Éireann is associated with the following nations, that is to say, Australia, Canada, Great Britain, New Zealand and South Africa, and so long as the King recognized by those nations as the symbol of their co-operation continues to act on behalf of each of those nations (on the advice of the several Governments thereof), for the purpose of the appoint-

ment of diplomatic and consular representatives, and the conclusion of
international agreements, the King so recognized may, and is hereby authorised to, act on behalf of Saorstát Éireann for the like purposes, as and when
advised by the Executive Council so to do.

Despite strong criticism by lawyers among the Opposition, the bill was
passed by 81 votes to 5. The minority consisted of Labour members.

The handling of the affair was a masterpiece of political opportunism
by de Valera. Without creating a crisis he had gone far to achieve the
constitutional position which he had put forward as his own alternative
to the Treaty. The removal of the Oath Bill had abolished the subordina-
tion of the Constitution to the Treaty. It is true that the amended
Constitution still retained the clause which stated that the Irish Free
State was a co-equal member of the British Commonwealth. It was not
long before he made it clear, however, that he would willingly repeal the
External Relations Act if it did not serve to secure the unity of Ireland.

The constitutional changes achieved in December, 1936, had made
easier the problems connected with the new Constitution, which was
still in process of being drafted. De Valera had stated in the debates on
the amendments to the Constitution in the Dáil:

> If I were proposing that we should declare either a twenty-six County
> Republic or a thirty-two County Republic, an occasion like the present
> would not be the occasion to do it. Neither is the present occasion one on
> which we should introduce a permanent constitution here.[7]

In the draft, indeed, he was carefully avoiding a direct challenge to
Britain. While the King and his representative had no place in it, and
while the new Constitution was a republican one, it did not specifically
declare that the State was a republic, but it did provide for the use of an
external organ or instrument.

In August, 1936, the title of the State had not yet been decided, for
in one of the drafts of a Foreign Relations Bill it was called 'Poblacht na
h-Éireann', the Irish of 'Republic of Ireland'. In an earlier draft, however,
the name 'Éire' was used. Hearne's first draft had used the form 'Saorstát
Éireann', the Irish for 'Irish Free State'. This, despite the use of the name
by the Republican Government before the Treaty, had by now a con-
notation completely unacceptable to Republicans and was early rejected.
The use of 'Poblacht na h-Éireann' would be a direct challenge to
Britain and was also rejected by de Valera, who later explained one of his
objections to it. He said that, while under the Constitution the State
would be a 'sovereign independent republic', it did not unfortunately
cover the whole of Ireland. For that reason he did not introduce into
the Constitution the name of 'Poblacht na h-Éireann' because that was

a name which was sacred. He deliberately excluded any clause referring to Ireland as a member of the British Commonwealth.

Professor Mansergh provides an authoritative summary of this aspect of the new Constitution: 'Relations with Britain and the Commonwealth had been taken out of the Constitution and had become matters of external policy for the government of the day. This was the most significant development in the whole period.' He continues:

> The oath had gone, appeals to the Judicial Committee of the Privy Council had gone, the Governor-General had gone, the Crown had been taken out of the Constitution, the Constitution itself had been replaced by a Constitution republican in all but name, with an elected President as its head, and all that remained on paper of dominion status was the permissive procedure sanctioned by the External Relations Act. Taken together [he concludes] the External Relations Act and the new Constitution destroyed the dominion settlement of 1921.[8]

It was de Valera's idea that the new Constitution should contain articles setting out the social principles which would actuate the State. Many of the principles which were included in the Constitution were not enforceable in law. It was not de Valera's intention that they should be. Central to his whole approach to the Constitution lay the sovereignty of the people and of their elected representatives in the legislature. He had no wish to tie them hand and foot by a rigid set of rules, which would either prevent useful legislation or lead to continuous litigation. He said of these social articles that they would form 'a general headline to the legislature.'[9]

The 1930s were years of ideological conflict in which any effort to frame a set of fundamental social principles was bound to run into trouble. On the Continent, the rise of Communism and National Socialism had widely affected social thought, and in Ireland a great variety of views were being propounded on the duties of the State towards its people. De Valera read carefully the writings of such Catholic professors as Dr Michael Browne and Dr Cornelius Lucey, of Maynooth College, both of whom were to become members of the Irish hierarchy, in *Studies* and other periodicals. Father Edward Cahill, s.j., of Milltown Park, was also in the forefront of Irish Catholic social writers at the time. The latter, in September, 1936, sent a rough draft of a statement on Catholic principles on which a constitution should be based. De Valera found them 'useful as indicating the principles which should inspire all governmental activity, so as to make it conform with Catholic teaching'. The difficulty, however, was to see how they could be included in a constitution. He asked Father Cahill to 'try to draft a preamble and a form of articles which it might be possible to incorporate'.

Father Cahill's draft was submitted in October, based on articles of the Austrian Constitution of 1934, and that of Poland of 1921, together with a wide range of other Catholic documents, including Papal encyclicals. De Valera, however, decided that he would have to draft the necessary articles in a form better suited to Irish conditions.

After the Abdication crisis, de Valera continued his work on the preparation and revision of the social clauses. In this work he consulted Father John McQuaid, C.S.Sp., who, in February, sent him 'an interesting and useful criticism of the French constitution of 1814 by Pius VII'. He also sent paragraphs relating to private property and to free competition, based on a close analysis of the Papal encyclical *Rerum Novarum* of Leo XIII, and *Quadragesimo Anno* of Pius XI. He gave de Valera two books, *Manuel Sociale* by Rev. A. Vermeersch, a Belgian Jesuit, published in 1909, and *Code Sociale Esquisse d'une Synthese Sociale Catholique*, issued by the Union International d'Etudes Sociales in Paris in 1934. The latter particularly was to prove of great help in de Valera's work on the Constitution, to which he was now devoting all his spare time.

Dr McQuaid's advice and suggestions continued through March. In the middle of that month he was given a copy of the printed draft by de Valera, who had received page proofs of all except one outstanding article on the previous day, March 15th. The subject left to last was one that, surprisingly, de Valera expected to present no trouble—religion. This, however, proved to be a delusion. In the drafting of an article, the problem was to reconcile Catholic claims with the just position of other churches. The first half of April was spent in discussion of the references to religion. On April 3rd, de Valera called on the Papal Nuncio, Pascal Robinson, bringing with him various submitted drafts. One of them was in the form which gave a special recognition to the Catholic Church, but would simply tolerate other churches. This de Valera certainly could not accept. No finality was reached at this meeting. As Cardinal MacRory was to be in the city on April 5th, the Nuncio suggested that de Valera meet him. The Cardinal felt that the omission of any mention of the special position of the Catholic Church would cause and lead to an attack on the whole draft. As an alternative, he proposed a draft mentioning that the Catholic Church represented 93% of the population, but de Valera would not accept it. His aim throughout was to produce a constitution which would not require any fundamental change when the unity of Ireland was accomplished.

Dr Byrne, the Catholic Archbishop of Dublin, consulted by de Valera, was greatly pleased by the draft preamble, which recognised God as the source of all authority. So much so, indeed, that he was prepared, if de Valera thought it necessary, to agree to the omission of any specific reference to the Catholic Church in the article relating to religion. On thinking the matter over next day, however, de Valera felt that it should be possible to put in a clause recognising the fact that the Catholic Church was the guardian of the faith of the majority of the citizens. This idea perhaps owed something to a clause in Father Cahill's draft of articles submitted in the previous October, but the draft evolved by de Valera was very different from any previous draft. For he was determined to recognise other churches besides the Church of the majority. Having discussed the question with the Nuncio, the Cardinal and the Catholic Archbishop of Dublin, de Valera felt that the time was ripe to see the heads of other churches. He saw his old friend, the Presbyterian, Dr Irwin, and discussed the questions involved with him, and on April 12th he called on Archbishop Gregg, the Church of Ireland Archbishop of Dublin.

Members of his own Church objected to being called Roman Catholics, while others were equally opposed to being called non-Catholics or Protestants. This problem was mentioned to Archbishop Gregg, who took down a book from his shelves, the *Records of the Council of Trent*, to see how the Church was described there. He found the phrase: 'Holy Catholic, Apostolic and Roman Church', which immediately suggested that the solution of the difficulty lay in giving each church the title which it had formally given to itself. In the next few days, de Valera saw the Rev. William H. Massey, President of the Methodist Church in Ireland, and the Right Rev. F. W. S. O'Neill, Moderator of Assembly of the Presbyterian Church in Ireland, and his successor, the Moderator-designate. All were very pleased with de Valera's fair-minded approach to the problems and with the draft which he submitted to them.

The final draft of the religious article of the Constitution read:

The State recognises the special position of the Holy Catholic Apostolic and Roman Church as the guardian of the faith professed by the great majority of the citizens. The State also recognises the Church of Ireland, the Presbyterian Church in Ireland, the Methodist Church in Ireland, the Religious Society of Friends in Ireland, as well as the Jewish Congregations and the other religious denominations existing in Ireland at the date of the coming into operation of this constitution.

A difficulty had been solved in a way which was to set an example to the framers of other constitutions, notably that of Burma a decade later. Even in its final form the article on religion was not welcomed by everyone, and it was to remain a subject of some controversy on the part of an extreme Catholic minority group for many years. De Valera was to admit later that this article gave him more anxiety than anything else in the Constitution. But he always maintained that, despite the critics, the document was a reasonably good one, more Christian and Catholic than any other democratic constitution in the world.

> If we want to give a lead as a Catholic nation [he wrote] the first essential is that we live, each individual citizen, more in accordance with the Christianity we profess, i.e. consciously and deliberately checking and directing our daily and hourly actions in accordance with Christian principles, particularly in our dealings with our neighbours.[10]

This was the spirit which lay behind de Valera's efforts to draft the religious article of the Constitution, a spirit which foreshadowed a later ecumenism.

The draft Constitution was published and circulated on May 1st. Immediately the leading Opposition newspaper commented:

> Apart from certain amendments which seem called for, he will naturally have the wholehearted support of the Opposition in enacting this document. It is at least to his credit that he has produced a Constitution in regard to which there will be no serious division of opinion.[11]

Such an optimistic view, however, was somewhat premature, for soon the document became the subject of attack. The *Church Times* in Britain was impressed with the Christian tone of the draft, but the British press as a whole was hostile, ranging from the churlishness of the *Morning Post* to the more dignified comments of the *Manchester Guardian*. This latter paper at least recognised the true meaning of the document, that it was 'as far as mere words go, a Constitution for an independent Republic', and made the suggestion that it should be possible to reform the British Commonwealth, so as to retain within it a republican state.[12] The American press, too, was somewhat unfriendly. The Hearst papers carried an interview with George Bernard Shaw, attacking the draft as creating a new post of President with dictatorial powers and reactionary in its attitude to women.

The fight for acceptance of the Constitution, however, had to be fought in Ireland, first of all in Dáil Éireann. The opposition to it centred not on the relations with Britain, which were accepted by all parties except a small minority, but on the two issues incidentally raised by Bernard Shaw, the rights of women and the powers of the President. A number of feminists objected to the clauses which recognised the importance of women's work in the home and made it a point of state policy to ensure that mothers would not be forced by economic necessity to go out to work. They claimed that these clauses implied that no women should work outside the home. To meet these objections, amendments were introduced and accepted, which recognised more definitely the equal rights of men and women, while not changing the fundamental position of mothers of families. The arguments on this matter were somewhat unreal, but undoubtedly influenced women voters.

The issue concerning the powers of the President was even more fanciful, because the opposition parties appear to have been convinced that the post was being created for de Valera himself and that he would use the powers obtained to set up a dictatorship. They seem never to have quite understood that de Valera held the sovereignty of the people as fundamental.

The Constitution was approved by Dáil Éireann on June 14th, and thereafter was submitted to a plebiscite. De Valera's purpose in submitting the Constitution to the people was to remove any doubts as to its basis. He wanted to make it clear that it was enacted by the people and not imposed on them, that it was truly Irish and depended on the people's will. He also felt that this form of enactment would disarm any lawyer who might be tempted to test the validity of the Constitution in the courts. Moreover, Dáil Éireann was held by some to be a Parliament tainted in its origin and not an appropriate base on which to build a new Constitution. 'We are going back to the sovereign authority, to the Irish people, or that section of the Irish people whom we can consult on the matter,' said de Valera.

In advance, too, he ensured that the judges accepted the new Constitution by requiring all of them to swear to uphold it. Any judge who declined to do so would be deemed to have vacated his office. This, of course, further discouraged any lawyer from arguing against the validity of the Constitution in any Irish court.[13] While neutralising the courts, de Valera hoped also to disarm the Republicans to his left. He had hoped to open the doors of the Dáil to them by the abolition of the oath, but they had remained outside constitutional politics. Their objection to the Free State was based on its origins in 1922. By his new Constitution, de Valera wanted to make a new beginning, based on the sovereign decision of the Irish people, and owing nothing to the dubious disputed character of the Free State.

It was, perhaps, expecting too much to hope that the draft Constitution would not be dealt with as a party measure in the Dáil and in the country. Perhaps de Valera contributed to making it a party issue, by deciding that the plebiscite should take place on the same day as a general election. De Valera himself said that he would have liked to see the Constitution 'put to the people independent of and separate from a general election.' The cost of a separate plebiscite was a factor on the other side. More important was the danger that the electorate might not vote in large numbers on an issue like the Constitution, unless they were attracted to the polls by the appeals of candidates in a general election.[14] It was important that the Constitution be voted on by a sufficient body of voters to give their decision authority.

In an address to the electors on the eve-of-the-poll, de Valera set out his own view on the Constitution:

> It is a renewed declaration of national independence and its enactment will mark the attainment of one definite objective in the national struggle. It consolidates the ground that has been gained and forms a secure basis from which we can move forward towards the recovery of the national sovereignty over our ports and the reunion of the whole national territory into one State.

He appealed to the people not to view it as a party measure, but to vote for it whether they favoured the continuance of Fianna Fáil in office or not. His plea was not without effect. The Constitution was passed by 685,105 votes in favour to 526,945 against. That it was not an exclusively party vote was shown by the fact that the total first preference votes cast for Fianna Fáil was 599,040. In thirty out of the thirty-four constituencies, a majority voted in favour of the Constitution. The four in which it failed to receive a majority vote were Cork West, Dublin Townships, Sligo and Wicklow.

The Constitution did not long remain a controversial topic. It automatically came into force on December 29th, 1937, and received considerable acclaim at home and abroad.

Cardinal MacRory described it as 'a great Christian document . . . a splendid charter—a broad and solid foundation on which to build up a nation that will be, at once, reverent and dutiful to God and just to all men.' The subject had become a barren one for the political tacticians and soon all were to give their adherence to the document. Internationally as well as nationally it won recognition and provided something of a model. The only strong critics were the Catholic minority whose religious susceptibilities were hurt by the fact that recognition should be given to any religion but their own. They were a vociferous and embarrassing group, but were finally silenced when Pope Pius XII received de Valera on the occasion of the centenary celebrations for Luke Wadding, o.f.m., and went out of his way to pay tribute to the Constitution.[15] And Britain had acquiesced. The British Government declaration of December 29th, 1937, stated that the Constitution did not affect membership of the Commonwealth. By the time the two governments reached the negotiation table early in 1938, it will be seen that the constitutional question in regard to the twenty-six counties did not need to figure, and did not figure in fact.

A very different kind of constitutional issue caused much concern for several years. When the results of the General Election of 1932 became known, a number of those who had been members of the Free State Army had formed, as we have seen, a body called the Army Comrades Association. It set itself up as an unofficial police force, to protect Cumann na nGaedheal meetings against the other 'physical force' group in the country—the IRA, which traced its history back to the army of the War of Independence.

After the 1933 election, de Valera removed from office General Eoin O'Duffy, Commissioner of Police. He was widely admired as an organiser, but his judgement was less formidable than his energy, and by the beginning of 1933 de Valera and his Government felt that O'Duffy was not a man on whom they could adequately depend. De Valera interviewed him and relieved him of office, offering him instead a post of equal salary in another government department. This O'Duffy rejected, becoming thus a martyr figure to whom the Army Comrades Association could turn for leadership.

For a time, the Army Comrades gained a new dynamism. They adopted the blue-shirt uniform which was to give them the name by which they are known to history—the Blue Shirts. But by August, a mass parade destined for the lawn of Leinster House was banned by de Valera. The Blue Shirts, who had now adopted the official title of 'National Guard', were declared an illegal organisation.

De Valera took firm and careful steps to deal with them. The military tribunal, which had been created by the Cosgrave administration and disbanded by de Valera, was now revived. De Valera felt that the Blue Shirts, as supporters of Cosgrave's régime, could not reasonably object to a tribunal which was established by his predecessors in office. All the more so as the members of the tribunal were the same officers who had been appointed by Cosgrave when the tribunal was first set up.

Within a few weeks, the Opposition parties, Cumann na nGaedheal and the smaller group, the Centre Party, merged with O'Duffy's followers. The new party was named 'United Ireland' or Fine Gael, and O'Duffy became its President.

The Blue Shirts themselves were not suppressed by the Government action of August, 1933. For months they continued to parade under a series of changing names. They aimed to bring down the Government by rendering impossible de Valera's stand against British economic pressure. The farmers were called upon to resist the payment of land annuities to the Government. When this campaign was extended to advocating the withholding of all local rates, many of the Blue Shirts realised that O'Duffy was leading the movement towards anarchy. In the Autumn of

1934, it split and the parliamentary Opposition purged itself of its military associates. Thereafter the movement fell asunder.

De Valera had no sympathy with the Blue Shirts—he looked on them simply as a body without roots whose sole object was to oust him from office. For the IRA he had greater understanding, although he objected vehemently then and later to their methods. They tried to intervene in the economic war by destroying British-made goods, in an effort to push de Valera ever deeper into conflict with Britain. They also took on themselves the indefensible task of harassing the public meetings of Treaty supporters.

The IRA had arms. As far as the Government knew, the Blue Shirts also had access to arms. For de Valera the situation was indeed grave. He was endeavouring to make constitutional changes which would remove the barriers between the IRA and a proper democratic function. His endeavours culminated in the Constitution of 1937 already described. But at no time could he allow the IRA or anyone else the right to take the law into their own hands. The military tribunal acted as firmly against them as it did against the Blue Shirts, and although both complained that de Valera favoured the other group, he made sure that as far as it lay within his power impartial justice was done.

The IRA was soon to fall into difficulties itself. It had split on social questions in 1934 and soon, like the Blue Shirts, was to become an impotent body. However, unlike the Blue Shirts, it was never to disappear and was to raise its head on a number of later occasions in de Valera's career—always to his extreme inconvenience.

TOWARDS A SETTLEMENT

1933 – 1938

Great Britain and Ireland settled down to economic war and official misunderstanding. Ordinary life and communications continued. Hope did not vanish. At the end of 1933, J. H. Thomas, in answer to a House of Commons question on the dispute, said that the Irish Free State was, as a member of the British Commonwealth, free to order its own affairs. De Valera wrote to him to make Ireland's position clear:

> The Irish people have never sought membership of the Commonwealth. Their association with Great Britain and the Commonwealth has never been on their side a voluntary association. In every generation they have striven with such means as were at their disposal to maintain their right to exist as a distinct and independent nation, and whenever they yielded to British rule in any form they did so under the pressure of overwhelming material force.

He went on to point out that the Treaty settlement had been imposed by force and would never be the basis of lasting friendship between the two nations:

> The Government of the Irish Free State infer from your statement of the 14th instant that the British Government also now realise the evils of a forced association and have decided not to treat as a cause of war or other aggressive action a decision of the Irish people to sever their connection with the Commonwealth.

This was so vital a point, he suggested that it should be stated in unequivocal terms and would be a first step towards free and friendly co-operation. Here he was going too fast for the British and he made no immediate progress.[1]

But in autumn, 1935, a crucial event occurred and one of immense benefit to Ireland—the advent (already referred to) of Malcolm MacDonald, then aged thirty-four, as Dominions Secretary in place of J. H. Thomas. De Valera already enjoyed friendly relations with the British ministers whom he had met at Geneva. In fact, however, a new departure was at hand.

As soon as MacDonald took over, he was determined to see whether it was not possible to break the deadlock and reach a settlement with de Valera. He was no doubt aware that just before the British elections Joseph P. Walshe, head of External Affairs, had indicated to Eden at Geneva that de Valera was favourably disposed to an initiative from the British side.

John Dulanty, a close friend of MacDonald, who was Irish High Commissioner, conveyed to de Valera in Dublin that MacDonald would very much like to meet him and make his personal acquaintance. De Valera, rather guardedly, agreed and said that every now and then he passed through London on his way to Switzerland to receive eye treatment. He suggested a date at the end of March, 1936, when he would next be in London. They could meet in his rooms in the Grosvenor Hotel, Victoria.

When the time came, John Dulanty waited for MacDonald at the hotel and conducted him unobtrusively to de Valera's rooms. From the beginning, de Valera was informal and charming, and within no time he had got down to business. They made a rough, general exploration of possibilities and both agreed that it would be useful to have another talk next time de Valera was in London. Subsequent talks took place on nights when de Valera was passing through.

De Valera was fully aware that MacDonald had initiated these talks with the authority of Stanley Baldwin and that he and other ministers were kept informed of the contents of his talks with MacDonald and of the major questions discussed. Baldwin was extremely shy and cautious about secret meetings. Although he gave MacDonald the authority, he did not commit himself at all. MacDonald remembers that early in the talks he told de Valera that H.M.G. could not change their attitude on Ulster, and de Valera replied that he could not change *his* attitude. They subsequently agreed that the whole question should be put aside for the moment and they would continue talking about other things. Soon they reached a point at which MacDonald felt able to go to Baldwin with a paper of recommendation. It went to the cabinet and was referred by them to the strong group of ministers called the Irish Situation Committee.

From this paper of May, 1936, it is possible to quote only the beginning and the end. The opening is unequivocal:

> The most serious aspect of Inter-Imperial relations at present is the absence of agreement between the United Kingdom and the Irish Free State on various important matters. This state of affairs between the United Kingdom and a Dominion is unsatisfactory in itself, and inevitably tends to weaken the moral authority of the British Commonwealth of Nations in world affairs. Moreover, if matters are allowed to drift they may well end before long in a more serious breach between the two countries. On the other hand, I think the time has come when, despite the well-known difficulties, a careful

effort to reconcile differences between the two countries has some prospect of meeting with success. Even if an agreement proves impossible, I believe that our own people expect the attempt to be made and that the Government will be criticised if it does not, in the near future, take the initiative in promoting discussions.[2]

And the conclusion is just as definite. Informal discussions should be opened with the Irish Free State High Commissioner or between officials of the two countries 'with a view to exploring the possibility of a general settlement of outstanding questions'.

It should be added that already in February of that year, 1936, the Chiefs of Staff had recommended a defence agreement with the Irish Free State. (For their general ideas, see below page 315.) When the time came, on May 12th, 1936, for the British ministers to discuss the problem, MacDonald made his case as persuasively as ever, one may be sure, but he was clearly to have no easy passage. Hailsham, the Lord Chancellor, came out in violent disagreement with a course 'which was destined to failure and which could produce no good result at home in Ireland or elsewhere.' The division bell rang and the cabinet had to go and vote, leaving Hailsham with the last word for the moment. Before they left the table the Prime Minister told them that the discussion was adjourned for the day. MacDonald accepted this, but was somewhat concerned that Hailsham's arguments should have gone without reply.

As the Ministers left the Prime Minister's room, Neville Chamberlain, Chancellor of the Exchequer, asked MacDonald to have a word with him after the vote. MacDonald went to his room and Chamberlain said to him: 'I should like to know what you would have said in reply to your critics if the discussion had continued this afternoon'. MacDonald was relieved. He put his case to Chamberlain as though they were in full cabinet. Afterwards Chamberlain said: 'MacDonald, I agree with you, and you can count on my support.' This was an all-important moment on the British side; Chamberlain was soon to be Prime Minister and had an immense influence just then over Baldwin, though MacDonald did not know this latter fact at the time.

Thenceforward the determining voices in the British cabinet favoured a settlement, but there were plenty of obstacles in the way.

We turn back to the story as seen from the Irish side. By September 7th, 1936, exploratory talks were taking place in the Treasury Chambers, Whitehall, between John W. Dulanty, the Irish High Commissioner and leading British officials, Sir Warren Fisher, Sir Horace J. Wilson and Sir Edward J. Harding. Their purpose was to see whether it was possible to find a solution of the questions at issue. The partition of Ireland was stressed as a fundamental difficulty by Dulanty. He pointed out that de Valera had explained recently to MacDonald that the British 'should not be misled into thinking that superficial modifications, instead of really fundamental changes, would lead to a satisfactory settlement.' The discussion centred on the constitutional issue, including the position of the King in relation to Ireland under de Valera's proposed new Constitution. Could not de Valera agree to retain not only the *external* link but also some link between the *internal* affairs of Ireland and the King? If that could be arranged, it was clear the British would be happy to meet him on the financial and economic questions.[3]

These secret conversations between Dulanty and British officials continued through September and October, 1936. Malcolm MacDonald was eager to have greater participation from the Irish side and to make some progress by meeting Dulanty himself. He said that he hoped to see de Valera at Geneva for a discussion and suggested that if Joseph P. Walshe and John Hearne were members of the Irish delegation to the League of Nations, they should stay a couple of days in London on their way, to participate in the official discussions. Dulanty found MacDonald sincere and anxious to reach a settlement. The officials were adamant; it was actually stated in a letter to Dulanty by Fisher, that 'final agreement could only be arrived at on the basis of a solution of *all* the matters involved.' [Our italics.] But the Minister was less rigid. Fisher had said on the morning of September 15th that if agreement were not reached on the constitutional question, then there could be no agreement on the other three issues. MacDonald, that same afternoon, told Dulanty that, as far as he was concerned, he would try to avoid a deadlock on any question. Even if the constitutional problem proved for the moment insoluble, he would seek a solution on the others, especially defence.[4]

The anxiety of MacDonald to bring Irish officials into the talks was further displayed in a personal letter to de Valera of September 17th. He reiterated the view which he had expressed to Dulanty. Regarding the talks which were in progress he wrote:

As you know, my hope was that all the questions outstanding between our two Governments should be fully examined, that either side should be free to raise any relevant subject and that on all these matters both sides should state and discuss their views and difficulties with complete frankness.

He felt that no individual could know enough of all the issues to engage in a close examination of them, and he reiterated his desire that Walshe and Hearne participate in them on their way to Geneva. He appreciated and shared de Valera's desire that the discussions should proceed, at this stage, without the public knowing of them and thought that his suggestion 'overcomes the difficulty of the presence of Dublin officials in London giving rise to suspicion and rumour'.

Dulanty visited Dublin and saw de Valera on September 23rd. They discussed the progress of the talks and in particular a further letter in which Sir Warren Fisher set out his views on the lines on which they should proceed. Allegiance to the Crown he considered vital. He had written to Dulanty:

> The constitution of a State would not be consistent with membership of the Commonwealth if it did not recognize the King as Head of the Commonwealth, of which the State forms part, and the special relationship of its citizens to the King. If this point were adequately provided for, we feel that there would be room for discussion about the part which the Crown takes in legislation as Head of the Executive.

On defence there could be no question, said Fisher, of the Irish ports *not* being available to Britain in time of war. The financial and trade questions were treated as open for discussion.[5]

In a note on his conversation with de Valera, which the latter approved, Dulanty recorded the disappointment which Fisher's letter produced in the Irish leader. 'It indicates all through failure on the part of the British to appreciate the real character of the problem,' noted Dulanty. 'Do the British really want a settlement that will be satisfactory? If so, they must face the issue of a United Ireland. No agreement on the basis of partition would be acceptable to the Irish people and no such agreement could bring active goodwill and co-operation.' His record continues:

> In the absence of any proposal for an all-Ireland settlement, President proposes to proceed with the Constitution on which he has already made unequivocal statements in public. The President's aim in this Constitution is to establish now such a relationship with the members of the British Commonwealth of Nations that, in the event of the Six Counties voluntarily accepting union with the rest of Ireland, the Constitution would not require amendment.

Regarding the Irish ports de Valera made it clear that no country could be given an automatic right to them. Neither could he accept an arrangement with Britain by which Ireland would be involved in hostilities whenever and wherever Britain was at war. His attitude was summed up by Dulanty: 'If no common interest were at stake, our attitude that of benevolent neutrality.'

De Valera noted on Dulanty's first draft of this record: 'The above notes only the President's personal views verbally expressed on the Fisher letter and indicate the lines on which solution should be sought. The Executive Council in the first instance and then the pol. party would have to be satisfied before any agreement could be brought to the Dáil.'

The record of the conversation as approved by de Valera was the basis of the instructions to Dulanty for subsequent meetings. Every effort was made by British officials to mollify the Irish High Commissioner regarding the form of Fisher's letter, but no real advance was forthcoming. 'Sir Warren Fisher', reported Dulanty, 'thought a good deal could be done on the question of defence, but he did not think we could make progress on that subject, nor on finance and trade policy, until we could get closer to some solution of the Constitutional question.'[6]

So far the new effort to solve the Anglo-Irish difficulties had ended in failure. And now came the Abdication and, as has been seen in the previous chapter, the Irish exploitation of it which might well have increased the tension.

Malcolm MacDonald did not allow himself to be discouraged or deflected. There are records in the British documents of two long meetings with de Valera at the beginning of 1937 when the latter was passing through London. About the same time MacDonald wrote to de Valera officially that he hoped to get his colleagues in the cabinet to agree that in making the post-Abdication reforms, Ireland had satisfied the requirements, albeit to a minimum degree only, of Commonwealth membership. He wished to avoid any controversy about what had taken place. He had asked Lord Craigavon to call, so that he could persuade Craigavon to use his influence with his Belfast cabinet to avoid trouble. Indeed, he said that if the atmosphere were favourable, Baldwin would take the opportunity of raising with Craigavon the question of a United Ireland.

The British cabinet, on January 25th, 1937, discussed the acts passed by Dáil Éireann in December, and decided tentatively that 'the recent Irish Free State legislation should not be regarded as having altered fundamentally the position of the Irish Free State as a Dominion.' In reporting this to Dulanty, MacDonald stated that the British cabinet were seriously concerned lest, in the new Constitution which was in preparation, Article 1 of the old Constitution be dropped. This stated that the Irish Free State 'is a co-equal member of the Community of Nations forming the British Commonwealth of Nations.' This clause had not been interfered with by de Valera's amendments, though he had no intention of including it in the new Constitution which he was drafting.

If it were omitted from the new document, said MacDonald, it would make the British Government's position more difficult. As an alternative he suggested that an amendment to the External Relations Act could include a clause to the same effect. From the point of view of his Government, some clause of this kind was considered vital. He also suggested some revision of the same act so that Irish 'recognition of the Crown as a symbol of the association should be brought into line with that of the other member states of the Commonwealth'. Finally, he stated that the references to the King in the External Relations Act as an 'organ' had led to raised eyebrows at the cabinet meeting. It was feared that it might hurt people on what was a very susceptible point.

British protests and anxieties were understandable, but de Valera was getting his changes through without any great crisis. He was gradually removing the main stumbling block to negotiations without allowing his constitutional plans to be altered by British pressure. He forged ahead with his new Constitution, the main principles of which the British had swallowed in January, 1937. He did not make the amendments they suggested. When the draft Constitution was published in April, it contained, as we have seen (page 295), no clause stating that Ireland was a member of the British Commonwealth. It was left to the British to decide whether it was in or out. Some months later, when the new Constitution had been approved by the Dáil and passed by plebiscite, the constitutional issue had settled itself in de Valera's favour.

That the British accepted the position became clear when de Valera was attending a meeting of the League of Nations in September. De Valera met Malcolm MacDonald, with whom he had two long informal discussions, on September 15th, and the following day at the Hotel de la Paix. The first day the topics which they covered included partition, the financial dispute, the treaty ports and defence and trade. De Valera in a note on the meeting summed up the position:

Before he [MacDonald] left, he had quite definitely my views on the following matters:
1. That the ending of partition was absolutely necessary for the good relations we both desired.
2. That we could not consent to paying a penny of the land annuity money.
3. That we could not consent to any commitment to invite the British to our ports for the defence of their supplies in time of war.
4. That the line to pursue for a solution was to find how our increased commitments in regard to defence (so as to make good the policy of preventing a foreign power from using our island as a basis of attack against Britain), would be held to equate the payments on which a compromise could be made.
I indicated that I was willing to meet representatives of their Government, for the purpose of hammering out the financial agreement, once the main lines were fixed and it was certain that an agreement could be arrived at.

This conversation was resumed the following day and the new Constitution and the External Relations Act were discussed. MacDonald stated that, when the Constitution came into operation at the end of the year, the British would have to protest at the second and third articles of it, which asserted that the national territory consisted of the whole island of Ireland. They did not want to appear to be acquiescing in the Irish claim put in those two articles. De Valera noted:

> I pointed out that we would have to reply fairly stiffly on that matter and that there could of course be no question of change.

He emphasised again that the most fundamental and vital question in Anglo-Irish relations was partition. He noted:

> that no agreements on other matters could bring about the good relations both he and I desired, so long as partition lasted. Settlement on the other matters would help to make the solution of partition itself easier, perhaps, by improving the relations and securing the good-will of Great Britain.

MacDonald insisted that they could do nothing about partition, which could only be ended by the South winning over the North. The British would do nothing to stand in the way. De Valera recorded:

> I pressed him on whether they desired partition or not. He said they did not desire it 'for its own sake'. They were committed to the North. I asked if they would publicly state that, so far as they were concerned, they would desire partition to end. He could not promise that such a statement would be made. His steadfast view was that the partition solution would have to wait. I said we would therefore have to consider a campaign to inform British and world opinion as to the iniquity of the whole position.

The meetings were inconclusive, but friendly. De Valera was impressed once more by the patent sincerity of MacDonald. Since it was the Dominions Secretary who had asked for the meetings, it was clear that he was anxious to do all he could to break the deadlock. When Anthony Eden, the Foreign Secretary, and MacDonald entertained de Valera to dinner two nights later at the Bois, to discuss the international situation generally, de Valera felt, not for the first time, that Eden also had real goodwill for Ireland.

MacDonald said that he would report back to Neville Chamberlain, who had taken over from Baldwin as Prime Minister early in the summer. He suggested that he might raise a discussion in a cabinet sub-committee and, if they could find a basis, put proposals to de Valera. 'I thought', wrote de Valera, 'that discussions by civil servants would be of no use, as the questions were essentially ones which would have to be decided by principals. I thought a delegation of British Ministers could meet ours either in Dublin or in London to hammer out a settlement finally, but that any such meeting would be worse than useless unless there was a reasonable prospect that a settlement could be made.'[7]

For the next two months, MacDonald worked on possible proposals. Hitherto, he had made most of the running and had worked long and hard on his own cabinet colleagues, as appears from the British records. But now de Valera stepped forward with an initiative. MacDonald was quite surprised to receive a despatch dated November 24th, 1937, from de Valera which suggested a meeting of members of the two Governments to consider important matters that would arise in case of war.

The British cabinet appear to have had no hesitation in responding favourably. They agreed on December 1st that the meeting should take place, although MacDonald suggested to Dulanty that it would be best to wait until the parliamentary recess. On January 7th the cabinet in Dublin approved a delegation consisting of the Taoiseach, Eamon de Valera; the Minister for Industry and Commerce, Seán Lemass; the Minister for Finance, Seán MacEntee, and the Minister for Agriculture, Dr James Ryan. These ministers represented in particular the departments involved in the financial and trade difficulties.

The request for a meeting of ministers had not been expected by Malcolm MacDonald, as we have seen. He had been under the impression that de Valera was against such a course, until it was fairly certain that a meeting would be successful. MacDonald himself was not at all sure that sufficient progress had yet been made. But de Valera's motivation is easily comprehensible. He had been impressed—and rightly so—by the real goodwill which had been shown by MacDonald at their various meetings. He might have been still more impressed if he had known the inside story of MacDonald's exertions in the cabinet. His Constitution was now safely on the Statute Book. He had become imbued with a sense of urgency under the growing threat of war. The arguments for a settlement with Britain were powerful.

For long he had seen the dangers of the existing position and had, indeed, been criticised by the Opposition in the Dáil for not taking steps to prepare for the defence of the country in case of hostilities. He felt that it was impossible to plan Ireland's defence while Britain occupied the ports and, under the Treaty, could claim other far-reaching facilities.

> So long as the British occupy certain points along our shores and so long as there is here an agreement which seems to give them a right to claim whatever facilities they want, is it not clear that it is not our will that would be effective in keeping a position of neutrality but the will of other people?[8]

Neutrality was his aim, but without a settlement which gave Ireland control of her own territory it was impossible.

In an interview published January 13th, 1938, de Valera stated that the questions which would be discussed at the forthcoming talks included partition, defence and the disputed monies. Immediately Lord Craigavon responded by calling a general election in the partitioned area. He was determined to stand by his policy of 'Not an Inch'. Two days later, the Irish delegation, together with senior civil service advisers, left Dun Laoghaire by boat and were met at Euston Station by Malcolm MacDonald and G. P. Humphries Davies, Neville Chamberlain's private secretary.

On January 17th, 1938, following an informal luncheon given by the Prime Minister, the talks commenced in No. 10 Downing Street at 2.30 p.m. The British representatives were, apart from the Premier, Sir John Simon (Chancellor of the Exchequer), Sir Samuel Hoare (Home Secretary) and Malcolm MacDonald (Dominions Secretary). Other Ministers who were brought in during the discussions included Sir Thomas Inskip (Defence), Oliver Stanley (President of the Board of Trade) and W. S. Morrison (Agriculture).

For de Valera, the second round had begun.

A QUALIFIED TRIUMPH

January – April, 1938

In many ways it was all reminiscent of October, 1921. There was one enormous difference. War, it is true, was once again in the air, but this time there was no question of hostilities between England and Ireland. War, if it came, would come from an external aggressor. It would be of a kind to jeopardise the very existence of Britain and, it might well be, of Ireland.

According to the cabinet records, Chamberlain asked de Valera to suggest an order of business. De Valera, in reply, began by stating the grave dangers from partition during a war. In the view of his Government there should never have been any partition at all. He was just as severe on the coercion of the minority in Northern Ireland.

There were parts of the country which by every test should be within the jurisdiction of his Government but which were subject to Belfast. Then there was the question of the presence of British troops in certain Irish ports. All of these would make the position of an Irish government difficult in wartime, just as they handicapped it in planning for war. If these difficulties were removed it would be greatly to Britain's advantage, because Ireland could then build up its defences with the enthusiastic support of its people. She would be able to prevent any enemy of Britain from using her as a base from which to attack her neighbour.

The objectives to be attained were, according to de Valera:

(1) the unity of Ireland and the ending of the state of affairs in the Six Counties under which one section of the population coerced another;
(2) the handing over of the Irish ports without reservation to the Irish Government and
(3) the dropping by Britain of the special duties on Irish goods, so that Ireland might be able to find the funds to equip her army.

Following this general statement the first topic discussed in detail was partition. Despite all de Valera's powers of argument, he could not make any real progress there. When they turned to the question of the ports, however, he made it clear that since there appeared to be no hope of any understanding on partition, he was going to stand out for absolute control of the bases on the Irish coast.

His disappointment at the lack of progress on partition was visible to all. As usual, however, he responded neatly to courtesies. MacDonald, for example, recalls that on one occasion during the conference, de Valera was still putting the Irish case at one o'clock. MacDonald himself had to write the press report. He scribbled something and handed it to Chamberlain. It stated that de Valera had started to state the Irish case and that the meeting had adjourned for lunch. Chamberlain threw this across to de Valera who looked at it and smiled. He suggested that if this went into the press the next day it might be said that de Valera had started making the Irish case way back in prehistoric times and by lunch had not yet got to Oliver Cromwell!

At the resumed meeting the following morning, January 18th, the ports were the main subject discussed. It gradually became clear that the British would concede *something*. De Valera sought the complete abrogation of the clauses of the Treaty under which they were held by Britain. Towards the end of the meeting there was still some distance between the two sides when Chamberlain suggested that officials should draw up a preliminary draft of an agreement. De Valera stated that it was beyond the wit of man to draw up a formula which would both hand the ports over to Ireland and yet lay it down that the United Kingdom had the right to use them in an emergency.

Here lay the kernel of the problem. Immediately Chamberlain replied that he had been misunderstood. He had accepted Mr de Valera's insistence that there could be no question of giving an assurance here and now that the ports would be made available for the use of the United Kingdom forces in the event of a major war. He was not pressing Mr de Valera further on that point.

De Valera might have been excused a sense of elation. As always he showed no sign of it. He remained as meticulous as ever. There was going to be a close study of every document to which he was asked to put his name. He warned that even after the ports had been conceded in principle, it would be far from easy to have agreed on a form of words defining a defence agreement. He could not, in any case, go further than put his initials to a text until it had been examined and approved by his cabinet in Dublin and by legal advisers. Nevertheless by one o'clock on Tuesday, January 18th, 1938, a historic step had virtually been taken. De Valera had effectively succeeded in obtaining full control of the Irish ports which had been retained by Britain under the 1921 Articles of Agreement.

When the agreement came to be announced, this item was almost universally accepted in Britain as necessary to a statesmanlike settlement. Later, during the war, its justification tended to be overlooked. Churchill at least was consistent throughout. His vehement criticisms in 1938 and later are well known. 'Personally', he wrote, *Second World War*, Volume I, 'I remain convinced that the gratuitous surrender of our right to use the Irish ports in war was a major injury to British national life and safety. A more feckless act can hardly be imagined and at such a time. Many a ship and many a life was soon to be lost as a result of this improvident example of appeasement.'

But quite apart from arguments, Chamberlain and his colleagues were resting on strong advice from the Chiefs of Staff. These can be traced in the British documents now available, and are set out succinctly and authoritatively in the Memoirs of Lord Chatfield, First Sea Lord and Chairman of the Chiefs of Staff at the time, to which Sir Winston Churchill refers the student. Chatfield explains that three 'alternatives' had to be faced:

(1) Ireland, as an active ally with a Defence Agreement to make the ports available in time of war.

(2) Ireland a friendly neutral.

(3) A hostile Ireland, with her possible use by the enemy, as a base against Britain and a possible over-running of Ulster and the seizure of her ports.

For Britain the best solution was clearly one which made the ports available in time of war, i.e. (1) above, the defensive alliance. The Chiefs of Staff were emphatic that the attempt to use the ports *without* Irish consent was, as would be said nowadays, just 'not on'. It would land Britain 'in a series of Gibraltars scattered round the Irish coast' and was divorced from reality, whereas the defensive alliance involved Irish consent and could not be imposed on Ireland against her will. If Irish consent were not forthcoming, the second course, friendly neutrality, was far the best objective; this could only be achieved if the ports were conceded to Ireland. (3), a hostile Ireland must be averted at all cost.

In what follows, therefore, we must assume that the expert British opinion would much prefer a defensive agreement which would make Ireland an active ally in wartime. But in the last resort it would come down in favour of making sure that Ireland was, at the worst, a friendly neutral. There were various possible arrangements between the two main alternatives which held out greater or less likelihood of Irish facilities being made available if war came. There could be, for example, a defence agreement providing for consultation which, in the event of war, left to Ireland the final decision between active alliance and neutrality. (Additionally, the Chiefs of Staff were anxious to free the army of its existing task of guarding the ports in peacetime, whatever the wartime provision.)

The agreement to hand over the Irish ports on certain conditions to the Irish Government did not abrogate all the clauses regarding defence in the 1921 Treaty. Chamberlain had, however, gone so far that it was clear that all British claims in relation to defence would, in practice, be rendered nugatory. The British planned at this early stage of the negotiations to make any concession dependent on a defence agreement between the two countries. But it was obvious that there were dangers to both sides.

Chamberlain was aware of the prospect of being severely criticised in Britain. 'It would be urged,' he said at the third session on Tuesday afternoon, January 18th, 'that at a very dangerous and critical time the United Kingdom had decided to hand over the defended ports in Éire and, in so doing, were running very grave risks.'

De Valera was equally aware that any defence agreement between the two nations, no matter how independent it left both parties, would inevitably be interpreted by outsiders as making them allies. When a draft agreement on defence was placed before the fourth session on Wednesday, January 19th, the Irish leader, according to the British record, stated that the powers of his delegation were limited. There was some difference of opinion inside his own cabinet. Some of his colleagues held that unless there was to be full co-operation in regard to partition, no commitments should be entered into regarding co-operation over defence questions. If a defence agreement was couched in the general form of effect being given to it on the initiative of the Government of Ireland he thought he might get agreement with his colleagues. Otherwise he anticipated difficulty in his cabinet, his Party and with the Dáil.

He agreed to take the draft agreement on defence back to Dublin with him, so as to allow the Irish Government an opportunity to study it. It is clear that any defence agreement regarded as tolerable by de Valera, would leave it within the discretion of the Irish Government to provide or not provide defence facilities in time of war. At this stage, moreover, he was still hoping for substantial progress towards the ending of partition.

By and large, however, good progress was being made on defence at these early meetings. If we may judge by British cabinet papers,[1] the aim on the British side was to promote the closest consultation with Ireland on defence matters while the ineluctable fact was recognised that Ireland must be allowed to make her own decisions in peace and war.

Progress could also be reported on the financial issues. At the first meeting de Valera made it clear that he could not and would not accept responsibility for paying land annuities to Britain. He maintained his point of view that they were not legally due. While he agreed, in the interests of peace between the two countries, to make some financial concessions on other matters, there could be no question of paying the land annuities themselves. At that very first meeting Chamberlain said that they proposed to wipe out these annuities and to substitute a lump sum. To this de Valera insisted that the Irish Government were not paying the annuities as such in any shape or form. This he foresaw might create difficulties for Chamberlain in Britain, but the latter did not object. Even leaving out the annuities, the difficulty lay in the calculation of the lump sum to be paid.

The basis on which calculations were made during the conference was on the capital value of the annual payments which the British maintained were due. It was accepted by the British representatives that a single capital payment without any label relating it to specific items would be acceptable. Chamberlain assessed the capital equivalent of the payments demanded by Britain as £104·05 millions. Of this total, £78 millions was on account of land annuities. If that were wiped out, it would leave a lump sum of £26,000,000 due. De Valera at an early stage offered a lump sum of £10,000,000 and the position still rested at that level by the end of the first series of meetings on January 19th.

De Valera had already begun to use the fact that the cost of defence in Ireland was to be much greater than before. He argued, on January 18th, that in order to prevent Ireland being used by some enemy of the United Kingdom as a base for attacking the United Kingdom, it had become necessary to contemplate the expenditure of very large sums of money in re-arming the country and people in Ireland would argue that this was much more a United Kingdom interest than an Irish interest. With this increased expenditure on defence it would be impossible to pay any sum which even remotely approached the reduced claim of £26,000,000.

The first round of negotiations ended on January 19th, with no progress made on partition, substantial progress on the disputed ports, considerable progress towards a settlement on the financial questions and some discussion of a trade agreement. There remained a big gap between the two sides, at that stage an apparently unbridgeable gap, but the talks had led to a mutual understanding of each other's position. De Valera was impressed with Chamberlain's sincerity and his wish to do all he could. The talks were adjourned to allow discussions to proceed at official level, and also to avoid coinciding with the General Election which Lord Craigavon had called in Northern Ireland.

When de Valera returned to Dublin, resolutions poured into his office denouncing any settlement which failed to solve the problem of partition. In London, Malcolm MacDonald worked without success on Lord

Craigavon in the direction of Irish unity. Craigavon appears to have been privately impressed, though publicly his attitude remained unaltered.

De Valera was never one to neglect a flanking movement in diplomacy. Frank Gallagher was despatched on a special mission to President Roosevelt. In a letter to the United States' President de Valera argued strenuously:

> Another great opportunity for finally ending the quarrel of centuries between Ireland and Britain presents itself. The one remaining obstacle to be overcome is that of the partition of Ireland. The British Government alone have the power to remove this obstacle. If they really have the will they can bring about a United Ireland in a very short time. I have pressed my views upon them, but it is obvious that they recognise only the difficulties and are not fully alive to the great results that would follow a complete reconciliation between the two peoples.

De Valera saw that the effect in America of a just and final settlement would appeal to Roosevelt. He wrote:

> Reconciliation would affect every country where the two races dwell together, knitting their national strength and presenting to the world a great block of democratic peoples interested in the preservation of peace.

De Valera continued on a more personal note:

> Knowing your own interest in this matter, I am writing to ask you to consider whether you could not use your influence to get the British Government to realise what would be gained by reconciliation and to get them to move whilst there is time. In a short while, if the present negotiations fail, relations will be worsened.[2]

Roosevelt remembered the time, in 1919, when de Valera had consulted him on the legality of the bond certificates being issued on behalf of Dáil Éireann. He recalled those days in the reply which he sent on February 22nd:

> As you will realise I am greatly in sympathy with the thought of reconciliation, especially because any reconciliation would make itself felt in every part of the world. It would also strengthen the cause of Democracy everywhere.

Goodwill, of course, was not enough and he was, despite difficulties, willing to back it by some action. He went on:

> You will realise, I know, that I cannot officially or through diplomatic channels, accomplish anything or even discuss the matter. But I have taken the course of asking my good friend, Mr Joseph P. Kennedy, who sails today for England to take up his post as Ambassador, to convey a personal message from me to the Prime Minister, and to tell the Prime Minister how happy I should be if reconciliation could be brought about. As an old friend I send you my warm regards.[3]

The dispatch of this letter coincided with the resumption of the ministerial talks, on February 23rd, in the Prime Minister's room at the House of Commons. The Irish delegates had arrived in London on February 19th, to find themselves in the middle of a British ministerial crisis. Anthony Eden had just resigned as Foreign Secretary. The plenary conference was postponed for some days. But, in the meantime, de Valera met Malcolm MacDonald on a number of occasions at the Piccadilly Hotel. Once again, de Valera stressed the importance of partition as the irritant in Anglo-Irish relations. As he waited for the resumption of the talks, de Valera received a strongly worded letter, signed by the Catholic Bishop of Down and Connor and others, which stressed their grievances arising out of discrimination and gerrymandering as well as their fundamental objection to partition in any form.

When de Valera went into the conference on Wednesday, February 23rd, his line appeared to have hardened. He came back determined to fight the partition issue even more strenuously than before. The draft defence agreement might seem to have offered favourable terms, but he and his cabinet colleagues had decided that they could not possibly assume responsibility for sponsoring it so long as no hope was held out of Irish unity. In detail he argued the injustice of the partition itself, the injustice of an arbitrary boundary which ignored the wishes of the inhabitants in the border areas, the injustice of discrimination against Nationalists in the North. Unless something were done, he said, it seemed that deadlock was inevitable. The British Government had a direct legal responsibility for what happened in the North, and while partition lasted the Irish would not tolerate a government in Dublin which signed a defence agreement with Britain.

De Valera's argument about Irish public opinion was answered by Chamberlain with a reference to opinion in Britain. It would be politically impossible, he maintained, for the British Government to put any pressure in regard to partition on the Belfast Government. It was quite out of the question. He asked de Valera whether he had any alternative suggestions. In the circumstances de Valera thought that there were two possible courses which might be taken. Finance and trade might be settled between the two governments, leaving the defence issues in abeyance. The alternative was the course which he and his Government would prefer— the three defended ports to be taken over by his Government without entering into any defence agreement with Britain. He would have to explain to his people that in assuming responsibility for these ports, neither he nor his Government had entered into any commitment to Britain. He would, however, be willing to repeat assurances which he

12

had already given in the Dáil that it was the intention of the Government
to protect their territory and prevent its use by any foreign hostile power.
Again he came back to partition. As long as it lasted, he warned, the
establishment of good and close relations between the two countries
could not be expected. He recognised the advantages of a defence
agreement, but it could only apply to a United Ireland. The whole attitude
of the government and of the people would be very different indeed if
partition could be got rid of and an entirely different spirit would
prevail.

Partition was a stumbling block. But it did not undermine the personal
relations between the ministers at the table. De Valera was impressed
once again by Chamberlain's sincerity and his real desire to help towards
ending partition. Privately, to de Valera, he admitted that it was an
anachronism but he felt that he would not have the necessary support to
move in the matter. That he was not alone in his view was confirmed by
Sir Thomas Inskip. In the course of the discussions he said that many
people in Britain were of the opinion that partition could not last. To
help towards ending it, and as a gesture of goodwill which would carry
conviction in Britain, it was suggested that de Valera make special
concessions to Northern Ireland in regard to trade. If this were done it
would be possible to persuade the British people that a settlement on the
ports and finance was not altogether a bad bargain. There was the grim
prospect that British ministers would have to inform the House of
Commons that they had handed over the Irish ports and got nothing in
return.

Despite the pressures to give way on one front or another, de Valera
remained adamant. He even warned that any statement which he made
across the table was no more than an indication of his Government's
policy on defence and not a commitment or an understanding. He made
it clear that in his statements to the Dáil on defence he would assert
Ireland's right to remain neutral in a war in which Britain might be
involved. Throughout he refused to be cornered into bargaining one
right against another. He stressed that Ireland had nothing tangible to
give way on; that her people regarded the defended ports and other items
which the United Kingdom were proposing to concede as theirs by right;
and that they were only recovering what had been wrongfully taken away
from them.

The meeting ended inconclusively. De Valera and his ministers
returned to Dublin on domestic business. The British delegates were to
consider the refusal of de Valera to conclude any defence agreement in
which the Government of Britain would be consulted on the adequacy of
Irish defensive measures. The Irish were to discuss the suggestion

that special trade arrangements should be made for the entry of Northern Ireland goods into the rest of Ireland. Before leaving for Dublin, the Taoiseach and Seán MacEntee received a deputation of Nationalist members of the Stormont Parliament at the Piccadilly Hotel. They strongly pressed the Irish leader to stand firm on the partition question. Cahir Healy issued a statement afterwards in which he said: 'We would regard it as a betrayal of all our interests if he ignored the problem of partition by getting Trade and Defence Agreements only'.

De Valera, however, had already been facing this dilemma. He was finding it impossible to get real concessions on partition. Should he or should he not reject proposals which were to Ireland's benefit simply because their heart's desire and his appeared to be unobtainable?

When he and his colleagues returned from Dublin to London to resume negotiations on Thursday, March 3rd, he showed more clearly than ever that as long as partition lasted he was not going to make many concessions. Anxious as he was to promote better feelings between the two governments in Ireland he did not feel that opening the market of the twenty-six counties to the products of the six counties would help in any way. The six-county Government had shown no inclination to treat its minority justly. Until it did so he saw no reason why it should be presented with free entry into the main Irish market. The infant industries which had been set up under protection would be bound to suffer. That could be faced if partition were ended; there was no justification for it while the Government in Belfast made no reciprocal move to meet Irish opinion. He thought, however, that it might be possible to consider a plan for an exchange of preferences. He desired nothing better than to persuade Northern Ireland to co-operate in this sense.

The British Prime Minister had been banking on a trade concession to Belfast, partly as a step towards ending partition and partly as a counter to the criticisms which concessions on other matters would meet in Britain. Indeed, he had already mentioned it as a possibility to the Belfast Government. He did not disguise his regret at the turn matters had taken. Nor were the issues of the Treaty ports and of finance by any means settled. De Valera pointed out that the British delegates spoke of handing the ports unconditionally to Ireland. It was not at all certain that the people of Ireland would welcome the gift without reserve, he said. They would be fully alive to the fact that it meant undertaking a heavy financial burden.

He was using the cost of defence to offset other British demands. He argued that it would be heavy and that the Irish people would object to any cut in social services to meet it. Chamberlain was taken aback. He asked:

Is Mr de Valera trying to make it appear that we were thrusting a burden upon Éire in making her take over the defended ports? I am lost in admiration of Mr de Valera's skill in dialectics.

De Valera retorted that the view which he had been expressing was not his own but that of the Irish people. They felt strongly about partition and in the event of war might not be very sympathetic to Great Britain. A shade ironically, Chamberlain suggested that it might be better 'to spare Mr de Valera the embarrassment of having the Treaty ports offered to him'.

There was really no question of going back on the previous offer regarding the ports. But the negotiations were now 'bogged down'. Meetings of ministers followed at various levels. De Valera was MacDonald's guest at his home at Little Waltham one weekend. He met Chamberlain privately on March 8th and 11th. In the meantime, the British ministers were in consultation with ministers in Northern Ireland. According to the British records of March 9th, the Prime Minister had addressed some well-chosen words to the Irish ministers. He had made it clear that there could be no question of handing back the ports unless something was done for Northern Ireland and that there would be no trade agreement and no finance agreement either. This, Chamberlain felt, had had a salutary effect. But it did not work out that way.

The Irish delegates returned to Dublin on the evening of March 12th. A meeting of the Irish Cabinet was held next morning. De Valera had in London been trying to get the British Government at least to make some public statement in favour of the ending of partition. At one moment it appeared that Chamberlain might agree. A few days after the delegation's return, de Valera received an unofficial British 'heads of proposals' from Joseph P. Walshe, who had remained behind to participate in talks at official level. This included a draft declaration on partition to be made unilaterally by the British. The harbour defences at Berehaven, Lough Swilly and Cobh were to be handed over to the Irish Government and Articles 6 and 7 of the 1921 Treaty were to be abrogated. The financial dispute was to be settled by a single payment by Ireland of £10,000,000 and, under a trade agreement to be operative for five years, the British levies on Irish goods were to be abolished while Ireland would promise a review of protective duties against British goods. Preference in regard to duties was to be accorded to British goods in some instances. There was also a proposal for immediate reductions in the duties on certain goods from Northern Ireland, and free entry for them to the Irish market after four years. This document was simply a clarification of one which had been given to de Valera before he left London. The Cabinet, after his return, instructed the Irish High Commissioner, J. W. Dulanty, by telephone, to inform Malcolm MacDonald informally that it was almost certain that the Irish Government would not be able to accept.

Dulanty did as instructed and reported back to Dublin what he had told MacDonald.

> The provisions put forward late in the negotiations about our making big concessions to the North had made the proposals completely impossible for the Government of Éire. It might well be that our people could have accepted the other items, even though nothing had been done on the question of partition, but so long as the minority in the Six Counties is treated as it is today, any concession to the Six Counties would be a sheer impossibility. The statement on partition, containing as it did nothing of a positive character, was altogether inadequate.[4]

MacDonald was dismayed. He maintained that it would be impossible to get the trade agreement through the House of Commons without special concessions for Northern Ireland goods. As far as partition was concerned, he emphasized that the proposed British statement was no pious hope. It was something on which the Government would act if they got acceptance of the agreement. The less they said publicly the more that they could do later.

Negotiations were now at a critical stage. The two outstanding issues were the attitude of the London Government towards partition and that of the Dublin Cabinet towards special trade concessions to the North. MacDonald reported to the Irish Committee of the British Cabinet on March 23rd that it was now known that the Irish Government had found it impossible to make the special concessions to Northern Ireland for which he had asked. Consequently there was the threat of a breakdown of all the negotiations. It was at this time that Dulanty met Joseph P. Kennedy, the new American Ambassador in London. The High Commissioner reported that Kennedy expressed the hope that the negotiations would bear fruit. 'Speaking in the strictest confidence,' reported Dulanty,

> 'he said that President Roosevelt's opinion was that a settlement between the Irish and British Governments was a matter of importance in regard to the question of Anglo-American relations. Whilst that was the President's opinion it could not be regarded as the opinion of the American government since the subject had not been fully considered by the State Department. Nevertheless he had himself spoken to Mr Chamberlain—a good friend of Éire the Ambassador thought—acquainting him with President Roosevelt's opinion.'[5]

This intervention was opportune for Ireland. It was fortunate for her that the American Ambassador in London at this stage was a man as proud of his Irish origins as Joseph P. Kennedy. How much actual

difference he made cannot now be determined. Each side recognised that
the other genuinely desired a settlement. A breakdown would perhaps
have been particularly repugnant to British ministers and, if one may
judge from subsequent press comment, British public opinion. There was
clearly nothing doing on partition on the British side or on concessions
to Northern Ireland on the other. The inevitable was accepted and with
it the lines of a settlement in principle. The details were smoothly disposed
of. On April 22nd it was announced simultaneously that the discussions
were at an end and that an agreement had been reached.

The next day de Valera and his colleagues left Dublin for London. He
spent the following afternoon and evening at Malcolm MacDonald's
country home. On April 25th delegates met at a luncheon given by
Neville Chamberlain at 10 Downing Street. Just three months had passed
since a similar, less relaxed luncheon party had preceded the first day's
discussion. That had been quite a pleasant occasion. But this time a new
spirit in Anglo-Irish relations was manifest. The ceremony of signing
followed. After Chamberlain had signed, he presented de Valera with his
pen as a souvenir of the occasion. De Valera signed with another pen and
gave it to Chamberlain.

The following day the texts of the agreements were published. Ireland
was offered possession of the ports and Britain gave up any other rights
which, in time of war, she might have demanded within the twenty-six
counties of Ireland. There was no defence agreement. The financial
dispute was to end on a single payment of £10,000,000. The special duties
imposed in 1932 by the two governments at the outset of the economic
war were to end, but this did not affect Ireland's right to protect its infant
industries. There were no special trade concessions to Northern Ireland.

The Agreement has often been described as a triumph for de Valera,
although he did not himself see it that way. The full implication of handing
back the ports and ending the defence clauses of the 1921 Treaty were
not yet wholly visible. But it was obvious to all that this would be a major
factor in Ireland's position in the event of another war. As a negotiator
de Valera had proved himself a tough man to bargain with, but one whose
integrity and consistency had made a lasting impression. He gave away
nothing because he spoke the truth when he said he had nothing to give.
What he was seeking was a rectification of injustices; about these there
was no question of bargaining. What he was getting he felt was only
Ireland's right and due.

He could be, and was, subtle in argument and as usual was ultra-careful
of every word he spoke. Throughout he showed himself not only an
excellent strategist, but a master of relevant detail. Under firm but human

leadership the Irish delegation had worked as a team. Most of the arguing
had fallen to de Valera, although on matters of finance, trade and agriculture he had very able support from the three ministers at his side. He
and they had ample grounds for personal satisfaction. To judge his
achievement fully, one should attend not only to the negotiations but to
the long preparation and exact timing.

But his mood as he came away from London was far from jubilant. He
knew the limitations of possible achievement at this stage. Yet he was
heartily disappointed at making no real progress on the partition question.
He had failed even to bring away a statement that the British Government
would welcome its abolition, although he knew that privately
Chamberlain hoped that it would end.

In a few years he would look back somewhat wistfully on the encouragement he obtained from his talks with Chamberlain. In Chamberlain he
found a British leader whom he could wholly trust. Neither man committed himself to anything beyond the published terms of the Agreement
—neither Chamberlain to ending partition, nor de Valera to providing
any facilities in the event of war which would be inappropriate in a
neutral. But each man was convinced that the other believed in the untold
blessings of a true Anglo-Irish understanding and friendship. No one
will ever know what this meeting of minds would have led to if war had
not intervened or had not come so pitilessly soon.

De Valera and MacDonald kept their personal contact during negotiations. On almost the last day MacDonald said to de Valera: 'Look, I
would be terribly pleased if you would accept some gift from me as a
souvenir of our association.' De Valera said he did not want any souvenir
but the memory, and MacDonald replied: 'Well I am sorry about this
because I would have liked to give you something to look at occasionally.'

As usual he was not easily put off. The British security men who had
accompanied de Valera, had noticed him looking carefully at a certain
book in Foyles in the Charing Cross Road—a first edition of a book by
Hamilton on the elements of quaternions. Learning of this, MacDonald
bought the book, had it rebound, and presented it to de Valera. It became
a treasured possession.

Some time fairly soon after the Anglo-Irish Agreement there was an
announcement in the newspapers that Sir Samuel Hoare, the Home
Secretary, was drafting a Penal Reform Bill. MacDonald received a letter
from de Valera saying that he had read about this with great interest. He
knew quite a lot about the prisons of England and had certain ideas on
prison reform. Did MacDonald think that Sir Samuel Hoare would care
to receive them? If not he would quite understand. Samuel Hoare said
he would be delighted. In MacDonald's recollection, some of de Valera's

ideas were incorporated in Sir Samuel Hoare's bill, which was postponed owing to the war, but became the basis of much subsequent penal reform.

MacDonald was struck by many aspects of de Valera's personality, but most of all perhaps by his magnanimity. He never allowed his memories of prison in England to prejudice his feelings towards her people.

THE MANY SIDES OF GOVERNMENT

1932 – 1939

Several strands of policy must now be brought together, beginning with economic and social affairs. The neglect of economic and social improvement under British rule had been a constant theme among leaders of opinion in Ireland. Some, like Horace Plunkett, thought that much could be done by the organized efforts of the people themselves in advance of any measure of political independence. Others, like the Irish Nationalist members of the House of Commons, sought to extract ameliorative legislation from the British Parliament while at the same time pursuing the agitation for Home Rule. Others again thought it best to concentrate their energies on the struggle for independence. This left economic and social advancement to be attended to by a free Irish Government and Parliament when their establishment had at last been secured.

The 1916 Proclamation laid down the general principles when it guaranteed equal opportunities and declared a resolve 'to pursue the happiness and prosperity of the whole nation and of all its parts'. More specific statements were made in the constitution of Sinn Féin when reorganized on a republican basis at the Ard Fheis of October, 1917. Arthur Griffith had always been a protectionist. For that reason alone, it was to be expected that a protective system for Irish industries would have a prominent place, as it did, among the aims of the organization. The other objectives included the establishment of an Irish mercantile marine, the carrying out of an industrial survey, the exploitation of Irish mineral resources, the development of transport by rail, road and water, the utilization of waste lands, the development of sea fisheries, the reform of public assistance services, the provision of employment on land reclamation, afforestation, and other public works, and the payment to workers of a living wage.

Although Ireland was in a virtual or actual state of war with Britain from 1919 to 1921 and the Dáil Cabinet and individual ministries were working under extraordinary difficulties, some efforts were made to improve social services through the agency of the local authorities and to frame policies in preparation for better times. During the period of controversy and civil war that followed the signing of the Treaty there was little that could be done in these directions. In the period from 1923 to the beginning of 1932, however, important measures were enacted by the Free State Parliament in relation to land settlement and agriculture. Also to arterial drainage, hydro-electric power and electricity supply, tourist development, currency, agricultural credit, transport and housing. Moderate protective measures were introduced for the encouragement of industries.

In de Valera's view, however, the progress that was being made during those years was too slow and the measures taken were inadequate or, in some cases, ill-advised. In his address at the inaugural meeting of Fianna Fáil in May, 1926, one of the most important speeches of his career, he declared his full sympathy with James Connolly's sentiment: 'Ireland, as distinct from her people, is nothing to me . . .' He spoke of the part which Republican deputies could take in the improvement of the social and material conditions of the people. Emigration would have to be checked; the condition of the unemployed and their dependants should be relieved. He recalled that in 1921, while he believed that the London negotiations might lead to an acceptable agreement, he had set out to plan for the future. He had seen the provision of employment as the most urgent need. Only organization and capital had been required for the solution of that problem. There was no lack of useful national work to be done. Road, rail and water transport, afforestation, land reclamation and drainage, the development of water and fuel power, fisheries, housing, the abolition of slums, land division—all would be embraced in the plans which he had in mind at that time. Financial resources were available. Vast deposits were being held in the banks and were being used chiefly to build up foreign countries. In 1921 he had had no doubt that the people, in the enthusiasm of their newly-won freedom, would not hesitate to make available by way of loan a large part of these deposits. Even if they had not been able to secure all the initial capital required at home, they could have placed a supplemental loan with people of Irish race abroad. The public capital programme (as it would now be described) would be productive in character. 'As it was proceeding the other essential industries would have been developing with protective tariffs to foster them, and would have absorbed labour gradually according as it was released from the more pressing State undertakings'. This was the economic programme he had had in mind for so long. 'It is', said de Valera, 'still largely capable of being put into effect, if the essential condition of enthusiasm can be restored and we have people with the will to do it.'[1]

So, in the spring of 1926, de Valera reaffirmed his faith in the economic policies which he had been pondering in 1921. Three years later he made a statement on the proposals for economic development which Fianna

Fáil would put before the people at the next general election. Having urged concentration, in the first place, on production for the home market and only in the second place on exports, he announced his party's intention to reserve a progressively increasing proportion, and ultimately the whole of the home market, for Irish agricultural products and, by import duties and quotas, to give Irish manufacturers reasonable security. The main requirements for the development of sea fisheries appeared to be training for fishermen in the handling of deep-sea craft, co-operative organization, and loans on easy terms for the purchase of boats and equipment. Peat was used elsewhere in the generation of electricity and, in a compressed form, as domestic and industrial fuel. The possibilities of making similar use of Ireland's great peat resources deserved investigation. The control of Irish currency and credit should be placed in the hands of Irishmen, to be exercised entirely in the interests of the Irish people. Road, railway and canal transport should be co-ordinated under a single management, with safeguards for the interests of the community.

By 1932, economic and social policy had already been settled in its main features and was understood and agreed upon by all the members of the Government. Its detailed application was, to a large extent, left to the individual ministers, but was reviewed in long discussions at cabinet meetings held twice a week or even more frequently. Seán Lemass was, as always, a man of strongly independent mind, quick to make a decision and to act, unlikely to bear with patience intervention in the administration of his department from any source. De Valera, who was well able to practise judicious delegation, respected Lemass's preference for a large degree of autonomy. He gave to his able young Minister for Industry and Commerce confidence and support, in full measure, which were invaluable throughout the years, particularly whenever doubts and reservations occurred on the part of other members of the Government. Yet the outlook of the two men on economic and social matters was not identical. De Valera's ideal of a society content with frugal comfort was not one to appeal with any great attraction to the urban mind of Mr Lemass. When the Constitution of 1937 was still in the form of an early draft, it was the Minister for Industry and Commerce who persuaded the President to modify the 'Directive Principles of Social Policy'. 'You know, Chief,' he said, 'we can't very well make the Constitution a manifesto of Fianna Fáil social policy'.

It would, of course, have been impossible to leave it to the courts to determine the application of the Directive Principles—these were properly and expressly set down for the general guidance of Parliament. Although in their final form they were less specific in some respects than in de Valera's original draft, they remain as an accurate expression of his social ideals. Justice and charity were to inform all the institutions of the national life. All citizens, men and women equally, should have the right to an adequate means of livelihood. Ownership should be distributed so as best to subserve the common good. The operation of free competition should not be unbridled. The welfare of the whole people should be the aim of credit control. As many families as practicable should be established on the land in economic security. Private enterprise should be favoured, but the public should be protected against its abuse. The economic interests of the weaker sections of the community were to be safeguarded with special care. In another part of the Constitution, the family was recognized as 'the natural primary and fundamental unit group of Society', as 'the necessary basis of social order' and as possessing 'inalienable and imprescriptible rights'.

Injustice and inequality still exist in Ireland as they do in every other country, but there can be no doubt that remarkable improvements have taken place. To a large extent the foundations for subsequent progress were laid in the relatively short period between Fianna Fáil's accession to office in March, 1932, and the outbreak of war in September, 1939.

Before the Dáil rose for the summer recess of 1932, legislation had been enacted for the stabilisation of dairy produce prices, for the protection by means of customs duties of various forms of agricultural and industrial activity, and for the emergency imposition of duties by government order, subject to parliamentary confirmation. An important Housing Act was passed. Before the end of the year a Control of Manufactures Act was passed, with the general object of keeping Irish industrial development, under protection, in the hands of Irishmen while not excluding external participation. Legislation for the control of prices was enacted almost on the eve of Christmas. Within the first eight months of 1933, provision had been made by law for the control of milling and encouragement of the growing of cereals, especially wheat; measures had been enacted regarding transport by road and by rail, for the establishment of a unified National Health Insurance Society, for the development of cement manufacture, for expansion of the manufacture of sugar from home-grown beet, and for the establishment of a company to provide industrial credit. The legislation passed during the remainder of the year included a Land Act, an Unemployment Assistance Act and a Sea Fisheries Protection Act.

So it went on in the succeeding years. In agriculture, the policy of encouraging tillage and stabilizing dairy produce prices was continued, while land annuities were reduced and grants in relief of agricultural rates were increased. In manufactures, protective measures—duties and quotas—to substitute home-produced for imported products of light industry were vigorously and successfully applied—too vigorously in the opinion of some economists. Considerably more rapid progress was made in house-building and reconstruction and in slum clearance. Provision was made for the regulation and improvement of farm workers' wages and conditions of employment. Irish neutrality in the war would scarcely have been possible if it had not been for the extent to which self-sufficiency had been achieved. One need only point to the greatly increased production of wheat and other cereals and of sugar beet; to the development of peat as an alternative to imported fuel; and to the growth and diversification of industrial output under the policy of protection. (For illustrations see below page 333.)

We must not seem to argue that the economic war with Britain was of immediate benefit to Ireland. De Valera admitted candidly (in October, 1932, for example) that 'the Tariff War is bound to impose considerable hardships on our people'.[2]

The disturbance of the normal trading relationships was added to the effects of the disastrous fall in world agricultural prices which had already been in progress before the beginning of the economic dispute. Although the British punitive duties were offset in part by export bounties and other benefits granted by the Free State Government, the cash income of the farmers declined, credit from banks and shopkeepers became more difficult to obtain, there was a significant reduction in the use of fertilizers and the standard of living in rural Ireland fell to a lower level.

All classes of farmers did not suffer in equal degree—many, for example, benefited by the new policy of encouraging the extension of tillage. There can be no doubt, however, that the agricultural community as a whole endured considerable hardship as a result of the dispute. It is not surprising, therefore, that the end of the 'economic war' was welcomed with profound relief, not only by those who had been most directly affected by it but by the people at large.

By the end of the thirties De Valera had established his position as a leader of decision and all-round practical ability. Within his own party, then and later, his personal position was unchallenged. He held throughout the devoted loyalty of his followers. His cabinets were not large; they were limited to about a dozen members. Anything more than that de Valera would have considered too large for intimate discussion, anything less would have failed to represent the necessary variety of opinion. In many ways de Valera felt that members of the cabinet were not so much picked by him as selected for him by circumstances. They had to reflect the opinions of a wide range of Irishmen.

Meetings of the cabinet were long. De Valera did nothing to curtail discussion. He believed in letting every aspect of a question be aired; he had unending patience. Indeed not all his ministers agreed with the amount of time spent on cabinet discussions. It helped, however, to produce united decisions. De Valera did not believe in reaching cabinet decisions by majority vote. He felt that, since there was combined cabinet responsibility, the opposition of even one member to a certain course of action had to be taken seriously. A vote on the course to be followed could only make for division within the cabinet. De Valera preferred to hear the opinion of each minister and then to attempt to reach a consensus.

He himself was adept at wearing down opposition for he could, and often did, argue interminably in favour of a certain course. If he failed to carry his cabinet with him on the first occasion, he would postpone the issue and raise it again and again until such time as by a process of attrition he had reduced the opposition to at least a silent acceptance.

Often, however, de Valera appears to have approached his cabinet meetings with a very open mind. He was frequently slow to reach final decisions and was known, on a number of occasions, to reopen discussions on matters apparently settled. He might feel that a point made by a minister had not been given proper weight. Indeed, he is remembered as having been very considerate to all individual ministers, particularly those who lacked assertiveness or found difficulty in convincing their colleagues. There were some decisions which were within the competence of the head of the government and no one else. Here de Valera guarded his own rights closely. His decision to go to the country in 1933 is a good example.

His relations with the Labour Party were good throughout. Regular fortnightly meetings were held with their representatives at which proposed legislation on social matters was discussed. Indeed, there was considerable agreement on social policy between the two parties, Labour and Fianna Fáil. De Valera said in the Dáil at this time:

> I am quite willing to admit that during my whole time in struggling for the freedom of this country I had only one object and that was to get free so as to be able to order our life for the benefit of our own people. I never regarded freedom as an end in itself, but if I were asked what statement of Irish policy was most in accord with my view as to what human beings should struggle for, I would stand side by side with James Connolly.

He regretted that there had been differences between the Fianna Fáil and Labour parties:

> These two parties had naturally the same programme and when I differed with the Labour Party after the Treaty it was because I thought that that Party was making a mistake and that they did not see what James Connolly saw, and what he told me he saw, that to secure national freedom was the

first step in order to get the workers of Ireland the living they were entitled to in their own country.[3]

There were many social welfare benefits introduced in this period, notably the first pensions for widows and orphans in Ireland, which were started in 1935. In 1932 there was no unemployment assistance available to those in uninsured occupations and little recognition of the State's obligations to the unemployed. In 1933 the Fianna Fáil Government introduced legislation to benefit those unemployed who had hitherto been excluded from State assistance. The housing programme produced in the first decade of de Valera's administration 132,220 newly-built or reconstructed houses, more than four times the number built or reconstructed in the previous ten years.

Protection of Irish industry might or might not have been politically acceptable otherwise, but Britain's economic sanctions gave it the justification of necessity. The central task was placed on the shoulders of the aforementioned Seán Lemass, Minister for Industry and Commerce, a Dublin deputy of exceptional drive. He was ultimately to succeed de Valera in 1959 as Head of the Irish Government and President of the Fianna Fáil Party. De Valera himself was no doctrinaire advocate of protection. 'I do not believe in tariffs simply as if they were some kind of religion', he said in 1932. 'I have regarded tariffs simply as a present means to an end. What is the end to be served? To protect our own industries to enable them to grow and to be built up'.

While in theory he believed that there were considerable advantages attaching to a free trade policy if all nations were at the same stage of development, yet he felt that protection was essential in the early stages of industrial growth. He gave great freedom to his Minister for Industry and Commerce in pushing forward an industrial policy. 'Our policy', said de Valera, 'is that we are going to produce for ourselves the things which we were unnecessarily paying others to produce for us.'[4]

The results were dramatic. One illustration only can be given here. In 1931 more than five million pairs of boots and shoes were imported. By seven years later this number had been reduced to one-twentieth. Supplies were, in 1938, coming from Irish tanneries and Irish footwear factories. The number of persons employed in the leather industry quadrupled between 1931 and 1938. Of course not all changes were of this order. But within the first six years of de Valera's administration the number of persons in industrial employment increased by fifty per cent.

This industrial development was based to some extent on a new policy in agriculture. The Minister for Agriculture during this period was Dr James Ryan and he was faced with the task of directing the agricultural industry towards supplying Irish needs first and the British market second. De Valera's attitude to the British market for Irish cattle was stated by him in the course of the economic war between the two countries:

> Now with regard to this foreign market for cattle, our attitude is the sensible attitude to it. We are anxious to have it provided that it is not purchased at too great a cost, and I claim that the development of the cattle industry here in this country in the past, as a corollary of the English free trade system, was purchased at an immense cost to our people and that it was not worth it . . .[5]

In one of his most vivid phrases:

> No longer shall our children, like our cattle, be brought up for export.

At another time he stated:

> If there is to be any hope of prosperity for this country it is by reversing that policy which made us simply the kitchen garden for supplying the British with cheap food.

A major change in agricultural policy was the extension of tillage and especially the growing of wheat for home consumption. In 1931 3,300,000 cwt of flour was imported. In 1938 only 100,000 cwt came from outside Ireland. Idle mills had been set working again. De Valera had set on foot a policy of self-sufficiency which was to be a crucial factor in the years of World War II.

The economic principles behind de Valera's policies were simple and straightforward. Early in his career he did allow himself to pose a challenge to the existing economic system as Head of the Government when he said:

> It may be that under the present system we cannot do the full work we would like to do, but we are going to try. I am going to say this, that if I try within the system as it stands and fail, then I will try to go outside the system, and I will go to the country and ask them to support me to go outside the system.[6]

But he never did go outside the system, although his Government had the whole question of currency, banking, credit and other aspects of the financing of State and other enterprises examined by a commission set up in 1934 by the Minister for Finance, Seán MacEntee. The result was a conservative report published in 1938.

In those first years of his administration de Valera sometimes found the delegation of authority difficult and involved himself somewhat too readily in matters in which he became interested. An extreme, though minor, example occurred early in 1933 when Patrick Nolan, a lecturer in

University College, Dublin, approached de Valera to ask his help. A heavy snow-fall had occurred and Professor John Nolan, a scientist, who had been studying ions in the Dublin mountains was cut off. De Valera understood that unless he were rescued quickly the professor could die of exposure and hunger. He got in touch with the Department of Defence and he understood that the army would go to the rescue. The following morning was Saturday and de Valera waited impatiently for news from Defence. None came. De Valera went home to lunch intent on doing something about the matter. He ordered his car to be ready for a journey into the mountains and after lunch he, together with his two eldest sons, Vivion and Éamonn, set out for the hills south of Dublin. At Enniskerry they saw an army lorry stopped outside a public house and a number of soldiers showing more interest in the premises than in the hills behind. When he asked whether they had gone up to rescue Professor Nolan, he was informed that the lorry had got stuck a short distance up the road and they had to return.

De Valera was angry. He decided to press on and his driver continued the ascent until his car too came to a halt in the snow. Persistent to the last de Valera went to a nearby farm. He left Éamonn by the fire while he and Vivion borrowed two horses to continue their mercy mission. At last they found Professor Nolan, but he was not suffering from exposure in an open shed as de Valera had envisaged, but was standing on the floor of a comfortable country kitchen, with a bright fire glowing on the hearth behind him and a bottle of whiskey in his hand as he poured a drink for two army officers in uniform who had made their way to the house on foot. De Valera realised that he had foolishly jumped to conclusions and that the officers had wisely sent back the lorry while they went the last part of the journey alone. He admired the spirit and initiative shown by the officer in charge whom he first met on that occasion. He was Major Dan McKenna whom de Valera was to select to be Chief of Staff of the Irish Army at the beginning of the second World War.

The supreme issues involved in External Affairs convinced de Valera that it was better that this portfolio should remain in his own hands. Thus it was that he represented Ireland every year at meetings of the League of Nations in the 1930s. He was fortunate in the circumstances of his first appearance at Geneva in September, 1932, but he used it to the fullest advantage. On that occasion he found himself President of the Council of the League of Nations. As such he took the chair at the opening of the thirteenth Assembly of the League. It was customary for the President to open the proceedings with a review of the work of the League during the previous year. Indeed it was usual for him to accept a script provided by officials of the secretariat. De Valera, however rarely delivered a speech which he did not carefully prepare and the importance of his platform did not daunt him now. He spent many hours working on his address.

When he rose to speak to the Assembly on September 26th, 1932, there was no handclap to welcome him. The formal politeness customarily shown to any chairman was absent. He did not miss it for he had a message to give. Twelve months before, Japan—a member of the League—had attacked the territory of China. De Valera saw in this a challenge to the basis of the League and he appealed for a frank consideration of the working of the international organization:

> Out beyond the walls of this Assembly there is the public opinion of the world, and if the League is to prosper, or even survive, it must retain the support and confidence of that public opinion as a whole. It is often said that, in a final analysis, the League has no sanctions but the force of world opinion. At the moment that is profoundly true . . . friends and enemies of the League alike feel that the testing time has come; and they are watching to see if that test will reveal a strength that will be the assurance of a renewal of vigour and growth. The eyes of all peoples are focused on Geneva today as perhaps they have never been focused on it before . . .

He insisted that there was only one effective way of silencing criticism of the League and of bringing to its support millions who at present stood aside in apathy or undisguised cynicism. This was to show unmistakably that the Covenant of the League was a solemn pact, the obligations of which no state, great or small, could ignore. The only alternative to competitive armament was the security for national rights which an uncompromising adherence to the principles of the Covenant could afford. 'Ladies and Gentlemen', he said, 'the avoidance of wars and of the burden of armaments is of such concern to humanity that no State should be permitted to jeopardize the common interest by selfish action contrary to the Covenant. No state is powerful enough to stand for long against the League if the governments in the League and their peoples are determined that the Covenant shall be upheld'.[7]

No speech he ever made impinged on a wider audience. Around the world it was acclaimed. The *Montreal Star* said 'it revealed with brutal frankness the seriousness of the situation confronting the League. It gave the delegates practically nothing to cheer about but plenty to ponder over'. That perhaps explains the stony silence which greeted the unusual speech which, according to the *New York Times*, made de Valera 'the outstanding personality' of the session. Yet his criticism of the League was moderate and its main importance lay in making known the opinion of countless millions on its activities. The *Manchester Guardian* called the speech 'the best ever yet made by a president of a League Assembly'. The *Daily Herald* concurred. The *News Chronicle* correspondent, A. J. Cummings, considered that de Valera was no orator: 'He keeps his chin down, mumbles and stumbles over his lines, has no sense of the dramatic phrase. . .' Certainly his statements tended to be complicated and involved, but then so also were the issues with which he dealt. Yet Cummings went on to record the reaction in Geneva to what de Valera had said. 'In the lobbies', he reported, 'the speech received nothing but praise; and in private many delegates expressed their envious admiration of Mr de Valera's courage'.

Not all sections of the press, however, accepted the speech in the spirit in which it was made. De Valera was, to some of them, an enemy of the League, an impression which he was at pains to correct in a broadcast from Geneva a few days later. He went on to warn:

> The League must stand or fall by disarmament. The League cannot stand still. It must go forward or disappear . . . But the League is as necessary for the world today as when it was held forth as the hope of despairing humanity during the war.[8]

De Valera displayed his hopes if he did not hide his fears! In the years which followed he spoke from time to time at League meetings, always in carefully weighed terms. He was fearless in the expression of his opinions, and on occasion did not hesitate to take a stand which would be seriously questioned in Ireland. Perhaps the outstanding instance was in the debate on the entry of Russia into the League in 1934. Despite the religious and political problems which his attitude might raise, de Valera stated that he would support and vote for Russia's being accepted by the League. The exclusion of a nation so important was, in itself, creating a danger to world peace. While casting his vote in favour of Russia he made an appeal that liberty of conscience and freedom of worship be accorded by that state within its borders.

The absence of major powers from the deliberations of the League detracted greatly from its authority. This was true, for some or all the time, of the United States, Russia, Germany and Japan. But the greatest weakness of the League in de Valera's eyes was its lack of power in making binding decisions. The League, he admitted was 'a precarious and imperfect instrument', but he strove to the uttermost to use it on behalf of peace. He contributed to the debates at Geneva on the Abyssinian crisis in September, 1935, and earnestly and forcibly demanded:

> Why cannot the Peace Conference which will meet in Europe when the next conflict has decimated the nations and disaster and exhaustion have tamed some of them into temporary submission—why cannot this Conference be

convened now, when calm reason might have a chance to bring the nations into friendly co-operation and a lasting association of mutual help?[9]

It was a vain hope as the world staggered helplessly from one crisis to the next. De Valera supported the use of economic sanctions by the League of Nations against the aggressor, but less than twelve months later he was to join the procession of speakers at a special session of the League who had to admit that the sanctions had failed. 'We have now to confess publicly', he said, 'that we must abandon the victim to his fate. It is a sad confession, as well as a bitter one. It is the fulfilment of the worst predictions of all who decried the League and said it could not succeed'.[10]

A crisis of confidence in the League was now manifest. But de Valera saw all too well the impotence of the small states. 'Peace,' he said, 'is dependent upon the will of the great states. All the small states can do, if the statesmen of the greater states fail in their duty, is resolutely to determine that they will not become the tools of any great power, and that they will resist with whatever strength they may possess every attempt to force them into a war against their will.'[11]

A role of neutrality he concluded was the only choice for a small nation if there was not united action by the League against aggressors. He was starkly realistic. By now he knew that there was no immediate hope of bringing about a change. But he was hoping to direct the statesmen of Europe to face the dangers of a bloody conflict—to act before the power passed into the hands of soldiers.

The Civil War in Spain which began in July, 1936, was an issue on which de Valera felt called upon to give a firm lead to his own people. There was much Catholic sympathy for General Franco's forces; a movement was organized by General O'Duffy—the former Blue Shirt leader—to recruit volunteers for that side. Despite many protests in Ireland, de Valera strongly supported the League of Nations in its attitude of non-intervention.

In September, 1938, de Valera was elected the nineteenth President of the Assembly of the League of Nations. It was a tribute to a man who had, through the previous six years, walked a path independent of the pressures of major powers. His election was no doubt the result of compromise among the nations. He had won himself an international recognition which was out of proportion to the size of his country. It was a moment of major crisis; German demands on Czechoslovakia had brought Europe to the brink of war. In accepting office de Valera appealed to all nations to cling to the League as an instrument of peace. He pointed out the shortcomings of international relationships as known hitherto:

We have been unable to bend our wills to sacrifice selfish advantage even when it conflicts with justice to others. We have been unable, no matter on what side we are, to apply to others the law we insist in having applied to ourselves. All history tells us that, in the long run, to be just is to be truly wise. But we seem unable to apply the lesson.[12]

It was now that Neville Chamberlain made his desperate efforts to find a way of peace with Hitler. De Valera sent him a telegram of encouragement. He urged him to let nothing deflect him from his attempts to avert catastrophe. Later he warned him in a letter that he would be blamed if his initiative proved unsuccessful, but assured him that it was overwhelmingly right that this one last great effort to save the world should be embarked on. The position of the Sudeten Germans was such that de Valera felt that there was some justice in Hitler's claims to this territory. He recognized that the Treaty of Versailles had created problems by somewhat arbitrary curtailment of German borders. 'The circumstances of war', he said, 'are such that the settlements imposed by it are almost inevitably unjust'.[13]

In a broadcast from Geneva to the United States he appealed for a general European peace conference. He was appalled at the apparent inevitability of war—at the fatalistic attitude of mind which the procession of crises had produced—at the fact that the will to make one further effort for peace was atrophied. In this he saw the gravest danger. 'Not always', he said, 'will we have someone to do what Mr Chamberlain has done, and we shall find that we shall have had one crisis too many.'[14]

On the morning of September 30th, 1938, the Munich Agreement was reached; war, which had till then appeared inevitable, was averted. Later on that same day de Valera spoke, as President, at the closing of the session of the League of Nations Assembly. It had been a session overshadowed by the international crisis. The international standing of the League had suffered an indubitable decline. The Assembly had performed its limited functions in Geneva while the fate of Europe was being decided elsewhere. De Valera, in his concluding speech to the Assembly, was not sanguine about world prospects. Yet he still felt that the League 'with all its acknowledged shortcomings', could be a basis on which to raise a genuine international organization for the future. It sounded, however, like an admission of failure.[15]

From his own point of view the years had been far from wasted. There had been a steady and imposing growth in his own international stature and Dr Conor Cruise O'Brien has testified to the effect of this at home. 'He had gained', he tells us, 'an authority not possessed by any Irish leader since the fall of Parnell nearly fifty years before. Much of his authority had been won by his activity in international affairs. His speeches at Geneva had caught the imagination of Irish people.'[16] That seems true beyond question.

The troubled international scene did not assist a solution of the partition question. De Valera had realized after his discussions with Chamberlain in the spring of 1938 that he could expect no British politician to take the initiative towards ending partition unless public opinion in Britain was willing to support such action. Yet, as he took over the Irish ports which the British evacuated in the summer of 1938 and raised the Irish tricolour over the defence post at Spike Island, Cobh, de Valera was far from discouraged. His political position had been further strengthened by a General Election in June, 1938.

The support which he had received in the early years of his administration had been wearing thin. His Government had been defeated on a snap vote in favour of arbitration on civil service salaries on the day he himself had been attending the funeral of his uncle, Patrick Coll, at Bruree. Arbitration for government employees was something which de Valera feared as a possible shirking of government responsibility. His Government had established an Agricultural Wages Board in 1937 and was to set up a Labour Court in 1946, but in these matters he himself was conservative. He felt that the Government itself was the arbitrator dealing with the whole Irish community. He had stated, in response to criticisms that his was a 'hairshirt policy':

> Our purpose as a Government is to see that . . . burdens rest heaviest on the shoulders of people who are best able to bear them and rest lightest on the shoulders of those least able to bear them. . . . Every member of the community has to bear his part of the burden.[17]

Be that as it may, a defeat by the Opposition within a few weeks of his completing the Agreement with Britain afforded de Valera an ideal opportunity for going to the country. The result was an overwhelming victory for de Valera and Fianna Fáil. His party won 77 seats out of 138 seats in the Dáil, an overall majority of 16 seats. This and 1944 were the only elections in which de Valera's party received more than 50 per cent of the total first preference votes cast.

With a government independent of all other parties de Valera now felt that he could go all out for Irish unity. He decided that the British public must, at all costs, be informed of the issues involved. Liam MacMahon of Manchester, who had helped in the establishment of the Irish Self-Determination League in 1919 was approached, and steps were taken to set up the Irish Anti-Partition League. In an interview with a special correspondent of the London *Evening Standard* on October 17th, 1938, de Valera set out his ideas about the solution to the problem:

> Taking into account the prevailing sentiment of the present majority in the Six Counties and bearing in mind also the sentiment of the minority there

and of the majority in the whole Island, here is what I propose. If I could have my own way, I would have immediately a single All-Ireland Parliament, elected on a system of proportional representation so as to be fair to minorities —this might entail a different form of executive.

But this he realized was wishful thinking. It could not be acceptable at that time unless some separate recognition were given to the Northern area. He therefore went on to put his practical proposal:

I would say to Belfast—keep all your present powers. We ask only one thing of you. We think the area you control is not the area which in justice you could claim, even for a local parliament, but we make the concession if you guarantee fair play for the minority and consent to the transfer to an All-Ireland Parliament of the powers now reserved to the Parliament at Westminster.

De Valera considered with some reason that he was going a long way to meet the situation. He had entered Irish public life originally and joined the Irish Volunteers in 1913 because of the threat of partition. He had this to say in 1939 about the development of his views in the quarter of a century which had elapsed:

It seemed to me that no more cruel wrong could be inflicted on any country than to divide its national territory, and from that to build up vested interests and prejudices which were going to keep that country divided. I can honestly say that in any thought that I have given to Irish political matters during the whole of the period that has elapsed since 1913 or so, I have always put one question to myself, and that is: Are we making towards having ultimately one State—one national State or not? Are the things that we are doing ultimately to mean a national State or not?[18]

By 1921 he had been willing to accept local autonomy under an Irish legislature in Dublin for the area where the majority were Unionist. At that time there was still hope that the areas with Nationalist majorities, two counties or more, would not be left under the jurisdiction of a government in Belfast.

Now, in 1939, he was putting forward a solution based on the existing boundary, despite the injustice of that boundary to the majorities in the border counties. This time, in other words, he did not appeal for a rectification of the boundaries. That, he felt, would be no more than tinkering with the basic question. A re-drawing of the boundary, while it might give a greater measure of justice, it would still be no more than a half measure or palliative.

The beginning of this campaign in Britain was unfortunately followed by a revival of activity on the part of a wing of the Irish Republican Army. The IRA had been divided and without a clear-cut policy for the last few years. Seán Russell, however, had rallied an activist group which later, in 1938, laid plans for a bombing campaign in England. In January, 1939, an ultimatum was served on the British Foreign Secretary, Lord Halifax, demanding the withdrawal of British troops from Northern Ireland and threatening reprisals if this was not done within four days. Shortly afterwards time bombs began to explode in a number of public places in England. In one explosion in Coventry in August, 1939, five people were killed and about seventy others wounded. The bombs also blew sky-high any hopes which de Valera had of convincing British public opinion of the justice of the Irish cause. He and his Government were forced to take steps to prevent the usurpation of the authority of the State. The Offences Against the State Bill became law on June 14th, 1939, and the Government issued an order declaring the IRA an illegal organization. It was, however, to be a thorn in the side of the Irish Government for some time, especially during the early years of World War II.

The IRA was not alone in dashing de Valera's hopes for an effective anti-partition campaign at this time. The situation was made more explosive on April 26th, 1939, when Neville Chamberlain announced his Government's decision to introduce compulsory military service. De Valera had arranged to leave Ireland two days later for the United States to open the Irish pavilion at New York's World Fair. He was to follow this with a tour, putting the Irish case against partition. In view of the possible consequences of the inclusion of Northern Ireland in Chamberlain's plans, de Valera cancelled his tour and sent Seán T. O'Kelly to New York in his place.

Conscription of Nationalists in Northern Ireland could only have led to resistance and to a strengthening of the IRA. The Catholic bishops whose dioceses lay wholly or partly within the area of Northern Ireland issued a statement that any attempt to impose conscription in the area would be disastrous. Lord Craigavon was requested by the British Government to go to London to give his advice. He pressed for the enforcement of conscription. In the meantime, de Valera protested vehemently against a threat which would have wrecked the peace of Ireland and which he considered an act of aggression against Irish people. In the Dáil his stand received unanimous support and the crisis was averted when Chamberlain, on May 4th, announced that it had been decided not to include Northern Ireland in the conscription plan.

Events of this kind were sufficient to block de Valera's anti-partition plans for the moment. The coming of the second World War was to cancel them for the six years of the conflict and to frustrate them for a long time thereafter.

But that is only part of the story of Anglo-Irish relations from the

Agreement of April, 1938, to the outbreak of war, September, 1939. The British documents published on January 1st, 1970 bring out the mounting anxiety of de Valera as nothing was done on the British side to end or mitigate partition, although nothing disturbed the very friendly relations built up between de Valera himself and Chamberlain.

No hint was ever dropped by de Valera to encourage the idea that Ireland would participate in the war. There is, however, one passage in the British records which might give rise to misunderstanding. Recording a conversation with de Valera at Chequers, on March 25th, Chamberlain wrote: 'I asked him to tell me honestly whether he thought the majority of the people in Ireland wanted to cut loose from the Empire, to which he replied that he thought they did because, mistakenly, they believed they would never have complete independence unless they were a separate republic.' To this Chamberlain replied that he, personally, was not afraid that the Irish would ever separate from the British Empire because, he said, in that case they would be a foreign country; and in the interests of their own safety they could not possibly afford to occupy that position. That is, unless they had secured British help by means of a treaty, which would place on them much closer restrictions than they would ever have to submit to if they remained within the British Empire.

'Mr de Valera said that he entirely agreed and that this was the argument he would use with those who wished for a republic. In the meantime, however, he pressed me to take some steps in the direction he wanted, in the general interest of the security of these islands.'

Mr Neville Chamberlain was the most accurate-minded of men, but his account of such a conversation could not fail to reflect, in its terms, his own hopes and fears for Britain and the Commonwealth. It is, however, more than likely that de Valera strongly emphasized on this occasion what he repeatedly stated publicly and privately: that a reunited Ireland externally and freely associated with the Commonwealth would have a greater interest in Britain's welfare in peace or war than a divided Ireland; that a united Ireland would, in fact, be freer to take its own decisions on matters of defence if it were externally associated with the Commonwealth than if it were not, and was compelled like many small nations to arrange for its defence in time of war by entering into detailed and binding defence arrangements.

That this was, indeed, de Valera's line of argument in the conversation of March 25th, 1939, is confirmed by his personal handwritten letter to Chamberlain two weeks later, on April 12th, and quoted in the British cabinet papers, in which he said that 'a free, united Ireland would have every interest in wishing Britain to be strong, but when Britain's strength appears to be used to maintain the division of our island, no such considerations can have any force.'

This was the burden of his message in good times and in bad in his discussions with British statesmen whom he trusted profoundly, and with others with whom he felt less at home.

Part IV

1939 – 1945
IF NECESSARY, ALONE

ONE OF THE NEUTRALS

1939 – 1940

For the first time in her modern history Ireland was free to enter or
abstain from a British war. De Valera himself was never an isolationist.
Since his first entry into politics he had an international outlook on Irish
affairs. In 1919 he wrote:

> So far are we from desiring isolation that our whole struggle is to get Ireland
> out of the cage in which the selfish statecraft of England would confine her—
> to get Ireland back into the free world from which she was ravished—to get
> her recognized as an independent unit in a world league of nations.[1]

The advantages of neutrality, however, had always been plain to him.
For a small nation, participation in a world conflict had few attractions,
with everything to lose and nothing to gain. Small nations were not
consulted beforehand about the necessity for the wars in which they
might be involved. They would be allowed no voice in the peace settlement which must follow the war and the chaos, through which they, with
others, must pass. For a small nation neutrality was almost certain to
represent the purely national interest, a neutrality guaranteed by all sides
if possible. There remained the question of international obligation. Had
World War II come from a joint decision of the League of Nations his
attitude would, no doubt, have been modified. We have noticed his
valiant efforts at Geneva on behalf of the principle of collective security
while it had any chance of operating. Later, when at last Ireland became
a member of the United Nations, he was able to practise what he had
preached. From 1936 it was clear to him that his efforts and those of
many others had been nullified by the attitudes of the great powers.
Collective security in the circumstances of the time had ceased to possess
any physical significance. For a small country neutrality seemed the only
course left open. It was the course pursued by all the small democratic
countries outside the Commonwealth until they were attacked themselves.
Also by all large ones except Britain and France who responded when,
but only when, it was clear to them that they must fight or surrender.

On August 31st, 1939, Dr Edouard Hempel, the German Minister in
Ireland, called on de Valera to find out what was likely to be the attitude

of the Irish Government in the event of a European war. Hempel said that he came on the instructions of Ribbentrop. He promised that Germany would respect Ireland's neutrality. De Valera had long seen the shadow of war over Europe and had many times thought over the issues likely to arise in just such an interview as this. He began by emphasizing Ireland's desire for peace with all nations, including Germany. He pointed out the evident difficulties arising out of the narrowness of the Irish Sea and the vital importance to Ireland of maintaining her trade with Britain. The Irish Government would have to show a certain consideration for Britain which, in similar circumstances, they would also show for Germany. He was explicit in his discussion of the dangers to Irish neutrality. These he saw as possible violations of territorial waters by either side, action against the partitioned area and the exploitation by Germany of 'the anti-British radical nationalist group'. He warned Hempel of the possible consequences of German action along any of these lines.

The German Minister was impressed by the sincerity of de Valera's decision to keep out of the war, but felt that he was apprehensive over the weakness of the Irish position. In his report to Berlin, he mentioned that de Valera went into the issues involved 'in his usual doctrinaire fashion'. Later, after the war, in denying the accuracy of the official translation of his report published by the Allies, Hempel explained that he simply used the word 'doctrinaire' to indicate that de Valera approached the problems in a theoretical way. This rings true of de Valera, who had a rare ability to divorce a problem from its personal elements and study it almost as a mathematical abstraction. It was a talent which could on occasion cause annoyance, but on the whole it led to judgements uninfluenced by personal prejudice.[2]

On the day following Hempel's visit to Government Buildings, Germany invaded Poland. War was now inevitable between Germany and Britain. De Valera convened the Dáil and Senate at once to meet the emergency.

> We, of all nations [he said], know what force used by a stronger nation against a weaker one means; . . . we are not forgetful of our own history, and as long as our own country, or any part of it, is subject to force, the application of force by a stronger nation, it is only natural that our people, whatever sympathies they might have in a conflict like the present, should, looking at their own country, consider what its interests should be and what its interests are.[3]

It was a pragmatic approach based on Ireland's interest and on the circumstances of Irish public opinion. De Valera recognized that Irish people had divided opinions on the belligerents but that the vast majority, despite their personal feelings towards one or other of the countries concerned, were agreed that Ireland should not get involved. That was the decision which could get almost unanimous support, and did in fact secure it. Any other course would have created a serious split in the country. Sympathy with the fate of Poland on the one hand was counterbalanced by Ireland's objection to partition of its own island for which Britain was blamed. Partition was, in itself, a sufficient reason for staying out. That does not mean that if partition had been abolished at that moment the reasons for neutrality would no longer have existed in Irish minds. The whole atmosphere would have been so completely transformed that one can only speculate as to what path Ireland would or would not have chosen.

As things were, neutrality was accepted wholeheartedly by the bulk of the Irish people. There are some indications that when de Valera announced his Government's policy it caused considerable discussion in the leading Opposition party, Fine Gael, who had previously stood for a policy of close association with the British Commonwealth. One of the leaders, Dr T. F. O'Higgins, stated in the Dáil in the early days of the war:

> I was never a firm believer in the feasibility or benefits of neutrality . . . I was prepared to adopt it and support it, however, as the policy that appealed to the vast majority and that, at all events, was worth trying.[4]

It is very unlikely, however, that Fine Gael, if they had been in office at the outbreak of war could have adopted any course other than neutrality. In the event, their general acceptance of the policy was a triumph for the party leader, W. T. Cosgrave.

For de Valera the war, and the policy of neutrality, created grave and immediate problems. He soon made clear the emphasis of his thoughts.

> Our attitude we hope to keep not by adherence to some theoretical, abstract idea of neutrality or anything like that, but by addressing ourselves to the practical question that we do not want to get involved in this war, and we merely want to keep our people safe from such consequences as would be involved by being in the war.[5]

The most immediate effect of the war was the threat to supplies from abroad. The self-sufficiency policy pursued by de Valera's Government in the preceding seven years was to pay ample dividends in the prolonged crisis. But there could be no question of Ireland escaping the consequences of the world conflict.

To meet the new situation de Valera recast his Government. He hived off a new department to deal with the vital question of supplies and put the energetic Minister for Industry and Commerce, Seán Lemass, in charge of it. A few other changes in a cabinet reshuffle included the appointment of Frank Aiken as Minister for the Co-ordination of Defensive Measures. De Valera added the portfolio of Education to his own offices of Head of Government and Minister for External Affairs. It was to this latter office that he had to give most of his attention in the struggle to maintain neutrality. On September 3rd came the inevitable British declaration of war on Germany. The diplomatic difficulties for Ireland were obvious. Within Ireland there were a number of diplomatic missions, but there was no British diplomat accredited to the Irish Government. For some time de Valera had been acutely aware of this lacuna and had wished to have in Dublin a counterpart to the Irish High Commissioner in London. There were, however, complexities of title which had hitherto deterred him from suggesting the appointment.

The title 'high commissioner', with its imperial history, was unacceptable in Ireland while, for Britain, the appointment of an 'ambassador' or 'minister' might be considered a recognition of Irish independence.

But now he had to take action. The Secretary to the Department of External Affairs, Joseph P. Walshe, was sent to London to explain Ireland's position to Anthony Eden, Secretary of State for Dominion Affairs. Walshe pointed out that de Valera wished to be as friendly as he could and to assist Great Britain as far as possible while maintaining the essentials of neutrality. Formal recognition of Irish neutrality by Britain would, he argued, be a great contribution towards good feeling in Ireland. Time and again de Valera was to seek this recognition of her neutrality from Britain, but it was never given during the war. Walshe's visit, however, had one result—a decision to have a British diplomat in Dublin.

Within a short time of Walshe's return from London to Dublin, he was followed by an envoy from the Prime Minister, Neville Chamberlain. This was Sir John Maffey, a former head of the Colonial Office, a man of commanding stature and personality, a public servant of the highest distinction. His mission at this stage was to meet de Valera and arrange for the establishment of diplomatic relations on a regular basis. He reported back to Chamberlain and on a second visit he brought a personal letter from Chamberlain to de Valera:

> Your suggestion that the United Kingdom representative in Dublin should have the name, and presumably the status, of Minister would raise most contentious issues for us here and is one which it would not be possible for me to accept. I hope, therefore, that you will see your way to help by accepting a solution which, in fact, represents a compromise between our respective points of view. The title 'Representative' would seem to be well suited to an appointment such as this which is essentially an emergency arrangement intended to meet a temporary but urgent situation.[6]

A characteristic photograph of de Valera, in a cloak, addressing a meeting.

Above: As President of the Council of the League of Nations, de Valera presided over the Disarmament Conference at Geneva in September 1932. *At the table, left to right:* Baron von Neurath (Germany), M. Paul Boncour (France), President de Valera (Irish Free State), and Sir Eric Drummond and Sir John Simon (United Kingdom).

Below: With Anthony Eden and Sean T. O'Kelly in Dublin, September 1938.

Opposite above: With Col Lindbergh at Baldonnel, November 1936.

Opposite below: With Jack B. Yeats and his wife at an exhibition of the artist's works.

Opposite above left: Greeted by Churchill in Downing Street, 1953.

Opposite above right: With Nehru during his visit to India in 1948.

Opposite below: With Attlee during his visit to London in 1947. Also in the picture are Sir Stafford Cripps (*left*), Ernest Bevin and John Strachey.

Two views of de Valera during the election of May 1951.

Opposite above: With President Kennedy on the latter's visit to Ireland, June 1963.

Opposite below: With President Johnson at the White House, May 1964.

Above: With Pope Pius XII in October 1958.

Below: With Pope John XXIII in March 1962.

De Valera 'has always revelled in physical exercise'.

When Maffey delivered that letter he also told de Valera that the full title for the proposed post would be 'United Kingdom Representative in Eire'. After studying it for a few moments, de Valera crossed out 'in' and substituted 'to'—the problem of title was solved.[7]

In his reply to Chamberlain's letter de Valera said:

> I have explained to Sir John Maffey the difficulties which the acceptance of your proposal will involve for us. He will, I am sure, make clear to you how much, in my opinion, will depend on the character of the person chosen to inaugurate the service. I have already informed my colleagues that I believe that Sir John Maffey has the experience and understanding necessary to make it a success.

To this he added a postscript:

> I would like you to know how much I sympathize with you in your present anxieties.[8]

Three days later Chamberlain thanked him for agreeing to accept the name 'Representative' and added:

> I am very glad to learn from your letter that, in your opinion, Sir John Maffey's qualities will enable him to make a success of his service and he has accordingly been appointed . . .[9]

The position of the British Representative was to be a difficult one. Historic causes could give rise to grave dangers. A new West Briton court in the centre of Dublin would not win the respect of the majority of the Irish people. Sir John Maffey was to prove an admirable choice, tactful, discreet and discerning. He won de Valera's confidence, the respect of all who met him and the friendship of many of the people of Ireland while remaining a thorough Englishman throughout. He was a key figure in the testing years of neutrality.

In terms of policy, however, the American Minister at that time, John Cudahy, was, naturally, more sympathetic to Ireland's neutrality. The call of the blood was strong and the descendant of famine emigrants from County Kilkenny was, at the height of the war, to write a public justification of de Valera's policy. His admiration for de Valera was exceeded only by his adulation of F. D. Roosevelt.[10]

The representative of Germany in Ireland was the aforementioned Dr Hempel—a gentlemanly diplomat who showed few of the traits of Nazi officials. He, of course, was concerned for Germany's interest, but saw no reason why that should conflict with Irish neutrality, which he did all in his power to protect. While the tide of war flowed in Germany's favour in the early war years he could be inflexible. Throughout the war, however, he acted with correctness and in a straightforward manner which

13

assisted de Valera's policy. There were, of course, various legations in Dublin too, representing Spain, France, Belgium, Canada and other countries, but inevitably the most provocative figures in British eyes were to be the Italian Minister, Vincenzo Berardis, and the Japanese Consul, Satsuya Beppu. It was not the personality of the representatives themselves which created controversy, but the fact that their countries were involved in the war on the same side as Germany.

The wisdom of Maffey was soon to be tested—as indeed was that of de Valera and the British leaders. October, 1939, saw strong approaches by the British Government 'with regard' as they put it 'to the use of facilities for the Royal Navy at Berehaven.' British cabinet papers for 1939 were published on January 1st, 1970, having been made available a few days earlier to the press. The *Times* immediately carried a full-length article under the heading: 'How Britain nearly invaded Ireland in 1939'— a misleading formulation as will appear in a moment. The distinguished and official British naval historian, Captain Roskill, at once challenged the implication that some new revelation had been vouchsafed, hitherto undisclosed in the British war histories. This, however, seems to be going too far in the opposite direction.

Students will, no doubt, read the British documents as published in full, the *Times* article, Captain Roskill's letter and, it may be, other contributions. In a life of de Valera one can only quote briefly. According to the official British war history, the First Lord

> took the matter up strenuously and repeatedly with his colleagues, and an approach was made to the Eire Government. But the desired result was not accomplished. Happily the bases in Northern Ireland at Londonderry and Belfast remained available to our use and when, in mid-1940, all our shipping had to be diverted round the north of Ireland the importance of the bases was reduced. But the handicap imposed by having to use Plymouth and Milford Haven, instead of Berehaven, as the bases for the escorts working in the south western approaches was serious. . . .
>
> The Naval Staff had, in October, explained very forcibly the benefit derived by German U-boats from the inability of our escort craft and flying boats to cover from English bases a sufficient area of sea in the Western Approaches. We should press for the use of one or more of the Irish ports, Berehaven being the most suitable. The British Government had approached Mr de Valera, but found him inflexible.[11]

True, no doubt, but the whole truth seems to have been more dramatic.

We must concentrate on the cabinet documents for October 21st, when Sir John Maffey saw Mr de Valera in Dublin, on very full instructions from the War cabinet, and about October 28th when the War cabinet in London received his report. It is understood, since the publication of the British documents, that Mr de Valera has raised no objection to the gist of this account. 'In accordance', wrote Sir John, 'with the instructions received in London, I approached Mr de Valera on the subject of facilities at Berehaven. His uncompromising answer to every line of approach was a categorical "non possumus".' De Valera told Sir John that he knew this issue would be raised and that no adjustment of his view, or of his answer, was possible, and Sir John's report continued:

> The creed of Ireland today was neutrality. No Government could exist that departed from that principle. The question of the ports was at the very nerve centre of public interest in that matter, and the public mood would react with intense violence to any action invalidating their integrity. *If a demand were made—he fully realized that no demand was being made* [Authors' italics]— he would be forced at whatever cost to treat such a situation as a challenge, and his Parliament would endorse his measures. If, on the other hand, facilities were voluntarily afforded in breach of neutrality, his Government could not live. No other Government which might endeavour to meet our request could survive for twenty-four hours.

That was the main outcome of the interview and summed up the attitude adopted by de Valera and by Ireland during the following six years. At least three other points emerge, of high interest. Maffey states emphatically that in de Valera's attitude 'there was nothing anti-British, though he indicated more than once that if we paved the way to Irish unity, Ireland today might—only "might"—have been able to co-operate with us'. He would greatly regret a German victory, his sympathies were with the Allies, but if there was on the whole perhaps a vague majority sentiment in favour of the Allies, any encroachment upon an Irish interest would create a swift swing over of opinion. Many people in Ireland were ready enough to acclaim a British defeat at any price. Though that view might be based on ignorance it had its roots in history.

On the moral aspect, de Valera maintained that there could have been no mental reservations on the British side justifying any belief that Ireland would adopt any particular course in the event of a world conflict. Maffey reports himself as saying, a shade surprisingly perhaps, that 'such mental reservations had existed.' The path of generosity had been followed as an act of faith, and in the belief that in the hour of need the hand of friendship would be extended. De Valera insisted strenuously that the British had no right to expect to derive advantage from what was not theirs. 'Such a view would justify encroachment by Germany on Holland or Belgium'.

Still on the moral aspect, de Valera stressed his admiration for Chamberlain, who had been genuinely helpful in regard to the Irish question. Not only that, he found himself in full agreement with everything that Chamberlain had done in Europe: 'England,' said de Valera, 'has a moral position today. Hitler might have his early successes, but the moral position would tell. Any action against the Irish ports would shake our position of moral strength.' Maffey said 'Not if help were voluntarily conceded'. De Valera replied: 'No, but that would stir up trouble which would quickly compromise your moral position'. Maffey suggested that he should discuss the matter personally with Chamberlain. But de Valera considered that 'it would be a pity to take this step, since it could not in any way alter matters'.

Additionally, de Valera pointed out, reported Maffey, that he had sought 'to help us within the limits of neutrality', to the full extent possible. 'The measures arranged with regard to information and liaison were all evidences of this, and of the fact that he was being helpful, perhaps beyond the strict definition of neutrality.' In a significant, and it may well have been influential letter accompanying his report, Maffey confirmed de Valera's last contention. 'In many ways the government of Eire and the set-back over the ports has obscured the bright side of the picture.'

On the credit side he records the instant reporting and signalling arrangement in regard to German submarines, the acceptance of a naval attaché with wide facilities for investigation, the holding-up at Maffey's request of a series of emergency orders implementing neutrality in detail, the retention of an Admiralty tug at Cobh. De Valera had also accepted the fact that British surface craft would pursue and attack hostile submarines in the territorial waters of Eire 'whatever the regulations may be'. Today moreover 'our aircraft are flying over the headlands of Eire and even inland and nothing is being said'.

Maffey's service to Ireland at this crucial moment did not end there. In the same accompanying letter, he said unequivocally that the policy of neutrality commanded widespread approval among all classes and interests in Eire. 'It is remarkable how even the "pro-British" group, men who have fought for the Crown and are anxious to be called up again, men whose sons are at the front today, loyalists in the old sense of the word, agree generally in supporting the policy of neutrality for Eire. They see no possible alternative.' That last opinion, coming from such a source, must surely have weighed heavily with any British cabinet.

The discussion there is of course of wide historical interest. From the Irish standpoint, it was mercifully one-sided. According to the cabinet documents, the Secretary of State for Dominion Affairs, Anthony Eden, set out three possible courses: '(1) To seek further discussion with Mr de Valera: he did not think this would serve any useful purpose. (2) To acquiesce in Mr de Valera's attitude and endeavour to secure what we could, bit by bit: he feared, however, that this would produce only minor concessions of comparatively little value. (3) To make forcible use of the harbours. If we did so, he did not think that Mr de Valera would oppose us with military force, but he would indict us before the world and rally his people against us. There would be serious repercussions in the United States and in the Dominions, and the passive support which we now received from great numbers of Irish people would be alienated. In addition, Eire might grant facilities to the enemy.' In other words, he favoured the second course, acquiescence in one form or another.

The First Lord of the Admiralty urged that 'we should challenge the constitutional position of Eire's neutrality . . . no doubt it would be advisable to postpone action until the United States neutrality Act had been repealed, but we should then having set out the juridical position and made clear to the world that we were not committing a violation of neutrality, insist on the use of the harbours.' But the Prime Minister, Chamberlain, Anthony Eden and, it would seem, the rest of the cabinet, would have none of it, and the idea of the 'showdown' was emphatically rejected. It would not be true, therefore, to say with the *Times*' headline that Britain 'nearly invaded Ireland'. On the evidence, it would not be quite true, though close to the truth, to say that Winston Churchill urged the invasion of Ireland. He got as far as suggesting that 'we should take stock of the weapons of coercion'. If it had not been for Chamberlain, Eden and Maffey, Ireland might have been faced with a very nasty situation. Lord Harvey records in his diary for October 30th, 1939: 'A. E. (i.e. Anthony Eden) says de Valera is doing all he can for us.'

Extreme delicacy in the diplomatic field was clearly essential. De Valera realized, however, that the most grievous danger to the policy of neutrality might come not from outside but from within. While scarcely a voice was raised against neutrality within the Dáil and the people were overwhelmingly in favour of it, there was an unreconciled element in Ireland whose policy was based on the traditional one that England's difficulty was Ireland's opportunity. These people were dissatisfied with the progress made by de Valera, since he took office in 1932, in removing the trappings of empire.

Some, indeed, might have been impossible to satisfy with any lesser constitutional change than an absolute reversion of authority to the Second Dáil which, in their view, had been illegally dissolved in 1922. But the main grievance which won them adherents was the continued partition of their country. Physical force was the solution which recommended itself to a number of these men.

It had appeared possible, after the passing of the new Constitution in 1937, that the ending of the British occupation of the forts at Cobh and

Berehaven the following year might cause the underground Irish Republican Army to decline. But these were premature hopes as we saw in the last chapter.

The IRA policy was, apparently, that they would refrain from open activities against the Irish Government provided that they were allowed to use Ireland as a declared base for their operations. But de Valera stood firmly by his declared policy of not allowing Ireland to be used as a base for attacks against Britain. He could see, in the summer of 1939, that, with a war on the not too distant horizon, such attacks carried the danger of British intervention. To deal with illegal armed actions the Offences Against the State Act had been passed (see page 342). It provided for the establishment of a special criminal court and for the internment of suspects on the authority of a ministerial warrant. Gerald Boland, the new Minister for Justice, was a man with strong views who could be relied upon to be firm without being vindictive. Immediately on becoming Minister he issued warrants for the internment of about seventy persons who were believed to be active members of the IRA. Though these warrants were duly executed, the statute was challenged in the courts and was found to be repugnant to the Constitution. All the internees were released. An amending statue was passed and became law in February, 1940. In the meantime other provision was made under Emergency Powers.

De Valera was determined that the security of the State should not be endangered by these young men, though he understood their motives and their dedication. He faced an immediate challenge when Patrick McGrath, a prisoner awaiting trial in Mountjoy Jail, and some others, went on hunger-strike on October 23rd, 1939. It rent his heart to see men die, but he faced it. In response to a resolution by the Labour Party, asking for the release of the prisoners, de Valera made a statement in the Dáil. The only way, he argued, that the Government could secure Ireland's safety was by the detention of those who were in a position to bring the country to disaster. The policy of hunger-strike was aimed to take away that power.

> We do not wish them to die [he said with emotion]. We would wish—Heaven knows I have prayed for it—that these men might change their minds, and that the people who are with them might change their minds, and realise what our obligations and our duties are. If we let these men out we are going immediately afterwards to have every single man we have tried to detain and restrain going on hunger strike.[12]

It was a terrible decision arrived at after the gravest consideration. There was tremendous pressure on de Valera not to let the men die. A bishop approached him to persuade him to relent. Then he received a doctor's report that McGrath was dying, that he could not recover, and that he was in great pain. De Valera weakened. He allowed him to be removed to hospital and, despite the doctor's report, he recovered.

The sequel was to be tragic and worse than de Valera feared. It was to have a profound effect on his future course of action. A second hunger-strike began some months later and two young men, Tony Darcy and Seán McNeela died in consequence in April, 1940. They had persisted in their hunger-strike in the face of the strongest warnings. In the following August two detective officers were shot dead in arresting Patrick McGrath and Francis Hart. Both the latter were executed. De Valera felt that six lives were lost because of his giving in when faced with McGrath's hunger-strike. Possibly he was too hard on himself. His gesture of patience and mercy in October, 1939, may well have helped him to win the support of a public opinion which might not at that time have been prepared for Draconian measures. His sorrow and self reproach remained. He showed one other striking example of leniency when he reprieved another member of the IRA, Tomás MacCurtain, who was sentenced to death in the summer of 1940 for the shooting of a detective officer in Cork. From August, 1940, however, he was determined, no matter how much his decisions pained him, that he would show no signs of weakness.

Before the outbreak of the war, de Valera had responded to a significant request from Sir Edward Harding of the Dominions Office in London. Harding had asked for the co-operation of the Irish authorities in preventing IRA actions against Britain from being planned in Ireland. This was forthcoming in the event, but de Valera wrote to Neville Chamberlain on the basic cause of the continuing trouble:

> I cannot refrain from writing to you. You and I have worked to bring about conditions which would make it possible to lay the foundations of good neighbourly relations between the British and Irish peoples. The agreement, a year ago, was a notable advance in that direction; but the failure to deal with Partition has largely offset what was then accomplished.

He assured Chamberlain that a free united Ireland would have every interest in wishing Britain to be strong. But when Britain's strength appeared to be used to maintain the division of the island, no such consideration could have any force:

> A large section of our people, particularly the young, are led to see hope only in Britain's weakness. Can something not be done, and without delay?

The consequences of failure in the past to act in time were clear to see and should be a warning:

Will the generation that succeeds us have again to deplore the unwisdom of those who did not act when action would have meant success? I know your difficulties and your present pre-occupation with events further afield, and deeply sympathise with you. But the intensification of feeling here, and amongst our people in the United States, makes it imperative to act quickly lest it be too late to save the situation.[13]

The cause of the contention was, however, not eradicated, and perhaps could not have been at that time. By 1940 the IRA was firmly set against the authority of the Irish Government. It was committed to the support of Germany, probably under the conviction that Hitler would win the war and would end partition. It had had contacts with Germany even in the years before the outbreak of the war and, once the policy of attacks on Britain failed, the principal objective appears to have been to involve Ireland in the war on the German side.

The German Minister in Dublin, however, was not very much impressed by their activities. Early in October, 1939, he warned the Foreign Minister in Berlin, Joachim von Ribbentrop, against any interference in the internal affairs of Ireland and strongly recommended a careful regard for Irish neutrality.[14] A month later he followed this up with a specific warning against giving any support to the IRA. Rumours of German contacts with that body were circulating and Hempel warned:

> Interference on our part would ... prematurely endanger the whole nationalist movement including groups which are not radical, because the latter would accuse the IRA of making national interests dependent on Germany; in view of the widespread aversion to present-day Germany, especially for religious reasons, this could rob the IRA of all chances of future success. England would be given a pretext for intervening—which she would probably welcome —and Irish neutrality as well as the possibility of a future utilisation of the Irish cause for our interests would be prematurely destroyed.[15]

This attitude of Hempel certainly dimmed the prospects of large-scale German meddling with the IRA, though agencies other than the Foreign Office in Berlin did continue to maintain some contact.

De Valera had no fear that the extremists were sufficiently strong on their own to present a real threat to his Government or to the State. His main concern was the fear that Germany might overestimate their strength and be tempted to use them or that Britain, if it determined to occupy Irish bases, might find a plausible excuse in the activities of the IRA. There was also another danger. Public opinion in Ireland had to be protected against violent swings in any direction. This was the reason for careful censorship of news throughout the war, but it could not, of course, prevent the publication of some items of news which stirred up the public. De Valera, in fact, tried, through Sir John Maffey, to influence the British Government against an action which he knew would rouse bitter feelings in Ireland—the execution of two Irishmen who had been sentenced to death for their part in the bombings in England in 1939. He also wrote to Anthony Eden, the Dominions Secretary, that he understood all the difficulties in the way of reprieve: clemency might well be misunderstood.

> Nevertheless [he continued], I am convinced that it will be a mistake if you let these considerations prevail. There are, in my opinion, considerations of higher policy which dictate the opposite course. The history of the relations between our two countries has already been much stained with blood. Each succeeding generation of your countrymen have deplored the unwisdom of their predecessors and themselves fallen into the very errors they condemned. Ought you not to make sure that you avoid doing likewise . . .?

He believed that if the British Government gave the matter full consideration, they would agree. If these men were executed, the relations between the two peoples would almost certainly deteriorate:

> It will matter little that Barnes and Richards have been found guilty of murder. With the background of our history and the existence of partition many will refuse to regard their action in that light. They will think only of the cause these men had it in mind to serve . . . The execution of these men will give rise to new and bitter antagonisms between us which countries who see their profit in them will not hesitate to exploit. Is it wise, with eyes open, to permit this thing to happen?[16]

It was a strong appeal and, to reinforce it, de Valera sent a personal letter to the Prime Minister asking him to use his influence to prevent the executions:

> I believe that you will be able to appreciate the full significance of what I have urged and that you will make your decision in the light of long-time policy to secure better relations between the people of Ireland and the people of Britain.[17]

Despite de Valera's appeal the British Government's decision was against reprieve. When he learned this, de Valera made a final effort, speaking to Eden on the telephone and sending through the Irish High Commissioner in London a message to Chamberlain expressing his regret at the outcome:

> I have received your decision with sorrow and dismay. The reprieve of these men would be regarded as an act of generosity, a thousand times more valuable to Britain than anything that can possibly be gained by their death. The latter will be looked upon as an act fitting only too sadly into the historic background of our relations. Almost superhuman patience is required on

both sides to exorcise the feelings which the knowledge of centuries of wrong-doing have engendered. I hasten with a final entreaty that this execution be not permitted to take place.[18]

Chamberlain's reply closed the door on further efforts:

I know how deeply you feel over this matter and I wish that we could have met your request. Our desire to do all that we can to promote good feelings between our two countries remains unchanged, and it is only for reasons which appear to us to be of overwhelming force that we have felt unable to act as you wish.[19]

Despite de Valera's failure to alter the decision of the British Government, he did not blame Chamberlain or Eden.

There was a slight difficulty with the British Government over the question of the appointment of an Irish minister to Germany. At the outbreak of the war William Warnock had been Irish Chargé d'Affaires in Berlin. De Valera wished to have a minister there and spoke about it to Maffey. Under the External Relations Act of 1936, diplomats were still accredited on behalf of the Irish Government by the British King. His functions were purely nominal, but the suggestion that he should accredit a diplomat to a country with which he was at war was one which caused acute embarrassment in Britain. So much so, in fact, that Anthony Eden wrote to de Valera: 'You will appreciate the difficulties arising over the formal procedure, such as asking the King to sign credentials addressed to Herr Hitler.'[20] De Valera had demonstrated the anomaly of the relationship which existed between Ireland and Britain. He felt it unwise to pursue the matter.

Any growth of anti-British feeling which arose over the two executions was offset to some extent by the feeling that the IRA was the tool of Germany. Once she launched her attack on Belgium and Holland, feeling turned strongly against her. De Valera was in Galway, engaged in a by-election campaign, when he got the news of the invasion. Quite deliberately he made a protest, not only from his own convictions but because the people of Ireland would have expected no less. He thought of his work at Geneva before the war and of the small nations who were represented there, but who had now disappeared:

Go over in your own minds the list of small nations, and ask yourselves how many of them are now with their old independence, or free from the horrors of war. The representatives of Belgium and the representatives of the Netherlands were people that I met frequently because we co-operated not a little with the Northern group of nations. Today, these two small nations are fighting for their lives and I think I would be unworthy of this small nation if, on an occasion like this, I did not utter our protest against the cruel wrong that has been done them.[21]

It was a brave statement as Hitler's forces drove westwards and one which brought a protest by the German Minister in Dublin. De Valera did not see him. F. H. Boland received him on de Valera's behalf. He poured oil on troubled waters and apparently instructed Warnock in Berlin to do the same. According to the German records—but not to the Irish—both expressed themselves in an 'apologetic manner'. However, there could be no doubt about the tone of de Valera's publicly delivered protest.

As the threat from Germany loomed large in the early summer of 1940, a drastic change occurred in the British Government which could only add to de Valera's anxieties. On the very day that Germany invaded Belgium and Holland, Winston Churchill replaced Neville Chamberlain as Prime Minister. To the latter de Valera wrote a letter of appreciation.

> Those of us who understood the problems with which in recent years you were faced have no doubt that the courses which you took were the best available and we are confident that, in calmer times, the importance of what you have achieved will be appreciated by all your countrymen.

The compliment which followed was deeply felt.

> I would like to testify that you did more than any former British statesman to make a true friendship between the peoples of our two countries possible and, if the task has not been completed, that it has not been for want of goodwill on your part.[22]

It was not the kind of tribute which he ever paid lightly.

The change of British Prime Minister could not be looked upon by de Valera as helpful to Irish neutrality. Churchill had shown little sympathy for Irish national aspirations since his long-forgotten Liberal Home Rule days before World War I. A speech of his in 1922 had been looked upon as the ultimatum which started the Civil War. In 1938, he had vigorously opposed the handing over of the occupied ports in Ireland. It was not till the publication, in 1970, of the British cabinet records for 1939, that it was realized quite how strenuously Sir Winston, as First Lord of the Admiralty, had pushed his demands for the grant of facilities at Berehaven.

But his general attitude was common knowledge. From the beginning of the war he had chafed at Irish neutrality. As First Lord he had felt most keenly the limitations imposed on British anti-submarine activities by the denial of the Irish ports to British naval vessels. Soon after the outbreak he encountered a young Irishman whom he had been kind to in the past and who was about to visit Ireland. 'You can tell your friend de Valera,' he impressed on him weightily, 'we have treated him with prodigal liberality, with unexampled generosity. And what does he do in return? He sinks the *Courageous*', and a good deal more to the same effect.

His indignation and sorrow were equally unmistakable. Wisely or foolishly, the message was not, in fact, passed on. 'I do not personally recognize Irish neutrality as a legal act,' he insisted in private. His memoirs revealed him castigating within the Admiralty, while still First Lord, what he called 'the odious treatment we are receiving'.[23]

Publicly Churchill had never gone as far as in private. Now, as Prime Minister, he was concerned not only with the military, but also the political implications, including far-reaching repercussions on Irish-American opinion and Anglo-American relations. His first message to de Valera after becoming Prime Minister was friendly: 'I look forward with confidence,' he wrote, 'to continued friendship between our two countries and you may rely upon me to do my utmost to ensure this.' De Valera's reply was simple: 'I thank you for your message of greeting, which I cordially reciprocate.'[24]

So far de Valera had been able to maintain a balance between the various sides in the conflict. His measures against the IRA had shown that he had the strength to control them and he had succeeded in convincing both the German and British Ministers in Dublin of his determination to maintain neutrality. Hempel reported to Berlin in May, 1940:

> De Valera, in my judgment, is still the only recognized political leader of large stature who has the nationalists firmly in hand. He will maintain the line of friendly understanding with England as far as it is at all possible, on account of geographical and economic dependence, which will continue even in the event of England's defeat, as well as *his democratic principles* [our italics], even in face of the threatening danger of Ireland becoming involved in war.[25]

He made it clear that German intervention in Ireland before Britain intervened would meet with strong Irish resistance which de Valera would lead.

At that time de Valera was showing the strength of the Irish determination to resist invasion no matter whence it came. He issued an invitation to the leaders of the Opposition parties in the Dáil to join in a consultative defence conference. There would be three members of the Government, three of Fine Gael and two of Labour. The leaders agreed and it was arranged that the conference should meet regularly. It demonstrated Irish solidarity in defence of her neutrality. Whatever doubts there may have been about the wisdom of the policy six months before, it now had almost unanimous support. With this new unity, which derogated in no way from the Government's executive authority, de Valera launched a recruiting drive for the army and auxiliary forces. Men who had not shared a platform since the pact election of 1922 and whose friendship had been broken by a cruel civil war, now joined together in an appeal to the young men of Ireland to make themselves ready to defend their country. Nobly they responded in their thousands, united in their resolution that they would fight the first country which invaded them.

The opening of an official means of contact with the Opposition was a major step in healing old wounds. It was high time. The relationship was still very distant. W. T. Cosgrave had, for example, early in the war, wished to pass on a suggestion about the opening of trade negotiations with Britain. The author was obviously unaware of the lack of contact between the leading Opposition party and the Government. Cosgrave passed it to General Mulcahy with the comment:

I cannot offer any advice on the matter of the Memorandum, knowing from experience that the Government's practice is not merely to turn a deaf ear to such advice but even to resent it. I should, therefore, simply ask you to see that the enclosed Memorandum is brought to their notice for any action that they think fit to take.[26]

Mulcahy passed it on to Gerald Boland, Minister for Justice, who gave it to de Valera. Now at last there was a drawing together. The new conference opened the lines of communication. De Valera, however, saw no benefit in handing over governmental powers to a coalition. The Government was strong and united and he was willing to take the full responsibility of leadership.

At this stage, as the Germans advanced westwards, a police raid on the house of a certain Stephen Karl Held in a Dublin suburb revealed that a German parachutist had been there. A number of documents, codes, a radio transmitter, a parachute, 20,000 American dollars and the equipment of a German officer were discovered. The German Minister was embarrassed; he thought at first to pass it off as a piece of English provocation. Soon, however, he saw that German responsibility was unmistakable. He made an effort to get the subsequent trial of Held dealt with quietly and kept out of the papers, but de Valera would not carry censorship that far.

Despite sweeping German military successes, the month of June was a somewhat uncomfortable one for Hempel. The German parachutist was later identified as Hermann Goertz. An assurance that he was on a special mission directed exclusively against England had little effect. De Valera was intent on showing to England that he would not allow Ireland to be used as a base for any attack on its security. In interviews with Joseph P. Walshe and F. H. Boland of the Irish Department of External Affairs, Hempel was pressed hard. Walshe suggested that the only way to undo the effect of the scare started by the Goertz affair was for Germany to give a guarantee that in no circumstances would the Germans invade Ireland. He got this guarantee. According to German records Hempel now went further. On instructions from Berlin, he gave a clear indication that a German victory would bring the ending of the partition of Ireland.[27] There is, however, no confirmation of this on the Irish side.

The German Minister was fully aware of the strength of de Valera's desire to end partition and surmised that his statement would lead to a meeting with the Irish leader. He was not mistaken. On de Valera's invitation Hempel came to him on June 20th, 1940. The British had been ejected from Norway, the Low Countries, and now from France. France herself had collapsed. Italy had joined in the war on the side of Germany. To many, Germany appeared invincible. Two days earlier, in the House of Commons, Churchill had called for a superlative effort. 'What General Weygand called the Battle of France is over—I expect that the Battle of Britain is about to begin. Upon this battle depends the survival of Christian civilisation. . . If we fail then the whole world will sink into the abyss of a new Dark Age. . . Let us therefore brace ourselves to our duties and so bear ourselves that if the British Empire and its Commonwealth last for a thousand years men will still say This Was Their Finest Hour.' And so it proved. But on an objective view, Britain's fortunes in her entire history had never seemed to be at a lower ebb.

Hempel reported to the Foreign Ministry in Berlin his conversation with de Valera:

> De Valera listened to my statements with interest, but obviously attached principal importance to assuring me of Eire's continued adherence to strict neutrality. He explained that at the beginning of the war anxiety about English intervention had been uppermost in his mind but Irish neutrality had so far been respected by the English. This could, of course, change.

De Valera admitted that with Germany's closer approach anxiety had increased concerning possible German intentions to use Ireland as a base for attacks on England. He had repeatedly declared publicly, that Ireland would not become a point of departure for an attack against England. To this he would adhere, whatever the threat or the temptation.[28] So ran Hempel's report, which left no doubt that the man of principle remainded himself.

Partition was not for de Valera a subject for bargaining, but there were others who thought that it might be at that time. Churchill would seem to have decided to use the good relations between Chamberlain and de Valera to put out feelers for a bargain of this very kind. Chamberlain was still a member of the Cabinet and had replied to de Valera's letter on his resignation as Prime Minister with a warning:

I trust you will consider very seriously the danger of enemy landings from troop-carrying planes. The Germans do not respect neutrality and the rapidity and efficiency of their methods are terrifying.[29]

Some weeks later he followed this with another. It was dated June 12th, 1940:

My dear de Valera,

You may remember that when I wrote to you recently I begged you to look into the possibilities of a sea and airborne invasion of Eire by Germany. Since then I understand that you have been giving a good deal of attention to the subject, but I have lately received additional information of such a character as to cause me the most serious anxiety, and I have come to the conclusion that the time has arrived when a personal consultation is the only satisfactory way of dealing with the situation.

I have therefore asked the Dominions Secretary to instruct Sir John Maffey to call upon you and hand you this note which he will supplement with some verbal observations.

Since the invasion of Ireland might take place on either side or on both sides of the border, and since in any case defence would require close collaboration between the forces in Eire and those in Northern Ireland, it seems to me essential that Lord Craigavon should attend any meeting which may take place between us, and as soon as I hear whether and when you could come to London I would arrange for his presence also. The meeting would thus be between yourself, the Dominions Secretary, Lord Craigavon and myself.

I very much hope you will be able to come at once and I shall look forward with great pleasure to seeing you again.

> Yours sincerely,
> (sgd.) Neville Chamberlain.

It is somewhat significant that, if de Valera went to London he was not to meet the new Prime Minister. Perhaps it was felt that such a meeting could end explosively.

A visit to London at this juncture by de Valera would only, he reckoned, endanger Ireland's neutrality. But he did not turn down the suggestion of talks. As we have seen, Malcolm MacDonald and de Valera had become trusted friends in the pre-war negotiations and settlement. It was arranged that MacDonald, by that time British Minister of Health, should go to Dublin. The proposals of the British Government, which are of high interest today and have never before been published, were presented to de Valera in Government Buildings on June 26th. They must be given at length:

(i) *A declaration to be issued by the United Kingdom Government forthwith accepting the principle of a United Ireland* [authors' italics].

(ii) A joint body including representatives of the Government of Eire and the Government of Northern Ireland to be set up at once to work out the constitutional and other practical details of the Union of Ireland. The United Kingdom Government to give such assistance towards the work of this body as might be desired.

(iii) A joint Defence Council representative of Eire and Northern Ireland to be set up immediately.

(iv) *Eire to enter the war on the side of the United Kingdom and her allies forthwith* [authors' italics], and, for the purposes of the Defence of Eire, the Government of Eire to invite British naval vessels to have the use of ports in Eire and British troops and aeroplanes to co-operate with the Eire forces and to be stationed in such positions in Eire as may be agreed between the two Governments.

(v) The Government of Eire to intern all German and Italian aliens in the country and to take any further steps necessary to suppress Fifth Column activities.

(vi) The United Kingdom Government to provide military equipment at once to the Government of Eire . . .

If this plan were acceptable to the Irish Government it would then be submitted to the Northern Ireland Government for their assent to those parts which affected them. These proposals had a certain allure, but, from the moment he studied them de Valera was not impressed.

Apart from his refusal to bargain about partition, he looked upon the offer as largely illusory. Speaking of it years later he mentioned that when he was a child it was customary for two boys swopping treasures to insist on 'equal holds'—that each should have a firm grip on what he was to receive before he loosened his grip on that with which he was parting. The offer, which he knew came from Churchill, did not give 'equal holds'. Ireland would be involved in the war and the ending of partition would be no more than a half promise over which Belfast would have the full right of veto. Redmond had responded to this kind of promise in 1914, but de Valera was not likely to do so in 1940. He made this plain at once. Chamberlain, however, did not give up easily. On the morning of June 29th, a copy of a letter from Chamberlain to de Valera was handed to Joseph P. Walshe. It had been sent by wire to Sir John Maffey:

Mr MacDonald has reported to me [wrote Chamberlain] upon his conversation with you, and upon the reasons why you and your colleagues are not disposed to give an affirmative answer to the plan outlined in the document which he handed to you.

It seemed that de Valera felt that the plan did not give any firm assurance that the unity of Ireland would definitely become an established fact.

I would remind you that the whole plan depends on our obtaining the assent of Northern Ireland. I cannot, of course, give a guarantee that Northern Ireland will assent, but if the plan is acceptable to Eire we should do our best to persuade Northern Ireland to accept it also in the interests of the security of the whole island.

He suggested a modification of the first clause of the proposals by the addition of the words:

This declaration would take the form of a solemn undertaking that the Union is to become at an early date an accomplished fact from which there shall be no turning back.

De Valera had suggested to MacDonald that, instead of a joint defence council, a meeting together of the two Irish Parliaments with sovereign powers to legislate for the whole of Ireland on matters of common concern would be necessary to demonstrate the genuineness of the British offer. But this did not mean that de Valera was willing even then to abandon neutrality, for Chamberlain continued:

I understand that you demur to the suggestion that the Government of Eire should enter the war on the side of the United Kingdom and her Allies forthwith . . . Mr MacDonald has further reported that your own suggestion is that the union of Ireland should be established on the basis of the whole country becoming neutral.[30]

The modifications suggested did not meet de Valera's objections to the original proposals. In a letter of July 4th, he told Chamberlain why:

The plan would commit us definitely to an immediate abandonment of our neutrality. On the other hand, it gives no guarantee that in the end we would have a United Ireland unless indeed concessions were made to Lord Craigavon opposed to the sentiments and aspirations of the great majority of the Irish people.

He referred to his proposal that the unity of Ireland should be established on the basis of the whole country becoming neutral; he regretted that it was unacceptable to the British Government. On the basis of unity and neutrality they could mobilize the whole of the manpower of the country for the national defence.

That, with the high morale which could thus be secured and the support of the Irish race throughout the world . . . would provide the surest guarantee against any part of our territory being used as a base for operations against Britain. The course suggested in your plan could only lead to internal weakness and eventual frustration.[31]

The approaches to de Valera from both sides had, therefore, come to nothing. Churchill, it is said, was particularly annoyed when MacDonald reported his lack of success. Henceforth it was the tempestuous Prime Minister who would face de Valera more directly. Chamberlain was moving out of the scene. When he retired through ill-health in October, de Valera sent him a letter of sadness and sympathy:

We here all regretted that you had to retire from the Government and we look forward to the time when you will be able to return. We sympathise with you in the anxieties which must continue to be yours whilst the war lasts. How cruel it all is. It must be some consolation to you to know that you did your part to prevent it.[32]

Within a few weeks he was to send a telegram of condolence to Chamberlain's widow:

Mr Chamberlain will always be remembered by the Irish people for his noble efforts in the cause of peace and friendship between the two nations.[33]

It was a message of profound sorrow at the death of a former British Prime Minister who, in de Valera's view, had both the sincerity and goodwill to eradicate the causes of difficulty between the neighbouring islands. Many years later, he made sure that the Irish Ambassador should represent him at Mrs Neville Chamberlain's funeral in Birmingham.

ON RAZOR'S EDGE

1940 - 1941

The summer of 1940 was a harsh one for neutrals. The pace of the German advance had increased the threat to Britain and had, no doubt, caused the Chamberlain approach to de Valera. Between Britain and Germany, and their respective diplomats in Dublin, de Valera had so far succeeded in keeping a somewhat uneasy balance. But British press criticism of Irish neutrality mounted at this time, causing grave concern to de Valera, as at subsequent stages of the war. He believed it to be a planned attempt to appeal to the people of Ireland over the heads of the Government. Censorship was designed to prevent this, but it could not stop the growing campaign which coincided with MacDonald's visit to Dublin.

When Walshe saw Sir John Maffey, on July 15th, he protested. Walshe made a report on the interview for de Valera:

> I spoke at length to Maffey about the anti Irish propaganda in the British Press up to Wednesday of last week, and its continuance in the American Press in the form of despatches or radio broadcasts from London. I referred in particular to the Press Association message about a supposed military pact between us. . . . Maffey was at first inclined to repeat the arguments with which British Ministers reply to the High Commissioner when he protests against anti Irish articles in the British Press, but, in the end, he admitted that the British Ministry of Information must have been doing things without consulting the Dominions Office . . .

Indeed Maffey had a rather uncomfortable session with Walshe. If Hempel had been embarrassed over the Held case, Maffey it seems was to be equally nonplussed by what Walshe had to tell him. Walshe reported:

> I . . . expressed my great regret at the discovery we had recently made relating to a highly placed Officer. . . . I emphasized that such an incident was bound, like the activities of the Ministry of Information, to provoke the deepest suspicion between the two peoples . . .
>
> He seemed to be genuinely horrified at the espionage episode, and he did not express any desire for the early release of the Officer concerned . . . [1]

As if this were not enough to discomfort the British Representative,

Walshe followed up with a protest against the activities of a British agent, who was directing his energies to trying to persuade members of the Dáil that neutrality was foolish. This agent was being used, apparently by the British Ministry of Information, to appeal to deputies.

Maffey was undoubtedly taken aback. Like Hempel, he was finding that government departments, other than that to which he belonged, were interfering in Irish affairs. He admitted that he was in a real difficulty about the agents from the Ministry of Information and thought that the best way to prevent their continued activities was for the Irish High Commissioner in London to go to the Minister responsible, Lord Caldecote, and protest. Maffey himself went to London a couple of days later for the express purpose of re-establishing good relations which, after much fencing, he admitted had been seriously disturbed by the operation of unofficial agents. Maffey's own good faith and understanding were never questioned at any time on the Irish side. In London J. W. Dulanty, the Irish High Commissioner, protested against the activities of British agents in Irish affairs. Lord Caldecote in fact named the principal offender and said that he would prevent the issue of travel permits to him. He denied, however, that he personally had anything to do with these activities. Press comments improved after Maffey's visit to London, and by the end of July there were indications that the British pressure on Ireland was being eased. In particular, the British Government expressed a willingness to supply some military equipment for the Irish forces.[2]

The month of July had placed a severe strain on de Valera. The flood of ominous rumours had been reinforced by a telegram from the Dominions Office to de Valera, on July 10th, stating that a German invasion of Ireland had been on the point of taking place six days before. On July 14th, Maffey sent him word that their intelligence reported that the invasion would take place next day. The climax seemed to be at hand.

The Leader of the Opposition wrote a long letter to de Valera, the first in eighteen years. He expressed the fears which many felt at that time concerning aggression from Germany. He did not feel that there was any danger from Britain. He feared that Ireland was ill-equipped to hold off a German invasion and that considerable loss of life and damage to property would occur before Britain came to Ireland's aid:

> We appreciate the difficulty of the Government in coming to a decision in the matter. They may feel themselves placed in the dilemma of taking a decision between adhering to neutrality for too long a period, or on the other hand abandoning neutrality too soon.

This was a question which should be discussed and he did not feel that the defence conference as it was being operated was serving its full purpose. It had discussed measures not policy and, though the members had been informed of the offer made through Malcolm MacDonald, he felt that they should be more fully informed on all proposals made to the Government regarding defence. The Fine Gael members of the defence conference had stated, on July 2nd, that:

> If the Government in changing circumstances feel it necessary to depart from the policy of neutrality in which they have had our support up to the present, my colleagues and I would be prepared to give them our fullest support in such a change of policy.[3]

But for de Valera in those all-too-long summer days, the anxieties mounted, coming as they did not only from one side but from both. He appreciated that both he and Cosgrave had a common interest in the preservation of national security, but he gained the impression that Cosgrave was, in fact, proposing an immediate abandonment of neutrality. He wrote that the Government's view had not changed regarding neutrality:

> We are fully aware that this policy does not guarantee the country immunity from attack. There is always the possibility of attack should one side or the other decide, during the progress of the war, that the circumstances are such that the resultant advantages to its interests outweigh the disadvantages. The assumption that hostile invasion need be feared from one side only is one which cannot in all circumstances be relied upon.

His conclusion remained firm.

> As long as we are neutral, there is a possibility that the danger of attack may be averted; whilst if we invite military assistance from one side, immediate attack by the other, with all its consequences, will be almost inevitable.

De Valera was willing to agree to further discussions on defence questions, in addition to those at the conference, with members of the Opposition, but he maintained the right of the Government to formulate its policy:

> The ultimate decisions as to any steps to be taken in the national interest must, of course, rest with the Government in office.[4]

Cosgrave's reply accepted this position. He emphasized that his letter had been written, not to suggest a change of policy but to indicate what would be his party's view if the Government felt obliged to abandon neutrality.[5]

On the strength of the Irish will to defend its neutrality largely depended the success of their policy. De Valera was well aware of this and reiterated time and again his determination to resist any and every attack. He realized, however, the weakness of Irish armaments and made every endeavour to get arms. Despite the stated willingness of Britain to supply some arms, nothing came. There was a great response to the appeal to Irishmen to join the armed forces in Ireland, but the army could not be expected to put up an effective resistance against attack without weapons. There was even a certain amount of dispute as to what was the best way of distributing the arms that were available. Some claimed that it was best to scatter them evenly through the army, so that a certain supply would be available in all areas. De Valera intervened to make sure that one division at least would be fully equipped.

In April, 1940, a new American Minister had been appointed in Dublin—a relative by marriage of Mrs Roosevelt, Mr David Gray, of whom more later. Shortly after his arrival in Ireland, de Valera took up with him the possibility of obtaining arms. At the same time, he asked that the United States, which was still neutral, should declare that the Irish *status quo* was vital to American interests. In neither of these instances did he succeed, though Gray undoubtedly did his best about arms. Ultimately, however, some twenty thousand American-made rifles, which had been sold to Canada, were obtained for Ireland with the goodwill of Britain.[5A]

With the Germans now in possession of the coast of France, the war entered a new phase. The German Minister gave warning of the course it would take when, on August 17th, he handed to Joseph P. Walshe a note from his Government, announcing a total blockade of Britain. The sea area all around Ireland was included in the zone of operations and the German Government warned neutral ships against entering it. Hempel said, however, that Germany would not attack ships sailing under the Irish flag if they were specially marked and their cargoes and sailing orders reported to Germany in advance, provided, that is, that they carried nothing which was to be transhipped to Britain. The Minister suggested that the details of the procedure could be settled in a formal agreement. An acute problem raised was the suggestion that de Valera's Government enter into an agreement with Germany. While the Germans might have been happy with whatever propaganda value such an agreement might give them, it was equally certain that it would cause a vigorous British reaction. There were, it is true, some possible benefits to be gained from it for Britain. If the Germans allowed freely the import of animal feeding-stuffs, it might have been possible to increase the supplies of finished livestock for sale to Britain. It was felt, however, that no agreement with Germany would protect shipping in mine-infested waters and that there would be little real benefit from entering into a formal agreement or even into a formal arrangement. Equally, there were strong reasons against rejecting the German offer out of hand. If the blockade were completely effective, it would be well to keep open the possibility of using some means of passing goods through it to Ireland, and it would be foolish to close that door too firmly.

It was a question of playing for time. Walshe saw Hempel a week after he had delivered the note. De Valera had instructed him to discuss the possible consequences of the blockade with the Secretaries of the Departments of Supplies, Agriculture, and Industry and Commerce. The principal conclusion which they reached was that the Government should take no step which would constitute an interference with Ireland's exports. Walshe explained all this to Hempel and pointed out to him the peculiar nature of Irish overseas trade which was mainly with England and in British ships. He indicated his Government's anxiety lest a German agreement give ground to Britain for a charge of unneutral behaviour. He suggested that this proposal be discussed through the Irish Chargé d'Affaires in Berlin. This was a diplomatic way of postponing the possibility of an agreement. The Foreign Office in Berlin would have more to think about than an Irish agreement and would scarcely be on the doorstep of the Irish Minister, William Warnock, every day regarding it. Warnock, too, would be able to plead difficulties of communication with Dublin as an excuse for delay. The matter was raised with him a couple of times in Berlin but was never pursued.[6]

For Britain the tension, and at the same time the exhilaration, accumulated as the people waited throughout the summer for Hitler's threatened invasion. From July to September raged the Battle of Britain. By the end of it emerged what seemed, and still seems, the miracle of the defeat of the Luftwaffe. Already, early in September, the blitz had started on the British cities; and de Valera had begun to feel that something might be and should be done for the suffering civilian population. On September 27th, he sent word to Sir John Maffey that the Irish Government would be glad to receive women and children from areas exposed to air-raids. A few days later, Maffey reported his Government's appreciation of the offer.[7] He assured him that it would be considered. The German menace to Irish neutrality receded. It was replaced, however, by increased tension with Britain. In a tough speech in the House of Commons on November 5th, Churchill adverted to the increased activity of the U-boats. He said:

> The fact that we cannot use the south and west coasts of Ireland to refuel our flotillas and aircraft and thus protect the trade by which Ireland as well as Great Britain lives, is a most heavy and grievous burden, and one which should never have been placed on our shoulders, broad though they be . . .

While de Valera did not construe this as an immediate threat to seize

Irish soil, he was alarmed at the campaign which it sparked off in the British and American press in favour of taking over the Irish ports. In the Dáil he replied to Churchill:

> We have chosen the policy of neutrality in this war because we believed that it was the right policy for our people . . . There can be no question of the handing over of these ports so long as this State remains neutral. There can be no question of leasing these ports. They are ours. They are within our sovereignty, and there can be no question, as long as we remain neutral, of handing them over on any condition whatsoever. Any attempt to bring pressure to bear on us by any side—by any of the belligerents—by Britain—could only lead to bloodshed . . .
>
> I want to say to our people that we may be—I hope not—facing a grave crisis. If we are to face it, then we shall do it, anyhow, knowing that our cause is right and just and that, if we have to die for it, we shall be dying in that good cause.[8]

In Aiken's opinion, it was the finest speech of his life. The language was less arresting than Churchill's 'We shall fight them on the beaches . . .' The spirit was precisely the same.

Sir John Maffey, who was in London at the time, was perturbed by the affair. When he returned to Ireland he called on Walshe and told him that he had found the Dominions Office worried about Churchill's statement of which they had known nothing beforehand. In general, he was reassuring, emphasizing that the statement itself carried no threat and that the press and other comments had no official significance. He regretted the whole matter and hoped that it had blown over.[9]

Privately, de Valera was not reassured. The possibility of a British attack, never out of his mind throughout the war, probably disturbed him more sharply at this moment than at any other. No one who reads Sir Winston's memoirs for November and December, 1940, will lightly dismiss de Valera's fears. Sir Winston's record lays bare the extremity of the apprehensions he entertained at that time about the U-boat menace, and his conviction that the Irish attitude, if allowed to continue, might prove fatal to the very survival of Britain.

> One evening in December I held a meeting in the downstairs War room with only the Admiralty and the sailors present. All the perils and difficulties about which the company was well informed had taken a sharper turn. My mind reverted to February and March, 1917, when the curve of U-boat sinkings had mounted so steadily against us that one wondered how many months more fighting the Allies had in them . . .

To the two men who, each in his own country, bore the chief burden, the situation seemed equally desperate.

The United States had always been considered a major factor in the struggle for Irish independence. Now, though still neutral, she was moving more and more towards war with Germany. It was crucial to discover if possible her attitude. In view of Churchill's statement, de Valera instructed the Irish Minister in Washington, Bob Brennan, to give to the Under-Secretary of the State Department, Sumner Welles, a copy of his reply. Brennan found Welles friendly and reported:

> He said it was very clear from both that Ireland could have no other policy and that Ireland's peace was an asset to Britain. Any clash between the two countries would be disastrous for both.[10]

So far, it seemed, so good. Ten days later, however, de Valera was disconcerted to receive a letter from David Gray, the American Minister to Ireland, who now comes increasingly into the story. From the time of his arrival in Ireland he had made no secret of his sympathies and had built up a considerable circle of friends. Since the re-election of President Roosevelt, he had been pressing on Joseph P. Walshe, Head of External Affairs, the view that Ireland should give Britain the use of the ports. This letter gave de Valera his assessment of American public opinion: 'Nations that are not co-operating with Britain have come to be regarded as not in sympathy with the interests of America.'[11] Gray was seeking an interview with de Valera, but in a report to Washington, following de Valera's reply to Churchill, he had already revealed a powerful dislike of him:

> His whole power is based on his genius for engendering and utilizing anti-British sentiment. His administration otherwise is generally unsuccessful. He is probably the most adroit politician in Europe and he honestly believes that all he does is for the good of his country. He has the qualities of martyr, fanatic and Machiavelli. No one can outwit him, frighten or blandish him. Remember that he is not pro-German, nor personally anti-British, but only pro-de Valera. My view is that he will do business on his own terms or must be overcome by force.[12]

The diplomat who wrote this had already aroused considerable criticism in Ireland and his attitude during the interview with de Valera was not calculated to win him a new friend. De Valera recorded the conversation thus:

> The American Minister prefaced his statements by saying that Americans could be cruel if their interests were affected and Ireland should expect little or no sympathy if the British took the ports. He added that, in any case, America herself was coming into the war in a short time and then Ireland would have to give the ports to America.

Gray gave quite a different version of Brennan's interview with Sumner Welles from that which de Valera had received from Brennan.

According to Gray, Welles had said to Brennan that the Irish Government, by its attitude, was jeopardizing Ireland's security; that the use of the Irish ports was essential to British naval success and that, apparently, the ports should be given to Britain. A minatory tone was clearly being adopted by Gray. He was deliberately showing his claws. De Valera informed Brennan:

> Gray is very imprudent. He repeats these views publicly in the diplomatic corps and amongst his ascendancy friends and has told them that he had been instructed to give the message in question to the Taoiseach. Since this attitude may give the impression here that America wants the British to seize our ports, it might be well to visit the Under-Secretary once more.[13]

When Brennan called on Welles for a clarification of the position, the latter claimed that Gray had got things mixed. He admitted that he had not said all that Gray had reported to de Valera, but Roosevelt had decided to let de Valera know of American public opinion. Gray had accordingly been instructed that 'We are anxious to do everything possible to prevent a British defeat; one factor is that the British should have the use of the ports.'[14] It would not be fair to Gray to hold him responsible for the confusion over what Welles had told Brennan. It was, however, clear to de Valera that he would be an unsympathetic reporter on Irish affairs to the State Department. The British Representative, Sir John Maffey, later said of his American colleague:

> Probably I could appreciate Mr de Valera's difficulties more sympathetically than Mr Gray was able to do. David Gray in that crisis of human affairs felt that 'those who are not with us are against us'. That was his stern unshakeable principle. In his diplomacy there was no room for compromises, God bless him . . .[15]

At this time Gray's own country was not at war, and did not enter into the conflict until twelve months later after an attack on her navy. He sought to set up a circle of pro-British elements in Ireland, in a way which Maffey would not have cared to do; and worked hard and unsuccessfully on the Opposition, in the hopes of forcing Ireland into the war.

His pressure certainly did nothing to ease the strains created by Churchill's speech. In a radio address, at the end of 1940, Roosevelt added to them by referring to the danger of Nazi Germany to Ireland. In the taut atmosphere of that Christmas, de Valera gave a token of his determination to defend Irish neutrality by setting up a defensive front against a possible attack by British forces from Northern Ireland. By Spring, 1941, however, the tension had eased somewhat, despite Churchill's instruction that Sir John Maffey should say nothing to reassure or mollify the Irish Government. 'He should not be encouraged to think that his only task is to mollify de Valera and make everything, including our ruin, pass off pleasantly.' The tactics were to play on Irish fears.

In February, indeed, de Valera had sought from Maffey a guarantee similar to that which he had received from Hempel, that his Government would not invade Ireland. But Maffey's reply was that he could not give such an assurance without a mental reservation. If the Germans had them by the throat, they wanted to be free to take whatever measures they might consider necessary to save themselves. On March 14th, Maffey told de Valera that the time might come—indeed he said that he believed it would come—when Britain or America, or both, would have to bring serious pressure on Ireland. Churchill, himself, had written: 'I think it would be better to let de Valera stew in his own juice for a while.'[16] This apparently was the policy being pursued for the time being.

In an atmosphere improved, but still uneasy, there was a conference between high-ranking officers of the British and Irish armies on March 10th, regarding the defence of Ireland in case of a German attack. Maffey spoke to the Irish Chief of Staff regarding the tension which had admittedly existed at Christmas. This time his reassurance was quite solid. If Britain were to take any action against Ireland it would be preceded by months of parley. The demand would be made by or through America.

At this stage, a new type of pressure began to be brought to bear. De Valera had shown his determination to resist any attack and had impressed on Gray that, in such circumstances, he and his ministers would be with the troops, that their resistance would only be overcome, not by imprisonment, but by death.[17] The alternative to military action was economic pressure. Churchill appeared to decide, at the end of 1940, to use the weapon placed in his hands by the shipping arrangements made between Britain and Ireland at the beginning of the war.

It had been understood that petrol supplies for civilian and commercial needs would be kept at the same level in the two countries and, on this understanding, ships had been transferred to the British from the Irish register. Churchill now showed, in a letter on December 1st to his Chancellor of the Exchequer, that he wished to end all the trading arrangements entered into with Ireland at the outbreak. He knew it could mean a loss to Britain's own food supply, but this would be compensated for by a saving in shipping space for 'the enormous mass of fertilizers and feeding-stuffs we have to carry into Ireland through the de Valera-aided German blockade'. Churchill was to reiterate his view to Roosevelt a fortnight or so later:

> We are so hard pressed at sea that we cannot undertake to carry any longer the 400,000 tons of feeding-stuffs and fertilisers which we have hitherto convoyed to Eire through all the attacks of the enemy. We need this tonnage for our own supply and we do not need the food which Eire has been sending us. . . . You will realise also that our merchant seamen, as well as public opinion generally, take it much amiss that we should have to carry Irish supplies through air and U-boat attacks and subsidise them handsomely when de Valera is quite content to sit happy and see us strangled.[18]

A supreme fighter is almost inevitably a partisan. No country was ever led by a greater fighter than Churchill. His view of the situation naturally was far removed from any held in Ireland. Despite his suggestion that the effect of cutting off Irish supplies might 'loosen things up and make him more ready to consider common interests', the pressure was to have no effect on de Valera's fundamental policy of neutrality.

The cancellation of the shipping arrangements which had been in operation since autumn, 1939, was, however, a serious blow to Ireland. She had no merchant navy and the ships transferred to the British register under the earlier understanding were not returned. Far-reaching fears about the continued supply of petrol in Ireland made themselves felt by Christmas, 1940, although the British had made no statement regarding their new policy. De Valera, in an interview with the German Minister on December 29th, mentioned 'the bilateral blockade' which seriously threatened Ireland's economic situation.[19] The policy of Britain became startlingly clear in mid-January when Lord Cranborne, in reply to a memorandum presented by the Irish High Commissioner in London, set out the British Government's view that the previous shipping arrangements had been simply a voluntary assistance to Ireland which neither imposed nor implied obligations. Both sides, he maintained, were at liberty to terminate the arrangements.[20]

It was in these circumstances that the policy of self-sufficiency pursued by de Valera since he attained office in 1932 was to prove of inestimable value. Had the land under wheat not been increased from 21,000 acres in 1932 to 220,000 acres by the outbreak of the war, it would never have been possible to increase the production of food on the scale required. On January 17th, 1941, de Valera told the Dáil of the possible need for rationing. He warned:

> We are very fortunate to have gone so far without suffering greater hardships. We cannot expect to get on for the future as well as we have done in the past . . . If this community is going to survive and come through it—and I hope with God's help, we shall—we will have to take a number of these problems much more seriously than we have taken them up to the present.[21]

Rationing might have to be introduced in regard to some commodities to conserve stocks, he stated. There was an immediate order to extend compulsory tillage so that one-fifth of the arable land would be under the plough. A ration-card system was devised. Tea was the first commodity put on it. The tea requirements of the country were drastically cut. The British Government had, in 1939, asked Irish ministers that tea for Ireland be bought through the British tea control; but within a few weeks the Irish ration was reduced to a half ounce per week for each person, less than 25 per cent of normal requirements, while British wholesalers' supplies were fixed at 85 per cent of normal purchases. This was a clear indication of British policy, despite the protestations of British ministers that the cut in Irish supplies was due simply to a deterioration in the shipping position.[22]

As soon as the danger of the British move to cut off supplies was appreciated, de Valera and his cabinet decided that the only means of countering it was to buy ships. He took up this question with the American Minister on January 6th, 1941, saying that he was anxious to purchase five or six ships, which he understood the United States were offering for sale. The imperative needs of the time were for arms to prevent invasion and for wheat to supplement Irish production. In a broadcast to America on St Patrick's Day he stated the position in which Ireland found itself: 'Both sides in blockading each other are blockading us.' By then he had sent Frank Aiken, Minister for the Co-ordination of Defensive Measures, to America to argue the Irish case for arms, ships and supplies and to defend Ireland's stand for neutrality. David Gray had, early in the year, suggested that an Irish cabinet minister should visit Washington, but the choice of Aiken for the task was not to his liking. Despite de Valera's assurance that Aiken was not pro-German, Gray's report to the Department of State was to the opposite effect.

In the United States, Aiken came up against a barrier which he found it impossible to overcome. While there was much goodwill for Ireland's request for shipping, arms and wheat, some officials and pressmen regarded Irish neutrality as pro-German, to which Aiken's reply was: 'We are neither pro-German nor pro-British, we are just pro-Irish.' The swing of American public opinion in favour of Britain was strong. Indeed, just as Aiken was leaving Ireland, Colonel William J. Donovan, the personal representative of Frank Knox, United States Secretary of the Navy, visited Dublin and impressed on de Valera the trends of American public opinion, which, he claimed, was critical of Irish neutrality. His main aim appears to have been to persuade de Valera to allow the British the use of the Irish ports. De Valera, however, was adamant in his adherence to neutrality. He was willing to co-operate with Britain, but not in any way to jeopardize the Irish stand.

He explained the position to the German Minister when the latter sought to extend the staff of the German Legation in Dublin. It had been considered as a piece of boldness for Ireland, in the particular political, economic and geographic situation of this country with respect to England, to have dared to make a neutrality declaration at the beginning of the war. He believed that no other Irish government would have risked this, and he had from the outset been aware of the great difficulties that this bold venture entailed and the prudent and cautious governmental policy it demanded. It was a matter of having a general policy that could give none of the belligerents even as much as a pretext for intervention.[23]

De Valera was undoubtedly under severe pressure from all sides, and concession to one might antagonize the other. It was often better not to refuse to do something in a manner to cause trouble, but rather to make it so difficult as to be impossible to practice. De Valera, when he saw Hempel, refused to allow the extra German staff to land in a Luftwaffe plane, but he agreed that they could come through the normal transport channels. This rule could be applied impartially but, like many of the rules devised during the war, it favoured the Allies. When Hempel had reluctantly agreed to this and the German Government decided to transfer some of its officials from America, the Irish Government insisted that the ordinary means of travelling to Ireland from the American continent was by the Pan-American passenger line to Lisbon and thence to England by British plane[24]—which, of course, killed the idea. Direct requests for the Irish ports could be parried in no such fashion. Refusal by de Valera on such a matter was always firm and absolute.

Frank Aiken's mission to the United States coincided with a hardening of the Roosevelt administration's resolve to give every possible assistance to Britain, short of declaring war. Gray, in Dublin, was not helping his mission by reporting:

> The Irish Government is exploiting Aiken's mission as American approval of its policy, at the same time making political capital out of inciting anti-British sentiment. Unless Aiken has made undertakings of co-operation of which we are ignorant, I believe the time has come for a firmer attitude and the demand that de Valera clarify definitely his position.

Gray suggested to the State Department that he be instructed to protest at a statement which de Valera had made in a broadcast to America on St Patrick's Day.[25] The statement in question (mentioned above) was that the belligerents 'in blockading each other are blockading us' and had first been made by de Valera in January without protest.[26] Now Gray objected to it as an accusation against Britain.

In America, too, despite every precaution, Aiken was being misrepresented. He carefully avoided contacts with senators and congressmen opposed to Roosevelt. Indeed, his main supporters were the Democratic House Leader, in Congress, John McCormack, and representative Jim McGranery of Philadelphia, both of whom had voted for the Lease-Lend arrangement to help Britain. When he met Roosevelt on April 7th, however, the President charged him: 'You are reported as having said that the Irish had nothing to fear from a German victory.' Denials were useless, though a challenge to produce any evidence of such a statement was unanswered. Aiken tried to pin down Roosevelt on one vital point. He asked him to say that the President sympathized with Ireland's 'stand against aggression'. Roosevelt's reply was 'against German aggression'. Aiken said 'or British aggression', to which Roosevelt answered that this was nonsense. There was no need to fear a British attack. Then Aiken asked the question which had been perturbing de Valera since the outbreak of the war: 'Why did the British refuse to give an undertaking on this point?' Roosevelt said the suggestion was ridiculous, but agreed that he would get in touch with Churchill about it.[27] This latter point was pressed afterwards, but Roosevelt evaded the question. To Senator Joseph O'Mahoney, of Wyoming, he went so far as to say: 'I can give you my personal guarantee and word of honour that they will never do anything of the kind', but there was no British assurance of their acceptance of Irish neutrality.[28]

On April 28th the American Minister, David Gray, called on de Valera and said that he was instructed to ask for an explanation of his statement about being blockaded by both sides. Gray stated that de Valera 'flushed angrily and shouted that it was impertinent to question the statements of a Head of State'.[29] De Valera's own note of the interview does not record the anger, but it confirms the lines of the conversation. His note was as follows:

Saw Mr Gray, who read for me two memoranda, which he said he had been asked to bring to me. I said I regarded the first document as a piece of impertinence. I said my statement had not been questioned when it was made and now only appears to be a rehash of the attacks which were made in the Dáil and Senate on it. What I had said was intended to indicate, as vividly as I could, the position in which Ireland was finding herself. After Mr Churchill's statement about the ports a new policy seemed to be adopted by the British Government. There was cumulative evidence of it. Officials who had been strongly pro-British in their attitude had reported it to me. Nobody suggested that Britain was sinking our ships. The action which Britain was taking was preventing us from getting ships. We had refrained from going into competition with Britain at the beginning, at her request, and now we were left without any, etc. I, of course, denied that I had any intention of trying to influence the American public against the American Executive.[30]

This last comment was made in reply to a charge from Gray that de Valera had made his statement at a time of tense feeling in America. Anti-British elements, to whom de Valera chiefly appealed, had attempted, according to Gray, to defeat the present administration and the Lease-Lend law and were now engaged in sabotaging the American aid for Britain policy.[31] Indeed, de Valera could have gone further in his reply and named the list of staunch Democrats on whose support both Roosevelt and Ireland relied—Senators Meade of New York, O'Mahoney of Wyoming, Murray of Montana and Congressman John McCormack (already mentioned)—to name a few.

Undoubtedly it came rather strangely from Gray to accuse de Valera of using the opposition in the United States against Roosevelt's administration. That was exactly what he himself was seeking to accomplish in Ireland. De Valera, at this interview, was recorded by Gray as stating that certain of his friends considered the American Minister as 'more British than the British' and that he 'would do better to mind American interests'.

The second document which Gray read to de Valera, at that interview, was an offer of two ships, but this was couched in terms which appear to have been devised to split the Irish Government. The offer was being made directly to him, and not through Aiken, because 'his point of view has appeared to be one of blind hostility to the British Government and to the British people.' De Valera recorded:

I said that that was a completely mistaken view; that he [Aiken] naturally resented the partitioning of his country and the cutting off of the people of the territory in which he was born from the main territory of the Irish nation. Mr Gray made it clear, however, that the offer was being made to me and that they would not do business with Aiken.[32]

This offer posed a problem. Ships were urgently needed, but to accept them implied a criticism of a cabinet colleague in whom de Valera had the utmost confidence. De Valera decided to refuse them and the Irish Minister in Washington informed the Department of State:

Ireland's needs for the ships, and possession of them, might well mean the difference between extreme hardship and a hardship which would be tolerable. The manner, however, in which the offer is made and the suggestion of certain implied conditions render it impossible for the Irish Government to accept. They cannot agree that the estimate of Mr Aiken's attitude and the criticism directed against him is just.[33]

Gray, at this time, was well aware that one of the Opposition leaders had approached de Valera to have Aiken recalled from the United States, on the grounds that he was antagonizing American opinion. De Valera, however, would not let down his colleague and ultimately succeeded in getting the two ships, the *West Neris* and the *West Hematite*, on charter. They became the *Irish Oak* and the *Irish Pine* of the fleet of Irish Shipping Ltd, a government-sponsored company set up in March, 1941, to defeat the British policy of economic pressure. In its first year the company bought eight vessels and chartered five others, and throughout the war the little merchant fleet, which included even ancient schooners, ran the gauntlet of the German blockade to bring vital supplies to Ireland.[34]

At the time that Frank Aiken was in America the first large-scale bombing of an Irish city by German planes took place. On the night of May 1st Belfast was attacked. Hitherto, although Northern Ireland was at war, being part of the jurisdiction of the United Kingdom, Germany had not subjected it to air-raids. Indeed, in the hope that this would continue, de Valera had let it be known to the German Minister that he appreciated the German attitude which, he suggested, was a recognition, despite partition, of the essential unity of Ireland.[35] Nevertheless, at about 2 a.m. in the morning of May 2nd, de Valera was wakened up by the ringing of the telephone beside his bed. The official in charge of the Dublin telephone exchange had got a message that Belfast had been bombed and was ablaze. De Valera's first reaction was that the victims of this bombing were Irishmen and he must send aid. However, he weighed the consequences. Germany had decided to bomb the city. If he interfered to prevent it, or to counter the effect of the bombing, he would be considered as interfering against Germany in the war. Normally he was not a man to take quick decisions, but that night he took what was possibly the fastest decision of his career—all the Dublin fire-engines, except one, were to go at once to Belfast. The fact that it was Irish men and women who were in danger overruled his caution.

The fires of Belfast were still warm when a new crisis arose for Ireland's neutrality. It was apparently suggested to Churchill that conscription should now be extended to the Six Counties. (They had hitherto been excluded from its operation.) On May 20th the Prime Minister announced that the question had been before his Government. On the following day, de Valera instructed the Irish High Commissioner to see Lord Cranborne, the Dominions Secretary, and to inform him that the Irish Government were seriously perturbed at the action contemplated by the British Government. Such a course would bring about a situation, the end of which no one could foresee. The British Government should recognize what an outrage it would be to force the Nationalist population in the Six Counties to fight for a freedom which they had not themselves been permitted to enjoy. The effect on Irish opinion all over the world would be disastrous. Dulanty found that the matter was out of Cranborne's hands, so he asked to see Churchill.

14

It was a crisis of the first magnitude, carrying a threat to the whole internal peace of Ireland. The IRA which had been rendered ineffective, though responsible for a few minor incidents, would be assured of an accretion of sympathy and strength if conscription were enforced. Its contacts with Germany had been cut by official action and the few German agents who did land in the country, apart from Hermann Goertz, were arrested within a remarkably short time and interned. Goertz himself had already reached the conclusion that his mission was hopeless and the Government was aware that he had made an attempt to return to Germany. Nevertheless he continued to evade capture, though having a number of narrow escapes. He was no great danger to Irish neutrality, cut off from his homeland and hunted as he was. The crisis of conscription, however, might have made him really dangerous. He was not arrested ultimately until the end of November, 1941, but by then the IRA had become disorganized, rent by internal disputes and personal recriminations. Members became suspicious of each other. They shot one of their members without trial. They tried and sentenced their own Chief of Staff. His supposed confession was to cause some confusion, but the methods by which it was obtained brought further discredit on the IRA. This is, however, to anticipate.

During the morning of May 22nd, the High Commissioner saw Churchill, who was quite amicable to start with. The friendship of these two went back to Churchill's candidature in N.W. Manchester in 1906 and to Dulanty's work under him in the Ministry of Munitions during the first war. Their mutual affection survived every tribulation. As the argument proceeded Churchill suddenly lost, or appeared to lose, his temper. He said that the demand for conscription had come from the Six Counties and that everybody there would be treated alike, though he added that 'no obstruction would be put in the way of those who wanted to run away'. He was not interested in any trouble that might occur in Ireland. There was trouble and bloodshed everywhere, and disturbance in Ireland would be just a small addition to the general welter. If Ireland refrained from giving Britain facilities, there were other ways of getting them. Churchill seemed to be at his most hostile. Though the Prime Minister calmed down before Dulanty left him, he made it clear that he had had no sympathy with Ireland since the Treaty was cast aside. 'Since that date he had drawn the sword.'[36]

The threat of conscription brought a strong public reaction. Cardinal MacRory in Armagh denounced it and warned that it would rouse Irishmen everywhere 'to indignation and resistance.' De Valera consulted the leading members of the Opposition parties on the crisis,[37] while David Gray, the American Minister in Dublin, sent a telegram to

Washington deploring the threat. He warned, 'It will . . . seriously hamper the opposition on which we must rely.'[38] The man who accused de Valera of appealing to the opposition to the Roosevelt administration was admitting, as now appears, his reliance on the Opposition in Ireland. Gray informed de Valera of the substance of his messages to America and de Valera was deeply grateful. Though he felt that Gray had done all in his power to sabotage the Aiken mission, he was glad to accept his good offices when available.

On the conscription issue, Gray was certainly a great help. He was approached by leaders of the Opposition who said that unless there was an escape clause by which the Nationalists in the North could opt out of conscription, the situation would damage American interests and strengthen de Valera's hands:

> They predict draft riots [Gray reported], the escape of draft dodgers to Southern Ireland who will be acclaimed as hero-martyrs by three-quarters of the population and the fomenting of trouble by Republicans and Fifth Columnists. The clearest headed leader predicts that de Valera will seize the opportunity to escape from economic and political realities by proclaiming himself the leader of the oppressed minority.[39]

It was not such a fantastic forecast as might appear, for, if conscription were applied, de Valera would have been compelled to take the part of the conscripted Nationalists. The whole equilibrium of neutrality would have been upset; the outcome could only have been turmoil.

In view of Gray's goodwill over the conscription issue, de Valera spoke to him urgently on the telephone. Gray suggested that, as Opposition leaders had proposed, an escape clause might solve the problem. De Valera, however, saw objections to it and later rang Gray saying that it was impossible. This second conversation ended on a note of tension, Gray apparently feeling that de Valera had shifted his ground. De Valera, thinking that the conversation had not been satisfactory, wrote Gray a letter setting out his view that, for historic reasons, nothing less than the total abandonment of conscription in the Six Northern Counties was a tolerable solution.[40] Though Gray had threatened to wash his hands of the whole affair, the American Ambassador in London, Mr John G. Winant, called on Churchill, on instructions from Washington, to let the Prime Minister know the anxieties of Roosevelt.[41]

Dulanty, too, was active, telephoning a number of members of the British cabinet. He found Attlee and Morrison, Beaverbrook and Sinclair reserved. Others were away for the weekend. On Monday, May 26th, he went to see Churchill again, this time to deliver a personal message from de Valera. Dulanty read the message to Churchill at No. 10 Downing Street. It was calm but powerful:

Mr Dulanty has reported to me your conversation on the subject of conscription in the Six County area. Before your final decision is taken, I feel that I should again put before your Government, as earnestly as I can, my view that the imposition of conscription in any form would provoke the bitterest resentment amongst Irishmen and would have the most disastrous consequences for our two peoples.

He went on to say that a feeling of better understanding and of mutual sympathy which held in it the promise of an ultimate close friendship had grown up between the two peoples in recent years. The existence of partition was the only stumbling block, and there was the hope that in the improved conditions it too would disappear. The imposition of conscription would inevitably undo all the good that had been done, and throw the two peoples back into the old unhappy relations.

The conscription of the people of one nation by another revolts the human conscience. No fair-minded man anywhere can fail to recognise in it an act of oppression upon a weaker people, and it cannot but do damage to Britain itself. The Six Counties have, towards the rest of Ireland, a status and a relationship which no Act of Parliament can change. They are part of Ireland. They have always been part of Ireland, and their people, Catholic and Protestant, are our people. [He ended with a plea from the heart.] I beg of you, before you enter on a course which can affect so profoundly the relations of our two peoples to take all these matters into the most earnest consideration.[42]

Churchill was furious. When Dulanty finished reading the text and handed it to him, he threw it on one side asking whether de Valera wanted a public answer. 'If he does,' he said, 'I will give it and it will resound about the world.' Furiously he paced about the room, denouncing the Irish vehemently and in the strongest language. They had broken faith about the Treaty. Ireland had lost her soul. When he thought of John and Willie Redmond, and of Kettle—one of the best minds Ireland had produced in recent times: when he thought of their courage and valour his blood boiled. Poor Dulanty was caught in the torrent of invective, unable to do more than throw in an occasional interjection which was swallowed up in the flood of words. No wonder he described the interview as 'exceedingly unsatisfactory'—it was the understatement of the period. He felt that Churchill had taken no notice of anything which he had said to him. He had sounded like the reincarnation of an old Victorian Tory. The only information which Churchill gave him was that, since the matter was to be decided by the Cabinet, de Valera's message would be put before it.[43]

Because of the gravity of the crisis, de Valera asked that a special meeting of the Dáil be summoned for Monday, May 26th. The leaders of the three major parties made careful speeches in which they showed the strength of their feelings against the threat. De Valera's speech reiterated much of what he had said in the message to Churchill. He spoke of his efforts for lasting peace between Ireland and Britain. It sums up so much of his attitude to Britain that it must be quoted at some length:

> No matter what political or economic changes may take place in the world, the people living on these two islands are destined for all time to live as neighbours upon the earth. They are certain at all times to have many more interests in common than they can have with other nations. Surely, then, it must be the aim of statesmen on both sides to make the relationship between the peoples of those islands that of friendly neighbours.

It was quite clear that such a relationship could only be built on the basis of mutual freedom. It was for that reason that for over twenty years he had sought to establish such a basis by removing the causes of quarrel which lay in any provision which would make the people of this island subject to the people of the other island.

> Should the British Government now go ahead with a proposal to enforce conscription upon the people of the Six Counties, the work which has been accomplished with the utmost patience, perseverance and goodwill, over a long period of years, will be undone and the people of the two islands will be thrown back again into the old unhappy relations.[44]

Though it was a stern warning of the dangers involved, de Valera's speech was couched in such a way as not to make it difficult for Churchill to take a decision against conscription. He was unutterably relieved when, the next day, Churchill announced that it had been decided that it would be more trouble than it was worth to enforce the policy. His public comment was reserved. Wisdom had prevailed and de Valera felt that this was not a time for claiming a victory. All he said was that he was very glad, and thanked God that the wise decision had been taken.[45]

THE LONELINESS OF A NEUTRAL

1941 – 1942

The uneasy balance which de Valera succeeded in maintaining during the first two years of the war gave him confidence, if not a sense of security. What had been a decision fraught with danger was vindicating itself in the testing of war. Nevertheless, none knew better than de Valera how easy it would be to upset the equilibrium which he was determined to maintain. He never knew whence the blow might come, when one or other of the belligerents might decide that the benefits to be gained from infringing Irish neutrality would more than offset the loss. The failure to obtain arms worried him unceasingly. The strength of the resistance which Ireland could put up against invasion might determine whether that invasion would take place or not. Sir John Maffey said, on March 14th, 1941, that the British could not give arms to Ireland, unless they were absolutely certain that they would not be used against themselves. He followed his statement with a heavy warning. The British could not omit from their calculations the possibility of having to use force in a vital emergency.[1]

The inability of Aiken to get much in the way of arms from America appeared therefore to carry a threat to Irish neutrality. It seemed to de Valera that the arms were not forthcoming because they might be used to prevent Britain from taking over Irish facilities. President Roosevelt justified the American attitude by saying that he had never received assurances that the Irish would defend themselves against German attack.[2] On instructions from de Valera, Brennan wrote a long memorandum to the State Department giving details of the numerous occasions on which Irish leaders had emphatically stated that any aggressor would be resisted. As a result, there was a shifting of ground. The American reply admitted that this attitude was well known, but that Roosevelt felt that Ireland would be unable to repel a German attack unaided. Talks between Irish and British military leaders had been proceeding for some months as to how an invasion might be repelled. Yet Sumner Welles dragged in, as a final reason for not giving arms, that no such consultations were in progress.[3] Indeed the argument about arms seemed to go round in circles. De Valera would not renounce his duty to resist aggression from whatever quarter. Neither America nor Britain would give him arms which might be used against themselves if they decided to take over the ports.

Another matter caused some misgivings in Dublin in the summer of 1941. The United States had decided to assume the defence of Iceland; for that purpose American technicians were said to be engaged in building a naval base in Derry. News of these events broke in July, 1941, and de Valera immediately asked David Gray whether the American Government intended to take over a base in the Six Counties. Such action would concern him since, while he recognized the *de facto* occupation of that part of Ireland, he could not waive Irish rights of sovereignty over it. Gray, of course, refused to accept de Valera's view and requested him to take it up through the Irish Minister in Washington. De Valera did not press ahead with a protest immediately but, within a couple of months, he decided to do so.[4]

When the *Daily Mail*[5] in London, under the heading 'Irish Base wants U.S. Marines', published an account of the progress of the American technicians at Derry, and suggested that Americans man the base, de Valera ordered Bob Brennan to ask the State Department about its intentions in relation to the Six Counties. This area, it was pointed out, is regarded in Ireland 'as part of the national territory'.[6] Not receiving any reply to this request, a formal note was addressed to the State Department. It was not so much a protest as a request for a statement of American intentions. But it had the clear purpose of stating Ireland's right to unity.[7] As expected, the American reply refused to admit that its Government was involved and insisted that the whole question was one between Ireland and Britain.[8]

In the meantime, the American Minister was in no way increasing his popularity in Ireland. He was the most candid or naïve of diplomats in many of his actions. He wrote to the Secretary of the Department of External Affairs, supplying the gist of answers which he was giving to American journalists regarding Irish neutrality. These replies were loaded with innuendoes which could do nothing but harm to Ireland. A few extracts are sufficient to show the tone:

> The Germans must presumably have tried unsuccessfully to interest the Irish Government, before turning to the Irish Republican Army movement. What proposals they have made, I have never heard.

A presumption passes over into 'proposals they have made!'

A fair presumption is that many parachutists have been captured.

To this presumption is added the definite statement 'they know the country and are taken care of by friends.' Regarding the possibility of newspaper censorship having a pro-German bias, Gray stated of an official:

I am told he spent a considerable time in Germany and presumably is sympathetic to the German cause.

The man in question had served in the British Air Force during World War I and had never been in Germany.

The head of the German spy system is presumably some agent unknown to the public . . .[9]

said Gray, starting from the presumption that there was a 'spy system' in Ireland. Was Gray simply naïve, or did he wish to draw comment? De Valera did not in fact comment, although the matter was submitted to him.

He was much concerned throughout the war as to how to avert injudicious statements by Irishmen which might be used in propaganda. Democratic procedures must be interfered with as little as possible. The deputies in general were careful and restrained. De Valera warned them, however, in the Dáil, of the dangers:

I am particularly anxious lest statements by public men here should be taken up by Press correspondents and sent abroad to cause misunderstanding of our position and increase our dangers.

He stressed that in July, 1941, the difficulties which might be encountered showed no signs of lessening and would only be met by courage and caution:

We are in an extremely difficult and delicate situation. The policy of neutrality is not by any means an easy policy and it is not a cowardly policy. It will require as much courage to put that policy through, and to stand by our national statements regarding it, as it would to put any other policy through. [He added, surprisingly perhaps]: It may be a more difficult policy, in the long run, than any other policy.[10]

As the summer of 1941 passed, some of the more immediate anxieties became less pressing. When the Germans bombed Dublin on May 30th, following an earlier bombing in January, it was at once clear that it was an error. No one was more perturbed than the German Minister, who had a month earlier pointed out to his superiors in Berlin the danger of building up anti-German feeling by a repetition of the Belfast bombings.[11] Churchill has later suggested, in his history of the war, that the Dublin bombing might have been caused by the deflection of the beams on which the Germans were flying, but this explanation was not known at the time.

Hempel was called to the Irish Department of External Affairs on de Valera's instructions and there Joseph P. Walshe, the Secretary, made a sharp protest. He told Dr Hempel that his Minister was deeply moved at the tragedy, which had cost a number of lives, and wounded many other people. Germany accepted full responsibility for the error and Hempel was anxious to do everything possible to make reparation.[12] The possible threat of invasion from Germany was, within a few weeks, weakened when Hitler, on June 22nd, turned his forces against Russia. The long awaited invasion of Britain was now set aside for the moment and with it the feeling of tension eased in Dublin.

The weakening of one threat, however, was balanced by the strengthening of another. De Valera never knew whence a blow might come. As he went about his duties in various parts of the country, encouraging farmers to produce more food, or warning people to be always prepared, he constantly felt the danger through which his country was passing. Every ring on the telephone appeared to him to spell danger. Then one night, when he was already aware of tremendous happenings on the world scene, the telephone rang as he lay in bed at his home in Blackrock, near Dublin. It was 1.30 a.m. on the morning of Monday, December 8th, 1941. Joseph P. Walshe was ringing up to say that Sir John Maffey had a message from Churchill, which he had been instructed to deliver personally to de Valera at once.

De Valera asked: could it not wait until the morning?, and was informed that it could not. Churchill had instructed that it be given to him immediately. Deeply perturbed, de Valera arranged to receive Maffey in half an hour. He rang up the Secretary to the Government, Maurice Moynihan, and the Chief of Staff, Major-General Daniel McKenna, and warned them to stand by for any instructions which might become necessary after the interview. De Valera knew, of course, that on the previous day there had been a savage attack on the American fleet at Pearl Harbour. He realized that this must almost certainly bring America into the war. What did this portend for Ireland? He could only believe that an ultimatum demanding the surrender of the ports was on its way.

Shortly after 2 a.m., Sir John Maffey arrived on the doorstep of Teach Cuilinn, de Valera's private house in Cross Avenue, Blackrock. De Valera made a note of what happened:

> He said that he had got a message from Mr Churchill which he was asked to deliver. I gathered from his introductory remarks before handing me the paper that he was rather surprised at the message; that he regarded it as Churchillian. I understood that it was an invitation to go over to see him. Before seeing the paper, I pointed out to him that I thought it would be

unwise; that it would probably be misunderstood by our people and regarded to have a significance beyond anything which it would in reality have.

He felt that, even though no agreements were arrived at, it might be suspected that there was some secret bargain, and that subsequent actions of the Irish Government might be considered the outcome. A visit to England could do nothing but increase the difficulties of the Irish Government.

Sir John Maffey handed the typewritten text to de Valera. It read:

> Following from Mr Churchill for Mr de Valera. Personal. Private and Secret. Begins. Now is your chance. Now or never. 'A Nation once again.' Am very ready to meet you at any time. Ends.

It was a peculiar, enigmatic message, an impulsive act from Churchill in an exuberant mood at the news from Pearl Harbour. Indeed, Churchill's war memoirs made it clear that he was highly excited that night and scattered telegrams both east of him and west of him. De Valera recorded his own reaction:

> On being handed the written text I concluded that it was Mr Churchill's way of intimating 'now is the chance for taking action which would ultimately lead to the unification of the country'. I indicated to Sir John Maffey that I did not see the thing in that light. I saw no opportunity at the moment of securing unity, that our people were determined on their attitude of neutrality, etc.

He pointed out that it was not because he did not wish to meet Mr Churchill that he was not in favour of going.

> I was not in favour of it because I considered it unwise; that I didn't see any basis of agreement and that disagreement might leave conditions worse than before and that my visit, in any case, would have the results that I had already indicated. Sir John Maffey urged that, whilst he understood my position, I should not turn the suggestion flatly down. I said that I would naturally consult my colleagues on the matter and would let him know.[13]

Then de Valera rang Moynihan and McKenna to tell them that they could go back to bed.

There is a small difference between the text of the message from Churchill and that which he published in his history of the war. It was really confined to the last sentence, which Churchill published as: 'I will meet you wherever you wish'.[14] The text delivered read: 'Am very ready to meet you at any time'. It was the time, not the place, of meeting which was in fact left open. To de Valera the message appeared to be an invitation to go to London.

Next morning, de Valera called a meeting of the Government. He had already heard from Joseph P. Walshe that the British Representative was leaving Dublin for a day or two, and felt that there was no need for an immediate reply to Churchill's message. Perhaps a couple of days' delay would indicate that he saw no point in being awakened out of his sleep to receive it. At 3.45 on the afternoon of Wednesday, December 10th, de Valera saw Maffey and, after sympathizing with him on the recent loss of the ships *Prince of Wales* and *Repulse*, handed him the following message:

> From Mr de Valera to Mr Churchill. Personal. Private. Thanks for your message. Perhaps a visit from Lord Cranborne would be the best way towards a fuller understanding of our position here. Details of the visit could be arranged through our High Commissioner or your representative here.[15]

Churchill's reply accepted this suggestion and Cranborne arranged to visit Dublin secretly the following week.

On Tuesday, December 16th, he arrived in Dublin, staying with Sir John Maffey. The following morning he met de Valera at Iveagh House and talked for two hours. De Valera noted his impression of the conversation. It should be mentioned that his relations with Cranborne were always based on mutual respect.

> I wasn't clear what Mr Churchill's message meant. He said that it was indeed vague (Sir John Maffey had previously told me that of course there was no question of a bargain about the North, as I had seemed to infer). C. thought that it might be possible for us to come in; referred to my influence and their feeling that I had not used that influence to get the Irish people to move towards war.
>
> I explained what I had tried to get their people to do, (1) to give arms so that this part of Ireland would be safe from invasion which, if successful, would of course affect them, and (2) to make use of our resources in supplying the things which we could supply while still remaining neutral—greater quantities of food and perhaps articles of clothing, etc.

De Valera pointed out that the Irish people had no wish to profiteer, but the prices paid should approximate to those paid to British producers if Irish production was to continue. From the British point of view, there were difficulties in this. The British Dominions would expect the same price as that paid for Irish goods. The result would be to send up prices all round. The question of partition, too, was discussed. De Valera noted:

> I said there was considerable goodwill for Britain here, but of course there was a section who, on account of our history and the existence of partition, were still strongly opposed. I discussed the nature of partition, the fact that only one half of the area would, on a plebiscite, be likely to vote itself away from this country. I referred to my suggested solution of a local parliament

having the powers of the existing parliament and the same boundary, with the Westminster powers transferred to an all-Ireland parliament. This gave the Northern minority more than justice. They could really only demand a local parliament for the area in which they had a local majority and not the whole of the Six Counties . . .[16]

De Valera spoke of the goodwill which Chamberlain had shown and of pre-war events in Geneva and Munich, and speculated on what would be the conditions of the world after the war. Cranborne pointed out that, if Ireland remained neutral, it would not be represented at the post-war peace conference. He had come back to his point of entry and he had not got de Valera to move an inch from the policy of neutrality. After the meeting, de Valera entertained Cranborne and Sir John Maffey to lunch. The Irish point of view had been demonstrated and the situation remained unchanged in respect of Irish neutrality.

But large changes were taking place in the warring world outside. The entry of the United States into the war was a completely new factor. It brought with it new dangers for Ireland and an increase in the activities of David Gray. 'The attitude of the Irish Government has become notably more friendly, although there is no suggestion of recession from neutrality' reported Gray.[17] Indeed, de Valera, in his first speech after the entry of the United States into the war, in Cork on December 14th, stated where Irish sympathy lay in the conflict:

Its extension to the United States brings a source of anxiety and sorrow to every part of this land. There is scarcely a family here which has not a member or a near relative in that country. In addition to the ties of blood, there has been between our two nations a long association of friendship and regard, continuing uninterruptedly from America's own struggle for independence down to our own. The part that American friendship played in helping us to win the freedom that we enjoy in this part of Ireland has been gratefully recognised and acknowledged by our people. It would be unnatural then if we did not sympathise in a special manner with the people of the United States and if we did not feel with them in all the anxieties and trials which this war must bring upon them.

But he was announcing no alteration in policy:

The policy of the State remains unchanged. We can only be a *friendly neutral*. Our circumstances of history, the incompleteness of our national freedom through the partition of our country made any other policy impracticable. Any other policy would have divided our people, and for a divided people to fling itself into this war would be to commit suicide.[18]

If de Valera's speech was only partially welcome in Washington, it was anything but welcome in the German Legation in Dublin. The German

Minister called on the Secretary of the Department of External Affairs the next day to ask what de Valera intended by the expression 'a friendly neutral'. Joseph P. Walshe pointed out that de Valera's speech had made it clear that Irish neutrality would be maintained but that there must, indeed, be 'a certain very real sympathy for America in a fight in which so many people of Irish blood would be taking part'.

Fortunately Hempel was not in a strong position for a protest. Little more than a fortnight before, Hermann Goertz, the German parachutist who had evaded arrest since May, 1940, had been captured in a Dublin suburb. The German Minister had, on December 4th, objected to any publicity about this capture, but the Irish Government felt that much of the propaganda against Irish neutrality dated from the arrival of Goertz and was given strength by the feeling that he was still at large. Publicity was a method of countering the continued propaganda.

Walshe had spoken very strongly to Hempel on the subversive activities of Goertz. Unless there was some promise that no further German agents would be sent to Ireland, it would be almost impossible to maintain a normal relationship. When Hempel took up the question of de Valera's speech, Walshe reopened the Goertz affair and asked whether Hempel had received any assurance from Berlin that nothing like it would happen again. Hempel was, indeed, in an unhappy position. He had known of Goertz's presence in Ireland, but had been consoled by the knowledge that he was endeavouring to leave the country. Walshe felt that Hempel's loyalty to his own Government had been placed under a considerable strain by the action of the Abwehr in sending agents to Ireland. In fact, after the entry of America into the war, the impact of Germany on the course of affairs in Ireland was to decline considerably.[19]

Neutrality was the basic fundamental fact of de Valera's policy and all his energies were devoted to maintaining it. The principal danger from the German Legation was that it might, by injudicious action, give just grounds for complaint to other belligerents. It might be represented not only as a centre of espionage, but also a transmitting station for information of military importance. The German Legation possessed a radio transmitter and the use which was made of it was closely watched by the Irish authorities. Indeed its use had ceased for some time before the end of 1941 and, when it was renewed, Walshe gave Hempel the full text of the three messages which had been sent out and warned him of the danger of again using the transmitter.[20]

This issue became more important when, in February, 1942, it was suggested that weather information transmitted on the legation radio had helped German battle units to get through St George's Channel. Walshe, on de Valera's instructions, faced Hempel once more with the texts of recent transmissions and with the opinion of the Irish meteorological service that weather information from Ireland would have been useful on that occasion to the Germans. Walshe reported the interview to de Valera:

> The time had therefore come for me to say to him—and I was acting on the formal instructions of my Minister, the Taoiseach—that he must cease absolutely using the transmitter. If he used it again, my Minister would have to require its transfer to the custody of the Department.[21]

While Hempel argued that he was legally entitled to use a transmitter, de Valera was equally adamant that Ireland would not be used as a base to damage Britain. That position was fundamental to neutrality. The wireless transmitter was always a plausible excuse for protests from the British or American governments. Hempel accepted the decision as inevitable but the story did not end there.

The control of German espionage in Ireland was completely effective. All the half dozen or so agents who had landed on the coasts or by parachute were interned, most of them having been arrested within a few hours of their arrival. At the end of 1943, two Irishmen were landed by parachute in Clare on a special mission to send meteorological reports to Germany. Walshe, on de Valera's instructions, at once protested to Hempel about the activities of his Government which violated Ireland's neutral status. They were bound to provoke something like an ultimatum from the British or the Americans about the legation's transmitter. In the circumstances de Valera had told Walshe to ask him to hand over or destroy the instrument. Hempel proposed an alternative solution. It should be lodged in a bank safe. He and the Department of External Affairs should both hold the keys. It was agreed that neither party should have access to the safe unless the other was present. This was the final solution, and the wireless issue was solved when the set was deposited in a bank on December 21st, 1943.[22]

The entry of the United States into the war had been followed, within a few weeks, by the landing of American troops in Northern Ireland. That area was *de facto* belligerent, but de Valera was anxious not to let the occasion pass without some statement as to Ireland's right to unity, though he also had no desire to rouse American opinion against his policy. Careful as always, he made no real protest except at the continuance of partition. He said:

> The people of Ireland have no feeling of hostility towards and no desire to be brought in any way into conflict with the United States. For reasons which I referred to a few weeks ago, the contrary is the truth, but it is our duty to make it clearly understood that no matter what troops occupy the Six

Counties, the Irish people's claim for the union of the whole national territory and for supreme jurisdiction over it, will remain unabated.[23]

It was the least which he could say on the occasion but privately, through the Irish Minister in Washington, he tried to extract some benefits from the situation. He sought a guarantee that the American action in sending troops to the northern area of Ireland was not an official sanction by the United States of partition, and that the neutrality of the rest of Ireland would not be infringed. He had failed to get this latter guarantee from Britain. If he could get it from America, it would be a considerable help to the policy of neutrality.

On the first point, partition, Sumner Welles assured Bob Brennan that the American action did not involve any question of principle. The second point, the danger that the United States troops were going to attack Irish forces and take over the whole country, was referred by Welles to President Roosevelt. The latter, in a personal message to de Valera, gave an assurance that there was not, and is not now, the slightest thought or intention of invading Irish territory or threatening Irish security.[24]

Although Roosevelt's message in late February, 1942, eased some of the tension caused by the uncertainty as to what might follow the American landing in the northern counties, it did not end de Valera's anxiety. Indeed, the entry of America into the war brought the first rift among Irish public representatives on the issue of neutrality. The deputy, however, who advocated an abandonment of the policy was disowned by his own party and was in a minority of one. The solidarity of the nation behind the policy had not been shaken. Some sense of relaxation prevailed. The liaison between British and Irish forces which had been built up in case of German invasion continued. It was even extended to include Americans, but the Irish doubted whether David Gray was fully informed by his British colleague of the extent of the liaison. It was felt among officials in the Department for External Affairs in Dublin that Maffey was allowing Gray to raise problems without fully informing him of the relations between the British and Irish security services. These feelings may or may not have been justified.

There were, of course, uncomfortable and disturbing incidents such as, for example, the seizure of the Irish diplomatic bag, destined for the Irish Legation at Lisbon, from an Irish boat at Swansea. The Irish High Commissioner in London took up the question with Mr Attlee, who was then in charge of the Dominions Office. He was genuinely shocked, yet it was only with difficulty that the bag was recovered from the censorship centre at Liverpool.[25] In fact, the whole question of the censorship of Irish mail caused some difficulty. After transatlantic flights were restarted in May, 1942, Gray tried to get the Irish Government to send all Irish mail to Britain for censoring, before putting it on the planes at Foynes.[26] There was no objection to mail ordinarily passing through Britain being censored by the British, but there was objection to having to send letters for America to Liverpool before being despatched.

These, however, were minor annoyances. Much graver issues arose from the conviction of six young men in Belfast for shooting a police constable on Easter Sunday, 1942. They were tried in the following July and all were sentenced to death. If any action could revive the IRA, a mass execution on that scale would be sure to do so. It would undoubtedly lead to renewed and increased activity. De Valera did all in his power to prevent the executions. He spoke earnestly to David Gray, then got the Irish Minister in Washington to approach the State Department and urge them to use their good offices. The United States Ambassador in London took up the matter with Anthony Eden, Secretary of State for Foreign Affairs. De Valera, indeed, used every diplomatic line possible to save the lives of the young men.

Five of them were reprieved and de Valera, who was in Cork when he heard this, instructed Joseph P. Walshe, by telephone, to send a personal message to Churchill regarding the one remaining. He said:

> The saving at this last moment, through your personal intervention, of the life of young Williams, who is to be executed on Wednesday morning in Belfast, would profoundly affect public feeling here. I know the difficulties, but results would justify, and I urge strongly that you do it.[27]

It was the only personal appeal which de Valera addressed to Churchill and it failed. Maffey told Walshe that he was certain that the addition of a fifth man to the four whom the British had decided to reprieve had been due to de Valera. But he was not to be consoled when, on September 1st, he received the final decision that the British Government had refused to intervene. There were some outbreaks of IRA violence the next day when Williams was executed, but the reprieve of the five had at least stabilized public opinion, and there was no increase in the strength of the militant movement. In fact, it was considerably weakened during that year.

MOUNTING PRESSURES

1942 – 1945

With Germany occupied in the east in 1942, the principal problems for Irish neutrality arose from relations with the United States. In July of that year, de Valera objected strongly to American publicity about the completion of the base at Derry. It was calculated, he felt, to draw German bombing raids on that part of Ireland and lead to loss of Irish lives in a manner which might endanger neutrality in the rest of Ireland. Despite this, however, from the first landing of American forces in the Six Counties, de Valera had shown a benevolent attitude towards them. On the day after the first Americans landed, he ordered that an American Eagle Squadron flier, who had landed at Dublin Airport by mistake, be secretly given fuel and sent off across the border.[1]

Connivance of this kind continued for some time until, at the end of the year, a new formula was suggested by the State Department which would regularize matters without infringing neutrality. Hitherto both German and British airmen who landed in Ireland had been interned. Now it was decided that only those who made forced landings during *operational* flights would be held. This, of course, was open to more favourable interpretation in the case of American and British pilots than in the case of Germans, who were less likely to be on training flights over Ireland.

The policy was not embarked upon without rousing the German Minister to make a protest. Time and again, during 1942 and 1943, he objected to the release of British and American airmen and on July 27th, 1943, he presented a formal note of protest. De Valera, however, stood by the policy which he explained publicly in the Dáil. Those who were engaged on operational flights were detained and their crews interned. The others were released.[2]

In the meantime, the relative peace and quiet of neutral Ireland tended to lull people into a false sense of security in a warring world. There were signs of this in the General Election which was fought in the summer of 1943. Some members of the Dáil urged that its life be extended beyond the five years laid down by law, but de Valera strongly opposed this. He was ever willing to consult the people; this time he was particularly anxious to test public feeling on such controversial issues as his handling of the IRA problem. By special legislation the existing Dáil was kept in being until the new Dáil was elected.

The election was held on June 22nd, under conditions less than favourable to de Valera and the Fianna Fáil Party. Ireland's neutrality by that date seemed assured. It had been respected by Great Britain when the temptation to infringe it was greatest and now, with war receding from the shores, the Government's claim to be the only safe custodian of neutrality lost its force. Against it were opened the gates of criticism, much of which had been previously curbed by a sense of national danger. Of course there were grievances arising out of all the shortages and restrictions of wartime, but de Valera was in no way deterred.

There were a number of extreme Republican candidates, including one internee, Seán McCool, Chief of Staff of the IRA. He was offered parole to carry on his election campaign in Donegal East, but refused it and went on hunger-strike instead. Nevertheless, he polled only 1,961 votes out of 34,472 valid votes cast. Indeed, all the candidates who might be considered extremist fared badly.

A new party, Clann na Talmhan, however, representing particularly the small farmers of Munster and Connacht entered the field and met with some success. It won ten seats, to which number may be added five others returned as independent farmers. Labour also made a substantial gain. The result was a disappointment for de Valera. His party, with 67 deputies returned, finished with ten seats less than it had won in 1938.

But if the result was a disappointment for him, it was nothing less than catastrophic for the leading Opposition party, Fine Gael. It won but 32 seats as against its previous 45. The principal point which emerged from the election was the growth of interest groups, such as those representing labour and farmers. The inherent weaknesses of the system of proportional representation were illustrated—in Fianna Fáil eyes at least.

De Valera's party remained by far the largest party in the Dáil and, when his name was proposed as Taoiseach, it was not opposed by any party except Fine Gael and a few independents. The position could scarcely be considered satisfactory. A coalition of the 71 deputies of the Opposition could at any time unseat the Government, but de Valera was determined to carry on without entering into any bargains with, or commitments to, other parties.

His precarious position did not make him deviate from his party's policies. He was as firm in withstanding the pressures of hunger-strikers as he had been in 1940.[3] The election, however, had brought in a more carefree attitude on the part of a very small number of deputies. DeValera, in March, 1944, protested that certain deputies were obviously specializing in asking questions which appeared to be aimed at embroiling the country with one or other of the belligerents.[4]

This was at the time of a particularly dangerous crisis which seemed to spring right out of the blue. Yet it had been maturing for a considerable time in the ever-active brain of the American Minister, David Gray. In May, 1943, he had put forward a series of suggestions to the American State Department, in the course of a long and tendentious memorandum on Ireland.[5] He suggested that a demand for the lease of air and port facilities be presented to de Valera on behalf of the Allies. He also proposed that de Valera be asked to remove the diplomatic representatives of Axis nations and that he be asked to clarify the position of Ireland in regard to the British Commonwealth. An unsatisfactory answer to any of these demands would be followed by the shutting off of raw materials for Irish industries. Finally Gray raised, as an effective means of forcing an issue with de Valera, the possibility of imposing conscription in the partitioned Six Counties. The proposals were sent to Roosevelt, who asked Cordell Hull, Secretary of State, for his opinion.

Cordell Hull favoured them, provided they had a sound military basis, and suggested getting the views of the United States Joint Chiefs of Staff on this question. Their opinion, signed by General George C. Marshall, is of much significance. They concluded that, while the ports of the Bay of Biscay were in German hands, it would be inexpedient to route convoys to the South of England, and that air or naval bases in Ireland would not appreciably alter that position. Indeed, they recommended that, if an approach were made to Ireland for naval or air facilities, no commitment should be made that bases would be established there.

This memorandum from the United States Joint Chiefs of Staff confirms the long-held opinion of the Irish Government as to the real military importance of the ports. In an exaggerated form, the issue had become a prime subject of anti-Irish propaganda.[5] Some Americans appear to have been eager, nevertheless, to take issue with de Valera. They envisaged a personal message from Roosevelt, saying that it would be helpful in planning their war strategy if they knew that naval and air bases in Ireland would be available to them. Gray discussed this with Sir John Maffey and with the Canadian High Commissioner in Dublin, John D. Kearney, and pointed out that the whole purpose which he had in mind was political and not military, that it was aimed to get de Valera on record as refusing the ports, so as to undermine any effort which he might make after the war to appeal to American public opinion on the partition question.[6]

The Americans submitted their proposed note to the British Government but, though Churchill was in favour of it, his cabinet was much divided. In fact, Gray felt that Churchill's only supporter on this issue was Herbert Morrison, Secretary of State for Home Affairs. The matter dragged on for several months, the British acting as a brake on American impetuosity. Just before Christmas, Anthony Eden emphasized the British view that the American proposal 'would be likely to give rise to acute difficulties.'[7]

As the years passed, Gray had grown more and more hostile to Ireland and he was not satisfied to let matters rest. Baulked on one line of attack on de Valera, he tried to open another. Even before the final decision against an approach on the air and naval facilities, he was already putting forward a draft note to be presented to de Valera, demanding the removal of German and Japanese diplomats from Dublin.[8] This suggestion received more support. It involved no military commitment and so met with no opposition from the Joint Chiefs of Staff. The American Ambassador in London, John G. Winant, found Lord Cranborne, the Dominions Secretary, favourable. By February 10th, 1944, the British Government had signified its approval and arrangements were made that a British note would be presented to de Valera a day or two after Gray presented the note from America.

On the afternoon of February 21st, David Gray called on de Valera at Government Buildings in Dublin. Gray recorded:

> He read and re-read certain passages slowly . . . He betrayed no anger as he often had done when confronted with an unacceptable proposal, but he looked very sour and grim. When he reached the next to the last page the purport of the note became clear, he paused and said: 'Of course, the answer will be no; as long as I am here, it will be no.' He read a few lines further and paused again, asking me: 'Is this an ultimatum?'[9]

Gray replied that he did not believe so. Nonetheless, Sir John Maffey called on de Valera the next day and presented a note stating that the British Government had been consulted by the Americans and approved of the demand.

De Valera was deeply concerned about possible steps which might be taken to force compliance. He saw in it a conspiracy to exert pressure on a weak neutral. He never doubted that interference with Ireland's neutrality was an infringement of the country's sovereignty.

The American note was framed in such a way as to charge Ireland with providing 'the opportunity for highly organized espionage'. 'Axis Agents', it said, 'enjoy almost unrestricted opportunity for bringing information of vital importance from Great Britain and Northern Ireland into Ireland, and from there transmitting it by various routes and methods to Germany.' It charged that the Axis representatives had used their diplomatic privileges 'as a cloak for espionage' and mentioned the

German Legation radio as evidence of this. It concluded by asking 'as an absolute minimum the removal of these Axis Representatives.'[10] It was these words which seemed to make the document an ultimatum.

In the circumstances of the time, de Valera knew that the war was drawing to an end. Information from the Irish Chargé d'Affaires in Berlin had told him that there were few optimists left in Germany. There was no sign of an immediate collapse, but the end was inevitable. De Valera could easily abandon neutrality without incurring much risk for Ireland. But that was not his way. Irish independence of action had to be preserved despite outside pressures. He knew, too, that the note was drafted with a purpose in mind, beyond that of getting rid of the legations in Dublin. In a draft for a reply he noted this when he said:

> The request was one to which it must have been known by the American Minister here, the Irish Government could not possibly accede . . . It seemed designed therefore to put the Irish people in the wrong before the American public, in the case of certain contingencies occurring.[11]

He was aware of the malevolent stories which newspapers in Britain and the United States might carry—the thousands of British and American lives lost in bringing food to Ireland, the diplomatic bags and couriers going to Berlin, the refuelling of German submarines in lonely Irish creeks, even the hundreds of Japanese tourists which were said to have reached Ireland. It would be impossible to catch up with the lies. The only answer would be to reveal the full extent of the collaboration which existed between the Irish intelligence service and those of Britain and America. In fact that co-operation could be jeopardized by the note. It was feared the information which had been discovered and given by the Irish service to the Allies might be published as proof of the use of Ireland as a base for espionage against Britain.

The first effort to deal with the situation, which de Valera made, was to call in the Canadian High Commissioner to ask him, as the representative of a friendly power not involved in the *démarche*, to ask his Government to intervene to have the notes withdrawn. This the Canadians refused to do, though the message which the High Commissioner gave de Valera on February 26th indicated that, had they been consulted beforehand, they would not have supported the presentation of a formal demand. Indeed, de Valera understood that they deplored the whole manner in which the American request had been conveyed. The Irish High Commissioner in London, John Dulanty, approached the Australian representative there, S. M. Bruce, in the hope of getting his support against the pressure, but again without success.[12]

In Ireland, de Valera kept leading members of the Opposition informed of the course which events were taking. There was strong support for a firm stand against pressure from the Labour and Clann na Talmhan spokesmen, William Davin and Michael Donnellan. The Fine Gael leaders, General Mulcahy, Dr T. F. O'Higgins and Patrick McGilligan, did not give any indication of their attitude, largely because de Valera was stating the policy of his Government, rather than trying to commit them to supporting it. Indeed, when Mulcahy asked that he and his colleagues be shown a copy of the reply which it was intended to send to the American request, de Valera thought this inadvisable. The responsibility for the reply must rest on the Government, but he agreed to let them see it shortly after it was sent.[13]

But he was determined to avoid provocation. He diplomatically endeavoured to obtain assurances that, in the inevitable event of his refusing the American request, there would not be an invasion of Irish territory. Bob Brennan, the Irish Minister in Washington, raised the question with the State Department, and was informed that the note was not an ultimatum and that Roosevelt's message of February, 1942, that there was no intention of invading Ireland, still stood.[14] This was confirmed by Gray who met de Valera on February 29th. Some of the anxiety was now removed from the crisis, but there remained the implicit threat of a publicity campaign against Ireland. However, Gray gave a clear indication that there was no intention of launching such a campaign.[15]

Armed with these guarantees, de Valera sent his carefully drafted reply on March 6th to the Irish Legation in Washington, for transmission to the State Department. Before him, as he prepared his reply, de Valera had drafts prepared by Joseph P. Walshe, Secretary of the Department of External Affairs, Maurice Moynihan, Secretary of the Government, and Frank Gallagher, Director of the Government Information Bureau. But, as usual, the document which he produced was completely his own. It avoided all details of the extent of Ireland's co-operation with American and British intelligence services, but pointed out the success with which the Government had dealt with espionage attempts. He did not corroborate these, as he might have done, by quoting the tributes which had been paid to the Irish Government on these grounds by Americans and Britons who were aware of the facts. His conclusion was firm:

> The Irish Government are . . . safeguarding, and will continue to safeguard, the interests of the United States, but they must in all circumstances protect the neutrality of the Irish State and the democratic way of life of the Irish people. Their attitude will continue to be determined, not by fear of any measures which could be employed against them, but by goodwill and the fundamental friendship existing between the two peoples.[16]

It was a reserved and diplomatic reply. It would have been strengthened by more information on the intelligence activities but if, by any chance, such details had been revealed, it could have given grounds for a German protest. When the note and the reply were published, the Germans had no grounds for grievance. But de Valera's reply was scarcely complete enough to persuade the American or British public that Irish counter-intelligence was an effective force.

As it happened, the publication of the notes caused considerable embarrassment to David Gray. He endeavoured to prove that the leakage of information which led to their publication occurred in Dublin. The evidence is inconclusive as to where and how it happened. De Valera was unable to resolve whether the leakage was a deliberate attempt to increase the pressure on him or not. Be that as it may, the publicity initiated a British and American press campaign, the Irish reaction to which caused David Gray an unhappy time. It was felt necessary to put a guard on the American Legation and to give the Minister a police escort, though this was withdrawn at his request.

Gray found that the note had caused both anger and alarm in Ireland, and had rallied the people around de Valera. He, who had been largely the cause of the note being sent, now did all in his power to prevent the State Department from sending a second one. He was particularly perturbed when Churchill, within a few days of the publication of the note and of the reply, announced measures isolating Ireland from Britain. 'No one, I think, can reproach us for precipitancy,' he said. 'No nation in the world would have been so patient.'[17] Churchill, at this stage was continuing his policy of playing on Irish fears. He wrote to Roosevelt on March 19th:

> It is too soon to begin reassuring de Valera. A doctor telling his patient that medicine prescribed for his nerve trouble is only coloured water is senseless. To keep them guessing for a while would be better in my opinion . . . I think that we should let fear work its healthy process, rather than to allay alarm in de Valera's circles.[18]

The British Government's measures were aimed at restricting all trade between Ireland and Britain, mainly as a safeguard against any leakage of information regarding the opening of the Second Front. The whole tone of Churchill's speech was to give the impression that these pre-cautionary measures were in the nature of sanctions. Joseph P. Walshe, on behalf of de Valera, took up this question with Sir John Maffey. The latter gave the impression that the series of events began under pressure from Eisenhower. He personally felt sure that there would be no sanctions and, in one of three interviews around St Patrick's Day, he even intimated that Lord Cranborne would resign if sanctions were imposed.

Maffey was eager to let matters cool off, but undoubtedly the general attitude of the British Government at this time helped to maintain the heat. The announcement by Britain, without any consultation or warning, of measures which to the public appeared punitive, though explained to the Irish Government afterwards as precautionary, was not calculated to maintain harmony. The same results or better could have been obtained by co-operation. The mere one-sided announcement itself was enough to give the measures the appearance of sanctions. Churchill's speech had been unrelieved by any tribute whatever to what the Irish Government had done by way of co-operation over the previous four years. In private he might admit to Roosevelt that the Irish measures to prevent espionage were 'not so bad', but he gave not the slightest inkling of this publicly. In fact de Valera did not get any definite guarantee that sanctions were not intended by Britain.

The measures adopted by Britain involved considerable hardship in Ireland. They included the cutting of coal supplies, already dangerously low, in half, with consequent repercussions on those dependent on gas for cooking. On the Irish side, the granting of travel permits to those who wished to work in England was suspended for a time. As Walshe explained to Maffey—

> It would hardly be fair of the Government to allow more workers to go over to England so long as the press and the radio were accusing them of being potential spies and a menace to British security. The presence of more workers could only make the situation worse.

In the end, the tension gradually eased off. The Americans, advised by their Ambassador in London and their Minister in Dublin, and by Lord Cranborne, decided against sending a second note to de Valera. Churchill, too, appears to have felt that a second note was not necessary. They might feel that they had gained something in the way of tightening security measures, but they had lost much goodwill. The one man to gain from it all in terms of further standing was the man whom Gray had hoped to damage. De Valera had emerged once more as the strong leader and the Irish people rallied behind him.

Internationally, too, despite the fever of war, his voice was heard. As the war progressed and the American and British troops moved into Italy, de Valera became anxious about the loss to civilization which might occur because of bombing attacks on Rome. In March, 1944, he sent an appeal to the principal belligerent countries, after consultation with the Papal Nuncio, Pascal Robinson. On behalf of his people, he called attention to:

> the deep distress which they feel, a distress shared by the three hundred million Catholics throughout the world, at the danger now threatening the

City of Rome and at the absence of any measures by the belligerent Powers to ensure its safety. It is clear to all that, if the City be militarily defended by the one side and by the other attacked, its destruction is inevitable.

He went on to request the belligerents to agree to save Rome, 'this great centre of Christian Faith and civilization.'[19] He wrote a letter to the German Minister, Hempel, enclosing a resolution passed by the administrative council of the Irish Labour Party on the same subject and received the reassuring information that the German authorities had issued strict instructions to keep Rome free from German soldiers. Even the railways of Rome were being by-passed by military traffic.

It is difficult to assess how far de Valera's intervention had led to this decision, but in the event Rome was saved indubitably from destruction. Some people in Rome, at least, felt that de Valera should be thanked and they sent to him an address of gratitude, signed by some hundreds of artists, scholars, scientists and musicians of the city:

> Rome . . . is for us the very reason of life, and it is easy to understand our emotion when we think that a son of such a far away country has tried to keep it from being harmed, just as if he himself felt himself to be a son of Rome. We Italians feel you to be a brother, and the attachments of affection and thanks between Italy and Ireland will never weaken. The memory of this noble gesture on the part of Ireland's Prime Minister will pass on also to future generations.[20]

Internally in Ireland, however, despite the solidarity of all parties on the neutrality question, de Valera saw continuous danger in carrying on a Government supported by a minority of the elected deputies. On May 9th, 1944, his Government was narrowly defeated on a vote on a transport bill and he resigned. He had carried on for eleven months as Leader of a minority Government. He had been reluctant to take the initiative of going to the country again so soon to resolve the difficulty. The defeat of his Government, however, gave him good reason for resigning, even though he might well have won a vote of confidence on the following day.

The election campaign was brief. De Valera had many advantages. The Opposition parties were badly disorganized. Indeed, Fianna Fáil was the only party to nominate sufficient candidates to win a majority. Labour had split into two groups in January, and Fine Gael had not recovered its confidence after the setback it had suffered the previous year. A greatly respected leader, W. T. Cosgrave, had just retired from politics owing to ill-health. And de Valera had another unwitting ally in the American Minister.

Not that David Gray ever saw himself as a canvasser for de Valera or his party. In 1941 and 1942, he reiterated time and time again that his main hopes rested on the Opposition. The 1943 election came as a sad blow. That summer, however, during a visit to Washington in which he laid the foundations for the American note, he informed Seán Nunan, who was on the staff of the Irish Legation there, that he saw a new chance of getting rid of de Valera and getting access to the Irish ports. This time he was resting his hopes, not on the Opposition, but on the emergence of Seán Moylan as an opponent to de Valera within the Fianna Fáil party itself.

Gray showed his naïveté in telling this to Seán Nunan, whose loyalty to de Valera was not only that of a civil servant to his Minister, but that of a fellow-patriot who had shared in every aspect of the Irish struggle since the 1916 Rising. He showed a complete lack of understanding of Irish affairs in thinking that Seán Moylan would either try to or succeed in ousting de Valera from the leadership of Fianna Fáil. Indeed, all Gray's plans reacted against him. The American note, however much Churchill might persuade himself that it led to the tightening of security arrangements, benefited nobody except de Valera. At the time of the 1943 election, neutrality was taken for granted. All danger seemed to have receded. This sense of security had been rudely disturbed by the American-British *démarche* which strengthened de Valera's prestige.

The 1944 election was to have a double effect. The calling of it put an end to any idea which the Americans might still have of sending a further note regarding the Axis representatives in Dublin. The result of it was to place de Valera's Government firmly in office. It was returned with 76 seats, fourteen more than all others combined. De Valera might well have thanked the American Minister. In one sense, international issues had played no part in the election campaign; all parties were united on neutrality, but voters were undoubtedly influenced by the certainty that de Valera would withstand all pressures.

The victory of de Valera's party strengthened him against the heavy weight being brought to bear on all neutrals as the Allies moved forward to final victory. There were minor concessions, but they were more than balanced by the firmness with which de Valera withstood the major demands. When David Gray, in September 1944, asked for assurances that what he described as 'Axis war criminals' would not be given asylum in Ireland, de Valera's reply was that his Government would 'give no assurance which would preclude them from exercising that right [to asylum] should justice, charity or the honour or interest of the nation so require.'[21] He did, however, point out that it was, since the war began, the uniform practice of the Government to deny admission to all aliens whose presence would be at variance with the policy of neutrality or likely to damage either Irish interests or those of friendly states. This practice was not likely to be altered. Gray was far from satisfied.

To the end, de Valera maintained Ireland's position of neutrality.
There was a sense of balance which annoyed the victors. When Roosevelt
died on April 12th, 1945, he sent a message of sympathy to President
Truman: 'America,' he said, 'has lost a great man and a noble leader'.
He moved the adjournment of the Dáil out of respect and called on the
American Minister. It was more than a formal gesture for he had held
Roosevelt in high esteem. He said in the Dáil:

> President Roosevelt will go down to history as one of the greatest of a long
> line of American Presidents with the unparalleled distinction of having been
> elected four times as head of the United States. That was the greatest tribute
> that could be paid to any man. It is also a measure of his loss. Personally, I
> regard his death as a loss to the world, for I believe his whole career has
> shown that he could ultimately be depended upon, when this war had ended,
> to throw his great influence behind and devote his great energy to the
> establishment of a world organisation which would be just and which, being
> just, could hope to save humanity from recurring calamities like the present
> war.[22]

But shortly afterwards, with the war a few weeks from its end,
de Valera took a step which caused outraged cries throughout Britain and
America. Hitler died on 30th April, 1945, and de Valera, accompanied
by Joseph P. Walshe, paid a formal call of condolence on the German
Minister. Nothing that he did at any time in the war was so unpopular
in allied countries. He wrote a personal letter to Bob Brennan in
Washington, to explain his point of view:

> I have noted that my call on the German Minister on the announcement of
> Hitler's death was played up to the utmost. I expected this. I could have had
> a diplomatic illness but, as you know, I would scorn that sort of thing . . .
> So long as we retained our diplomatic relations with Germany, to have failed
> to call upon the German representative would have been an act of unpardon-
> able discourtesy to the German nation and to Dr Hempel himself. During
> the whole of the war, Dr Hempel's conduct was irreproachable. He was
> always friendly and invariably correct—in marked contrast with Gray. I
> certainly was not going to add to his humiliation in the hour of defeat.

He went on to add another reason for his action.

> It would establish a bad precedent. It is of considerable importance that the
> formal acts of courtesy paid on such occasions as the death of a head of a
> State should not have attached to them any further special significance, such
> as connoting approval or disapproval of the policies of the State in question,
> or of its head. It is important that it should never be inferred that these
> formal acts imply the passing of any judgments, good or bad.

He was anxious that Brennan should know his mind; he had carefully

refrained from attempting to give any explanation in public. 'An explanation would have been interpreted as an excuse, and an excuse as a
consciousness of having acted wrongly. I acted correctly, and, I feel
certain, wisely'.[23] There was probably never a moment when de Valera
was quite so unpopular in England. As the war passions have faded, a
better understanding has manifested itself, and even a reluctant admiration. Once again, as when he refused the German offer of a deal on
partition, when their victory seemed certain in 1940, he acted according
to principle.

A week after de Valera visited the German Minister, the latter called
to make arrangements for an announcement that the legation had been
vacated, and that it was being placed in charge of the Irish Government
'until the assumption of the government of the Reich by the new
authority'. By this time the war was over.

De Valera's policy of neutrality had achieved its purpose in face of
endless hazards. It was a remarkable group effort in which Joseph P.
Walshe and his colleagues of the Department for External Affairs played
an important role, as did the Irish representatives abroad, especially
J. W. Dulanty, who occupied a post of danger in London, and Bob
Brennan, who weathered many storms in America. Not less important in
this fulfilment was the character of two diplomats in Dublin, Sir John
Maffey and Edouard Hempel.

There were also the military and economic factors. Ireland's position
never became one of absolute military importance to either set of
belligerents. The bases in the North protected the only convoy route
possible as long as Germany held the French ports. But nothing could
detract from the diplomatic skill and leadership of de Valera and his
unshakeable nerve. It was he who gave the Irish representatives their
instructions. He was aided by the solidarity of Irish public opinion behind
his policy and by the support of the Opposition parties. Many press
campaigns in Britain and America were made and resisted. To give only
one example, even a normally moderate paper like the *Economist* called
on the British Government in 1940 to invade Ireland and seize the ports
by force.

Persistence was the keynote of de Valera's diplomacy, persistence in
keeping the lines of communication open, even with the most difficult of
diplomats in the most serious of crises, persistence too in asserting
Ireland's right to neutrality and the Irish determination to protect it
against any attack.

Realism, too, marked his whole approach to the problems. Neutrality
was a realistic policy in Irish circumstances, as one on which the nation
could unite. There was realism, too, in the lack of rigidity in the successive

adaptations of policy. De Valera could bend a little under pressure, but never give an inch on anything he judged essential. Always he impressed the diplomats with whom he dealt with his absolute integrity.

The war was over, but there was to be a final climax in the battle of wills between Churchill and de Valera. The British Prime Minister broadcast a victory speech on May 13th, 1945, in the course of which he made a bitter attack on de Valera. 'Had it been necessary,' he said, 'we should have been forced to come to close quarters with Mr de Valera.' He went on:

> With a restraint and poise to which, I venture to say, history will find few parallels, His Majesty's Government never laid a violent hand upon them, though at times it would have been quite easy and quite natural, and we left the de Valera government to frolic with the German and later with the Japanese representatives to their hearts' content.

All Ireland waited for de Valera's reply. It came three days later in an address from Radio Éireann, though de Valera had the first draft of his speech ready the evening after Churchill's broadcast. The morning of Wednesday, May 16th, he spent at work on the manuscript. He approached the radio station in Dublin's main thoroughfare without difficulty. Everyone was near a radio to listen. Speaking at first, as was his custom, in Irish and then in English, he thanked God for the end of the war which had devastated Europe and for the fact that Ireland had been spared. He thanked all who had contributed to saving the nation, the political parties and sections of the community, members of the defence forces and other services whose united stand had been so important. He warned of trials ahead, shortages and restrictions which could pass but slowly. Help must be given to nations less fortunate than Ireland. Many a listener wondered when he would reach the section which all awaited. Then it came, about two-thirds of the way through:

> Certain newspapers have been very persistent in looking for my answer to Mr Churchill's recent broadcast. I know the kind of answer I am expected to make. I know the answer that first springs to the lips of every man of Irish blood who heard or read that speech, no matter in what circumstances or in what part of the world he found himself. I know the reply I would have given a quarter of a century ago. But I have deliberately decided that that is not the reply I shall make tonight.

Throughout Ireland, ears strained to hear the calm and simple voice which made excuses for Churchill's statement in the first flush of victory. 'No such excuse could be found for me in this quieter atmosphere'. Then he continued dispassionately:

> Mr Churchill makes it clear that, in certain circumstances, he would have

violated our neutrality and that he would justify his action by Britain's necessity. It seems strange to me that Mr Churchill does not see that this, if it be accepted, would mean that Britain's necessity would become a moral code and that, when this necessity became sufficiently great, other people's rights were not to count. It is quite true that other great powers believe in this same code—in their own regard—and have behaved in accordance with it. That is precisely why we have the disastrous succession of wars—World War No. 1 and World War No. 2—and shall it be World War No. 3?

He even turned to praise Churchill for resisting the temptation, which he knew must have been strong at times, to infringe Irish rights:

It is, indeed, hard for the strong to be just to the weak. But acting justly always has its rewards. By resisting his temptation in this instance, Mr Churchill, instead of adding another horrid chapter to the already blood-stained record of the relations between England and this country, has advanced the cause of international morality an important step . . .

De Valera mentioned how partition poisoned Anglo-Irish relations and then adverted to Churchill's pride in Britain's stand alone after France had fallen:

Could he not find in his heart the generosity to acknowledge that there is a small nation that stood alone not for one year or two, but for several hundred years against aggression; that endured spoliations, was clubbed many times into insensibility, but that each time on returning consciousness took up the fight anew; a small nation that could never be got to accept defeat and has never surrendered her soul?

It was a speech of deep sincerity as well as of considerable skill. A little tribute within it to Neville Chamberlain appealed even to some English consciences, for they had been harsh in their judgements. But the speech fell first on Irish ears and it raised Irish hearts as they had seldom been raised. A large crowd had flowed out to O'Connell Street from listening to his speech, to cheer him as his car left the radio station. His secretary, Kathleen O'Connell, noted in her diary, 'Phone was ringing all night'. The next day the telegrams and letters of congratulations flowed in. 'No speech ever made such an appeal,' noted Kathleen O'Connell. As he entered the Dáil the following afternoon there was an unprecedented demonstration of enthusiasm. Never had he spoken so clearly for the nation and never had the nation been so proud of him.

INTERLUDE

INTERLUDE

THE FAMILY MAN

Seven children were born to Eamon and Sinéad de Valera between 1910 and 1922. Between 1916 and 1924, there were only two very hectic years, 1917–18, and from July, 1921, to the first six torturing months of 1922, when he was neither in jail, nor on the run, nor in America. A strange atmosphere to be reared in. Yet as parents, Eamon and Sinéad de Valera passed with flying colours the two most obvious tests—the devotion of the children and the success of these children in life. The first of these emerges at every point from notes supplied to the authors by various members of the family. It is symbolized by the image of Vivion, the eldest, taking his father's place, as a boy of twelve, with the young Erskine Childers at a great meeting during his father's imprisonment in 1923.

Nine years later, it is Vivion again who acts as bodyguard, revolver showing through his overcoat, when his father takes his place as the new Head of the Government. The worldly success of an unworldly family has been astonishing, and possibly unequalled. Out of six surviving children, three are professors, one married a professor, four hold university doctorates and one is Taxing Master of the High Court and a leading solicitor. But they are all very modest in their appraisal of their own abilities, compared with those of their father. In mathematics, only Vivion is credited with a comparable gift. Yet Brian, who died in a riding accident, also showed promise in this direction and the fact that the eldest grandchild—Emer's daughter, Nora—won a travelling studentship in mathematics was a source of much satisfaction to her grandfather.

There is no doubt among them about their father's profound concern for their welfare and education as children; some differences exist as to his power of communication with them, when they were small. Máirín has already been quoted several times: 'Among the pleasant memories of my later school days', she writes, 'are drives in the car with my father at the wheel. My mother has never been a good traveller, but she enjoyed Sunday afternoon drives around Dublin and Wicklow. She often teased my father about forcing the car to take hills. She called him Eamon An Chnuic (Ned of the Hill).

'My mother never went on long drives down to the country; she was too busy making home comfortable, and helping us with home lessons, but she wanted us to see as much as we could of the "little country". She believed that Ireland is much more beautiful, and much more fertile, than any other country on the face of the earth.'

Máirín loved those long drives when her father had to go to meetings and conferences in remote parts of the country. It was a family joke that he charged a fare by making his passenger recite long mathematical formulas and listen to tedious oral solutions of mathematical problems. 'But we really loved the trips', says Máirín, 'especially when he decided to take a detour, in order to show us some ruin or some interesting feature of the countryside.'

Emer, whose husband is today a professor and Director of the School of Celtic Studies, again seems to have found it easy to get close to him from early days. A very early recollection of hers is being brought to Arbour Hill Military Prison to visit her father. 'My mother took the two girls with her, and it now seems strange to me that I took it so much for granted that my father was in jail.'

He was in jail in Belfast just before she was confirmed, and apparently he asked the chaplain for a life of St Theresa. The great St Theresa was intended, but he was brought a life of the 'Little Flower'. He was disappointed at first, but when he read it, he was very much taken with her great strength and wonderful courage. 'He wrote to my mother, to say that he would like me to take Theresa as my name in confirmation which, of course, I did. Ten years later, he took me with him to Lisieux, where we had the privilege of meeting the sisters of the "Little Flower" in Carmel—my father had continued to be devoted to her.'

Her baptismal names were always a joke at home. 'I had three, which was considered a lot: Íde, for my father's County of Limerick, Emer, because my mother loved it as a name, and Clare, because I was born in 1918 after the Clare by-election, and when it was suggested that I should have a Clare Saint's name, someone said: "why not the County name?"' She often got quite indignant as a child, when nuns at school tried to make out that her patron Saint was St Clare. 'I used to protest that I was called after the County'.

When she was about ten years of age, she had taken to walking to and from school, instead of going by train. Her father measured the distance in the car; the fact that she walked four miles a day gave her great satisfaction and a great feeling of achievement. She was very proud of his interest and praise. 'He then took to walking in with me in the mornings (for perhaps a month or two), and to teaching me my tables on the way, and also telling me *Séadna* in the folk version he had heard at home in Limerick.'

Later on—in 1934—he was very proud of a certificate which she gave him, to say that for several weeks he had risen at 7.45 each morning, and had brought her into school in town, leaving home at 8.40. In fact, he kept the certificate and finally returned it to her quite recently.

A great, but sensible, love of animals was evident in the home always. 'We had a really beloved dog called Nessa. She came to us on July 12th and so had to have a Northern name.' Both parents taught them to love and observe the plants and animals around them. Their father especially liked to watch the stars and to point out the more important constellations.

Ruairí tells many stories of his father which should one day see the light. There is room for only three of them here. 'One day, Daddy came in with two men, Harry Boland and Michael Collins. We went out with them in a car. We stopped below a steep wooded slope—perhaps the Glen of the Downs, or Glencullen. Daddy and the other men went up the hill. After a while, they came back with what seemed to me to be a Bovril packet. They were discussing how well Daddy had hit the target.' De Valera, in fact, was always fond of shooting with shotgun, rifle or revolver and was reckoned an excellent shot. 'That night', goes on Ruairí, 'we were allowed to stay up late. There was talk of putting me to bed, but one of the men—I think it was Michael Collins—said: "only bad boys go to bed early". I think I was let stay up.'

Another tale, of possibly more significance. 'In 18, Claremont Road, I think, soon after Daddy came out of jail, one evening Daddy was having his tea and I was playing with toy soldiers on the floor. He took an empty egg shell and threw it at some of the soldiers, saying: "There's a shell". I said: "Daddy you hit the wrong soldiers—these are the Irish". He said: "Who are the others?", and I said "the English". He said gently, "No, just call them the enemy". I think he did not want me to hate the English, or any other people. The enemy was impersonal.' It will be recalled that Malcolm MacDonald was struck by his lack of bitterness towards the British, in spite of his years in prison.

Ruairí recalls that 'Daddy always took Mummy's little teasing stories very well. There was one in particular I remember him using frequently. She had an old song: "I'll be there love at half-past nine", which described a man and his sweetheart arranging to meet at the end of the lane. The girl waited at one end, while the man waited at the other, so they did not meet. When Daddy heard the song for the first time, he remarked: "That's what comes from not giving specific instructions". Mummy often quotes the phrase still.'

'My first recollection of a normal situation', writes Terry, 'was to have my father in America and my mother at home, in gentle but firm control, not only of the day-to-day running of the house, but very much in command of the school-work. Father, on the other hand, meant little more than the tall, dark-haired, bespectacled, severe figure who occasionally appeared on the home scene.

'I have a very early recollection of my mother wanting me to take a certain medicine, which I had found extremely disagreeable. Childlike I, of course, protested, but that very tall dark figure was at home and he decided otherwise. Amid much struggling and protest, I was all too soon aware of a slimy, foul-smelling substance sliding down my throat. He had won.

'Later', says Terry, 'as I climbed the stairs, I remembered calling out "dirty fellow . . . filthy fellow, I wish he'd go back to jail again".'

His father used to tell this story with enormous gusto in after years. Jail, of course, seemed to the children to be a place where a self-respecting father might find himself from time to time.

The children vie with one another in tributes to their mother's nobility and dedication to them, and hardly less to her gifts of instruction. 'I know', says Terry, the youngest son, 'that my father would be the first to agree that such success in life as we all have enjoyed, is due in great part to her industry, management and sheer devotion to duty. What wonderfully kind memories I have, as she encouraged me on the stage, in the Gilbert and Sullivan operas in Blackrock College. Her love and knowledge of the stage is of course now well-known. It was then that she first wrote her plays for children. To her I owe so much, and my first liking for poetry.'

She would recite line after line, verse after verse of Byron, Shelley, Keats, Wordsworth and many others. The Irish poets such as Mangan, Rooney and Griffin, were specially dear.

Shakespeare had, of course, his rightful position. Perhaps her great favourite of those days was Gray's Elegy, which she would recite from beginning to end, as indeed she still can at the age of ninety-two. So deep was the impression which she made upon Terry, that he twice visited Stoke Poges, just to relive the poem. 'Mother encouraged me', he says, 'in every way as far as music is concerned and, while she never claimed to be musical, she had in fact a splendid ear and a sweet voice.'

'She loved singing', says Ruairí, 'and sang a lot herself; often sad, romantic songs: "In the gloaming", "We met, 'twas in a crowd", "Juanita".' She liked all her children to sing. Ruairí was very proud when he heard her say that he had a voice like a thrush. As might be expected, she was a great story-teller and read endlessly to her children, often in Irish. Each had his or her own special items. 'That was a thing about Mum'.

She spoke often about her father, mother and family. Odd little incidents were recalled. One uncle who was only late twice in his life. Her mother's good humour—how she used to see the funny side in everything. One Hallowe'en, an old woman in Balbriggan who did not want her door banged took it off the hinges and put it beside her near the hearth. 'Granny, that is Mummy's mother, came into the house and talked in her winning way to the cross old woman, then suddenly took a cabbage stalk from behind her back and dealt the door a resounding blow. Mummy half disapproved, yet wholeheartedly enjoyed the idea.'

Mrs de Valera was very ecumenical, in the modern phrase. She always emphasized how saintly her Protestant friends were.

'Old Miss Hawkes, who loved Brian—I remember her sitting outside the door, and Mummy telling me afterwards that she was a saint. Seoirse Irvine, Miss Wilson. . . Looking back on it, I think she saw these people as especially valuable, good, Irish and Christian.'

She held family life to be all-important. The children remember how sorry she was in Greystones for the little boy next door, who used to stand at the top window, looking wistfully down as they played in the back garden. He was an only child. 'Mummy pitied only children.' She considered food much more important for the family than respectability in dress. Not that the children lacked warm clothing, or were badly dressed in public. But the boys could get as untidy and dirty as they liked in the garden. She used to cite unnamed, respectable suburban families, who starved themselves for respectability and clothes. Ruairí remembers a cotton nightdress with red stripes which she made for him. An aunt remarked unfavourably on the cut. He replied: 'Sure, You wouldna' mind the shape'. It was comfortable. His mother quoted him for years after, in support of her prowess with the needle.

Mrs de Valera was frequently plagued with visitors. We have already heard of this from Máirín. 'We often laughed at how bothered she was when she heard the door bell, and then how charmingly she welcomed the caller, even though we knew well she would much prefer to be at her work and minding us.'

And then there were the cats: Pangur, Connie and Dinny, in turn. Cats loved her. They rolled for her, when she sang to them. They were very much part of the household. They could talk or, at least, she used to use a special voice and speak in their name. Sometimes, in this fashion, they used to interject quite devastating asides. 'Daddy was often slyly chided by them.'

'One day', remembers Terry, 'Mother wished to impress my father with some particular view or point, so she addressed father in Dinny's voice. Dinny, of course, was sitting dreamily in an armchair nearby. At once their father reacted, and like a flash turned round to look the dozing cat straight in the eye. With some force he exclaimed: "It is certainly not so!"'

Emer adds this footnote from later days: 'When we went away on holidays, we used to leave our cat at home and my father would call every day with food and milk for it, and he always made sure that the cat was in good health. In this way, the cat got to know him well.'

By common consent, Eamon and Sinéad were wonderful grandparents. Emer remembers Granny as a most important person in her children's lives. 'Sunday, in Blackrock' is something that the seven eldest talk of with love, and not a little nostalgia. Granny made all the cakes, scones and bread herself for the grandchildren's tea. 'She kept a big box of dressing-up clothes and jewellery, and in summer produced a series of memorable plays in the garden.'

Finally, some systematic notes from Éamonn who, as a doctor, came to have special opportunities of insight. He does not shut his eyes to early tensions. 'As a child, I feared my father, and resented his intrusion into our lives. He had been in prison and in America, and on his return I found it hard to accept the stricter discipline he enforced.' His mother was, he thinks, over-protective, and in some ways too easy on the children. He does not know how she was able to manage with so little money.

'Although my father loves children, he has not been able to communicate well with them. Looking back, I realize that he has never really appreciated the difficulties and shortcomings of minds less gifted than his own.' His father felt that he could grasp and follow mathematical arguments when, in simple fact, he had not this ability. In his mature years he remembered wistfully, and with regret, his father's attempts to teach him.

As he grew older, he gradually came to know and love his father. He was always very proud of him and shared his mother's intense loyalty to him. He found, in a sense, a security and complete trust in him and in his judgement.

Éamonn came to know his father best during his father's first serious illness in Zurich, in 1936, when, as a final medical student, he remained with him for six weeks. His younger brother had been killed on Sunday, February 9th, of that year, following a riding accident in Phoenix Park. 'Brian', says Terry, 'was a splendid horseman and riding was his pride and joy. For his part, I am sure he would have wished to die in no other way.' But his death, at the age of twenty, was shattering to the family. 'The effect upon my parents', says Terry, 'was immense, especially on my mother who had come through so much, and must now lose a son in this way.' In time to come, she would console another bereaved mother with the message, deliberately imparted: 'I would not have him back.' But that was years later. At the time, life had to go on, and they returned to the duty of living with renewed resolution and ardour.

It so happened, that this tragic loss was followed in de Valera's case by the severe trouble with his eyes.

During his father's illness, Éamonn learned how extraordinarily sensitive he was, and how well he concealed his feelings. 'Tears and laughter are very close to the surface of his character. The commonly-held view that he is aloof and austere is untrue. His natural reserve and self-discipline have so been misinterpreted.

'During this same illness, I made it a point to collect amusing stories for him, and I still do. He can laugh so heartily and the same jokes do over and over again. But I have seen him hard put to repress the tears. I remember reading a story of A. Conan Doyle's for him and it brought back memories of old comrades who had died in troubled times. His eyes filled with tears—eyes that, at that time, could see clearly only in memory.

'My father', he concludes, 'is a gentle person who abhors violence and brutality. He loves life and has no wish to die. Yet I know he does not fear death.' He remembers vividly when driving with him, his father said: 'You know, Éamonn, dying will be a wonderful adventure'. 'My mother, on her side, has always been "half in love with easeful death". Both have been given a luminous faith which has always supported them.'

Part V

1945 - 1970
THE STABLE YEARS

IN OFFICE AND OUT OF IT

1945 – 1951

The years 1945 to 1951 in Ireland have been dealt with in a series of Thomas Davis lectures of much perspicacity.[1] On the economic side, Dr Lynch distinguishes two distinct phases—the first under Mr de Valera up to 1948, and the second under the Coalition from 1948 to 1951. Professor Mansergh, however, who deals with foreign policy, is not alone in discovering an underlying unity. He finds two dominant preoccupations in Europe, the building-up of the military strength of peace-loving nations in the Western world, and the employment of every means to ensure rapid economic recovery from the devastation of war. The Irish Government withheld from the one and participated in the other. Ireland, though frankly anti-Communist and pro-Western, was not a signatory to the new defensive alliances in the West from the five-power Brussels Treaty of March, 1948, to the North Atlantic Treaty of April, 1949. But from the outset she was associated with plans for economic and social reconstruction in Western Europe, stemming from the historic initiative of General Marshall, on June 5th, 1947. She was active in the work of the Organization for European Economic Co-operation and was a founder member, moreover, of the Council of Europe.

On all these developments in Irish policy, positive and negative, de Valera, in office or out of it, must be held to have exercised a major influence.

In Ireland herself there was little relief from wartime shortages and restrictions. Dr Lynch points out that the immediate economic objectives of the Government were to restore the economy from the effects of the war and to avoid inflation. The first objective was attained more easily and more quickly than many had expected. But the second, the defeat of inflation, proved more elusive.

De Valera's policy was intended to prevent an inflationary spiral. Wages had been pegged back by controls during the war. Prices had also been controlled and kept down by food subsidies. Restraints were still demanded and dissatisfaction grew rapidly, especially among those employed by the State.

The most pressing demands were made by the Irish National Teachers' Organisation. Their representatives were received by de Valera in

September, 1945, but he gave them little hope that their grievances would be met. Ultimately the teachers in primary schools in Dublin embarked on a long and bitter strike, supported by subscriptions from members throughout the rest of Ireland. It was a strike which went a long way towards undermining the goodwill which de Valera had won by his success in maintaining neutrality.

Admittedly the Opposition parties were not at the moment very formidable. Fine Gael had been reduced at the previous election to the lowest point in its history, thirty deputies in a Dáil of 138 seats. Labour was split into two warring parties.

Clann na Talmhan, a farmers' party, which first entered the political scene in the 1943 General Election, had failed to win any widespread support outside Connacht and Munster. But in 1946 the situation was rapidly changed by the emergence of a new republican party, called Clann na Poblachta. At its head was Seán MacBride a former Chief of Staff of the IRA, at this time a prominent member of the Irish Bar. This new movement gave an outlet for energies which had hitherto been pent up; it gathered support not only from many Republicans who had been interned during World War II and their sympathizers, but also from many other dissatisfied elements. Their diversity was to contribute to the ultimate decline of the party, but in 1947 they appeared to constitute the first real challenge to de Valera since the early 1930s.

The new party won seats in by-elections late in 1947 and its progress was watched with some anxiety by de Valera. For the first time a party had begun to eat into the Republican vote which had always been solidly behind Fianna Fáil. Some of the older Republicans, but not only they, were dissatisfied with the subtle relationship with Britain which de Valera had brought about. Questions were asked in the Dáil about the constitutional position. James Dillon was particularly anxious for a precise statement as to whether the State was or was not a Republic. De Valera tended to adopt the view of Joseph de Maistre that 'in all political systems there are relationships which it is wiser to leave undefined'. But the issue could not be altogether evaded. On July 17th, 1945, in the course of a speech on the vote for the Department of External Affairs, he set out to answer questions posed by Dillon.

His exposition smacked very much of the classroom. He pointed out that the constitution of the State and its institutions were the factors which made the State a Republic or otherwise. It did not depend on a reply from him or anybody else. He pointed to the Constitution passed in 1937, to the fact that the State had an elected President and that by every test which could be applied this Constitution made the State a Republic. He went on:

Let us look up any standard text on political theory, look up any standard book of reference and get from any of them any definition of a Republic or any description of what a Republic is and judge whether our State does not possess every characteristic mark by which a Republic can be distinguished or recognised. We are a democracy with the ultimate sovereign power resting with the people . . .

This is a representative democracy with the various organs of State functioning under a written Constitution.

The executive authority was controlled by Parliament, an independent judiciary functioned under the Constitution and the law. A Head of State was directly elected by the people for a definite term of office. Not content with this statement de Valera then quoted the definition of the word Republic from a number of dictionaries and encyclopedias and concluded:

If anyone still persists in maintaining that our State is not a Republic, I cannot argue with him for we have no common language.

The nub of the question, however, lay in the External Relations Act of 1936. Under this statute, for so long as Ireland was associated with the nations of the British Commonwealth the King was permitted and authorized to act in matters regarding the appointment of diplomatic and consular representatives on the advice of the Irish Government in the same way as he acted on behalf of the Governments of Australia, Canada and other Commonwealth countries. This External Relations Act was not part of the Constitution, but a simple statute repealable at any time. De Valera agreed that the arrangement which it expressed was a unique one, but then he argued: 'The situation which it was designed to fit, and for a number of years has effectively fitted, was likewise unique.' He summed up the situation: 'We are an independent Republic associated as a matter of our external policy with the states of the British Commonwealth.'

De Valera then turned to the second question as to whether Ireland was a member of the British Commonwealth or not. He was much less definite here. He simply quoted the statement issued from 10 Downing Street on the day on which the Irish Constitution came into force, which treated that event 'as not effecting a fundamental alteration in the position of the Irish Free State . . . as a member of the British Commonwealth of Nations'.[2]

In all, it was a somewhat pedantic statement which gave the Opposition a chance to refer to de Valera's 'dictionary Republic'. At a time when there was a growing demand, somewhat stimulated, for a clarification of the constitutional position, the public were confused by the subtlety. The new Clann na Poblachta party was capitalizing on Republican disappointment at lack of progress on the partition issue and on the complexities of external association. De Valera, however, had not been idle in regard to either matter. As early as in spring of 1939, he had warned that the experiment of external association was not a permanent solution to Anglo-Irish relations. It retained a bridge which might help to solve partition, but if that bridge did not serve its purpose, then it would have to go.

After the war he had embarked on a last effort to use the 'bridge' to solve partition. He had invited the British Representative to Ireland, Lord Rugby (formerly Sir John Maffey) to see him and told him informally that he intended to repeal the External Relations Act. Rugby begged him to refrain. De Valera, however, was adamant. It was not serving its intended purpose; instead of helping to solve partition it was creating confusion and controversy in Irish politics. One development only might persuade him to hold his hand—an initiative by the British Government towards the revival of the Council of Ireland. This Council, representative of both parts of Ireland, had been provided for in the 1920 Government of Ireland Act. But the idea had never operated and was later scrapped. Its revival now might be the first step towards reunification if Britain were willing to press the Government in Belfast.

De Valera left the matter in the hands of Lord Rugby while a draft bill for repeal of the External Relations Act was prepared by his own legal advisers. He proposed to inform Lord Rugby officially of his intentions and to ask him whether the British Government had reacted in any way to the suggestion of reviving the Council of Ireland. Time for action was, however, running out. The result of by-elections at the end of October, following an unpopular supplementary budget, was the election of two deputies representing the new party, Seán MacBride and Patrick Kinane. De Valera had committed himself to going to the country in the event of a reversal for his party and, though Fianna Fáil had retained their seat in Waterford, he announced that a General Election would take place early in 1948.

Not all de Valera's party agreed with his decision. A number felt that the Government could have weathered the crisis of confidence by retaining office until the auspices were more favourable. De Valera, however, was determined to put the question before the people at the earliest possible moment. He felt, for the first time, that a party had arisen in the State, which was actually winning over solid Fianna Fáil supporters. Delay in going to a general election would have been all to Clann na Poblachta's advantage. A quick contest would prevent further losses by Fianna Fáil.

The winter election campaign was vigorous. The main catch-cry of all the Opposition parties was 'Put them out'. It was a slogan which appealed to all who, after sixteen years of Fianna Fáil rule, wished for changes. De Valera was a man to show little emotion in his political life and he showed none at this time. Nevertheless, that slogan hurt more than all the wild charges which had been made in the previous four years. He was being told that he and his Government had done nothing for the country. He was very sensitive on this point.

Did he remember that the same slogan was used by Fianna Fáil against W. T. Cosgrave and his Government in the 1932 election? The result in 1948 was that Fianna Fáil was returned as the largest single party in Dáil Éireann, but it got the lowest number of first preference votes that it had received at any general election since 1927. It no longer had an overall majority; the future depended on the efforts of the Opposition parties to reach agreement and to form a coalition.

In the days following the General Election, alliances and bargains were explored with eagerness—based less on compatibility of policy than on intense opposition to de Valera, much of it highly personal. The multiplicity of small parties and the large number of independent deputies made actual agreement difficult. The strong feeling between the two Labour parties was one severe stumbling block. Even on the day when the Dáil assembled a coalition seemed far from certain.

De Valera understood up to a short time before the meeting that National Labour had refused to participate. Then he was told that agreement had been reached. There was a hustle to prepare his office for his departure. His personal papers had to be bundled up hurriedly. When the Dáil met, his name was put forward for Taoiseach, but he was defeated by seventy-five votes to seventy, and an eminent barrister, John A. Costello, was elected to the office. He had not been leader of his own party, Fine Gael, but he was prevailed upon to accept office as an acceptable compromise candidate for the post of Taoiseach.

Out of office, de Valera continued to have the devoted services of Kathleen O'Connell. She resigned her civil service post, to help the man whose personal secretary she had been for just twenty-nine years. He himself was keenly aware of his changed situation and loss of power. Occasionally he intervened in debates, sometimes becoming involved in altercations with the new Government. But there was, for the time being, little which he could do, except act as watch-dog and occasional critic.

One issue of the highest importance on which de Valera had been working intensively came to a head in the first year of the new Government's term. This was the status of Ireland under the External Relations Act. On August 6th, 1948, in closing an adjournment debate in the Dáil the Tánaiste (Deputy Premier), William Norton, said: 'I say now that I think it would do our national self-respect good both at home and

abroad if we were to proceed without delay to abolish the External
Relations Act'. De Valera replied: 'You will get no opposition from us'.[3]

There was known to be more than one view in the Government. The
Labour members had opposed the External Relations Act from the time
it was passed. Clann na Poblachta was committed to its repeal, but had
promised to leave such matters in abeyance. Other parties were also
critical of its provisions, including Fine Gael. The latter had, however,
differed from the others sharply; its policies had, at all times, called for
closer and clearer association with the British Commonwealth; the others
had demanded the precise opposite.

The surprise, therefore, was considerable when, early in September,
the *Sunday Independent* announced that the Government intended to
repeal the External Relations Act. The Taoiseach, John A. Costello, was
in Canada and faced a press conference a couple of days later. In answer
to a question, he confirmed the newspaper report.

There has been considerable dispute about the sequence of events, for
it is often thought that the decision had not been formally taken before
Costello's announcement in Canada, but in a number of interviews he
has emphatically stated the opposite.[4] It is clear, in any case, that the
policy had been effectively agreed on by the time he left Ireland. The
circumstances of the announcement, clearly set out by Professor Lyons,
were not understood at the time. It appeared strange in Ireland that an
announcement of such national importance should be made several
thousand miles away. Many felt, irrespective of its merits, that if this
was to be the new Fine Gael line it should have been put before the public
at the recent election. On his part, de Valera had stated in August, as we
have seen, that if the Government decided to repeal the External Relations
Act, Fianna Fáil would not oppose it. This did not prevent many Fianna
Fáil deputies from making every kind of uncomplimentary reference to
the dramatic change in Fine Gael policy.

The best friends of the Government could hardly deny that the
matter was handled with little attempt at diplomacy and in a manner
liable to arouse the indignation of the Labour Government in England.

De Valera, however, dwelt on none of those things when he spoke on
the second reading of the bill for repeal of the External Relations Act.
Instead he rejoiced as one who saw in the action of the Government the
ending of a long controversy. He saw in it the general acceptance of the
1937 Constitution by all parties and the new unanimity regarding the
Republican status of the country which that Constitution bestowed. He
welcomed the Taoiseach's action, but could not refrain from recalling
the steady opposition to his own efforts to liberate Ireland from
constitutional restrictions in the 1930s:

I would like to think but I am afraid that even my goodwill in that matter, however great, will not get me to believe that if we had proposed this Bill when on the opposite side of the House we would have got unanimity. But you will get unanimity from us because we have been in public life not to retard, not to put barriers to the onward march of the nation.[5]

He did have certain criticisms of the Bill. Its title was, he felt, dictated by politics. It was not called, as it should have been, a bill to repeal the External Relations Act, not the Description of the State Bill. It was more flamboyantly styled the Republic of Ireland Bill. De Valera pointed out:

The Bill does not purport to be establishing a new State. We are simply giving a name to what exists—that is, a Republican state.[6]

The Taoiseach, John A. Costello, pointed out that the *name* of the State (Éire or Ireland) remained the same as it was in the 1937 Constitution. The Bill changed the *description* of the State which would be 'the Republic of Ireland'. It was possible to achieve this without any amendments to the Constitution. 'We were not, since 1936', he added later, 'a member of the Commonwealth of Nations'. It is often supposed that the Costello Government formally withdrew from the Commonwealth; strictly speaking that is not so. They took certain steps which, not surprisingly, led the British and the rest of the Commonwealth to the conclusion that Ireland was no longer a member, whereas up to that point they had treated Ireland as such. De Valera made another thing clear when he warned:

I want the country and every representative here to see that we are, by doing this, burning our boats. I do not say it is a bad thing to do. There are times, but rare times, when it should be done. I hope there is to be no further disestablishment of the Republic. It must be on the basis of that Republic, existing as a State, that the relationship and the association, whatever it may be, whatever its form, with the states of the British Commonwealth will be founded.[7]

It was inconceivable that there should be no passage of arms during the debate. De Valera's followers were irate at the manner of Fine Gael's change of policy. It took some persuasion on de Valera's part to achieve unanimity in his party and to prevent some of them from voting against the bill.

On one matter he and his party declined to co-operate. The great achievements of the 1930s, including the passing of the 1937 Constitution, had never been the cause of national celebrations by de Valera. He and his Government had, as he claimed, 'done things in our usual way without fanfares'. They had strong feelings against celebrating any political or constitutional event short of the final reunification of the whole island as a Republic. In the celebrations on Easter Monday, 1949, which greeted the coming into operation of the Republic of Ireland Act, de Valera and his colleagues did not participate.

The Irish Government's handling of the final break with the British Commonwealth brought inevitable repercussions from the British Government. The Prime Minister, Clement Attlee, complained that he had no notice of Mr Costello's intention, and he gave assurances to the Northern Ireland Government that, while citizens of the Twenty-Six Counties would not be regarded as foreigners by Britain, there would be no question of ending the partition of Ireland without the consent of the Belfast Parliament. Rightly or wrongly, however, it came as a shock to the Irish Government when, early in May, 1949, it learned that this guarantee was to be enshrined in a law to be passed at Westminster.

The Taoiseach put a resolution of protest before the Dáil. De Valera spoke firmly in favour of it. He dwelt on the patent injustice of the border; it was drawn without consideration for the opinions of the people in two of the six Northern counties who would much prefer to be in the South. He asserted Britain's responsibility for partitioning Ireland originally and protested:

> Every time . . . this question of the partition of our country loomed up as a question to be considered between the Irish and British governments you had immediately an election call to pretend that the people in the Six Counties were democratically supported in their attitude. They told us that it is only by the will of this Northern Ireland Parliament that we can ever hope to get our unity—through the will of a Parliament that is specially designed to deny it. We are told that no part of that territory can be taken from them except by the will of that Parliament—a Parliament that is empowered to gerrymander, as they have done in many cases, to any extent they wish.[8]

He deplored the action of the British Government, as it was a further proof of the poisoning effect of partition on Anglo-Irish relations. He did not see any hope of a solution out of a tripartite conference between the Belfast, Dublin and London Governments as long as one member had the right to veto decisions. The British had the power to undo the injustice which they had perpetrated. 'They have the power to do it', he said. 'If they really want to they can tell this minority in our country, that is not a fifth of the population of this country and not a fiftieth of the population of Britain, "we are not going to support you in your claim for privilege. We are not going to permit this small minority of the two peoples to continue to set the two peoples by the ears and to stir up and continue the old antagonisms between them".' He himself had no doubts: 'If you had properly informed public opinion in Britain and a Parliament and a government that responded to the feelings of the fair-minded people in Britain we would have reached the stage when this would be done.'⁹

An all-party anti-partition conference now followed under the chairmanship of the Taoiseach. De Valera participated in it as one of the representatives of Fianna Fáil. His activity was not, however, confined to Ireland. Since becoming Leader of the Opposition he had made use of his freedom to travel extensively throughout the world, expounding the partition question at every opportunity. In 1948 he visited Australia and New Zealand and the United States as a guest of the Irish Societies. On the last night of British rule in India he was the guest of Lord and Lady Mountbatten, and early next morning, before leaving for the airport, saw the troops rehearsing for their last review. Early in the following year it fell to his lot, in conjunction with the Taoiseach, to lead Pandit Nehru to a seat in the Dáil. (MacDonald found much to compare and appreciate in the two statesmen.)

In 1950, the Holy Year, he was invited to attend ceremonies at Luxeuil, in France, to commemorate Saint Columbanus, a missionary of the early Irish Church. Thence he set off as a pilgrim, first to Rome and then to the Holy Land. When he landed at Lydda Airport he was greeted by representatives of the Israeli Government and put up as their guest at the King David Hotel in Jerusalem, looking out on Mount Zion and the Cenacle. He visited many of the places about which he had read so often in the Gospels. But one joy was denied him. He could not travel to Nazareth along the route which the Holy Family would have followed. Now it was crossed by the line dividing Jews from Arabs and therefore barred to travellers. When he left Israel he made sure to cross into Jordan. He was *persona grata* with both sides and felt sympathy for both.

These were not the only journeys which he undertook during this period, 1948–51. The long isolation which had started in the years of neutrality had begun to break. De Valera's efforts to get Ireland accepted as a member of the United Nations in the post-war years had so far been rendered futile by the veto of Russia. His attendance, however, at the Marshall Aid meeting in Paris in 1947 and his discussions with British ministers in London at that time were of considerable value. The beginning of the European Movement and of the Council of Europe, brought him to Strasbourg in 1949. There, for the first time, he saw one with whom his fortunes had been at certain moments so intimately linked —Sir Winston Churchill. What followed can be told in the words of de Valera, whose tribute to Churchill as 'a great War Minister' will be quoted later.

'At Strasbourg, Churchill was treated as a hero and honoured accordingly. When I approached the foot of the series of steps leading to the entrance to the hall, I noticed Churchill was at the top of the steps and surrounded by photographers and newspaper reporters. Some of the photographers looked over at me and wanted me to go up and be photographed with Churchill. This I refused as I did not want to run the risk of being snubbed publicly by Churchill'. One is reminded of something said by Dr Adenauer, later the German Chancellor, to one of the present authors. Seeing Churchill for the first time at the Hague in 1948, he also declined to make the first move towards him. 'I had heard that he had said that "Germans are either at your throat or at your feet". In the hour of my country's humiliation I was not going to risk a rebuff'.

De Valera's narrative continues: 'Later, when I was speaking in the hall, Churchill was seated on the ground seat of the gallery of seats that were arranged in a semi-circle around the stage. As I was speaking he was looking at me and put his hand behind his ear to try to hear more distinctly. I suspected that this was an act. After a few moments he left his seat and came over to the seat just under the one from which I was speaking; another part of the act, I thought.' De Valera seems to have been partly right but basically mistaken. From later happenings it appeared that Churchill's feelings towards him were by this time genuinely warm. Being Churchill, however, he inevitably—some would say delight-fully—dramatized them. The more histrionic type of British statesman, Lloyd George for example, seldom appealed to de Valera. His favourite was Neville Chamberlain whom no one could call over-dramatic.

In Ireland there were limits to what a Leader of the Opposition could accomplish. One success of this period out of office lay in the establish-ment by the *Irish Press* of a Sunday newspaper which was soon to acquire the largest circulation in Ireland. The party itself did not lose its vigour in opposition; it was ready to fight an election campaign should oppor-tunity offer. The opportunity came unexpectedly in May, 1951, following on the disruption of the Coalition Government over the health scheme planned by the Minister for Health, Dr Noel Browne.

The cabinet, and indeed at least one party within the Coalition, Clann na Poblachta, broke up in bitter dispute. The resigning Minister for Health made a personal statement which laid the blame on the Catholic bishops for thwarting his plans for a free-for-all maternity scheme and on the Taoiseach for not giving him full support. In fact it appears that it was the doctors who played the crucial part. Their opposition was intense and proved decisive. Be that as it may. . .

The Taoiseach replied to the Minister, and a number of deputies entered into the debate. Many of the Opposition would, no doubt, have willingly stirred up further trouble in the broken ranks of the Government parties. But de Valera kept a tight rein on his followers. He took no part in the debate apart from a disdainful comment: 'I think we have heard enough'.[10] A couple of Fianna Fáil deputies did manage to throw in a few interjections but the row was left to the disputants. Tactically it was the shrewdest way. The Coalition was falling apart. From Fianna Fáil's point of view it was better to let events take their course.

The inevitable dissolution came in May, 1951, and in the General Election which followed, Fianna Fáil gained back many of the first preference votes lost three years before. The party which had been a threat in 1948, Clann na Poblachta, was decimated. It had ten deputies returned in 1948 and two in 1951. Fianna Fáil's gain in votes, however, was not reflected to any great extent in seats. It still had not got an overall majority. But with independent support de Valera was re-elected to power.

HANDING ON THE INHERITANCE

1951 – 1959

De Valera emerged a somewhat Pyrrhic victor, confirmed in his objection to proportional representation. Admittedly, it secured an adequate representation of minorities, but it seemed to make it almost impossible for a single party to win an overall majority. The multiplicity of small parties which had grown up, particularly since 1943, appeared to him to militate against effective government. The system was, however, fixed by the Constitution. It could not be changed except by plebiscite. The years which followed were to make him more and more certain that his criticisms were well-founded.

The dependence of his Government on a handful of independent deputies meant that it was always vulnerable. In no case, however, did he bargain for support. He and his Government pressed forward with their own policies for good or ill. Fianna Fáil distrusted the inflationary tendencies of the three Coalition years and returned to a more staid policy of balanced budgets. De Valera deliberately selected, as Minister for Finance, Seán MacEntee, a man of recognized character and ebullient charm, but definitely, so it was thought, a conservative choice.

In general he relied on those on whom he had depended for years. Half of them had been members of his first cabinet in 1932. There were fresh faces in the lower reaches, for example a new Parliamentary Secretary in Jack Lynch, later to become Taoiseach in succession to Seán Lemass. On the whole, however, it was the old team back at work again, though there was some reshuffling of portfolios.

Notable was the appointment of Frank Aiken as Minister for External Affairs. A new departure this, for de Valera had previously retained the portfolio in his own hands. The rapid growth of Ireland's international activity persuaded him that this was no longer possible. De Valera was always to look back with satisfaction on his choice of Aiken, a man of massive physique, soft-spoken but firm, with a sense of humour that fitted in well with de Valera's own. While they were in opposition he had accompanied de Valera on many of his journeys.

Aiken was to hold his new office in successive Fianna Fáil governments until his retirement in 1969. After Ireland's entry into the United

Nations, he was to play a notable role on the world scene, assisted by outstanding officials such as the sage F. H. Boland, later President of the United Nations Assembly, and, in the earlier stages by Dr Conor Cruise O'Brien, a writer of immense distinction.

In 1951 de Valera reached his sixty-ninth birthday without showing many signs of age. His energy was still greater than that of the majority of younger men. Then came the blow which was to rob him suddenly of his sight. His eyes had long caused him trouble and in 1970 he recollected the details. It will be recalled that he had worn glasses since he was a young man. For some time, he remembers (after 1927 and in the early thirties), 'I had noticed that luminous objects, such as a lamp, at a distance appeared to me as if there were three lamps. I was becoming more and more disturbed by this. The climax was reached when one morning, as I turned into St Stephen's Green, I saw two girls like identical twins, dressed exactly alike, walking across the street in front of St Vincent's Hospital. I said to myself "I have never seen two such identical twins", and then oh horrors! there was a third girl walking as it were in the air between them, on top of their heads, at the apex of an equilateral triangle. As I was driving my car at the time, I realized that the condition was very dangerous, and went to see specialists in Dublin and in London. The lens in the better of my eyes appeared to have three symmetrical foci, and there seemed to be no practical cure.'

Later, at Geneva, he consulted an ophthalmic diagnostician, and on his advice went to Zürich to see a specialist there, Dr Vogt. The latter said the condition was an unusual one, and produced a large book which he had written and in which he described similar cases. When de Valera next went to Zürich, in the spring of 1936, he saw Dr Vogt again. He was told that the only cure was to remove the lens, and that if he waited over, Dr Vogt would operate next morning. This he did, and from that operation on de Valera was treated as for simple cataract.

His sight then, with the proper glasses, became extremely good. 'I could read the smallest print, and when travelling at sea and testing my sight with the Captain on the bridge, he said he would have no hesitation in granting me a full seaman's certificate!' Later on a film seemed again to cover the iris, and de Valera began to see very indistinctly. Dr Joyce operated for this at the Mater Hospital, Dublin (1940), and once more his vision was restored.

This remained the position 'until one day I was bending down, sorting some documents which I had spread out on the floor; I noticed that something new had happened. I went to see my son, Éamonn, at his surgery at 33, Fitzwilliam Square. Next door to him was the eye specialist, Dr Werner. We got in touch with him immediately, and he diagnosed my condition as that of detachment of the retina. In consultation with Dr Joyce, he suggested I should go at once to Utrecht, to Professor Weve. This I did. It was only after six operations that the retina was re-attached. My prayer finally was that I would be left with sufficient sight to distinguish dark from light. Since then I have been left with only peripheral vision. Although I have not been able to read, I was left with sufficient sight to enable me to move about freely in places with which I have been acquainted. The condition has remained the same since.'

For eighteen years he has been almost blind, but he has used his patch of sight with incredible skill and energy.

To return to the latter part of 1952. His secretary many times feared that after his severe ordeal the Taoiseach would not survive. But through everything de Valera showed the determination, the will to live which had marked his entire existence. Nor did anyone, then or at any other time, hear him say one bitter word about the fate which imposed on him so much affliction and so much apparent interference with his precious freedom.

His seventieth birthday was celebrated in a hospital bed and he was awakened to see candles round him. His sight, though heavily impaired, was not completely lost. He could see the hospital staff in white around him and they were chanting. Do they think I am dead, he thought, before he woke up to the tune they sang—'Happy Birthday To You'!

Messages poured in on him, including one quite unexpected from Sir Winston Churchill. A number of Irish friends visited him in Utrecht —Kathleen O'Connell, Seán Moynihan, and his son Doctor Éamonn de Valera, were with him much of the time. The hospital provided a birthday cake in the shape of Ireland which de Valera was supposed to cut. He refused. He would not be a party to carving up his native land.

On his return to Ireland, shortly before Christmas, 1952, de Valera resumed the duties of his office. During his illness he had, naturally, contemplated and assessed the handicap under which he would have to work in future. He thought that perhaps he might not be able to perform his tasks. But back at work, with unfailing assistance from all those around him, he became more optimistic. He found that he could satis-factorily fulfil the duties of his office.

He was soon faced with a critical issue. The Catholic hierarchy were sensitive about the principle of State medicine; as previously indicated, their intervention had been a factor, if by no means the critical one, in the break up of the Coalition Government. In April, 1953, de Valera learned that a letter from the hierarchy had been given to the Dublin newspapers protesting against the Health Bill proposed by the Minister,

Dr Ryan. This came as a complete and unpleasant surprise to de Valera. He had no wish to embark on a public confrontation with the Church; he felt that there was no reason why objections to a health scheme could not be met without resort to a controversy in the papers. In an urgent telephone call to Cardinal Dalton, he asked why the difficulty could not be settled by discussion, and set off for Drogheda to meet the Cardinal, who withdrew the statement from the newspapers. An amicable solution followed.

The incident was an example of de Valera's tact and natural gift for diplomacy in handling a delicate situation. It also reflected his attitude to the vexed question of Church/State relations. He believed that there were certain areas where the authority of the Church and of the State overlapped. In those areas, the views of religious leaders had to be given proper weight in the consideration of government policy. Yet he was no clerical instrument. On this occasion he avoided a clash with the hierarchy without giving offence to any section of the Irish people. He did not need to speak in the subsequent debates. The bill was steered through the Dáil by the Minister for Health, the knowledgeable and prudent Dr Ryan. The essence of Dr Browne's bill was secured.

The Taoiseach himself, despite his handicap of sight, soon found that not only was he able to get through his office work in satisfactory style but he was able to fulfil his parliamentary duties. His speech on financial affairs on July 23rd, 1953, revealed that his memory was sufficiently good to allow him to speak without notes and at the same time give details of facts and figures. He was even able to deal quickly and effectively with interruptions, for he asked no quarter and expected none. He had rapidly proved that his disability did not necessitate retirement.

During that year, as he passed through London, he was invited by Winston Churchill to lunch at 10 Downing Street. Lord Moran has recorded the British Prime Minister's keen desire to meet his old adversary, and his efforts to make the lunch a success.[1] Friendly messages had been passing between the two statesmen on more or less formal occasions. At the time of the death of George VI, Churchill thanked de Valera for what he called 'a most kind message of sympathy', and added a personal and private message: 'It gives me much pleasure to receive this telegram from you. You know, I am sure, that I bear sincere goodwill to your country and admire the faith and culture of the community you have built amid so many difficulties.' De Valera took care to congratulate Churchill on receiving the Garter and on various birthdays. His last message of all, some years later ran: 'Congratulations on your reaching your ninetieth birthday. May you make the century in good health and wonted vigour'.

In 1953 de Valera, on his side, was pleased to meet Churchill face to face at the Downing Street lunch. His own record goes as follows: 'I had lunch with Churchill at Downing Street. He went out of his way to be courteous. After lunch, we retired with other guests to the far end of the room where I spoke to him about matters of most immediate concern. I spoke first of a possible unification of the country. To this he replied that they could never put out of the United Kingdom the people of the Six Counties so long as the majority wished to remain with them. There were also political factors which no Conservative would ignore.'

De Valera then urged the return of Casement's body. 'On this point Churchill said that personally when a man was dead, he was dead as far as he was concerned, and what was done with his body did not matter. The people of the Six Counties and other members of his Government might hold a different view; he would have to consult his Government.' That sounded encouraging, but the sequel was a big disappointment. Churchill wrote to de Valera when he had looked into the matter: 'I am sorry to tell you that we cannot comply with your request as the law on the subject is specific and binding'. No exception had ever been made to it. 'There is no doubt that we should be led into great difficulties were we to seek to amend the law now. But apart from these legal considerations, I am sure that we should avoid the risk of reviving old controversies and reawakening the bitter memories of old differences.'

These second thoughts could certainly not seem better thoughts in de Valera's eyes. He insisted in reply that the Irish Law Officers gave contrary advice to that referred to by Churchill, and went on to add: 'With regard to the non-legal considerations, your own first personal reaction was the natural and human one, and I am convinced—with a view to good relations between our two countries—the right one. So long as Roger Casement's body remains within British prison walls, when he himself expressed the wish that it should be transferred to his native land, so long will there be public resentment here at what must appear to be, at least, the unseemly obduracy of the British Government. I would urge you, therefore, to look into the matter again'. In de Valera's recollection Churchill was on holiday on the Continent about the time he would have received de Valera's letter. 'I got no reply.'

It is significant that the legal objections to returning Casement's body seem to have evaporated by 1964 when Harold Wilson came to power in Britain. One of his first acts was to return Casement's body. Perhaps no single British gesture has ever gone so quickly and decisively to Irish hearts. De Valera never doubted that this was the course which Churchill personally would have favoured.

The weakness of the Irish Government's position was at this time irremediable. They found it necessary to go to the country in May, 1954, lost four seats and were duly defeated. For the next three years de Valera was again Leader of the Opposition. A Fine Gael–Labour–Clann na Talmhan Coalition was supported by some independent deputies and the remnants of Clann na Poblachta. Economic difficulties mounted. Not surprisingly Fianna Fáil laid all the blame on those in office. De Valera found further confirmation of his existing disapproval of coalition governments. He now considered that they not only led to weak and indecisive government, their policies were never put before the people at election time but arrived at in backstairs bargaining afterwards. He felt that he had but to bide his time till the Coalition fell asunder in the same way as before.

In that same period there began a revival of IRA activity in the form of cross-border raids into Northern Ireland. The partition of Ireland was indeed a running sore. It was in Irish eyes based on injustice and lived on injustice. Britain had ignored all the proofs of discrimination and injustice within Northern Ireland. British governments had done nothing to protect the Nationalist majorities of Tyrone, Fermanagh, Derry City, and other large parts of the partitioned area, from the practices of Unionist rule. Efforts to raise the question at Westminster were ruled out of order. It was hardly surprising that quite a few young Irishmen decided that the only way to solve the problem was by the use of force. They were inspired for the most part by a sincere love of country, but their knowledge of political reality was minimal.

Some of them met de Valera in 1956 and asked him to assist in their attacks or at least connive at them. De Valera gave them not the slightest encouragement. He was indeed extremely forthright with them and impressed upon them his belief, often stated publicly, that partition could not be solved by force of arms. Their movement, he said, was bound to fail; it would cause great suffering without any visible weakening of partition. Events proved him right beyond question. The IRA raids led to a number of deaths before they were abandoned in 1962. They did nothing but harm to the cause they were intended to benefit.

In the meantime the second Coalition Government tottered and fell. In the General Election of March, 1957, de Valera led his party to its first overall victory since the wartime election of 1944—a majority of nine seats over all others in the Dáil. He had in this, his last General Election, won more seats than he had ever won in any election during his political career. He also was returned by his own constituency of County Clare by the highest number of votes ever given to him.

De Valera once again became Taoiseach. He was now in his seventy-fifth year. His cabinet still contained a number of the old guard who had served with him since 1932, but he was obviously intent on giving younger men a chance. Among them were Jack Lynch, Neal Blaney and Kevin Boland. At the same time, de Valera continued his loyalty to older comrades. Seán Moylan, a former minister, had lost his seat in the election, but de Valera went out of his way to bring him into the cabinet by making him a senator. It was a time, however, in which one generation, and a long-lived one at that, was handing over to another. Within the next two years, de Valera was to promote two other younger men to cabinet rank, Micheál Ó Móráin and Gerald Bartley.

It was inevitable, in the circumstances, that his own retirement should have come into his mind, and it must have been reinforced from time to time by the loss, by death and ill-health, of some of those around him. One of the great blows was the death, in 1956, of Kathleen O'Connell, his personal secretary for thirty-eight years. Her niece, Marie O'Kelly, took her place and continued with him, not only while he remained Taoiseach, but also in the years which followed. De Valera's immediate thoughts, however, turned to one major political task which he felt needed to be accomplished—a change in the electoral system, responsible so largely in his eyes for the political instability of the preceding decade. Dáil deputies had been elected, since 1921, by a complex method—the single transferable vote in multiple constituencies. If the main purpose of the general election was to elect a stable government, acceptable to the people as a whole and one which would accept responsibility for all its acts, de Valera felt that proportional representation militated against that end.

But this was not by any means his sole preoccupation. He interested himself deeply in the study of economic problems which had been prepared by the Secretary of the Department of Finance, Kenneth Whitaker, and agreed that the document should be published, not anonymously as would have been usual, but over its author's name. The Government decided that Whitaker should get the full credit. A five year Government programme issued after consideration of Whitaker's conclusions laid the basis for a new organized development of the economy and more rapid economic growth.

The system of election was also a special interest. As already mentioned, a change could only be made by plebiscite. But before this stage was reached, the measure had to be placed before the Dáil and Senate. None of this could come about until de Valera had persuaded both his cabinet and his party that the abolition of proportional representation was necessary. There was no doubt among the members of the cabinet about the correctness of de Valera's views. Many of them feared that no party would ever again win a working majority once 'the Chief' departed from the political scene. Even 'the Chief' had succeeded in winning clear majorities in only four out of twelve general elections.

What hope was there for the lesser mortals who would succeed him? As for the Opposition parties, not one of them had ever won an overall majority in the same period.

The Fianna Fáil Party, however, was made up not only of men who headed the polls in multiple constituencies, but also of deputies who came in on the second and third preferences of other candidates. They undoubtedly were less than enthusiastic in their reception of the proposed changes. Yet their consent was won without much difficulty.

On November 2nd, 1958, de Valera introduced in the Dáil the bill which would initiate the necessary amendment of the Constitution. It was opposed by the Opposition parties even on the first reading—an indication of the strength of the effort which would be made to stop its passage. The succeeding months were to be given over to hectic parliamentary and public debate. De Valera did not argue against proportional representation on the grounds of its known consequences in other countries so much as on its consequences in Ireland as he saw them. His principal public argument against the complicated system of voting which existed in Ireland was that it led to weak government and indecisive coalitions which perished on the rocks of internal divisions. In fact he was more influenced than he admitted by the history of France in the preceding years. There continuous changes of government had wrecked all prospects of progress and he feared a similar situation arising in Ireland where governments might change not only every few years but every few months.

De Valera saw the struggle about the electoral system as his last major political battle. At seventy-seven years of age he felt that it was time he handed over the reins of office to a younger man. He had kept his counsel on this matter since the General Election of 1957, but he went to a meeting of the Fianna Fáil Parliamentary Party in mid-January, 1959, and told them of his determination to retire from office. Immediately after the meeting, his secretary recorded his account of what he had said:

An Taoiseach had said that there was no use in beating about the bush in this matter. Most deputies knew the position. He had for a considerable time made up his mind that it would not be in the interests either of the country or the Party that he should lead Fianna Fáil in the next general election. For that reason he thought that it would be necessary for him, in any case, at least a year before the general election was due, to resign so as to enable the new leader of the Party and the Party to decide on policy and prepare their plans and organisation for the election. There was something more to come. Recently since the Presidential election became a matter of general public interest he had been approached by some members of the Party urging him to consent to go forward if the Party so desired. He was in this matter completely in the hands of the Party.[2]

This bald statement conceals a dramatic incident. Despite his age, few members of the Fianna Fáil organization had visualized their party without their founder. There was no movement to unseat him from his undisputed leadership and no ambitious rival emerging from the wings to push de Valera aside. All accepted him as their leader. As far as most of them were concerned he would be with them until death.

A few, notably Oscar Traynor, Minister for Justice, had noted that Seán T. O'Kelly's second term of office as President of Ireland was due to expire in the following June. Under the Constitution he could not be elected for a third term. It was obvious that a successor must be found. Traynor's suggestion to de Valera that he should allow his name to go forward was in the circumstances natural. He was an obvious Fianna Fáil nominee. Nevertheless, de Valera's own announcement of his intention to resign the leadership of the Party and of the Government came to most of the members as a bombshell. It resulted in the most moving scenes. After following him throughout their political lives the party members were, in general, dumbfounded that he should ever think of retiring. Cabinet ministers and others emerged from the meeting with tears in their eyes; for the first time the years seemed to have suddenly caught up with their well-nigh indestructible leader. The man who had always been 'the Chief' to them was determined on his course, but they could visualize no other 'Chief' than he.

The choice of de Valera as a candidate for the presidency was automatic, but his immediate concern was to pilot through the legislature his bill to amend the Constitution. Despite the handicap of his almost total blindness he bore the brunt of the parliamentary exchanges. Indeed he appeared to revel in dealing with a critical Opposition, and while he might feel that his ear was unable to identify interruptors he was in fact able to reply by name to some of them. On occasion he used his disability with dramatic effect, as when he waved in his hand a photostat of an Opposition criticism of proportional representation made thirty years before, and added that he wished he could read it to them. He had memorized sufficient extracts to embarrass his opponents effectively.

Despite his best efforts the bill had a stormy passage through the Dáil. In the Senate it foundered and was rejected by a single vote on March 19th, 1959. Just six weeks later the bill came before the Dáil again; de Valera proposed that the House pass a resolution to the effect that the bill be deemed to have been passed by both Houses of the legislature. Under the Constitution, such a resolution would undo the Senate decision. There followed a renewal of the debate which had taken place in the previous November and succeeding months. The delays, however, introduced a new element. It was becoming clear that the election of

16

President and the referendum on the system of voting would be held on the same day, early in June. 'When two decisions have to be made', said de Valera, 'the public convenience is best met by having the two on the one day'. An Opposition speaker interjected: 'And you will be in the scales.'[3]

This was indeed the position. De Valera was impelled to put the issue to the people at this stage because he considered that it had the best hope of success if it were clearly seen that he had no intention of leading the next government. After he had succeeded in piloting his resolution through the Dáil, he turned himself to the task of persuading the voters that they should vote for his alternative to proportional representation; that is to say for the system which operated in Britain. For de Valera the election campaign hinged on this issue. Up and down the country he travelled, impressing on all and sundry his fear of the existing system. Never did he speak in favour of himself as President. His last appearance on a party political platform was at the final rally on the eve-of-polling day in College Green in Dublin. It was a dramatic occasion which marked the passage of time. One of the young men on the platform to speak that night was Kevin Boland, the nephew of Harry Boland who had stood by de Valera's shoulder forty years earlier. Kevin Boland was already a cabinet minister, but he could speak for a younger generation whose admiration for de Valera was as strong as that of his uncle. College Green was thronged. People were massed from the gates of Trinity College to Dame Street. All recognized the historic moment. De Valera alone seemed unmoved by any sentimental reactions. He put his heart into driving home his argument in favour of a new electoral system.

The Fianna Fáil slogan in the double election had been simple, 'Vote Yes and de Valera'. 'Yes' was to indicate a wish for electoral change. The meaning of 'de Valera' was obvious. His opponent was General Seán MacEoin, the famed leader of the Irish Midlands in the war of independence and minister in the coalition governments of the previous decade. It was one of the sad quirks of politics that de Valera's opponent should have been the man who proposed him as President of the Irish Republic in 1921. The divisions of the Treaty threw long shadows, though the bitterness was now much mitigated.

De Valera fought his campaign up to election day. Then he retired from politics. Before the ballot-boxes were collected, he had resigned as Taoiseach. He did not await the result. He had decided that, no matter what happened he was retiring from the leadership of both the Government and the party. When the results came in they gave a mixed result. De Valera had failed to win a majority for amending the Constitution, but by a comfortable majority he had been elected President. He was not, however, to take office until the end of the term of Seán T. O'Kelly later in the month. In the meantime, his place in Fianna Fáil and in the Government had to be filled. The choice fell naturally and properly on Seán Lemass, who had been Tánaiste (Deputy Premier) for fourteen years. He was to be the link between the old and the new generation in Irish government, a man of loyalty, force and business acumen, who could be relied on to continue the tradition he inherited.

PRESIDENT OF IRELAND

1959 onwards

The election of de Valera as President of Ireland was the climax of a long career. The office which he now held was one which he had helped to institute under the Constitution of 1937. His predecessors in that office had been Dr Douglas Hyde, one of the founders of the Gaelic League, and Seán T. O'Kelly, a leading minister in de Valera's governments. In many ways de Valera had himself set a pattern during the preceding decades for the relations between the government and the President. The Constitution itself laid down basic rules by which the holder of the office must abide. He could not, for example, hold any other paid position. Since de Valera held no paid posts other than his Dáil seat and his office in the Government, from which he had already resigned, he was not affected by this condition. He did, however, divest himself of the unpaid position which he had held of controlling director of the *Irish Press* newspapers. His son, Vivion, succeeded him. The other unpaid position which he held, that of Chancellor of the National University of Ireland, he continued to fill. It was not likely to clash in any way with his presidential functions.

The inauguration of the President took place in St Patrick's Hall, in Dublin Castle, on June 25th, 1959, before a large and representative gathering. Solemnly de Valera made the declaration of office, promising to maintain the Constitution and to fulfil his duties faithfully and conscientiously. He concluded: 'I will dedicate my abilities to the service and welfare of the people of Ireland. May God direct and sustain me.' It was a declaration which in fact summed up his life for the best part of half a century. It was to continue to be his aim in the years still left to him.

He had retired from the political arena but he was still, in his seventy-seventh year, intent to give what service he could to his country. He took up residence in the official home of the President, Áras an Uachtaráin, in Phoenix Park. His wife, ever shy of the public eye, was reluctant to leave her home in Blackrock. She was also anxious for the welfare of her eldest son's two children. Since the untimely death of Vivion's wife, when they were infants, it was she who had reared them. Even when she and her husband went to live in Phoenix Park, she was often to say that a rope of sand was all that was ever needed to drag her back to the home in Black-rock. She continued to pay regular visits there, and the two grandchildren whom she had cared for through their tender years, Ann and Eamon, were to spend much of their free time with their grandparents in Phoenix Park.

Their sons and daughters had all by now won recognition in their chosen fields. Vivion, an active member of the Dáil, was still the only son to take any public part in politics. He was also controlling director of the *Irish Press*, with strong scientific interests. Máirín, the eldest daughter, was a botanist of note and Professor of Botany in University College, Galway, while Éamonn was an eminent Dublin gynaecologist and a professor in University College, Dublin. Among his colleagues on the staff there was his brother, Ruairí, who had become Professor of Archaeology a few years before. Also with him was his brother-in-law, Brian O Cuív, Professor of Classical Irish Language and Literature, who was married to Emer de Valera. He was later to become Director of the School of Celtic Studies, in the Dublin Institute for Advanced Studies. Terry de Valera was establishing himself in practice as a solicitor in Dublin. The grandchildren were growing up.

The post of Secretary was soon filled by Máirtín O Flatharta, de Valera's private secretary many years before, when he was Head of the Government. Marie O'Kelly, de Valera's personal secretary since the death of her aunt, Kathleen O'Connell, maintained a family tradition of dedicated service. His aides-de-camp included Colonel Seán Brennan who had been his aide when Head of the Government since the 1930s. There were others, long associated with the President, who were also attached to the new office. He was not to be cut off from all those who had given him and the country such faithful and unswerving loyalty.

Although as President he was outside politics, de Valera was entitled under the Constitution to be kept generally informed by the Taoiseach on matters of domestic and international policy. While he had been Head of the Government, during the presidency of Dr Douglas Hyde, de Valera had started the custom of the Taoiseach calling on the President once a month. These regular visits continued under the premiership of Seán Lemass, and under his successor, Jack Lynch. On occasion there might be reasons for visits more frequently but, in general, these monthly meetings kept the President in touch with government activity and policy, and national affairs in general. Like other Irish Presidents, he had no part in the policy-making processes. Indeed at all times he has been careful, even in private, to avoid any expression of a party political viewpoint.

Money never seems to have caused him great anxieties, though one sometimes wonders what he and his family lived on in times of misfortune. He grew up with scant resources and for a long time his income was most precarious. As President of Ireland, he received a salary of £5,000 a year, together with an allowance for expenses of £6,500 a year. The salary of President has not changed since it was fixed by de Valera in 1937 for the first President. Since that time the expense allowance has once been increased from £5,000 to £6,500 (before de Valera became President). Out of this he pays the domestic staff of Áras an Uachtaráin, the upkeep of his car, the wages of his driver, among other expenses of his office. De Valera would not wish to take more; for money itself he had no great longing. His family have established themselves through their own ability and the education which he was able to give them. He himself must be far from being a rich man, but he is content with what he has, having been ultra-careful at all times to make no profit out of anything connected with his political career. Royalties due to him from the sale of recordings or printed collections of his speeches have been made over to the Irish Red Cross of which as President he has been an active patron for many years.

The official duties of the President are largely mandatory. They are laid down in the Constitution and are performed on the advice of the Taoiseach in some instances, on that of the Government in others. He appoints the Taoiseach on the nomination of the Dáil, and the other members of the Government on the nomination of the Taoiseach, previously approved by the Dáil. The ceremony at appointment has been to give members of the Government seals of office though, in fact, there is no legal authority attaching to the actual seals. The President has, however, some functions in which he can act independently of the Government and of the legislature. These are strictly limited; de Valera has only twice made any effort to use his powers independently of the Government. Both occasions related to the formal signing of bills which had been passed by the legislature.

In June, 1961, de Valera consulted the Council of State as to whether the Electoral Amendment Bill of that year should be referred to the Supreme Court for a decision on whether any of its provisions were repugnant to the Constitution. It was adjudged constitutional and the President signed it. The second occasion on which he held up a bill was in March, 1967. He was not satisfied that certain powers of entry and arrest being granted to revenue officers under the Income Tax Bill were constitutional; he again called the Council of State together to get advice. In this case, the bill was not referred to the Supreme Court, but an Income Tax Amendment Bill was passed at once by both Houses of the legislature. This repealed the repugnant sections of the original bill.

De Valera signed the Income Tax Bill first and the amending bill immediately afterwards. The action of the President in the case of the Income Tax Bill was acclaimed not alone as a proof of the value of the presidency as a guardian of constitutional rights, but also of the continuing clarity of mind of a President who was already in the eighty-fifth year of his age.

As President, de Valera's public duties naturally included the reception of important visitors, those who came on state visits occupying pride of place. There was a long stream of visitors calling on the venerable statesman. Among those whom he had as guests at Áras an Uachtaráin, in this way, were the President of India, Dr Sarvepalli Radhakrishnan, the President of Pakistan, Ayub Khan, President Kaunda of Zambia, Prince Rainier and Princess Grace of Monaco, King Baudouin and Queen Fabiola, King and Queen of the Belgians, and John Fitzgerald Kennedy, President of the United States; and U Thant, head of no State, but more significant than most if not all of the kings and presidents.

General de Gaulle came with his wife to stay there, after he retired from the presidency of France. As the General was no longer in office, his was not a state visit, but it was all the more intimate a meeting between the two statesmen who found that they had so much in common. There was no detailed and heavily-loaded schedule of events attached to this visit; there was a greater opportunity for the exchange of ideas than when time was limited by a succession of official functions. De Valera's admiration for de Gaulle had always been great and it was not lessened during the time they spent together.

The visit of President Kennedy to Ireland was somewhat different in character, for he was caught up in a ceaseless round of duties. Also he stayed not in Áras an Uachtaráin, but in the American Embassy, a short distance away. Nevertheless, in a few days he won the hearts of the entire country. 'He was welcomed', said President de Valera in his address in the following year to the American Congress, amid applause, 'not merely because he was of Irish blood, not merely because of his personal charm and his great qualities of heart and mind, not even because of the great leadership which he was giving to the world in critical moments; but he was honoured because he was regarded by our people as the symbol of this great Nation, because he was the elected President of this great people.'[1]

He seemed to be completely at home in Ireland. A guest at the large reception who watched the two Presidents standing or strolling together throughout the afternoon, both equally relaxed and happy-looking, could not help thinking of de Valera as the father, and President Kennedy as the favourite son. He became a captive of Mrs de Valera's gentle grace during his short visit, and as we have seen embraced her affectionately as he took his leave.

In receiving foreign notables, de Valera filled his office of President with dignity and charm. This charm, however, a quality which he had selected so emphatically in his description of President Kennedy, was not confined to heads of state from abroad. He received countless ordinary visitors each year; he was, and is, the most approachable of men. His interest in people has never flagged; his courteous unaffected manner, less formidable perhaps than in his days of controversy, puts his visitors —no matter who they are—at their ease. He has the directness of the countryman in many ways, despite his long absence from rural life. He lives an austere life from choice, though he plays his part generously when called upon by the duties of his office to entertain.

During his presidency, de Valera represented the Irish nation on memorable occasions abroad. He attended the Coronation of Pope Paul VI in Rome, and he undertook, when eighty-one years of age, the sad and arduous task of attending the funeral of the assassinated President Kennedy, whom he had entertained but a few months earlier. He portrayed in full measure the horrified sorrow of the Irish people. They had warmed to President Kennedy as they did to no other visitor.

Two years later, de Valera was to return to the United States on a much happier mission. He was the invited guest of President Johnson, on a state visit from the land of his adoption to the land of his birth. It was a nostalgic journey which brought back memories of the year and a half which he had spent in the United States in 1919 and 1920, as President of a Republic seeking recognition. Now that Republic was internationally recognized, and the rare honour was accorded him of addressing Congress as a guest. His own pride was shared by the Irish people who saw and heard his remarkable speech on television. For twenty-five minutes he spoke without a note to guide him and to repeated applause.

He introduced more than one theme, apart from the courtesies which he would be the last to neglect and which, in the case of the United States, came unaffectedly from the heart. He paid effective tribute to the American initiative in begetting the League of Nations and now the United Nations. 'Most thinking people will admit that if we are to look forward to anything like a lasting peace in this world, it can only be secured by the working of such an organization.' But he was not likely to end without a reference to partition and, sure enough, he testified indomitably. 'When I was addressing you here, in 1919 and 1920, our ancient nation, our ancient Ireland, was undivided. Since then, it has been divided by a cruel partition. I salute here in prospect the representative of Ireland who will be able, with full heart, joyfully to announce

to you that our severed country has been re-united and that the last
source of enmity between the British and Irish peoples has disappeared,
and that at last we can be truly friends.'[2]

Throughout his career, de Valera was a man of great compassion,
especially conscious of first and last things. He who stood beside the
graveside of an American President at Arlington Cemetery was, during
his years as President of Ireland, to participate in the funeral services of
many whose relations were in mourning. By his kindness on such
occasions, by the very unexpectedness of his presence, he helped those
whose grief was crushing. He did not confine himself to attending the
funerals of leading public figures or their relatives. He also attended those
of persons whose relatives were almost surprised to know that he was
aware of their existence.

During his presidency the last of his colleagues in the cabinet of the
First Dáil, W. T. Cosgrave, died. His death brought a special pang, for the
division over the Treaty had kept them apart for more than forty years.
De Valera had wished to restore the relations which had been broken.
The divide was deep and the friendly meeting he had hoped for was long
delayed. Eventually, however, Cosgrave accepted an invitation to meet
the Papal Nuncio under the President's roof. The two statesmen, at a
certain point, were observed to be standing apart and chatting amicably
—a matter of much satisfaction to so many who admired them both.

De Valera could understand and appreciate the deep-seated differences
which had divided himself and Cosgrave. It was always, however, a cause
of regret to de Valera that the years of division were to stand as a barrier
against the restoration of former relations.

Funerals are sad occasions usually, but there was one graveside at
which de Valera was present with some satisfaction. This was in 1965
when the remains of the executed Roger Casement were exhumed in
Pentonville Prison and were taken to Ireland for burial in a plot set aside
in Glasnevin Cemetery. No public announcement of the bringing of the
remains to Ireland was made until they were already well on their way
from England. The British Prime Minister, Harold Wilson, had agreed
to grant a request which de Valera had pressed in vain on successive
prime ministers. It was a national surprise and thousands flocked in
spring sunshine to the little church at Arbour Hill, near where the remains
of Pearse, Clarke, Connolly and the other executed leaders of the 1916
Rising lay buried.

The day of the State funeral, however, saw a freak change in the
weather. The cortège passed with full military honours through sleet and
snow to the cemetery. Despite his age, de Valera insisted on standing

bare-headed at the graveside. His doctor, Senator Bryan Alton, had advised him against exposing himself, but he was determined to do what he considered his duty on that occasion. He paid a final tribute to Casement, whom he had met at Tawin, in County Galway, more than half a century before, and beside whose prison grave he had stood in Pentonville in 1917. Here was an Irishman who had given his life for his country and whose character had, in de Valera's eyes as well as in those of many others, been blackened by forgery.

> I ask then, each one of you [he concluded], when you pray for the eternal repose of his soul, to pray that you will be true to the end to noble ideals, as he was. But every one of us must believe, and I do not think it presumption on our part to believe, that a man who was so unselfish, who worked so hard for the downtrodden and the oppressed and who so died, that that man is in Heaven with, I hope, all the other Irishmen who have given their lives for our country.[3]

De Valera's years of office coincided with a succession of golden jubilees. He had lived long enough to see the fiftieth anniversary of the founding of the Irish Volunteers in the Rotunda Rink. He unveiled a plaque to mark the occasion, which had been for him not only a turning point in the life of the nation, but also in his own. He had already, in 1961, spoken at Howth when the Erskine Childers' yacht, *The Asgard*, was handed over by the Irish Government as a training vessel for naval cadets. He recalled the day in 1914 on which he helped to take from its decks some of the guns which were to make the 1916 Rising possible.

Then came the great commemoration of 1966, fifty years after the Easter Rising. De Valera was, week after week, involved in some event to mark the occasion. He paid tribute at the General Post Office to the single-mindedness and unselfishness of those who by their sacrifice had inspired a national resurgence, and he set out the vision which he was sure had been their inspiration. It was, had been and remained his own: Political freedom alone was not the ultimate goal. It was to be, rather, the enabling condition for the gradual building-up of a community in which an ever-increasing number of its members, relieved from the pressure of exacting economic demands, would be free to devote themselves more and more to the mind and spirit, and so be able to have the happiness of a full life. The nation could then become again, as it was for centuries in the past, a great intellectual and missionary centre from which would go forth the satisfying saving truths of Divine Revelation, as well as the fruits of the ripest secular knowledge.[4]

The second great commemorative occasion came after his re-election as President. This was the Jubilee of the founding of the First Dáil, the first native legislature in Ireland since the extinction of the Irish Parliament in 1800, the occasion therefore which marked the establishment of the democratic Irish State. After consultation with the Council of State, as required by the Constitution, the President proceeded to address a joint meeting of the Dáil and Senate on January 21st, 1969, fifty years exactly after the first meeting of the Dáil.

The speech which he made in Irish to the combined Houses, meeting in the Mansion House, Dublin, where the first meeting had been held, was not only a tribute to those who had helped to found the State, but also an expression of his conviction that the age of nationalism was not gone. Irish nationalism would last, he felt, and the ancient nation would retain and preserve its characteristics and its culture. But this must go hand in hand with international co-operation for the benefit of all mankind. It was because of the work of the heroes of the past that Ireland was able to take her place among the nations of the earth. She could and must work with them, without losing any of her distinctive qualities.[5]

De Valera was happy looking back on the past. He always had an interest in the history of Ireland. He was also conscious that much that had happened during his own lifetime was misunderstood. He had always been eager to make available the fullest possible information about the controversies in which he had been involved. In the 1920s he had envisaged a huge documentary history of the years of the struggle, from the 1916 Rising to the end of the Civil War, as the only answer to partisan narratives. He did succeed in getting Dorothy Macardle to write her impressive volume *The Irish Republic* which remains one of the essential sources for any study of the period.

Frank Gallagher was, in later years, to embark on a biography. The author, very dear to de Valera, died before the work had progressed very far. Then it was that the publisher suggested that the present book should be undertaken, and President de Valera agreed. For him this has been an arduous and exacting task; he suffered many a severe and searching cross-examination with the utmost patience and understanding.

His life-long absorptions did not weaken. Dr A. J. McConnell, Provost of Trinity College, Dublin, himself an eminent mathematician, has had for more than thirty years a close knowledge of President de Valera's interest in mathematics. While his busy life left de Valera but little time for its study in depth, it remained always a passion with him and he turned to it on every available opportunity. He continued to subscribe to the great mathematical journals and not only did he take them, but the numerous notes on the margins in his hand show that he read them. He carried on a correspondence on mathematical subjects with eminent mathematicians and even after the almost complete loss of his eyesight, in 1952, he continued to take great pleasure from having mathematical books and journals read to him. He still also uses the dark green linoleum, which covers the top of his large desk in his private study, as a blackboard on which he draws geometrical figures and pursues such algebraical expressions as he finds difficult to visualize otherwise.

Mathematics was always his relaxation and while he was not, and would never pretend to be, an original mathematical writer he was deeply interested and had read widely, especially in the fields of quaternions and tensor calculus. In Dr McConnell's opinion, had his life not been directed into other channels, President de Valera would have been a teacher of mathematics of a high order for he had always an exceptionally keen interest in post-graduate research. It was this interest and his interest in Dunsink Observatory which motivated him in establishing the Dublin Institute for Advance Studies, especially the Schools of Theoretical Physics and of Cosmic Physics.

Looking back, de Valera was all too well aware that the two prime issues which drew him into public life, the cause of the Irish language and the threat of partition, were still unsettled matters of concern and controversy. Of the two, the Irish language was, he thought, the more urgent. If the Irish language were to be lost, it could never be revived, whereas partition was a transitory thing which could never endure. The island of Ireland was a natural territorial unit in which its people could not stay separated for ever. In this he echoed a conviction once expressed by Lord Craigavon, Prime Minister of Northern Ireland, when he said: 'We are too small to be apart or for the border to be there for all time.'[6]

He had little doubt about the measures which governments must take to help in restoring the national language. The problem 'had not really been tackled yet, because the nation as a whole had not yet put its back into it.' It was essential that it remained as a subject taught in every school, that it be a necessary qualification for official positions. He saw the difficulties of maintaining official correspondence in Irish, but even here there were things which could be done to help—for example, the provision of a 'sample book of correspondence'. Above all, it needed the will of the people to be directed clearly to the aim of making Ireland a bilingual nation; and to make that will strong enough to face the sacrifices and overcome the difficulties involved in pursuing the aim. In this he was more realistic than those whose aim was to make Irish the sole language spoken in the country. He himself would have Irish and English as the two languages, with Irish as the home language, while English remained the language which gave most ready access to the outside world.

He had no fear that his dream of restoring Irish would run counter in any way to his other dream—the reuniting of the country. His view would be that the Northern Unionists were, at bottom, proud of being Irish; that the history, tradition and culture of the historic Irish nation could not fail to attract them; that the language was a mine of this tradition and culture, as well as being in itself a beautiful and well-developed language capable of expressing in characteristic idiom the thoughts that might enter the mind of man.

He regretted some missed opportunities of the past; the failure of his efforts in 1924 and 1925 to provide an independent endowment for the Irish language movement from the remains of the loan raised by him in the United States on behalf of the First Dáil. His regrets included the time which he had to spend on other affairs of state when he might have been doing even more than he did for the language. The cause remained as close as ever to his heart. In his message to the people of Ireland, at Easter, 1966, he foresaw the task of the young men and women of this generation when he said:

> Our national language has a vital role. Language is a chief characteristic of nationhood—the embodiment, as it were, of the nation's personality and the closest bond between its people. No nation with a language of its own would willingly abandon it. The peoples of Denmark, Holland, Norway, for example, learn and know well one or more other language[s], as we should of course for the sake of world communication, commerce and for cultural purposes; but they would never abandon their native language which enshrines all the memories of their past. They know that without it they would sink into an amorphous cosmopolitanism—without a past, or a distinguishable future.

Then he put forth the challenge:

> To avoid such a fate, we of this generation must see to it that our language lives. That would be the resolve of the men and women of 1916. Will it not be the resolve of the young men and women of 1966?[7]

He himself never weakened in his personal attitude to the national language. He had begun his work for the language, as we have seen, when he joined the Gaelic League and later when he directed a summer school at Tawin, Co. Galway, before he joined the Irish Volunteers. He had done an immense amount for its development and tried to make it an easier medium for modern use by encouraging standardization of grammar and spelling. He had also endeavoured whole-heartedly during his time as Taoiseach to do what he could for the economic benefit of areas where Irish continued to be spoken as the normal daily language. Meetings connected with its revival had first call on his time. He never missed an occasion to show his solidarity with the ideal of restoring Irish. Above all, he had set the example of using it on every occasion on which

he could appropriately do so during his career. Yet he admitted the
difficulties which he himself, who came to learn it when he was already
twenty-six years of age, had found in making it the daily language of his
household and of his office.

He had no time for sham and make-believe. For example the embroidered ring on the lapel of each of his suits was put there as a token
of his attitude towards the Irish language. It replaced an earlier gold ring,
the Fáinne, the wearers of which promised that they would speak nothing
but Irish to others who wore a similar Irish Fáinne. De Valera found that
he could not express himself accurately enough in a language which he
had learned in adult life, to ensure that a famous native speaker, Seán
a Chóta Caomhánach, understood fully an official task to which de Valera
was assigning him. This was the compilation of a dictionary of Irish
words in use in West Kerry, but not generally used throughout the
country. Reluctantly de Valera turned to English, but before he did so
he took off the gold Fáinne, conscious that he was breaking the promise
which he had made when he first wore it. The embroidered ring on his
lapel was retained simply to show that he desired to speak the language,
and would speak it to those who spoke to him in Irish, but was not
pledged to do so in all circumstances.

De Valera, since 1921 particularly, has been a man of controversy, but
he was never one to lower the flag. His determination has always been
pre-eminent. It was seen in big things and in small. It was seen in his
bearing on special occasions, in the way he has overcome the handicap
of near blindness. It was seen in the way in which he endured imprisonment and obloquy for the cause of freedom and no less in his persistent
championship of the Irish language.

When the end of his first term of office in 1966 was drawing near,
many people thought that it might be unanimously agreed that he be
asked to carry on as President for a second term, like Seán T. O'Kelly
in 1952. De Valera, however, was still too controversial a figure to be
allowed this honour. The Fine Gael Party, at its Ard Fheis, announced
that it was putting up a candidate of its own choice for the office. President
de Valera had no great desire to serve a second time, but he was persuaded
by Seán Lemass, the Taoiseach, that he should allow his name to be put
forward. At this time, de Valera was in his eighty-fourth year. Full,
however, of vigour. Since there was to be a contest, it was necessary that
de Valera have the organized support of a party and it was natural, in the
circumstances, that he should be nominated by the party which he had
founded.

In the election campaign as such, de Valera did not participate, though

he certainly found no handicap in the blaze of publicity which attended
the commemorations of the 1916 golden jubilee. His opponent, Thomas
F. O'Higgins, was the nephew of Kevin O'Higgins, the Free State
Vice-President assassinated in 1927. O'Higgins' campaign was principally
based on the need for a young and active President, one who, for example,
would be prepared to go abroad to help the Irish export drive, with the
Government's concurrence. Criticism and dissatisfaction with Government policy were played upon. These were matters for which de Valera,
now President, could not be held responsible, but they were also matters
on which he, being outside party politics, could not speak.

The Irish language was also used as a basis for criticism in the Fine
Gael presidential campaign.

In the event, de Valera won the election by a short head. As he
commented: 'it is better to win by a short head, than lose by it'. In his
second inaugural, he dwelt as undeviatingly as ever on his two 'cherished
aims not yet realized.' The unity of Ireland, of course and, more surprisingly to some in view of the election controversy, the restoration of
the language. No one present will forget the firm, but kindly, tone, the
absolute conviction, the restrained display of an unconquerable spirit.

Out of a million votes cast, de Valera's majority was but 20,000. There
are those who would see in this a commentary on the divided attitude of
Irish people to de Valera in terms of voting since the 1920s. It could be
pointed out that one half of the people had always been behind him;
another half, admitting the magnitude of his personality, had never been
able to accept him when it came to the ballot-box. But bearing in mind
the relative unpopularity of his party at that particular moment, his
personal performance in 1966 was no mean achievement. All the more
so when in Ireland, as in many other countries, there was a demand to be
governed by the young.

In any democracy, a party leader who consistently wins half the votes
is a rare phenomenon; if he manages this feat for half a century, he can
fairly be described as unique.

As the years passed, even those who had strenuously opposed him for
so long had come to appreciate what he had accomplished, and to adapt
words used many years earlier by Patrick Pearse of J. M. Synge, they had
come to recognize that in his brave heart there glowed a true love of
Ireland.

EPILOGUE

It is impossible to exaggerate the extent to which de Valera submitted all his actions to a criterion which was at once intellectual and moral. (In the nineteenth century, Gladstone provides a kind of analogy.) It was not only his practice to study every proposed decision from the point of view of conscience—the same could, presumably, be said of quite a few Christians of various denominations—but he always had to satisfy himself that a powerful argument could be constructed and presented for the course he chose. A temperament of this kind in the harsh conditions of politics leads easily to accusations of casuistry. His attitude to the oath of allegiance, when he eventually led his party back into the Dáil in 1927, is a striking case. It can be studied at length in the text. One thing is certain: de Valera never reached any of his more ingenious and controversial conclusions without much striving of intellect and spirit.

Frank Aiken served in de Valera cabinets from 1932–59, with short intervals of opposition, and in later cabinets from 1959–69. Though many years younger, he might be thought of as de Valera's closest friend and as knowing him exceptionally well, if biased in his favour. Having represented Ireland very successfully at the United Nations and in the Council of Europe for many years, he had ample opportunities of assessing contemporary statesmen. Asked privately how any of these compared with de Valera, he replied emphatically: 'They are nowhere with him. The nearest I ever met were de Gasperi and Schuman. In Britain, Sir Stafford Cripps.'

As suggested earlier, de Valera stands out as a Christian, rather than a peculiarly Catholic, statesman. A list of pious Catholics who have helped to build the modern world must include Schuman and de Gasperi, but just as inevitably Franco and Salazar. De Valera never showed the slightest sympathy for dictatorship in any shape or form. (Hempel, the German Minister in Dublin during the war acknowledged this in reporting to Hitler.) He has been *par excellence* the democratic Christian.

De Gaulle was hardly a democrat in the same sense as Schuman and de Gasperi, though not a dictator like Franco and Salazar. De Valera has gone on record privately as admiring him. 'Before I met General de Gaulle he was France to me. I believed that, without him, France would have been pushed aside and regarded as a second-rate nation in Europe. His great work was to make sure that that would not be so. Meeting him confirmed me in all my previous views. I found him a great French patriot. We did not have much time together for really intimate conversation. In so far as I had an opportunity of judging his character, I did not cease to admire him. The more I got to know him, the more I liked him.' But it is inconceivable that he would ever have wished to govern Ireland as de Gaulle governed France. His basic humility alone would have made it impossible.

The apparent paradox of his career is that he was at once a great revolutionary and a great constitutionalist. 'He assumed power,' says Professor Desmond Williams, 'as an apparent revolutionary, in a potentially revolutionary situation and, having gained most of his political objectives by constitutional means, was to become outside a lasting symbol of representative democracy.'

No one can question that he presided over, and in a large way inspired, the violent Irish Revolution of 1916–21. It is just as undeniable that, supported by devoted followers, he further revolutionized by peaceful means the relationship between Ireland and Britain between 1932 and 1937.

'Taken together, the External Relations Act and the new Constitution', says Professor Mansergh, 'destroyed the dominion settlement of 1921. Relations with Britain and the Commonwealth had been taken out of the Constitution, where Mr de Valera felt that they had no place, and had become matters of external policy for the Government of the day. This', he concludes (see above, p. 295), 'was the most significant development in the whole period' (1926–39). After the Agreement of 1938, and six years of neutrality in the war, it was manifest to all that total independence for the Twenty-Six Counties had been secured.

Yet Frank Aiken can find the most decisive of all his achievements in his treatment of the Irish military, the civil service and the police when he came to power in 1932, after so many years in a most disagreeable wilderness. He was pressed hard on his own side to make sweeping changes in the personnel of the State services who, during and after the Civil War, had served his bitter and frequently contemptuous opponents. But his clear and unshakeable determination was to reunite the men who had been divided in the Civil War and he rigidly declined to retaliate for the past, or to adopt the spoils system. From this policy Ireland reaped handsome dividends in the rapid subsidence of Civil War bitterness and the steadfastness of the people, army and civil service in the testing days of the 1930s and the 1940s. It was only a matter of years (in spite of a Great War intervening) before Churchill could call Southern (sic) Ireland 'A society independent, Christian, cultured and law-abiding'.

Aiken finds what we have called his constitutionalism to be the product of his Christianity and his mathematics. Asked what was the most striking feature of de Valera's statesmanship, he said simply: 'You couldn't imagine him doing anything opposed to the Sermon on the Mount'. (Almost in the same breath he mentioned his 'wonderful humour', his day-to-day capacity for seeing the funny side of things—this might surprise outsiders.) But he considered the calm, methodical and persistent manner in which he sought to identify and weigh all the factors in complex political and constitutional problems was a vital factor in the achievement of the progress made during his leadership.

De Valera began adult life as a professional teacher of mathematics. When in prison in 1923–24, for instance, we find him calling for mathematical works as the real solace of his confinement. Aiken finds his insistence on *order* in human affairs (and his prolonged search for the appropriate phrase in which to express an idea), to be a counterpart of his joyful discovery of *order* in the world of mathematical symbols.

De Valera himself did not find anything particularly significant in this revolutionary constitutional antithesis, when it was discussed during the preparation of this book. 'Ours', he said, 'was not a revolution in the ordinary sense—it was not an internal revolt. It was a revolt against external domination. Constitutionalism? Difficult to know what constitutionalism means. I would describe myself as a Democrat, as far as our people are concerned.' He once described himself as a 'reformist'. In constitutions he came to take a passionate interest. Did any prime minister ever carry out so much personal constitutional research as he did, when he was formulating the Irish Constitution of 1937? But he would prefer the label democrat, and that in itself is of interest.

What made him a democrat? No particular studies in political thought can be pointed to. He is known to have read Machiavelli. But neither Machiavelli, who was not a democrat, nor Abraham Lincoln, who was a very great one, nor the Irish nationalist writers who at various times fired his imagination, can be said to have provided him with ideological origins. Bearing in mind, as we always must, that his own mental training was mathematical, we cannot be sure that any particular books, apart from religious books, went far to form his standpoint. Pearse was one of his greatest heroes, but Pearse's writings did not mean so much to him before 1916 as they did after. 'You can write from an idealistic view', he said, 'but your action may not come up to your writings.' Pearse proved in every possible way that he meant what he said. It is clear that he did what he did deliberately, that he foresaw the consequences of what he was proposing. De Valera gave far more weight to Pearse's writings after 1916, not just because of the nobility of Pearse's death, but because what followed proved the wisdom and foresight of the author.

Aiken described de Valera as the greatest political thinker he had ever known. Malcolm MacDonald generously referred to the invaluable lessons he had learnt from him in politics. What is meant here, surely, in the first place is that he possessed and developed an exceptional power of thought applied to actual problems in the political world. The kind of political thought that forms the basis of university lectures absorbed a relatively small degree of his attention, except in the sense that his love of learning never faltered. The truth is that he was always a democrat in the bone. He applied his democratic principles to very urgent and often unprecedented problems with the aid of his personal intelligence, rather than the theories of others. In the world of political thinking, we cannot say that he was the heir of anyone. Alike on the plane of theory and practice, he did his thinking for himself.

This question, therefore, 'What made him a democrat?' is somewhat fruitless. He grew up in an atmosphere where it was taken for granted. But a qualification must be quickly inserted. The Fenian tradition of Irish revolt was by no means obviously democratic. No doubt there was some rather vague conception of a democratic régime to be established, once Ireland was free. But Irish freedom came a long way before everything. The only question was how it was to be achieved. And it came to be assumed that it must, in fact, be achieved by a heroic minority whatever the majority attitude. The men of 1916 would never have struck their immortal and triumphal blow for freedom if they had waited for a majority verdict.

There was a concealed dilemma here which was to haunt de Valera for many years and, indeed, was never finally disposed of while he led the Government, though his own mind became clear enough. If the heroes of 1916 were entitled to put the Irish Republic before the apparent or immediate wishes of the people, why should not their successors do likewise? That was how the new IRA reasoned, and continued to reason. It will be seen that from the signature of the Treaty, December, 1921, till he re-entered the Dáil in 1927 this, in one form or another, was for de Valera the most awkward of all the problems confronting him. Gradually he established a Republican tradition which was genuinely democratic rather than military. The new IRA denounced him bitterly, although when he came to power he was widely accused of being far too soft towards them. In the war, his Government was compelled to execute members of the IRA—the exteme and utterly poignant expression of the democratic principle.

In 1916, it should be added, he was very much the soldier. This aspect of him has never been appreciated in Britain, where he is type-cast as the professor or schoolmaster. In the Rising, he took orders and carried them out with the utmost efficiency and a determination, faithful unto death, if need be. In his whole career the most striking transformation came between his military obedience in 1916 in a subordinate role, and his self-confident acceptance of national leadership spontaneously and popularly acclaimed a year later. (The Irish were wont to canonize their own saints without waiting for Rome.)

Thenceforward he appeared to have no doubts that he had been 'born to be king'—not, of course, an expression he ever used, but it was as an unanimously-elected leader and president that he led the country from 1917. From then on, it would be his mission to give effect to the real wishes of the people of Ireland and he believed that he knew how to discover them. 'When I want to know what the people of Ireland want, I examine my own heart.' That famous saying, often ridiculed, does not look quite so ridiculous when one measures his forty odd years of leadership. Some years later, he said to one of the present authors: 'It is not what I want. It is what the people of Ireland want'. The soldier's idea of unquestioning obedience to some civil authority had given way to the democratic statesman's idea of himself as part of the authority guiding, but at the same time responding, to the popular will.

Long before he became President, he had proved himself a great man of action, a man capable of forming and carrying out far-reaching policies and acting dramatically in crises. Yet the word decisiveness applied to him more happily in later, than in earlier, days. From the beginning it was apparently impossible to shift him once his mind was made up on fundamental issues, or issues which appeared to him to be fundamental. But his control of policy was for a long time far from complete in those days. It was one thing to make up his mind what needed doing and another to get it done. Collins, certainly, and in some ways Griffith, an older man and till 1916 infinitely better known, possessed an influence which rivalled his among certain sections of the people. Cathal Brugha occupied a much more formidable position than anyone in his later cabinets. Throughout his whole career, he was much concerned with promoting unity. In the early days he had often to seek it as best he could. No one who praises or blames him for the events of 1922 can neglect the fact that at that time neither side in the Civil War paid much attention to his wishes. By 1932 it was totally different. He was still a democratic leader, but he was indisputably 'the Chief'.

The course of Irish politics might not have been so very different without de Valera from 1916 to 1924. From 1924 to 1932, when a lesser man would have been crushed to extinction, he created a democratic Opposition and framed its strategy and tactics. From 1932 to 1948, he inspired and controlled the Irish Government, sustained by ministers whom he had himself selected, some of them men of the highest ability— all of them devoted to him.

The series of intricate and interlocked steps by which Ireland passed from dominion status to external association between 1931 and 1937 were his own conception and, since he was Minister for External Affairs as well as Head of the Government, Taoiseach, largely his in deed. The economic war with Britain in 1932–38 may not have come about in quite the way he expected. It was made to fit in with his long-premeditated plans for economic self-sufficiency. The London agreements in 1938, including the return of the ports, were a personal triumph. He never ceased to pay tribute to Chamberlain and Malcolm MacDonald. He never wavered in insisting that his ultimate aim was genuine friendship between Britain and Ireland.

Looking back on the war and Ireland's neutrality, he often thanked the Almighty for sparing his country from the horrors suffered by the combatants. He never called attention to the strain under which he himself must have laboured, but in fact his burden must have been almost intolerable. The decision to remain neutral may have sounded easy to take, but he was under no illusions; standing up, year after year, to great powers who might invade and overwhelm him at any moment; the ever-delicate balance involved in preserving peace within and without the State; the endless interferences with ordinary life, often misunderstood by the public. All these would have broken an ordinary statesman. Here again, he was sustained by devoted colleagues. The supreme responsibility rested on him alone.

When Belfast was bombed by the Germans, it took him only a few minutes to decide to send the fire-engines from Dublin, whatever the possible bearing on neutrality. When America entered the war Sir John Maffey, the British Representative, requested an interview in the middle of the night. De Valera immediately took it upon himself to warn the Chief of Staff to prepare to resist a British invasion.

Left to himself, he liked to proceed slowly—step by step—inflexibly pursuing his end but causing as little antagonism as possible at any one moment. Sometimes, as in 1932, he was compelled to depart from this rule, and when speed was of the essence he made up his mind and acted.

If one has a regret, it must be that a man cut out so clearly for states-manship on the widest stage should have been confined for the most part to one small country, Ireland. The transformation of Ireland in his lifetime from a subordinate position in the United Kingdom to one of freedom for Twenty-Six Counties, might be held a sufficient monument. Nevertheless, the impression he made in Geneva before the war, as President first of the Council and later of the Assembly of the League of Nations, leave one speculating wistfully as to the role he might have played as a champion of world peace if his opportunities had been less restricted. Part of the price for Irish neutrality was Irish exclusion from the United Nations for the first ten years after the war and the consequent muffling of de Valera's voice in world affairs. Between 1957 and 1959 he had time, but not much time, to lend a strong support to Frank Aiken and the notable Irish initiative at UNO.

In international politics he was no utopian. He did not believe that Connemara could be suitably governed from Strasbourg or, for that matter, from New York. He believed in patriotism as a social virtue akin to family feeling, but he saw it as something which ought to be restrained by international morality. This last he sought untiringly to promote in good times and bad, with arguments based on reason and common sense couched in no rancorous language. He himself has said that 'such respect as we were able to acquire in Geneva was largely due to the fact that on every question that arose we were able to express our own views independently.' But behind the style and the tactics lay always the moral approach.

Looking back from the relative tranquillity of his years as President, he was reluctant to criticize anyone in the recent past whether for publication or otherwise. When pressed very hard, he was ready to say this about Sir Winston Churchill:

> I regard Churchill as one of the old-time Victorian statesmen who looked upon Britain as the foremost world power, and was prepared to take every step necessary to maintain Britain in that position. He was, in every way, a great war minister, resolved not to let anything stand in the way of Britain's being on the victorious side.
>
> He was opposed to the freedom of this country admitted by Chamberlain, and would not have hesitated had he thought that Britain's victory depended upon it, to invade this country. He was regarded by many of the States of Europe as their saviour, and was greeted by them as such after the war.

De Valera then and at other times tried to set aside any feelings derived from the period of the Civil War, or Churchill's role in the events leading up to it. The ultimate difference lay between his own code of international behaviour and that of Churchill, as expressed in the latter's broadcast at the end of the war. It was not what Churchill or Britain did, but what Churchill said in certain circumstances they would have been entitled to do to Ireland, that represented in de Valera's eyes a philosophy lower than the highest. Chamberlain, Malcolm MacDonald, Eden and Cranborne (now Salisbury) always appealed to him more, as closer to himself in scruple. Yet he has been inclined to feel that, if he had been an Englishman, he would have voted for Churchill at the end of the war.

The lack of progress towards Irish unity was, no doubt, after the Civil War, the great tragedy in his political life. It was, after all, the Ulster question before 1914 which led him into public affairs. It would, however, be grossly and manifestly unfair to hold him responsible in any way at all for the continuance of partition. There was nothing effective he could 'do about it' till he was returned to power in 1932, though he bitterly denounced the agreement of 1925. Whatever the justification of duress, this indubitably abandoned the prospect held out under the Treaty of large gains for Southern Ireland from the Boundary Commission. The economic war followed. It was not, therefore, till the settlement of 1938 that a real opportunity of tackling partition began to present itself.

De Valera clearly came away from his talks with Chamberlain with a strong hope that Chamberlain would find a way of ending partition, Chamberlain with a hope—equally strong—that under certain circumstances Ireland would be at Britain's side if war came. Neither was in the faintest degree committed, nor ever claimed that there was a commitment on the part of the other. In the event, war came before either hope had any chance of being realized. The war set back the cause of Irish unity for many more years than the six for which it lasted. The part played by the Six Counties in the war inevitably strengthened their claims compared with those of the South in the mind of the British Labour Government of 1945–51. That phase also has passed. At the moment of writing the whole future of Northern Ireland lies in the melting pot.

The last two years in that area have seen much turmoil, fear and suffering. But we can believe that we are witnessing the birth pangs of a modern democratic community in which at last there are no second-class citizens and all enjoy equality of rights, in which no section persecutes or dominates another. Since passing to the Presidency de Valera has strictly interpreted the rule which forbids the President to make public comments on current political events or controversies. It can be taken for granted that any responsible movement for civil and political rights in Northern Ireland has his heartfelt support, as have any effective steps towards a peaceful restoration of the unity of Ireland. Half a century ago he laid it down that Irish unity must be restored by peaceful means. He has never wavered in his insistence that unity must come about by consent and not by force. As Roger Casement said from the dock, 'Loyalty is a sentiment, not a law; it rests on love not on restraint.'

Intrinsically in de Valera's eyes the problem has always been an Irish issue to be settled between Irishmen. He has given conclusive proof by his actions and by his public assertion that to him a Northern Irishman is as Irish as one from any other part of Ireland.

During his years of office de Valera strove to promote good-will and economic co-operation between both parts of Ireland for their mutual benefit. In spite of manifest obstacles he made some progress; during his time came about the linking of the electricity grids, the establishment of the joint Foyle Fisheries Board, co-operation in the prevention of farm stock disease and other developments. Later the present Lord O'Neill courageously embarked on more far-reaching initiatives with de Valera's successors, Seán Lemass and Jack Lynch. Certainly the need for ever-growing co-operation and friendship demands urgent action by all who can assist in Britain as well as Ireland.

Englishmen of today carry in de Valera's eyes an inescapable responsibility for playing a constructive part and setting right the grievous wrong done to their country's neighbour. Long before he went to the Presidency he called earnestly for English good offices in ending partition and, at the least, for an emphatic statement from British Ministers that Irish unity is regarded as a British interest and British objective. It can be taken as certain that he believes that more than ever today.

When tributes are paid, as increasingly they are in these latter days, to his immense sagacity, what is usually meant is that he was capable of looking much further ahead than ordinary statesmen; of biding his time and winning his point by peaceful means when the occasion happened to suit it. His use of the Abdication crisis of 1936 to further his constitutional ends is a good illustration. He is rightly seen, moreover, as a master of the political arts required to maintain the leadership of a nation over such an immense period. The technical expertise was never denied him even by his harshest critics. But as time has passed, the deep moral strength based on religion which has given consistency in retrospect to so many fine-spun calculations, is more and more widely recognized. Thirty-five years ago his integrity was widely challenged. He would be a rare bird and a foolish one who would talk in that fashion today. He has added much to the dignity of the presidency, as to every post he has occupied.

An Irish immigrant mother—a Spanish-American father dying while he was very small—a return to Ireland, his mother remaining in America

—an upbringing by an uncle in what he himself has called a labourer's cottage—no psychiatrist could forecast the outcome of such an inheritance and early environment. The President never tired of expressing his gratefulness to his grandmother and his uncle Pat, but from his earliest years, without father or mother to guide him, he had to fend for himself compared with others. One cannot say what effect this must have had on a small boy's formation. In fact, he grew up with a strong confidence in himself, powerful family affection and a surpassing love of Ireland.

His deepest feelings about Ireland have for many years been intertwined with his dedication to the Irish language. No one who heard his references to the language, or for that matter his words in Irish when re-elected President, could doubt that this was an attachment which would only end with death. But it did not *create*, it articulated his passion for the Irish people, which was part of his deepest being before he studied the language or entered politics.

The estimates of his quality as a public speaker have varied considerably. Timothy Patrick Coogan, in his valuable book, *Ireland since the Rising*, asserts that 'he was not a good orator as far as delivery went and he had a marked tendency to repetition.' Yet if the test of an orator is his ability to communicate effectively with all kinds of audiences under all sorts of conditions, de Valera passes it easily. He was a successful lecturer before he was pitchforked in 1917 into large-scale public speaking in the full gaze of Ireland, Britain and later, America. He responded like a veteran. Some of his appeal in early days was attributed to his 1916 halo. But Coogan gives a generous picture of the President fifty years later leaving a nursing home and delivering 'a long, strong-voiced oration standing bare-headed by the grave of Roger Casement.' No man could have sustained the legend unless he himself contained some element of magic.

His technique as a speaker suffered, it may well be, from a certain school-masterly approach. He said himself, looking back, that he seems always to have been certain that he could convince anybody of anything he himself believed in, given time and goodwill. Hence no doubt the repetition referred to. But his edited speeches, those of 1939–45, for instance, read extremely well. And on various great occasions, at Geneva for example in 1932, as President of the League Council, or in his radio reply to Churchill, he left an ineffaceable mark.

Criticism of his delivery cannot obscure the thrill which he was able to impart at dramatic moments with apparently simple words. A man then young, who stood at the back of the Dáil gallery at a tense moment in 1932, could ever afterwards recall the tremor that passed through the assembly as he pledged himself: 'When I negotiate—when I negotiate, it will be on the basis of a united Ireland.'

He has known how to coin or exploit a vivid or revealing phrase, or produce a tart rejoinder. 'I am not going to be an engine running away without the train.' When Lloyd George said that negotiating with him was like trying to pick up mercury with a fork, de Valera replied: 'Why doesn't he use a spoon?'

He has shown an almost obsessional interest in dictionaries and exact meanings. As Professor Desmond Williams has written: 'Few politicians have paid more attention to the significance of detail in the use of words.' But sometimes this turned into a scrupulosity—an over-reluctance to use an expression that could possibly be turned against him. He was always aware, some would say, too aware—of the infinite complexity of the future. He was known to fall back on long, involved paragraphs when others less meticulous would have used an arresting, if ambiguous sentence. Always behind the words, and this has given them much of their force, lay the ever-active brain and the hunger and thirst for righteousness.

The crowd saw and approved the bare-headed veteran (aged eighty-two) on the sleety day at the grave of Casement. What they could not know was that that morning his internal pains had been diagnosed as jaundice, a disease for him of particular ill-omen. All around him begged him not to go to the ceremony. Finally, they insisted that if he went at all he must keep his head covered throughout. He would not have it. 'Casement', he said, 'deserved something better than that.' When his vigorous declamation was over, he was assisted away by Aiken. When he got home, he collapsed.

President de Valera has been admired by very many, from far and near. But those who have known him best always admired him most.

In old age, he creates an impression of unruffled calm, except in face of public or private mourning. At all times, his self-control has been phenomenal. Seán McEntee, so great a friend afterwards, met him for the first time in prison, after the 1916 Rising, and recognized his self-control at once as a vital element in his natural leadership of men. But deep down he was hot-blooded. He was not using a *façon de parler* when he told the world in his famous reply to Churchill: 'I know the answer that first springs to the lips of every man of Irish blood who heard or read that speech. I know the reply I would have given a quarter of a century ago.' He had deliberately decided, 'That is not the reply I shall make tonight.'

It had taken him the best part of a life-time to bring under full restraint his passionate nature, and integrate it with his higher purposes. In one form or another, crude or sublimated, it would always be an essential part of him. Without that underlying counterpart to his ascetic principles he would have been a very different and far less inspiring leader of his people.

Such a man in theory might have been set down anywhere. In fact he has lived his life in Ireland. His universal principles have been worked out in an Irish context and drawn their inspiration thence. He has been at once a product and a creator of Ireland's destiny.

SOURCE REFERENCES

SOURCE REFERENCES

Prologue pages xv to xix

1 F. Pakenham, *Peace by Ordeal* (1935).

Chapter 1 The Early Years (pages 1 to 10)

1 E. de V.'s Vere Foster copy book, April 13th, 1891. 2 E. de V. to his Aunt Hannie, March 2nd, 1896. 3 *Blackrock College Athletic Sports . . . May 22nd, 1901.* 4 Original text of speech dated February 18th, 1903.

Chapter 2 Youth (pages 11 to 18)

1 Rev. James Mellett, *If any man dare*, pp. 2–5. 2 N.L.I. MS. Holloway diaries, November 28th, 1905. 3 E. de V., *Examples of arithmetic and mensuration*. 4 Dr Mannix to E. de V., October 2nd, 1912. 5 Draft lecture by E. de V., undated but *c.* 1910. 6 Holograph of lecture by E. de V., November, 1910. 7 Roger Casement to E. de V., August 14th and September 1st, 1912.

Chapter 3 The Irish Volunteers (pages 19 to 28)

1 Original in E. de V.'s handwriting in National Museum of Ireland (E.W. 1047). 2 P. H. Pearse to E. de Valera, March 11th, 1915, in National Museum of Ireland (E.W. 1045).

Chapter 4 The Rising (pages 31 to 50)

1 The Rose Tree (*Selected Poems of W. B. Yeats*, 1938). 2 J. O'Connor, 'The rising by the river', in *Irish Press*, April 14th, 1950. 3 *Ibid.* April 13th, 1950. See also a similar tribute in *An tÓglach*, April 17th, 1926, p. 25. 4 E. MacNeill to E. de V., April 23rd, 1916, 1.20 p.m. 5 Rev. F. X. Martin, *ed.*, 'Eoin MacNeill and the 1916 Rising', in *Irish Historical Studies*, xii. 269 (March, 1961). 6 *Catholic Bulletin*, vii. 330–1 (May, 1917). 7 'Easter diary' by L. Stokes published in Non-Plus, no. 4, p. 25 (Winter, 1960). 8 Seán T. Ó Ceallaigh, *Seán T.* (pp. 203 et seq.).

Chapter 5 Felons of our Land (pages 51 to 61)

1 Frank L. Polk, Acting Secretary of State, to Senator J. W. Wadsworth, July 14th, 1916. 2 E. de V. to C. Murphy, Dispatch 2. 3 *La recente insurrezione in Irlanda* (Rome, 1916). 4 E. de V. to S. Donnelly, Easter, 1917. 5 E. de V. to C. Murphy, Dispatch 2. 6 E. de V. to S. Donnelly, Easter, 1917. 7 E. de V. to S. Donnelly, April 23rd, 1917. 8 Final orders by E. de V., Whit Monday, 1917. 9 R. Brennan, *Allegiance*, pp. 131–2; P. Béaslaí, *Michael Collins*, i. 155–6. 10 Rev. John Cooney to E. de V., July 4th, August 6th, 1917; S. Ua Dubhghaill to Peadar [Clancy] n.d. 11 P. Béaslaí, *Michael Collins*, i. 158.

Chapter 6 National Resurgence (pages 63 to 75)

1 *Irish Times*, June 27th, 1917. 2 *Irish Independent*, June 25th, July 2nd, 9th, 1917. 3 *Cork Examiner*, July 9th, 1917. 4 Draft speech in E. de V.'s hand, July, 1917. 5 *Irish Independent*, July 6th, 1917. 6 Draft speech of election address in E. de V.'s hand.

7 Draft speech in E. de V.'s hand. 8 *Freeman's Journal*, July 12th, 1917. 9 *Irish Independent*, July 13th, 1917. 10 *Daily Express*, July 12th, 1917. 11 *Ibid.*, July 11th, 1917. 12 D. Ó Hegarty to E. de V., July 17th, 1917; P. Ó Caoimh to E. de V., July 21st, 1917. 13 *Irish Independent*, September 24th, 1917. 14 *Daily Mail* quoted in *Northern Whig*, October 8th, 1917. 15 *Daily Mail* quoted in *Freeman's Journal*, October 20th, 1917. 16 *Irish Independent*, October 26th, 1917. 17 *Hansard debates*, October 23rd, 1917. 18 *Weekly Despatch*, quoted in *Sunday Independent*, October 28th, 1917. 19 *Irish Independent*, October 29th, 1917. 20 *Irish Independent*, November 2nd, 5th, 1917. 21 *Ibid.*, November 26th, 1917. 22 Draft speech for South Armagh by-election. 23 William O'Brien, *The Irish Revolution*, pp. 361–2. 24 *Daily Chronicle*, April 24th, 1918, quoted in *Irish Press* (Philadelphia), May 18th, 1918. 25 *Irish Independent*, May 6th, 1918. 26 *Christian Science Monitor*, May 15th, 1918. 27 E. de V. to G. Lansbury, March, 1919.

Chapter 7 Lincoln Jail (pages 77 to 93)

1 *Irish Independent*, May 20th, 1918. 2 *Documents relative to the Sinn Féin movement* (Parliamentary Papers, H.C., 1921, XXIX, Cmd. 1108). 3 *Irish Independent*, January 12th, 1921. 4 *Freeman's Journal*, May 20th, 1918; *Irish Independent*, May 20th, 1918. 5 *Irish Independent*, June 7th, 1918. 6 *Freeman's Journal*, June 13th, 1918. 7 *Irish Independent*, June 20th, 1918. 8 Lavelle, *James O'Mara*, pp. 123–4. 9 E. de V. to his mother, November 28th, 1918. (Third Irish Race Convention, programme). 10 John O'Mahony to Father Kavanagh, December 24th, 1918. 11 C. Brugha to E. de V., November 28th, 1919. 12 *Irish Press* (Philadelphia), March 15th, 1919. 13 Draft speech in E. de V.'s handwriting. 14 P. S. O'Hegarty to H. Boland, March 25th, 1919. 15 Quoted in P. Béaslaí, *Michael Collins*, i. 282–4. 16 April 2nd, 1919. 17 *Dáil Éireann, Minutes of Proceedings, 1919–21*, pp. 72–4, 76. 18 *Ibid.*, pp. 45–7, 67–9. 19 *Ibid.*, p. 78. 20 *Ibid.*, p. 151; M. Collins to E. de V., August 25th, 1919. 21 *Dáil Éireann, Minutes of Proceedings, 1919–21*, p. 83.

Chapter 8 American Mission (pages 95 to 104)

1 E. de V. to M. Collins, June 21st 1919. 2 H. Boland to E. de V., May 24th, 1919. 3 H. Boland to E. de V., June 4th, 1919. 4 E. de V. to A. Griffith, July 9th, 1919. 5 *Leader* (San Francisco), July 5th, 1919. 6 E. de V. to A. Griffith, July 9th, 1919. 7 Liam Mellows' diary, July 8th, 1919. 8 E. de V. to A. Griffith, August 13th, 1919. 9 E. de V. to trustees, Friends of Irish Freedom, September 20th, 1919. 10 E. de V. to M. Collins, August 13th, 1919. 11 E. de V. to A. Griffith, August 13th, 1919. 12 H. Boland's diary, October 18th, 1919. 13 *Ibid.*, January 31st, 1920; K. O'Doherty, *Assignment—America*, p. 39. 14 *Westminster Gazette*, February 7th, 1920.

Chapter 9 The Mission under Strain (pages 105 to 114)

1 *Gaelic American*, February 14th, 1920. 2 *Ibid.*, February 21st, 1920. 3 *Ibid.*, March 13th, 1920. 4 E. de V. to Cabinet, February 17th, 1920. 5 J. Devoy to John A. McGarry, February 26th, 1920 (Printed in P. MacCartan, *With de Valera in America*, p. 165). 6 E. de V. to Judge Cohalan, February 20th, 1920. 7 Judge Cohalan to E. de V., February 22nd, 1920. 8 E. de V.'s comments on Cohalan's letter for the information of the Dáil Cabinet, March, 1920. 9 A. Griffith to E. de V. (*c*. March 11th, 1920). 10 E. de V. to Cabinet, *c*. March 1st, 1920. 11 Draft letter from E. de V. to Cabinet. 12 'Inside story of the Republican National Convention' by J. E. Milholland, in *Irish Press* (Philadelphia), October 8th, 15th, 1921. 13 Draft letter from E. de V. to Cabinet.

14 Drafts of statements for San Francisco Convention, June, 1920. 15 *Public Ledger* (Philadelphia), July 13th, 1920. 16 E. M. Borchard to E. de V., October 2nd, 1920; *Ireland's claim for recognition as a sovereign independent state* (Washington, 1920). 17 *Irish Press* (Philadelphia) and *Irish World* (New York), November 27th, 1920. 18 M. Collins to E. de V., October 11th, 1919. 19 A. Griffith to E. de V., December 8th, 1919. 20 D. O'Hegarty to E. de V., June 8th, 1920, and to H. Boland, October 13th, 1920.

Chapter 10 A President in Hiding (pages 115 to 125)

1 Public Record Office, London: F.O. 371/4249. 2 Public Record Office, London: Cab. 23/24; Cabinet decision, January 14th, 1921. 3 Memo of meeting kept by E. de V., January 3rd, 1921. 4 E. de V. to M. Collins, January 6th, 1921 and undated letter. 5 *Dáil Éireann, Minutes of Proceedings, 1919–21*, pp. 236–41. 6 E. de V. to M. Collins, undated but January, 1921. 7 Quoted in P. Béaslaí, *Michael Collins and the making of a new Ireland*, p. 146. 8 E. de V. to A. Stack, February 10th, 1921. 9 E. de V. to P. Béaslaí, April 2nd, 1921. 10 Press statement by E. de V., March 30th, 1921. 11 E. de V. to H. Boland, April, 1921. 12 E. de V. to Judge O'Connor, May, 1921. 13 E. de V. to E. Childers, May 9th, 1921.

Chapter 11 Fencing with the Welsh Wizard (pages 127 to 144)

1 E. de V. to D. O'Hegarty, June 23rd, 1921. 2 D. O'Hegarty to E. de V., June 23rd, 1921. 3 *Dáil Éireann: Correspondence relating to peace negotiations, June–September, 1921* (Dublin, 1921) contains the official correspondence quoted in this chapter. 4 S. Millin, *General Smuts*, ii. 329. 5 M. Collins to E. de V., July 16th, 1921; K. O'Connell's diary, July 11th, 1921. 6 Beaverbrook, *The decline and fall of Lloyd George*, pp. 85–6. 7 W. S. Churchill, *The Aftermath*. 8 E. de V. to M. Collins, July 15th, 1921. 9 *Freeman's Journal*, July 18th, 1921. 10 E. de V. to Lloyd George, July 19th, 1921, and reply same date. 11 E. de V. to M. Collins, July 19th, 1921. 12 M. Collins to E. de V., July 20th, 1921. 13 Beaverbrook, *op. cit.*, pp. 88–9. 14 E. de V. to J. C. Smuts, July 21st, 1921. 15 Report by H. Boland and J. McGrath, *c.* September 15th, 1921. 16 K. Middlemas, ed., *Sir Thomas Jones—Whitehall Diary*, Vol. I.

Chapter 12 The Best Laid Plans (pages 145 to 156)

1 E. de V. to J. McGarrity, December 27th, 1921. 2 F. O'Connor, *The Big Fellow*, p. 132. 3 e.g. F. Pakenham, *Peace by Ordeal* (1935); F. Gallagher, *The Anglo-Irish Treaty* (1965). 4 F. Gallagher, *op. cit.* 5 E. Childers to E. de V., October 22nd, 1921. 6 A. Griffith to E. de V., October 24th, 1921. 7 E. de V. to A. Griffith, October 25th, 1921. 8 Delegation to E. de V., October 25th, 1921; E. de V. to A. Griffith, October 27th, 1921. 9 *An Phoblacht*, January 24th, 1922.

Chapter 13 The Thumbscrew (pages 157 to 170)

1 F. O'Connor, *op. cit.*, p. 135. 2 R. Taylor, *Michael Collins*. 3 F. Pakenham, *op. cit.*, p. 245. 4 E. de V. to J. McGarrity, December 27th, 1921. 5 F. Gallagher, *op. cit.* 6 *Freeman's Journal*, December 5th, 1921. 7 *Irish Independent*, December 6th, 1921. 8 *Ibid.* 9 See *Sir Thomas Jones—Whitehall Diary*, ed. K. Middlemas, Vol. I, p. 177. 10 W. S. Churchill, *The Aftermath*. 11 E. de V. to J. McGarrity, December 27th, 1921. 12 Frank Gallagher, *op. cit.*

Chapter 14 Peace v. Principle—the Treaty Debate (pages 171 to 180)

1 E. de V. to J. McGarrity, December 27th, 1921. 2 *Ibid.* 3 R. Taylor, *op. cit.*, pp. 176-7. 4 F. O'Donoghue, *No other law*, pp. 193-4. 5 *Dáil Éireann, Official report, Treaty debate*, pp. 24-5, 274. 6 *Freeman's Journal* and *Irish Independent*, January 5th, 1922. 7 *Dáil Éireann, Official report, Treaty debate*, p. 203. 8 *Ibid.*, p. 281. 9 *The Times*, January 6th, 1922. 10 *Dáil Éireann, Official report, Treaty debate*, p. 344. 11 *Ibid.*, p. 347.

Chapter 15 The Drift to Disaster (pages 181 to 193)

1 *Iris Dháil Éireann: Official report, Debate on the Treaty*, p. 399. 2 *Dáil Éireann, Official report, Treaty debate*, pp. 399-411. 3 *Irish Independent*, February 13th, 1922. 4 *Ibid.*, February 27th, 1922. 5 K. O'Connell's diary, February 22nd, 1922. 6 E. de V. to A. Stack, March 31st, 1922. 7 November 11th, 1959. 8 *Irish Independent*, March 17th, 1922. 9 *Ibid.*, March 23rd, 1922. 10 W. S. Churchill to M. Collins, April 12th, 1922. 11 *Irish Independent*, February 22nd, 1922. 12 *Ibid.*, April 12th, 1922. 13 *Ibid.*, April 7th, 1922. 14 E. de V., *A national policy* (Fianna Fáil Pamphlet No. 1), pp. 9-10. 15 *Poblacht na hÉireann*, April 20th, 1922. 16 *Irish Independent*, May 24th, 1922. 17 *Ibid.*, June 22nd, 1922. 18 H. Boland to J. McGarrity, July 7th, 1922.

Chapter 16 The War of Brothers (pages 195 to 201)

1 *Poblacht na h.Éireann, War News*, No. 2, June 29th, 1922. 2 *Irish Independent*, September 14th, 1922. 3 H. Boland to J. McGarrity, July 13th, 1922. 4 E. de V.'s diary, August 9th, 11th, 1922; K. O'Connell's diary, August 3rd-11th, 1922. 5 E. de V.'s diary, August 13th, 1922. 6 *Ibid.*, August 13th-14th, 1922. 7 T. de Vere White, *Kevin O'Higgins*. 8 Peter Golden, *Impressions of Ireland*, pp. 54-6. 9 E. de V.'s diary, September 6th, 1922. 10 E. de V. to James K. McGuire, October 19th, 1922. 11 *Dáil Éireann: Correspondence of Mr Eamon de Valera and others*, p. 13. 12 E. de V. to J. McGarrity, October 19th, 1922.

Chapter 17 The Emergency Government (pages 203 to 213)

1 E. de V. to Dr Amigo, November 6th, 1922. 2 E. de V. to Dr Mannix, November 6th, 1922. 3 K. O'Connell's diary, November 10th, 1922. 4 *Dáil Éireann, debates*, i. 859. 5 K. O'Connell's diary, November 17th, 1922. 6 *Dáil Éireann debates*, i. 2267. 7 E. de V. to M. Comyn, undated. 8 R. Brennan to E. de V., November 18th, 1922. 9 K. O'Connell's diary, November 24th, 1922. 10 E. de V. to J. McGarrity, November 28th, 1922. 11 *Ibid.* 12 E. de V. to M. P. Colivet, March 17th, 1923. 13 F. O'Donoghue, *No other law*, p. 291. 14 E. de V. to Liam Lynch, November 27th, 1922. 15 E. de V. to P. J. Ruttledge, December 15th, 1922. 16 E. de V. to L. Lynch, December 12th, 1922. 17 L. Lynch to E. de V., December 14th, 1922. 18 E. de V. to L. Lynch, January 18th, 1923. 19 Operation order, No. 17, February 3rd, 1923. 20 E. de V. to M. Twomey, March 14th, 1923. 21 E. de V. to P. J. Ruttledge, December 15th, 1922. 22 E. de V. to Chief of Staff and all members of the Ministry, February 9th, 1923. 23 E. de V. to Rev. L. McKenna, S.J., January 18th, 1923. 24 *Irish Independent*, March 10th, 1923; E. de V. to Edith M. Ellis, February 26th, 1923. 25 E. de V. to M. MacSwiney, March 17th, 1923. 26 E. de V. to R. Brennan, January 15th, 1923 and reply, January 19th, 1923. 27 D. Macardle, *Irish Republic*, pp. 830-1. 28 E. de V. to J. McGarrity, February 5th, 1923 (quoted in *Irish Independent*, March 15th, 1923). 29 F. Fahy to A. Stack, December 9th, 1922; E. de V. to F. Fahy, December 12th, 1922; E. de V. to L. Lynch, December 11th, 1922; L. Lynch to E. de V., December 11th, 1922. 30 L. Lynch to E. de V., January 30th, 1923. 31 E. de V. to L. Lynch, February 2nd, 1923 (two memos). 32 E. de V. to L. Lynch, February 7th, 1923.

Chapter 18 The Darkest Hour (pages 215 to 223)

1 *Freeman's Journal*, February 17th, 1923. 2 L. Lynch to E. de V., February 28th, 1923. 3 E. de V. to L. Lynch, March 7th, 1923. 4 E. de V. to P. J. Ruttledge, March 9th, 1923. 5 E. de V. to M. MacSwiney, March 14th, 1923. 6 E. de V. to M. MacSwiney, February 24th, 1923. 7 *Irish Independent*, March 12th, 1923. 8 *Ibid.*, February 9th, 1923. 9 E. de V.'s diary, March 18th–27th, 1923. 10 Minutes of executive meeting, March 23rd–26th, 1923; F. Aiken's draft of minutes of same; F. O'Donoghue, *No other law*, pp. 299–301. 11 K. O'Connell, Diary, April 3rd, 1923. 12 E. de V. to P. J. Ruttledge, April 9th, 1923. 13 E. de V. to A. Stack, April 10th, 1923. 14 E. de V. to P. J. Ruttledge, April 11th, 1923. 15 *Daily Bulletin*, No. 165, April 13th, 1923. 16 E. de V. to Monsignor O'Hagan, May 19th, 1923. 17 E. de V. to Monsignor Luzio, April 30th, 1923. 18 Minutes of meeting, May 13th–14th, 1923. 19 Letter from E. de V., May 21st, 1923. 20 E. de V. to M. MacSwiney, May 26th, 1923. 21 E. de V. to Monsignor O'Hagan, May 19th, 1923. 22 E. de V. to Monsignor Luzio, May 23rd, 1923. 23 E. de V. to F. Aiken, May 24th, 1923. 24 E. de V. *Peace and War*, p. 72.

Chapter 19 De Profundis (pages 225 to 231)

1 E. de V. to manager of *Éire*, June 19th, 1923. 2 General order, No. 22, July 14th, 1923, signed F. Aiken. 3 E. de V. to F. Aiken, June 22nd, 1923. 4 Address to E. de V. from Co. Clare convention, July 22nd, 1923. 5 *Irish Independent*, July 23rd, 1923. 6 *Ibid.*, July 24th, 1923. 7 E. de V. to Mrs E. Childers, July 31st, 1923. 8 Michael Carolan, Director of Intelligence (IRA), to E. de V., August 10th, 1923. 9 National Library of Ireland, MS. 10 Orders by Minister for Defence, August 9th, 19th, 24th, 1924. 11 Mrs de Valera to K. O'Connell, undated but *c*. August 24th, 1924; *Irish Independent*, August 25th, 1924. 12 E. de V. to K. O'Connell, January 19th, February 2nd, 1924. 13 Mrs de Valera to K. O'Connell, May 7th, 1924.

Chapter 20 In Search of a Path (pages 235 to 243)

1 D. O'Callaghan to F. Aiken, June 2nd, 1924. 2 Minutes of Comhairle na d'Teachtaí, August 7th, 1924. 3 Minutes of executive meeting, August 10th–11th, 1924. 4 Mrs de Valera to K. O'Connell, August 11th, 1924. 5 Typescript of E. de V.'s speech at Ennis, August 15th, 1924. 6 Typescript of speech at Dundalk, August 24th, 1926. 7 *Irish Independent*, October 14th, 17th and 21st, 1924. 8 Typescript of speech at Gorey, December 14th, 1924. 9 E. de V. to A. Ford, May 27th, 1926. 10 E. de V. to Adjutant-General (P. Murray), January 13th, 1925. 11 Agreement signed by E. de V. and F. Aiken, February 20th, 1925. 12 F. Aiken to Chairman of Army Council, November 18th, 1925. 13 Quoted in D. Macardle, *Irish Republic*, pp. 893–4. 14 Speech by E. de V. at the Rotunda, Dublin, December 10th, 1925. 15 *Ibid.* 16 Report of Sinn Féin Ard Fheis, March 10th, 1926.

Chapter 21 Founding a New Party (pages 245 to 258)

1 E. de V. interviewed by United Press representative, April 17th, 1926. 2 E. de V., *National Policy*, pp. 6–7. 3 E. de V. to A. Ford, May 27th, 1926. 4 J. McGarrity to E. de V., November 7th, 1926. 5 Typescript of E. de V.'s speech at Ennis, June 29th, 1926. 6 *Irish World*, August 28th, 1926, Peadar O'Donnell, 'There will be another day', pp. 36–7. 7 E. de V.'s speech at Fianna Fáil Ard Fheis, November 24th, 1926. 8 E. de V. to J. McGarrity, January 22nd, 1929. 9 Testimony of E. de V. before Supreme Court, New York, March 22nd to 24th, 1927 (typescript). 10 Statement by E. de V., May 12th, 1927. 11 *Boston Sunday Post*, May 1st, 1927. 12 *Dáil Debates*, xix, 992. 13 *Irish Independent*, June 8th, 1927. 14 Statement by E. de V., June 14th, 1927.

15 Statement by E. de V. for *New York Tribune*, June 14th, 1927. 16 Opinion dated June 21st, 1927, signed by Arthur C. Meredith, Albert E. Wood and George Gavan Duffy. 17 *Irish Independent*, June 30th, 1927; Minutes of National Executive of Fianna Fáil, June 23rd, 1927. 18 *Nation*, July 16th, 1927. 19 *Evening Mail*, July 25th, 1927. 20 E. de V. to Frank P. Walsh and others, August 3rd, 1927. 21 Minutes of National Executive, Fianna Fáil, August 9th, 1927. 22 E. de V. to O. W. Bohan, August 10th, 1927. 23 Draft of statement for newspaper by E. de V., August 11th, 1927. 24 Statement by F. Aiken and J. Ryan, September 23rd, 1927. 25 Statement by P. Ó Caoimh. 26 *Dáil debates*, xli. 1387–91. 27 *The Advocate* (Melbourne), August 25th, 1927. 28 *Nation*, August 27th, 1927. 29 F. MacManus, ed., *The years of the great test, 1926–39.*

Chapter 22 Leader of the Opposition (pages 259 to 271)

1 Statement by E. de V., August 25th, 1927. 2 Typescript of speech by E. de V., August 22nd, 1927. 3 Draft by E. de V. for election address (published in *Irish Independent*, September 12th, 1927). 4 *Irish Independent*, September 7th, 1927. 5 *Ibid.*, September 10th, 1927. 6 *Ibid.* 7 *Ibid.*, September 12th, 15th, 1927; *Dublin Evening Mail*, September 12th, 1927. 8 *Irish Times*, September 21st, 1927. 9 *Ibid.* 10 *Dáil Éireann debates*, xxviii. 1398–1400 (March 14th, 1929). 11 *Ibid.*, xl. 51–61 (October 14th, 1931). 12 S. T. O'Kelly to E. de V., January 5th, 1930; national executive of Fianna Fáil, minutes, January 7th, February 11th, 1930. 13 *Ibid.*, July 9th, 1931. 14 *Ibid.*, August 4th, 1931. 15 *Ibid.*, October 6th, 1927. 16 A. C. Meredith to E. de V., March 17th, 1929. 17 E. de V. to A. C. Meredith, June 23rd, 1934. 18 *Irish Times*, January 28th, 1929. 19 *Ibid.*, May 4th, 1929. 20 *Dundalk Examiner*, June 22nd, 1929. 21 *Dáil Éireann debates*, xxiii. 2270–1 (May 30th, 1928). 22 *Ibid.*, xxi. 1455 (November 16th, 1927). 23 E. de V., *Fianna Fáil and its economic policy* (1928). 24 Director of Publicity to E. de V., November 16th, 1922. 25 K. O'Connell to J. T. Ryan, February 5th, 1929. 26 E. de V. to J. T. Ryan, March 26th, 1929. 27 E. de V. to J. T. Ryan, July 15th, 1931. 28 *Irish Press*, September 5th, 1931.

Chapter 23 The Collision Course (pages 273 to 288)

1 *Dáil Éireann debates*, xli. 146 (March 15th, 1932). 2 E. de V. *Recent speeches and broadcasts* (1932), pp. 9–14. 3 *Saorstát Éireann: text of notes exchanged . . .* (P. No. 650). 4 Conor Maguire to E. de V., April 15th, 1932. 5 *Seanad debates*, xv. 938 (June 2nd, 1932). 6 *Ibid.*, xv. 1320 (July 18th, 1932). 7 D. Gwynn, *Eamon de Valera*. 8 *Dáil Éireann debates*, xlii. 1688–1700 (June 17th, 1932); *Saorstát Éireann: text of further notes exhanged* (P. No. 829). 9 Hansard debates, July 4th, 1932. 10 *Evening Press*, July 5th, 1932. 11 Seán Lemass to E. de V., July 15th, 1932. 12 *Dáil Éireann debates*, xliv. 138–42 (October 19th, 1932); *Seanad debates*, xv. 935, 1320–1 (June 2nd, July 18th, 1932); Note of meeting between E. de V. and MacDonald, July 15th, 1932. 13 *The Times*, August 5th, 1932. 14 *Irish Times*, September 29th, 1932. 15 E. de V. to J. H. Thomas, September 9th, 26th, 1932; J. H. Thomas to E. de V., September 14th, 27th, 1932. 16 *Dáil debates*, xliv. (October 19th, 1932). 17 Correspondence between E. de V. and J. McNeill, *Irish Times*, June, 1932. 18 S. T. O'Kelly to E. de V., November 19th, 1932; Telegram from S. T. O'Kelly to E. de V., November 22nd, 1932. 19 Memorandum by J. P. Walshe, October 30th, 1932, and enclosures. 20 Hansard debates, July 10th, 1935. 21 *Dáil Éireann debates*, xliv. 141 (October 19th, 1932). 22 *Irish Independent*, August 15th, 1932. 23 *Irish Press*, January 3rd, 1933.

Chapter 24 Framing a New Constitution (pages 289 to 302)

1 *Irish Press*, April 24th, 1933. 2 *Dáil Éireann debates*, xlviii. 2752–4 (July 14th, 1933). 3 S. MacEntee to E. de V., November 13th, 19th, 1936; S. Ó Muimhneacháin to E. de V., October 6th, 1936 (unsigned). 4 S. Baldwin to E. de V., November 28th, 1936. 5 E. de V. to S. Baldwin, November 29th, 1936. 6 Memorandum by J. P. Walshe on interview with Sir H. Batterbee, December 10th, 1936. 7 *Dáil Éireann debates*, lxiv. 1277 (December 11th, 1936). 8 N. Mansergh, The implications of Eire's relationship with the British Commonwealth of Nations. *International Affairs* (January, 1948). 9 *Dáil debates*, lxviii. 216–7 (June 9th, 1937). 10 E. de V. to a correspondent, July 4th, 1949. 11 *Irish Independent*, May 1st, 1937. 12 *Manchester Guardian*, May 3rd, 1937. 13 *Dáil Éireann debates*, lxvii. 416 (May 13th, 1937). 14 *Ibid.*, lxviii. 287–8, 417 (June 10th, 14th, 1937). 15 *L'Osservatore Romano*, October 5th, 1957.

Chapter 25 Towards a Settlement (pages 303 to 312)

1 E. de V. to J. H. Thomas, November 29th, 1933. 2 Public Record Office, London: C.P. 124 (36). 3 J. W. Dulanty to J. P. Walshe, September 8th, 1936. 4 J. W. Dulanty to J. P. Walshe, Memos 74 and 75, September 15th, 1936. 5 Sir N. F. Warren Fisher to J. W. Dulanty, September 14th, 1936. 6 J. W. Dulanty to J. P. Walshe, October 14th, 1936. 7 Memorandum by E. de V., dated September 17th, 1937, on meetings with Malcolm MacDonald. 8 *Dáil Éireann debates*, lxvii. 721–2 (May 19th, 1937).

Chapter 26 A Qualified Triumph (pages 313 to 326)

1 Public Record Office, London: Cabinet Papers, COS 690. 2 E. de V. to F. D. Roosevelt, January 25th, 1938. 3 F. D. Roosevelt to E. de V., February 22nd, 1938. 4 J. W. Dulanty to J. P. Walshe, March 14th, 1938. 5 J. W. Dulanty to J. P. Walshe, March 15th, 1938.

Chapter 27 The Many Sides of Government (pages 327 to 344)

1 E. de V., *A National Policy* (Fianna Fáil Pamphlet I). 2 *Dáil debates*, xliv. 141 (October 19th, 1932). 3 *Dáil Éireann debates*, xli. 906–7 (April 29th, 1932). 4 *Ibid.*, liv. 1748 (December 19th, 1934). 5 *Ibid.*, liv. 1752 (December 19th, 1934). 6 *Ibid.*, xli. 917–8 (April 29th, 1932). 7 E. de V., *Peace and War*. 8 *Ibid.* 9 *Ibid.* 10 *Ibid.* 11 *Ibid.* 12 *Ibid.* 13 *Ibid.* 14 *Ibid.* 15 *Ibid.* 16 C. C. O'Brien, *Ireland*, p. 117. 17 *Dáil Éireann debates*, xli. 908–9 (April 29th, 1932). 18 *Senate debates*, February 9th, 1939.

Chapter 28 One of the Neutrals (pages 347 to 368)

1 *Daily Herald* (London), April 2nd, 1919. 2 E. Hempel, to E. de V., May 1st, 1957; E. Hempel to a friend, May 22nd, 1957. 3 *Dáil Éireann debates*, lxxvii. 1–8 (September 2nd, 1939). 4 *Ibid.*, lxxvii. 463, 1197 (September 28th, November 9th, 1939): J. Hogan, *Election and Representation*, pp. 33–35. 5 *Dáil Éireann debates*, lxxvii. 592 (September 29th, 1939). 6 Neville Chamberlain to E. de V., September 19th, 1939. 7 'Lord Rugby Remembers' (*Irish Times*, July 3rd, 1962). 8 E. de V. to N. Chamberlain, September 22nd, 1939. 9 N. Chamberlain to E. de V., September 25th, 1939. 10 J. Cudahy, *The armies march*, pp. 28–9. 11 Roskill, *The War at Sea*, i. 46. 12 *Dáil Éireann debates*, lxxvii. 1210 (November 9th, 1939). 13 E. de V. to N. Chamberlain, April 12th, 1939. 14 *Documents on German Foreign Policy, 1918–45*, Ser. D., viii. 241–2. 15 *Ibid.*, 405–6, 545. 16 E. de V. to Sir A. Eden, January 29th, 1940. 17 E. de V. to N. Chamberlain, February 2nd, 1940. 18 Telephone message from E. de V. for N. Chamberlain, February 5th, 1940. 19 Message from N. Chamberlain for E. de V.,

February 6th, 1940. **20** A. Eden to E. de V., April 6th, 1940. **21** E. de V., *Ireland's stand*, pp. 17–18. **22** E. de V. to N. Chamberlain, May 15th, 1940. **23** W. S. Churchill, *The Second World War—the Grand Alliance*, iii. 725. **24** *The Times*, May 17th, 1940. **25** *Documents on German Foreign Policy, 1918–45*, Ser. D., ix. 423. **26** W. T. Cosgrave to R. Mulcahy, November 27th, 1939. **27** *Documents on German Foreign Policy, 1918–45*, Ser. D., ix. 573–4, 601–3; x. 184–5. **28** *Ibid.*, ix. 637–8. **29** N. Chamberlain to E. de V., May 18th, 1940. **30** N. Chamberlain to E. de V., June 29th, 1940. **31** E. de V. to N. Chamberlain, July 4th, 1940. **32** E. de V. to N. Chamberlain, October 23rd, 1940. **33** *Irish Press*, November 15th, 1940.

Chapter 29 On Razor's Edge (pages 369 to 387)

1 Report from J. P. Walshe to E. de V., July 16th, 1940. **2** Ditto, July 25th, 1940. **3** W. T. Cosgrave to E. de V., July 9th, 1940. **4** E. de V. to W. T. Cosgrave, July 13th, 1940. **5** W. T. Cosgrave to E. de V., July 16th, 1940. **5A** R. Brennan, 'War-time mission in Washington', *Irish Press*, May 5th, 1958. **6** *Documents on German Foreign Policy, 1918–45*, Ser. D., x. 420–21; Memo from J. P. Walshe to E. de V., August 19th, 1940. **7** Memo. from J. P. Walshe to E. de V., October 2nd, 1940. **8** *Dáil debates*, lxxxi. 583–6 (November 7th, 1940). **9** Memorandum by J. P. Walshe, November 13th, 1940. **10** R. Brennan's telegram report, No. 258, received November 11th, 1940. **11** D. Gray to E. de V., November 21st, 1940. **12** *Foreign relations of the U.S., diplomatic papers, 1940*, iii. 169–70. **13** Telegram, E. de V. to R. Brennan, No. 193, December 4th, 1940. **14** Telegram, R. Brennan to E. de V., No. 305, received December 10th, 1940. **15** 'Lord Rugby remembers', *Irish Times*, July 4th, 1962. **16** W. S. Churchill, *The Second World War—Their Finest Hour*, ii. 690. **17** Memorandum by D. Gray of interview with E. de V., January 6th, 1941. **18** W. S. Churchill, *The Second World War—The Commonwealth Alone*, iv. 254–6. **19** *Documents on German Foreign Policy, 1918–45*, Ser. D., xi. 972. **20** J. P. Walshe to Kathleen O'Connell, January 16th, 1941 and enclosures. **21** *Dáil debates*, lxxxi. 1645 (January 17th, 1941). **22** *Irish Press*, February 1st, 1941. **23** *Documents on German Foreign Policy, 1918–45*, Ser. D., xi. 973. **24** Memorandum by J. P. Walshe, January 6th, 1941. **25** *Foreign relations of the U.S., diplomatic papers, 1941*, iii. 225. **26** E. de V., *Ireland's Stand*, p. 41. **27** Report by R. Brennan, April 10th, 1941. **28** Telegram from R. Brennan, April 23rd, 1941. **29** *Foreign relations of the U.S., diplomatic papers, 1941*, iii. 230. **30** Memorandum by E. de V. of interview with D. Gray, April 28th, 1941. **31** *Foreign relations of the U.S., diplomatic papers, 1941*, iii. 230. **32** Memorandum by E. de V. of interview with D. Gray, April 28th, 1941. **33** *Foreign relations of the U.S., diplomatic papers, 1941*, iii, 233. **34** B. Peterson, *Turn of the Tide*, pp. 133–40. **35** *Documents on German Foreign Policy, 1918–45*, Ser. D., xi. 805. **36** J. P. Walshe to E. de V., May 22nd, 1941. **37** *Irish Times*, May 22nd, 1941; *Irish Press*, May 23rd, 24th, 1941. **38** *Foreign relations of the U.S., diplomatic papers, 1941*, iii. 235. **39** *Ibid.* **40** E. de V. to D. Gray, May 25th, 1941. **41** *Foreign relations of the U.S., diplomatic papers, 1941*, iii. 238–9. **42** Message from E. de V. to W. S. Churchill, May 25th, 1941. **43** J. P. Walshe to E. de V., May 26th, 1941. **44** *Dáil debates*, lxxxiii. 971–2 (May 26th, 1941). **45** *Irish Independent*, May 28th, 1941.

Chapter 30 The Loneliness of a Neutral (pages 389 to 399)

1 Notes by E. de V. on moments of crisis during the war. **2** Telegram from R. Brennan, June 30th, 1941. **3** *Foreign relations of the U.S., diplomatic papers, 1941*, iii. 240–6. **4** *Ibid.*, p. 244. **5** *Daily Mail* (London), October 13th, 1941. **6** Aide memoire handed to State Department by R. Brennan, October 15th, 1941. **7** Note by R. Brennan to

Secretary of State, November 6th, 1941. 8 Under Secretary of State to R. Brennan, November 17th, 1941. 9 D. Gray to J. P. Walshe, September 3rd, 1941 and enclosures; J. P. Walshe to D. Gray, September 11th, 1941. 10 *Dáil debates*, lxxxiv. 1905 (July 17th, 1941). 11 T. D. Williams, 'Irish neutrality', *Irish Press*, July 9th, 1953. 12 J. P. Walshe to E. de V., May 31st, 1941. 13 W. S. Churchill to E. de V., December 8th, 1941, and memorandum by E. de V. 14 W. S. Churchill, *The Second World War*. 15 E. de V. to W. S. Churchill, December 10th, 1941. 16 E. de V., memorandum on conversation with Lord Cranborne, December 17th, 1941. 17 *Foreign relations of the U.S., diplomatic papers, 1941*, iii. 252. 18 *Ibid*., pp. 250–2. 19 J. P. Walshe to E. de V., December 4th, 15th, 1941. 20 J. P. Walshe to E. de V., December 15th, 1941. 21 J. P. Walshe to E. de V., February 17th, 1942. 22 J. P. Walshe to E. de V., December 20th, 1943. 23 E. de V., *Ireland's Stand*. 24 *Foreign relations of the U.S., diplomatic papers, 1942*, i. 755–9. 25 J. P. Walshe to E. de V., May 28th, 1942. 26 J. P. Walshe to E. de V., May 23rd, 1942. 27 J. P. Walshe to E. de V., August 31st, September 1st, 1942; *Foreign relations of the U.S., diplomatic papers, 1942*, i. 764–7.

Chapter 31 Mounting Pressures (pages 401 to 414)

1 *Foreign relations of the U.S., diplomatic papers, 1942*, i. 754. 2 *Dáil debates*, xci. 1555 (November 4th, 1943); Unsigned memorandum, November 29th, 1943. 3 *Dáil debates*, xci. 600–606. 4 *Ibid*., xcii. 1911–16 (March 1st, 1944). 5 *Foreign relations of the U.S., diplomatic papers, 1943*, iii. 132–44. 6 *Ibid*., p. 146. 7 *Ibid*., pp. 152–68. 8 *Ibid*., pp. 164–5. 9 *Ibid*., 1944, iii. 216–22. 10 *Ibid*., p. 223. 11 Draft reply to American note in E. de V.'s handwriting. 12 *Foreign relations of the U.S., diplomatic papers, 1943*, iii. 226–40. 13 Memoranda of conversations, February 25th, 26th, 28th, 29th, 1944, initialled by M. Ó Muimhneacháin, February 29th and April 4th, 1944. 14 *Foreign relations of the U.S., diplomatic papers, 1944*, iii. 226–7. 15 *Ibid*., p. 234. 16 *Ibid*., pp. 232–3. 17 *Ibid*., pp. 238–40. 18 *Ibid*., p. 243. 19 E. de V., *Ireland's Stand*, pp. 87–8; *Irish Independent*, March 13th, 1944. 20 E. Hempel to E. de V., April 15th, 1944; Address dated May, 1944. 21 Aide memoire handed by E. de V. to D. Gray, October 9th, 1944. 22 *Dáil debates*, xcii. (April 12th, 1945). 23 E. de V. to R. Brennan, Whit Monday, 1945.

Chapter 33 In Office and Out of it (pages 427 to 437)

1 T. D. Williams and K. B. Nowlan, edd. *Ireland in the war years and after*. 2 *Dáil debates*, xcvii. 2568–75 (July 17th, 1945). 3 *Ibid*., cxii. 2441 (August 6th, 1948). 4 *Irish Times*, September 1967. 5 *Dáil debates*, cxiii. 410–11 (November 24th, 1948). 6 *Ibid*., 410 (November 24th, 1948). 7 *Ibid*., col. 414 (November 24th, 1948). 8 *Ibid*., cxv. 814 (May 10th, 1949). 9 *Ibid*., 813 (May 10th, 1949). 10 *Dáil debates* (April, 1951).

Chapter 34 Handing on the Inheritance (pages 439 to 449)

1 Lord Moran's diaries, *Winston S. Churchill—The Struggle for Survival*, pp. 471–3. 2 Account of meeting of Fianna Fáil Parliamentary Party, mid-January dictated by E. de V. 3 *Dáil debates*.

Chapter 35 President of Ireland (pages 451 to 462)

1 *Irish Press*, May 29th, 1964. 2 *Ibid*. 3 *Ibid*., March 2nd, 1965. 4 *Ibid*., April 11th, 1966. 5 *Ibid*., January 22nd, 1969. 6 G. C. Duggan, *Northern Ireland, success or failure?* p. 21. 7 *Irish Press*.

INDEX

18

INDEX